Lecture Notes in Computer Science 9073

Commenced Publication in 1973
Founding and Former Series Editors:
Gerhard Goos, Juris Hartmanis, and Jan van Leeuwen

Editorial Board

Brian Donnellan · Markus Helfert
Jim Kenneally · Debra VanderMeer
Marcus Rothenberger · Robert Winter (Eds.)

New Horizons in Design Science: Broadening the Research Agenda

10th International Conference, DESRIST 2015
Dublin, Ireland, May 20–22, 2015
Proceedings

Springer

Editors
Brian Donnellan
Maynooth University
Maynooth
Ireland

Markus Helfert
Dublin City University
Dublin
Ireland

Jim Kenneally
Intel Labs Europe
Leixlip
Ireland

Debra VanderMeer
Florida International University
Miami, Florida
USA

Marcus Rothenberger
University of Nevada
Las Vegas, Nevada
USA

Robert Winter
Universität St. Gallen
St. Gallen
Switzerland

ISSN 0302-9743
Lecture Notes in Computer Science
ISBN 978-3-319-18713-6
DOI 10.1007/978-3-319-18714-3

ISSN 1611-3349   (electronic)

ISBN 978-3-319-18714-3   (eBook)

Library of Congress Control Number: 2015938111

LNCS Sublibrary: SL3 – Information Systems and Applications, incl. Internet/Web, and HCI

Springer Cham Heidelberg New York Dordrecht London

Printed on acid-free paper

Springer International Publishing AG Switzerland is part of Springer Science+Business Media
(www.springer.com)

Preface

This volume contains selected research papers and descriptions of prototypes and products presented at DESRIST 2015 – the 10th International Conference on Design Science Research in Information Systems and Technology held during May 20–22, 2015, at Clontarf Castle, Dublin, Ireland.

The DESRIST Conference continued the tradition of advancing and broadening design research within the information systems discipline. DESRIST brings together researchers and practitioners engaged in all aspects of Design Science research, with a special emphasis on nurturing the symbiotic relationship between Design Science researchers and practitioners. As in previous years, scholars and design practitioners from various areas, such as information systems, computer science, industrial design, design thinking, innovation management, service science, and software engineering, came together to discuss and solve design problems through the innovative use of information technology and applications. The outputs of DESRIST, new and innovative constructs, models, methods, processes, and systems provide the basis for novel solutions to design problems in many fields. The conference further built on the foundation of nine prior highly successful international conferences held in Claremont, Pasadena, Atlanta, Philadelphia, St. Gallen, Milwaukee, Las Vegas, Helsinki, and Miami.

The title of this volume, "New Horizons in Design Science: Broadening the Research Agenda," reflects the need for a discussion to broaden the research agenda of Design Science Research, if it is to flourish and grow as a research activity. The agenda of DESRIST 2015 conference reflected this inclusive approach. By accommodating a range of diverse design perspectives, the intent of the conference was to stimulate discussion and enable cross-discipline collaboration.

Overall we received 111 submissions (61 research manuscripts, 11 prototypes and products, and 39 research-in-progress and poster papers) to the conference for review. Each research paper was reviewed by a minimum of two referees. For these proceedings 22 full papers and 11 short papers were accepted together with 10 short papers describing prototypes and products.

The program also included two panels, two keynote presentations, as well as poster presentations. The accepted papers were distributed between ranges of diverse design perspectives. As in previous years, a substantial number of papers discussed methodological aspects of Design Science and described the application of Design Science research to real-world design problems.

We would like to thank the authors who submitted their papers to DESRIST 2015 conference and we trust that the readers will find them as interesting and informative as we did. We would like to thank the members of the Program Committee as well as the additional referees who took the time to provide detailed and constructive reviews for the authors. We appreciated the efforts of the other members of the Organizing Committee, as well as the volunteers whose dedication and effort helped bring about another successful conference. We would like to take this opportunity to thank

Prof. Alan Hevner for his encouragement and guidance. And our special thanks to Dr. Rob Gleasure as Proceedings Chair. Furthermore, we thank the sponsoring organizations, in particular Science Foundation Ireland, Irish Design 2015, Intel, Maynooth University, and Dublin City University for their support.

We believe the papers in these proceedings provide several interesting and valuable insights into the theory and practice of Design Science, and they open up new and exciting possibilities for research in the discipline.

May 2015

Markus Helfert
Brian Donnellan
Jim Kenneally
Robert Winter
Monica Chiarini Tremblay
Debra VanderMeer
Marcus Rothenberger

Organization

Program Committee

Stephan Aier	University of St. Gallen, Switzerland
Andreas Auinger	Upper Austria University of Applied Sciences, Austria
Liam Bannon	University of Limerick, Ireland
Richard Baskerville	Georgia State University, Atlanta, USA
Marian Carcary	Innovation Value Institute, Ireland
Sven Carlsson	Lund University, Sweden
Kevin Casey	Dublin City University, Ireland
Samir Chatterjee	Claremont Graduate University, USA
Roger Chiang	University of Cincinnati, USA
Monica Chiarini Tremblay	Florida International University, USA
Gabriel J. Costello	Galway-Mayo Institute of Technology, Ireland
Martin Curley	Intel Corporation, Ireland
Edward Curry	Digital Enterprise Research Institute, Ireland
Dave Darcy	Florida International University, USA
Brian Donnellan	Maynooth University, Ireland
Kaushik Dutta	National University of Singapore, Singapore
Rob Gleasure	University College Cork, Ireland
Goran Goldkuhl	Linköping University, Sweden
Shirley Gregor	The Australian National University, Australia
Riitta Hekkala	Aalto University, Finland
Markus Helfert	Dublin City University, Ireland
Alan Hevner	University of South Florida, USA
Keumseok Kang	Florida International University, USA
Dimitris Karagiannis	University of Vienna, Austria
Jim Kenneally	Intel Corporation, Ireland
Bill Kuechler	University of Nevada, Reno, USA
Subodha Kumar	Mays Business School, Texas A&M University, USA
Jan Marco Leimeister	University of Kassel, Germany
Peter Loos	Saarland University, Germany
Jan Mendling	Vienna University of Economics and Business, Austria
Andreas Oberweis	Karlsruhe Institute of Technology, Germany
Rory Oconnor	Dublin City University, Ireland
Balaji Padmanabhan	University of South Florida, USA
Claus Pahl	Dublin City University, Ireland

Tero Päivärinta	Luleå University of Technology, Sweden
Jinsoo Park	Seoul National University, Korea
Jeffrey Parsons	Memorial University of Newfoundland, Canada
Jan Pries-Heje	Roskilde University, Denmark
Hajo A. Reijers	Eindhoven University of Technology, The Netherlands
Michael Rosemann	Queensland University of Technology, Australia
Matti Rossi	Aalto University, Finland
Gerhard Schwabe	University of Zurich, Switzerland
Alexander Simons	University of Liechtenstein, Liechtenstein
Jonas Sjöström	Uppsala University, Sweden
Henk Sol	University of Groningen, The Netherlands
Oliver Thomas	University of Osnabrück, Germany
Tuure Tuunanen	University of Jyväskylä, Finland
Karthikeyan Umapathy	University of North Florida - School of Computing, USA
Vijay Vaishnavi	Georgia State University, USA
Debra VanderMeer	Florida International University, USA
John Venable	Curtin University of Technology, Australia
Joseph Walls	Ross School of Business at the University of Michigan, USA
Axel Winkelmann	University of Würzburg, Germany
Robert Winter	University of St. Gallen, Switzerland
George Wyner	Boston University, USA

Additional Reviewers

Ahmed Elragal	Markus Salo
Ala Alluhaidan	Martin Meyer
Andreas Kiesow	Michael Cahalane
Andrew Pope	Moutaz Haddara
Anna-Liisa Syrjänen	Mouzhi Ge
Ciara Fitzgerald	Nikolaos Tantouris
Ciara Heavin	Novica Zarvic
Colin Ashurst	Owen Foley
Constantin Houy	Patrick Brandtner
Denis Dennehy	Peter Heinrich
Fred Adam	Phelim Murnion
Giovanni Maccani	Plamen Petkov
Howard Duncan	Rajendra Prasath
Inkyoung Hur	Robert Johnston
JB McCarthy	Tadhg Nagle
Julian Krumeich	Taekyung Kim
Karen Carey	Thoa Pham
Louise Veling	Tobias Mettler

Organization Committees

General Chairs

Robert Winter	University of St. Gallen, Switzerland
Monica Chiarini Tremblay	Florida International University, USA
Debra VanderMeer	Florida International University, USA
Marcus Rothenberger	University of Nevada Las Vegas, USA

Program Chairs

Markus Helfert	Dublin City University, Ireland
Brian Donnellan	Maynooth University, Ireland
Jim Kenneally	Intel Labs Europe, Ireland

Panel Chairs

Par Agerfalk	Uppsala University, Sweden
Jonas Sjöström	Uppsala University, Sweden

Local Organizing Chairs

Carol Travers	Innovation Value Institute, Ireland
Sarah Hetherington	Innovation Value Institute, Ireland
Aline Dijon	Intel Corporation, Ireland

Industry Chairs

Martin Curley	Intel Corporation, Ireland
Glenn Wintrich	Dell, USA
Arkin Efeoglu	SAP, Germany

Proceedings Chair

Rob Gleasure	University College Cork, Ireland

Doctoral Consortium Chairs

Henk Sol	University of Groningen, The Netherlands
Jan vom Brocke	University of Liechtenstein, Liechtenstein

Sponsoring Organizations

Science Foundation Ireland
IRISH DESIGN 2015

Contents

Design Science Research in Action

Meta Perspectives

Data Mining and Analytics

Emerging Themes

Design Practice and Design Thinking

Prototypes

Short Papers

Design Science Research in Action

Designing an Enterprise Social Questions and Answers Site to Enable Scalable User-to-User Support

Oliver Gass[1], Gülcan Öztürk[1], Silvia Schacht[1,2(✉)], and Alexander Mädche[1,2]

[1] Chair of Information Systems IV, University of Mannheim, Mannheim, Germany
[2] Institute for Enterprise Systems, University of Mannheim, Mannheim, Germany
{gass,oeztuerk,schacht,maedche}@es.uni-mannheim.de

Abstract. Nowadays, the information technology infrastructure within organizations is getting more and more heterogeneous. Recent trends such as bring-your-own-device or choose-your-own-device satisfy user requests for diverse devices they already know from their private life. On the other hand, following these trends results in an increased complexity of the organizations' infrastructure and a substantial rise in required effort for supporting users. In order to address this increased support demand, the establishment of a user-to-user support culture seems promising. An established concept to provide user-to-user support is the concept of social questions and answers (SQA) sites. SQA sites have been shown to be successful in the private context. Users can seek and provide knowledge and thereby support each other. This paper presents the design and evaluation of an enterprise SQA platform aiming to support employees in solving problems with processes or technologies. Building on already derived design principles, we discuss the design and implementation of the SQA prototype within an existing Customer Relation Management platform. The resulting system was then evaluated within five focus group sessions with professionals from various industries. The evaluation results show the validity of our design principles and the usefulness of the implemented prototype.

Keywords: BYOD · User-to-user support · Social questions and answer sites

1 Introduction

Only few years ago, companies' information technology (IT) infrastructures have been adapted to organizational rather than individual needs [1]. Thereby, organizations maintained control over devices, access points, interfaces and security controls. However, such rigid IT infrastructures are no longer up-to-date due to increased mobility and people are becoming more and more tech-savvy. Even in their private life, people started to solve problems and fulfill tasks with the aid of *"complex and relatively large-scale individually owned IS"* [1, p. 252]. Now, they are transferring their IT experiences collected in private life to organizational settings [2]. In doing so, people prefer to adapt their IT landscape not only to their tasks and problems, but also to their skills and experiences. Another reason why rigid IT infrastructures are outdated is the increased mobility resulting in an increased amount of remote work and

© Springer International Publishing Switzerland 2015
B. Donnellan et al. (Eds.): DESRIST 2015, LNCS 9073, pp. 3–18, 2015.
DOI: 10.1007/978-3-319-18714-3_1

people remain connected [3] not only with their friends and family, but also with their colleagues. Thus, the borders between private and professional life are getting blurred. When companies insist to maintain standardized IT infrastructure, their employees are forced to wear multiple devices and separate their two worlds. The separation of private and professional life, however, can result in loss of efficiency [3]. In order to address these trends, companies should adapt their IT infrastructure to more flexible forms in order to meet the needs of their employees.

Examples for such modern and flexible strategies are bring-your-own-device (BOYD) respectively choose-your-own-device (COYD) initiatives [4]. By applying these strategies, employees are able to choose their preferred technology for work purposes by themselves. However, in addition to obvious challenges such as security issues, BYOD respectively CYOD also result in a high heterogeneity of a company's IT landscape. As Gens et al. [5] already highlighted *"more devices, times more apps, equals exponentially more complexity for IT support"* [5, p. 4]. In private life, people deal with their need for support by consulting experts and expertise for example via the internet. In social questions and answers (SQA) sites users give support to each other and can receive expert assistance [6]. While SQA sites perfectly fit to explorative problem solving, they are inadequate to support specific problems, e.g. in the context of organizational processes. SQA sites base on indirect communication resulting in a delayed assistance. However in companies, ad-hoc problem solving is often necessary in order to achieve efficiency and effectiveness. Nevertheless, we strongly believe that SQA sites can address the issues of BYOD and CYOD strategies when adapted to organizational needs. Therefore, our research aims to design an enterprise SQA site that allows to support employees to handle not only technological issues related to a highly heterogeneous IT landscape, but also to fulfill their tasks and solve their work-related problems by applying the IT of their own choice. Consequently, our research aims to answer the following research question:

How to design an enterprise SQA site to enable efficient and effective user-to-user-support for employees?

The remainder of this paper is structured as follows: In Chapter 2, we will briefly discuss the related work on social software in organizations and SQA sites. After describing our research methodology in Chapter 3, we will present in Chapter 4 the design of our enterprise SQA platform by discussing the meta-requirements and design principles and outlining the implementation of the platform. In Chapter 5, we report the evaluation of our platform before discussing its results in Chapter 6. Finally, we will utilize Chapter 7 to reflect our research, its limitation and to outline our future work.

2   Related Work

2.1   Social Network Sites in Organizations

Every organization operating in the online and/or offline space should be aware of social media [7]. Social media categorizes a group of applications or web sites, building on concepts such as Web 2.0 and user generated content. Social media enables people to form online communities and to share their knowledge [8]. The term 'social network sites' is generally associated with the web-based services allowing users to construct a public or semi-public profile maintaining a list of other users they are connected to and the possibility to browse these user connections within this network of users [9]. Using the concepts 'social network sites' and 'social media' within organizations is considered as 'enterprise social software' [10].

Various scholars investigate the usage and acceptance of social software in organizations as well as private settings. Some of this research (e.g. [11], [12]) applied established constructs from technology acceptance literature (such as TAM [13] or UTAUT [14]) to explain the users' intention to use the social software on an individual level. Other researches, for example Zhou and Lu [15], found that one important antecedent for the acceptance of social software is the perceived network size, such as the total number of members of the social software or total number of peers of the user. The total number of peers in turn was found to influence the perceived usefulness and the perceived enjoyment of the investigated platform [16].

The usage behavior in the context of social software has also been analyzed on a group level with respect to the we-intention to use the system (see [17], [18]). In his study, Muller [19] identified two use types of enterprise social media: the passive ("lurking") and active ("contribution") usage. On the contrary, Pöyry [20] differentiate between participation and browsing as social media use types in a private context. Whereat, the adoption of social software depends on a balanced mixture of both use types ("lurkers" and "contributors"), the participation in social software often follows the 90-9-1 rule meaning that 90 percent of the users are pure consumers ("lurkers") while 9 percent are contributing few content and 1 percent contributes the lion share of content [21]. Therefore, the contribution and sharing of user generated content (such as knowledge) is an antecedent of the success of social software. The attitude towards the sharing of knowledge is positively influenced by subjective norms and a sense of self-worth [22].

2.2 Social Questions and Answers Sites

Harper and Raban [23] distinguish three types of internet-based questions and answers sites: (1) Digital reference services, (2) Expert services, and (3) Social Question and Answer (SQA) sites. SQA sites are defined as *"a Web-based service for information seeking by asking natural language questions to other users in a network"* [24]. They leverage the time and effort of everyday users to ask and answer questions [23] using various algorithmic strategies to allow for collaborative assessment of the quality of the submitted content [25]. SQA sites typically focus on individuals' information needs and do not explicitly consider the collaboration information accumulation of a group [25]. Many SQA sites have little structural or role-based organization, but share characteristics of online communities. These sites have a base of regular users who engage in off-topic discussions, reply to another instead of just asking or answering questions or take the role of a moderator [23]. Gazan [26] identified two roles of question answerers on SQA sites (specialists and synthesists) and two types of questioners (seekers and sloths). Specialists are knowledge experts who provide answers without referencing other sources, while synthesists are the ones who do not claim any expertise and provide answers with references to existing solutions. Seekers demonstrate active engagement with the community and pursue communication regarding their questions. Sloths do not pursue further interaction with community members after receiving answers to their questions [26].

Other researchers focus on design characteristics of SQA sites and their evaluation with regards to usage behavior and answer quality. For example, it has been shown that systems which prevent social interaction among users suffer from underuse or were abandoned outright [27]. In contrast to this, the prominent example of an SQA site Yahoo Answers[1] has been found to be successful, because of its sophisticated reward features which intensify the user participation [24]. However, Yahoo Answers and some of its design characteristics have been critically evaluated and discussed in research. The feature to allow exactly one answer as best is a potential weakness, because there could be several answers which may be equally good or even better for a given question [28]. Another feature of Yahoo Answers, the possibility to annotate previous answers, contributes to a higher user engagement as it creates a sense of collaborative information seeking [29].

3   Research Design

In order to design an SQA site which enables an user-to-user support in an organizational context, our research applied the design science research (DSR) approach [30]. Thereby, we followed the design research cycle methodology as introduced by Vaishnavi and Kuechler [31]. The methodology defines five sub processes, which are executed iteratively: (1) awareness of problem, (2) suggestion of key concepts to address the problems, (3) development of a solution design, (4) the evaluation of the solution and (5) the conclusion to decide which elements of the solution to adopt.

Aiming to identify key requirements on the enterprise SQA site – also called meta-requirements [32] – we analyzed key literature already existing in related research areas. Next, we investigated existing SQA solutions existing in the internet to identify typical capabilities and derive design principles. Based on the design principles accounting for public SQA sites, we suggested additional principles that need to be considered in an enterprise SQA site. In the third step of the design cycle, we applied the identified design principles to develop an enterprise SQA instance in the form of a prototype. The final design was implemented as an extension module of an existing customer relationship management (CRM) software package in cooperation with a software company being the practice partner of the DSR project. Having a solid prototype, we initiated the evaluation phase. Therefore, we presented the prototype to several focus groups being formed by representatives of various companies. In this focus groups, the participants were asked to discuss the usefulness of each design principle. The findings were used to further refine the design of the enterprise SQA site.

---

[1] https://answers.yahoo.com/

4   Solution

While we intensively discussed the first two steps (awareness of problem and suggestions of key concepts to address the problems) of the DSR cycle in another article (see [33]), this article presents the design of the enterprise SQA site and its evaluation. In order to give the reader an overview, we will briefly summarize our key findings, before describing the artifact and its evaluation in detail.

4.1   Awareness of the Problem

In order to understand the problem domain (being the first step of our DSR project), we consulted existing literature on challenges of SQA sites. SQA sites implemented in private contexts are – as outlined in the related work section – subject of research. However, for organizational contexts we did not find any design principles informing the design of an enterprise SQA site. Therefore, we identified research areas that can inform the design of our solution based on existing research related to public SQA sites.

Table 1. Meta-requirements of an Enterprise SQA Site

Meta-Requirements		Exemplary Sources
Knowledge Management	1: Provision of an integrated access to both, experts and externalized experience e.g. in form of documents	[34]–[37]
	2: Monitoring of user context in order to provide access to knowledge based on current needs	
Social Networking	3: Information of users with regard to changes in the SQA site in order to speed up the support process by pointing out recent changes	[26], [38]–[41]
	4: Implementation of measures for self-regulation in order to increase the overall quality of both, structure and content	
Social Presence	5: Stimulation of users to include many social cues in their profiles by providing users enough room for self-expression	[9], [35], [42]–[45]
	6: Provision of options for direct communication reflecting the continuum for basic text message functions up to the technological state-of-the-art	
Motivation	7: Inclusion of emotional, gameful design elements that activate user behavior to support the use objectives of the platform	[19], [46]–[48]
	8: Provision of gamified services that lead to a new cognitive, emotional, social use of the core functionalities	

In total, we identified four main research areas: The first research area being of interest for our design is the knowledge management research field, since the SQA platform aims to serve for knowledge exchange and transfer in order to support employees in solving their problems. Because the platform connects its users for communication and knowledge transfer, we identified research and theories related to social networks as the second important stream. In order to motivate users of an organizational SQA platform, we also investigated various research fields examining important antecedents of user participation in such networks. Thus, a third research field being of interest related to social presence, since the feeling of human warmth and sociability plays a major role in social networks. Another modern way of ensuring motivation to participate in social platforms is the implementation of emotional and affective functionalities (e.g. by Gamification mechanisms).

Based on the four research fields, we identified in total eight meta-requirements that need to be considered when designing an organizational SQA site. While an extensive discussion of the literature and the identified meta-requirements can be found in [33], summarizes the meta-requirements and some exemplary sources identified in the four **Table 1** research areas.

4.2   Design Principles

Having the meta-requirements, we identified in a next step the design principles for an enterprise SQA site. Thereby, we approached two steps: First, we analyzed popular SQA sites in the internet and extracted the principles behind their design. Second, we again consulted the literature to derive the design principles for an enterprise SQA site.

In total we identified 24 design principles – 18 extracted from public SQA sites and six additional design principles examined by analyzing existing literature. The analysis of the popular SQA sites like stackoverflow.com or yahooanswers.com and the identification of additional design principles being important for an enterprise SQA site is presented in [33]. **Fig. 1** provides an overview on the identified design principles (DP).

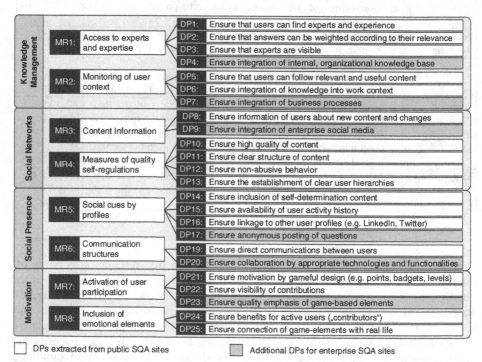

Fig. 1. Design principles for an Enterprise SQA Site

4.3   Design Decisions and Artifact Realization

While the formulation of the design principles serves for providing guidelines for an class of IS, the third phase of the DSR cycle specifically aims to create the solution to a problem through a more concrete specification of the functionality and architecture [49]. Therefore, we translated the design principles to design decisions being concrete functionalities of the enterprise SQA artifact. In the following paragraphs, the key design decisions are described and illustrated by screenshots (see **Fig. 2** and **Fig. 3**) of the realized enterprise SQA artifact.

The core element of the enterprise SQA site is the *multi-dimensional matching algorithm*, since it links knowledge seekers to appropriate knowledge providers. Thereby, the multi-dimensional approach aims to address different problem dimensions. Gorelick and Tantawy-Monsou [50] realize two main problem dimensions: either people are struggling in using the technology, or they have difficulties in performing the processes facilitated by the technology [50]. In order to address the large variety of problems, the matching algorithms has to monitor the context where the user experiences issues. Therefore, a *categorization of the problem context* is necessary where the characteristics of a problem will be specified.

In our SQA artifact, the system automatically illustrates in which problem context the user can find existing solutions (marked by a yellow question mark). After clicking the yellow question mark, selection of various given contexts is provided where the user can refine the context he/she is interested in. In addition, the user is able to specify the problem context by selecting additional characteristics provided in a check-box list. Based on the categories, the enterprise SQA artifact is able to match

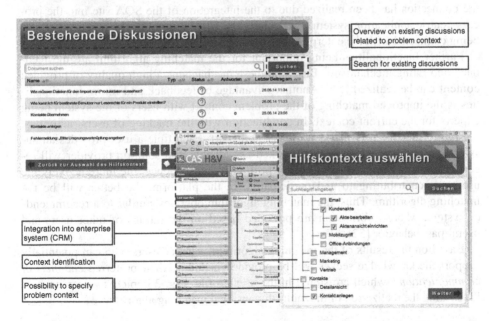

Fig. 2. Screenshots of the Enterprise SQA Site and context-related functionalities

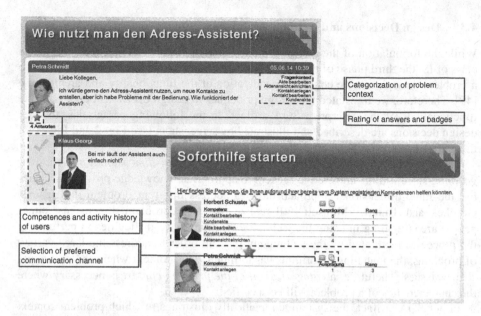

Fig. 3. Screenshots of the Enterprise SQA Platform and the profile-related functionalities

the current problem to categories and characteristics of existing solutions. Because the platform does not only connect knowledge seekers to experts, but also documented knowledge, a *connection to the enterprise knowledge base* is required. In our artifact, the connection has been realized due to the integration of the SQA site into the process-centric application system (particularly the CRM system of the practice partner) being connected with the enterprise knowledge base.

Further functionalities being important for the matching algorithm are the feedback and rating mechanisms. Based on these mechanisms a high quality of provided content can be realized [51]. Another advantage of feedback and rating functionalities is the improved matching of the problem context with users of the system being experts for the current context. In combination with the tracking of users' activities, the rating functionality marks a user as an expert. Each time a user provides an answer to a problem which is then marked as valuable, the solution provider will receive points of competence in his/her profile. In consequence, the more actively the users are contributing to and participating in the platform, the better will be the matching algorithm. Thus, the matching algorithm operates similar to a recommender system, where information are provided based on the ratings of other users and users' past behavior [52].

Based on the results of the matching algorithm, a list of users who can potentially support the knowledge seeker will be provided including their preferred *channels of communications*, which are stored in the user profile. **Fig. 3** depicts two screenshots illustrating the realization of the multi-dimensional matching algorithm.

5   Evaluation

5.1   Methodology

In order to evaluate the design principles, we implemented a qualitative approach using focus groups. Stewart et al. [53] define a focus group as *"a moderated discussion among six to twelve people who discuss a topic under the direction of a moderator whose role is to promote interaction and keep the discussion on the topic of interest"* [53, p. 600]. Scholars identified focus groups as an appropriate method for DSR artifact evaluations, in particular for enhancing the artifact design, and demonstrating the artifact's utility [53]. Focus groups can take an exploratory stance if their main purpose is to incrementally improve an artifact design, or a confirmatory stance if their main purpose is to confirm the utility of the design [54]. Our implementation of the focus group approach followed the proposal of Tremblay et al. [54] with the slight modification that we set a stronger emphasis on the confirmation of the utility of the design principles rather than their improvement. Thereby, our evaluation focused on the design principles being identified as an additional guideline for enterprise SQA platforms (in particular: DP4, DP7, DP9, DP17, DP19 and DP22). Altogether, we conducted five focus groups. The focus groups consisted of participants from different industries, including car manufacturing, software engineering and consulting. Each focus group comprised between three to eight participants and all of them were familiar with CRM systems. The majority of the participants were end-users of the CRM system, mostly sales and back office personnel. In particular, some of the focus groups even were customers of the practice partner of the DSR project. In order to consider additional perspectives, we also made sure that each focus group included IT professionals, such as IT support employees. Each focus group was held on premise of the corresponding company. Each session started with a 30 minutes introduction to the prototype and a subsequent question and answer session. Afterwards the participants discussed each design principle. The moderator guided the discussion by making sure the participants remained focused and that each design principles was addressed properly.

Collected data included audio recordings of the whole session and notes that were taken during the sessions by two researchers. Subsequent to each focus group discussion, the data were analyzed and key findings and statements were extracted and linked to a particular design principle. Similar statements were then grouped and generalized. Afterwards, we applied the dimensions of the SWOT matrix to categorize each statement as a strength, weakness, opportunity or thread. While the first two dimensions provided confirmatory input in whether the design principles had the anticipated utility, the latter two dimension provide exploratory insights into potential improvements of the artifact design.

5.2   Findings and Discussions

The evaluation of **DP4 – integration of organizational knowledge base** – supported the need for the integration of user-to-user support with organizational knowledge management. Participants criticized the increasing heterogeneity of current knowledge management solutions in their companies which requires additional effort to identify relevant documented knowledge. With regard to the integration of the user-to-user support by the yellow question mark in the Enterprise System, one participant stated *"When individuals face problems, it can happen that they feel alone; maybe they even cannot cope with clicking a button or opening another support system."* Some participants argued that a platform which centralizes and standardizes access decreases the effort of finding existing knowledge and in turn would become more useful to them. The focus group discussions further shed light on the type of knowledge required. Besides immediate knowledge to a particular problem, the participants expressed their need to access supporting knowledge, for example, manuals or process descriptions that allow them to better understand the context of a problem. However, participants also pointed out various issues related to amount and relevance of the documented knowledge. In particular, outdate knowledge poses a significant thread to the usefulness of the platform. The management of the actuality of the knowledge should be supported or handled by the system. The participants suggested several opportunities for improvement, such as alerts requesting the knowledge provider to update the knowledge item or the possibility to mark knowledge items as invalid. In her work, Allee [55] already realizes that knowledge *"has a limited shelf live and can quickly become obsolete"* [55, p. 10]. Therefore, researchers [e.g. 56] of the knowledge management community suggest to consider the maintenance as an important process phase within the knowledge management process. Thereby, feedback and rating mechanisms can ease the maintenance of knowledge, since these mechanisms enable the identification of knowledge that is rated by other users as important and up-to-date, while outdated knowledge will be rated as less important [57].

The evaluation of **DP7 – integration of business processes** – was two-fold. On the one hand, participants consider the integration of user-to-user support into the business processes as a major strength. A participant underlined this strength by stating *"A big advantage – I see – is the direct linkage to the knowledge base so that I can jump from the process I am actually working at to the according discussion – to the 'world of information'"*. In general, the participants argued that the easier it is for users to ask a question, to seek support, and/or to answer a question, the greater will be the acceptance and motivation to use the platform. In contrast to this, participants criticized the categorization of the problem along the proposed dimensions. First, they argued that the need to manually adjust or extend the semi-automatic categorization of a problem creates additional effort, and therefore may create additional barriers to seek or provide help. This barrier to seek or provide help will be even higher if the usability of the implementation is poor, according to a participant. Another point of critique was the current granularity of problem categorization. The opinions within the focus groups varied on the optimal level of granularity. Participants raised the concern that a low level of granularity might result in an unspecific set of problem solutions, where at a high level of granularity might be too specific to find appropriate solutions to a problem. Summed up, the design principle was perceived as useful. However, the details of its implementation require additional reasoning regarding usability, and can furthermore benefit greatly from advanced recommender algorithms to classify a problem.

The focus group also confirmed the necessity of **DP 17 – anonymous posting of questions**. Participants argued that such a feature will lower the barriers to ask and answer questions in an organizational context. They reason that knowledge seekers or experts can avoid potential negative consequences if they are not exposed to the organization in their posts. However, the focus groups also pointed out that anonymity impedes the evaluation of the quality of posts because users do not know the person providing the solution and therefore require an alternative quality indicator.

All focus group discussions confirmed the integration of enterprise social media (DP 9) as well as the provision of appropriate technologies and functionalities for collaboration (DP19) for the usefulness of the enterprise SQA site. According to the focus groups, many knowledge seekers, for example less tech-savvy users, feel more comfortable when solutions are explained systematically. The main weakness of these design principles are the potential distraction from actual work. The possibility to imitate a direct communication between knowledge seeker and knowledge provider can lead to a high amount of communication requests for distinguished knowledge experts, resulting in less time for their actual work. Participants remarked that experts should be able to select whether they are available for direct communication or prefer non-direct communication methods. Additionally, some focus groups suggested different levels of escalation in which direct-communication serves as the last resort when no other support, such as manuals and documented users posts, is available or sufficient to solve the problem at hand.

The evaluation of **DP23 – quality emphasis of game-based elements** – showed that the majority of the participants view game-based design elements as generally beneficial. The focus group discussions highlighted in particular the importance of the checkmark mechanism to validate the helpfulness of the provided knowledge. However, the groups evaluated the ranking of experts derived from the checkmark mechanism critically. Here, they remarked that companies could easily abuse the information on competences to identify incompetent users. While most participants agreed with regard to the potential risk of assessing employees purely based on their participation at the enterprise SQA site, one participant commented *"As I understood the system, I first formulate a question and then receive a list of users listed in keeping with the motto: 'Based on their experiences, these users can help you'. Thus, in fact there is no assessment of people"*. Nevertheless, despite the apparent importance of the rankings for the selection of an expert from a list of potential experts, most focus groups rather prefer fewer exposed details, even though their own capability to select an appropriate expert for direct communication suffers. Interestingly, the participants where less worried about the information on competences stored in the system than about the information on competences visible in the user interface. Furthermore, the participants suggested that users are also incentivized for continuous contributions to the platforms, for example, by designating badges or states. Thus, as already realized by researchers such as Lawley [58] or Laschke and Hassenzahl [59] the participants recognize the need to connect the gameful elements implemented in the system with a real-world outcome being meaningful for its users and the organization. Failing to do so will result in the opposite effect, the "pure pointification" [60] will not sustainably increase the users' participation in the system, as shown by Thom et al. [61].

To summarize, enterprise SQA sites are perceived as beneficial, since the IT infrastructure and the IS landscape is getting more and more complex and the SQA site actively supports employees in fulfilling their tasks. The support platform acts as a mediator between knowledge seekers and knowledge providers as well as between knowledge items and individuals. Consequently, the presented version of the enterprise SQA is desired by all participants of the focus group workshops. One participant, being a customer of our practice partner, even declared to introduce the enterprise SQA in his company in order to test the long-term effects of the platform because he was entirely convinced by the SQA usefulness for his company. Consequently, we forwarded the feedback collected in the focus groups to our industry partner in order to improve the design of the SQA platform.

6   Conclusion

In this paper, we present our research on the design and evaluation of an enterprise SQA site. While there exists quite some SQA sites for the private context (also referred to as public SQA), we could not identify research reporting the design of a SQA platform for an organizational context. In order to design an enterprise SQA site, existing knowledge on the design of public SQA cannot be used directly. Instead, the existing knowledge needs to be adapted and additional requirements addressing the specialties of the organizational context need to be considered. Therefore, we identified design principles for an organizational SQA site (also referred to as enterprise SQA site) by analyzing public SQA sites and literature discussing related concepts. Based on the identified design principles we designed a prototype of the enterprise SQA site being integrated in an Enterprise System offered by our practice partner. In our evaluation phase, the resulting enterprise SQA site has been assessed within five focus groups where participants provided feedback on the strengths, weaknesses, opportunities and threats of the design with regard to the underlying design principles.

At the moment, our practice partner refines the enterprise SQA by integrating the feedback received in the focus group. Subsequently, the enterprise SQA platform will be implemented within the company of one focus group participant. Because the participant was delighted to be integrated in the design and development process of the enterprise SQA platform, he agreed to conduct follow-up research within his company. Therefore, we plan to conduct a longitudinal study observing the usage of the refined enterprise SQA platform, the quality of the content (e. g. knowledge items) provided in the system, and users' satisfaction with the system.

We are aware that our research comes with some limitations. First, the design principles has been evaluated in a qualitative approach by conducting focus groups. While the application of focus groups is a feasible approach in order to receive first indications of strengths and weaknesses of the system, a long-term study is necessary in order to investigate the effects of the platform with regard to its real usage. We plan to mitigate this limitation in the next cycle of our DSR project by conducting a longitudinal study in the mentioned case company. Another limitation refers to the limited generalizability of our research results. At the moment, the design principles are extracted from public SQA sites and literature of related research areas, and qualitatively evaluated. However, in order to make statements regarding the generalizability of the design principles further research is needed.

Although having some limitations, we perceive our research as a valuable contribution for both, researchers and practitioners. Our research extends the existing body of knowledge by introducing evaluated design principles for an enterprise SQA platform. To our knowledge, there are currently no attempts to design enterprise SQA platforms in research. However, we perceive the implementation of such a platform as beneficial, since it addresses the issues stemming from modern IT infrastructure strategies of organizations such as BYOD or CYOD. Due to such strategies, the IT infrastructure in companies is getting increasingly heterogeneous making the support for employees from a technical and a procedural perspective highly complex. Consequently, our research addresses issues being relevant for practitioners. In addition, by evaluating our artifact within focus groups consisting of different representatives of practice, our research follows the call of Peffers et al. [62] for more research in collaboration with practitioners. By integrating practitioners in the evaluation and (re-)design phase, design theories can demonstrate their applicability in real-world environments [62]. The conducted focus group evaluation reported in this paper is the first step in proving the applicability of our findings on enterprise SQA in a real-world environment.

Acknowledgments. This paper was written in the context of the research project WeChange (promotional reference 01HH11059) which is funded by the German Federal Ministry of Education and Research (BMBF). Although, they did not co-authored this article, we would like thank our researcher colleagues Björn Niehaves, Kevin Ortbach, Sebastian Koeffer and Nikolai Walter of the WeChange project and our industry partner CAS Software AG.

References

[1] Baskerville, R.: Individual information systems as a research arena. Eur. J. Inf. Syst. 20(3), 251–254 (2011)

[2] Harris, J., Ives, B., Junglas, I.: IT Consumerization: When Gadgets turn into Enterprise IT Tools. MIS Q. Exec. 11(3), 99–112 (2012)

[3] Chamakiotis, P., Whiting, R., Symon, G., Roby, H.: Exploring Transisitions and Work-Life Balance in the Digital Era. In: ECIS 2014 Proceedings (2014)

[4] Forrester, Key Strategies to Capture and Measure the Value of Consumerization of IT, A Forrester Consulting Thought Leadership Paper Commissioned by Trend Micro, Cambridge, MA, USA (2012)

[5] Gens, F., Levitas, D., Segal, R.: 2011 Consumerization of IT Study: Closing the Consumerization Gap. IDC, Framingham (2011)

[6] Von Hippel, E., Lakhani, K.R.: How Open Source Software Works: 'Free' User-to-User Assistance? Res. Policy 32, 923–943 (2003)

[7] Kaplan, A.M., Haenlein, M.: Users of the world, unite! The challenges and opportunities of Social Media. Bus. Horiz. 53(1), 59–68 (2010)

[8] Kim, W., Jeong, O.-R., Lee, S.-W.: On social Web sites. Inf. Syst. 35(2), 215–236 (2010)

[9]   Boyd, D.M., Ellison, N.B.: Social Network Sites: Definition, History, and Scholarship. J. Comput. Commun. 13(1), 210–230 (2007)

[10] Kügler, M., Smolnik, S., Raeth, P.: Why Don't You Use It? Assessing the Determinants of Enterprise Social Software Usage: A Conceptual Model Integrating Innovation Diffusion and Social Capital Theories. In: ICIS 2012 Proceedings (2012)

[11] Meyer, P., Dibbern, J.: An Exploratory Study about Microblogging Acceptance at Work. In: AMCIS 2010 Proceedings (2010)

[12] Shipps, B., Phillips, B.: Social Networks, Interactivity and Satisfaction: Assessing Socio-Technical Behavioral Factors as an Extension to Technology Acceptance. J. Theor. Appl. Electron. Commer. Res. 8(1), 7–8 (2013)

[13] Davis, F.D.: User Acceptance of Information Technology: System Characteristics, User Perceptions and Behavioral Impacts. Int. J. Man. Mach. Stud. 38(3), 475–487 (1993)

[14] Venkatesh, V., Morris, M.G., Davis, G.B., Davis, F.D.: User Acceptance of Information Technology: Toward a Unified View. MIS Q. 27(3), 425–478 (2003)

[15] Zhao, L., Lu, Y.: Enhancing Perceived Interactivity through Network Externalities: An Empirical Study on Micro-Blogging Service Satisfaction and Continuance Intention. Decis. Support Syst. 53(4), 825–834 (2012)

[16] Lin, K.-Y., Lu, H.-P.: Why People Use Social Networking Sites: An Empirical Study Integrating Network Externalities and Motivation Theory. Comput. Human Behav. 27(3), 1152–1161 (2011)

[17] Cheung, C.M.K., Lee, M.K.O.: A Theoretical Model of Intentional Social Action in Online Social Networks. Decis. Support Syst. 49(1), 24–30 (2010)

[18] Cheung, C.M.K., Chiu, P.-Y., Lee, M.K.O.: Online Social Networks: Why Do Students Use Facebook? Comput. Human Behav. 27(4), 1337–1343 (2011)

[19] Muller, M.: Lurking as Personal Trait or Situational Disposition? Lurking and Contributing in Enterprise Social Media. In: Proceedings of the ACM 2012 Conference on Computer Supported Cooperative Work, pp. 253–256 (2012)

[20] Pöyry, E., Parvinen, P., Malmivaara, T.: Can We Get from liking to buying? Behavioral differences in hedonic and utilitarian Facebook usage. Electron. Commer. Res. Appl. 12(4), 224–235 (2013)

[21] Palmisano, J.: Motivating Knowledge Contribution in Virtual Communities of Practice: Roots, Progress and Needs. In: AMCIS 2009 Proceedings, Paper 198 (2009)

[22] Pi, S.-M., Chou, C.-H., Liao, H.-L.: "A Study of Facebook Groups Members' Knowledge Sharing," Comput. Comput. Human Behav. 29(5), 1971–1979 (2013)

[23] Harper, F., Raban, D.: Predictors of answer quality in online Q&A sites. In: Proc. SIGCHI (2008)

[24] Shah, C., Oh, J.S., Oh, S.: Exploring characteristics and effects of user participation in online social Q&A sites. First Monday 13(9), 18 (2008)

[25] Gazan, R.: Social Q&A. J. Am. Soc. Inf. Sci. Technol. 62(12), 2301–2312 (2011)

[26] Gazan, R.: Specialists and synthesists in a question answering community. Proc. Am. Soc. Inf. Sci. Technol. 43(1), 1–10 (2007)

[27] Tiwana, A., Bush, A.: Continuance in Expertise-Sharing Networks: A Social Perspective. IEEE Trans. Eng. Manag. 52(1), 85–101 (2005)

[28] Adamic, L., Zhang, J., Bakshy, E., Ackerman, M.S.: Knowledge sharing and yahoo answers: everyone knows something. In: Proceedings of WW 2008, pp. 665–674 (2008)

[29] Gazan, R.: Social Annotations in Digital Library Collections. D-Lib Mag. 14(11/12) (2008)

[30] Hevner, A.R., March, S.T., Park, J., Ram, S.: Design Science in Information Systems Research. Mis Q. 28(1), 75–105 (2004)

[31] Vaishnavi, V.K., Kuechler, W.: Design science research methods and patterns: innovating information and communication technology. Auerbach, New York (2007)

[32] Walls, J.G., Widmeyer, G.R., El Sawy, O.A.: Building an Information System Design Theory for Vigilant EIS. Inf. Syst. Res. 3(1), 36–59 (1992)

[33] Ortbach, K., Gaß, O., Köffer, S., Schacht, S., Walter, N., Maedche, A., Niehaves, B.: Design Principles for a Social Question and Answers Site: Enabling User-to-User Support in Organizations. In: Tremblay, M.C., VanderMeer, D., Rothenberger, M., Gupta, A., Yoon, V. (eds.) DESRIST 2014. LNCS, vol. 8463, pp. 54–68. Springer, Heidelberg (2014)

[34] Gregor, S., Benbasat, I.: Explanations from intelligent systems: Theoretical foundations and implications for practice. MIS Q. 23, 497–530 (1999)

[35] Petter, S., Vaishnavi, V.: Facilitating Experience Reuse Among Software Project Managers. Inf. Sci (Ny). 178(7), 1783–1802 (2008)

[36] Petter, S., Randolph, A.B.: Developing Soft Skills to Manage User Expectations in IT Projects: Knowledge Reuse Among IT Project Managers. Proj. Manag. J. 40(4), 45–59 (2009)

[37] Al-Alawi, A.I., Al-Marzooqi, N.Y., Mohammed, Y.F.: Organizational culture and knowledge sharing: critical success factors. Journal of Knowledge Management 11, 22–42 (2007)

[38] Agichtein, E., Castillo, C., Donato, D., Gionis, A., Mishne, G.: Finding high-quality content in social media. In: Proc. Int. Conf. Web Search Web Data Min., WSDM 2008, p. 183 (2008)

[39] Anderson, A., Huttenlocher, D.: Discovering value from community activity on focused question answering sites: A case study of stack overflow. In: Proc. of the 18th ACM SIGKDD International Conference on Knowledge Discovery and Data Mining (2012)

[40] Gyarmati, L., Trinh, T.: Measuring user behavior in online social networks. IEEE Netw. 24(5), 26–31 (2010)

[41] Gazan, R.: Microcollaborations in a social Q&A community. Inf. Process. Manag. 46(6), 693–702 (2010)

[42] Goffman, E.: The Presentation of Self in Everyday Life. Anchor Books (1959)

[43] Walther, J.B., D'Addario, K.P.: The Impacts of Emoticons on Message Interpretation in Computer-Mediated Communication. Soc. Sci. Comput. Rev. 19(3), 324–347 (2001)

[44] Short, J., Williams, E., Christie, B.: The Social Psychology of Telecommunications. John Wiley & Sons, Ltd. (1976)

[45] Julian, J.: How Project Management Office Leaders Facilitate Cross-Project Learning and Continuous Improvement. Proj. Manag. J. 39(3), 43–58 (2008)

[46] Bista, S.S.K., Nepal, S., Colineau, N., Paris, C.: Using Gamification in an Online Community. In: Proceedings of the 8th IEEE International Conference on Collaborative Computing: Networking, Applications and Worksharing, pp. 611–618 (2012)

[47] Deterding, S., Dixon, D., Khaled, R., Nacke, L.: From game design elements to gamefulness: defining 'gamification. In: Proceedings of the 15th International Academic MindTrek Conference on Envisioning Future Media Environments, MindTrek 2011, pp. 9–15 (2011)

[48] Huotari, K., Hamari, J.: Defining gamification: A service marketing perspective. In: Proceeding Int. Acad. MindTrek Conf., pp. 17–22. ACM (2012)

[49] Peffers, K., Tuunanen, T., Rothenberger, M., Chatterjee, S.: A Design Science Research Methodology for Information Systems Research. J. Manag. Inf. Syst. 24(3), 45–77 (2007)

[50] Gorelick, C., Tantawy-Monsou, B.: For performance through learning, knowledge management is critical practice. Learn. Organ. 12, 125–139 (2005)

[51] Geister, S.: Effects of Process Feedback on Motivation, Satisfaction, and Performance in Virtual Teams. Small Gr. Res. 37(5), 459–489 (2006)

[52] Adomavicius, G., Tuzhilin, A.: Toward the next generation of recommender systems: A survey of the state-of-the-art and possible extensions. IEEE Transactions on Knowledge and Data Engineering 17, 734–749 (2005)

[53] Stewart, D.W., Shamdasani, P.N., Rook, D.W.: Focus groups. Theory and practice 20, 188 (2007)

[54] Tremblay, M.C., Hevner, A.R., Berndt, D.J.: Focus Groups for Artifact Refinement and Evaluation in Design Research. Commun. ACM 26, 599–618 (2010)

[55] Allee, V.: The Knowledge Evolution: Expanding Organizational Intelligence. Butterworth-Heinemann (1997)

[56] Tan, H.C., Carrillo, P.M., Anumba, C.J., Bouchlaghem, N.D., Kamara, J.M., Udeaja, C.E.: Development of a Methodology for Live Capture and Reuse of Project Knowledge in Construction. J. Manag. Eng. 23(1), 18–26 (2007)

[57] Dellarocas, C.: The Digitization of Word Digitization Feedback Mouth: Promises and Challenges of Online Feedback Mechanisms. Manage. Sci. 49, 1407–1424 (2010)

[58] Lawley, E.: Games as an Alternate Lens for Design. Interactions 19(4), 16–17 (2012)

[59] Laschke, M., Hassenzahl, M.: Mayor or Patron? The Difference Between a Badge and a Meaningful Story. In: Proceedings of the CHI 2011 Workshop on Gamification, pp. 72–75 (2011)

[60] Sjöklint, M., Constantiou, I., Trier, M.: Numerical Representations And User Behaviour In Social Networking Sites: Towards A Multi- Theoretical Research Framework. In: ECIS 2013 Proceedings, Paper 167 (2013)

[61] Thom, J., Millen, D., DiMicco, J.: Removing Gamification from an Enterprise SNS. In: Proceedings of the ACM 2012 Conference on Computer Supported Cooperative Work - CSCW 2012, pp. 1067–1070 (2012)

[62] Peffers, K., Rothenberger, M., Tuunanen, T., Vaezi, R.: Design Science Research Evaluation. In: Peffers, K., Rothenberger, M., Kuechler, B. (eds.) DESRIST 2012. LNCS, vol. 7286, pp. 398–410. Springer, Heidelberg (2012)

Real Time Bidding in Online Digital Advertisement

Shalinda Adikari and Kaushik Dutta

National University of Singapore, Singapore, Singapore
shalinda.adikari@gmail.com, duttak@nus.edu.sg

Abstract. Real time bidding (RTB) is becoming the key to target marketing where it could optimize advertiser expectations drastically. Not like the conventional digital advertising, in the process of RTB, the impressions of a mobile application or a website are mapped to a particular advertiser through a bidding process which triggers and held for a few milliseconds after an application is launched. To carry out the bidding process a special platform called demand side platform (DSP) provides support to advertisers to bid for available impressions on their behalf. This process has turned into a complex mission as there are many applications/websites that have come into the market. Mapping them to advertisers' target audience, and bidding appropriately for them is not a simple human mediated process. The complexity and the dynamic nature in the RTB process make it difficult to apply forecasting strategies effectively and efficiently. In this paper we propose an autonomous and a dynamic strategy for bidding decisions such as bidding price. We applied our proposed approach on a real RTB bidding data and demonstrated that our approach can achieve higher conversion rate with the target spend for a DSP.

Keywords: Real time bidding · Demand side platform · Bid price · Bid request · Impressions · Advertiser expectations · Target audience · Forecasting · Dynamic programming

1 Introduction

Real-time bidding (RTB) is considered as the new era of digital advertising. RTB is autonomous and algorithm driven, which completes a full transaction in milliseconds on pre-set parameters. RTB is a programmatic instantaneous auction, which allows impression buyers to launch their advertising campaigns via multiple ad-networks. It enhances online advertising while providing higher opportunities for advertisers to publish their ads and increasing the publishers' gain through competitive advantage. According to the recently published Online Advertisers Survey Report [5], among 650 advertisers 62% of them see improved performance as the main advantage of RTB; in addition, the trading desk spent on RTB, globally stands at 40%. Mainly, RTB helps to reduce the wastage of manual intervention; also it facilitates better target marketing strategies. Therefore, compared to static auction of digital marketing, RTB can add dynamism to the bidding process where advertisers are bidding for a specific single impression to optimize their expectations.

© Springer International Publishing Switzerland 2015
B. Donnellan et al. (Eds.): DESRIST 2015, LNCS 9073, pp. 19–38, 2015.
DOI: 10.1007/978-3-319-18714-3_2

RTB consists of many different challenges compared to the currently offered buying and selling policies in advertising. Mainly, as the name itself implies, RTB is a real time process that we need to decide our offer within less than 120 milliseconds [11], thus it makes obscure to practice highly complex and time consuming techniques for the decision making. Therefore, this study recommends a novel approach to decide the bid price of the RTB in ad platforms. The proposed model follows a dynamic programming (DP) algorithm to adjust the bid price based on the advertiser's target goals. We have tested our approach on the real mobile RTB campaign data and demonstrated its effectiveness.

1.1   Background

As shown in Fig. 1, RTB ecosystem has two sides, that is, advertiser side and publisher side. Each side has its own components and techniques in the bidding process [11]. The RTB allows purchasing individual impressions through a bid engine that unfolds within milliseconds when an application is launched by a consumer. Each step of the bidding process is demonstrated in Fig. 1 [11, 15].

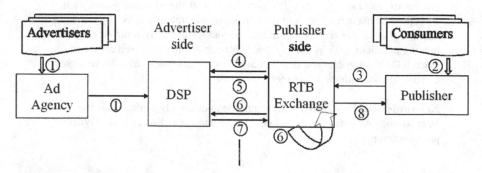

Fig. 1. High-level communication diagram between parties in the Open RTB Ecosystem

The RTB process can be explained further via the following steps,

Step 1:   Advertiser request a DSP to run an ad campaign for a particular product based on predefined campaign budget, target audience and campaign duration.

Step 2:   When the user interaction originates, the mobile app or the web browser sends user preferences, context, location and the mobile device/browser information to the publisher to fill up the impressions in the mobile app or the website.

Step 3:   Then the publisher will check whether there is a contracted advertiser available for the mobile app or the website based on the previous agreement and if that is still valid. Then the ad request is sent to that particular advertiser. If the quota is not available or the contracted advertiser is not interested in the new impression, then the ad request is sent to the RTB exchange.

Step 4: RTB exchange or sell side platform will create a bid request for the incoming ad request and send it to all subscribed DSPs (See Table 1 for content of a bid request).

Step 5: DSP will decide the bid price based on an anticipated ad campaign of a particular ad agency. All DSPs send their bid responses with the bid price for the relevant RTB exchange (See Table 1 for the content of a bid response).

Step 6: After a predefined fixed time period has elapsed, RTB exchange apprehends the auction and decides the bidder who has made the highest bid price as the winner through second bid price auction [6]. Then RTB exchange will send the win note to the winning DSP with the winning bid price (See Table 1 for content of a win note).

Step 7: DSP requests the ad from the ad agency and sends the ad response to the RTB exchange.

Step 8: The RTB exchange will forward the advertisement to the germane publisher and then users can see the advertisement on their mobile application or web page.

Table 1.0 provides essential details which are included in the bid request, bid response, win note and conversion note [11]. The bid request "id" is a unique identifier for each bid request which is created by RTB exchange and used throughout the RTB process. Additionally, DSPs create another unique identifier (adid, see Table 1.0) to track ad conversions.

Table 1. Details of the bid request, bid response, win note and conversion note in the RTB process

Field	Description
Bid request (Step 4)	
id	Unique ID of the bid request, provided by the RTB exchange.
timestamp	Time of the bid request initiated
imp	Describes the ad position or impression being auctioned.
site/app	Whether the ad supported content is part of a website or mobile application. Also, it includes information such as identifier, name, Domain, publisher, content and keywords which describe the site/app
Device	Information pertaining to the device including its hardware, platform, location, and carrier.
Geo	Describes the current geographic location of the device (e.g., based on IP address or GPS), or it may describe the home geo of the user (e.g., based on registration data).
User	Describes the user details such as year of birth, gender and user interests
tmax	The maximum amount of time in milliseconds to submit a bid (e.g., generally the bidder has 120ms to submit a bid before the auction is complete)
Bid response (Step 5)	
Id	Relevant bid ID which the response is mapped
Price	Bid value which is decided by the DSP

Table 1. (*Continued*)

currency	Type of the currency, which the bid is made
nurl	Win notice the URL
adid	An identifier that references the ad to be served if the bid wins and it is stated by the DSP.
Win note (Step 6)	
id	Same identifier as adid in the bid response
winPrice	Winning bid value which is decided by the RTB exchange
currency	Type of the win price currency
Conversion note	
impression_id	Same identifier as adid in the bid response
timestamp	Time which is the conversion happened (the time user views the advertisement)

As per the work flow of publishers and ad agency communication, DSP is bidding on behalf of the ad agency, to buy impressions from applications which have similar target audience as an advertiser is expected. An advertising agency is seen as any third party or in-house team which works on behalf of advertisers to broadcast their advertising performance. An ad exchange is responsible for deciding the winning criteria and delivering the winning notification, to the relevant advertisers through a DSP. The DSP facilitates the agencies by planning and executing the ad campaigns and analyzing the best possible investments on bidding, to improve the returns on investments (ROI) of advertisers. Among the different type of ad platforms which practice RTB strategies, the main two streams are web and mobile. Thus, almost all the RTB systems facilitate both platforms in parallel without much differentiation. Consequently, in this paper, we have used the term "application" as a common term to address any mobile applications or web sites that are incorporated with an ad platform. Before describing the details, we define several other common terms which are important in understanding the RTB ecosystem and is used throughout the paper. The advertiser target is a common term to denote advertisers' target spend, target audience and target number of conversions, all together. The target spend is the total dollar value an advertiser can spend in buying impressions during a particular campaign. The target audience of an application can be determined based on the characteristics of users, such as age, income, ethnicity, languages, has children, gender, education, etc. The conversions are also called actions and they reflect how users interact with the advertisements, such as clicks, calls, SMS, views, etc. The campaign period is the total duration of an ad campaign. To further understand the aforementioned terms let's consider an example. A DSP runs an ad campaign for a day targeting a Unilever Shampoo product called "Dove" towards a female audience. Here Unilever is the advertiser and Dove is the product. In this instance, Unilever will decide the target spend as $1000, the campaign period as a day, target audience as 100% female and target number of conversions as 2000 clicks.

1.2   Problem Specification

As explained earlier, at the step 5 in the RTB ecosystem, the DSP needs to determine the best bid price which can win the impression. If the DSP is not interested in winning the impression, then the bid price is mentioned as zero in the bid response. The key problem that we address in this research is, how to determine this bid price while achieving advertiser target. In relation to the above example, DSP needs to decide the most appropriate bid prices for selected set of bid requests which enable Unilever to achieve its target, among many such bid requests from many different applications with a different target audience and different wining rates, such that maximum return is achieved. The return is the numbers of actions (clicks) by the target audience at a given target spend.

As depicted in Fig. 2, we are able to gather information about applications' historical winning bid price, target audience and conversion rates using past ad campaign data. The objective is to target, applications which have the correct target audience, highest historical conversion rate and lowest historical winning bid price.

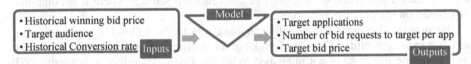

Fig. 2. Inputs and outputs

Currently, most of the DSPs carry out RTB via a greedy approach, where they try to achieve a higher number of conversions by bidding for the applications which have a relevant target audience. To increase their probability of winning, they manually decide a higher price than the known WBA (winning bid average). However, this is a very suboptimal strategy. Other prior researches focus on deciding the best bid price through a prediction algorithm [13], but as we demonstrated in this paper, due to the unpredictability and rapid variation in the RTB context, it becomes harder to predict.

1.3   Challenges

The main challenge of the research is the different dynamic aspects of the RTB process. The conventional bidding strategies completely depend on the number of bidders and their bids [4]. But in the RTB process, the dynamism exists over the number of bid requests received from each application; the different types of active applications in a particular period of time, the number of advertisers and their target spend and target goals. The target goals refer to the required number of conversions, duration of the campaign and the target audience. For example, in our dataset we identified that some mobile applications are highly active in a particular day with larger number of incoming bid requests, but in the next day, some of them didn't even appear and others had very less number of bid requests. Fig. 3 demonstrates the average number of applications that appear in DSP during different hours of the day in two adjacent weeks. As, can be seen, it is difficult to deceive any patterns out of it and so applying

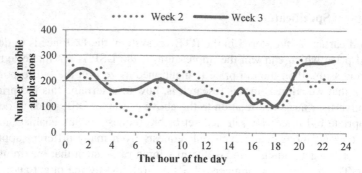

Fig. 3. The average number of distinct mobile applications which offer bid requests for DSP, in different hours of the day

any predictive logic could be futile. The difficulty of forecasting bid prices and number of impressions from the past data is elaborated in one of the following sections. Consequently, the bid price should be decided based on the advertisers' target spend, target audience and winning rate, not like conventional settings where it is computed only based on the previous bid price.

The problem becomes additionally complex due to the following two reasons of partial data accessibility [12]. First, unlike other auction systems in the RTB process, every winning bid price is not published to all the DSPs. Therefore a particular DSP have the data related to its winning bid prices only. RTB exchanges also publish the WBA for each application. However the WBA is computed at less frequency (such as every 24 hours) and is based on a longer duration of data (such as a week), which does not add much value other than aiding the current approach of DSP bidding – bidding higher than published WBA of a desired application. Secondly, the RTB exchange doesn't send all the bid requests to every DSP. The bid requests distribution is based on the agreement between the DSP and the RTB exchange. Both the above reasons make the global view of the RTB exchange unavailable to DSPs. As a result, we cannot develop a solution which considers the global view of the data. Any solution we design should be bound to the local view of the data i.e. from a particular DSP perspective only and will be run the DSP system.

The rest of the paper is organized as follows. The next section provides an overview for the prior researches on real time bidding strategies. Then, it explains the methodology and the dataset which is used to test the proposed models. After that each of the sections describes forecasting approach and dynamic programming approach in detail, including the problem formation. The following section describes the analysis of the dynamic programming model and its results. The last section provides the conclusion for the study.

2   Related Work

Rogers et al. [14] have proposed a probabilistic model while taking into account both the behavior of the users (advertisement viewers) and the advertisers. Their model endows a better exposure to the advertisers on the bidding strategy. The evaluation of the model was carried out via a simulation mechanism and its objective is, to identify the most appropriate bid value for each auction and to maximize the probability of having a larger number of impressions. In other research, impressions are allocated in a randomized fashion [7]. Hegeman et al. [8] have emphasized the important criteria to build a bidding strategy based on historical value of the impression, the time or date of the impression, total allocated budget, the identity of the entity requesting, the predicted likelihood the ad will be selected, the presence of social functionality, available budget, total number of impressions of the ad, and the remaining number of impressions to be achieved etc. Besides, in other research, a bidding strategy was developed by optimizing both the budget and the bid price, which guarantees the convergence to a locally envy-free equilibrium via greedy strategy [2]. A detailed elaboration is made by Yuan et al. [16] about the RTB strategy and comprehended on how temporal behaviors, the frequency and recency of ad displays would be nontrivial. Chakraborty et al. [3] have come up with a joint optimization framework through online algorithms and stochastic model to optimize the allocation and solicitations. Their solution is an online recurrent Bayesian decision framework with bandwidth type constraints. The work carried out by Li et al. [13] is very similar to the work which we proposed in this paper, except they did not consider an advertiser's target goal as a key parameter for the model. They also tried to predict the bid value while acquiring an impression at a lowest cost. Their strategy is based on a win rate model which predicts the win rate and the winning price based on a logistic regression model and then, they derive the bidding strategies from the resulted model. As, we have discussed under the challenges, none of the aforementioned research completely admit the dynamism which is embedded in the RTB process. These past solutions do not bind with the rapid real time decision making. In addition, all these solutions try to simulate the process of the ad exchange, but there is no solution which looks at the DSP perspective which is the key business entity in the RTB ecosystem.

3 Methodology and Dataset

Initially we have evaluated the feasibility of applying forecasting approach via Autoregressive Integrated Moving Average (ARIMA) to predict the bid prices and number of bid requests. Due to dynamism in the RTB process, the accuracy of the predictions was very low. Next, we developed a dynamic programming (DP) algorithm to bid for the impressions that operates over a set of consecutive time periods which are called bid periods spread across the total campaign duration. To achieve the best outcome, the algorithm follows a model which adjusts its properties for the next bid period based on the prior period behavior. The model consists of three steps – (1) budget allocation strategy, (2) bid price adjustment strategy and (3) application allocation strategy. The model will execute all these three steps at the beginning of a particular bid period and its outcome will be applied to the campaign execution during that bid period. Such a dynamic programming approach can adapt the bidding process in the RTB successfully. The performance of the algorithm can be adjusted by reducing the duration of each bid period.

To develop a model and test it empirically, we have preserved certain huge amount of data from an ongoing RTB process of a leading mobile DSP. Compared to previous studies where the model is examined with the synthetic data, the factual data has given a proper insight into the model. The dataset includes the data for three campaigns, each of 10 days duration, run by the DSP in August 2014. It includes 6,317,443 bid requests which are spread across month of August 2014. Table 2 depicts some of the details of these three campaigns and Table 3 provides an example actual data values from our dataset for the fields listed in the Table 1.

Table 2. Data difference among three days

	Campaign X	Campaign Y	Campaign Z
Total number of bid requests	2,209,864	2,113,487	1,994,092
Total distinctive applications	240	205	160
Winning bid average for the whole campaign $	1.06	1.15	1.08

Table 3. Actual values for the fields of bid request, bid response, win note and conversion note

Field	Actual values
Bid request	
id	9026174797775044599
timestamp	1402724400154
imp	"banner": {"top-frame":1,"id":"1","w":320,"btype":[1,4],"battr":[3,8,9],"hmin":50,"api":[4,3,5],"wmin":300
site/app	"id":"81134", "name":"AcacdemMedia Nail Manicure", "publisher":{"id":"194507","name":"AcademMedia"}, "domain": {"com.games4girls.NailManicure"}
device	"os":"Android","model":"SPH-M830"
geo	"zip":"10030","lon":-73.88476,"lat":40.73874,"city":"New York"
user	"gender":"M"
tmax	200
Bid response	
id	9026174797775044599
price	1.50
currency	USD
nurl	http://inneractive.mobilewalla.com/inneractive/win/${AUCTION_ID}/${AUCTION_BID_ID}/${AUCTION_IMP_ID}/${AUCTION_SEAT_ID}/${AUCTION_AD_ID}/${AUCTION_PRICE}/${AUCTION_CURRENCY}
adid	inneractive-9026174797775044599
Win note	
id	inneractive-9026174797775044599
winPrice	0.66
currency	USD

Table 3. (*Continued*)

Conversion note	
impres-sion_id	inneractive-9026174797775044599
timestamp	1402724433677

4   Forecasting Approach

In this section we verify whether the forecasting based approach can be used to determine the average winning bid price and number of incoming bid requests for applications. We segment the total campaign period in multiple bid periods. Next, to forecast the average winning bid price and the number of incoming bid requests of applications in a bid period, we fit time series to the historical values for all previous bid periods up to maximum one week.

We have considered Autoregressive Integrated Moving Average (ARIMA) technique for forecasting among many time series analysis techniques. This technique is a generalized version of Autoregressive-Moving-Average (ARMA) which can only applicable with time series data. Since the average bidding price of an application is a non-stationary series, we have to apply ARIMA while taking its successive derivatives until it meets a stationary one. In this technique lags of the differenced series appearing in the forecasting equation are called autoregressive terms, lags of the forecast errors are called moving average terms, and a time series which needs to be differenced to be made stationary is said to be an integrated version of a stationary series.

A non-seasonal ARIMA model can be written as

$$y_t' = c + \phi_1 y_{t-1}' + \cdots + \phi_p y_{t-p}' + \theta_1 e_{t-1} + \ldots + \theta_q e_{t-q} + e_t$$

where y_t' is the differenced series (it may have been differenced more than once). The "predictors" on the right hand side include both lagged values of y_t and lagged errors (e_t or white noise). c is a constant. This can be further classified as an ARIMA (p,d,q) model where:

- p is the number of autoregressive terms,
- d is the number of non-seasonal differences, and
- q is the number of lagged forecast errors in the prediction equation.

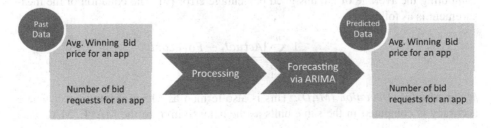

Fig. 4. RTB forecasting strategy

Initially we have begun the analysis by identifying the order of differencing needed to stationeries the series and remove the gross features of seasonality, in conjunction with a logging which leads to variance-stabilizing transformation.

In this approach, selecting appropriate values for p, d and q is difficult. Therefore, we have used the auto.arima() function in R which will automatically identify the best ARIMA model based on the dataset. This function uses a variation of the Hyndman and Khandakar algorithm [10] which combines unit root tests, minimization of the corrected version of the Akaike information criterion (AIC) for ARIMA model and the Maximum Likelihood Estimator (MLE). The reason to find the AIC is because it can help to determine the order of an ARIMA model. It can be written as follows,

$$AIC = -2log(L) + 2(p + q + k + 1)$$

Where L is the likelihood of the data with, $k = 1$ if $c \neq 0$ and $k = 0$ if $c = 0$. Moreover, the corrected AICc can be written as

$$AICc = AIC + 2(p + q + k + 1)(p + q + k + 2)T - p - q - k - 2$$

Once the model order has been identified (i.e., the values of p, d and q), we need to estimate the parameters $c, \phi_1 ... \phi_p, \theta_1 ... \theta_q$. To estimate them R uses MLE, because this technique finds the values of the parameters which maximize the probability of obtaining the data that we have observed.

Based on the output model, the prediction of the next bid period's average win price is carried out through the one-step forecast technique. One-step forecast can facilitate to predict the value of an endogenous variable in the current period by using the estimated coefficients, the past values of the endogenous variables, and any exogenous variables. In simple terms it can predict next period values while giving higher weight to the previous period value of the time series.

The forecasting experiment was carried out using the dataset which was described earlier with 15 minutes bid periods, i.e. bid price and number of bid request for each application are predicted at every 15 minutes based on time series fitted on past data. To generate the accurate time series data, we relied on at least one week's (seven days) of historical data. The predicted value at each bid period is compared with the actual value using few accuracy measurement techniques as described below. In each equation, t represents the bid period and n the number of total bid periods in a week.

Mean Absolute Percentage Error (MAPE): This determines the size of the error by computing the average of the unsigned percentage error [9]. The equation of the measurement is as follows:

$$MAPE = \frac{1}{n} \sum_{t=1}^{n} \frac{|Actual_t - Forecast_t|}{Actual_t}$$

Mean Absolute Deviation (MAD): This is also termed as Mean absolute error where accuracy is computed in the same units as the data. Similar to the MAPE, MAD also helps to conceptualize the amount of error [9]. The calculation can be carried out using following equation:

$$MAD = \frac{\sum_{t=1}^{n}|Actual_t - Forecast_t|}{n}$$

Root Mean Square Error (RMSE): This can be used to measure the differences between predicted values and actually observed values. RMSE is the standard deviation of the differences between predicted and actual values [9]. Following equation depicts how it can be computed,

$$RMSE = \sqrt{\frac{\sum_{t}^{n}(Forecast_t - Actual_t)^2}{n}}$$

Table 4 exemplifies the accuracy calculation statistics for the forecasting on both bid price and number of bid requests received for each of the 4 weeks in the dataset.

Table 4. Accuracy measurement for forecasting results

	Week 1	Week 2	Week 3	Week 4
Bid Price Forecast				
Mean Absolute Percentage Error (MAPE)	14.55	20.51	65.78	9.02
Mean Absolute Deviation (MAD)	0.11	0.14	0.41	0.11
Root Mean Squared Error (RMSE)	0.13	0.17	0.56	0.12
Bid request count forecast				
Mean Absolute Percentage Error (MAPE)	34.54	24.98	78.97	24.71
Mean Absolute Deviation (MAD)	20.05	19.64	17.44	12.66
Root Mean Squared Error (RMSE)	26.88	28.78	21.49	13.72

As per the results listed in Table 4, all the three accuracy measurements have very high values which reflect that the accuracy of the forecast is very low. Additionally, there is a considerable difference between the weeks' results, for an example, week 3 has smaller accuracy values than other weeks. This also indicates the unreliability of forecasting based approach in RTB bidding.

Thus above analysis demonstrates that forecasting the number of bid requests and winning bid price based on historical values has very low accuracy. Such forecasted values can't be reliably used for bidding by DSP in RTB exchange.

Following this we propose a dynamic programming based approach to determine the bid price and the number of bid requests from the each selected applications.

5   Dynamic Programming Approach

In this section we present a dynamic programming based approach, where we determine the bid price of each application to optimize the advertiser's target click (or other actions) with a given spending at each bid period. Before probing the details of the approach, a list of notations which are used throughout the rest of the paper is declared in Table 5.

Table 5. Notation for the model descriptions

Indices	
j	index for applications $j = 1, \ldots, J$
b	index for the selected applications for bidding $b = 1, \ldots, B$
x	index for applications' target audience characteristics $x = 1, \ldots, X$
d	index for advertiser's desired target audience characteristics $d = 1, \ldots, D$
t	index for a bid period $t = 1, \ldots, T$
Parameters	
S_t	remaining budget of an advertiser at bid period t
I_{jt}	total number of impressions available for application j at bid period t
P_{jt}	bid price for application j at bid period t
C_{jt}	conversion rate for application j at bid period t
Y_{xj}	target audience options for characteristic x on application j
Y_d'	advertiser's target audience option for characteristic d
J	total number of available applications to bid
X	total number of target audience characteristics
T	total number bid periods performed during an ad campaign period
B	total number of applications which have selected to bid
A_j	accessible target audience for application j
W_{bt}	target winning rate for application j at bid period t
P_{bt}	bid price for application b at bid period t
S_t'	budget allocation for bid period t
M_t	moving average on total bid requests at bid period t
MAR_t	moving average ratio at bid period t
V_{bt}	number of impressions won in application b at bid period t
Decision variables	
K_{bt}	number of impressions selected to bid from application b at bid period t

The Dynamic programming model is developed to achieve advertiser target by running the ad campaign during the whole campaign period. To utilize the full campaign period properly, dynamic programming approach divides the campaign period into equal multiple intervals which are called bid periods. As explained in Fig. 2, when the campaign is running, based on the previous bid period's data, the proposed dynamic programming model will determine the next bid period's target bid price, target applications and number of bid requests per app. The model mainly consists of three steps (see Fig. 5). Firstly, the campaign budget is distributed and allocated to the next bid period, based on the remaining number of periods and prior period's number of received bid requests. Secondly, based on the bid price(s) of the selected application(s) during the previous bid period, it adjusts the bid prices to obtain the target winning rate in the next bid period. Thirdly, the application selection strategy facilitates to identify the best possible applications which optimize the advertiser target through maximizing advertiser utility value with respect to the accessible target audience, conversion rate and the bid price. Since, these three steps are required to be executed, during each bid period; it depicts an autonomous and dynamic bidding strategy for the whole campaign. The duration of a bid period will be decided by the DSP, thus it could be on a daily, hourly, 30, 15 or 5 minutes, etc. Next we describe each of these steps.

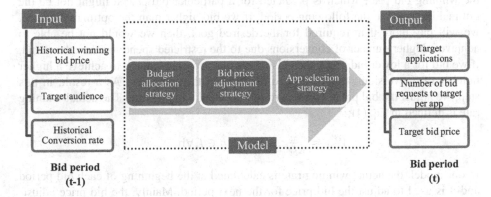

Fig. 5. Three steps of the auto pricing strategy

5.1   Budget Allocation Strategy

When a new bid period is starting, we need to allocate the target spend for each remaining bid period, depending on the previous periods' total number of bid requests received and the remaining target spend. As, real time bidding is a very rapidly changing environment; the number of bid requests which is received to a DSP can fluctuate in adjacent bid periods capriciously. To enforce this dynamism, we have calculated the moving average value of the total bid requests for each bid period until the last executed bid period.

$$M_{t-1} = \frac{\sum_{t-1} \sum_j I_{jt-1} \times t-1}{\sum_{t-1}} , \forall j \tag{1}$$

According to the Eq. (1), we have considered the index of the bid period as the weight of each period's total bid request. As a result, the current period has the highest weight compare to the previous bid periods. Using moving average value of the last period $(t-1)$ and the bid period before the last period $(t-2)$, we compute the Moving Average Ratio (MAR) for the current period as shown in Eq. (2). This will help to apply the recent changes of the received bid requests in the last bid period in the model with respect to the previous bid periods.

$$MAR_t = \frac{M_{t-1}}{M_{t-2}} , \forall t \tag{2}$$

Whilst, we have MAR for current period, then we can compute the budget for the next period as shown in Eq. (3),

$$S'_t = \frac{S_t \times MAR_t}{T} , \forall t \tag{3}$$

5.2   Bid Price Adjustment Strategy

In RTB, the winning bid price has a dynamic behavior which varies frequently. Thus the winning bid price which is predicted for a particular bid period might not be the optimal bid price in the following period. If we bid higher than the optimal bid price, we will pay more than required for the desired goal, then we would not be able to achieve a higher number of conversions due to the restricted spend; on the other hand, if we bid for a lower bid price, then also we would not win enough to achieve a higher number of conversions, due to limited duration of the campaign. As a result, in this step, we adjust the bid price with regard to the actual winning rate. The actual winning rate is defined in Eq. (4):

$$W_{bt} = \frac{V_{bt}}{K_{bt}} , K_{bt} > 0, b \in J, \forall b \tag{4}$$

In our model, the actual winning rate is calculated at the beginning of each bid period and it is used to adjust the bid price for the next period. Mainly, the bid price adjustment strategy is developed on the idea of maintaining a higher winning rate for a lower bid price. For instance, in a particular application, in a particular bid period if the numbers of actual winning bid requests are equal to the number of expected winning bid requests, it is possible to reduce the bid price. However, in many situations, the actual winning rate is lower than the expected winning rate, hence, to increase the wining rate for the subsequent bid period, we increase the last period bid price with respect to the actual winning rate for the last period. Furthermore, if the actual winning rate for the last period is zero for a particular application, then we increase its bid price for the next period by a constant value multiplication.

The new target bid price for the next bid period is computed as Eq. (5),

$$P_{bt} = \begin{cases} P_{bt-1} \times \alpha, & W_{bt-1} = 0, \ 1 \le \alpha \le 2 \\ \frac{P_{bt-1}}{W_{bt-1}}, & 1 > W_{bt-1} > 0 \\ P_{bt-1} \times \beta, & W_{bt-1} = 1, \ 0.5 \le \beta \le 1 \end{cases} \tag{5}$$

In the Eq. (5), we have defined two constants α and β, as thresholds to limit the scope of bid price adjustment. We have tested and proved their boundaries. Furthermore, as per the experimental results we have identified the best possible values for the α and β, as respectively 1.5 and 0.8. Apart from the bid price adjustment on the selected applications, the system also should keep track of all the applications and their details which generated the bid requests in the previous period. We apply the price adjustment strategy to all the targeted applications during the last bid period. Therefore, to condense the effect from applications which was not targeted in the previous period, we have updated their total number of bid requests in the last period as 1. Even the model selects such applications to bid in the next period, it can expect only one bid request to be bid. Resultantly, if such bid requests couldn't win, then the model will adjust their bid prices for the next bid period $(t + 1)$ and it will increase the probability of winning for the next period. The Eq. (6) defines this constraint. This strategy has been experimentally evaluated and the results are explained in the analysis section.

$$I_{jt} = 1 \quad j \notin B, \forall j \tag{6}$$

5.3   App Selection Strategy

Accessible Target Audience

In most cases, publishers provide the target audience for their applications to the DSPs based on user characteristics such as a percentage of males use the app, a percentage of different age groups use the app, etc. With such information and the advertiser's preferences, the following process defines the strategy to identify the accessible target audience. For example, if an advertiser requests to target his advertising campaign towards female users, then the best impressions to be published for such advertisements, are those, which belong to an application with target audience gender as 100% female and the worst case scenario is an application with 100% male target audience. In a similar way, if there is an advertiser who requires targeting his ad campaign for females who are aged under 30. Also, if there is a particular application with 60% female and 80% aged under 30 years as target audience, then accessible target audiences will be computed by the product of female and age group percentages (48%). Hence, the accessible target audience for a particular application is captured based on the product of relevant advertiser's target audience characteristics and it can be defined as Eq. (7),

$$A_j = \prod_x Y_{xj}, \quad Y_{xj} \in Y_d', x \in d, \forall j \tag{7}$$

Optimization Strategy

In the RTB process, the advertiser is looking for higher returns, through a higher number of conversions for his investments. Therefore, the goal of the model is to increase the advertisers' returns on investments (ROI) of buying impressions, by optimizing their target in all the available listed applications at a certain bid period. In the process of establishing the model, we can define a utility value to demonstrate the effectiveness of achieving conversions with regard to the advertiser target. The utility value can be determined based on the return rate. By multiplying conversion rate and accessible target audience, we can calculate how many conversions of the required target audience can be obtained for a particular bid value of an impression. Then, to identify the exposure or return per dollar, the return rate can be estimated as Eq. (8),

$$\text{Return rate} \quad RR_{jt} = C_{jt-1}A_j/P_{jt}, \quad \forall j, t \tag{8}$$

Since we have the return rate per impression, the value of an effective number of conversions per dollar can also be computed. This value reflects the utility value for an advertiser. Eq. (9), defines the utility value for the advertiser on a particular application j.

$$\text{Utility value } U_{jt} = \frac{C_{jt-1}A_jK_{jt}}{P_{jt}}, \quad \forall j,t \tag{9}$$

When maximizing the utility value we can increase the return rate and effective number of conversions that can be attained for a lower bid price. In simple terms, when maximizing the utility value we can access to higher conversion rate, higher accessible target audience, lower bidding price and higher number of selected impressions. However, when identifying the highest utility value among all the applications' utility values, we have to endure following constraints of the advertiser.

The first constraint, Eq. (10), is the number of impressions chosen from a particular application is limited to its total number of available impressions. As per the results of earlier section, we consider predicted value of the number of available impressions for the next bid period. Therefore, when selecting impressions to bid, the total number of impressions which can be selected is limited to the number of available impressions of that particular bid period. This should be true for all the listed applications.

$$K_{jt} \leq I_{jt}, \quad \forall j,t \tag{10}$$

The next constraint, Eq. (11) is, when selecting applications, the spending for all the impressions should be less than or equal to the target spend for the period. The mathematical formulation for this constraint can be defined as follows:

$$S_t' \geq \sum_j P_{jt}K_{jt}, \quad \forall t \tag{11}$$

However, since impressions are selected only from the applications which have maximum utility value, for the remaining applications, the number of selected impressions could be zero. Therefore, the constraint, Eq. (12) should hold,

$$K_{jt} \in \mathbb{Z}^*, \quad \forall j,t \tag{12}$$

Based on the above three constraints, the utility values can be maximized to find the most suitable applications which could optimize the advertiser expectations. As a fact, we can define the Eq. (13) to maximize the sum of the utility value across all applications at a particular bid period (t) while bonding through the constraints.

$$Maximize \sum_j U_{jt} \rightarrow Maximize \sum_j \frac{C_{jt-1}A_jK_{jt}}{P_{jt}}, \forall t \tag{13}$$

According to the value of K_j, we can find the actual number of impressions to bid for each application. The applications whose impressions are not selected will not be considered for the bid price adjustment strategy of the next bid period.

6   Analysis and Results

As we discussed in the prior section, the problem has been formulated using mathematical modeling, and we have developed a DP algorithm [1] to test the model. Since the model is developed in such a way that, each bid period's inputs are set based on the previous bid period's output, this can be implemented incrementally while adjusting the bid prices and target spend dynamically during the algorithm execution. The algorithm was coded using Java programming language and solution to the optimization problem is implemented using existing free and open-source Java library called Java Optimization Modeler (JOM). It offers a full pledged platform to model Java programs and solve optimization problems.

To evaluate the efficiency and effectiveness of the model, the metric, i.e. Target Spend per Conversion (TSPC), as Eq. (14) has been defined,

$$TSPC = \frac{\text{Target spend per campaign}}{\text{Total number of conversions}} \tag{14}$$

Align with formulated metric in the above; the objective of our analysis is to demonstrate that, the proposed model can accomplish lower TSPC while achieving higher number of conversions. According to Table 6, TSPC values for each different target spends increase, when the bid period is increased. To further understand this scenario, we have demonstrated it in Fig. 6. Comparing Fig. 6, (a) and (b), we can determine that, when the bid period is small (this means that higher number of bid periods), we can achieve a higher number of bids for a lower TSPC value.

Table 6. Model behavior at different bid periods

Campaign X		5 minutes		15 minutes		30 minutes		60 minutes	
		TSPC	conversions	TSPC	conversions	TSPC	conversions	TSPC	conversions
Target spend	$ 1000	0.14	6621	0.21	4555	0.28	3879	0.46	1988
	$ 2000	0.19	8961	0.23	6878	0.31	5006	0.51	2731
	$ 3000	0.22	9877	0.27	7543	0.33	5766	0.54	3104

However, when a particular bid period is considered, TSPC increases with respect to the target spend. That is because, when we allocate a higher budget for a campaign, the allocation for a particular period is also high. Since, the model has a lower granularity to select applications; it will also bid for the applications with higher bid prices to maximize the number of conversions.

As per the above scenario, we can demonstrate that, when the bid period is less, the model accuracy will be increased. Nevertheless, when the target spend is high, it will try to achieve more conversions from the applications with the higher bid prices. The insight from this analysis is, *when an advertising campaign is running in RTB, it is needed to maintain the bid period at a minimum level.*

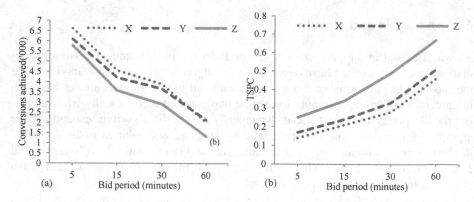

Fig. 6. (a) Conversions achieved vs. Bid periods and (b) TSPC vs. Bid periods in X, Yand Z campaigns

To validate the model with Eq. (6), we primarily look at how the model behavior would change based on the number of bid requests of the inactive applications, during the previous bid period. Resultantly, we test the model based on their last updated bid requests and updating them to single bid request and 100 bid requests. The analysis is performed for three campaigns when the bid period is 5 minutes. The results are listed in Table 7.

Table 7. Model behavior based on the number of bid requests of the applications which are not active during the previous period

	Based on last updated bid requests		Based on single bid request		Based on 100 bid requests	
	TSPC	# conversions	TSPC	# conversions	TSPC	# conversions
Campaign X	0.18	4883	0.14	6621	0.19	4412
Campaign Y	0.21	4411	0.17	6103	0.28	3631
Campaign Z	0.27	3867	0.25	5789	0.32	3347

As depicted in Table 7, we can get a better outcome, when the number of bid requests is adjusted to 1 for all the inactive applications during the previous period. Moreover, this provides added advantage, if the applications with a single bid request are selected by the optimization strategy, then based on their winning outcomes, the model can further adjust their bid prices and optimize the winning outcome for the next bid period. In parallel, when the bid price is increased, by 1.5 times for an application which couldn't win any impressions during the previous period the model provides two advantages. The first advantage is, its return rate will be reduced according to Eq. (13). This will increase the probability of bidding for another application with a higher return rate. Secondly, if it is still selected by the optimization strategy, then there is a high likelihood to win its impressions due to the high bid price. Insight of the analysis is to understand two techniques which help to increase the model performance; the first technique is, *assign the number of bid requests to 1 for all the inactive applications in the previous bid period* and the second technique is, *increase the bid price for all the unsuccessful applications in the previous period.*

7   Conclusion

In conclusion, we have made a few clear contributions in this study. First, we explained the problem of bid price determination from the DSP perspective in a RTB system. Second, we demonstrated that due to inherent dynamism in the RTB ecosystem, the forecasting based approach to determine the bid price based on historical WBA values will not work. Third, we presented a dynamic programming based approach to adjust the bid price of applications. We demonstrated how the parameters such as bid period and spend can affect the performance of applications. The proposed dynamic programming approach addresses the dynamism inherited in RTB process with a novel and effective solution while embedding autonomous bidding decisions into the RTB in advertising.

References

1. Bertsekas, D.P., Bertsekas, D.P.: Dynamic programming and optimal control, vol. 1(2). Athena Scientific, Belmont (1995)
2. Chaitanya, N., Narahari, Y.: Optimal equilibrium bidding strategies for budget constrained bidders in sponsored search auctions. Operational Research 12(3), 317–343 (2012)
3. Chakraborty, T., Even-Dar, E., Guha, S., Mansour, Y., Muthukrishnan, S.: Selective call out and real time bidding. In: Saberi, A. (ed.) WINE 2010. LNCS, vol. 6484, pp. 145–157. Springer, Heidelberg (2010)
4. Cui, X., Lai, V.S.: Bidding strategies in online single-unit auctions: Their impact and satisfaction. Information & Management 50(6), 314–321 (2013)
5. Econsultancy 2013. Online Advertising Survey (2013), https://econsultancy.com/reports/online-advertising-survey/
6. Edelman, B., Ostrovsky, M., Schwarz, M.: Internet advertising and the generalized second price auction: Selling billions of dollars worth of keywords. National Bureau of Economic Research (2005)
7. Ghosh, A., McAfee, P., Papineni, K., Vassilvitskii, S.: Bidding for representative allocations for display advertising. In: Leonardi, S. (ed.) WINE 2009. LNCS, vol. 5929, pp. 208–219. Springer, Heidelberg (2009)
8. Hegeman, J., Yan, R., Badros, G.J.: Budget-based advertisement bidding, US Patent US20130124308 A1 (2011)
9. Hyndman, R.J., Koehler, A.B.: Another look at measures of forecast accuracy. International Journal of Forecasting 22(4), 679–688 (2006)
10. Hyndman, R.J., Khandakar, Y.: Automatic time series for forecasting: the forecast package for R (No. 6/07). Monash University, Department of Econometrics and Business Statistics (2007)

11. IAB 2014, Openrtb api specification version 2.2., http://www.iab.net/media/file/OpenRTBAPISpecificationVersion2_2.pdf
12. King, M., Mercer, A.: Problems in determining bidding strategies. Journal of the Operational Research Society, 915–923 (1985)
13. Li, X., Guan, D.: Programmatic Buying Bidding Strategies with Win Rate and Winning Price Estimation in Real Time Mobile Advertising. In: Tseng, V.S., Ho, T.B., Zhou, Z.-H., Chen, A.L.P., Kao, H.-Y. (eds.) PAKDD 2014, Part I. LNCS, vol. 8443, pp. 447–460. Springer, Heidelberg (2014)
14. Rogers, A., David, E., Payne, T.R., Jennings, N.R.: An advanced bidding agent for advertisement selection on public displays. In: Proceedings of the 6th International Joint Conference on Autonomous Agents and Multiagent Systems, p. 51. ACM (2007)
15. Yahalom, et al.: Bidding for impressions, U.S. Patent Application 13/282,489 (2011)
16. Yuan, S., Wang, J., Zhao, X.: Real-time bidding for online advertising: measurement and analysis. In: Proceedings of the Seventh International Workshop on Data Mining for Online Advertising, p. 3. ACM (2013)

Information System Design Space for Sustainability

Moyen Mohammad Mustaquim$^{(\boxtimes)}$ and Tobias Nyström

Uppsala University, Uppsala, Sweden
{moyen.mustaquim,tobias.nystrom}@im.uu.se

Abstract. The interdisciplinary nature of human-computer interaction (HCI) makes it possible to contribute towards an improved thinking in design and the process of information system designs. It is, however, a challenging aim, because the transformation of different gathered knowledge from HCI to information system designers is not easy, there being multiple design solutions available. In this paper a design space for designing an information system aimed at sustainability is introduced and discussed. The design space could be seen as part of a new design process, or correlating with an existing design setting and consisting of nine different components that are explored elaborately through a design space analysis. Differently selected dimensions of the proposed design space imitate knowledge from HCI and the result thus reflects a support for successfully transferring knowledge from HCI to the information system (IS) designers for improving a design process.

Keywords: Information system design space · Sustainability · Design space

1 Introduction

The quest for sustainability is an omnipresent theme in research today. The sustainability problem could hence be undertaken by many research fields and many partial solutions developed in these fields could together make an impact and a significant change. The designing of artifacts, e.g. socio-technical systems like the information system (IS), is one of the predominant duties of human-computer interaction (HCI) and HCI is considered to be multidisciplinary. While HCI and IS can greatly use each other's knowledge, some cultural problems in fact prevent this from happening and even IS itself has its own research issues to handle regarding HCI [5]. Using design science to construct artificial creations is prescriptive research aimed at increasing system performance [19] and also may be used to solve human problems [15]. Thus, not only the HCI research community but also the IS research community stress the importance of design, e.g. Benbasat and Zmud [1] state that design is important. The designed system could therefore extend our problem-solving capabilities or, as Engelbart [4] writes, might bootstrap human intelligence. With a goal like sustainability to be achieved by IS design, there could be numerous design options in the hands of a designer. To realize different design dimensions is therefore important for the quality and success of a design for achieving the associated goals. The various available possibilities of design are seen within the concept of a design space, which

© Springer International Publishing Switzerland 2015
B. Donnellan et al. (Eds.): DESRIST 2015, LNCS 9073, pp. 39–54, 2015.
DOI: 10.1007/978-3-319-18714-3_3

is usually specifically intended for a particular product or process. The satisfactory formation of a design space is crucial for the success of a design and it is possible to explore different capabilities in design by making an analysis of design space [8]. Although there has evidently been research on how to design IS for sustainability, the focus has primarily remained within the scope of formulating new design principles, frameworks, and processes [17]. An absence of design space thus limits the scope for IS designers, who could otherwise resolve system design with sustainability. This was the rationale behind the research question of this paper: 'What are the dimensions of the design space of an IS design for sustainability?' As an answer to this question we conceived the proposal of a design space for IS design for sustainability by using a design space analysis. The proposed design space is structured and supported by the theoretical foundation and design concepts from HCI, thereby indicating the possibility of using knowledge from HCI to assist the issues of IS design. Theory, as a desirable output of design research, was identified by Walls et al. [24], and this paper contributes a matter of concept in this respect. Evaluation of the design is essential [21] which in this paper is made by following Halsteadt [6] in quantifying the properties of design process in a complexity measurement. This paper is structured into six sections. After this introduction, Section 2 briefly provides the background of sustainability within the context of IS design and elaborates the notion of design space. Section 3 displays the analysis of design space, illustrating and describing our proposed design space. Section 4 demonstrates a complexity analysis as an evaluation of the proposed design space. Discussions and future work possibilities are then presented in Section 5, followed in Section 6 by the conclusions drawn.

2   Background

2.1   Information System Design for Sustainability

The essential concept of this paper is to understand the design of an IS for sustainability by using a multidisciplinary HCI approach. The definition of 'sustainability' is not consistent everywhere, but varies depending on the research field and personal cognition and context. The focus of HCI and IS research is frequently one-dimensional and preoccupied with environmental sustainability [17]. In previous research the notion of Elkington's triple bottom line (TBL) [3] and Walker's quadruple bottom line (QBL) [23] have been acknowledged since many dimensions of sustainability must be considered. For example, the QBL acknowledged that sustainability could be related to social, environmental, practical, personal, and spiritual needs and that economic concerns only mediate the ability to satisfy those needs. Also, the dynamic interplay between the different dimensions is important. It is thus easy to harvest obvious low haning fruits, such as the reduction of energy in a device or system, but on the other hand, we might use it more and thereby not act in a totally sustainable fashion. For example, a smart home is often viewed to be sustainable at first glance [7], [18], [20] although the cost of the whole system is not always considered. It is possible to reverse or minimize the effects of different processes that impact sustainability. The rationale for this research is, therefore, that the knowledge of design space is crucial, giving options on how to design IS for sustainability, moving the IS design research frontier forward. To achieve this, a multidisciplinary approach like HCI is needed, since sustainability issues are very complex and dynamic. A holistic viewpoint is thereby needed. Therefore, establishing the design space for IS for sustainability could have huge implications for future systems and their ability to reach a specific set of sustainability goals.

2.2   Design Space and Its Importance

One of the primary reasons for using design space is the assurance of quality when a design space itself defines the operational flexibility. The design space could also be seen as a conceptual space of various plausible design possibilities. Bisjakar et al. [2], defined "design space" as a construct which is developed by the designer's own knowledge and experience in response to diverse external conditions. Design space analysis (DSA) is an established approach of looking into a design to act as a bridge between theoretical and practical design issues. DSA is an argumentation-based approach to design [8]. Frequently DSA is used in design rationale as a method of discovering why some possibilities were chosen during the design process [2] by using a protocol called "QOC" (questions, options, and criteria [9].) However, a design space is not a static construct and it may change through the cumulative knowledge learned by the designers together with the different conditions of a design project [2]. Therefore, understanding the proper combination and different interactions of variables as process parameters may be seen as the most important rationale behind creating a proper design space. The designers must decide how the design space should be described; it might vary from simple representation of changeable combinations to numerous complex mathematical relationships. However, the addressed design space in this paper is a reflection of the use of interdisciplinary HCI design knowledge for helping IS designers to realize how IS could be designed for sustainability. The design space described below is therefore in the form of a combination of different variables to achieve the success of IS design for sustainability.

3   Proposed IS Design Space for Sustainability

By using DSA, it would be possible to explore and comprehend the requirements of a design space aiming at IS design for sustainability (nine dimensions were identified as important for this). These dimensions were structured into four top-level dimensions' categories and were the results of a QOC analysis that was followed as in Figure 1. The QOC analysis for deriving the four top-level dimensions is displayed in Figure 2.

During a QOC analysis three operands are used, namely: questions, options, and criteria. Questions are taken from the information drawn from the scenario to explore. In our research the scenario consists of designing IS for sustainability. Often the hardest task in the QOC analysis is to find the question and help making it possible to use options to generate the questions in a heuristic way. We have used four ontological dimensions for the DSA, namely: information-collection, information-transformation,

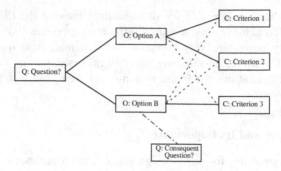

Fig. 1. Components of a design space using QOC notation (from [9])

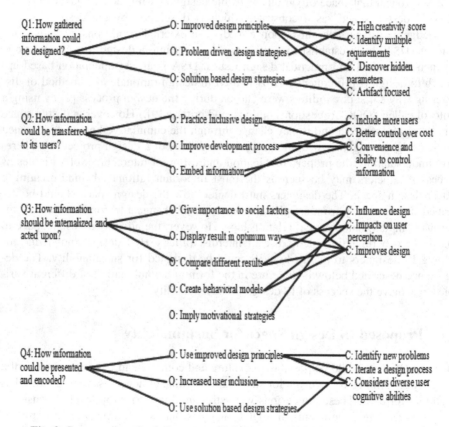

Fig. 2. Construction of a design space of IS for sustainability using QOC notation

processing of information, and information-presentation. These were selected as based on the standard information-processing method as the foundation. Questions were therefore drawn as based on these foundations. Next, we have "Options" that can be seen as answers to the questions. In Figure 1 we can see two different options to choose from: Option A and Option B. Option B generates a follow-up question that furthers more aspects of the design that may be considered. Options A and B have three different criteria that argue either for or against the possible options extended by the question (a solid line is positive and a dotted line is a negative relationship). Different IS design criteria were used to answer these questions, resulting with options from which it was possible to use heuristics to analyze criteria for selecting the correct options for a specific question. A total of thirteen criteria was used in this analysis (Figure 2). No negative criteria were used, since the scope of finding dimensions in a design space was focused on sustainability for IS, and not the opposite.

Based on our four ontological dimensions and the QOC analysis as presented in Figure 2, the four top-level dimensions of the proposed design space were summarized as follows:

How gathered information could be designed: Design Principles Dimension.

How information could be transferred to its users: User-inclusion, Development Process, and Embedding Information Dimensions.

How information should be internalized and acted upon: Behavioral models, Motivational Strategies, Social Factors, Presenting Results, and Comparison of the Result Dimensions.

How different information could be presented and encoded: User-Inclusion Dimension.

These four ontological dimensions and the identified nine principle dimensions were then shown to be supported by the seven sub-dimensions which the authors have identified from their previous studies of sustainability and system design in Table 1. These identified seven sub-dimensions should be considered to be the knowledge of HCI that could contribute to building IS design.

Table 1. Sub-dimensions of the design space and their sources

Sub-dimensions	Research Paper Sources	Research Contribution Type
Universality	[13]	Human-centered
Open Innovation	[12]	Human-centered
Persuasiveness	[14]	Human-centered
Cognitive Dissonance	[14]	Design Research
Design Life Cycle	[17]	Design Driven
Sustainable System	[10]	Design Research
Open Sustainability Innovation	[13]	Human-centered

The rationale behind using these seven sub-dimensions is that by their use human-centered design might be practiced in our design space. According to the design research quadrangle presented by Norman and Verganti [16], although the novel interpretation of meaning is not always possible, human-centered design (HCD) considers the practicality of design problems, which in return initiates and triggers incremental innovation. In this research our focused problem is the achievement of sustainability through an improved IS design. The meaning of sustainability is highly contextual, and to specify a novel meaning or to interpret this notion precisely is very difficult, if not impossible. Rather, it would depend on users and their current use of different artifacts. Diverse requirements would increase due to their use of the artifacts. On the other hand, our aim in this paper was never to innovate something totally new, but instead to make a contribution to the existing nature of the process of sustainability in IS design by supporting the argument of Norman and Verganti [16] on HCD, in that: '... the focus on current meanings and needs combined with the iterative, hill-climbing nature of the process, this approach serves to enhance the values of existing categories of products, not to derive entire new categories.' Besides, sustainability could be seen as a result of the different incremental development processes, justifying the rationale of using HCD for incremental innovation. Figure 3 below illustrates the design space resulting from our QOC notation. The four top-level dimensions supported by different sub-dimensions are discussed from Subsections 3.1 to 3.4. A theoretical framework for the design space is then shown in Subsection 3.5.

Fig. 3. A design space of information system design for sustainability

3.1   Information-Gathering

This dimension deals with the issue of information-gathering for the designing of the IS for sustainability. This could in a way be seen as the foundation of the design since the gathering of information will establish the designer's cognition and understanding of the context that surrounds the system. It is critical to identify the multiple requirements that probably will require comparison and must be weighted against each other because sustainability is a very complex issue. Something positive from one aspect could prove to be negative from another. It is also good to maintain high creativity since fresh solutions might be needed in order not to be rooted in obsolete thinking patterns. By using this unrestricted approach it should be possible to discover hidden parameters that might have an impact on the IS for sustainability, although it should also be stressed that the designer should not lose the focus of the design goal, namely the artifact that in the end will be the result of the design. The following dimensions in the process beginning with the information-transferring and ending with the information-presentation could require being iterated and returning to this dimension. Table 2 lists the associated sub-dimensions and their contexts with information-gathering.

Table 2. Sub-dimensions and their activities in information-gathering

Sub-dimensions	Actions in the Principle Dimension
Universality	Transferring views on universal design from a pragmatic to idealistic view
Open Innovation	Expanding the open innovation concept from simple to complex arrangements
Persuasiveness	Different cognitive model creation using focused and unfocused persuasion
Cognitive Dissonance	Controlling user's dissonance, through design to make information- gathering flexible
Design Life Cycle	Work on the definition phase of the design life cycle to understand the requirement
Sustainable System	Realize the meaning of sustainable system through the contextual information-gathering
Open Sustainability Innovation	Use an open innovation strategy for sustainable design outcome and imply the knowledge to understand users and their need in an improved way

3.2   Information-Transferring

The information-transferring dimension is about how the information from the IS for sustainability can be transferred from the system to the user (the reverse, how to transfer the information from the user to the system, is of course also important.) Here the practice of universal design is a cornerstone, since it will allow most users the ability to use the system with little effort and to find accurate information that they can use in their cognition; information that may be transformed into useful knowledge and will act towards the scheduled sustainable goal. It is crucial that the user has the possibility to control the information given to the system, such as security and anonymity since some information could be sensitive and should not be shared with others. Another issue concerns how to deal with the problem concerning control of expense, since information-gathering and storage of data could become costly. On the one hand, the technology to store data becomes cheaper, but on the other hand the process of collecting data becomes more intense and detailed, needing more storage. It might in that respect be seen as not acting in a sustainable way. Another problem is the amount of data that needs to be transferred. This issue could cause users not to use the system under certain circumstances, e.g. if high-speed internet were not available it could become costly and time-consuming to use the system. Table 3 lists the associated sub-dimensions and their contexts with information-transferring.

Table 3. Sub-dimensions and their activities in information-transferring

Sub-dimensions	Actions in the Principle Dimension
Universality	Practice inclusive design and make the information available for possible user groups
Open Innovation	Use open innovation policy as a method for information transformation
Persuasiveness	Design and develop persuasive system, keeping wide ranges of user groups in mind
Cognitive Dissonance	Control user's dissonance to act accordingly towards the sustainability cause
Design Life Cycle	Use design and development phase; iterate to go back to requirement phase if needed
Sustainable System	Embed the identified sustainability parameters into the system during design
Open Sustainability Innovation	Use open sustainability innovation to recognize information that is required to be embedded into the design of an information system

3.3   Internalizing Information and Acting Upon It

This dimension is concerned with how the user will proceed once the accurate information is delivered. Here social factors such as norms are important. If the delivered information is not consistent with the user's attitude and behavior it will create cognitive dissonance. Such a dissonance could be useful in some IS to initiate a change, e.g. persuasive systems (see Mustaquim and Nyström) [14] but in other kinds of system the dissonance could be damaging and might lead to people avoiding the use of the system since it has caused discomfort for users. Such issues could probably be analyzed by creating behavioral models and implying different motivational strategies. Table 4 lists the associated sub-dimensions and their contexts with information-processing.

To act upon gathered information and the internalization of information, universal design can play a different role. Although universal design will not be used to design something in this dimension, it still may be viewed in a pragmatic way to analyze and centralize the gathered information in an improved way leaving an impact on changing user behavior. Understanding different types of users is important and universal design can be of use to the designers in realizing this. While open innovation in this dimension can make more people be involved in the process, open sustainability innovation can create new norms for triggering the preferred behavior. Realizing how a cognitive model would influence persuasion is important and will require iteration in the design life cycle to align different parameters for sustainability according to the user's requirements and views.

Table 4. Sub-dimensions and their activities on information internalization and action

Sub-dimensions	Actions on the Principle Dimension
Universality	Universal design could be used in a pragmatic way to find effective and efficient ways to change the behavior
Open Innovation	Use open innovation to get more people involved in reaching the sustainable goal
Persuasiveness	Understand cognitive model influence persuasion
Cognitive Dissonance	Depending on the system's function and goal it could trigger a change of behavior
Design Life Cycle	Changes in the context could make it needed to update or change information in the system requiring a need of iteration
Sustainable System	Make the sustainability parameters align with the user's beliefs
Open Sustainability Innovation	Use open innovation strategy to include external stakeholders and thus put an emphasis on creating a new norm that accentuates the preferred behavior

3.4   Information-Presenting

Information-presentation is crucial since the wrong demonstration of information could make it impossible for the user to acquire the information. The user could hence act incorrectly and opposed to how the system's sustainability goal was set. There is probably no optimum way in which to present the information; instead many optimum ways exist, and the system must be ready for depending on the users. Some users might require a lot of text information while others might prefer a visual display of the information. Here it would be of uttermost importance to include as many users as possible to be able to analyze their behavior and their differences in cognitive abilities. Based on this, the cognitive model could be redesigned by focusing on multiple user needs. Using diversified information-presentation the persuasion of the users becomes easier. Universal design concept in this case thus plays an important role for user inclusiveness. Open innovation can discover different users' choices for the specific product or goal regarding information, and how users would like to be presented with the result. Open sustainability innovation at the same time could be a key to realizing this in the context of sustainable products or design. If any information needs to be updated a change in the design is consequently required. The system development life cycle can be used in the evaluation phase for altering any design issues for achieving specific goals. One example would be when a system is used in different devices that present information in different screen resolutions; the text may be easily read on one device but become very difficult to read on another. Table 5 lists the associated sub-dimensions and their contexts with information-presentation.

Table 5. Sub-dimensions and their activities on information presentation

Sub-dimensions	Actions on the Principle Dimension
Universality	Use universal design to fully comprehend all the difference and obstacles that information-presentation could cause for some users
Open Innovation	More stakeholders involved should make the presentation of information better and more diversified for users to grasp
Persuasiveness	Keep the presentation diversified to make the persuasion more easy
Cognitive Dissonance	Difference in cognitive preference of information-presentation will be needed to be carefully considered and observed
Design Life Cycle	Make the maintenance, needed updates, and changes easy to do for improved result presentation
Sustainable System	Use the information-presentation in a positive way to commit the user to the system
Open Sustainability Innovation	Keep the information as simple as possible without losing its importance

3.5   A Theoretical Framework for the IS Design Space

In Figure 4 a theoretical framework for the proposed design space was presented. The problem-identification phase initiates information-gathering and thorough infor-mation-presentation in a design; the sustainability goals aimed at by IS are reflected (the gathered information is transformed and processed before the presentation.) We also have the discussed HCI Knowledge Space that is built from the seven sub-dimensions to support four top-level ontological dimensions. It is important to note that new knowledge gathered from the HCI Knowledge Space contributes to each of the four top-level information phases (see Sections 3.1 to 3.4.) It is not important, however, to follow different phases of the design space sequentially and a specific dimension from the HCI Knowledge Space can start any of the four phases to contin-ue further. The proposed framework should not be interpreted as a design process. This framework, however, can be used to support the design process of an IS for sus-tainability. Also, it is here important to mention the nature of sustainability goals which should be considered to be contextual. As mentioned earlier, sustainability is a complex and contextual issue. The proposed design space is certainly inadequate to cover all aspects of sustainability issues for IS. This theoretical framework should thus not be interpreted as a universal framework for design space. Therefore, rather than narrowing the scope exclusively within the economic or social dimensions of sustainability, the specification of sustainability problems could be contextualized according to the need for the successful use of the proposed design space.

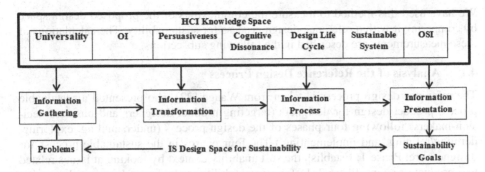

Fig. 4. A theoretical framework for the IS design space for sustainability

4   Complexity Measurement

The properties of a design process can be quantified by identifying the possible associated operators and operands as described by Halstead [6]. For a finite set of operators and operands denoted by Ω, the standard measure in a design is described as follows:

ρ: unique number of operators, N: unique number of operands
N_1:   total number of occurrences of operators
N_2:   total number of occurrences of operands
The size of the string is defined by,

$$\eta = \rho + N .\tag{1}$$

The length of the design form is,

$$L = N_1 + N_2 .\tag{2}$$

Structural information content,

$$H = L \log_2 \eta .\tag{3}$$

Minimal information content for denoting a design's most compact representation is,

$$H^* = (N+2) \log_2 (2+N_2) .\tag{4}$$

The level of abstraction for a design form is,

$$A = H^*/H .\tag{5}$$

The effort required to comprehend the design form is,

$$E = 1/A . H .\tag{6}$$

The time complexity measure is,

$$T = H^2/H^* . S .\tag{7}$$

We have used this method to measure the complexities of the proposed design space by comparing it with a reference design process for sustainability. The calculations of these measurements are described in the following subsections.

4.1   Analysis of the Reference Design Process

The reference design process is taken from Waage [22] who presented a sustainable process-product design for designers (targeting product designers and business decision-makers) following four phases of the design process (understanding, exploring, defining/refining, and implementing.) The four phases in the sustainable process for designers are: Phase 1: Establish the sustainability context by looking at issues related to a product or client. Phase 2: Define sustainability issues by analyzing and mapping sustainability. Phase 3: Assess by considering different pathways and their relation to a set sustainable goal. Phase 4: Act and receive feedback by making the product or service and then evaluate and assess it in terms of sustainability.

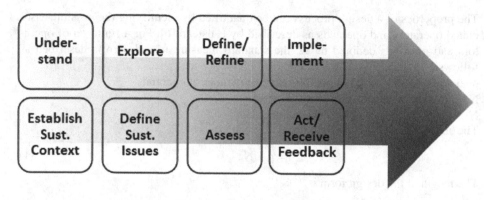

Fig. 5. A reference design process for sustainability (from [22])

The design process in Figure 5 can be represented using the following form of first-order predicate calculus:

$(\forall x)(\text{UNDERSTAND}(x) \Rightarrow \text{CONTEXT}(x)) \wedge (\forall x) \text{SUSISSUES (EXPLORE, x)} \wedge$
$((\forall x) \text{DEFINE (ASSESS, x)} \vee (\forall x) \text{REFINE (ASSESS, x)}) \wedge (\forall x \text{ (IMPLE-}$
$\text{MENT}(x) \rightarrow \exists y. \text{ ACT (y, x))}, \wedge \forall x \text{ (IMPLEMENT}(x) \rightarrow \exists y. \text{ FEEDBACK (y, x)))}$
From the equations 1 to 7 we calculate the following:

$\rho = 9$, $N = 11$, $N_1 = 61$ and $N_2 = 22$
$\eta = \rho + N \Rightarrow 9+11 \Rightarrow 20$
$L = N_1 + N_2 \Rightarrow 61+22 \Rightarrow 83$
$H = L \log_2 \eta \Rightarrow 83 \log_2 20 \Rightarrow 358.643$
$H^* = (N+2) \log_2 (2+N_2) \Rightarrow 22 \log_2 24 \Rightarrow 100.76$
$A = H^*/H = 100.76/358.643 \Rightarrow 0.280$
$E = 1/A.H \Rightarrow (1/0.280)X 358.643 \Rightarrow 1280.86$
$T = H2/H^*S \Rightarrow (358.643)2/ (100.76 \text{ x}18)$ [considering $S=18$]
$\Rightarrow 128625/1813.68 \Rightarrow 70.91$

4.2   Analysis of the Proposed Design Space Framework

The theoretical framework of our proposed design space (Figure 4) could be summarized as the following first-order predicate calculus form:

$(\exists x. PROB(x) \wedge \forall x.(PROB(x) \rightarrow IG(x)) \wedge \forall x.(IG(x) \rightarrow IT(x)) \wedge \forall x.(IT(x) \rightarrow IP(x)) \wedge$
$\forall x.(IP(x) \rightarrow IPR(x))) \wedge (\forall x.(PROB(x) \rightarrow HCIKS(x))) \rightarrow (\forall x.(IPR(x) \rightarrow$
$SUSGOALS(x))$

Therefore by following the equations from 1 to 7 we get:

$\rho = 7, N = 8, N_1 = 82$ and $N_2 = 29$

$\eta = \rho + N \Rightarrow 7+8 \Rightarrow 15$

$L = N_1 + N_2 \Rightarrow 82+29 \Rightarrow 111$

$H = L \log_2 \eta \Rightarrow 111 \log_2 15 \Rightarrow 423.9$

$H^* = (N+2) \log_2 (2+N_2) \Rightarrow 10 \log_2 31 \Rightarrow 49.5$

$A = H^*/H = 49.5/423.9 \Rightarrow 0.116$

$E = 1/A.H \Rightarrow (1/0.116).423.9 \Rightarrow 3654.31$

$T = H2/H^*S \Rightarrow (423.9)2/ (49.5 \times 18)$ [considering S=18]
   $\Rightarrow 179693/891 \Rightarrow 201.67$

Table 6. Complexity measurement parameters for two design processes

Cases	ρ	N	η	N₁	N₂	L	H*	H	A	E	T
Using Reference Process	9	11	20	61	22	83	100.76	358.643	0.280	1280.86	70.91
Using Proposed Design Space	7	8	15	82	29	111	49.5	423.9	0.116	3654.31	201.67

As seen from Table 6, measurement of time complexity and the effort required to comprehend the design form of the proposed model is higher than the reference model as expected. However, the level of abstraction and the structural information content values for the proposed design space do not indicate a bigger margin when compared with the reference framework. It could be concluded from this analysis that since adding new dimensions from HCI in our proposed model increases its complexity and therefore more effort and time will be needed to imply the design space, it would still be possible to see the different dimensions from an abstract point of view of the design, keeping the structural information content-value controlled. Empirical analysis in quantitative study with statistical operations on data will further this conclusion.

5   Discussions

The design space of IS design for sustainability, structured using a DSA in this paper, has revealed some interesting points. As mentioned in the introduction, there may be many possibilities in designing IS for sustainability, and selecting the right one is a challenge. The proposed design space adds value to this issue by showing that there could be several alternatives showing different relations between them. An improved design solution was concluded here in the form of our proposed design space. It should be noted that the goal here was to represent the structure of a design only, and as McLean et al. [8] stated, QOC should not be considered as a stand-alone representation. The proposed design space should instead be considered to be a tool for the designers—at least at this stage of the research.

One weakness about the QOC analysis worth indicating here is that we considered only positive criteria. It would be interesting to see how different criteria that are considered to be obstacles to the design of IS for sustainability might change the QOC analysis. It would also be an interesting topic to explore whether it would be possible to categorize the negative criteria or not. Our research question could therefore be answered by stating that the dimensions in a design space of an IS designed for sustainability could be seen from our proposed design space, for which different sub-dimensions from HCI knowledge were used in a HCD approach to support the ontological dimensions of a design process.

A few words about evaluation are also worth mentioning here. The design space concept is extremely complex, but at the same time is a useful thing. It is important to note that the evaluation process as shown in this paper did not involve any users and was performed using complex mathematical models only. It was not within the scope of this paper to involve a large study of users.

The focus of the design space as presented in this paper could easily be generalized and contextualized, as mentioned earlier. Although our theoretical frameworks supporting the nine identified dimensions have originated from HCI research, we believe that the design space still should not be exclusively generalized to be HCI-focused. We believe that this paper is an example of how the multi- and interdisciplinary powers of HCI could be used as a cross section with other research disciplines like IS. The research question in this paper was formulated within the context of IS and sustainability, in which the domain of HCI research and the knowledge acquired from it was seen as a tool for resolving the addressed problem. Example of similar work could be seen in [11].

Similarly, the application and usefulness of the proposed design space also could be seen as a contextual subject matter. One typical example may be to use the design space in different phases of a system development life cycle aimed at sustainable IS development. Identifying new requirements may be seen as an important use of the design space, which can be applied to both the existing and new system developments. What a particular IS is able to do for different sustainability goals could also be identified and evaluated using this design space. It is, however, important that different parameters to the evaluation or identification should be limited within the selected or identified context of sustainability for IS.

One of the significant challenges of sustainability and its achievement by IS design might be the maintainability of the outcome. While the future work built in this paper's design space of IS for sustainability may be in the form of used case studies of existing systems and by analyzing them with the proposed design space, one important research would be in maintaining the design space itself. In doing this, verification of the design space would thus be the first step. The complexity measurement we have illustrated is based on mathematics and not on any user data, which might be seen as another weakness and therefore should be taken to the next step by running empirical studies. There is a large gap associated with a design space developed in a research lab and transforming the knowledge to a commercial scale. Therefore, during maintenance and the verification of the design space, new important variables could be identified. Further verification or maintenance study will introduce complex mathematical relationships, function, etc. for realizing the critical dimensions that must be either included or excluded. Only then could the design space be taken a step ahead within the context of multi-scale sustainability problems that could be achieved by designing IS accordingly.

6   Conclusions

In this paper a design space of IS design for sustainability was structured and proposed. The DSA method was used to identify a set of variables that were included in the design space. The design space was built on four principle ontological dimensions and supported by seven sub-dimensions originating from the previous research knowledge from HCI. The proposed design space was preliminarily evaluated in terms of the measurement of its complexity by using first-order predicate logic to comprehend it by comparison with a reference model. The rationale behind the formulation of design space lies in using interdisciplinary design concepts from HCI. The proposed design space is specifically for IS design for sustainability, which, according to the knowledge of the authors, is not evident at present. The proposed design space in this paper can bridge the gap between designers and policymakers to support the improved application of an IS for sustainability. Additional verification of the proposed design space would therefore be the next research step to advance the knowledge for IS designers.

References

1. Benbasat, I., Zmud, R.W.: Empirical Research in IS: The Practice of Relevance. MIS Quaterly 23(1), 3–16 (1999)
2. Biskjaer, M.M., Dalsgaard, P., Halskov, K.: A constraint-based understanding of design spaces. In: Proceedings of the 2014 Conference on Designing Interactive Systems (DIS 2014), pp. 453–462. ACM, New York (2014)
3. Elkington, J.: Enter the Triple Bottom Line. In: Henriques, A., Richardson, J. (eds.) The Tripple Bottom Line: Does it All Add Up?, pp. 1–16. Earthscan, London (2004)
4. Engelbart, D.C.: Augmenting human intellect: A conceptual framework, SRI Summary Report AFOSR-3223, Stanford Research Institute (1962)
5. Grudin, J.: Three faces of human-computer interaction. IEEE Annals of the History of Computing 27(4), 46–62 (2005)
6. Halstead, M.H.: Elements of Software Science. Operating and Programming Systems Series. Elsevier Science Inc., New York (1977)
7. Heller, F., Borchers, J.: Physical prototyping of an on-outlet power-consumption display. Interactions 19(1), 14–17 (2012)
8. McLean, A., Belloti, V., Shum, S.: Developing the Design Space with Design Space Analysis. In: Byerley, P.F., Barnard, P.J., May, J. (eds.) Computers, Communication and Usability: Design Issues, Research and Methods for Integrated Services, pp. 197–219. North-Holland, Amsterdam (1993)

9. McLean, A., Young, R.M., Bellotti, V.M.E., Moran, T.P.: Questions, Options, Criteria: Elements of Design Space Analysis. Human-Computer Interaction 6(3), 201–250 (1991)
10. Mustaquim, M.M., Nyström, T.: Designing Sustainable IT System – From the Perspective of Universal Design Principles. In: Stephanidis, C., Antona, M. (eds.) UAHCI 2013, Part I. LNCS, vol. 8009, pp. 77–86. Springer, Heidelberg (2013)
11. Mustaquim, M., Nyström, T.: An Iterative Information System Design Process for Sustainability. In: CHI 2015 Extended Abstracts on Human Factors in Computing Systems (CHI EA 2015), ACM, New York (2015)
12. Mustaquim, M.M., Nyström, T.: Design principles of open innovation concept: universal design viewpoint. In: Stephanidis, C., Antona, M. (eds.) UAHCI 2013, Part I. LNCS, vol. 8009, pp. 214–223. Springer, Heidelberg (2013)
13. Mustaquim, M.M., Nyström, T.: Designing Information Systems for Sustainability – The Role of Universal Design and Open Innovation. In: Tremblay, M.C., VanderMeer, D., Rothenberger, M., Gupta, A., Yoon, V. (eds.) DESRIST 2014. LNCS, vol. 8463, pp. 1–16. Springer, Heidelberg (2014)
14. Mustaquim, M., Nyström, T.: Designing Persuasive Systems For Sustainability – A Cognitive Dissonance Model. In: Proceedings of the European Conference on Information Systems (ECIS 2014), Tel Aviv, Israel, June 9-11. AIS Electronic Library (2014)
15. Newell, A., Simon, H.A.: Human Problem Solving. Prentice-Hall, Englewood Cliffs (1972)
16. Norman, D.A., Verganti, R.: Incremental and radical innovation: Design research versus technology and meaning change. Design Issues 30(1), 78–96 (2014)
17. Nyström, T., Mustaquim, M.: Sustainable Information System Design and the Role of Sustainable HCI. In: Proceedings of the 18th International Academic MindTrek Conference (MindTrek 2014), ACM, New York (2014)
18. Pierce, J., Fan, C., Lomas, D., Marcu, G., Paulos, E.: Some consideration on the (in)effectiveness of residential energy feedback systems. In: Proceedings of the 8th ACM Conference on Designing Interactive Systems (DIS 2010), ACM, New York (2010)
19. Simon, H.A.: Sciences of the artificial, 3rd edn. MIT Press, Cambridge (1996)
20. Strengers, Y.: Smart energy in everyday life: are you designing for resource man? Interactions 21(4), 24–31 (2014)
21. Venable, J., Pries-Heje, J., Baskerville, R.: A Comprehensive Framework for Evaluation in Design Science. In: Peffers, K., Rothenberger, M., Kuechler, B. (eds.) DESRIST 2012. LNCS, vol. 7286, pp. 423–438. Springer, Heidelberg (2012)
22. Waage, S.A.: Re-considering product design: A practical "road-map" for integration of sustainability issues. Journal of Cleaner Production 15(7), 638–649 (2007)
23. Walker, S.: The Spirit of Design: Objects, Environment and Meaning. Routledge, London (2011)
24. Walls, J.G., Widmeyer, G.R., El Sawy, O.A.: Building an information system design theory for vigilant EIS. Information Systems Research 3(1), 36–59 (1992)

Visionary Design Research:
Renewing e-government Support for Business Set Up

Göran Goldkuhl[✉], Anders Persson, and Annie Röstlinger

Department of Management and Engineering, Linköping University, Linkoping, Sweden
{goran.goldkuhl,anders.persson,annie.rostlinger}@liu.se

Abstract. To set up a new business can be a complex and demanding task in a
highly regulated society. There is a need for many contacts with and applications for permits to different public authorities. There exists e-government support for new businesses, e.g. business link portals with information and services
based on a life-event approach. This presented research contains formulation of
a vision for a renewed e-government support for business set up (an assemblage
information system; joined-up support for application processes; a reversed application process). This is characterized as visionary design research, which is
argued to be a legitimate research approach. The paper articulates a visionary
design research approach based on multi-grounding principles. Grounding of
the emergent vision is done in theoretical pre-knowledge, internally through vision coherence and empirically in identified problematic situations, articulated
goals and opinions/assessments from knowledgeable practitioners.

1 Introduction

Governments strive to support the setting up of new businesses. This general aim is
expressed in policies, advisory support and in IT tools of diverse kinds. In highly
regulated societies (as the European countries) it can be a demanding task to set up a
new business. For several types of businesses there is a need for many different permits in order to set up and run a business. A consequence of this is that many governments work with administrative simplification as a strong reform idea. To decrease
the administrative burdens for businesses is one pivotal governmental strategy, both
on a super-national level (confer e.g. a European initiative [1]) and a national level
(confer e.g. a Swedish initiative [2]). On the European level this has been partially
regulated in the Service Directive [3].This regulation states that, in each country, there
should be digital "Points of Single Contacts" (PSC) for service businesses when interacting with public authorities. This means that business link portals have been established and developed in most European countries[1] as significant tools for government
to business interaction (G2B).

In Sweden there exists, since several years, a business link portal, verksamt.se,
which contains information and services for businesses, especially in the set up phase.

---

[1] An overview of such single points of contacts can be found at:
http://ec.europa.eu/internal_market/eu-go/index_en.htm.

© Springer International Publishing Switzerland 2015
B. Donnellan et al. (Eds.): DESRIST 2015, LNCS 9073, pp. 55–70, 2015.
DOI: 10.1007/978-3-319-18714-3_4

However, this web portal has had a rather limited use. It has several visitors obtaining general information about how to start and run a business, but the use of different application services seems to be fairly low. One conclusion is that the service level on this business link portal is too low. Although the web portal is conceived to be a national portal that assembles and contains information and service to businesses, there exist many other websites with information and services to businesses. Verksamt.se operates in a complex digital landscape with many competitive digital resources. Business users need to navigate between different websites from different organizations (on national, regional and local level) in order to find adequate information and service opportunities.

The research presented in this paper has a concrete project background in a research endeavor on development of governmental information systems for businesses [4]. This project has been working with development of proposals for new digital solutions for governments' services to businesses. A specific type of business (restaurants) was selected as study object, since this type of business was considered to be especially demanding in setting up, due to many required permits from authorities on national (agencies) and local level (municipalities). The project started from knowledge about current unsatisfactory situation concerning governmental web solutions for businesses. Based on this knowledge, visions for a new web portal were formulated. This vision has been documented and presented for decision-makers and designers.

In what way can such visionary development be seen as research? It is a kind of idea generation, but is the formulation of new ideas to be seen as legitimate research? Idea generation and vision formulation has been the core of this research, but this is not the whole story. The project was designed in order to create credible knowledge. The development of visions of new digital services has been seen as a kind of design research. The project has not created any factual digital solutions. There are not any "instantiations" [5] in terms of running systems or prototypes. How can we claim any credibility of the formulated visions? In this paper we argue for a research approach of *visionary design research*. This visionary development has been conducted following the principles of multi-grounded design research [6, 7, 8].

This paper has *dual purposes*: 1) It articulates *visionary design research*, based on multi-grounding principles, as a legitimate research approach. 2) It presents and motivates *principles for an integrative business link portal with high service value for businesses* (a vision of an assemblage information system). The first purpose gives methodological justice to the second purpose. The second purpose gives an empirical illustration of and support to the proposed research approach as stated in the first purpose.

The content/structure of this paper follows the guidelines of the design science research publication schema [9] with some important extensions. This introduction has framed the research and stated the over-all purposes. Section 2 contains the description of the chosen research approach with special articulation and argumentation for a multi-grounded visionary design research. Section 3 describes some parts of prior theoretical work. The "artifact description" as a design vision is found in section 6. Since we apply a multi-grounding approach it is important to explicitly clarify the empirical bases of problematic situations (section 4) and goals (section 5) as bases for the proposed design. These descriptions/sections are additions in relation to the suggested publication schema of [9]. These empirical parts are also used in the grounding of vision (section 7) which is the explicit evaluation part. Discussion and conclusions are found in section 8.

2   Research Approach: Multi-grounded Visionary Design Research

2.1   Visions as Elements of Design Research?

To develop something new should be understood in the context of design science research [5, 10]. This type of research is contrasted to the study and explanation of what already exists ("behavioral research"). We will use the concept of *design research* (and its abbreviation DR) below. Through design research, new artifacts are created. In DR theory, different types of artifacts are considered as valid outcomes; constructs, models, methods and instantiations [11, 5]. However, the primary outcome of IS design research is conceived to be an IT artifact: "The result of design-science research in IS is, by definition, a purposeful IT artifact created to address an important organizational problem" [5, p 82]. Visions can be thought of as a kind of DR outcome, including and manifested as constructs and models. Is it valid design research to stop with visions/models? Should the design researchers not try to instantiate the visions in IT artifacts?

We stopped, in this case, at *visions* only *linguistically expressed*. These visions were expressed in text and models (diagram figures). There were both practical and principal reasons for stopping at the visionary level and not trying to implement the ideas into artifacts of prototype character. We wanted to direct the discussions on *fundamental design issues*, not how something is solved in some prototype artifact. Our aim was to stimulate principal considerations and thus to think away concrete and specific digital solutions. The primary target groups for our visionary design proposals were policy-makers, designers and other practitioners. Even if our starting point for analysis was the existing business link portal verksamt.se, we did not want to restrict the design to making improvements in this portal. We wanted to be *innovative* and *radical* in our thinking and move *beyond limited adjustments* (see section 6.1 below for further motives).

In this design research we addressed real and highly relevant problems and concerns. This has required a strong orientation towards problem understanding and awareness [7, 10, 12]. We have made in-depth investigations of current practices and artifacts. This can be seen as a kind of *exploratory research* within a DR frame [13]. Based on a deep problem and practice understanding, we have formulated visions for future digital interaction in terms of principle design proposals. Such design proposals can be seen as proof-of-concept models.

Gregor & Hevner [9] discuss explicitly what kind of outcomes from DR that can be seen as legitimate ones. They state that a valid contribution can be 1) an instantiated artifact and/or 2) a nascent design theory (constructs, methods, models, design principles) and/or 3) a well-developed design theory. Our contribution belongs clearly to the second of these types of contributions as a visionary model using new/improved constructs and expressing design principles.

2.2   A Multi-grounded Design Research Process

We claim that visionary design research can be seen as a legitimate research approach. This does not mean that we claim that any projection of ideas should be labelled as research. Idea generation and vision formulation can be part of research if there are other arrangements and considerations made. What are the warrants for making vision development a legitimate research process? To design and justify visionary development as a research process, we turn to the principles of multi-grounded design research (MGDR). The general principles of multi-grounding were originally formulated in [6]. These principles have later been further developed and refined by several scholars [7, 8, 14]. Multi-grounding comprises three types of grounding of some specific knowledge item:

- Theoretical grounding; i.e. grounding in theory sources
- Empirical grounding, i.e. grounding in sources of empirical data
- Internal grounding, i.e. establishing internal coherence and grounding within the knowledge item itself

Concrete results from a design process are, in MGDR, labelled situational design knowledge. There can be diverse kinds of situational design knowledge, following general principles of DR, like models and manifestations in concrete IT artifacts. Situational design knowledge, in a MGDR process, should be grounded in three kinds of sources; in theory, in empirics and in itself (i.e. through internal coherence). This means that visions can be legitimate results if they are theoretically, empirically and internally grounded. Theoretical grounding means that we need to find some theory that could give warrant to the vision. Internal grounding means that different elements of the vision need to be harmonious. The claims for empirical grounding are more multi-facetted. "The produced situational design knowledge should be informed and governed by practical knowledge as for example problems, goals and needs. The proposed design should be a conscious and reflective response to these practical needs: a practical grounding of purpose, relevance and compliance." [8, p 56]. It is stated that the design proposals should be assessed against anticipated and observed use-effects. In the case of design visions there will only be anticipated use-effects.

The concept of grounding comprises both *generation* and *validation*. This means that the external sources are used for informing the design process and as well as for justifying the design results. Validation means in this context to check the correspondence between the design knowledge and the identified knowledge sources/warrants [6].

In MGDR, there is a differentiation between situational/concrete design knowledge (as result from a situational design process) and abstract design knowledge (as result from design theorizing). The aim of multi-grounded design research is to produce both situational design knowledge and abstract design knowledge (design principles or design theories). Abstract design knowledge can be formulated as "classes of problems", "classes of goals" and "classes of solutions" [10, 15].

In the presented design case, the visions are formulated as principles for proposed digital solutions. The principles are fairly general and abstract, which means that this design knowledge can be seen as both situational and abstract at the same time. As said in section 2.1 above, we have formulated a principle digital solution and there are no concrete illustrations in lo-fi or hi-fi prototypes. In figure 1, we have depicted the multiple sources for grounding in this case. The empirical bases are divided into 1) problematic situations of current practices ("problems"), 2) desired situations of future practices ("goals") and 3) opinions and assessments of proposed principles by knowledgeable practitioners including estimates of use-effects ("assessments and estimated use-effects"). The new design (i.e. the design vision) is a response to the problems in the current situation. It is also a way to operationalize the goals for an improved future situation. The relations between problems and goals (and their formulations) can be said to be dialectical. Problems exist as deviations from desired states. These desires can be tacit goals, which can, based on problem formulations, be articulated as explicit ones. Explicit goals can be used to evaluate current situation in order to detect (other) problems. Empirical methods and sources for problems and goals are described in section 2.3 below.

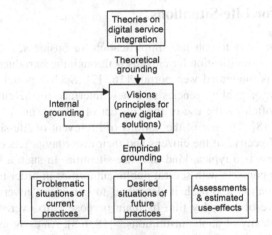

Fig. 1. Multi-grounding of visionary design knowledge

Since the design knowledge is stated in terms of not yet realized visions, there cannot be any factual use-effects. We have, however, collected views and opinions on the proposed new design from knowledgeable practitioners. The visionary knowledge has also been informed and justified by theoretical knowledge on digital service integration and the concepts of web portal and life-event.

2.3 Diverse Kinds of Data for Grounding

In order to pursue a multi-grounded design research process there was a need for diverse kinds of empirical data. Different empirical sources have been investigated. One kind of important data was different *descriptions of goals and rules*, as e.g. the EU Service Directive [3]. In this category, other documents were also included such as the corresponding Swedish legislation and different goal documents concerning administrative simplification and web-based support to entrepreneurs. An obvious data source was the *existing web portal verksamt.se*, with its different web pages. There existed also *other websites* with information and services for businesses, e.g. different municipal websites. Such websites were also investigated. *Digital forms* for applications existed on the verksamt website as well as on other websites. We have also studied *paper-based forms* for applications, since these forms give knowledge about the information demand on entrepreneurs.

Besides these digital artifacts and documents, we have collected data from interviews. We have *interviewed entrepreneurs* (business owners, business executives) about their problems during setting up of businesses. We have also *interviewed public administrators* about their views on interaction with businesses. *Workshops* and meetings have been arranged with policy-makers, executives, designers and administrators for discussing and assessing different problems, goals and design proposals.

3   Theoretical Pre-knowledge: Web Portals with Integrative Services for Life-Situations

E-government is one way to enhance simplification for businesses and citizens. One approach to address simplification for citizens is through the introduction of "one stop government", that is integrated web portals [16, 17]. Such a portal is an integrated digital tool in front of public agencies as a new interface to the citizens. The egov portal idea builds often on the use of the concept of a life-event of a citizen (as an external user) [16, 18]. The use of the notions of life-event or life-situation [19] implies taking the perspective of the citizens and their everyday practices and situations. Setting up a business is a typical kind of a life-situation. In such a life-situation the citizen may require contacts with several public authorities in order to reach different services. A life-situation approach is described to consider "government operation from the perspective of everyday life. Its main purpose is to overcome the existent structure and complexity of public institutions." [18, p 3]. An egov web portal should contain information and services related to a life-situation which makes it possible for citizens to have "a simple access to all services they need in one place" [ibid]. The importance of a "unified entry point" is emphasized [ibid, 16].

A web portal is seen as a new integrating interface between the citizens and public agencies. Behind this portal/interface there are back-office processes going on [16, 18]. A key issue in web portals is the degree of service integration. There is an important difference if the portal is 1) only simplifying the interface for the citizen (just one access point) or 2) if it builds on an integration of services from different public agencies behind the portal [17, 18]. In the first case it will be easier for the citizen to find information and services and in the second case it should also be easier to perform the required information tasks. The type of portal in situation 1 does not provide any real service integration: "the single portal … looks like integrated government, in reality it is just a layer covering the fragmented organizations behind it." [17, p 280].

With inspiration from e-government maturity stage models [e.g. 20], there are many scholars who write about the need for service integration in e-government. Integrated services are seen as the most mature stage in many such models. However, there are not much said in detail concerning how services are to be integrated. There are suggestions for back-office process re-organization [18] and information sharing among involved authorities [20]. There are also proposals for explicit guiding functions for the users. "A (web) portal ... will then locate the relevant services and make a recommendation, after which customers can use the portal to request the services they require." [17, p 281]. Digital guides seem to be important tools and there might also be needs for improved information sharing and process re-organization among involved public authorities. These proposals seem, however, to be insufficient for reaching a high degree of egov service integration. There is more knowledge to be added. Below, we will, through our design case, give more details concerning principles for service integration.

4   Problem Analysis

The existing web portal verksamt.se can be seen as a response to the demands for administrative simplification. Different kinds of information for businesses are assembled in one place. There are also several services co-located on the website, e.g. different forms for permit applications. We characterize verksamt.se as a first generation innovation of digital tools for businesses in their contacts with the public administration. The co-location of information and services (figure 3) is a clear improvement in relation to the fragmented situation of many authority websites with content limited to their "own" information and services (figure 2).

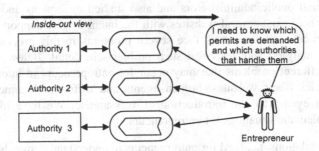

Fig. 2. Fragmented support for entrepreneurs (before/besides verksamt.se)

However, the fragmented and co-located solutions exist side by side. Not all application forms (and accompanying information) are located on the national business link portal verksamt.se. It is not mandatory for municipalities and other authorities to place their application forms on verksamt.se. In many cases there exist web links from verksamt to another website where some kind of form (completely digital or just a down-loadable pdf form) can be found. It is a complex digital landscape for entrepreneurs to navigate in.

The EU Service Directive [3] is one important impetus for a business link portal like verksamt.se. The Service Directive states that it should be possible and easy for service entrepreneurs to complete all procedures and formalities (declarations, notifications or applications necessary for authorization). These procedures should be possible to conduct through electronic means (a digital point of single contact). However, these regulations are not sufficient to enforce simple digital communication for the entrepreneurs in contacts with public authorities. It is even the case that the situation has been harder in business set up endeavors. The introduction of a digital PSC (like verksamt.se) adds partially more complexity and fragmentation to the digital landscape for entrepreneurs. The Swedish legislation (transforming the Service Directive to national rules and circumstances) has several dysfunctions making the communication between entrepreneurs and public administrators unnecessary complex and cumbersome [21].

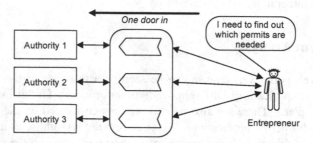

Fig. 3. Co-located support for entrepreneurs (current verksamt.se)

We have made empirical inquiries concerning the interaction between (restaurant) entrepreneurs and public authorities. As described in section 2.3, we have interviewed entrepreneurs and public administrators and also studied documents and digital artifacts. Even if there exist several websites with the intent to give support in the business set up process, entrepreneurs face severe problems in this process. We have elsewhere [4] analyzed and described such problems in detail. Below, we give an overview of different problems that may occur for entrepreneurs in interaction with public authorities (their websites, human agents and different documents). These problems exist even after the introduction of verksamt.se. We have identified the following problematic situations for entrepreneurs:

- Complex regulations, i.e. hard for entrepreneurs to understand demands for permits and operations
- There exists a mix of national and local regulations for businesses
- Information is provided by many different authorities/websites; hard to obtain a proper overview
- Information from different authorities to businesses can be contrarious
- Insufficient adaptation of authorities' information to certain types of businesses
- Bureaucratic (unintelligible) language with many synonyms and homonyms
- Many permits are demanded for business set up and operation

- The entrepreneurs usually lack knowledge about which permits are demanded for the planned practice
- The entrepreneurs usually lack knowledge about which authority that is responsible for a specific permit
- It is hard for the entrepreneur to get information about the case handling process of different applications and when to get a response to a submitted application
- Motivations and explanations for information demands (of applications) are often missing; it is hard for entrepreneurs to understand why certain information items are needed
- Some applications are hard to fill out; especially when multi-purpose forms are used
- Some information demands are fuzzy; especially in general descriptions in free text supplements to application forms
- Repeated information demands in different applications exist; authorities do not re-use already submitted information from entrepreneurs
- Hard for entrepreneurs to know the suitable sequence of filling out different application forms
- Sometimes, the entrepreneurs do not have (simple) access to the demanded information

5   Goal Articulation

There exist several policy documents concerning administrative simplification for businesses [e.g. 1, 2]. This includes also legislative documents such as [3]. We have studied such documents and detected many valuable ideas. However, when basing our analysis on the severe problems that entrepreneurs encounter when trying to set up a new business, we wanted to sharpen the goals further. We present below some goals aiming for *radical simplification* in the business set up concerning permits and other information from public authorities. This goal articulation is thus based on existing policy documents and our empirically based problem and practice analysis (summarized in section 4 above).

Instead of starting from public agencies and how they want to inform businesses and obtain applications from them ("inside-out"), we want to make a radical shift in the view. We want to start with the businesses and their needs for communication with public authorities ("*outside-in*"). We also adopt one collective view on public authorities treating them as *one compound actor*; the public sector as a whole. The entrepreneurs do not need to know how the public sector is organized in separate authorities. The goal is to have a *simple communication tool for* businesses when interacting with the public sector. Such a tool should enhance *communication quality* between the parties and give *mutual benefits*. The tool should also, with structured and accessible information, contribute to *knowledge development* among entrepreneurs; to support them to be more knowledgeable with *better grounds for decision-making* and having *better control* over the setting up process. Radical simplification is aimed for; a guided setting up process that is *transparent, coordinated, maneuverable* and *predictable*.

6   A Vision of an Assemblage Information System

6.1   Choice of Visionary Knowledge

We claim that our knowledge contribution is to be seen as vision development. What do we mean by visionary knowledge? A vision is a *desired state*. It should have an *attracting force*. The vision should *stimulate* and *inspire* people to strive towards it. In visions we *disregard* unnecessary *limitations* of current situations. Visions should be the result of a *radical* and *innovative re-thinking* aiming for knowledge of a *prospective* character with great *potentialities*.

We have, when forming a vision for the digital communication between entrepreneurs and public authorities, *intentionally disregarded many restricting aspects of the current situation*. We have put aside many organizational, technical, administrative and economic circumstances. We had, as a basis, knowledge about the current digital solutions (verksamt.se and other digital artifacts), but these different digital features of the current situation were disregarded in the visionary development. We did *not* work with *marginal modifications* of the current digital artifacts. It was rather a *clean slate* approach. We strived for an *ideal solution*. Even if we disregarded many aspects of the current situations, the vision should *not* be seen as *unrealistic*. We have for example taken into account the current legislation. The vision should be in alignment with current laws since we cannot just wish for new laws and we know that the legislation process usually takes quite a long time. We have based our vision on general *potentials of information technology* and an explicit view of a *free flow of information*. We have above emphasized (in text) different aspects of our visionary development. These aspects are to be seen as potential features of any visionary development, but DR designers need to take into account situational circumstances.

In using our vision for digital development, designers need to take into account current solutions and make choices how to adapt the vision and the current artifact to each other. Realizing a vision-based IS should probably be done in a step-wise fashion.

6.2   Proposal for a New Web Portal for Restaurant Businesses

We have formulated a vision for a web portal for restaurant businesses in their interactions with public authorities [4]. We describe three main principles of this vision here:

1. An assemblage information system
2. A joined-up support for application processes
3. A reversed application process

Following the goals (section 5) with one communication tool close to restaurant businesses, rather than close to public authorities, we put forth the principle of one information system for such businesses. We describe it as an *assemblage IS* for restaurants in their planning and communication with the public sector during both the set up phase and the operational phase. This should be a web portal in the meaning of gathering diverse kinds of information and services to be a meaningful assemblage. However, the emphasis is to see it as the entrepreneurs' IS, only provided by public authorities. This is a shift from a traditional view of seeing the public websites as digital faces of public authorities. To gather all information and services in one system is a radical simplification compared with the complex digital landscape of the present. Everything that is needed should be in one place for the restaurant entrepreneur.

It is not the case the separate things are put together just besides each other. Information and services are integrated when there are reasons for simplification and support for the entrepreneurs. The existing business link portal (verksamt.se) is mainly driven by the principle of co-locating (figure 3). Different communication services exist together at the same place but no real integration is made. On the contrary, we strive, in our vision for a new IS, to fuse services together when there are reasons and possibilities for that. This is the second principle of our vision and we call it a *joined-up support* for entrepreneurs (figure 4). The process of completing different application forms should not be treated as separate fragments. There is an administrative burden for the entrepreneur to find out what permits are needed and where and how to apply for them. This administrative burden should be relieved. Instead of separate permits, we have used one "restaurant permit" as a figure of thought. Metaphorically, the entrepreneur should apply just for one (restaurant) permit instead of many different permits. We call this approach, a figure of thought, since we do not mean literally and judicially that the separate permits should be formally integrated into one single permit. What we mean is that the application process should not appear for the entrepreneur to be a fragmented process, navigating between separate application forms. It should appear to the entrepreneur as he/she applied just for one permit, although there will exist different parts of this composite permit.

This integrative process should be pursued through the third principle of our vision: *a reversed application process.* The existing procedure working with separate application looks like this: 1) find out what permits are needed, 2) select one permit and fill out the application form including parts of the planned practice, 3) submit the application. There can be digital support for all three phases of this process. In the first phase there can be guiding support to identify needs for permits. In the second phase, there can be digital forms to fill out and in the third phase there can be a digital procedure for signing and submitting.

As a radical alternative we suggest a reversed application process. Such a process can be described consisting of the following phases: 1) the entrepreneur is prompted by the digital tool to describe the planned and desired practice of the business, 2) the tool identifies from this practice description needs for a permit and 3) generates an application proposal for the entrepreneur to be reviewed and 4) possibly submitted. The entrepreneur does not need to know beforehand which permits are needed. The IS helps the entrepreneur to describe the planned business and based on these descriptions generates which applications are needed. This is why we call it a reversed application process. In the existing process there is first an identification of permit needs and then description of (parts of) the business practice. In our visionary alternative there are first prompted practice descriptions and then digitally supported identification of permit needs. Compare the speech bubbles in figure 2/3 (traditional application processes) and figure 4 (reversed application process) concerning the demands on the entrepreneur in the application process.

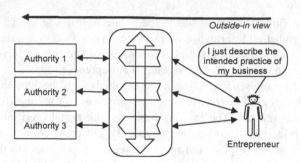

Fig. 4. Joined-up support for entrepreneurs (vision for an assemblage IS)

As a consequence of such a reversed application process there will be an automatic re-use of information between different applications. The current situation is characterized by multiple registering of the same information in different applications (section 4 above). The entrepreneur will only register one specific information item once.

We characterized verksamt.se above as a first generation of innovation for business support. Our design proposal can be characterized as a second generation of innovation.

7   Vision Grounding

7.1   Multi-grounding Principles

The design vision of a web-based IS for restaurant entrepreneurs, described in the previous section, is not just taken out of the blue. It has been developed based on empirical and theoretical knowledge. This visionary knowledge (in terms of design principles) can be justified through matching it with empirical and theoretical knowledge. Principles of multi-grounded design research [6, 7, 8] in relation to visionary design knowledge was described above in section 2.2. Theoretical grounding means an investigation how well the design principles correspond to established theoretical knowledge, that is relating it to what is sometimes called a kernel theory [7, 22, 23].

Even if the design principles have not been instantiated in real digital artifacts, it is possible to assess them empirically through knowledge of different epistemic types. The vision (as a proposed solution) can be assessed in relation to (figure 1):

- Problematic situations, which it is intended to reduce
- Goals, which it is intended to realize
- Opinions/assessments made by knowledgeable practitioners, including estimated use-effects

The grounding relations between the vision and its empirical warrants are specified in figure 5. The basic empirical justificatory scheme in DR is that a designed artifact leads to some positive use-effects [5, 8]. These use-effects should be factual. However, as said earlier in this paper, there cannot be any factual effects when we stopped at a visionary and linguistic level. The use-effects are anticipated, but not in a groundless fashion. The anticipated use-effects are grounded in an analysis of different empirical sources (problems, goals, assessments, estimates).

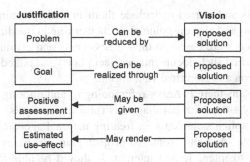

Fig. 5. Different types of grounding of the vision (proposed solution)

7.2   Empirical Grounding

The three main design principles in the vision are grounded in problematic situation as described in section 4 above. The first principle (an assemblage IS) is a response to the difficulties for entrepreneurs to comprehend the different demands from public authorities (e.g. complex regulations, fragmented information, several permits). The second and the third principle (a joined-up and reversed application process) can be seen as responses to several problems for the entrepreneur: Lack of knowledge of permits and responsible authorities, unclear information demands, difficulties to fill out applications, repeated registration of information, and unclear sequence for application submission.

The three design principles are operationalizations of the articulated goals for digital interaction between businesses and government (section 5 above). They are based on the outside-in view on arranging G2B interaction. The proposed IS is rather the restaurant entrepreneurs' IS than the public authorities. The public agencies will of course use the system as providers of information and services and receivers of applications. But the main and primary users are the entrepreneurs and the web portal will be fully adapted to their needs. The portal hides to a large degree the organizational structure of the government (different authorities). The public sector is mainly treated as one collective actor as stated in one goal. A joined-up and reversed application process is a way to create a transparent, coordinated, maneuverable and predictable process, which was stated as an important goal.

The vision (design proposal) was presented and discussed with several municipal administrators working with support for business set up. The reactions were very positive. They exclaimed: "This is what we want, but we don't want to wait too long". After our design research project was completed, we started discussions with executives and designers of the existing website verksamt.se. Our design orientation in the project had been to present something independent from this website, although with knowledge and inspiration from it. We did not take for granted that a new web portal for restaurant entrepreneurs, if realized, would be built through a redesign of verksamt.se. The executives and designers had general plans for expansion of verksamt through better inclusion of municipal information and services. These plans were, however, not as distinct as our design proposals. The practitioners became positive to our design proposals and started to include them in their planning. There exist now concrete project plans and also on-going projects working in the direction of our design proposals. Their plans were based on their assessments and estimates of positive use-effects. We have studied such documents (project plans) and talked with participants as parts of data collection and empirical validation.

In their project plans there is heavy referencing to and quoting from our vision report [4]. They totally agree with our diagnosis (problem analysis) as a basis for future designs. There are explicit statements for treating national agencies and municipalities as a collective whole. A quote from the project plan illustrates this: "Verksamt.se provides the ability to integrate and interact. It should be able to reuse information and e-services. This becomes particularly clear if you emphasize the perspective of the entire public sector that also includes the municipalities." There are also clear statements in their roadmap for improved process support, reuse of information, joined-up support for services. It is very clear from this and another project plan that our visions have had great impact on the planning for the future verksamt.se as a more comprehensive business link portal.

7.3   Internal and Theoretical Grounding

The three design principles form together a coherent whole. There is a clear hierarchic structure between the principles in the order they are stated. This is to say that they are well grounded internally.

We now turn to theoretical grounding. In section 3 above, some parts of prior theoretical knowledge has been reviewed. The assembly IS approach is a typical example of a one stop government (a web portal) based on a life-event approach. However, the existing portal (verksamt.se) is also an example of a one stop government. The proposed web portal does not only co-locate information and services in one place. There is a clear design strategy to integrate services. It utilizes some principles known from the literature like guiding functions and information sharing. However, the call for back-office reorganization has not been prioritized in this proposed design solution. This was not considered essential for improved quality for service delivery. The focus has been towards procedural reorganization and simplification for entrepreneurs. To change work with applications to a joined-up and reversed process has been our design focus. This concept gives new meaning to service integration.

8   Conclusions

There is no standard template for design research [9]. Such research can be conducted in many diverse ways. However, what is common to all of them is an ambition to *improve practice* [5]. This presented research has worked with real and complex problems. The roles of the researchers have been to generate visions and principle solutions, and not to construct IT artifacts. This research need to be understood in a *context of dialogue and argumentation*. There have been dialogues between practitioners and researchers in order to establish reliable knowledge on problematic situations and to furnish a basis for goal development. There have been dialogues between researchers and practitioners concerning proposed design principles based on a thorough argumentative base.

As all knowledge development, this piece of DR has been conducted in the becoming. What has been achieved is at the same time justified and provisional. There are needs for future studies for further development and justification of design principles for e-government support for business set up. There is also a need for inquiries concerning this kind of visionary design research. We have presented different arguments for conducting a visionary DR. These arguments are based on a multi-grounding perspective [6, 7, 8]. Further research (including more examples with elaborated reflections) is needed concerning different warrants for the creation and use of visions in design research endeavours.

Acknowledgements. This research has been conducted with financial support from the Swedish Governmental Agency for Innovation Systems (VINNOVA). It has been conducted in close cooperation with the Swedish Association of Local Authorities and Regions. Members from The Agency for Economic and Regional Growth, The Swedish Companies Registration Office, The Swedish Tax Agency and from several municipalities have participated in our workshops during the project. We are grateful for their input and assessment.

References

1. EC: Europe can do better. Report on best practice in member states to implement EU legislation in the least burdensome way. The European Commission (2011)
2. Ministry of Enterprise: Continued work to simplify matters for business. Government Offices of Sweden (2013)
3. EU: Directive 2006/123/EC of the European Parliament and of the Council of 12 December 2006 on services in the internal market. Official Journal of the European Union(2006)
4. Goldkuhl, G., Persson, A., Röstlinger, A.: DUKAT för restaurangföretagare – visioner om ett samlat informationssystem. Department of Management & Engineering, Linköping University (2012) (in Swedish)
5. Hevner, A.R., March, S.T., Park, J., Ram, S.: Design science in information systems research. MIS Quarterly 28(1), 75–115 (2004)
6. Goldkuhl, G.: Design theories in information systems – a need for multi-grounding. Journal of Information Technology Theory and Application (JITTA) 6(2), 59–72 (2004)
7. Kuechler, B., Vaishnavi, V.: A Framework for Theory Development in Design Science Research: Multiple Perspectives. Journal of AIS 13(6), 395–423 (2012)
8. Goldkuhl, G., Lind, M.: A multi-grounded design research process. In: Winter, R., Zhao, J.L., Aier, S. (eds.) DESRIST 2010. LNCS, vol. 6105, pp. 45–60. Springer, Heidelberg (2010)
9. Gregor, S., Hevner, A.: Positioning and presenting design science research for maximum impact. MIS Quarterly 37(2), 337–355 (2013)
10. Sein, M., Henfridsson, O., Purao, S., Rossi, M., Lindgren, R.: Action design research. MIS Quarterly 35(1), 37–56 (2011)
11. March, S.T., Smith, G.F.: Design and natural science research in information technology. Decision Support Systems 15(4), 251–266 (1995)

12. Beck, R., Weber, S., Gregory, R.W.: Theory-generating design science research. Information Systems Frontiers 15, 637–651 (2013)
13. Briggs, R.O., Schwabe, G.: On Expanding, the scope of design science in IS research. In: Jain, H., Sinha, A.P., Vitharana, P. (eds.) DESRIST 2011. LNCS, vol. 6629, pp. 92–106. Springer, Heidelberg (2011)
14. Ågerfalk, P.: Grounding through Operationalization: Constructing Tangible Theory in IS Research. In: Proc of the 12th European Conference on Information Systems, Turku (2004)
15. Lee, J.S., Pries-Heje, J., Baskerville, R.: Theorizing in Design Science Research. In: Jain, H., Sinha, A.P., Vitharana, P. (eds.) DESRIST 2011. LNCS, vol. 6629, pp. 1–16. Springer, Heidelberg (2011)
16. Wimmer, M., Tambouris, T.: Online One-Stop Government: A working framework and requirements. In: Proceedings of the IFIP World Computer Congress, Montreal (2002)
17. Klievink, B., Janssen, M.: Realizing joined-up government - Dynamic capabilities and stage models for transformation. Government Information Quarterly 26, 275–284 (2009)
18. Vintar, M., Kunstelj, M., Leben, A.: Delivering better quality public services through life-event portals. In: The 10th NISPAcce Annual Conference, Cracow (2002)
19. Bleek, W.-G.: Situations in life to support the use and modelling of municipal information systems. In: The European Conference on e-Government (2001)
20. Layne, K., Lee, J.: Developing Fully Functional E-government: A four-stage model. Government Information Quarterly, Vol 18(2), 122–136 (2001)
21. Goldkuhl, G., Röstlinger, A.: Intentions for simplicity and consequences of complexity: A diagnostic case study of an e-government portal and its back-office processes. In: The 1th Scandinavian Workshop on E-government. Linköping University (2014)
22. Walls, J.G., Widmeyer, G.R., El Sawy, O.A.: Building an information systems design theory for vigilant EIS. Information Systems Research 3(1), 36–59 (1992)
23. Gregor, S., Jones, D.: The Anatomy of a Design Theory. Journal of AIS 8(5), 312–335 (2007)

Design Science in Practice: Design and Evaluation of an Art Based Information System to Improve Indoor Air Quality at Schools

Paul Rigger[✉], Felix Wortmann[✉], and André Dahlinger[✉]

University of St. Gallen, Dufourstrasse 40,
9000 St. Gallen, Switzerland
{paul.rigger,felix.wortmann,andre.dahlinger}@unisg.ch

Abstract. Indoor air quality has a significant effect on human performance. In addition, many health issues can be traced back to bad indoor room-climate. However, especially in Europe, pupils spend a majority of their learning life in school classes affected by poor room climate. Without an automatic heating, ventilation and air conditioning system these pupils and their teachers have to rely on manual ventilation by opening windows. Thereby, they often lack fundamental room climate quality information to effectively guide their behavior. Information systems (IS) and sensor technology can be a remedy to these challenges. Existing room climate monitoring systems regularly reveal major shortcomings, e.g. in respect to user interfaces, presentation of data, and systematic engagement. We want to address the aforementioned shortcomings and present an art IS, which reflects room conditions in real time through modifications of depicted art. The artifact is evaluated in a field experiment, conducted in an Austrian grammar school. The evaluation reveals that room climate measured in CO_2 can indeed be improved significantly. In addition, pupils also perceive a significant room climate improvement.

Keywords: Human-computer interaction · Ambient displays · Art information systems · Pervasive computing

1 Introduction

The negative effect of poor indoor climate conditions on occupants is a well-researched phenomenon. In 1983 the World Health Organization defined this phenomenon as the sick building syndrome (SBS). SBS refers to symptoms such as skin reactions, non-specific hypersensitivity, mental fatigue, headache, nausea, and dizziness among people staying in respective buildings [1] [2]. Those negative effects have been regularly detected in office buildings [3] or schools [4]–[8]. Research primarily conducted in school environments show that, apart from effects on health, room climate additionally influences concentration and attendance [8]. More specifically, negative effects on simple calculations, word processing [3] as well as general math results [7] have been demonstrated.

© Springer International Publishing Switzerland 2015
B. Donnellan et al. (Eds.): DESRIST 2015, LNCS 9073, pp. 71–86, 2015.
DOI: 10.1007/978-3-319-18714-3_5

One of the key root sources for SBS is ventilation. Heating, ventilation and air conditioning systems (HVAC) ideally guarantee good room climate. However they are often poorly installed, setup and operated. Moreover, older professional buildings and residential homes, especially in Europe, are rarely equipped with an automatic ventilation system. Proper manual ventilation is therefore crucial to improve indoor air quality. This also holds true for the majority of European schools, where fresh air is usually provided by opening windows.

Sensing room climate can be very hard for humans as the human body is unable to sense important room climate parameters. Although we have a good sense for temperature, carbon dioxide levels, for example, cannot be sensed directly at all. This problem is known and room climate sensors are used in office buildings as well as in residential buildings to control the settings of HVACs or the users' own ventilation behavior. Monitoring Systems, like the commercial products Netatmo even allow detailed data analysis provided through a smartphone application. Furthermore, those applications provide user guidance, for example calculating an aggregated room climate index generated on the basis of temperature, carbon dioxide, humidity and noise, and having a traffic light indicating how good the overall room climate is. However, engaging people in tracking their room climate on a regular basis is far from being easy. While starting up a smartphone app on a regular basis is cumbersome, reading the values on a standard gauge is not very appealing. Furthermore, providing enough help to interpret room climate data is challenging. This is noteworthy, as people still have difficulties in understanding scientific notations such as carbon dioxide level expressed in ppm (parts per million).

In this paper we present and evaluate an IS to promote pupils ventilation behavior in classrooms via a visual feedback system – the "CO_2-Albert". We developed CO_2-Albert enabling pupils to overcome a lack of information availability and -processing that makes it hard or even impossible for them to direct their behavior (ventilation to improve CO_2 conditions) within a given feedback system. CO_2-Albert is a feedback system being equipped with standard room climate sensors for temperature, humidity, and carbon dioxide. In contrast to conventional monitoring systems a display embedded in a standard art frame presents the current room climate on the basis of a picture of Albert Einstein. Changing room conditions are reflected in modifications of the picture in real-time. While the focus of this paper is on CO_2 and ventilation we want to transfer the design of this art monitoring system to other cases like diabetes, i.e. we want to visualize HbA1c and Hypoglycemia in a CO_2-Albert-like feedback system.

The paper is structured as followed: Having outlined the motivation, section two depicts the existing knowledge base. Section three presents our research methodology. Section four outlines the design process. By demonstrating the artifact in a field test we evaluate its performance (section five). Finally, in section six we conclude our findings and present implications as well as limitations.

2   Knowledge Base

2.1   Fostering Health Behavior on the Basis of IS-Enabled Feedback

The rise of IS in the 90's also found its way to health care as IS proved to be cost-efficient and quality increasing [2–4]. The possibilities in processing information were soon used to give patients individualized feedback in order to support them improving their health behavior. This computer-tailored feedback was found to be effective in dietary [5], smoking [6], cancer [7] and health risk appraisal [8]. For an overview see [9].

In general, four stages of feedback IS can be distinguished. First-stage approaches provide general information about health issues. With email emerging as a vivid communication tool, attempts were made to use this channel for low cost and high reach information provisioning [10]. Second-stage approaches provide behavior-directed information personalized for a specific patient. There is broad evidence, that such second-stage information provisioning has a significant impact on physical activity, dietary behavior and alcohol consumption [11]. Third-stage approaches use multiple feedback loops in order to repeatedly readjust behavior [12]. This strategy proved powerful to increase physical activity [13], dietary [5], weight [14, 15] and diabetes self-management. For an overview see [16]. Latest research focuses on a fourth stage of feedback that comes constantly and in real-time. A very prominent example is biofeedback [17], [18]. The work presented in this paper can be attributed to the latter fourth stage type of feedback IS.

Research provides evidence that higher-level feedback approaches building upon more interactive interventions have a higher impact than lower level approaches. Brug et al. found that people ate more fruit and vegetables given second-stage feedback compared to the simple provision of general information [5]. This effect could even be enhanced with iterative feedback. Similar results were obtained in weight reduction [15] and risk behavior [8].

2.2 Feedback as a Means to Drive and Direct Behavior

There are several theories explaining the causes for behavior change in the field of health [9]. In the context of feedback IS, Control Theory [19] provides a powerful lens to understand the impact of these systems. Control Theory uses the basic cybernetic concept [20] of the negative feedback loop (NFL). A NFL starts with comparing an input capturing information on the present state to a desired reference value, the target state. Any discrepancy leads to behavior decreasing that discrepancy. The new present state then initiates a next NFL.

The origin of the reference value may stem from superordinate goals, such as beliefs ("fresh air will make me be able to concentrate better"), norms ("one should always breathe fresh air") or desires ("I would like better room climate") [19],[21]. Superordinate goals can influence subordinate goals in a hierarchical feedback system, e.g. "I love good room climate and therefore room temperature has to be 20°C." The means to achieve a superordinate goal via its subordinate goals is a script. A script is defined as a "general course of action, that incorporates a series of implicit if-then decisions" [19], e.g. "if room temperature is above 20°C, I have to open the window."

In order to make a feedback loop drive someone's behavior towards a certain goal, three requirements have to be fulfilled. First, the information of the present state has to be available. Second, the goal has to be appealing. And third, the individual needs to know what action to take to decrease present-target discrepancy, i.e. one has to have an effective script. The latter is an issue of knowledge and may therefore be solved with education. When it comes to health behavior present information is often far from perfect [22]. Moreover, the goal to be achieved may be discounted due to temporal distance, may get out of focus due to distraction, or may simply lack of importance [23]. The key to keep someone "on track" therefore lies in the format of the presentation to facilitate information processing and to increase awareness and goal attractiveness.

2.3   The Role of Information Visualization, Storytelling and Awareness in Feedback

Information visualization is a process that transforms data into a form that the human visual system can perceive the embedded information [24]. Its goal is to foster the observation and the understanding of data. Therefore information is made easier to process and thus more appealing [25]. There are no limits of how feedback is visualized. This offers the possibility of letting users work on a cover-feedback system that is more attractive than the original one [26]. In a first technical test setup, pupils behavior seemed to focus on restoring the natural state of the displayed modified portrait. Vital feedback and lively discussions were focused on how to make the displayed person ("cover"-feedback system) look "normal". Hardly any feedback was directly related to improving room climate (original feedback system). The pupils' actions were driven by a need for balance and order for the displayed manipulated picture of Albert Einstein [27–29].

A key research area for information visualization involves creating visual metaphors. Metaphors to represent and support the tasks of understanding of the visualized information [26]. Raw data and information are often complex, high-volume and time-dependent. Therefore, visual metaphors can foster compliance, motivation and help direct behavior. One key concept of information visualization in feedback systems is storytelling [26]. Storytelling is a universally present feature of human communication. Furthermore, it is a proven way to convey great quantities of information in a compelling, effective and efficient way [26], [30]. Technology now provides us with the means to convey information in a story-like fashion thereby leveraging the advantage of traditional storytelling. The paper at hand, for example, builds upon art visually telling a story about a suffering genius (Albert Einstein getting pale green).

Providing information is not enough for an internal feedback loop to drive behavior. Carver and Scheier propose that engagement in a loop "partially depends on the person's focus of attention" [19] (p. 120). While attention makes sensory inputs available for action, memory or thought, awareness is based on attention and implies that there is neural activity that produces conscious experience [31]. Shifting attention to the salient standard, i.e. increasing awareness, leads to "a tendency to compare one's perceptions of one's present state or behavior against the standard, leading (when possible) to a reduction of perceptible discrepancies between the two" (p.120). Awareness should further lead to "increased conformity to salient behavioral standards" (p.121). This holds for several behaviors like aggression [32–34] or resource allocation [35]. In the context of visual feedback discrete alerts in the form of caution or warning lights are commonly used as proven means to raise awareness [24]. In our case the attention-raising modified Albert should therefore motivate pupils to take action regulating room climate.

3   Research Methodology

The objective for this research is to develop, implement and evaluate an artifact that is novel and innovative. Therefore the proposed methodology is Design Science Research (DSR) [36]. We follow the DSR process suggested by Peffers et al. [37] outlined in Figure 1.

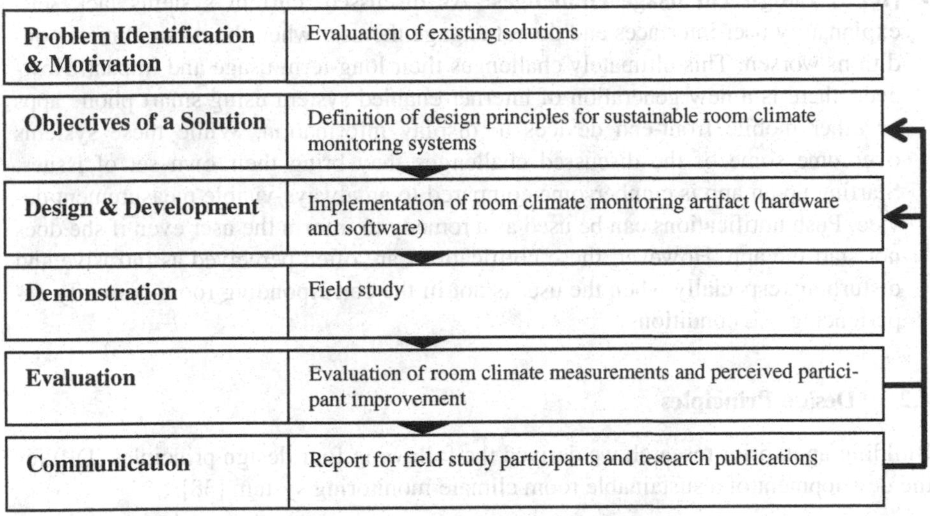

Problem Identification & Motivation	Evaluation of existing solutions
Objectives of a Solution	Definition of design principles for sustainable room climate monitoring systems
Design & Development	Implementation of room climate monitoring artifact (hardware and software)
Demonstration	Field study
Evaluation	Evaluation of room climate measurements and perceived participant improvement
Communication	Report for field study participants and research publications

Fig. 1. Research methodology based on [37]

The first three steps of the process are "problem identification & motivation", "objectives of a solution" and "design & development". These phases have been outlined extensively in previously research [38]. Thus, section 4 of this paper will outline essential findings of these three steps. The fourth step is the demonstration of the artifact. We demonstrate our artifact in a field setup by installing 10 artifacts in a grammar school. The evaluation of the artifact (step five) is presented in section five.

4   Design and Development

4.1   Evaluation of Existing Solutions

As part of the DSR process we have tested multiple solutions that are currently available to monitor indoor room climate. Systems are available from standard gauges to more sophisticated internet-enabled sensors [39]. We identified the following three key problems [38]:

- **[KP1] Lack of systematic engagement:** Room climate is specific for each individual room and has to be measured continuously when the user is present. Furthermore, the room climate IS should specifically engage the user in case of poor room climate conditions. Standard room climate systems tend to keep the level of engagement constant, thereby losing the users intention already during periods of good room climate.
- **[KP2] Complex, non-intuitive user interfaces:** Displaying blunt data on a gauge or a digital display requires a lot of prior user knowledge to be effective. Data has to be interpreted and compared against known target values. While an average user can perform interpretation of temperature, e.g. interpreting CO_2 values in parts per million (ppm) can indeed be very challenging.
- **[KP3] Long-term usage challenges:** As discussed, current systems lack self-explanatory user interfaces and do not engage the user when the room climate conditions worsen. This ultimately challenges their long-term usage and impact. However, there is a new generation of internet-enabled system using smart phone apps or other mobile front-end devices to display information. While these systems overcome some of the discussed challenges they bring their own set of issues. Starting up an app is cumbersome compared to an always-visible measurement device. Push notifications can be used as a remedy to inform the user even if she does not start the app. However, these notifications are often perceived as intrusive and disturbing, especially when the user is not in the corresponding room currently experiencing bad conditions.

4.2   Design Principles

Building upon prior research we derived the following four design principles (DP) for the development of a sustainable room climate monitoring system [38]:

- **[DP1] Draw attention only when necessary:** We want to build a monitoring device that is unobtrusive and remains so unless attention is really necessary. Without the need of the users attention the device displays art in its natural form integrate seamlessly into the surroundings addressing KP1 [40]. With decreasing room climate conditions the continuous modifications enables the attentive user to react. When attention is necessary the modification to the art is in full forming, drawing attention of the whole surrounding.
- **[DP2] Connect to people emotionally:** We want to go beyond designing a system that builds upon rationality and cognitive thinking, i.e. leverage emotions and psychological incentives [29]. By creating a visual metaphor through the modification to the art the user easily perceives the connection between room climate and humans health addressing KP2.
- **[DP3] Provide choice:** The design of the artifact is supposed to foster usage and post acceptance (KP3). Therefore, we want to leverage the advantages of personalization [41] and allow the user to customize the solution to a specific taste [42].

- **[DP4] Learn from the past:** Apart from having the current room climate displayed on the spot with the display, the analysis of historic room climate data is possible via a platform. Thereby, users can adjust the settings of their heating and ventilation system or conduct construction measures to improve indoor room-climate.

4.3   Design and Features of the Artifact

The goal of this research is to build a room-climate monitoring system that fosters sustainable ventilation behavior by integrating an innovative user interface. We do so by implementing a hedonic user-interface by incorporating art, which seamlessly blends into the surroundings (DP1). Therefore we build a standard wooden art frame that is equipped with standard room climate sensors, and internet-capable minicomputer and a LCD display to illustrate art. In contrary to a standard framed picture, the displayed art gets modified in real time according to the continuously measured room climate.

Our first prototype showed Marilyn Monroe (Albert Einstein was introduced later) and manipulated. As pointed out by [42] the idea behind using a face is that it is easily recognized, including changes in the appearance following DP2. In general, low temperature is presented by coloring the lips of the portrayed person blue. Likewise high temperatures, exceeding a predefined threshold, transform the lips neon yellow. The intensity of the lips color reflects the extent that the threshold is being exceed/fallen below. Humidity levels are presented by modifications to the skin. Values below a threshold are depicted as a dry skin with cracks. Exceeding the optimal humidity value forms sweat like droplets on the skin. Likewise, the indoor carbon dioxide level is also presented by a modification to the skin. The level of exceedance of each measurement is presented by the intensity of the modification. Figure 2 shows all the modifications in full intensity.

Fig. 2. Modifications according to room-climate conditions (from left: 1. Low temperature, high temperature, low humidity, high humidity, high carbon dioxide level)

This section will further outline the hardware used for the implementation of the design. A wooden art frame was equipped with standard room climate sensors, an internet-capable minicomputer and a LCD display to illustrate art. The artifacts display is a 23-inch TFT-LCD panel. Having a brightness of $250cd/m^2$ and viewing angles of $89°$ in each direction the displays are not recognized as displays but as a normal print of art. The wooden frame hides the metallic edges of the panel and provides enough space in the back of the display to house the sensors, the computer and electrical power supply. The Raspberry Pi, a Linux based small computer, in the back of the display was used to interact with the sensor and display the art using the built in graphic chip. Sensing room climate levels we used the K33 OEM module from Sense Air measuring carbon dioxide concentration with a no dispersive infrared sensor.

Fig. 3. Image showing the back of the prototype; Legend: Raspberry Pi [1], Wooden Frame [2], K33 OEM [3], LCD Display + Display Controllers [4]

Communicating with the Raspberry Pi the sensor provides a UART interface. Figure 3 shows the artifacts inner life with the mentioned hardware.

Beside the display we provide a web portal to change settings. This way the display itself stays a true plug and play product without a complicated user interface. On a web platform the users can change the displayed art to the individual choice (DP3) as well as adapt the behavior of the art. Further it provides the user with historic room climate data (DP4). A comprehensive system-architecture enables the described functionalities. A SQL database (PostgreSQL) stores all the art content that is available for download. A second database stores historical data, handles user administration and provides threshold data.

5   Demonstration and Evaluation

To evaluate the artifact, we conducted a field study in an Austrian Grammar School. The goal of this test is to improve the indoor air quality. We want to show that our system improves indoor air quality (IAQ). As shown in various previous research activities carbon dioxide levels are a good indicator for IAQ [43–45]. Hence we hypothesize:

Hypothesis 1 (H1): Classrooms with an artifact depicting room climate have a better IAQ in respect to carbon dioxide than classrooms with a dummy artifact only measuring IAQ.

Unlike other countries, Austria, the location of the field test, has no binding CO_2-regulations for schools. However local authorities issued three official CO_2-recommendations. The targeted carbon dioxide concentration for mechanically ventilated classrooms (de facto standard in Austria) is below 800 parts per million (ppm). The average over a single lesson shall not exceed 1'000 ppm. Single measurements during lessons should not be above 1'400 ppm.

By focusing the artifacts design on the depicted design principles we further hypothesize, that the students like and use the system, hence ultimately "feel" the improved air quality. We thus hypothesize:

Hypothesis 2a (H2a): The perceived improvement of well-being is higher in classes with the artifact depicting IAQ.

Hypothesis 2b (H2b): Students' level of engagement in improving indoor air quality is higher in classes with the artifact depicting IAQ.

5.1   Pre-test

Before the start of the field-test we pre-tested the first version of the artifact. We installed Marilyn Monroe in a single classroom to test robustness of the system and general system acceptance. The pre-test lasted for 22 days (550 hours), including 65 hours of occupancy during classes. The recorded data revealed CO_2 levels that, even with our feedback system, in 18% of the time CO_2 concentration exceed 1000ppm. Additionally in 5% of the recorded time the concentration exceed concentration levels of 1500ppm. Figure 4 shows the time series of a typical school day with occupancy of pupils during classes (depicted in green).

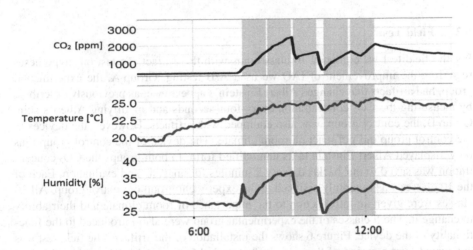

Fig. 4. Time series of room climate level during typical school day

The time series in Figure 4 further reveal that humidity and carbon dioxide levels show similar behavior. This is due to the fact that in buildings without humidifiers the exhaled air is the only source of humidity (increase of humidity goes along with increase of CO_2). Opening a window for fresh air leads to decreasing CO_2 concentrations as well as decreasing humidity (in winter outside air is very dry).

After receiving first feedback from students as well as teachers, we adapted the IS in accordance with the introduced DPs. First, after a discussion with students and on the basis of DP3 we chose a portrait photograph of Albert Einstein for the context of a grammar school. We then adapted the changes of the appearance of Albert Einstein according to the proposed regulations as shown in Figure 5.

Fig. 5. Albert in corresponding CO_2-concentrations; from left: < 800, 1000, 1400, >1500 ppm

Second, we removed monitoring temperature and humidity and the corresponding modifications to the art. This is done following DP1. As shown in previous research [38] it is also possible to modify the face on the basis of multiple room climate parameters, e.g. also color the lips according to the temperature. But it is not the purpose of the monitoring system to draw attention to conditions when the ability to react is not available. Having no control over the heating system and not having a humidifier in classrooms, pupils cannot react to these conditions in the setting at hand. According to the theory of self-efficacy [46] we assume that students' motivation to engage with the system would decrease showing temperature and humidity without appropriate means to react.

5.2   Field Test

For the field test we equipped 10 classrooms with the artifact. To test our hypotheses regarding the improvement of IAQ we used A/B testing. Group A, the experimental group, had artifacts that changed Albert Einstein's appearance, as previously described, by measuring the CO_2 concentration every four seconds and modifying Albert's skin. Group B, the control group, was also equipped with artifacts. However, the devices in the control group did not react on room climate. The device of the control group thus only displayed Albert Einstein in its unmodified form. In both groups the CO_2 concentration was saved to our backend every 5 minutes for analysis and evaluation. Each of the 10 classes was randomly assigned to the experiment group or control group. All 10 classes were given an introduction to the importance of room climate and their ability to change it. The 5 classes of the experimental group were also introduced to the functionality of the device. Figure 6 shows the installation of the artifact. The field test was conducted over a period of 8 weeks. In that period 519 school lessons where held all together: 255 in the experimental group and 264 in the control group.

Fig. 6. Photograph of the installed prototype in a classroom of a secondary school in Austria

We applied multiple regression analysis to examine the impact of the artifact on the improvement in IAQ during the experiment. This method was chosen for three reasons. First, the field test's overall goal was to prove that the system works and has a positive impact on room climate. Hence the average carbon dioxide (dependent variable) should be lower in school classes with an artifact than in the control group classes with a dummy artifact. Second, multiple regression analysis allows us to reflect potential confounds, i.e. outside temperature and numbers of students. And third, because it also allows us to incorporate the individual classrooms in the analysis. Thereby, we can rule out effects that root in the characteristics of the classroom.

The latter two reasons require further explanation. The field test was done in the last two months of the school year, May and June. In May and June the outside temperature varies strongly both over different days, and also within the course of a day. After cold mornings (minimal temperature during the period: 6°C) the temperature rises quickly from lesson to lesson (maximum measured temperature 28°C). Therefore opening a window in the cold mornings is correlated with a discomfort due to the cold and solely done to provide fresh air. At higher temperatures, the windows can remain open providing constant fresh air, erasing the artifacts impact on IAQ. The number of students was taken into the model because for certain lessons, the classes are divided, resulting in a smaller number of students and smaller decrease in IAQ during lessons. The individual rooms were modeled into the analysis because of the different physical characteristics (size, exposition, number of windows).

Table 1. Results of multiple regression analysis

	Coef.	Std. Err	t	P > t
Artifact	-149.59	70.03	-2.14	0.016
Outside Temperature	-23.96	2.95	-8.12	0.000
Number of Students	4.85	2.28	2.12	0.017

The results of the analysis, shown in table 1, support our first hypotheses (H1). There is a significant positive relationship between the artifact and measured CO_2. In addition, the outside temperature has a positive impact on CO_2. Finally, number of students is negative related to CO_2.

To test the robustness of the key findings of the field test and to further examine H2a and H2b we collected qualitative feedback via a questionnaire at the end of the 8 weeks field study. We obtained the data of 181 students (97 female, 84 male) from the age of 14 to 17 (M_{age}= 15.1, SD=1.2). Via a 7-point Likert scale, ranging from 1 (absolutely not) to 7 (absolutely) we measured the level of agreement to statements concerning students' perceived improvement of IAQ. Furthermore, students' perceived engagement to improve room climate was collected.

To examine H2a, i.e. perceived level of improvement, students had to evaluate 4 easy statements like: "Indoor air quality has improved since Albert was installed in the classroom" or "Since Albert was installed in our classroom, I feel more comfortable in our classroom". A t-test, shown in Figure 7, revealed that students in classes with the artifact had a significantly higher perceived improvement of well-being, t(180)=-9.17, p<0.001.

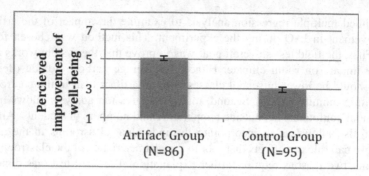

Fig. 7. Mean perceived improvement of well-being by group members

With H2b we wanted to test students' perceived engagement to improve room climate, an indicator on the usage of the system. Students were asked for their level of agreement to statements such as: "Since Albert was mounted in our classroom, I take care that our classroom is well ventilated" or "Also in the future, I will take care that our classroom is well ventilated". A second t-test depicted in figure 8, revealed that the students perceived level of engagement is also significantly higher in classes with an installed and functioning artifact, $t(179)=-5.26$, $p<0.001$.

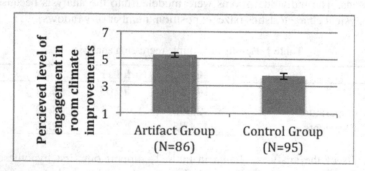

Fig. 8. Mean perceived level of engagement in room climate improvement by group members

Summing up, the results of the field test support the three hypotheses. Over the period of 8 weeks the group with the artifact depicting IQA had a better room climate in respect to CO_2. The results of the questionnaire also support the effectiveness of the artifact in respect to subjective artifact perception.

6   Conclusion

In this paper we suggested a novel design for a monitoring system to help the user comprehend and further improve indoor air quality, in order to prevent negative effects correlated with poor indoor air quality. Although prior research in domains such as "informative art systems" [47] or "ambient information systems" [48] also present innovative systems, the depicted designs focus on showing what is technically possible rather than finding reliable empirical evidence for their effectiveness. Commercially available systems reveal severe limitations, especially in respect to sustainable user engagement. By incorporating art, the proposed design of our artifact connects with the user on an emotional level, helps understanding the monitored values and integrates perfectly into the surroundings. The evaluation of the artifact was done by a demonstration in a field experiment.

The field study in this paper has various limitations. The experimental design was not a double blind study. Therefore a Hawthorne Effect [49] cannot be fully excluded, i.e. the behavior of the students could have been influenced due to the fact that they knew they were part of an experiment. We tried to diminish an eventual bias with randomized group allocation [50]. In addition, the restricted duration of our field test limits the generalizability of our findings. Indeed, in summer, when windows can stay open, the need for our artifact is not given. We tried to address the mentioned issues by taking the outside temperature explicitly into our model. Future studies following the proposed design principles should also consider ethical implications. In the case of our study with young people in schools, the artifact must not depict images that could trigger strong negative emotions, such as disgust, fear or anger.

The field experiment provides evidence for the positive impact of the artifact. More specifically, the study contributes to research on IS-enabled visual feedback systems. Our research shows evidence, that storytelling in a negative feedback loop as well as real time feedback contributes to the theoretical knowledgebase in the design and the effectiveness of a visual feedback system. The results though do not allow disentangling the effect of each given theory. Consequently, future work should focus on disentangling. In the course of our study we highlighted the importance of small details on feedback design and implementation, e.g. the effect of art modifications on the basis of temperature and humidity, which have substantial impact on behavior.

Following the DSR Methodology, the findings of this research approve the design for this specific use-case of an IAQ IS and provide motivations for future adaptions to the artifact. In the context of the school, we are going to extend the field test over the course of a whole school year. This allows us to evaluate the long-term system engagement and further evaluate the impact on student performance and health, as measured in yearly grades and in sick students over the course of a year. Furthermore, future experimental setups will be dedicated to a more fundamental research questions, i.e. "Are hedonic, art-based IS superior to utilitarian, non-art-based IS in respect to (long-term) usage and impact?" Therefore we want to compare the improved art-based artifact to a non-art based, utilitarian monitoring system. Ultimately, we intend to derive a design theory for art-based IS.

While the focus of this paper is on room-climate and ventilation, other data can be monitored in real-time. Data produced by the increasing number of connected sensors in everyday life could also modify similar art devices. Apart from the school context, we are currently also investigating the applicability of our solution to the case of diabetes through visualizing glucose levels as well as HbA1c. By providing a similar feedback system, we hope to help patients manage their diabetes mellitus more effective.

Acknowledgements. This research was supported by the Bosch IoT Lab at the University of St. Gallen, Switzerland. The authors would further like to thank the anonymous reviewers for their valuable comments and suggestions to improve the quality of the paper.

References

1. Skov, P., Valbjorn, O., Pedersen, B.V.: Influence of Indoor Climate on the Sick Building Syndrome in an Office Environment: The Danish Indoor Climate Study Group. Scand. J. Work. Environ. Health. 16, 363–371 (1990)
2. Chaudhry, B.: Systematic Review: Impact of Health Information Technology on Quality, Efficiency, and Costs of Medical Care. Ann. Intern. Med. 144, 742 (2006)
3. Shekelle, P.G., Morton, S.C.S., Keeler, E.E.B.: Costs and benefits of health information technology. Evid. Rep. Technol. Assess (Full. Rep). 132, 1–71 (2006)
4. Goldzweig, C., Towfigh, A., Maglione, M., Shekelle, P.: Costs and benefits of health information technology: new trends from the literature. Health Aff. 28, 282–293 (2009)
5. Brug, J., Glanz, K., Van Assema, P., Kok, G., van Breukelen, G.J.P.: The Impact of Computer-Tailored Feedback and Iterative Feedback on Fat, Fruit, and Vegetable Intake. Heal. Educ. Behav. 25, 517–531 (1998)
6. Strecher, V., Kreuter, M., Den Boer, D., Kobrin, S., Hospers, H.J., Skinner, C.S.: The effects of computer-tailored smoking cessation messages in family practice settings. J. Fam. Pract. 39, 262–268 (1994)
7. Baker, A., Wardle, J.: Increasing Fruit and Vegetable Intake Among Adults Attending Colorectal Cancer Screening The Efficacy of a Brief Tailored Intervention. Cancer Epidemiol. Biomarkers Prev. 11, 203–206 (2002)
8. Kreuter, M.W., Strecher, V.J.: Do tailored behavior change messages enhance the effectiveness of health risk appraisal? Results from a randomized trial. Health Educ. Res. 11, 97–105 (1996)
9. Noar, S.M., Benac, C.N., Harris, M.S.: Does tailoring matter? Meta-analytic review of tailored print health behavior change interventions. Psychol. Bull. 133, 673–693 (2007)
10. Abrams, D.B., Orleans, C.T., Niaura, R.S., Goldstein, M.G., Prochaska, J.O., Velicer, W.: Integrating individual and public health perspectives for treatment of tobacco dependence under managed health care: a combined stepped-care and matching model. Ann. Behav. Med. 18, 290–304 (1996)
11. Webb, T.L., Joseph, J., Yardley, L., Michie, S.: Using the internet to promote health behavior change: a systematic review and meta-analysis of the impact of theoretical basis, use of behavior change techniques, and mode of delivery on efficacy. J. Med. Internet Res. 12, e4 (2010)
12. Glasgow, R.E., Bull, S.S., Piette, J.D., Steiner, J.F.: Interactive behavior change technology: A partial solution to the competing demands of primary care. Am. J. Prev. Med. 27, 80–87 (2004)
13. Richardson, C.R., Brown, B.B., Foley, S., Dial, K.S., Lowery, J.C.: Feasibility of adding enhanced pedometer feedback to nutritional counseling for weight loss. J. Med. Internet Res. 7, e56 (2005)
14. Wing, R.R., Tate, D.F., Gorin, A.A., Raynor, H.A., Fava, J.L.: A self-regulation program for maintenance of weight loss. N. Engl. J. Med. 355, 1563–1571 (2006)
15. Tate, D.F., Jackvony, E.H., Wing, R.R.: Effects of Internet behavioral counseling on weight loss in adults at risk for type 2 diabetes: a randomized trial. JAMA 289, 1833–1836 (2003)

16. Fjeldsoe, B.S., Marshall, A.L., Miller, Y.D.: Behavior change interventions delivered by mobile telephone short-message service. Am. J. Prev. Med. 36, 165–173 (2009)

17. Nestoriuc, Y., Martin, A.: Efficacy of biofeedback for migraine: A meta-analysis. Pain 128, 111–127 (2007)

18. Nakao, M., Yano, E., Nomura, S., Kuboki, T.: Blood Pressure-Lowering Effects of Bio-feedback Treatment in Hypertension: A Meta-Analysis of Randomized Controlled Trials. Hypertens. Res. 26, 37–46 (2003)

19. Carver, C.S., Scheier, M.F.: Control theory: A useful conceptual framework for personali-ty-social, clinical, and health psychology. Psychol. Bull. 92, 111–135 (1982)

20. Wiener, N.: Cybernetics: Control and communication in the animal and the machine. Methuen, Cambridge (1948)

21. Dignum, F., Kinny, D., Sonenberg, L.: From desires, obligations and norms to goals. Cogn. Sci. Q. 2, 405–427 (2002)

22. Kenkel, D.: Health behavior, health knowledge, and schooling. J. Polit. Econ. 99, 287–305 (1991)

23. Myerson, J., Green, L.: Discounting of delayed rewards: Models of individual choice. J. Exp. Anal. Behav. 3, 263–276 (1995)

24. Gershon, N., Eick, S.G., Card, S.: Information visualization. Interactions 5, 9–15 (1998)

25. Davis, F.: Perceived Usefulness, Perceived Ease of Use, and User Acceptance of Informa-tion Technology. MIS Q. 13, 319–340 (1989)

26. Gershon, N., Page, W.: What storytelling can do for information visualization. Commun. ACM 44, 31–37 (2001)

27. American Psychiatric Association: Diagnostic and Statistical Manual of Mental Disorders. DSM-IV-TR. American Psychiatric Association, Washington, DC (2000)

28. Nakajima, T., Lehdonvirta, V., Tokunaga, E., Kimura, H.: Reflecting human behavior to motivate desirable lifestyle. In: Proceedings of the 7th ACM Conference on Designing Interactive Systems, DIS 20008, pp. 405–414. ACM Press, New York (2008)

29. Nakajima, T., Lehdonvirta, V.: Designing Motivation Using Persuasive Ambient Mirrors. Pers. Ubiquitous Comput. 17, 107–126 (2011)

30. Brown, J.S., Denning, S., Groh, K., Prusak, L.: Storytelling in Organizations: Why Story-telling is Transforming 21st Century Organizations and Management. Elsevier, Burlington (2005)

31. Lamme, V.A.F.: Why visual attention and awareness are different. Trends Cogn. Sci. 7, 12–18 (2003)

32. Carver, C.S.: Facilitation of physical aggression through objective self-awareness. J. Exp. Soc. Psychol. 10, 365–370 (1974)

33. Carver, C.S.: Physical aggression as a function of objective self-awareness and attitudes toward punishment. J. Exp. Soc. Psychol. 11, 510–519 (1975)

34. Fenigstein, A., Scheier, M.F., Buss, A.H.: Public and private self-consciousness: Assess-ment and theory. J. Consult. Clin. Psychol. 43, 522–527 (1975)

35. Greenberg, J.: Attentional focus and locus of performance causality as determinants of equity behavior. J. Pers. Soc. Psychol. 38, 579–585 (1980)

36. Hevner, A., March, S., Park, J., Ram, S.: Design Science in Information System Research. MIS Q. 28, 75–105 (2004)

37. Peffers, K., Tuunanen, T., Rothenberger, M.A., Chatterjee, S.: A Design Science Research Methodology for Information Systems Research. J. Manag. Inf. Syst. 24, 45–77 (2007)

38. Rigger, P., Wortmann, F.: An Art-Based IS for Improving Room-Climate. In: Tremblay, M.C., VanderMeer, D., Rothenberger, M., Gupta, A., Yoon, V. (eds.) DESRIST 2014. LNCS, vol. 8463, pp. 413–417. Springer, Heidelberg (2014)

39. The Netatmo Wheater Station, http://www.netatmo.com/en-US/product
40. Hallnäs, L., Redström, J.: Slow Technology – Designing for Reflection. Pers. Ubiquitous Comput. 5, 201–212 (2001)
41. Kulkarni, A.: Design Principles of a Reactive Behavioral System for the Intelligent Room. Bitstream MIT J. EECS Student Res., 1–6 (2002)
42. Ferscha, A.: A Matter of Taste. Ambient Intell., 287–304 (2007)
43. Scheff, P.A., Paulius, V.K., Huang, S.W., Conroy, L.M.: Indoor air quality in a middle school, Part I: Use of CO2 as a tracer for effective ventilation. Appl. Occup. Environ. Hyg. 15, 824–834 (2000)
44. Scheff, P.A., Paulius, V.K., Curtis, L., Conroy, L.M.: Indoor air quality in a middle school, Part II: Development of emission factors for particulate matter and bioaerosols. Appl. Occup. Environ. Hyg. 15, 835–842 (2000)
45. Ferng, S.-F., Lee, L.-W.: Indoor air quality assessment of daycare facilities with carbon dioxide, temperature, and humidity as indicators. J. Environ. Health. 65, 14–18, 22 (2002)
46. Bandura, A.: Self-efficacy: Toward a unifying theory of behavioral change
47. Holmquist, L., Skog, T.: Informative art: information visualization in everyday environments. In: Proc. 1st Int. Conf. Comput. Graph. Interact. Tech. Australas. South East Asia. (2003)
48. Pousman, Z., Stasko, J.: A Taxonomy of Ambient Information Systems. In: Proceedings of the Working Conference on Advanced Visual Interfaces, AVI 2006, p. 67. ACM Press, New York (2006)
49. McCarney, R., Warner, J., Iliffe, S., van Haselen, R., Griffin, M., Fisher, P.: The Hawthorne Effect: A randomised, controlled trial. BMC Med. Res. Methodol. 7, 30 (2007)
50. Clark, R.E., Sugrue, B.M.: Research on instructional media. Educ. media Technol. Yearb. 14, 19–36 (1978-1988)

Designing a Report Recommendation Assistant: A First Design Cycle

Martin Kretzer[✉], Maximilian Kleinedler, Christian Theilemann, and Alexander Mädche

Institute for Enterprise Systems, University of Mannheim, Mannheim, Germany
{kretzer, kleinedler,theilemann,maedche}@es.uni-mannheim.de

Abstract. Employees often supplement their organization's Business Intelligence (BI) system with individually tinkered reports. Unfortunately, these supplements bear numerous threats such as limited report reuse across all users of the BI system. Therefore, we established a design science research (DSR) project by exploring impediments of existing BI systems, building meta-requirements and suggesting design principles. In particular, we propose a Report Recommendation Assistant (RRA) for improving reuse of reports across potential users.

In this paper, we present our DSR project and focus on the first evaluation cycle. Our results indicate that the RRA has a positive impact on perceived ease of use and perceived usefulness of the BI system. Furthermore, we find that these effects are negatively moderated by user's expertise in using the BI system and are not biased by the underlying BI system. Finally, we leverage results from BI expert interviews and existing literature to refine the proposed RRA.

Keywords: Business intelligence · Design science research · Diffusion of reports · Report reuse · Recommendation assistant

1 Introduction

Over the last decade, many organizations made large investments into implementing standardized software products with the expectations that the resulting information systems (IS) integrate data and processes, allow control and reduce costs [1]. However, research indicates that these systems oftentimes do not achieve the expected goals due to numerous reasons such as missing flexibility and long implementation times necessary to change them [2]. To mitigate this problem, end users tend to supplement their IS with additional artifacts. This phenomenon has recently gained momentum because individuals today may choose from, and are able to use, an unlimited pool of advices and services [3].

However, these individually supplemented systems come along with dangerous threats such as limited reuse of data and functionalities [4]. Therefore, literature embraces them only within defined boundaries [2]. Rather than continuously installing additional supplementary systems, organizations should target stable systems that empower users and provide them with the flexibility to create new output [5]. This

© Springer International Publishing Switzerland 2015
B. Donnellan et al. (Eds.): DESRIST 2015, LNCS 9073, pp. 87–103, 2015.
DOI: 10.1007/978-3-319-18714-3_6

applies especially to Business Intelligence (BI) systems because (1) many users of BI systems frequently develop supplementary, individually tinkered reports [6] and (2) reuse of these reports across potential users is typically very low [4]. Consequently, an examination of possibilities for simultaneously increasing report reuse and users' flexibility with regards to report development would be highly interesting for industry and academia.

Our overall research project aims at designing such a BI system. As part of this research project, we address the following research question in this paper: *How to design a BI system that improves reuse of reports across employees without limiting employees' abilities to individualize their own reports?*

To answer this question, we first present our DSR project and then present two quantitative evaluation and one qualitative refinement study. In particular, the remainder of this paper is structured as follows: Section 2 shortly introduces related work. Section 3 briefly summarizes our overall DSR project. Upon our previous work [7], we now present instantiations of the proposed design principle as well as testable hypotheses for confirming or rejecting the proposed impact of the design principle. Furthermore, section 4 outlines our research methodology and section 5 presents our results. Section 6 discusses and refines the proposed design principle. Finally, section 7 concludes our work and outlines the next steps of our DSR project.

2   Related Work

In this paper, we investigate reuse of reports across users. Extant literature indicates tensions between reuse of reports and development of new reports that needed to be balanced by organizations [2], [4]. On the one hand, BI systems need to foster user's "ability to create, generate, or produce a new output, structure or behavior without any input from the originator of the system" [5, p. 750]. That is, they need to be flexible and empower users to quickly make use of this flexibility [8]; e.g. through quickly developing new reports [9], [10]. On the other hand, however, BI systems need to be stable because stability is a precondition for reuse of reports across users as well as a precondition for being able to develop new reports in the long run [5]. As a consequence, BI system designers need to balance the tensions [11] between developing additional reports within the BI system and reusing existing reports across users [12].

In particular, our work aims at increasing diffusion of reports. That is, reuse of reports across different employees or, more precisely, the number of employees who are using a certain report [13].

Diffusion of reports is important for organizations because more employees can benefit from the same report; thus generating scale effects (e.g., with regards to report development, maintenance and execution) and ultimately increasing the report's value for its organization. Diffusion emphasizes how new technologies, practices and ideas are adopted within a population of potential adopters [14]. The major underlying assumption is that diffusion starts slow but accelerates with each additional adopter until the innovation is adopted by the majority of the population. After this point, diffusion slows down, thus leading to an S-shaped curve as cumulative adoption function. Early studies on diffusion deemed available knowledge about a technology to be a major driver of diffusion of that technology. Knowledge about a technology, which is available within an organization, decreases knowledge barriers and improves adoption of the technology. New adopters in turn generate and provide additional knowledge about the technology, which progressively lowers the knowledge barriers for others to adopt and use the same technology [15]. Furthermore, research found an impact of socialization on diffusion. For instance, Dinev and Hu [16] draw on diffusion theory to explain socialization effects. They assume that individuals build up knowledge and become aware of new technologies through interacting with the society. This socialization effect then influences the individual's preferences and perceptions, for example, attitude formation, perceived behavioral control as well as social preferences, such as subjective norms. Similarly, Mustonen-Ollila and Lyytinen [17] determined organizational and environmental factors that cause a technology's diffusion within an organization and Siponen et al. [18] applied diffusion theory to investigate how the social context affects individuals' adoption decisions.

Synthesizing related work, we infer that diffusion refers to the increasing number of users who adopt a certain technology over time. Upon this understanding, we adopt the notion of report diffusion to refer to the number of employees who use a certain report at a certain minimum frequency. Although little report diffusion is a problem many organizations are facing, existing research does not yet prescribe how to tackle it while preserving employees' abilities to individualize their own reports.

3   Design Science Research Project – An Overview

The work presented in this paper is part of a larger research project with the goal of designing a BI system which facilitates balancing report reuse and development of new reports. Specifically, we established a design science research (DSR) project to address our research questions because DSR is particularly suited to theoretically prescribe how to do something [19]. In particular, this paper focuses on improving reuse of reports across users of the BI system without limiting their ability to develop new, individual reports.

Researchers have recommended DSR to investigate complex, non-decomposable research and business problems [20-21], understand and change generative events [22], and highlight knowledge creation based on rigorous validations [23-24]. According to Hevner [25], researchers first need to become aware of the relevant business problem they intend to investigate. The results of this stage are typically formulated as impediments of the current system [26]. Second, researchers should rigorously make use of the extant scientific knowledge base and theorize meta-attributes of the pursued future system [25]. These meta-attributes are usually referred to as meta-requirements (MRs; [27]) because they reflect generic requirements that need to be met. Finally, a system needs to be designed that fulfills the identified meta-requirements. Therefore, design principles (DPs) are proposed that describe how the new system should be implemented in order to meet the identified meta-requirements. Finally, these DPs should be implemented, evaluated and refined iteratively during multiple cycles [20], [25].

As a part of our overall DSR project, in this paper we focus on the instantiation, evaluation and refinement phases of the first design science cycle. Therefore, we only briefly present impediments to existing BI systems and only briefly introduce one of our identified meta-requirements and one of our proposed design principles [7].

3.1   Problem Awareness and Suggestion

As the exploration of impediments requires flexibility for examining aspects of report diffusion that may not be completely identifiable at the outset of the study, we conducted an exploratory interview study [28]. This is a common approach for establishing DSR projects [26]. Four sites were selected on the basis of theoretical relevance and to ensure an adequate foundation for comparison and to maximize variation [29]. Specifically, we selected two organizations that focus on stability and two organizations that focus on flexibility. Furthermore, since literature indicates a beneficial effect on balancing stability and flexibility from establishing additional specialized organizational units between end users and IT professionals [30], we assured that exactly one organization of each group had established a BI Competency Center (BICC). BICCs are specialized organizational units that perform cross-functional tasks regarding development, operation and support of BI systems across a company [30]. Furthermore, in order to mitigate industry biases, all four organizations are vehicle manufacturing companies. In total, we interviewed 20 employees in order to reveal impediments of current BI systems. [7] provides details about the selected organizations, the chosen snowball sampling approach, participants, semi-structured interview questions, data triangulation and the step-wise coding process.

The interview study indicated that diffusion of reports across the users of a BI system represents a major challenge for organizations. Moreover, the interview study revealed impediments to diffusion of reports across the users of a BI system. For instance, a BICC expert at one organization explained how he believes that the reason why end users tailor their own individual reports would not be a lack of reports or a misfit of existing reports to users' needs. Rather, the problem would be that users would not be able to retrieve the reports they were looking for: *"We have very detailed possibilities for analyses. [...] I fear it is less a problem that a required report does not exist. Rather the user gets buried by the bulk of options for selecting the report."*

This impediment adversely affects diffusion, because the ability to find a report is a precondition for an employee to reuse another employee's report. Too many options create huge complexity and intransparency over existing reports. To work around this impediment, end users start creating new reports instead of searching and reusing existing reports. Ultimately, this fuels a vicious circle. If employees create new reports because they cannot find their required reports, they further increase the number of reports and, thus, make retrieval of reports even more difficult. This is bad for their organizations because if existing reports are less often reused across individual teams and departments, achieving scale effects and operational efficiency becomes more difficult [2], [4-5].

Similarly, it is difficult for BI experts and administrators to identify reports that were developed by a specific employee but might also be useful to further employees. For instance, an interviewee at another organization who focuses on maintaining the organization's BI system complaints about the increasing number of reports: *"The problem I see is this identification. [....] How do you identify 'Oh, this is so great that others need it too'. You somehow have to provide a possibility to make this public."*

To tackle issues of little diffusion, extant literature has shown that diffusion increases through social influence [31], [32]. Potential new users typically turn to prior users as socially influential referents for determining the appropriate adoption choice [31]. However, contagious social influences of different prior users are not constant [33-34]. Therefore, they should be made visible to potential new users. Building on the findings from our exploratory interview study and extant literature, we derive a first meta-requirement which should be addressed in order to improve diffusion of reports across all users of the BI system.

> **MR1.** *In order to increase diffusion of a report, a BI system should make the social influence of previous users on a potential new user visible.*

As explained above, a BI system needs to improve visibility of the social influence of prior report users in order to improve diffusion of a specific report. Building on literature, a key factor for improving visibility is user guidance as it allows focusing a user's attention on desired information and functionalities. In the 1990s, Silver [35] started examining possibilities for decisional guidance and their potential impacts. Briefly after that, Dhaliwal and Benbasat [36] developed a framework for knowledge-based system explanations. Ever since, guidance studies have examined manifold application areas and have been conducted on individuals as well as groups [37]. More recently, guidance studies highlighted the need for recommendation assistants. Especially in the field of e-commerce, recommendation assistants who provide additional information and explanations have been found to focus customers' attention and affect their shopping behavior [38]. The goal of affecting online customers' shopping behaviors is conceptually similar to our goal of improving diffusion of reports. In both situations a user's attention is being focused on a particular information (e.g., a shopping item or the infectiousness of a report's prior users) in order to lead the user into performing a certain action (e.g., buying the item or executing the report). Therefore, we propose the usage of a report recommendation assistant (RRA) as a response to MR1.

> **DP1.** *In order to increase diffusion of reports, the BI system should recommend reports upon the social influence of previous users on the user.*

3.2   Instantiations

Design principles usually can be implemented in multiple different ways. This particularly accounts to BI systems because they are also composed of different architectural layers (e.g., database system, data warehouse, and reporting client). Thus, we first had to decide on which layer the RRA should be implemented. We opted for the client layer because only an extension to the BI client may sense the user's environment and, thus, analyze the user's currently selected data. Server-side layers (e.g., database and data warehouse) can only analyze which queries are executed by the user; but not which subset of all the data returned by a particular query is actually being filtered for analysis.

As a first running prototype, we implemented the aforementioned RRA as an extension to the BI client *SAP BusinessObjects Office Analysis*. Since this BI client itself is an extension to *Microsoft Excel*, the RRA looks and feels like an extension to *Microsoft Excel*. Regarding its capabilities, this RRA is able to access metadata from the central BI system and combine this information with contextual information such as currently filtered dimensions. The RRA recommends frequently used reports developed by prior users who have been investigating similar dimensions and are using similar data filters and, thus, have a high social influence on the current user [31]. Fig. 1 shows a screen-shot of our prototype.

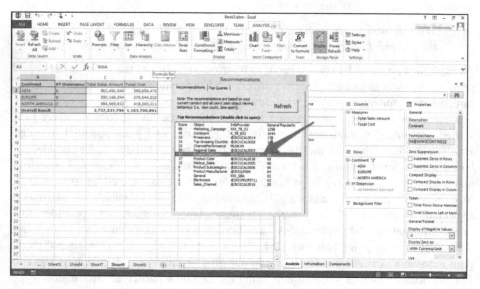

Fig. 1. Instantiation of a working RRA prototype

In addition, we developed alternative user interface mockups of three popular BI clients that were extended by the same RRA. Thus, we were able to control for potential biasing effects resulting from the BI client. Specifically, we instantiated the RRA as a side panel to three common types of BI clients [39]: First, we instantiated the RRA as an extension to a BI client which is typically used for agile business analysis and accessing data from rather small and medium BI systems, i.e., *Tableau Desktop*. Second, we instantiated the RRA as an extension to a BI client which is typically used for accessing data from a large, global BI system, i.e., *SAP BW/BO*. Finally, third, we instantiated the RRA as an extension to a BI client which itself extends *Microsoft Excel*. *Microsoft Excel*-based BI clients are provided by all large BI vendors in order to offer users ways to access large, global BI systems in familiar ways. We extended each of the three BI clients with a side panel that recommends additional reports based on the social influence of previous users and similarity to the currently viewed data. Fig. 2 and Fig. 3 show the RRA (i.e., the panel at the right side of the screen) as an extension to the three BI clients.

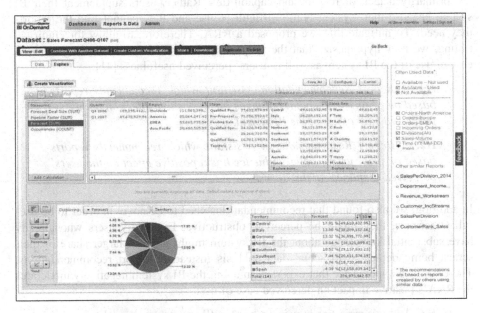

Fig. 2. SAP BW/BO extended with the RRA (panel on the right side)

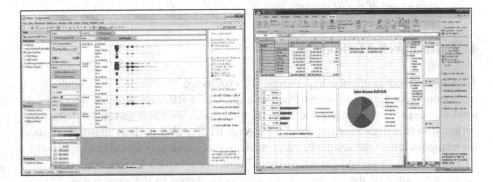

Fig. 3. Tableau Desktop (left) and MS Excel-based BI client (right) extended with the RRA

3.3 Testable Hypotheses

The goal of our work is to design a BI system that increases diffusion of reports. However, as empirically measuring diffusion of reports requires measuring usage of reports at multiple points in time [13], the work presented in this paper focuses on measuring antecedents of usage in a first step. In particular, we focus on perceived ease of use (PEOU) and perceived usefulness (PUSF) as antecedents of usage because numerous research studies have already confirmed the positive impact of PEOU and PUSF on intention to use, e.g. [40-41]. Besides, when we explored impediments of current BI systems, we found that the reason why users supplement their BI system is not primarily a lack of reports and capabilities. Rather, users supplement their BI system because their system is too difficult to use and they cannot find the reports they need. To mitigate this, we proposed a RRA. Therefore, to allow for empirical testing, we now hypothesize that the proposed RRA will improve users' perceived ease of use of the BI system as well as users' perceived usefulness [41]:

> **H1.** *A Report Recommendation Assistant which recommends reports based on prior users' social influence has a positive effect on the users' perceived ease of use of the BI system.*

> **H2.** *A Report Recommendation Assistant which recommends reports based on prior users' social influence has a positive effect on the users' perceived usefulness of the BI system.*

In addition, we also found that recommendations need to be novel in order to be useful. Otherwise, they might be perceived obstructive. Especially users who already have substantial knowledge about the BI system might prefer a larger share of their screen being dedicated to actual data analysis instead of report recommendations. Therefore, we hypothesize that expertise in using the BI system negatively moderates the RRA's positive impact on perceived ease of use:

> **H3.** *A user's expertise in using a certain BI system weakens the positive effect of a Report Recommendation Assistant on that users' perceived ease of use of the BI system.*

4   Research Method

To test the aforementioned hypotheses, we conducted two evaluation studies. First, we conducted a survey to investigate the impact of a RRA on students who have 12 weeks of experience in using the BI system. Second, we conducted a laboratory experiment to investigate the impact of a RRA on BI consultants. This approach allowed for triangulation of the results because novices (i.e., students) as well as experts (i.e., BI consultants) evaluated the RRA. In addition, we conducted semi-structured interviews with some of the BI consultants who participated in the experiment. This allowed us to explore how the proposed RRA should be further refined.

4.1   Confirmatory Studies for Evaluating Design Principle 1

As part of the first evaluation study, 100 graduate students, aged 22-29, who are specializing in "Business Intelligence and Management Support Systems" used a BI system for 12 weeks to explore a retail store's sales data [42]. Students were equipped with and trained in using the aforementioned BI client *SAP BusinessObjects Office Analysis* (Fig. 1) [43]. During the 12 week period, students were using the BI client without a RRA in order to familiarize themselves with the "standard" BI client. Afterwards, we surveyed them about their experienced [40] ease of use and usefulness of the BI client without a RRA. Furthermore, we showed them screen-shots of the BI client with the RRA and asked them about their expected [40] ease of use and usefulness of the BI client with a RRA. Furthermore, we surveyed participants whether they would intend to use the BI client with RRA or the BI client without RRA. All question items were based on the question items of the Technology Acceptance Model [41] because this model and its question items have been validated in numerous studies. Following recommendations in literature [40], question items were only adjusted to capture the difference between experiences and expectations. Finally, we received 98 completely answered questionnaires.

In order to triangulate our findings with experienced BI experts, we selected BI consultants for the second experiment and conducted a scenario description experiment. Scenario description experiments show and describe different scenarios (typically different user interfaces) to participants who then are asked to answer questions about those scenarios. Scenario description experiments are a specific type of laboratory experiments [44]. Since they allow for high control over potential confounding factors (i.e., high internal validity), scenario description experiments are particularly suited as evaluation technique before conducting expensive field experiments [44]. All participating BI consultants worked for one of two large international technology and management consulting companies. Specifically, we provided five BI consultants from each company with a link to the scenario description experiment website who then forwarded the link to further colleagues. Finally, 37 BI consultants answered all scenarios.

The scenario description experiment represented a mixed experiment design with recommendations (on, off) as within-subjects variable and the specific BI client (Tableau Desktop, SAP BW/BO, Microsoft Excel-based BI client) and expertise (self-reported on a Likert scale ranging from 1 to 5) as between-subjects variables. In particular, we first asked participants about their experiences in the usage of the three BI clients. Afterwards we provided four scenarios. Three of those four scenarios showed typical screens of the three BI clients (without RRA) and asked participants about their PEOU of each of them. The fourth scenario randomly selected one BI client, showed a screen of that BI client with a RRA implemented as a side panel (Fig. 1) and asked participants about their PEOU of the shown BI client with RRA. Additionally, in order to focus participant's attention on the shown recommendation assistant, the fourth scenario also included a sentence indicating that the side panel had been added. Again, all question items were adopted from previous literature: three items measuring expertise were adopted from Bhattacherjee and Sanford [45] and four items measuring PEOU were adopted from Davis [41]. Furthermore, to mitigate bias due to carry-over effects, learning effects and decreasing motivation, we counterbalanced the order in which the scenarios were presented to the study participants.

4.2   Subsequent Exploratory Study for Refining Design Principle 1

In order to refine the proposed design principles, we conducted semi-structured interviews with five BI consultants who also participated in the experimental evaluation.

BI consultants were suited for refinement due to their extensive knowledge about organizations' challenges with BI systems. Besides, these interviews also allowed us to qualitatively confirm the experiment findings. Table 1 provides detailed descriptive statistics about the interviews.

During the interviews, we showed the instantiated RRA mockups to the interviewees. Furthermore, we developed an interview guideline which focused on (1) the interviewee's opinion about recommending reports in order to increase reuse of reports, (2) the instantiated interface mockups, (3) ideas for alternative approaches, (4) issues that might occur during a real world implementation of a RRA, and (5) ideas for refinement.

Table 1. Interviews for exploring refinement requirements and opportunities

Interviewee Level	Quantity	Avg. duration	Avg. transcript length
BI Consultant	4	33 min	12 pages
BI Senior Manager	1	54 min	15 pages
Total	5	37 min	13 pages

5   Results

5.1   Confirmatory Evaluation Study 1

First, we compared experienced usefulness and experienced ease of use of the BI client without RRA against the expected usefulness and expected ease of use of the BI client with RRA [40]. Results indicate that both usefulness as well as ease of use are significantly higher with RRA; thus confirming H1 and H2. Table 2 provides detailed statistics. In addition, we asked participants, whether they would prefer to use the BI client without a RRA or with a RRA if they had to choose. On a scale ranging from -3 "strong preference for the BI client without RRA" to 0 "neutral" and to 3 "strong preference for the BI client with RRA", participants on average rated 1.33 (with a standard deviation of 1.19). Therefore, based on the results of this study, we conclude that there seems to be a preference for the BI client with RRA as opposed to the BI client without RRA.

Table 2. Evaluation Study 1: Survey with Graduate Students

Dependent Variable	BI Client		Mean abs. difference	t-value
	without RRA	with RRA		
Perc. usefulness	4.52 (1.15)	5.41 (0.92)	1.09	9.34 ***
Perc. ease of use	4.80 (0.99)	5.23 (1.13)	1.02	10.17 ***

N=98; values in brackets show std. dev.; t-value calculated using paired t-test).
Significance levels: ***p<0.001 (two-tailed).

5.2   Confirmatory Evaluation Study 2

To triangulate the first evaluation study's findings, we conducted a second study with BI consultants. We first gathered information about the expertise of participating BI consultants in using the three BI clients. While participants showed similar experiences in using the BI clients *SAP BW/BO* and the *Microsoft Excel*-based BI client, they had less experience in using *Tableau Desktop*. Table 3 provides detailed descriptive statistics on expertise per BI client.

Table 3. Participants' expertise in using the three BI clients

BI Client	Expertise Mean (Std. dev.)
Tableau Desktop	2.19 (1.41)
SAP BW/BO	3.32 (1.56)
MS Excel-based BI client	3.22 (1.38)
Total	2.91 (1.26)

Following widespread experiment research [44], we conducted analysis of variance (ANOVA) and F-tests to confirm or reject our hypotheses. As statistical analysis tool we used the statistical programming environment R. Our results indicate that report recommendations have a positive impact on PEOU (H1). Furthermore, our results indicate that the positive effect of report recommendations is reduced by users' prior experience in using the BI client (H3) at $p<0.05$. Although the positive effect of report recommendations on PEOU is "only" significant at $p<0.1$, we view H1 as being confirmed for the following two reasons: First, PEOU increased for all experience levels and all BI clients except for the highest experience level (i.e., experience level 5; see Fig. 3). This indicates that as long as users do not have very strong knowledge about the BI system, a report recommendation assistant increases PEOU. Second, since our evaluation serves as first evaluation cycle, the sample size is rather low and thus moderate significance levels of $p<0.1$ can already indicate interesting effects. Detailed statistics are provided in Table 4.

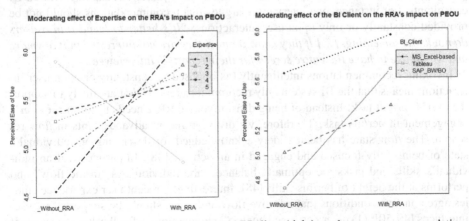

Fig. 3. Moderating effect of expertise (left) and BI client (right) on the report recommendation assistant's (RRA) effect on perceived ease of use (PEOU)

Table 4. Evaluation Study 2: Mixed Design Experiment with BI Consultants

	Df	Sum Sq	Mean Sq	F value	P(>F)
Between-subjects:					
Expertise (EXP)	4	0.42	0.106	0.048	0.995
CLIENT	2	6.93	3.464	1.587	0.227
EXP*CLIENT	8	24.23	3.029	1.387	0.256
Residuals	22	48.03	2.183		
Within-subjects:					
Recommendation (REC)	1	4.879	4.879	4.010	**0.058+**
REC*EXP	4	14.629	3.657	3.006	**0.040***
REC*CLIENT	2	0.496	0.248	0.204	0.817
REC*EXP*CLIENT	8	13.952	1.744	1.433	0.238
Residuals	22	26.769	1.217		

Dependent variable: PEOU;   N=37. Significance: *p<0.05; +p<0.10
[expertise (EXP); BI client (CLIENT); recommendation (REC)]

6   Refinement and Discussion

In addition to the confirmatory studies, we conducted semi-structured interviews with BI experts in order to refine the proposed RRA. While none of them disputed the results of our evaluation studies, some interviewees raised concerns about the RRA's usefulness for experienced users. For instance, one of them mentioned that it would be *"difficult to find an appropriate algorithm to really suggest something relevant"* (Interviewee 3). According to the interviewed BI experts, the greatest challenge would be the invocation of the RRA – that is, the decision when exactly should a report recommendation be displayed on the user's screen. At first sight, reports may either be suggested to the user upon specific user interactions or constantly through, e.g., a side panel [46]. However, alternatively, the RRA could also be invoked intelligently [47]. This form of invocation fits closest to the opinions of the interviewed BI consultants. For instance, one interviewee argues that recommendations should not be provided constantly or only upon user interactions: *"It's better to blend it in if users do not know something. [...] If they know it once, they are not interested in it anymore and would like to have the entire screen for their report."* (Interviewee 1)

Invoking recommendations intelligently (as opposed to constantly or upon user interaction) means that the BI system only recommends reports that are likely to support the user's current task. Instead of being disruptive, the RRA needs to foster the user's engagement in her/his task. Therefore, we draw on recent advancements in *flow* research. The *flow* state has been widely acknowledged for describing an individual's state of being fully focused and engaged in an activity [48]. In particular, if an individual's skills and tasks are optimally balanced, the individual is "in the flow" and performs at the height of her/his skills [48]. Interestingly, recent user experience studies agree on five conditions that improve flow and, thus, should be supported by user interfaces [49-50]: (1) clear perceived goals, (2) unambiguous feedback, (3) a sense of control, (4) a balance between the challenge of the task and skills of the individual, and (5) intrinsic motivation. Since the latter two conditions do not directly refer to the points in time when specific information such as report recommendations should be displayed, we do not consider them for refining the RRA. Furthermore, we assume that a user's sense of control is generally highest if the user is not interrupted with a report recommendation at all. Hence, report recommendations should be avoided in general and should only be displayed if their probability for being helpful is above a pre-defined minimum certainty. As a consequence, we suggest that in order to intelligently provide recommendations and support users' flow state, the BI system should only display recommendations if goals can be supported with a minimum certainty and recommendations are not contradictory among themselves. Specifically, we refine DP1 with the complementary design principles DP1a and DP1b as follows:

> *DP1a. The BI system should only recommend a report if the goals of the user can be supported with a pre-defined minimum certainty.*

> *DP1b. The BI system should only provide recommendations that are not ambiguous to other recommendations displayed simultaneously.*

We specifically looked at social influence of prior users as a driver of diffusion. While this is consistent with many research articles, specific types of social influence may be distinguished [31]: infectiousness, social proximity and susceptibility. First, infectiousness refers to the influence of prior adopters. This includes factors such as the size, performance, status, success of prior adopters as well as the overall number of prior adopters. Second, social proximity refers to the social distance between two actors and determines how easily information is transmitted between them. Marsden and Friedkin [32] even further distinguished social cohesion and role equivalence as two dimensions of social proximity. While social cohesion defines proximity in terms of the number, length, and strength of the paths that connect actors in a network, role equivalence defines proximity in terms of the similarity of two actors' profiles [31]. For instance, if a software designer and a requirements engineer would share an office and frequently work together, their social cohesion would be relatively high. However, role equivalence between them would rather be low because the requirements engineer would gather and describe requirements while the designer would draw mockups. In other words, role equivalence would be much higher between two software designers – even if they were working on different projects and would be located in different offices. Finally, third, the impact of social influence on diffusion is shaped by susceptibility. Susceptibility of a new adopter to social influence describes the adopter's experience and skills. As a consequence, future research may further refine our RRA by distinguishing between various types of social influence.

7   Conclusion

In this paper, we investigated how to design a BI system that improves diffusion [13] of reports (i.e., reuse of reports across different users) without limiting users' abilities to develop new reports. We built on our previously established DSR project in which we explored four organizations in order to identify impediments to diffusion of reports. Upon identification of impediments, we generalized the need for making social influence of prior report users visible (MR1) and subsequently proposed a RRA which recommends reports based on social influence of prior report users (DP1). Building on this work, in this paper we presented three mockups of the RRA based on different types of BI clients [39] as well as a working prototype. We also developed testable hypotheses in order to be able to evaluate the RRA through empirical confirmation or rejection.

We conducted two quantitative evaluation studies. While the first study focused on graduate students who are specializing in BI, the second study focused on BI consultants. Thus we were able to triangulate findings from novice users with findings from experienced users. The results showed that the proposed RRA improved perceived ease of use and perceived usefulness of the BI client that it extends. Since broad literature confirmed the impact of PEOU and PUSF on employees' usage intentions and ultimately their usage [40-41], [45], we conclude that the RRA increases usage and, thus, diffusion of the recommended reports. However, we did not yet collect longitudinal usage data as part of our evaluations. Thus, in the future, we intend to test diffusion of reports more rigorously by collecting usage data at different points in time in real field settings [13]. Finally, we interviewed BI experts who participated in our experiment. Findings revealed the challenge of recommendation invocation; that is, the decision when to display a report recommendation. To address this challenge, we suggested intelligent invocation of recommendations. Specifically, we draw on *flow* state research and refined DP1 by highlighting that recommendations should only be invoked if they can support the user's goals (DP1a) and if they are not ambiguous to further recommendations (DP1b). Furthermore, insights gained qualitatively confirmed the findings from the quantitative evaluation studies.

Throughout our DSR project we had to make decisions – for instance when deriving meta-requirements from empirical interview findings or when proposing and refining design principles or when instantiating the RRA. We acknowledge that these decisions are not without alternatives. In fact, it is likely that other scholars would have proposed different principles for tackling the identified impediments of current BI systems. Therefore, in order to back our decisions and make our work reproducible, we constantly referred to recent findings in literature. For instance, we focused on improving visibility of social influence in order to increase diffusion of reports because social influence has been widely recognized as a strong driver for diffusion [31], [34]. However, we do neither view our RRA as being "finished" or the only possibility for improving diffusion of reports. Thus, future research should complement and discuss our work. In addition, future research should address the following limitations of our work. First, we investigated BI systems at four organizations. Therefore, studying BI systems in additional organizations might reveal further impediments. Second, DP2 and the refined DP1a and DP1b are still tentative since they are still subjects for evaluation and refinement [20], [25]. Therefore, future work may center on further evaluation and refinement cycles. Third, evaluation study 1 compared experienced PEOU and PUSF of the BI client without RRA with expected PEOU and PUSF of the BI client with RRA. Although this has been done in other studies too [40], those studies mentioned that the two are not always suited for comparison. Therefore, we are currently implementing a RRA in a real organization's BI system and intend to investigate the RRA's impact on actual usage and diffusion over time. Finally, we conducted a scenario description experiment to evaluate DP1. While scenario description experiments allow for high control over potential confounding factors (high internal validity), they typically have little authenticity (low external validity) [44]. Thus, future research should complement our work by examining the impact of DP1 in a real world setting.

References

1. Maas, J.B., Fenema, P.C., Soeters, J.: Information System Infusion: The Role of Control and Empowerment. In: ICIS Proceedings (2012)
2. Györy, A., Cleven, A., Uebernickel, F., Brenner, W.: Exploring the Shadows: IT Governance Approaches to User-Driven Innovation. In: ECIS Proceedings (2012)
3. Baskerville, R.: Individual IS as a Research Arena. Europ. J. Inf. Sys. 20, 251–254 (2011)
4. Behrens, S.: Shadow Systems: The Good, the Bad, the Ugly. Com. ACM 52, 124–129 (2009)
5. Tilson, D., Lyytinen, K., Sørensen, C.: Digital Infrastructures: The missing IS Research Agenda. Information Systems Research 21(4), 748–759 (2010)
6. Davenport, T.H.: Big Data@Work: Dispelling the Myths. Uncovering the Opportunities. HBS Publishing, Boston (2014)
7. Kretzer, M., Gaß, O., Mädche, A.: Design Principles for Diffusion of Reports and Innovative Use of Business Intelligence Platforms. In: WI Proceedings (2015)
8. Bernardes, E., Hanna, M.A.: Theoretical Review of Flexibility, Agility and Responsiveness in the Operations Management Literature. Int. J. Op. Prod. Mgmt. 29(1), 30–53 (2009)
9. Li, X., Hsieh, J.J.P.-A., Rai, A.: Motivational Differences Across Post-Acceptance Information Usage Behaviors: An Investigation in the Business Intelligence Systems Context. Information Systems Research 24(3), 659–682 (2013)
10. Burton-Jones, A., Straub, D.W.: Reconceptualizing System Usage: An Approach and Empirical Test. Information Systems Research 17(3), 228–246 (2006)
11. Farjoun, M.: Beyond Dualism: Stability and Change as a Duality. Academy of Management Review 35(2), 202–225 (2010)
12. Zittrain, J.L.: The Future of the Internet and How to Stop It, New Haven (2008)
13. Rogers, E.: Diffusion of Innovations. Simon and Schuster, New York (2010)
14. Bhattacherjee, A.: Social Science Research: Principles, Methods, and Practices (2012)
15. Attewell, P.: Technology Diffusion and Organizational Learning. Org. Sc. 3(1), 1–19 (1992)
16. Dinev, T., Hu, Q.: The Centrality of Awareness in the Formation of User Behavioral Intention toward Protective Information Technologies. J. AIS 8(7), 386–408 (2007)
17. Mustonen-Ollila, E., Lyytinen, K.: Why Organizations adopt IS Process Innovations: A Longitudinal Study using Diffusion of Innovation Theory. Inf. Sys. J. 13(3), 275–297 (2003)
18. Siponen, M., Pahnila, S., Mahmood, M.: Compliance with Information Security Policies: An Empirical Investigation. IEEE Computer 43(2), 64–71 (2010)

19. Gregor, S., Hevner, A.R.: Positioning and Presenting Design Science Research for Maximum Impact. MIS Quarterly 37(2), 337–355 (2013)
20. Kuechler, W., Vaishnavi, V.: A Framework for Theory Development in DSR: Multiple Perspectives. J. AIS 13(6), 395–423 (2012)
21. Gill, T.G.: Reflections on Reshaping the Rugged Fitness Landscape. Int. J. Emerging Transdiscipline, 165-196 (2008)
22. Carlsson, S.A.: DSR in IS: A Critical Realist Approach. In: Hevner, A., Chatterjee, S. (eds.) Design Research in IS, pp. 209–233. Springer (2010)
23. Goes, P.B.: Design Science Research in Top IS Journals. MIS Quarterly 38(1), ii-viii (2014)
24. Nunamaker, J., Derrick, D., Elkins, A., Burgoon, J., Patton, M.: Embodies Conversational Agent-Based Kiosk for Automated Interviewing. J. Mgmt. Inf. Sys. 28(1), 17–48 (2011)
25. Hevner, A.R.: A Three Cycle View of DSR. Scand. J. Inf. Sys. 19(2), art. 4 (2007)
26. Day, J.M., Junglas, I., Silva, L.: Information Flow Impediments in Disaster Relief Supply Chain. J. AIS 10(8), 637–660 (2009)
27. Walls, J.G., Widmeyer, G.R., El Sawy, O.A.: Assessing IS Design Theory in Perspective. JITTA 6(2), 43–58 (2004)
28. Myers, D.M.: Qualitative Research in Business & Management. Sage Publications (2009)
29. Lapointe, L., Rivard, S.: A Triple Take on Information Systems Implementation. Organization Science 18(1), 89–107 (2007)
30. Unger, C., Kemper, H.-G., Russland, A.: Business Intelligence Center Concepts. In: AMCIS Proceedings (2008)
31. Singh, P.V., Phelps, C.: Networks, Social Influence, and the Choice Among Competing Innovations. Information Systems Research 24(3), 539–560 (2013)
32. Marsden, P., Friedkin, N.: Network Studies of Social Influence. Social Methods Research 22(1), 127–151 (1993)
33. Angst, C., Agarwal, R., Sambamurthy, V., Kelly, K.: Social Contagion and Information Technology Diffusion. Management Science 56(8), 1219–1241 (2010)
34. Fichman, R.G., Dos Santos, B.L., Zheng, Z.E.: Digital Innovation as a Fundamental and Powerful Concept in the IS Curriculm. MIS Quarterly 38(2), 329–354 (2014)
35. Silver, M.S.: Decisional Guidance for Computer-Based Decision Support. MIS Quarterly 15(1), 105–122 (1991)
36. Dhaliwal, J.S., Benbasat, I.: The Use and Effects of Knowledge-based System Explanations. Information Systems Research 7(3) (1996)
37. Limayem, M., DeSanctis, G.: Providing Decisional Guidance for Multicriteria Decision Making in Groups. Information Systems Research 11(4), 386–401 (2000)
38. Zhang, T., Agarwal, R., Lucas, H.C.: The Value of IT-Enabled Retailer Learning. MIS Quarterly 35(4), 859–881 (2011)
39. SAP. SAP BusinessObject BI Clients (2013), http://tinyurl.com/lmvaj7o
40. Brown, S.A., Venkatesh, V., Goyal, S.: Expectation Confirmation in Information Systems Research. MIS Quarterly 38(3), 729–756 (2014)
41. Davis, F.D.: Perceived Usefulness, Perceived Ease of Use, and User Acceptance of IT. MIS Quarterly 13(3), 319–340 (1989)
42. Microsoft: Contoso Retail Store Business Intelligence Dataset (January 01, 2015), http://microsoft.com/en-us/download/confirmation.aspx?id=18279
43. SAP: SAP BusinessObjects Analysis, edition for Microsoft Office (January 27, 2015), http://scn.sap.com/community/businessobjects-analysis-ms-office
44. Homburg, C.: Marketingmanagement, 5th edn. Springer, Gabler (2014)

45. Bhattacherjee, A., Sanford, C.: Influence Processes for Information Technology Acceptance. MIS Quarterly 30(4), 805–825 (2006)
46. Silver, M.: Decisional Guidance: Broadening the Scope. Advances in Management Information Systems 6, 90–119 (2006)
47. Gregor, S., Benbasat, I.: Explanations from Intelligent Systems: Theoretical Foundations and Implications for Practice. MIS Quarterly 23(4), 497–530 (1999)
48. Csikszentmihalyi, M.: Flow: The Psychology of Optimal Experience, New York, NY (1990)
49. Hamari, J., Koivisto, J.: Measuring Flow in Gamification: Dispositional Flow Scale-2. Computers in Human Behavior 40, 133–143 (2014)
50. Procci, K., Singer, A.R., Levy, K.R., Bowers, C.: Measuring the Flow Experience of Gamers. Computers in Human Behavior 28(6), 2306–2312 (2012)

Communication Artifacts for Requirements Engineering

Miloslava Plachkinova[1(✉)], Ken Peffers[2], and Greg Moody[2]

[1] Claremont Graduate University, Claremont, CA, USA
`miloslava.plachkinova@cgu.edu`
[2] University of Nevada Las Vegas, Las Vegas, NV, USA
`{ken.peffers,greg.moody}@unlv.edu`

Abstract. The current study aims to improve the requirements engineering (RE) communication, as often times projects fail due to poorly specified or misunderstood requirements. We use design science methods to build and evaluate a conceptual model which can add value to managers by offering them a set of guidelines and best practices for facilitating the RE communication. We did a qualitative study to investigate what the criteria are for selecting communication artifacts and we discovered that organizational culture plays a key role in this process. We demonstrate that the used artifacts need to adequately reflect the dynamic and intensity of the communication. Finally, we extend the RE process by adding two transitional phases to avoid requirements slipping through the gaps. Our findings indicate that such transitions are more distinct in traditional waterfall organizations and less salient in agile companies. The current study approaches the RE communication process from a design science perspective which adds more knowledge on the topic and addresses some existing issues leading to project failure.

Keywords: Communication artifacts · Requirements engineering · Design science · Qualitative research

1 Introduction

Requirements engineering (RE) is the process of eliciting individual stakeholder requirements and needs and transforming them into detailed, agreed upon requirements documented and specified so that they can serve as the basis for all future systems development [1]. This process is important because it provides team members an opportunity to discover the needs and requirements of the end-users at an early stage, so the final product or service can meet those predefined specifications.

Successful communication among the individuals involved in the RE process is of key significance to the overall development of information systems (IS) [2]. Thus, engagement and active participation of the team members are essential to effective transfer of knowledge and information across the various activities performed during RE.

The successful integration of RE and communication is problematic. Poorly specified requirements are considered to be a major factor for project delays and failures [3]. Differing motivations and expertise are additional factors contributing to poor

© Springer International Publishing Switzerland 2015
B. Donnellan et al. (Eds.): DESRIST 2015, LNCS 9073, pp. 104–118, 2015.
DOI: 10.1007/978-3-319-18714-3_7

communication during the RE process [4]. This problem is often caused by the varying backgrounds of the participants in the RE process. Prior studies have established that end-users, systems analysts, developers, and managers frequently face challenges when working together [5]. Such miscommunication can lead to significant challenges in adequately translating user context and needs into user requirements [6].

The goal of this study is to investigate how communication is occurring throughout the RE process and to establish some good practices and guidelines for successful requirements elicitation. We focus on communication artifacts and metaphors [7], as prior research has established a connection between the success of the IS and the value of tools for communication [8]. The research question guiding this study is: "What are the factors leading to the selection of communication artifacts for information systems requirements engineering?"

We follow design science research methods proposed by Hevner and Chatterjee [9] and Hevner et al. [10] because they consider IS from a more practical perspective. We use qualitative methods and more specifically, we apply a case study approach. We conducted semi-structured interviews with nine participants to investigate the RE process in seven projects across four different organizations. One of the respondents was an independent consultant who performs requirements elicitation on a regular basis and has a much broader perspective of the process. This qualitative method provided us with deeper and more meaningful information regarding the selection of communication artifacts for the RE process and allowed us to compare and contrast practices across a number of organizations.

The current study extends knowledge on requirements engineering in several aspects. First, we address the existing gap in the RE communication process, as we offer some input on the rationale of selecting certain artifacts and their use. Second, we explore how the project methodologies adopted in various environments reflect the selection of communication artifacts for the RE process. Third, we explore the communication metaphors suggested by Putnam and Boys [7] and we provide more insight on their application for RE. And fourth, we employ a design science methodology and propose a theoretical solution to a common problem in the practice of IS development, thus bridging the gap between theory and practice. These findings are significant, as they shed more light on the problem of RE communication and provide practical recommendations for improving the process by matching each stage of the RE process with specific communication artifacts which would add more value to the individuals involved.

2   Background

2.1   Requirements Engineering

Requirements engineering occurs at the start of software development and involves the analysis and negotiation of what capabilities and features a new IS should possess [11]. The RE process has been extensively investigated by researchers in the past. Sommerville and Kotonya [11] suggest that it consists of a number of stages - from elicitation, validation, and management to non-functional specification, classical techniques, viewpoint-oriented techniques, and interactive specifications. Wieringa et al. [12] propose the following sequence of activities involved in the engineering cycle: problem investigation, solution design, solution validation, solution selection, solution implementation, and implementation evaluation. Browne [13] discusses information gathering, representation, and verification as the three main steps performed to gather requirements. Nuseibeh and Easterbrook [14] identify elicitation, modeling and analysis, communication, agreement, evolution and integration as the six main phases of the RE process. A model for differentiating the RE activities proposed by Scacchi [15] involves: inception, initial development, productive operation, upkeep, and retirement. For the purposes of this study, we are adopting the RE activity differentiation proposed by Browne [13], as it is more general and we expect to find it in the case studies we are conducting. Further, its has much wider application which demonstrates its universality. The remaining studies are of no lesser value but they are too specific and may not be as widely used by practitioners.

2.2   Communication Metaphors

Communication can be conceptualized in terms of communication metaphors. A metaphor is a way to link abstract concepts to concrete things or to tie the familiar to the unknown [16]. One method to categorize metaphors for communication processes is within and across organizations on the basis of selected sentences from academic articles [7]. De-contextualizing the use of particular metaphors (at the linguistic level) within individual academic articles can be done to bring them together in coherent categories of conceptual or cognitive meaning [16]. The eight metaphors proposed by Putnam and Boys [7] include:

1. Linkage – organizations as networks of relationships in which information connects individuals, groups and institutions;
2. Performance – communication as social interaction;
3. Symbol – sensemaking through rituals and narratives;
4. Voice – expression or supression of the voices of the organizational members;
5. Discourse – language in use, words and signifiers that constitute an organization as inter-relationships among text;
6. Conduit – channel that transmits messages;
7. Lens – information processing by focusing on the nature and flow of information;
8. Contradiction – opposing forces or binary relationships between contradictory messages.

For the purposes of the current study, we are considering only the first five, as the other methaphors are more generic and do not directly relate to the RE process.

2.3   Communication Artifacts

The design of IS involves many communication activities occurring through different channels. Each of these channels utilizes certain artifacts which are more or less applicable based on the context. For example, interviews and conversations provide very detailed information and personal interaction with the participants but they are time and resource consuming [18]. Surveys and questionnaires, on the other hand, are cheap and easy to conduct because participants are familiar with the format but at the same time researchers have no control over the participants and there may also be issues related to the quality of the data [19]. Conceptual models are used to represent non-functional aspects of the new IS but they are time and resource consuming and there is no guarantee they will provide the necessary specifications requested by the end-users [20]. Ideation workshops are used to generate ideas from a large talent pool but it is often times very difficult to coordinate the schedules of multiple participants [17]. Prototypes are appropriate because they increase user confidence and involvement but they can also be very expensive and time consuming [21]. Narratives or stories are useful for keeping track of activities and participants are familiar with the format. However, they require constant updates and sometimes employees can feel overwhelmed with information and can experience cognitive overload [22]. Spreadsheets are familiar to many but in some cases users need specific skills to understand and interpret the presented data. Diagrams and animations are easier to visualize and comprehend but they are typically used as supplemental materials and not as a main form of communication. Meetings provide instant feedback and they are relatively inexpensive which makes them very widely used in the corporate world. The disadvantage is that they require an agenda and a moderator to keep everyone on track [17]. Finally, observations provide detailed information on user behavior but they require time in the field which makes them expensive, as often the researchers would need specific training and skills to remain objective [23].

2.4   Levels of Interaction

Based on the characteristics of these communication artifacts, we can attribute a certain level of interaction to each of them. To classify the levels of interaction, we refer to a differentiation proposed by Leonard-Barton and Sinha [24]. They organize the interaction in terms of low, medium or high depending on its intensity and frequency. The following is a differentiation of the communication artifacts we developed based on the levels of interaction:

- Low – narrative/story, spreadsheet, diagram/animation, observation;
- Medium –prototype, survey/questionnaire, conceptual model;
- High – interview/conversation, ideation workshop, meeting.

3   Conceptual Model

Based on the summarized information from prior literature on the RE process, communication metaphors, and artifacts we expect to observe a certain pattern or rationale for the selection of some communication artifacts over others. The current study investigates what factors are leading to the selection of communication artifacts for information systems requirements engineering.

We hypothesize that the level or amount of interaction among participants during each phase of the RE process is a key factor for determining the communication artifacts used for that phase. Matching the level of interaction is a factor when selecting artifacts because it can provide the most effective and efficient communication among the participants [25]. Thus, we expect to observe a connection between the levels of interaction and communication artifact selection as they are related to improving user satisfaction with new IS. To classify the levels of interaction, we refer to a differentiation proposed by Leonard-Barton and Sinha [24].

We use design science principles [9, 10] to develop our conceptual model. More specifically, we follow the iterative approach consisting of design, rigor, and evaluation cycles. The current study addresses a practical problem many individuals and organizations are facing. The proposed conceptual model emerged from a thorough understanding of prior studies and it was then tested in a number of real projects to evaluate its applicability and utility. As a result, we refined the model to better correspond to the environment and meet the needs of practitioners.

We propose a conceptual model of categorizing communication artifacts, metaphors, and levels of interaction that would be likely to correspond to the different phases of the RE process. The model represents the three phases of the RE process: discovery (D), analysis and verification (A&V), and decision making (DM) [13]. We extend the RE process by adding two transitional phases (T1 and T2), as often times requirements are slipping through the gaps and our goal is to encompass RE as a more comprehensive process and improve the existing communication. Based on these five phases, we hypothesize what would be the expected level of interaction among participants and we provide a list of artifacts which would allow a corresponding amount of intensity and frequency of the communication. We also provide a short rationale for our expectations.

In addition to the assumptions we have made, we also expect to observe that the organizational culture or existing project methodology plays a role for the selection of communication artifacts. For example, agile companies would prefer more flexible methods for communication which provide more dynamic and are easy to perform more frequently. On the contrary, the traditional waterfall method would suggest communication artifacts which are more structured and support more robust interactions. Further, we expect to observe more distinct transitional phases in waterfall projects, as in agile methodology there are typically more iterations and overalapping between RE phases.

Based on the conceptual model presented below (Table 1), we develop the following hypotheses to answer our research question:

H1: The organizational culture and established methodology influence the selection of communication artifacts for RE.
H2: Communication artifacts should be corresponding to the level or amount of interaction among participants.
H3: There is gradual transition between the different phases of the RE process.

Table 1. Conceptual Model

Phase	Artifacts	Metaphors	Interact.	Rationale
D	Interview, Conversation, Survey, Questionnaire, Meeting	Linkage, Discourse	High	Intensive communication, multiple participants and viewpoints, defining and asking the right questions
T1	Conceptual model, Meeting	Performance, Discourse	Medium	Additional feedback before designing the prototypes, verification that requirements are understood correctly
A&V	Workshop, Prototype, Meeting	Performance, Discourse	High	Highly interactive communication, gathering additional requirements, remodeling the initially elicited requirements if needed
T2	Narrative, Spreadsheet, Diagram, Animation, Meeting	Symbol, Discourse	Low	Structured and organized information, easy to measure and compare objectives
DM	Meeting, Observation	Voice, Discourse	Medium	More structured and static communication, supporting graphical and text tools

4   Methodology

To test our conceptual model and find support for our three hypotheses, we follow the design science methodology proposed by Hevner and Chatterjee [9] and Hevner et al. [10]. Since this is an exploratory study on such a broad topic, we used a qualitative approach to gather deeper and more meaningful information from the participants. We conducted a total of nine semi-structured interviews with participants across five different organizations within the US. We discussed seven projects to better understand how the RE communication process was occurring and to evaluate our model. We used a case study approach to be able to more adequately compare and contrast RE communication practices across the organizations and increase the generalizability of the findings.

Participants in the interviews represent a large public university, a local government, an international gaming corporation, and a private company for supplying geographic information systems (GIS) software. In addition, we conducted an interview with an expert working for a private consulting company specialized in requirements definition and management.

Interviews were conducted in person and via phone in cases when the individuals were geographically dispersed. Each interview took about 30-45 minutes and it was recorded for data analysis purposes. We strived to contact multiple participants from each organization to increase the validity and reliability of the collected data but due to high turnover and the fact that some projects were completed several years ago, this was not possible in all cases. We contacted key informants and using the snowball technique we were able to identify other members who took part in the projects. We chose a convenient sampling method in order to find participants who were familiar with the RE communication process and were actively engaged with the projects in their respective organizations. Using the information provided by the respondents regarding the RE communication, we assigned metaphors to each RE phase based on the definitions provided by Putnam and Boys [7]. Finally, we compared the results of the case studies with the proposed conceptual model to evaluate it and to demonstrate its utility.

5   Data Analysis and Results

5.1   Public University

We conducted three interviews with members of a large public university in the Western US. We discussed two projects – one on copyright violations related to peer-to-peer downloads using the campus network, and the other on email notifications to students. Participants in the interviews were the Vice Provost of Information Technology (IT), a Network Operations Center Manager, and an Administrator at the Student Housing Complex. The university did not have a specific project methodology and the IT team used best practices from both agile and waterfall based on the needs and complexity of the projects.

Copyright Project

The purpose of the copyright project (Table 2) was to create a notification system for responding to violations of copyrights by students, to store information about the violators in a database, and to provide input to university representatives about these violations on a regular basis. The project was initiated by changes in legislation and the team members involved in the RE process were concerned mostly with eliciting requirements from the official documention and transforming them into functional specifications.

Table 2. Copyright Project

Phase	Artifacts	Metaphors	Interact.	Rationale
D	Interview, Narrative, Meeting	Linkage, Symbol, Discourse	High	Very intense interaction, employees from various departments working together
T1	Narrative, Meeting	Symbol, Discourse	High	Additional features of the system kept emerging along the way
A&V	Narrative, Diagram, Meeting	Symbol, Discourse	High	Team members were pressed by time
T2	Narrative, Meetings	Symbol, Discourse	Medium	Requirements continued to emerge and changes were constantly made
DM	Narrative, Meeting	Symbol, Voice	Medium	Creating a consensus about the technology used for developing the system

Email Announcements Project
The purpose of the email announcements project (Table 3) was to consolidate all important announcements to students (i.e. dealines, workshops, events, etc.) in a weekly newsletter format. For a long time students felt overwhelmed by the constant daily notifications sent to them and they were the ones who initiated a new announcement system. Students also took part in shaping the features and specifications of the system, as well as in the development of the business processes – how to collect the announcements, which ones to be sent, who should send them, when is the best time for the bulletin to be distributed, etc.

Table 3. Email Announcements Project

Phase	Artifacts	Metaphors	Interact.	Rationale
D	Narrative, Meeting	Symbol, Discourse	High	Provide justification for the project and discuss possible solutions
T1	Narrative, Diagram, Meeting	Symbol, Discourse	High	Clarifying the initially gathered requirements
A&V	Narrative, Meeting, Prototype, Observation	Symbol, Performance, Discourse	High	Develop detailed procedures and guidelines, students testing the prototype, OIT observing and improving the system
T2	Narrative, Meeting, Prototype	Symbol, Discourse, Performance	High	Debug the prototype before implementation, make sure all features are implemented
DM	Narrative, Meeting	Symbol, Voice	High	Make a decision which requirements are out of scope and eventually implement them in separate systems

5.2   Local Government

We conducted two interviews with members of a local government in the Western US. We discussed two projects – one on online business licensing, and the other on online submission of plans for licensing and building permits. The goal of both projects was to save citizens time and money by providing them a number of online services. Participants in the interviews were the IT Portfolio and Applications Manager and the Systems Manager. The local government relied on established project management guidelines, had a handbook of approved procedures, and waterfall was the typical project methodology used.

Licensing Project
The purpose of the licensing project (Table 4) was to allow customers to submit their business licensing applications online which would save them time and resources. The city would also be able to track each application easier and faster, so the system would prevent document loss and accidental destruction.

Table 4. Licensing Project

Phase	Artifacts	Metaphors	Interact.	Rationale
D	Interview, Conversation, Meeting	Linkage, Discourse	High	Users were most familiar with the features of the system and they explained it to the team
T1	Meeting	Discourse	Medium	Initial requirements were refined based on existing paper form
A&V	Narrative, Meetings	Symbol, Discourse	Medium	Routine procedure, official approval required
T2	Prototype, Observation, Meeting	Performance, Discourse	High	Users and analysts were working together
DM	E-mail, Phone call	Voice	Medium	Customers' agreement was required before implementation

E-Plans Project

The purpose of the E-Plans project (Table 5) was to provide customers with the ability to upload plans for building permits online. In the past, they were required to print 15 sets of plans, one for each department which was costly and inefficient because for every single change all 15 sets had to be replaced. Developers from the local community were actively participating and providing their requirements for the new system.

Table 5. E-Plans Project

Phase	Artifacts	Metaphors	Interact.	Rationale
D	Interview, Conversation, Meeting, Diagram	Linkage, Discourse, Symbol	High	Gather ideas from as many users as possible
T1	Meeting, Diagram, Narrative	Discourse, Symbol	Medium	Refine initial requirements and gather more information
A&V	Meeting, Diagram, Narrative	Discourse, Symbol	Medium	Routine procedure, user feedback was collected before submitting the requirements to the vendor
T2	Prototype, Observation, Meeting	Performance, Discourse	High	Users and analysts were working together, the vendor was also involved
DM	Meeting, E-mail, Phone call	Voice	Medium	User feedback was used to decide which features to be included

5.3   Gaming Corporation

We conducted one interview with a systems analyst at a large international gaming corporation. We discussed two projects – one on reward cards system, and the other on a loyalty program for customers. The purpose of these projects was to increase satisfaction and provide better and more customized services to customers. Waterfall was the typicall methodology used for developing new systems in the organization. Due to the high turnover in the gaming industry we were not able to obtain another person to participate in the data collection.

Reward Cards Project

The purpose of the reward cards project (Table 6) was to improve customer service and add more value to the guests. This was the first project to allow employees to sign-up customers for its loyalty program via a mobile device. This project was phase two of a larger project aiming to increase customer satisfaction across over 40 casinos and resorts.

Table 6. Reward Cards Project

Phase	Artifacts	Metaphors	Interact.	Rationale
D	Interview, Narrative, Spreadsheet, Meeting, Diagram	Linkage, Symbol, Discourse	High	Intense interaction, many team members involved, strict deadlines
T1	Phone call, E-mail	Discourse	Low	Translate initial requirements into functional and feature specifications
A&V	Meeting, Narrative	Discourse, Symbol	Low	Single session to approve the requirements document
T2	Meeting, Narrative	Discourse, Symbol	Low	Official approval from the business owner
DM	Meeting, Narrative	Voice, Symbol	Low	Decision had to be made in the beginning of the project, either to meet a deadline or to implement more requirements

Loyalty Project

The purpose of this project was to integrate the customer loyalty program with an online ticketing website (Table 7). The customers using the program would receive tier credits every time they purchase a ticket from that website and would be able to spend their money at the casino or resort. This system was part of a larger project and it had to be integrated with the online ticketing system as well as with the company's existing systems.

Table 7. Loyalty Project

Phase	Artifacts	Metaphors	Interact.	Rationale
D	Interview, Narrative, Spreadsheet, Meeting, Use Case Diagram	Linkage, Symbol, Discourse	High	Intense interaction, people from different organizations involved

Table 7. (*Continued*)

T1	Meeting, Narrative	Discourse, Symbol	Low	Refine requirements and develop an interactive prototype based on them
A&V	Meeting, Narrative, Interactive Prototype	Discourse, Symbol, Performance	High	Test prototype, confirm specifications and business logic
T2	Meeting, Narrative	Discourse, Symbol	Low	Confirm end-user workflow processes
DM	Meeting, Narrative	Voice, Symbol	Medium	Official approval of the requirements documentation

5.4   GIS Supplier

We conducted two interviews with members of the Spatial Analysis team at an international supplier of GIS software products. We discussed one project which was representative of the RE process for that organization – development of online analysis tools. The company relied on agile methods for IS development and it had embraced scrum as its main approach. Due to the methodology used, the participants did not have official titles within the company.

Online GIS Analysis Project

The purpose of the online GIS analysis project (Table 8) was to add customer value and provide a web-based solution for spatial analysis. This project would allow multiple users to collaborate on the same project and would extend the current product offerings.

Table 8. GIS Analysis Project

Phase	Artifacts	Metaphors	Interact.	Rationale
D	User conference, Workshop, User request	Linkage, Symbol, Discourse	Low	Routine activities, user feedback is gathered on a regular basis
T1	Design meeting, Mock design	Discourse, Performance	Medium	User requests are transformed into possible specifications
A&V	Meeting, Observation	Discourse, Symbol	Medium	Unofficial release of the software update
T2	Meeting, Online training	Discourse, Symbol	High	Gathering input from the user community
DM	Meeting	Voice	Low	Software updates are quite frequent and decisions are informal

5.5   RE Consultanting Company

In addition to the case studies, we also conducted an interview with an expert working at a private company which provided consulting expertise, methodologies, standards and resources to the IT and business community in medium to large corporations and governments worldwide. This was a different approach compared to the case studies, as an external organization was used to facilitate the RE process. Employees may not always have the necessary experience and knowledge on requirements gathering, thus using a consulting service could increase the success of the project. Such a perspective can also be useful to avoid office politics. The consulting company used predominantly agile methods and recommended this approach to their clients. During the interview, the participant outlined a common scenario for outsourcing the RE process (Table 9).

Table 9. Common RE Process

Phase	Artifacts	Metaphors	Interact.	Rationale
D	Checklist, Meeting	Linkage, Symbol, Discourse	High	Heavy interaction, engaging the customers in the RE process
T1	Test script, Scorecard, Wiki, Repository/ Track system	Discourse, Symbol, Performance	Medium	Iterative process with constant client feedback and vendor input
A&V	Meeting, Observation	Discourse, Symbol	Medium	Reviewing gathered content and getting multiple perspectives
T2	Meeting, Report, Wiki	Discourse, Symbol	Low	Most of the work has been done already, traceability purposes
DM	Balanced scorecard, Meeting	Symbol, Discourse, Voice	Low	Information is gathered already, customer is making an informed decision

6   Discussion and Future Work

Based ont the data from these case studies, we were able to find support for our hypotheses and to answer the research question driving this study. H1 was supported, as the studied organizations demonstrated significant influence of the organizational culture on the selection of communication artifacts. The agile companies had a preference for faster turnover and results, more frequent meetings, and design iterations on a regular basis. On the other hand, the more traditional businesses were looking for more structured artifacts which could support long term projects with heavy reliance on documentation and reports. These findings correspond to previous studies. More specifically, they confirm the notion that agile methodologies focus on individuals and interactions rather than processes, working software rather than comprehensive documentation, customer collaboration rather than contract negotiation, and responding to change rather than following a plan [26]. The current study extends these concepts by identifying artifacts which are more commonly used in the requirements communication process and focuses on differences and similarities between agile and waterfall project methodologies.

H2 was partially supported. During the interviews, the participants confirmed the importance of a relationship between the levels of interaction in the RE process and the communication artifacts but admitted that the selection was made mostly based on already established principles and methodologies within the organization. Further, employees are familiar with the most common artifacts such as meetings, documentation or prototypes and there is no need for additional training or resources.

H3 was also partially supported. We found that transitional phases were more distinctive in organizations using traditional waterfall methodologies while in more agile companies the transitions from one RE phase to another were more seamless due to constant iterations and frequent software releases. In addition, participants in more agile organizations reported to have less communication issues during the RE process. This can be also related to the relatively small teams working on each project and the geographic proximity of the team members.

In addition, we can draw several inferences from the evidence in the case studies. First, some metaphors are more common in certain RE phases. The linkage metaphor is more frequently used in the discovery phase which supports the notion that there is a need for a network to recruit end-users for collecting initial requirements. The voice metaphor is also observed predominantly towards the end of the RE process which suggests that there is a relationship between making a decision on which requirements need to be implemented and the demonstration of power and superiority within the team.

Second, there are two metaphors (discourse and symbol) which are more universally adopted and are not tied to a particular RE phase. These metaphors represent meetings, conversations, and document exchange which are occurring across all RE phases. One explanation for the widespread utilization of these communication artifacts and metaphors, respectively, is their ease of use and general acceptance in all organizations regardless of the implemented project methodology.

And third, the fact that participants identified a number of important activities which took place during the transitional phases implies that RE is a much more complex process with many underlying layers of communication. Thus, it is important to further investigate how the RE activities gradually change and how knowledge and information can be more successfully transferred from one phase to another. Such insights can be used to improve the RE communication and avoid the problem of requirements slipping through the gaps [6].

Overall, the conceptual model we proposed has an application in organizational strucures and can add value to the RE communication process. Following the best practices in design science research [9, 10], we demonstrated the utility and usability of our artifact. We were able to establish a pattern for selecting RE communication artifacts and tie these artifacts to certain metaphors and levels of interaction. Such a relationship can be beneficial for both researchers and practitioners, as it provides a solution to the existing communication gap in requirements gathering and addresses the problem of misinterpretation of user needs and input in the initial stages of the IS development process.

This is an exploratory study on such a broad topic and more research needs to be done in this area. We recommend that others extend our study by considering all communication metaphors proposed by Putnam and Boys [7]. Using a much larger sample size would increase the generalizability of the findings. We suggest looking at small and mid-sized organizations, since they may have a different approach to the

RE communication process. And finally, while the current study considers only the communication between individuals, it may be beneficial to examine the RE process from a technological perspective as well.

7   Conclusion

The current study presents a design science method for solving the existing problem of misinterpreting and misunderstanding end-user requirements. By taking a more rigorous scientific approach, practitioners can improve the communication during the requirements gathering process. Such practices can lead to higher user satisfaction with the final products or services and can provide much richer and more meaningful communication among the participants.

We developed a theoretical model to answer the research question driving this study. We found that there are several factors leading to the selection of communication artifacts for RE. First, the organizational culture plays an important role and determines to a great extent the communication artifacts used by the team members. Second, we discovered that it is important for the artifacts to match the intensity and frequency of the communication, but this is not a primary concern for most participants. Instead, they follow established practices and project management guidelines, as the employees are already familiar with them and there is no need for training or additional costs associated with the adoption of new methodologies. Finally, the preferred organizational approach (agile or waterfall) determines the need for more distinctive transitional phases during the RE process. In agile organizations, processes typically overlap and there are no clear boundaries between the phases, while in traditional companies transitions are more clearly differentiated and a significant number of activities are performed in those in-between phases. These differences helped us to outline the need of a conceptual model which can be used to facilitate the RE communication and to offer practitioners a more scientific perspective to perform the requirements elicitation process.

References

1. Pohl, K.: Requirements engineering: fundamentals, principles, and techniques. Springer Publishing Company, Incorporated (2010)
2. Gallivan, M.J., Keil, M.: The user-developer communication process: A critical case study. Information Systems Journal 13(1), 37–68 (2003)
3. Maruping, L.M., Venkatesh, V., Agarwal, R.: A control theory perspective on agile methodology use and changing user requirements. Information Systems Research 20(3), 377–399 (2009)
4. Zin, A.M., Che Pa, N.: Measuring Communication Gap in Software Requirements Elicitation Process. In: 8th WSEAS Int. Conference on Software Engineering, Parallel and Distributed Systems (2009)
5. Abelein, U., Paech, B.: A Proposal for Enhancing User-Developer Communication in Large IT Projects. In: 5th International Workshop on Cooperative and Human Aspects of Software Engineering (CHASE 2012) 2012. at the ICSE 2012 Zurich. IEEE (2012)

6. Bjarnason, E., Wnuk, K., Regnell, B.: Requirements are slipping through the gaps – A case study on causes & effects of communication gaps in large-scale software development. In: IEEE 19th International RE Conference, pp. 37–46 (2011)

7. Putnam, L., Boys, S.: Revisiting Metaphors of Organizational Communication. In: Clegg, S.R., et al. (eds.) The Sage Handbook of Organization Studies, Sage, London (2006)

8. Wolf, T.V., et al.: Dispelling Design as the 'Black Art' of CHI. In: SIGCHI Conference on Human Factors in Computing Systems 2006. ACM, New York (2006)

9. Hevner, A., Chatterjee, S.: Design research in information systems: theory and practice, vol. 22. Springer (2010)

10. Hevner, A., et al.: Design science in information systems research. MIS Quarterly 28(1), 75–105 (2004)

11. Sommerville, I., Kotonya, G.: Requirements Engineering: Processes and Techniques. John Wiley & Sons, Inc., New York (1998)

12. Wieringa, R., et al.: Requirements engineering paper classification and evaluation criteria: A proposal and a discussion. Requirements Engineering 11(1), 102–107 (2006)

13. Browne, J.G., Rogich, M.B.: An empirical investigation of user requirements elicitation: Comparing the effectiveness of prompting techniques. Journal of Management Information Systems 17(4), 223–249 (2001)

14. Nuseibeh, B., Easterbrook, S.: Requirements engineering: A roadmap. In: Proceedings of the Conference on the Future of Software Engineering. ACM (2000)

15. Scacchi, W.: Process models in software engineering. Encyclopedia of soft+++ware engineering (2001)

16. Cornelissen, J.P.: Making sense of theory construction: Metaphor and disciplined imagination. Organization Studies 27(11), 1579–1597 (2006)

17. Peffers, K., Tuunanen, T.: Planning for IS applications: a practical, information theoretical method and case study in mobile financial services. Information and Management 42(3), 483–501 (2005)

18. Klein, H., Myers, M.D.: A Set of Principles for Conducting and Evaluating Interpretive Field Studies in Information Systems. MIS Quarterly 23(1), 67–93 (1999)

19. Russ-Eft, D., Preskill, H.: Evaluation in Organizations: A Systematic Approach to Enhancing Learning, Performance, and Change. Surveys and Questionnaires, pp. 224–267. Perseus Publishing, Cambridge (2001)

20. Cysneiros, L.M.: A Framework for Integrating Non-Functional Requirements into Conceptual Models. Requirements Engineering Journal 6, 97–115 (2001)

21. Mohapatra, P.K.J.: Software Engineering: A Lifecycle Approach. New Age International, New Delhi (2010)

22. Martin, J.: Stories and scripts in organizational settings. In: Hastorf, A., Isen, A. (eds.) Cognitive Social Psychology. Routledge, London (1982)

23. Myers, M.D.: Qualitative Research in Information Systems. MIS Quarterly 21(2), 241–242 (1997)

24. Leonard-Barton, D., Sinha, D.K.: Developer-User Interaction and User Satisfaction in Internal Technology Transfer. The Academy of Management Journal 36(5), 1125–1139 (1993)

25. Burgoon, J., et al.: Testing the interactivity model: communication processes, partner assessments, and the quality of collaborative work. Journal of Management Information Systems 16(3), 33–56 (1999)

26. Fowler, M., Highsmith, J.: The agile manifesto. Software Development 9(8), 28–35 (2001)

Meta Perspectives

Entering Action Design Research

Matthew T. Mullarkey[✉] and Alan R. Hevner

Information Systems and Decision Sciences Department, MUMA College of Business,
University of South Florida, Tampa, FL, USA
{mmullarkey,ahevner}@usf.edu

Abstract. In the execution of an Action Design Research (ADR) project, we experienced challenges in how to enter into the ADR research stages effectively. In this paper, we present how we addressed these challenges by extending the ADR model with two expanded up-front activities and multiple entry points. Our research on inter-organizational social networks is briefly described as the project context for application of the extended ADR model.

Keywords: Action design research · Design science research process · Social networking information systems

1   Introduction

In our research on inter-organizational social networking, we conducted an Action Design Research (ADR) [12] project with a mid-market private equity (MMPE) firm. In the project, we evaluate existing online MMPE networks and propose a set of design principles for an innovative inter-organizational social network information system (IO SNIS) artifact [9]. The goals of the research project are to extend existing streams of research on digitally embedded inter personal (IP) SNIS [1] into the domain of inter-organizational social behaviors.

In the course of our research, we discovered an interesting disconnect in the fundamental assumptions and definitions of the ADR method. ADR tends to suggest a single design science research entry point focused on an existing information system using an action research cycle from Problem Formulation (Stage 1) to Build, Intervention, and Evaluation (BIE) (Stage 2) [12]. In our IO SNIS research, no information system artifact existed in the problem domain being studied [9]. We needed to apply ADR at a much earlier point in the design science research process. Consequently, we drew from the multiple entry points proposed in the design science research model (DSRM) found in [11] to extend our ADR thinking.

The execution of this IO SNIS research project produced an extended ADR model that compliments the work of Sein et al. [12]. In the following sections, we motivate and describe the extended ADR model with details from the IO SNIS project and other ADR exemplars.

© Springer International Publishing Switzerland 2015
B. Donnellan et al. (Eds.): DESRIST 2015, LNCS 9073, pp. 121–134, 2015.
DOI: 10.1007/978-3-319-18714-3_8

2   Extending the Action Design Research Process Method

Sein et al. [12] focus their ADR model development with an emphasis on the DSR paradigm advanced by Venable [15] that the invention of the information system (IS) technology was the key activity that "distinguishes" DSR. The ADR method is their response to "a need for a research method that explicitly recognizes artifacts as ensembles emerging from design, use, and ongoing refinement in [the organizational] context." [12, p. 39]

In the four stage ADR method, the first stage – Problem Formulation (PF) - consists of two principles of IT design (Practice-Inspired Research and Theory-Ingrained Artifact) and requires the execution of four tasks to complete. The PF stage yields a confirmation that the problem under consideration addresses a class of problems and "inscribes theoretical elements in the [initial design of] ensemble artifact." [12, p. 41]

In our IO SN research, we were faced with applying ADR to a complex, "wicked" problem where no artifact exists to address the problem of replicating offline interorganizational social behavior in an online environment. Thus, we were forced to reexamine the PF stage and focus on an earlier point of entry than that discussed in the ADR method [12]. We needed to identify and define the problem and then demonstrate its importance to IT research and to practice. We determined at the outset that ADR must generate design knowledge that creates an innovative artifact and addresses an organizational need for intervention. This effort required the researcher to identify requisite theory and verify with practitioners the need for an as yet un-designed innovative artifact. As in AR, we conducted this investigation of the phenomenon through the interaction and intervention of the researcher-practitioner in the problem domain.

Once we had agreement as researchers and practitioners and before we could "realize" (i.e. build) the design, we then found that we needed to elaborate and evaluate the principles and features of a proposed artifact. We observed in the ADR method that this step in the process was assumed to have occurred as a function of the artifact build, intervention and evaluation (BIE) stage of the method. We found that before the organization (or researchers for that matter) were willing to invest in the realization of the design, a significant step was required that focused on the design theory stage in a fully elaborated DSR method. After conducting this intervention, we realized that the ADR method could benefit from a more explicit separation of the PF stage into a Problem Diagnosing (PD) stage and a Concept Design (CD) stage. Thus, we included these two new stages in our conduct of ADR.

The more fully elaborated ADR method is described in Figure 1 and adds these two important dimensions we found necessary to a robust ADR approach. This model of the ADR method adds emphasis to the Problem Diagnosing and Concept Design process steps prior to Building and Implementing an innovative artifact. We find that ADR must begin by demonstrating a rigorous PD stage informed by theory and an expressed need in practice. We then demonstrate a CD stage for the rigorous evaluation of design principles and features. These two distinct stages are essential to insure that a fully elaborated IO SN design emerges from the iterative interaction of researcher and practitioner. All of this is needed before we presume to build (the BIE stage in ADR) an IO SN artifact.

Second, as we reflected on our actual practice of the ADR method, we realized that the ADR method as proposed tended to emphasize the artifact build, potentially at the expense of a robust design theory CD activity in situ with practitioners. In the Sein et al. [12] article, in fact, the authors suggest a certain "tentative" nature to their exploration of the definition of a problem as an instance of a class of problems. We found that the definition of the first stage as a whole was somewhat inconclusive and could benefit from further elaboration. Moreover, we found that intervention and evaluation occurs at every stage in a robust ADR method. Each stage involves the researcher-practitioner intervention in situ to avoid the development of any part of the artifact in isolation from the organization problem setting.

Third, the extended model emphasizes the need for a cycle of researcher-practitioner evaluation to occur in situ (intervention in the organizational problem setting) at each step in the ADR method. We found it imperative to not only cycle from PD through CD to Build and, ultimately, Implementation (and back) but to also emphasize a disciplined reflection and evaluation cycle within the PD and CD stages before an artifact Build stage occurred. Each stage has an intervention (I) and an evaluation (E) activity so we simplified BIE to Build.

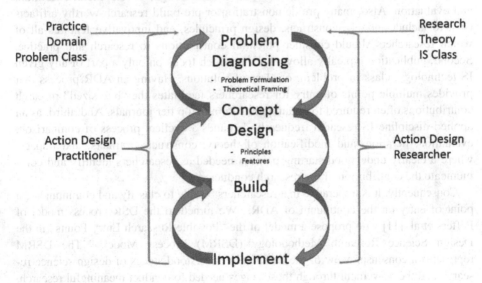

Fig. 1. Elaborated Action Design Research Method

3   Finding Points of Entry for ADR

We also realized that the ADR method as described and especially as it is diagramed in Sein et al. [12, Figure 1, p. 41] could predispose researchers to consider only realized artifacts for ADR. Stage 4, Formalization of Learning (FL), is shown to occur only upon the iterative completion of Stages 1, 2, and 3. We asked ourselves if, in fact, formalization of learning could occur as a result of each stage of the ADR method. More importantly, learning that informed researchers and practitioners alike should be an output from each stage in a robust application of ADR. Given our addition of stages in the more fully elaborated ADR in Figure 1, we believe that for any given problem class and innovative technology the research point of entry could occur at any one of the stages in an ADR investigation in situ.

A research effort could clearly start, as ours did, at the PD stage of ADR. An iterative effort to formulate a problem definition and theoretically frame the technology domain could be a research contribution in and of itself and require the robust application of ADR – even if no further stage of ADR ever occurred. The same could be said for an ADR research contribution with each stage. In fact, given the nature of research publication, space constraints and time to acceptance, it appears logical that a compelling application focused on a robust, iterative study of an artifact in just one stage might be the most likely form of published research using the method. How innovative technologies emerge from the interaction of researchers and practitioners in situ is, after all, the purpose of the ADR method.

We find the acknowledgement and communication of multiple entry points for ADR researchers to be significant for several reasons. First, new artifacts may be interesting to researchers at different stages of their design, development, execution, and evaluation. Also, many pre-demonstration or pre-build research-worthy artifacts exist to include models, constructs, design principles, and innovative features all of which researchers should consider potential contributions to research and practice. Second, publication typically allows for a research focus on only a part of any given IS technology, class of problem, or class of solutions. Having an ADR process that provides multiple points of entry for researchers facilitates the "bite-sized" research contributions often required to obtain publication in top tier journals. And, third, as an applied discipline IS research frequently demands a cyclical process of comparison, evaluation, iteration, and modification of theory, constructs, artifacts, and impacts where a clearly understood starting point is needed as researchers identify and communicate the contribution of the research conducted.

Consequently, it is imperative that researchers be able to classify and communicate a point of entry on the continuum of ADR. We turned to the DSR process model of Peffers et al. [11] who propose a model of the "Possible Research Entry Points" in the Design Science Research Methodology (DSRM) Process Model. The DSRM represents a consensus view of the commonly understood stages of design science research and the movement through those stages needed to conduct meaningful research. Having outlined at least four possible entry points for DSR, the authors provide a means for future researchers to identify the starting point of their research on the timeline of the DSRM process. This enables the researcher to better position the research and communicate its contribution to research, practice, and innovative artifact development.

We believe that ADR can be shown to be effective at the earliest possible entry point in the DSRM process and prove its value to an iterative, practice-inspired, theory-ingrained artifact with research contributions at every stage in the process of DSRM. To accomplish this, we can superimpose the fully elaborated ADR method on the DSRM as shown in Figure 2.

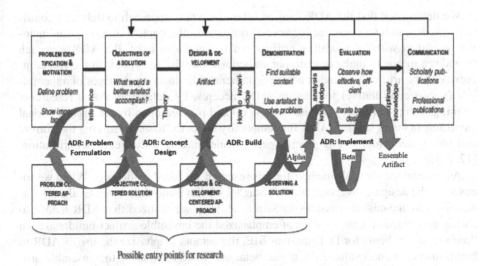

Fig. 2. Positioning of ADR's elaborated stages on a continuum of DSRM's entry points for Research

Next, we give an example using our extended ADR model with the design of digitally embedded social networks for organizations as a case for encouraging researchers using the method to identify their ADR point of entry. We demonstrate the value we achieved from separating the PF stage into two distinct stages of PD and CD before entering the B stage. We follow that section with an analysis of a number of published cases of ADR to provide examples of the positioning of the research on the ADR continuum and to propose reasons as researchers for doing so.

4   Applying the Extended ADR Model: Inter-Organizational Social Network Information Systems (IO SNIS) Case

In our research project we were faced with a unique organizational context demanding the design and development of an innovative artifact that replicated in the digital domain the offline social behavior that exists between organizations. Our prior research [8] found evidence of a clear gap in the replication of this type of social behavior (Inter-Organizational) in the online, digital domain - a need we described as the "Facebook of Inter-Organizational Social Networking." We also identified a motivation for Inter-Organizational (IO) Social Networks from existing social science research in a number of organizational domains. We chose one domain, Mid-Market Private Equity (MMPE) where practitioners confirmed (1) the essential need for a strong social network to achieve the primary organizational goal (PE business deals), (2) an attraction to many of the perceived connectivity and networking advantages of the Inter-Personal Social Network Information Systems (IP SNIS) (e.g. Facebook, LinkedIn), and, (3) a "fear" of many of the perceived risks to the organization inherent in uncontrolled digital connectivity and interaction [9].

We determined that the ADR method offered the best approach to deliver a contribution to research and practice for several reasons. In the context of a proposed innovative artifact where no existing artifact can be shown to exist, the ADR approach provides a means to make practitioner embedded knowledge explicit in the full complexity of the artifact's intended use environment while insuring the rigor of a theoretical (versus consultative) foundation. ADR accepts, by definition, that a researcher working with practitioners "in situ" acts upon and is acted upon by the organizational environment being studied. ADR fundamentally seeks to "assist in solving the current and anticipated problems of practitioners" while making a theoretical contribution. [12, p 38]

As we adapted an ADR method for this research we faced a dilemma. When we focused on the design conversion in ADR Stage 2 – BIE (Build, Intervene, Evaluate) – as described by the case discussions in Sein et al. [12], we realized that ADR tended to anticipate a research entry point that emphasized the ensemble artifact build stage. In their Generic Schema for IT-Dominant BIE, the authors emphasize the use of ADR to build, intervene and evaluate the alpha, beta, and final versions of the ensemble artifact. In their framework, the contributions occur post-BIE as shown. However, our research required us to choose a research entry point that was much earlier in the problem identification and diagnosing phase of new business process artifact development.

4.1   The Problem Diagnosing Activity

We began our study faithfully with the first stage in the ADR method - Problem Formulation. We intended to look at web-based digitally embedded social networks [1] or social network information systems (SNIS) that have emerged through the recreation and replication of offline inter-personal (IP) social networks (SN) online. Our observation was that many organizations also behave socially on an inter-organizational level in the normal conduct of business. Many examples exist, but a prime example turns out to be the inter-organizational (IO) social behavior predominant in Mid-Market Private Equity - MMPE. We reviewed the theory-ingrained research of Social Network Theory and the practice-inspired empirical research on existing IP SNIS artifacts with PE practitioners in the MMPE setting [9]. Following Baskerville and Myers [2], our theoretical purpose in this research was to build a nascent design theory that would guide the emergence of a practically useful IO SNIS artifact.

As researchers, our observations of our activities and the requirements of the first phase of the ADR lead us to realize that within the Problem Formulation phase of ADR we went through a number of iterations of diagnosing both the theory and the practice at work in this research. For example, the practical problem was considered in the general context of a "Facebook" of organizations and then in the specific context of the research opportunity for PE organizations. Our Problem Diagnosing step framed the Problem Formulation and nascent Design Theory, insured researcher-practitioner Knowledge Sharing, a common language for the research model and its design constructs, and evidenced that the domain and the artifact under consideration were appropriate for each other and could provide novelty. Table 1 summarizes the goals and data gathered in the Problem Diagnosing step.

We realized that we were entering the DSR process at an early stage with the Problem-Centered Entry Point [11]. Consistent with an environment where we were not replacing or improving an existing IS artifact but, in fact, confirming that a problem really existed that required an innovative artifact for resolution. Our experience was that the first activity in a fully elaborated ADR can be described as a Problem Diagnosing of existing theory and practice through an iterative problem formulation and design theory development. This emphasis on diagnosing often leads the researcher and practitioner to spend more time and effort in initiating ADR. This emphasis is consistent with the "four pragmatic premises" outlined by Baskerville and Myers [2] if we are to insure that the artifact that is eventually researched and built informs research and practice. This emphasis on Problem Diagnosing also supports a more abductive reasoning approach as proposed by Lee et al. [6] where more than one possible solution – and even a "do nothing" solution - to a given problem may exist in the design and build of a useable and useful IS artifact.   As such, a good Diagnosing step to start ADR will include problem formulation [14] and a theoretical component about the design artifact [6].

Table 1. Problem Diagnosing in ADR

Stage 1:   Problem Diagnosing
Purpose: Confirm Problem Formulation with Practitioner including introduction of relevant theory, prior existing technologies research, the proposed research model, and a novel artifact creation as a desired outcome.
Knowledge Transfer • Practitioner – understanding of existing research on theory and practice for the class of problem and reflection on most important features in successful artifacts. • Researcher – understanding of the chosen Action Research Domain, generally, and the Practitioner's organization, specifically.

ADR research cases similar to ours will inevitably need to enter the research at this Problem Centered point and should be able to use the fully elaborated ADR paradigm to describe their point of entry. ADR conducted just at this point in the process may yield important insights that inform research and practice – even if further research is unwarranted.   Knowing what not to build and which problems do not warrant further exploration can be a very useful means to avoid wasted effort designing and building unwarranted information systems.

4.2   The Concept Design Activity

The second step in our research project focused on the identification and elaboration of the proposed artifact design. We propose this step of Concept Design as a set of activities over the search space of possible design candidates. Via these activities, design principles emerge that address the problem class identified in PD. (Note that these design activities will come before the Build activities in the existing ADR model.) Our design goals include the abstraction and reflection on the IO SNIS purpose and the identification of the scope and constructs to elaborate (through guided emergence) the design features essential to each design principle for the desired artifact.

In our project, these design activities evolved through an iterative look at social theories and existing IP SNIS artifact design elements (i.e. social network design features in Facebook) to theorize key design principles for a novel IO SNIS artifact. The output of this step was our fully elaborated IO SNIS Design with well-established design principles (described in a separate article being prepared for journal submission). This step focused on the iterative evaluation of design principles through research and elaboration with practitioners (in the ADR approach) to establish completeness and parsimony in the innovative artifact design. This CD stage also ensured the requisite depth of understanding of the design principles needed to evaluate existing artifacts in the problem domain as possible solutions. We note that if our core research started in this CD stage, we would consider this an Objective Centered ADR study.

Table 2. Concept Design in ADR

Stage 2:   Research Model Testing & Design Principle Emergence
Purpose: Evaluate and refine the artifact Design Research Model including modification or addition of propositions.   Conduct Design Principle Emergence and Development of the fully Elaborated Design Artifact.
Abstract and Reflect • Abstract each Design Concept into a Design Principle;   Review existing artifacts design features; Compare to Practitioner's Experience; Evaluate in situ for problem class and problem domain; Derive Conclusions • Reflect on Key Design Features for each Design Principle: Practitioner-Researcher iterative reflection; Feature definition and elaboration; Simplify for Parsimony; Discussion of Interactions

5   Discussion – An ADR Research Continuum

In addition to our research into SNIS, the "reinterpreted" (authors' description) Volvo IT case described in the Sein et al. [12] article provides an ideal case to understand the extended ADR model. The authors use the case to describe their execution of the ADR method in detail. In this particular case, the authors explore a domain where the IT class has produced artifacts that are in use in the organization under study. In the case, the researchers collaborate with practitioners in situ to pursue an intervention that first critiques the existing instance (a Competence Management System (CMS)), identifies gaps in performance, investigates a means to modify and reimagine the artifact in an innovative way, prototype and test the artifact, and propose a generalizable set of design principles for the instance that inform research and practice.

Our observation of this case is that the build, intervene, evaluate iterative cycle of interaction with the practitioners makes perfect sense. The BIE cycle conforms to their Development Centered research entry point along the ADR continuum. In their case, they describe their iterations of artifact build with an intervention that leads to reflection, evaluation and documented learnings that inform research and practice. We find that the case, as presented, influences their definition of the ADR method but must be understood in the context of the DSR point of entry. The activities – evaluation, reflection and learning – are critical to each stage of the ADR process, regardless of point of entry.

As we considered the BIE cycle described, we observed that in Action Research, in the ADR article, and in DSR literature the Intervene, Evaluation, and Reflection on Learnings cycle can exist across stages as well as at each stage in the artifact development. As we considered the evaluation of ADR cases, we realized that we could construct a modified version of the BIE triangle model used by Sein et al. [12, p. 49] to describe the activity at each stage of the fully elaborated ADR (PD, CD, B, I) and with each entry point. Figure 3 provides a fully elaborated ADR method showing the iterative process within and between stages with entry points positioned appropriately along the innovative artifact design continuum.

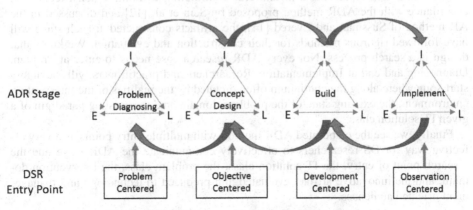

Fig. 3. ADR Continuum with Stages and Entry Points

If we use the fully elaborated ADR method as displayed, we see that the Volvo IT case described by Sein et al. [12] focuses on the Build stage with a Development centered entry point for the research. The original research conducted [7] was interested in developing an innovation adaptation of CMS for a new class of practitioners (knowledge workers instead of HR staff) using an innovative skill-based paradigm. In the execution of the research, the researchers and practitioners collaborated in an intervention in situ. Their iterative process led to the evaluation and rejection of the existing CMS. Experience with the existing CMS led to attempts to modify and adapt it which also failed. At that point, the intervention considered a new paradigm from the CD perspective, the new design principles were developed, the principles led to the emergence of new CMS features, and this version of the CMS was built and implemented.

Working with the ADR method in Figure 3, we see that the Volvo IT ADR entered the continuum at the Development Centered point. The initial testing and attempted adaptation occurred through an iterative intervention, evaluation and learning sequence. Once a new paradigm was determined to be necessary, the ADR moved to the earlier Concept Design stage where design principles and features were instantiated through guided emergence. These principles and features were then reintroduced into the Build stage and the new CMS was constructed, evaluated, and, ultimately, Implemented in situ.

We are able to consider our elaborated ADR method with multiple entry points in the context of the DSR guidelines [5]. We also observe that the ultimate goal in this research paradigm is the production of an innovative artifact. The artifact may be the output of any one of the stages described. When performed in adherence with the ADR method, the artifact will be constructed as a function of researcher-practitioner intervention in the problem space and be relevant to the problem at that point on the research continuum.

A clear contribution of the new ADR model is that researchers can enter the research continuum at multiple points. Moreover, the learning gained from iterative evaluation and reflection through intervention in a stage can inform research and practice alike and represents a meaningful contribution to both. When executed in accordance with the ADR method proposed by Sein et al. [12] and discussed in the AR method of Sussman and Evered [14], the artifacts constructed at each stage will have followed rigorous methods for their construction and evaluation. We know that design is a search process. Not every ADR research case needs to enter at Problem Diagnosing and end at Implementation. Researchers and practitioners will inevitably start somewhere along the continuum often dictated by the realities of the intervention environment, the existing state of the problem domain, and the existing paradigm of a given IT solution class.

Finally, we see the elaborated ADR method with multiple entry points as a very effective way for DS researchers to effectively communicate the ADR stage and the research point of entry, the IT solution class, the problem class, the intervention domain, and the innovative artifact evaluated and produced to technology and management oriented audiences.

6   An Analysis of ADR Cases

Our research suggests that any ADR research case conducted can be located on the continuum of the iterative ADR process in Figure 3. Admittedly, there is a fairly limited number of examples of ADR cases in the existing literature. A survey of proceedings and publications does provide a collection of cases that can be considered in light of our proposition that multiple points of entry are not only possible with ADR but that it is essential that DSR authors specify the point of entry. In this section we position several cases in the context of our elaborated ADR model from Figure 3. In

Table 3, we present a list of ADR cases by their ADR stage (as we elaborate the ADR method) and by our observation as to their entry points (EPs).

Table 3. ADR Case by ADR Stage and Entry Point

ADR Case	Stage	Entry Point	Discussion
Mullarkey et al. 2013 [9]	Problem Diagnosing	Problem-Centered	IT Solution Class: Social Networking Information Systems Problem Class: Social network dependent organizations Intervention Domain: A US Mid-Market Private Equity firm Artifact: Innovative ensemble artifact in a new problem domain.
Sein et al. 2011 [12] (Lindgren et al. 2004 [7])	Build	Development-Centered	IT Solution Class: Competence Management Systems Problem Class: Knowledge intensive organizations Intervention Domain: Volvo IT, HR, Workers Artifact: Innovative adaptation of CMS using a new skill-based paradigm
Bilandzic and Venable 2011 [3]	Problem Diagnosing	Problem-Centered	IT Solution Class: Urban informatics Problem Class: Shared community or societal issues (non-profit) Intervention Domain: Ubicomp Artifact: Innovation and application To Be Determined (TBD)
Coenen et al. 2015 [4]	Diagnosing	Problem-Centered	IT Solution Class: Virtual reality Problem Class: Living labs where new systems are tested in simulated "real-life" Intervention Domain: Societal (non-organizational) context Artifact: TBD
Noce and Carvalho 2014 [10]	Concept Design	Objective-Centered	IT Solution Class: Integrated Business Intelligence management systems Problem Class: Public sector business management practices Intervention Domain: Public institution – the Court of Auditors of the Mato Grosso state, Brazil Artifact: BI to support Financial Management of the Court
Sherer 2014 [13]	Implement	Observation Centered	IT Solution Class: Electronic Medical Record/Electronic Health Record Problem Class: Healthcare effectiveness Intervention Domain: Health Care Providers Artifact: EMR/EHR improvement

Our SNIS case demonstrates that when no instance of an artifact exists for comparison, modification or adaptation we as researchers must find an earlier entry point in the research process. In the case of IO SNIS, we needed to take a Problem Centered point of entry where we needed to evaluate, reflect and document learnings –first and foremost – as to whether an IT solution class was even warranted for the problem class identified. In the Sein et al. [12] case, the need for a CMS was not in debate. Thus, there was no need for a problem centered research entry point that questioned the existence of the problem class or the solution class. In the Volvo IT case as presented, questioning centered on the innovation of the artifact to fit the context.

The case discussed in Bilandzic and Venable [3] is one where the authors are formulating their adaptation of the ADR method to a specific research case where they understand the urban informatics problem class and hope to address the problem, ultimately, with an innovative IT solution class identified through their ADR intervention. In this case, we perceive a Problem-Centered research entry point that will require a significant effort that starts in the Diagnosing Stage of ADR.

In the Coenen et al. [4], the authors describe the IT solution and problem class but make no representation of the artifact to be considered or the specific intervention domain anticipated. Our observation is that their pursuit of research in this space is less dependent on the ADR variant chosen and more dependent on their selection of an interaction with a specific intervention domain beginning with a Diagnosing stage and a Problem-Centered point of entry. Thus application of the topology we suggest, with the requisite activites surrounding evaluation, reflection, and learnings, will lead to a rigorous exploration of this problem and IT class as desired by the authors.

In the Noce and Carvalho [10] case, the researchers sought to respond to an effective vote of no confidence in the exsting IT artifacts (represented by Business Intelligence Models such as Canvas, e-value, and Work Systems or by Enterprise Architectures such as TOGAF, FEA, etc). To do so the researchers employed the ADR approach. Our observation of their method suggests that researchers and practitioners ask the question: what would a better artifact accomplish? This Objective-Centered approach lead to an intervention where pratitioners and researchers, in situ, critiqued the design features of existing artifacts and developed an new set of features in an iterative process of evaluation, reflection and documentation of learnings. The resulting artifact was then proposed for build. The authors believe that the ADR method followed yielded an artifact design that should be built and tested in the next stage of ADR.

In the Sherer [13] case, the researcher identifies in Table 2, p. 867, that an ADR intervention in situ involving researchers and practitioners will be able to address a variety of functionality in EMR/EHR systems (such as payment structure, information control, information asymmetry, and privacy concerns) in a manner not currently addressed by the IT systems in place. Through ADR the author suggests that the researcher-practitioner interaction will propose, evaluate, reflect and learn different IT features, processes, practices, and/or system constraints that will improve the effectiveness of existing EMR/EHR artifacts. We observe that this application of ADR fits squarely in the Implement stage and enters the DSR at the Solution Observation point on the ADR continuum.

Taken collectively, these recent ADR cases illustrate the reality and the value of specifying as researchers the stage and point of entry for any given ADR research. We discovered the need to apply this discipline in our ADR research. We recognize the benefit to the DSR field when the discipline is applied to describe the ADR performed. And, we realize that defining points of entry along the ADR continuum also encourages researchers to iteratively evaluate, reflect on, and document learnings not just at the artifact Build stage as in Sein et al. [12], but also at every other stage in the ADR method.

7 Conclusions

Digitally embedded social network information systems are a new phenomenon in information systems that are steadily moving into the web-enabled business processes of organizations. Our challenge was to determine the most effective approach to the study and design of these innovative artifacts. We chose to integrate the relatively recent research paradigm surrounding ADR into our DSR exploration of IO SNIS. We found that we needed to extend the ADR method to emphasize the Problem Diagnosing and Concept Design stages and the possibility of multiple DSR entry points. We determined that doing so encouraged us to pose much more fundamental research questions that anticipate or propose innovative technologies not yet resident in business practice.

Our research suggests that IS research can benefit from our elaborated ADR method. Our analysis of cases conducted to date with the ADR method, confirms the need to clearly communicate the ADR stage and the entry point with every study. As our research into the IO SNIS domain highlighted, we found this to be particularly important when the research concerns innovative technologies where no prior instance exists. Using our elaborated ADR method helps when researching in complex business environments where we as researchers seek to conduct theory-ingrained, practice-inspired rigorous and relevant research to make practitioner embedded knowledge explicit in the full complexity of a novel artifact's intended use environment. Moreover, we establish that at every stage in ADR and regardless of the point of entry into DSR, the activities surrounding evaluation, reflection and learnings must be documented.

Our goal in this paper is to share a high quality research method that we found helpful in extending the boundaries of research in design science so that it can be applied to DSR. We provide a novel extension to the ADR method and suggest the approach that can be taken to effectively conduct ADR using this method.

References

1. Agarwal, R., Gupta, A.K., Kraut, R.: Editorial Overview, The interplay between digital and social networks. Information Systems Review 19(3), 243–252 (2008)
2. Baskerville, R., Myers, M.: Special issue on action research in information systems: making IS research relevant to practice – foreword. MIS Quarterly 28(3), 329–335 (2004)
3. Bilandzic, M., Venable, J.: Towards participatory action design research: adapting action research and design science research methods for urban informatics. Journal of Community Informatics 7(3), 1–17 (2011)
4. Coenen, T., Donoshe, V., Ballon, P.: LL-ADR: action design research in living labs. In: Proceedings of the 2015 48th Hawaii International Conference on Systems Sciences, pp. 4029–4038. IEEE (2015)

5. Hevner, A.R., March, S.T., Park, J., Ram, S.: Design science in information systems research. MIS Quarterly 28(1), 75–115 (2004)
6. Lee, J.S., Pries-Jeje, J., Baskerville, R.: Theorizing in design science research. In: 6th International Conference on Design Science Research in Information Systems and Technology (DESRIST), Milwaukee (2011)
7. Lindgren, R., Henfridsson, O., Schultze, U.: Design Principles for Competence Management Systems: A Synthesis of an Action Research Study. MIS Quarterly 28(3), 435–472 (2004)
8. Mullarkey, M.T.: Socially Immature Organizations: A typology of social networking systems with organizations as users. In: Proceedings of CSCW 2012, pp. 281–292. ACM (2012)
9. Mullarkey, M.T., Hevner, A., Collins, R.: Inter-Organizational Social Networks: An Action Design Research Study. In: Proceedings of SIGPRAG Workshop, Milan, pp. 1–11 (2013)
10. Noce, I., Carvalho, J.A.: Business and technology integrated management: a case of e-government for assessing the impact of policies. In: Proceedings of ICEGOV2014, Guimaraes, Portugal, October 27-30, pp. 1–4 (2014)
11. Peffers, K., Tuunanen, R., Rothenberger, M.A., Chatterjee, S.: A design science research methodology for information systems research. Journal of Management Information Systems 24(3), 45–77 (2007)
12. Sein, M., Henfridsson, O., Purao, S., Rossi, M., Lindgren, R.: Action Design Research. MIS Quarterly 35(1), 37–56 (2011)
13. Sherer, S.: Advocating for action design research on IT value creation in healthcare. Journal of the Association for Information Systems 5(12), 860–878 (2014)
14. Susman, G., Evered, R.: An assessment of the scientific merits of action research. Administrative Science Quarterly 23(4), 582–603 (1978)
15. Venable, J.: The role of theory and theorizing in design science research. In: Proceedings of the First International Conference on Design Science Research in Information Systems and Technology, Claremont, CA, USA, February 24-25, pp. 1–18 (2006)

Proposal for Requirements Driven Design Science Research

Richard Braun[✉], Martin Benedict[✉], Hannes Wendler,
and Werner Esswein

Chair of Wirtschaftsinformatik, esp. Systems Development,
Technische Universität Dresden, 01062 Dresden, Germany
{richard.braun,martin.benedict,hannes.wendler,
werner.esswein}@tu-dresden.de

Abstract. Design Science Research (DSR) still reveals several methodical shortcomings, which need to be remedied in order to enhance the maturity of DSR and its derived artifacts. For instance, there is a remarkable lack in methodical support for problem formulation. Also, DSR does not provide detailed procedure models, which can be operationalized appropriately. This compromises rigor within the design process and hampers demarcation from professional practice. In order to tackle these issues, we propose the adaptation of Requirements Engineering for structuring the problem space and deriving design decisions systematically. Requirements are also intended to work as glue between single design stages in order to keep the design process comprehensible and transparent. We therefore justify an ontology-based analogy between requirements analysis and DSR parts and provide a requirements-driven DSR framework based on a four-part ontology that especially focuses problem analysis and design preparation. Moreover, a detailed state of the art is presented and our approach is discussed within a critical appraisal.

Keywords: Design science · Requirements analysis · Requirements ontology · Analogy · Design rigor · Design science framework

1 Introduction and Motivation

Design Science (DS) is defined as the innovative, rigorous and relevant design of information systems for solving important business problems or improving the effectiveness or efficiency of existing solutions [1–4]. Relevance describes whether an artifact satisfies the identified problems from theory or professional practice [1, 5]. The rigor aspect covers the systematic, incessant and reasonable usage of appropriate research methods as well as the consideration of both the theoretical and practical state of the art [5, 6]. DS includes the investigation of technical, organizational or human components and primarily aims to develop prescriptive knowledge and means-end relations for a class of similar business problems in the form of artifacts [2–4]. Artifacts can be classified into constructs, models, methods and instances [7, 3, 8]. While design-oriented research is traditionally applied within the European BISE (Business and Information Systems

© Springer International Publishing Switzerland 2015
B. Donnellan et al. (Eds.): DESRIST 2015, LNCS 9073, pp. 135–151, 2015.
DOI: 10.1007/978-3-319-18714-3_9

Engineering) community due its roots in IT engineering, it is rather new within the more natural science based NAIS (North American Information Systems) community [2, 9]. Within the NAIS community, DS has been introduced by the works of [10], [11], [12] and the often cited contribution of [1]. Due to this kind of a clash between two research directions, it is still difficult to consolidate a common understanding of DS, its application and evaluation [1]. Thus, Design Science Research (DSR) is still in a pre-paradigmatic phase; lacking in the sense of commonly accepted methods, techniques and reference procedures [15, 8]. We therefore aim to provide means for better methodical support by adapting Requirements Engineering for better problem formulation and design conception within DSR. In preparation of that, the next subsections provide current deficiencies motivating our proposal and state desirable requests for improvement.

1.1   Deficiencies in Design Science Research

Problem Description: While some authors stress creativity within design processes [13], we agree with [16] stating that "it is very unlikely that new and fruitful ideas come out of the blue" [16, p. 749]. Clear and precise problem formulations are of high importance in order to construct effective design solutions systematically, minify the level of creativity at all and avoid unwanted side-effects (referring [12, p. 254]). Problem representation has a profound impact on the addressed artifact and makes its solution comprehensible [17, 12]. A profound problem description further enables both the rational consideration of the state of the art and the applicability of existing theories and preliminary works. However, there is still a remarkable lack in methodical support for problem formulation and representation within DS (see Section 2 in detail) and the "initial stage of the designing process is seldom satisfactorily formulated" [16, p. 749]. Although a straightforward problem formulation is not trivial as the problem domain affects complex socio-technical organizations [18, p. 20] and the level of novelty and uncertainty is usually high [1, p. 84], we think that it is necessary to provide means for describing both the initial problem and its possible revisions during the research progress.

Request for improvement: It is necessary to provide capabilities for representing the core concepts and interrelations of the problem and their sources from theory and practice [12, p. 253]. It should be possible to explicate particular "maturity levels" in the sense of describing the level of knowledge (or confidence) about a particular problem.

Operationalization and Comprehensibility: Following the idea of falsificationism, capacity for (temporal) truth requires refutability. Within DS, truth comes mainly from evaluation in the sense of fulfilling some sort of identified needs and requirements. Hence, it is necessary to ensure refutability by the comprehensive and clear presentation of the design process, its assumptions and decisions which allow design replicability and comparability (essentials in science [10]). However, many DS works lack such an appropriate presentation of their

---

[1] See the debates in [3], [13] and [14], for instance.

research method which hampers rigor to a considerable extent. Indeed, many researchers pretend to apply DS, but only very few explicate its implementation reasonably [19]. Apparently some researchers tend to use DS as a pretty "research method label" for the ex post legitimization of designed artifacts. We suppose that this is caused by an insufficient methodical support in terms of operationalization [20, 19, 21, 22] [2]. While providing general orientation, the majority of existing procedure models disclose deficiencies regarding to the permanent and consistent consideration of specific methods and techniques in single stages [23, 24]. Exceptions are the approaches of [20], [25] and [22]. The stated lack of concreteness may lead to neither objective nor replicable design decisions [2, 22, 26]. We therefore argue that a transparent presentation of the DS process (especially regarding the conception of the artifact) is crucial for ensuring comprehensibility, replicability and comparability.

Request for improvement: We need some kind of an anchor element which supports the operationalization of procedure models, ties design phases together and facilitates the integration of objectives, decisions, selected methods and evaluation criteria. Thus, it might be also possible to explicate research progress and revise assumptions (as DS is iterative research, e.g., [6]).

Professional Design vs. Design Science: Due to similarities to professional design, DS is compelled to demarcate its field; especially when designing IT artifacts. [8] and [2] state that DSR aims for results having practical relevance and rigorous generation. Of course, also practitioners can produce innovative, original and sophisticated artifacts, if they apply the same rigor as researchers would do. However, researchers generally intend to reach a certain level of generalizability for a class of similar business problems [22] and focus merely on the *way* of designing. Practice-based solutions usually address a single, business-specific issue. However, they can define rather precise requirements from a limited set of stakeholders. In contrast, research-based works often take multiple sources such as design theories into account. Consequently, DS can differentiate itself by strict rigor and a maximum of objective method selection [27, 8, 2], intended generalizability and also by rigorous evaluation [22, p. 115] [3].

Request for improvement: As already stated above, there is a need for methodical support in terms of providing a detailed design process and integrating several aspects from artifact planning, designing and evaluation.

The described shortcomings demonstrate that DSR suffers from limited problem formulation and poor design process representation. Hence, we aim to provide support for better structuring and representation of the design process with special consideration of the problem formulation phase. We therefore adapt the method of Requirements Engineering (RE). As RE itself is a complex and multilayered method, it might be too ambitious to conduct its entirety to DS at once.

---

[2] Operationalization is understood as detailing a rather abstract procedure model into a set of tasks, activities or techniques.

[3] A research process is understood as "application of scientific method(s) to the complex task of discovering answers to questions" [10] with the aim of increasing knowledge [18, p. 33].

Thus, we focus on appropriate adaptation of requirements formulation and specification. We aim to use requirements both as operationalization of research objectives and as glue within the process in order to explicate the research progress comprehensively. Requirements can contribute to DSR as follows:

- *During pre design phase:* Problem and domain description; conceptualization; base for design decisions and selection of appropriate methods.
- *During design and post design:* Decision justification; integration of research steps; visualization of research progress; revision of initial assumptions.
- *DSR community:* Comparability, replicability and generalizability.

Based on the stated objective, two research questions should be answered. First: How can fragments of RE be mapped and adapted to DSR? Second: How can we adapt these features to a DS reference framework in order to make the entire process more integrated? Within the research community, we see our approach as possible contribution to general DSR [8], respectively meta design [25]. We apply the analogy technique as it is a promising source for innovation (e.g., [2]) and especially relevant in DS [3, p. 9]. Hence, this research paper consists of three main parts. First, Section 2 provides RE fundamentals by consolidating a requirements ontology and summarizing the state of the art regarding problem analysis and possible requirements usage in current DS. We then propose the adaptation of requirements concepts and discuss their possible usage by proposing our ontology-based framework in Section 3. Afterwards, our proposal is critically reflected and related work considered in Section 4. The paper ends in Section 5 with an outlook to further research.

2   Requirements Engineering

2.1   Fundamentals

RE is a discipline which focuses on the gathering, management, validation and documentation of requirements primarily in the context of systems. The general objective of RE is to achieve a *requirements specification* that represents stakeholder needs [28]. The specification for a system is formulated with requirements. According to IEEE, a *requirement* is defined as a condition or a capability of a system or a person to solve a problem or to reach an objective [29]. [30] defines three orthogonal dimensions of RE: *Specification dimension, representation dimension* and *agreement dimension*. The first describes the degree of understanding (opaque to complete), the second the degree of formalization (informal to formal) and the third the degree of agreement (personal to common) between different stakeholders. All activities that increase the different degrees are part of the RE process. There are different sources for requirements, which can be analyzed using different elicitation methods (interview, questionnaire etc.) [28]. [31] distinguishes early phases and late phases of the RE process, whereby requirements in the early phase have low degrees in the dimensions defined by [30]. The early phases are characterized by a view on the domain context and the business need. Therefore they are less formal, the agreement between stakeholders is low and a comprehensive system understanding is not given in this phase. This view helps to understand the tasks which will be supported by the system. An approach for the classification of the discipline of RE is to differentiate between *problem-oriented* and *solution-oriented* RE. Problem-oriented RE focuses on the description of existing problematic phenomena, solution-orientied RE focuses on the description of the system and its context [32]. Important concepts that should also be created in the early phase of the RE process are *acceptance criteria*. They describe the conditions that must be met to lead to stakeholders acceptance of the system [29].

Requirements Classification: There are different approaches for classifying requirements. An often used approach classifies requirements into functional and non-functional requirements (quality requirements) as well as constraints [28, 29]. *Functional requirements* specify a behavior or a feature of a system. *Non-functional requirements* describe the quality of the features and *constraints* describe limitations and aspects that cannot be influenced during system development. Sub classes for non-functional requirements can be built [33]. This kind of classification does not consider the requirement process, as it has a more structural view to requirements. Furthermore, this classification approach does not consider different levels of granularity. A granularity-oriented view on requirements has been proposed by [34]. The authors define four requirements abstraction levels and an eliciting process. The most abstract level is the *product level* where the requirements can be directly linked to the strategy and goal of a product. The *feature level* requirements describe specific features of a desired system without specifying detailed functions. These functions are defined on the next level, the *function level*. The lowest level, *component level*, defines requirements that constraint the solution space to specific design requirements. The higher levels can be assigned to the phases of the RE process where the system specification is more abstract and goal-focused.

Goal Oriented Requirements Modeling (GORE): GORE is a specific method family in problem-oriented RE. It focuses on the objectives (goals) a potential system user wants to achieve [35]. Goals help to elicit requirements and to explore and evaluate alternative solutions to a problem [36]. [35] states that goals can be defined on different levels of abstraction and that the use of GORE is not inherently top-down. Two approaches for formalizing requirements are commonly used: KAOS modeling [37, 35] and the i^* modeling [31]. The i^* approach is an actor-centric modeling approach [38, 31], which allows the assignment of different intentions to actors (goals, beliefs, abilities and commitments). Further, the modeling approach differentiates between strategic dependency models and a strategic rationale models. The first should help to get an understanding of the reasons to specific questions and focuses an extrinsic view between actors. The second model focuses on intrinsic relationships between intentions of one actor [31]. Because i^* focuses more on actors and their intentions, this approach was not applied in the context of DS, as the intention of our approach is to describe the research objectives, break them down to fine-grained objectives and to structure them within the design process. Thus, we rather focus on objectivity instead of subjective actor-dependency.

Hence, we rather adapt the KAOS (Knowledge Acquisition in autOmated Specification) modeling method. KAOS defines a metamodel with different model types. Its central model type is the goal model where different goals with different levels of abstraction (strategic, technical etc.) are formulated and interrelated. The goal model represents goals, having particular relationships to each other (conflict, dependency, supporting). Goals can be decomposed to subordinated goals. *Obstacles* are conditions that prevent the goal achievement. KAOS also considers *agents* which are classified as software agents (as part of the software system) and environment agents (e.g., a human being). The assignment of agents to goals is realized within the responsibility model. For the description of concepts in the problem space there is furthermore an object model, which defines a *domain* ontology with specific *entities*. The behavior of agents which contribute to the fulfillment of goals is described in an operation model. This model assigns specific *operations* to software agents [39, 40].

2.2 Consolidated Requirements Ontology as Base for Adaptation

[40] compares six different KAOS metamodels. They found that each of these metamodels does not consider and formalize the full set of KAOS concepts. They propose a composite metamodel, which they use as an abstract syntax for a modeling method. Our approach considers this metamodel as a basis for the construction of an ontology for requirements engineering.

Motivated by the stated requests for improvement from Section 1, we propose the adaptation of RE (especially requirements analysis) to DSR in order to apply its capabilities in goal and problem formulation for solving or at least improving the stated issues. We suppose that the better the initial problem is described,

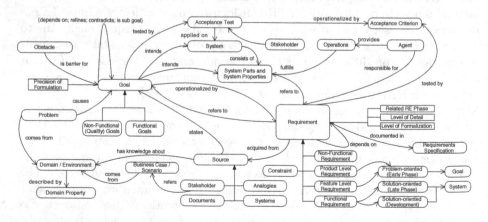

Fig. 1. Requirements ontology as base for the adaptation in Section 3

the better is the final artifact [12, p. 251]. We also strongly agree with the necessity of dovetailing descriptive and constructive research techniques in DS [14]. We aim at making the design process less designer-depended (purely creative) and more objective [16, p. 734]. Further, we argue that requirements facilitate the pre-design phase differentiation between scientific and professional design [20, 22]. Within the design phase requirements can be used for design specification in the sense of a rational selection of methods and decision explanations [26]. Revising requirements could also be useful for the explication of research progress and even as indicator for stopping the research process. The derivation of evaluation criteria seems to be reasonable in the post-design phase. From an outside perspective, requirements are powerful concepts for the replication of research settings and comparability between artifacts and their construction. Consequently, they could be used for justifying and presenting originality [41].

2.3 Requirements in Design Science - State of the Art

In order to examine the state of the art of requirements in DSR, we analyzed a range of frameworks or procedure models from the literature. We especially focused on the pre-design phase in order to identify advices concerning problem analysis, design preparation and method configuration. In order to prove the possible revision of these initial assumptions, we also considered the construction phase. Finally, the post-design phase was considered in order to find reasonable integration between evaluation criteria and activities to initially stated objectives.

Problem Analysis: The relevance of the context in the sense of stakeholders, opportunities and domain laws is often emphasized (e.g. [6]). It is common sense, that analyzing and describing both the research problem and the problem domain are important parts of the entire design process [10, 12, 1, 3]. In this context, [4] recommends some kind of atomization of the research problem into better manageable entities. [10] emphasizes the importance of domain understanding by identifying constraints and requirements to the aimed system. Several authors proclaim requirements as suitable means for goal refinement [26, 5], problem explication [42, 16] or as indicators for practical relevance [5]. In detail, different requirement types are stated in literature: [16] specifies functional, user-related and contextual requirements of an artifact. [22] adds organizational requirements such as required skills, tools and competences, which need to be fulfilled by the designer itself. [26] introduces theory-driven requirements and outlines the possibility of requirement conflicts. [42] distinguishes between specific and generic requirements. Finally, requirements can be used for reasons of justification and demonstrating artifact originality [18, 26].

Preparation and Method Configuration: Construction preparation contains the artifact design and configures appropriate methods and techniques. [41] proposes requirements as base for design and several authors indicate their relevance for functional and structural specifications [16, 10, 22]. Also, a refinement of requirements into design criteria and metrics is considered [16, 22]. [20] emphasizes the possibility of assessing the actual relevance of the aimed artifact. [41] brings up the comparison of requirements for justifying originality. [26] applies requirements for the selection of appropriate design theories.

Construction: Since the majority of DS frameworks and models lacks a detailed design support, there is only weak consideration of the impact and usage of requirements in the design phase. While explicit documentation of the construction process is needed [20], only very few authors consider requirements for that: [26] understands requirements as representations of designed constructs and [16] facilitates early evaluations based on requirements. Although a few authors stress the importance of iterative and incremental system specifications [4], there is neither a detailed methodical support for that nor some kind of requirements re-engineering, which would be necessary for design iteration.

Evaluation: Evaluation should primarily prove goal achievement [12, 16, 6, 3], as the designed artifact is "complete and effective when it satisfies the requirements and constraints of the problem it was meant to solve" [1, p. 85]. Consequently, requirements need to be defined precisely and measurable [10, 41]. [26] proclaims requirements-related indicators for conducting evaluations.

Further, requirements play a role in some research articles from the field of Design Theory: For instance, *meta requirements* are understood as a "class of goals to which the [design] theory applies" [11, p. 42]. [43] considers the possible implementation of theory-based requirements of design-oriented research in general. However, it has to be concluded that there is a general lack of specificity regarding artifact conception and design. Consequently, also the identification, formulation, management and revision of requirements before, within and after the artifact design remains vague and scattered. Only a few articles address the integration of requirements with evaluation processes and criteria. There is also no deeper consideration of requirements and goal representations at all.

3   Requirements Driven DSR Framework

Figure 2 presents our framework as ontology. The most concepts are derived from the previously introduced requirements ontology and aligned to DSR. The derivation was conducted by analogical conclusion based on a rational discourse. We therefore examined the semantics of requirement concepts in regard of an appropriate application in DS. In addition, typical DS concepts are integrated and the entire ontology aligns with typical DS stages: analysis (Figure 2a), preparation and method configuration (Figure 2b), construction (Figure 2c) and evaluation (Figure 2d). Below, the ontology is explained in detail.

3.1   Problem Analysis

The initial impulse for designing artifacts comes from an *idea source* like a specific *practical problem* which is identified in daily business. Even already *existing artifacts* can inspire DS activities; for instance in the sense of improving their effectiveness or efficiency. As we already stated within this paper, *analogies to*

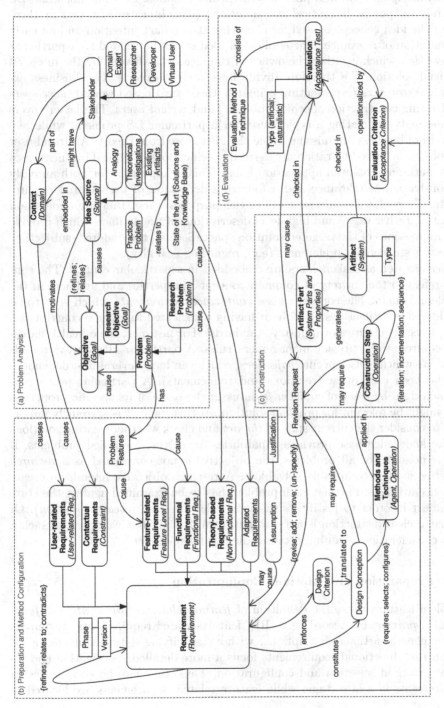

Fig. 2. Ontology for requirements driven DSR. Analogous or adapted concepts from RE are stated in brackets.

related disciplines can also provide worthwhile stimulus. Last but not least, DS can rely on purely *theoretical investigations* (e.g., literature reviews or theories). The idea concept is used for clarifying the artifact intention and an early presentation of relevance. The explicated idea might be related to a particular *stakeholder*, which is either the owner of the idea or is affected by the intended artificial solution. We therefore divide into *domain experts* (i.e., business experts), *researchers* (representing primarily theoretical-based works), *developers* (addressing construction-specific problems) and *virtual users*. The latter covers the necessity of creating a typical user for a particular DS problem, while real users from business are missing, since the idea arose from theory. A virtual user can be characterized by rationally derived specifications of typical business cases or by outlining potential application fields. This is important for both an early demonstration of relevance and a following derivation of user-related requirements. *User-related requirements* have two purposes: First, they are understood as initial, rather vague and high-level descriptions of the artifact, which provide first impressions of the targeted solution space. Second, they address subjective, more soft stakeholder preferences (e.g., regarding usability).

Ideas as well as stakeholders are embedded in a particular *context*. The context refers to the entirety of common concepts, properties and artifacts in the problem domain. The context causes *contextual requirements*, which need to be considered in artifact design without having a dedicated functional contribution (e.g., laws, regularities or industry standards). For instance, the e-health industry requires strong privacy management rules. A particular idea always reveals *problems* which cause specific *objectives*, which can have several interdependencies between each other (relations and refinements). A particular problem is characterized by a set of *problem features* in the sense of its specific properties that might be relevant for problem solution. At this stage, it is extremely important to consider the current *state of the art* and check whether existing solutions or the knowledge base provides capabilities for solving identified problems. If this is possible for all problems, the objective is not considered as a *research objective* as it is completely solvable [4]. A research objective intends to create or revise artifacts. Further, each problem has to be examined against the state of the art in order to justify its scientific relevance (see *research problem*). Of course, a clear distinction is not straightforward at all, but we proclaim such a deep consideration as an important indicator for relevance.

3.2   Preparation and Method Configuration

Problem features cause the definition of *feature-related requirements* and *functional requirements*. According to RE, feature-related requirements encompass rather general artifact descriptions, without specifying detailed functionality. In contrast, functional requirements focus a more detailed specification and facilitate method selection and configuration. Thus, they can be seen as design requirements in a late stage, while feature-related requirements are located in

---

[4] Reformulating or focussing the objectives can cause new research problems.

the very early design stage and are less specified or formalized. Non-functional requirements are adapted in order to integrate the aspect of quality. As quality in DS is tightly coupled to rigor, guidelines [1, 18] can cause requirements to the target artifact. Furthermore, design theories or research methods itself can set constraints or limits to artifacts [26]. Both directions are condensed within the concept *theory-based requirements*. Besides, *adapted requirements* stand for any kind of requirements, which are adapted or reused from previous works in order to benefit from comparable and reliable solutions. The stated requirement types are sub types of the central *requirement* concept. As stated at the beginning of the paper, requirements are primarily used for structuring, formulating and describing the problem space and the target artifact from several perspectives in order to achieve an integrated picture of the problem. Requirements are intended to operationalize research objectives, make the design process more transparent and constitute intermediate results of the design process. As depicted in Figure 2b, it should be also possible to represent refinements, relations and even contradictions between requirements in order to systematize the pre-design phase.

As mentioned above, requirements have different levels of detail or formality in relation to the artifact. This aspect is explicated by the *phase* property. The *version* property implies the actual state of revision, as DS often starts with some vague requirements, which need to be refined or even redefined during the research process. Consequently, requirements should enforce the definition of *design criteria* [16] in order to constitute the entire *design conception*. As this stage is close to the construction phase, the design conception actually represents the set of all late-phase requirements. Afterwards, appropriate *methods and techniques* for the fulfillment of these requirements are selected and configured [5]. In contrast to RE, agents are understood as research methods and techniques which are able to resolve a requirement rigorously. A particular method is then applied within *constructions steps*, producing an *artifact part* or the final *artifact*. Thereby, the concept of artifacts is similar to the RE concept of systems.

3.3 Construction and Evaluation

Generally, DS is seen as an iterative and incremental procedure [4, 5]. As we see requirements as the first intermediate result of the entire design process, their iterative re-engineering has to be considered. Revision is also necessary, as design problems are "wicked" by definition with rather vague initial requirements and straightforward constructions are rarely possible (e.g., [18]). We proclaim four reasons for requirements revision: First, there is no suitable method for requirements fulfillment. This would actually lead to the definition of a new research problem owning separate requirements. Alternatively, the requirement can be defined in a broader way by generalizing. Second, the requirement is defined too generic and needs specification in order to apply a method usefully. In this case,

---

[5] Actually, this is a point where the "creativity" of the researcher still plays an important role [13, 16].

the scope of the artifact is naturally limited, but rigor and quality are enhanced. Third, there can be an increase of knowledge thanks to the progress of the design process (see the artifact parts). This could lead to adding, specifying or even removing particular requirements. Fourth, updated knowledge can also be caused by new solutions or comparable approaches. Thus, a continuous consideration of the state of the art is indispensable. Revisions can be triggered at several points in the design process and are summarized with the *revision request* concept.

Finally, the designed artifact is tested within the *evaluation* phase, which has strong similarities with acceptance tests from RE. The evaluation is operationalized by particular *evaluation criteria*, which are associated with corresponding requirements (cf. [26]). Thus, it is possible to utilize the concept of requirements as design glue from analysis to evaluation.

4   Critical Appraisal and Related Work

4.1   Possible Reasons for Critique

We assume that there is some reservation to our proposal. Hence, two issues that are worthy for discussion are considered below.

Complete Problem Description: [41] criticizes the "mechanic world view" that is implicated in the popular approach of [1], as the approach presupposes the existence of both a clearly definable problem space and a translation into a design of the solution space. [41] merely negates the complete describability of the problem space and states its contingency due to the immanent uncertainty and novelty of research. Hence, the author also considers requirements as contingent. The author justifies his objection with the underlying positivistic position in [1], which refers to the subject-independent existence of a completely describable reality (i.e., that there is one complete set of correct requirements). However, we follow the constructivist approach that stands for a subjective re-construction of the reality. This is more suitable for DSR due to the consideration of stakeholder dependencies both in problem and solution space (referring to [6]). Consequently, a *complete description* of the problem and its requirements is neither possible nor necessary per se, since the correspondence to participated stakeholders is essential. Moreover, consensus on an acceptable level of detail and completeness is only possible iteratively by reusing as much knowledge sources as possible. Further, we understand requirements primarily as means for the *representation* of goals, design decisions and design progress in order to describe "hard describable" aspects at all.

Creativity in Design Processes and Possible Worlds: It is quite often stated in literature that design thinking primarily requires a high level of creativity and does not allow pure analytical solutions (e.g., [20, 42]). Although we generally agree to [2] stating that the definition of an appropriate, creativity-independend design method is very hard, we think that the great majority of DS projects can be conceptualized and planned in a very strict manner, since artifacts are usually build incrementally or by the usage of analogies (as IS research is a inter-disciplinary field of research; e.g., [3]). It is very rare that a design artifact comes out of the blue and provokes a disruptive, break-through innovation. Thus, we think that creativity merely refers to method selection, adaptation and configuration. Therefore, we postulate the codification of design work by the usage of requirements (referring to [44]). This is mainly driven by a better design explication and justification in the great majority of DS projects.

[41] also criticizes the affirmative character of [1] as the authors only address explicit problems from business. Although this aspect is slightly corrected in later works, this is an important aspect as DS can overemphasize the business relevance and "close the doors" for normative artifacts such as reference models [41] or problems that are not even recognized in practice [2]. Consequently, it might be hard to explicate requirements since the related problems are yet missing. We therefore consider multiple problem sources (see Figure 2a). Herein, spontaneous ideas need to be motivated reasonably and a translation into possible business cases is required due to the derivation of requirements.

4.2 Related Work

A review of the literature reveals only one research article having a similar approach - namely the approach of [16]. The authors present a six stage design and evaluation cycle having an elaborated pre-design phase. First, during the hunch phase a small set of stakeholder goals is described. Second, functional, user-related and contextual requirements as well as design-related assumptions are formulated and integrated with the previously defined goals. Third, these requirements are transferred into structural systems specifications, which enable the prototypical design subsequently. After real life implementation, the designed product is evaluated against the initial goals [16]. Although the classification of requirements and the throughout integration of them are very promising and similar to our approach, there are some differences: The authors mainly focus on practice-driven problems and omit theoretical motivations. Also, there is no consideration of changing or incomplete requirements and the authors suppose fully describable design problems categorically.

[42] introduces the *Soft Design Science* approach combining DS and the soft systems methodology. The authors emphasize the general relevance of requirements [42, p. 5] and propose the definition of specific requirements for a specific problem. These requirements are then transformed into a more generic set of requirements in order to provide the base for a class of problems. However, the research paper does not provide deeper specification of requirements formulation and management and remains a little sketchy in this respect.

[26] aims to provide methodical support for better design justification by deploying design theories as there is usually "no guidance [...] on how to relate design decisions to suitable theoretical justification" [26, p. 3]. The authors propose the decomposition of goals into requirements that are measured by indicators. Requirements are than matched to existing theories (or theoretical constructs) based on a comparison of their indicators and consistency rules [26, p. 5]. This

implies that both requirements and theories can be described completely. Hence, there is no consideration of requirements redefinition or an integration into an existing framework. Also, the approach mainly focus IT artifacts [26, p. 2].

[45] proposes *Action Design Science* and emphasize the interaction between organizational context and design. Thus, research is practice-inspired and tries to generate knowledge by generalization from a specific problem that is seen as an instance of a class of problems. Focusing the issue of problem formulation, [45] aims to incorporate action in the DS approach instead of sequencing both approaches. This is done in order to emphasize that "the artifact emerges from interaction with the organizational context, even when its initial design is guided by the researchers' intent" [45, p. 40]. Within problem formulation, [45] proclaims the principles of practice-inspired research and theory-ingrained artifacts. In the first, the practice problem is seen as a trigger and a knowledge creation opportunity. In the second, the researcher brings in theoretical elements to the artifact. Unfortunately a systematic approach to identify and describe the generalized class of problem is not described, which leaves a gap that could be filled by a systematic requirement analysis. Also, there is still a need for a description of the resulting problem class that incorporates the practice driven requirements and the ingrained theory requirements.

5   Conclusion and Further Research

This research article outlines the adaptation of RE for DSR in terms of representing the research objective and corresponding artifact requirements systematically. The incentive for that comes from methodical lacks within current DS frameworks, which can hamper rigor and the quality of artifacts at all. We have chosen requirements as they can work as appropriate means for the integration of objectives, decisions, methods and evaluation criteria. Thus, the entire design process can be presented transparently and more comprehensible. The researcher is supported by providing concepts for explaining or explicating parts of his research process in accordance to the proposed concepts. We therefore presented respective concepts within the ontology-based framework in Section 3 and briefly introduced their usage. This should also facilitate communication within the research community and push a discussion on common concepts in order to enhance the maturity of the DS discipline itself (cf. [15]). Furthermore, the ontology itself can be seen as functional requirement for DSR frameworks and procedure models.

This article was mainly intended to both motivate and introduce requirements to DSR in general. Hence, there are several topics for further investigation and extension: Due to the limited size of this article, a worthwhile demonstration of the proposed framework was not feasible. Therefore, a separate research article is written. This article also presents integrations of our approach into existing DS frameworks (e.g., into [5]). It is furthermore important to address the issue of very innovative artifact ideas (see Section 4.1), which can only be described by rough requirements (as we used *requests for improvement* in Section 1). At least, it is required to explicate such first intentions and describe their emergence precisely. Besides, it is very promising to analyze a possible adaptation of requirements elicitation techniques in order to provide further methodical support during design. As this article focuses on structural aspects (*what* are the requirements), the procedural aspects (*how* to elicit requirements) should be intensified. Last but not least, epistemological questions in the context of design requirements have to be elaborated, as different positions on that might cause serious misunderstandings within the research community.

Acknowledgement. This research was funded by the German Research Foundation (DFG) within the research project "SFB Transregio 96". The authors are grateful for the funding and the research opportunities.

References

1. Hevner, A.R., March, S.T., Park, J., Ram, S.: Design science in information systems research. MIS Quarterly 28(1), 75–105 (2004)
2. Iivari, J.: A paradigmatic analysis of information systems as a design science. Scandinavian Journal of Information Systems 19(2), 39 (2007)
3. Österle, H., Becker, J., Frank, U., Hess, T., Karagiannis, D., Krcmar, H., Loos, P., Mertens, P., Oberweis, A., Sinz, E.J.: Memorandum on design-oriented information systems research. European Journal of Information Systems 20(1), 7–10 (2011)
4. Peffers, K., Tuunanen, T., Rothenberger, M.A., Chatterjee, S.: A design science research methodology for information systems research. Journal of Management Information Systems 24(3), 45–77 (2007)
5. Hevner, A.R.: The three cycle view of design science research. Scandinavian Journal of Information Systems 19(2), 87 (2007)
6. Hevner, A., Chatterjee, S.: Design science research in information systems. In: Design Research in Information Systems, pp. 9–22. Springer (2010)
7. Gregor, S., Hevner, A.R.: Positioning and presenting design science research for maximum impact. MIS Quarterly 37(2), 337–356 (2013)
8. Winter, R.: Design science research in europe. European Journal of Information Systems 17(5), 470–475 (2008)
9. Buhl, H.U., Müller, G., Fridgen, G., Röglinger, M.: Business and information systems engineering: a complementary approach to information systems–what we can learn from the past and may conclude from present reflection on the future. Journal of the Association for Information Systems 13(4), 236–253 (2012)
10. Nunamaker Jr., J.F., Chen, M.: Systems development in information systems research. In: Proceedings of the Twenty-Third Annual Hawaii International Conference on System Sciences, vol. 3, pp. 631–640. IEEE (1990)
11. Walls, J.G., Widmeyer, G.R., El Sawy, O.A.: Building an information system design theory for vigilant eis. Information Systems Research 3(1), 36–59 (1992)
12. March, S.T., Smith, G.F.: Design and natural science research on information technology. Decision Support Systems 15(4), 251–266 (1995)
13. Baskerville, R., Lyytinen, K., Sambamurthy, V., Straub, D.: A response to the design-oriented information systems research memorandum. European Journal of Information Systems 20(1), 11–15 (2011)

14. Frank, U.: Die konstruktion möglicher welten als chance und herausforderung der wirtschaftsinformatik. In: Wissenschaftstheorie und gestaltungsorientierte Wirtschaftsinformatik, pp. 161–173. Springer (2009)

15. Loos, P., Mettler, T., Winter, R., Goeken, M., Frank, U., Winter, A.: Methodological pluralism in business and information systems engineering? Business & Information Systems Engineering 5(6), 453–460 (2013)

16. Verschuren, P., Hartog, R.: Evaluation in design-oriented research. Quality and Quantity 39(6), 733–762 (2005)

17. Simon, H.A.: The sciences of the artificial, vol. 136. MIT Press (1969)

18. Frank, U.: Towards a pluralistic conception of research methods in information systems research. Technical report, ICB-research report (2006)

19. Indulska, M., Recker, J.: Design science in is research: a literature analysis. Information Systems Foundations, 285 (2010)

20. Offermann, P., Levina, O., Schönherr, M., Bub, U.: Outline of a design science research process. In: Proceedings of the 4th International Conference on Design Science Research in Information Systems and Technology, p. 7. ACM (2009)

21. Ostrowski, L., Helfert, M.: Commonality in various design science methodologies. In: 2011 Federated Conference on Computer Science and Information Systems (FedCSIS), pp. 317–320. IEEE (2011)

22. Alturki, A., Gable, G.G., Bandara, W.: A design science research roadmap. In: Jain, H., Sinha, A.P., Vitharana, P. (eds.) DESRIST 2011. LNCS, vol. 6629, pp. 107–123. Springer, Heidelberg (2011)

23. Otto, B., Österle, H.: Relevance through consortium research? Findings from an expert interview study. In: Winter, R., Zhao, J.L., Aier, S. (eds.) DESRIST 2010. LNCS, vol. 6105, pp. 16–30. Springer, Heidelberg (2010)

24. Venable, J.R.: Design science research post hevner et al.: Criteria, standards, guidelines, and expectations. In: Winter, R., Zhao, J.L., Aier, S. (eds.) DESRIST 2010. LNCS, vol. 6105, pp. 109–123. Springer, Heidelberg (2010)

25. Ostrowski, L., Helfert, M., Xie, S.: A conceptual framework to construct an artefact for meta-abstract design knowledge in design science research. In: 2012 45th Hawaii International Conference on System Science (HICSS), pp. 4074–4081. IEEE (2012)

26. Gehlert, A., Schermann, M., Pohl, K., Krcmar, H.: Towards a research method for theory-driven design research. Wirtschaftsinformatik (1), 441–450 (2009)

27. Venable, J.: A framework for design science research activities. In: Proceedings of the 2006 Information Resource Management Association Conference, Washington, DC, pp. 21–24 (2006)

28. Pohl, K., Rupp, C.: Requirements Engineering Fundamentals: A Study Guide for the Certified Professional for Requirements Engineering Exam - Foundation Level - IREB compliant (Rocky Nook Computing). Rocky Nook (2011)

29. IEEE: Systems and software engineering – vocabulary. ISO/IEC/IEEE 24765:2010(E), 1–418 (December 2010)

30. Pohl, K.: The three dimensions of requirements engineering: a framework and its applications. Information Systems 19(3), 243–258 (1994)

31. Yu, E.S.: Towards modelling and reasoning support for early-phase requirements engineering. In: Proceedings of the Third IEEE International Symposium on Requirements Engineering, pp. 226–235. IEEE (1997)

32. Wieringa, R.: Requirements engineering: Problem analysis and solution specification (Extended abstract). In: Koch, N., Fraternali, P., Wirsing, M. (eds.) ICWE 2004. LNCS, vol. 3140, pp. 13–16. Springer, Heidelberg (2004)

33. Chung, L., do Prado Leite, J.C.S.: On non-functional requirements in software engineering. In: Borgida, A.T., Chaudhri, V.K., Giorgini, P., Yu, E.S. (eds.) Conceptual Modeling: Foundations and Applications. LNCS, vol. 5600, pp. 363–379. Springer, Heidelberg (2009)
34. Gorschek, T., Wohlin, C.: Requirements abstraction model. Requirements Engineering 11(1), 79–101 (2006)
35. Van Lamsweerde, A.: Goal-oriented requirements engineering: A guided tour. In: Proceedings of Fifth IEEE International Symposium on Requirements Engineering, pp. 249–262. IEEE (2001)
36. Monteiro, R., Araujo, J., Amaral, V., Goulao, M., Patricio, P.: Model-driven development for requirements engineering: The case of goal-oriented approaches. In: 2012 Eighth International Conference on the Quality of Information and Communications Technology (QUATIC), pp. 75–84 (September 2012)
37. Dardenne, A., Van Lamsweerde, A., Fickas, S.: Goal-directed requirements acquisition. Science of Computer Programming 20(1), 3–50 (1993)
38. Quartel, D., Engelsman, W., Jonkers, H., Sinderen, M.V.: A goal-oriented requirements modelling language for enterprise architecture. In: IEEE International Enterprise Distributed Object Computing Conference, EDOC 2009, pp. 3–13. IEEE (2009)
39. Respect, I.: A kaos tutorial (2007)
40. Nwokeji, J.C., Clark, T., Barn, B.S.: Towards a comprehensive meta-model for kaos. In: 2013 International Workshop on Model-Driven Requirements Engineering (MoDRE), pp. 30–39 (2013)
41. Frank, U.: Ein vorschlag zur konfiguration von forschungsmethoden in der wirtschaftsinformatik. Wissenschaftstheoretische Fundierung und wissenschaftliche Orientierung der Wirtschaftsinformatik, 158–185 (2007)
42. Baskerville, R., Pries-Heje, J., Venable, J.: Soft design science methodology. In: Proceedings of the 4th International Conference on Design Science Research in Information Systems and Technology, p. 9. ACM (2009)
43. Goldkuhl, G.: Design theories in information systems-a need for multi-grounding. Journal of Information Technology Theory and Application (JITTA) 6(2), 7 (2004)
44. Archer, L.B.: Systematic method for designers. Council of Industrial Design (1964)
45. Sein, M., Henfridsson, O., Purao, S., Rossi, M., Lindgren, R.: Action design research. MIS Quarterly, 37–56 (2011)

A Postmodern Perspective on Socio-technical Design Science Research in Information Systems

Andreas Drechsler[✉]

Institute of Computer Science and Business Information Systems,
Universitätsstr. 2, University of Duisburg-Essen, 45141 Essen, Germany
andreas.drechsler@icb.uni-due.de

Abstract. This paper presents a critical account of the current state of design science research (DSR) of socio-technical artifacts in the information systems discipline as viewed through a postmodern lens. The paper offers a novel perspective to reflect on DSR and socio-technical artifacts, especially in terms of their limitations and boundaries of application. To achieve this, I critically appraise the current state of DSR practices, based on postmodern researchers' key stances. The findings offer new perspectives on artifact effects, their application contexts, artifact utility, artifact audiences, the roles of the languages in which artifacts are specified, the design researcher's role in the DSR process, and the political dimension of artifact design and evaluation. Design science researchers working on all types of socio-technical artifacts can use this paper's findings to reflect on their artifacts' limitations and potential real-world consequences before, during, and after artifact design and instantiation, and to subsequently improve these artifacts.

Keywords: Design science · Socio-technical artifacts · Postmodernism · Postmodern

1 Introduction

In recent years, design science research (DSR) has become an established research paradigm in the IS field [1]. Its goal is to design and evaluate socio-technical artifacts (or design theories) that provide potential solutions for classes of real-world problems. The purpose of artifact evaluation is to assess an artifact's impacts and utility in solving the problems for which it was designed, to assess its superiority to other solutions (if applicable), and to derive future artifact improvements based on its application experiences. Over the past decade, DSR has seen substantial development concerning its theoretical and methodical foundations [2–8]. Pries-Heje et al. [9] stated that methodical support for DSR evaluation research was still thin, but a few years later, Peffers et al. [10] provided an extensive analysis and overview of existing artifact evaluation methods. Recently, Venable et al. proposed a comprehensive framework to guide artifact evaluation throughout its development in an entire research project [11]. However, these approaches and methods have one thing in common: They take a positivist stance on research. Consequently, researchers using these

© Springer International Publishing Switzerland 2015
B. Donnellan et al. (Eds.): DESRIST 2015, LNCS 9073, pp. 152–167, 2015.
DOI: 10.1007/978-3-319-18714-3_10

methods for artifact evaluation – at least implicitly – assume an ontological and epistemological objectivism [12, 13]: That there is one reality out there and that they are able to objectively perceive the artifacts and their impacts in this reality, i.e. without distortions, biases, or alternative interpretations. This can lead to a narrow perspective, as well as to misleading ex ante and ex post assessments of potential or de facto artifact impacts and their utility.

However, there are other research paradigms in the IS field, namely interpretivism and critical emancipatory research [13]. The latter is often simply called *critical research*, but with the recent emergence of critical realism in the IS field [14–16], the adjective *emancipatory* is added throughout this paper to distinguish them clearly. Both interpretivism and critical emancipatory research take a more subjective stance on reality [12, 17], which lead to a more differentiated picture of reality (and sometimes even to the questioning of the existence of objective reality). However, both need suitable research questions in order to be useful; consequently, simply switching to different methods would not be a viable solution to gain a more thorough understanding of artifact impacts and their utility. In addition, non-positivist approaches are far less common in the IS field than positivist ones [18]. Stahl's appraisal of DSR takes a critical emancipatory stance [19]. According to him, the key contributions of a critical emancipatory perspective of DSR include 1) the risk of unconsciously following the *heroic design ideology* that unidirectionally shapes artifact users' realities as a projection of managerial power, 2) a prescriptive perpetuation of extant ideologies codified in predominant artifacts (leading to conservatism instead of innovation), and 3) the neglect of moral and ethical aspects of DSR.

Besides the positivist, interpretivist, and critical emancipatory research paradigms, social scientists often mention postmodernism as a fourth extant paradigm [20]. Postmodernism acts as an umbrella term for a number of diverse stances that social researchers take; it challenges the foundations of traditional research interested in generalizations and progress – two goals DSR also strives for. Novel artifacts (or design theories) should be applicable to more than a single local context and should have greater utility than existing artifacts or solutions [1]. Since applicability and utility are both crucial constituents of progress and contribution in DSR, additional lenses through which researchers can question the extent to which they can reliably argue for artifact generalizability and superiority can help justify the resulting artifacts. In addition, analogous to theories' boundaries, these lenses may help improve discussions of, or reflection on, an artifact's boundaries [21, 22].

This is especially relevant for socio-technical artifacts that explicitly include the social context and, thus, affect individuals and society. The extent to which an artifact affects people and society can be rather limited, such as a novel business information system that allows its users to work more efficiently or has a more user-friendly user interface. On the other end of the scale, there are the individual and societal impacts of other IS DSR endeavors, such as assisted living [23], or smart cities [24]. Here, the artifacts' impacts have more far-reaching – positive and negative – applications in terms of the extent to which they intend to and in fact affect individuals and society as a whole.

For an extreme illustration of the negative consequences that artifacts' unintended side-effects may have, I draw on a prominent example from another design-related context: architecture. Jencks uses the following example to denote the end of the modern architecture era and, thus, the beginning of postmodern architecture [25]: In 1952, a housing complex called Pruitt-Igoe in St. Louis, MO was planned with great expectations regarding contributing to urban renewal and inhabitants' quality of life. A renowned, successful architect designed and built the complex according to state-of-the-art functionalist architecture principles. However, it soon became clear that these design principles and goals did not hold in reality. First, the complex's inhabitants quality of life and safety were low, and occupancy dropped rapidly, despite costly countermeasures on the part of the city and the federal administration. Eventually, having become a slum, the entire complex was dynamited in 1972. There is little in the current IS design science discourse for socio-technical design projects that encourages, or even guides, researchers to prevent their artifacts from triggering similar (or worse) consequences and, metaphorically speaking, from meeting the same fate as Pruitt-Igoe. Yet socio-technical design artifacts may affect people or society as strongly as, or even stronger than, a failed housing project of 2,870 apartments.

Against this backdrop, it is worth taking a more in-depth look at what postmodernism, as a critical lens, can contribute to the current state of IS DSR discourse. However, postmodernism has generally only been covered in the IS discipline to a very limited extent [26–28], nor has any of its previous contributions covered design science. In this light, this paper seeks to provide a critical yet constructive appraisal of the current state of the DSR discourse through a postmodernism lens. The findings allow design researchers to take new angles and lenses to view and reflect on – and subsequently improve – their artifacts during their design and during their instantiation in practical settings. The postmodern research stances challenge traditional research's fundamental assumptions and may even appear 'impertinent' in this regard but nonetheless provide a useful lens for becoming aware of the boundaries of current DSR.

The remainder of this paper is structured as follows: Section 2 provides a brief overview of common research streams within postmodernism, Section 3 discusses the implications of each research stream on IS DSR designing socio-technical artifacts, and Section 4 highlights the primary impacts on the design science discourse, while Section 5 provides a conclusion and an outlook for future research.

2   Postmodernism as Research Paradigm – An Overview

My overview on postmodernism as a research paradigm in this section follows Alvesson and Sköldberg's summary [20], since it covers many streams of a disjointed and fragmented research field. Their overview also provides a critique of postmodernism and poststructuralism (in this paper, labeled *postmodernism*) while keeping in mind applied and empirical social science, which one would rely on in order to evaluate socio-technical artifacts. Alvesson and Sköldberg use postmodernism as an umbrella term for a wide variety of research streams and schools that follow the same ideas, and emphasize that the two umbrella terms of postmodernism and poststructuralism do not have a clear and unified relationship in the literature. All postmodern research approaches have in common a fundamental opposition to structuralist and functionalist principles. The summaries I provide below only capture the key elements of each postmodern research stream. In a detailed view, each stream and each author within each stream offer a more multifaceted perspective. Space restrictions do not allow for such a detailed level here. The same applies for a more detailed differentiation between postmodernist and poststructuralist perspectives.

2.1   Postmodernism as a Lens for the Deconstruction of Texts

A first stream within postmodernism is concerned with the *deconstruction* of texts. In short, the deconstruction of a text means, in a first step, to turn its predominant meaning around to an opposing one through weaknesses in the text (*destruction* of its principal meaning). Afterwards, the two opposing meanings are then placed in a wider context in which they are just gradual differences. In other words, in this second step, the opposing difference between the meanings is also *destructed* and, finally, a new context is *constructed* into which the two former extremes fit as mere special cases – hence, *deconstruction* [29].

Derrida introduces the concept/non-concept[1] of *différance* in language – a neologism of *difference* and *deferral* [30] – on the basis of this deconstruction of texts. In his view, there is a *difference* between every word's intended meaning and its opposite meaning, which should be deconstructed. Further, the sense of an entire text composed of words is not yet clear when a word is written (or spoken); its overall meaning is thus *deferred*. Thus, for Derrida, there is never an absolute meaning, only relative and temporary ones.

On this relativist foundation of an *absence* of meaning, Derrida further argues against the concept of *presence*, which is dominant in Western metaphysical thinking [31]. For him, there are no principles, causes, goals, intentions, or other forces *present* behind the observable surfaces of real-world phenomena. Therefore, only the observable surfaces should be considered.

2.2   Postmodernism as a Stance against *Grand Narratives*

Another stream in postmodern research turns against what proponents such as Lyotard call *grand narratives* [32]. Grand narratives are a label for all theories, approaches, methods, or paradigms that are – to a limited or greater extent – of a coherent, comprehensive, and unified nature. This postmodern research stream rejects the existence of such grand narratives and dismisses them as 'myths.' Instead, Lyotard advises that we seek out fragmented local histories, the specifics of a situation or a context, emergent instead of regular phenomena, contradictions, and paradoxes.

---

[1]   Différance is called a concept and a non-concept due to a self-referential application of deconstruction / différance to différance in a postmodern spirit, cf. [20 p. 187, 224].

In science, Lyotard approves of Feyerabend's [33] methodological pluralism/anarchism and is of the view that, with their elements of unpredictability and randomness, chaos and catastrophe theories are superior to classic theories that strive for order, harmony, and regularity. This especially refers to theories and methods that follow a positivistic paradigm. Interestingly, Lyotard values pragmatic technologic criteria where applicability – or *utility*, as used in design science discourse – dominates aspirations towards a universal truth. He further criticizes critical emancipatory theory. While he values free communication and dialogue, Lyotard prefers disturbances and contradictions that lead to fruitful disagreement instead of striving for consensus and harmony.

2.3   Postmodernism as Criticism of the (Humanistic) Subject of Research

A third postmodern research stream consists of authors who reject the idea and the existence of a coherent individual – who acts consciously, autonomously, and rationally – as a research subject [34–37]. Consequently, these authors also reject the idea of a unified subjectivity. Further, language constitutes and influences all subjectivity. For instance, subjective perceptions of *work* may cover different facets of work, such as "heavy demands, stress, opportunity, or challenge" [20, p. 195]. In addition, subjectivity is not considered stable over time, since language triggers ideas and emotions that may differ over time, even within the same individual. Thus, proponents of this research stream advise one to de-center the human subject in research and to problematize his or her predominant role. In other words, they challenge the assumption that people behave consistently and predictably over time. Combined with the role of language, which influences subjectivity in essentially unpredictable ways, these authors treat subjectivity as a highly volatile concept, which essentially acts as a potential destabilizer of any discourse between subjects – including conversations, interviews, and surveys.

2.4   Postmodernism Questioning the Role of the Researcher as Author

Other postmodernists problematize the role researchers play in the research context. From this postmodern perspective, research is not supposed to explain, verify, and seek truth, but should foster a critical conversation between researchers [38]. Postmodernism questions researchers' authority and ability to objectively determine the relationships between identified elements, or to offer a simple synthesis of individual, more complex, findings at all [39]. Further, the differing styles of the authorship of intermediate or final texts, of interpretations, or of individual values lead to different researchers – at least subconsciously – using different languages to present their research, conveying different messages even though they followed the same goals and adhered to the same procedures and methods [40, 41]. Empirical researchers thus face two representational challenges [42]: First, researchers reproduce or reconstruct a particular fragment of reality (epistemological dimension). Second, by doing so, researchers implicitly select, interpret, and frame their real-world object(s) of interest in subjective ways (ethical-political dimension). In this light, any seemingly objective data or facts are in fact individual researchers' subjective accounts. Consequently, in this postmodern view, research, "constructs rather than depicts what is being researched" [20, p. 200]. To avoid a single subjective lens, research should therefore seek out alternative accounts, or voices, of an empirical situation; it should also be self-reflective on its limitations in this regard.

2.5   Criticism Directed at Postmodern Research

Alvesson and Sköldberg [20] summarize criticism of postmodernism as follows:

Lack of Constructivity. A researcher applying a postmodern perspective does not solely attempt to create knowledge, to contribute to a cumulative body of knowledge, or to provide meaningful and substantial contributions for someone else than other (postmodern) researchers.

Textual Reductionism. In several postmodern streams, the emphasis is on text and language, instead of on the social phenomena in a text. Taken further, there is a danger that postmodern research is only concerned with research for its own sake, with self-referential positions and arguments. Postmodern research can thus lose its connection to phenomena beyond the text.

Relativism. Taken seriously and literally, many postmodern streams advocate a stance of "anything goes" – to quote Feyerabend [33], who directed this criticism at methodological anarchism in research. Postmodernism takes *anything goes* one step further and extends it to research subjects. In other words, not only are there no limits to irrelevance in postmodernist research, but it would also be impossible to argue about research topics that are not worthy of attention in the first place. This leads to an overall impression of postmodern research's arbitrariness and relativism.

2.6   Recommendations for Non-postmodern Empirical Research

Against the backdrop of these four identified postmodern research streams and their limitations, Alvesson and Sköldberg [20] draw the following implications for non-postmodern empirical research. They intend to stimulate researchers' reflections on the limitations of their research. Section 3.2 will draw on these implications to derive and discuss corresponding implications for DSR artifact evaluation research as an instance of empirical research.

Pluralism as an Empirical Research Principle. Taking seriously postmodern ideas in empirical research means that researchers need to deliberately seek out multiple voices and facets of a real-world setting. The 'raw data' they seem to have gathered may not be as raw as it seems. In addition, moving towards pluralism means deliberately looking for voices that contradict the messages the dominant voices convey and paying special attention to conflicting or paradoxical statements in the data. Furthermore, acknowledging a complex environment and developing suitable categories for the multitude of observed phenomena is a solution as much as a problem: Researchers who categorize reality construct their own reality and base their subsequent analysis on their subjective interpretations and categorizations of reality.

Well-grounded Process of Exclusion. Since not all unique – dominant and marginal – voices in a real-world setting can be realistically captured during empirical research, the process of consciously excluding voices can help researchers become aware of their perspective's limitations and implications for their subsequent research.

Cautious Interaction with Empirical Material. Postmodernism highlights the strong influence that the researcher as a subjectivity-inducing individual has on all facets of empirical research. The recommendation here is not to shy away from shaping research and drawing bold conclusions, but to do this consciously and deliberately. Researchers can achieve this by actively seeking a wide range of possible theories or metaphors to frame and guide the selection and analysis of empirical material.

Differentiated Role of Theory. Postmodernism reminds us that moving from theory to data to analysis to interpretation to text and back does not happen seamlessly. The choice of one theory/piece of data/analysis/interpretation/set of words excludes all others (including, but not limited to, their various opposites). If researchers are aware of this, they can avoid locking themselves into a specific frame of reference.

Problematization of Authorship and Language. When, in a postmodern view, nearly all of a research endeavor's properties influence – or even shape – its process and outcome, such a view emphasizes that researchers must take responsibility for their findings and their 'blind spots' in any case and may not hide behind methodological (and conformist) procedures and protocol. Furthermore, the exposed role that language plays in nearly all stages of empirical research, regardless of setting and method, severely limits the extent to which one can strongly justify arriving at specific interpretations and conclusions. While this should not stifle a researcher and nor promote relativism or nihilism, being aware of and sensitive to differing interpretations and conclusions can lead to greater awareness of the limitations of one's research.

Awareness of Political Aspects of Research. Finally, when authorship implies authority, it also implies power and, in turn, politics. Consequently, readers can interpret politically any statement or conclusion (or the absence of these) drawn by researchers. Again, this should not stifle researchers, but should make them aware of this issue underlying their research.

3   A Postmodern Lens on IS DSR

Section 2 showed that, taken to their extreme, postmodern thoughts may lead to research having a very limited contribution potential. At the same time, such thoughts allow for a focused and structured reflection on research content and practices before, during, and after an empirical research project. In this way, postmodern thoughts can help empirical researchers to increase their awareness of their work's limitations and boundaries. This section now shows how postmodern thoughts can also act as helpful lenses to reflect on the limitation and boundaries of artifact design, instantiation, and evaluation in IS DSR. Two separate subsections cover the (constructive) artifact design and (empirical) artifact evaluation phases. In this section, *organization* is not limited to traditional business organizations, but encompasses all types of socio-technical systems for which IS DSR may develop socio-technical artifacts.

3.1 Implications of Postmodernism for Artifact Design and Instantiation

This subsection highlights the implications of the four postmodern research streams outlined in Sections 2.1 to 2.4 for the artifact design process and its application/instantiation in one or more real-world contexts.

Indeterminism of Artifact Effects during Design Time. The general principles behind Derrida's deconstruction of texts and *différance* are also applicable to artifacts. Usually, each socio-technical artifact has a specific purpose: to solve an existing problem (in case of a local artifact/design theory), or a class of problems (in case of a mid-range artifact/design theory) in a real-world organization [1]. Likewise, each word in a text usually also has a specific meaning. When applied/instantiated in a specific socio-technical application context (organization), an artifact should trigger one or more effects within that context, in order to achieve the intended solution. This may include the provision of a technical infrastructure (an information system), as well as changes to an organization's processes and the required human behavior. Deconstructing this intended effect in the first step opens up the possibility that the artifact's instantiation may in fact lead to the opposite effect. Such effects are well known in social policy research, for instance, requiring car passengers to wear seatbelts leads to increased fatalities owing to the heightened feeling of increased security [43]. In the second step, the deconstruction tasks researchers with finding a spectrum of possible outcomes with the two opposites now mere dots on the spectrum. This opens up a perspective on a much wider range of possible artifact effects. In addition, organizations continuously change and evolve over time. Therefore, organizational dynamics may reinforce, sidestep, or counteract the initial effect that an artifact triggered. Consequently, a stable and sustained artifact effect is indefinitely deferred.

Thus, design researchers can use Derrida's concept of *différance* to reflect on their artifacts' possible effects in a static (deconstruction) and a dynamic (deferral) perspective beyond the desired and intended effect an artifact has, or may have, on an application context. They can do so not only right before the de facto introduction of an artifact into an application context, but already during a very early stage of the design and during intermediate evaluation phases. In turn, the results of their reflection can serve to improve the artifacts so that unintended side-effects can be minimized. Since the second deconstruction step can specifically yield a multitude of possible effects, it is not possible to anticipate each possible artifact effect and develop countermeasures. Instead, this step can prepare design researchers for organizations' effectively unpredictable reactions when an artifact is introduced. The effective deferral of de facto sustainable artifact effects also has implications for artifact evaluation, as discussed in Section 3.2.

Artifacts as Grand Narratives. Viewed through a postmodern lens, the current understanding of artifact utility in DSR as the 'dependent variable' constitutes a rationalistic and functionalistic construct. In addition, artifacts promising to solve (a class of) real-world problems through their application fit all the characteristics of grand narratives. They are of a coherent nature, generalized, and disregard the specifics of each local application context. Postmodernism is highly critical of such grand narratives and challenges them on a fundamental level.

Thus, neither design researchers nor future artifact users should expect artifacts to be 'turnkey solutions' for the problems they want to tackle. Instead, they should anticipate the need to tailor the socio-technical artifact elements to their specific contexts, in order to be successful. This is in line with Pandza and Thorpe's warnings to treat DSR outcomes' introduction into organizations as a trigger for change processes and not as an engineering-like application [44]. The context-specific adaption issue is already reflected as in the 'mutability' and 'principles of implementation' aspects in a design theory [3], and in proposals to also consider artifact fitness (adaptability to the specifics of application contexts) in addition to artifact utility [2].

Moreover, viewing artifacts as grand narratives emphasizes the importance of particular aspects of an application context for artifact success and thus points to the limitations of generalizing across artifact application cases. This is especially relevant when moving from local to mid-range artifacts/design theories or trying to generalize as a final step in an action design research project [45].

Subjectivity and Artifacts. At first glance, artificial entities – socio-technical artifacts – and not people are the center of attention in IS DSR. Therefore, the issues concerning subjectivity do not at first seem to be of particular relevance for conducting IS DSR. However, subjectivity enters DSR in four different ways. First, by definition, socio-technical artifacts (excluding purely technical IS DSR artifacts) contain a social component, which immediately connects socio-technical artifacts to the realm of human subjectivity. Second, all artifact users have their own subjective perceptions of how and how well an artifact can solve their problems (or may create new ones in the process). This relates to the concept of *affordances* in design research [46], but goes one step further. In this postmodern-inspired lens, affordances – as expressions of artifact users' subjectivity – should not be regarded as stable over time. Consequently, neither should (perceived) artifact utility be regarded as stable. Third, when postmodernists posit that (textual) language triggers ideas and emotions – and thus influences subjectivities; this not only also applies to DSR artifacts, but even leads to an extension of the postmodernist perspective. Commonly, DSR artifacts' specifications are not limited to textual language, but also employ semi-formal graphical depictions, which may or may not conform to modeling languages such as BPMN or UML. In turn, this requires attention to the kinds of ideas and emotions triggered by artifact specifications or representations in the different textual and modeling languages when potential or designated future artifact users view the artifacts. In turn, these ideas and emotions may influence these users' perceptions of artifact utility. The role of design researchers, which is problematized in a separate paragraph below, is a fourth source of subjectivity in a DSR context.

Design science researchers can already draw on the above conclusions during their artifacts' design time to reflect who their artifacts' audiences are (which arises from their artifacts' social component) and how the artifacts they create influence the different individuals in their audiences. This influence not only comprises the subjective perceptions of an artifact's utility, but also the perceptions of – and, in a second step, attitudes towards – an artifact. In sum, design science researchers can therefore use this postmodern lens to extend their focus beyond their artifacts, to consider individuals whom their artifacts are likely to affect in differentiated ways.

The Design Science Researcher's Role. While postmodernist criticism of empirical research practices is limited to questioning the role of the researcher as an author, the multiple roles design science researchers take during a DSR project require more extensive problematization. DSR researchers are first and foremost designers and therefore take an intentionally active stance in shaping possible future realities [47]. They therefore figuratively *and* literally construct what is being researched, regardless of whether they choose an action design research approach [45], or whether they choose to design abstract artifacts that will be instantiated and applied to specific application contexts later on. Simultaneously, design science researchers change roles during the evaluation phase and seek to become passive observers of artifact effects. Design science researchers are thus authors of artifacts, as well as authors of empirical research accounts. Empirical researchers' afore-mentioned double representation problem is therefore even more multifaceted concerning design science researchers. They not only – subjectively – select, interpret, and frame a real-world problem, but do the same with their proposed solution – the artifact. Likewise, Stahl [19] also highlights that the ethical-political dimension extends to the artifact as well as its evaluation. In addition, creativity's role in DSR clarifies that different designers come to different solutions/artifacts for the same problem and context [48]. Moreover, a published artifact only retains an indirect connection to its creators (through formal authorship), but still embodies all the afore-mentioned sources of researcher subjectivity. When an artifact is instantiated in a new organization, all these subjectivities are also applied to this application context, possibly even without its original designer's involvement.

Therefore, it seems even more imperative for design science researchers than for empirical researchers to (self-)reflect on the roles they take and the limitations they are responsible for in any DSR effort. The call to seek multiple voices in empirical research also applies to design science research in the form of intentionally seeking multiple solutions. In this regard, Boland and Collopy provide an illustrative report on how an architect working for the star architect Frank Gehry deliberately sought another solution by discarding the first workable solution for a challenging architectural problem, starting from scratch [49]. Since writing a DSR publication constitutes decoupling an artifact from the persons of its designer(s), covering the afore-mentioned issues in the resulting text can raise future artifact users' awareness of the hidden issues of subjectivity. In addition, DSR projects – especially those concerning socio-technical artifacts with a potentially high impact on individuals' lives and society – can generally benefit from an intensive reflection on the political and ethical dimensions of artifact design.

3.2   Implications of Postmodernism for Artifact Evaluation

This section now applies Alvesson and Sköldberg's [20] recommendations regarding empirical research (see Section 2.6) to artifact evaluation in a DSR context.

Pluralism as an Artifact Evaluation Principle. Transferring the first principle to artifact evaluation leads to the recommendation to deliberately seek multiple voices within an affected organization to evaluate artifact utility in practice. During artifact evaluation research, it may be convenient to limit interviews, for instance to IT, or business executives, or the end-users selected by executives – with the executives typically in the role of the gatekeepers. A thorough reflection on the different artifact audiences during design time (see above) should yield a comprehensive list of the different stakeholders – and thus, relevant voices – that design researchers can cover during artifact evaluation.

Well-Grounded Process of Exclusion. It may not be feasible – especially for socio-technical artifacts with large-scale impacts on society – to listen to representatives of all artifact audience groups during an artifact evaluation cycle. In such cases, the second principle recommends a conscious selection process of the audiences that researchers exclude from the artifact evaluation process.

Cautious Interaction with Empirical Material. In addition to the general recommendations by Alvesson and Sköldberg [20] in their third principle for all empirical research, there is an additional aspect of particular relevance for artifact evaluation research. The application of the deferral part of *différance* to socio-technical artifacts in Section 3.1 highlighted that there may not be any point in time in which artifact utility takes its final shape. This implies that any evaluation of artifact utility is likely to remain a snapshot in time, and that subsequent later evaluation rounds may well yield a different utility evaluation or show additional – positive or negative – side-effects that only manifest in an organization after the first evaluation.

Differentiated Role of Theory. As theories form important foundations for both artifact design and evaluation [6], the choice of theories constitutes a crucial decision for any DSR effort. The choice of different theoretical lenses may lead to different solutions and different artifact utility criteria. However, the chasm between explanatory-oriented theories and actionable knowledge has been discussed extensively in DSR [50]. Therefore, it is important to keep this chasm in mind when deriving theoretical implications and discussing theoretical contributions during artifact evaluation.

Problematization of Authorship and Language. Since an artifact's designers usually also conduct evaluation in artifact evaluation research, the design researcher's pronounced role – as discussed in Section 3.1 – gains an additional facet. It is easy to imagine that the same biases and frames of mind that influenced artifact design decisions are also likely to influence artifact evaluation. In addition, as noted, artifact evaluation research presents researchers with the additional obstacle of evaluating their subjectivity – or themselves, to a certain extent – as embedded in a particular artifact. While 'ideal' researchers would not shy away from questioning their previous decisions and would be open to the increased potential to learn from a failed artifact application, a research project's realities could simultaneously be a powerful force to bias artifact evaluation research towards artifact success. Here, the postmodern lens helps raise the awareness of the researchers conducting artifact evaluation. Further, textual and modeling languages' previously discussed roles and influences also apply to artifact evaluation research.

Awareness of Political Aspects of Design Research. Artifact evaluation research becomes a political instrument, especially when an artifact has been developed in close collaboration with and/or has been funded by powerful persons in the target organization. In this context, the challenge of an unbiased evaluation now extends from the individual person(s) of the researcher(s) to the joint collective responsible (and perhaps even accountable) for an artifact's design and ultimate success. Artifacts are thus more than a mere political statement published as an isolated research finding outside an organizational context. Taken further, as soon as seemingly neutral researchers enter an organization in order to design, apply, or evaluate an artifact with the potential to influence the organizational context, they instantly become political entities. Therefore, ample awareness of this issue can help design researchers to prevent or at least reduce the circumstances of the political setting from compromising the artifact evaluation. This should be seen in addition to design research's other political aspects, which Stahl [19] has pointed out – as mentioned in the Introduction – which should also be the subject of artifact evaluation.

4   Discussion

A postmodern perspective such as the one taken up in this paper has rarely been applied in the IS field and its application to DSR is, to my best knowledge, the first of its kind. This paper therefore offers several novel lenses from other research disciplines for IS research and IS DSR in particular. At first glance, the 'unconstructive' nature of the postmodern paradigm does not constitute an attractive proposition for a field with a cumulative tradition. However, the in-depth consideration of each postmodern research stream and extant recommendations for empirical research have yielded several novel and, given the nature of postmodern research, surprisingly structured implications for the design and evaluation of socio-technical artifacts. While this appears somewhat ironic, given the nature of postmodern research, irony is another common trait in postmodern research [20]. A further ironic consequence of postmodern criticism of the humanistic subject of research and its subsequent advice to de-center the human subject from research is the advice that DSR researchers should go beyond a singular artifact focus and should deliberately consider the individuals whom the artifact are likely to affect as the artifact audiences.

Some of the implications – such as the importance of adapting artifacts to application contexts' specifics, the necessity for artifacts to keep up with changing environments, and IS DSR's political-ethical dimension – have been considered in other DSR papers and contexts. However, to my best knowledge, other implications have not yet been discussed in the literature. These include the role artifact audiences and artifact languages play in the design and evaluation process, design science researchers' multifaceted role over the course of a DSR project, the issue of artifacts' unintended side-effects, artifact utility's unstable nature in social contexts, the challenge of seeking many voices on artifact effects during artifact evaluation, and the perspective on socio-technical artifacts as *grand narratives*. While some researchers may, in fact, address some or all these issues during their DSR consciously or sub-consciously, the lack of comprehensive coverage in the extant literature leaves the extent to which they actually address these issues to researchers' (and their reviewers') common sense.

Here, this paper makes another major contribution by turning the 'unconstructive' nature of postmodern research into constructive implications for DSR. Taking postmodernism as grounds for reflection, this paper provides multiple perspectives from which one can reflect on DSR's limitations and artifact boundaries. These perspectives for reflection complement researchers' common sense as well as existing theoretical and methodological DSR guidance, and each perspective contributes a distinct lens for artifact criticism and the enhancement of particular areas. The reflection process allows design researchers to explicate and discuss issues that would otherwise stay hidden, would be tackled subconsciously if at all, or would be taken for granted. Most factors are induced by or related to the social application context of socio-technical artifacts. Hence, the reflection processes will probably be more extensive and will also have greater effects if artifacts' social component and the social application context affected by the artifacts are large.

Returning to the architecture example of the Pruitt-Igoe housing complex mentioned in the introduction, such a reflection process would not prevent a similar 'disaster' with one's own IS DSR artifacts. Nevertheless, it is conceivable that more unintended side-effects and artifact limitations may be uncovered, taken into account, and prevented during the reflection process than without such a structured and thorough reflection process. Such reflection should at least mean that one is better prepared for negative side-effects during artifact evaluation and can pinpoint possible reasons for this failure more easily and in a more structured way.

5   Conclusion and Outlook

Overall, this paper provides design researchers and DSR publication readers – and, thus, future artifact users – with a number of additional perspectives through which they can view and evaluate artifacts, as well as DSR in general. Design researchers can draw on these perspectives during the various stages of artifact development, instantiation, and evaluation over the entire course of a DSR project, in order to further improve their artifacts. However, owing to space restrictions, this paper only covers each perspective in brief. Future research can expand on each of the perspectives and can illustrate the benefits of appropriate reflection in the context of past or ongoing DSR projects in greater detail. Another direction for future research is, analogous to the boundaries of theories, to develop a more coherent artifact boundary concept [21] based on the various limitations of artifacts I have pointed out in this paper. This could further strengthen the foundations of the fundamental entity *artifact* in the IS DSR meta-discourse.

References

1. Gregor, S., Hevner, A.R.: Positioning and Presenting Design Science Research for Maximum Impact. MIS Q. 37, 337–A6 (2013)
2. Gill, G., Hevner, A.R.: A Fitness-Utility Model for Design Science Research. ACM Trans. Manag. Inf. Syst. 4, 5:1–5:24 (2013)
3. Gregor, S., Jones, D.: The Anatomy of a Design Theory. J. Assoc. Inf. Syst. 8, 312–335 (2007)
4. Hevner, A., Chatterjee, S.: Design Research in Information Systems: Theory and Practice. Springer, New York (2010)
5. Hevner, A., March, S.T., Park, J., Ram, S.: Design Science in Information Systems Research. MIS Q. 28, 75–105 (2004)
6. Kuechler, W., Vaishnavi, V.: A Framework for Theory Development in Design Science Research: Multiple Perspectives. J. Assoc. Inf. Syst. 13, 395–423 (2012)
7. Peffers, K., Tuunanen, T., Rothenberger, M., Chatterjee, S.: A Design Science Research Methodology for Information Systems Research. J. Manag. Inf. Syst. 24, 45–77 (2007)
8. Vaishnavi, V., Kuechler, W.: Design Science Research Methods and Patterns. Auerbach, Boca Raton (2008)
9. Pries-Heje, J., Baskerville, R., Venable, J.: Strategies for Design Science Research Evaluation. In: Proc. ECIS 2008 Conf. Galway Irel (2008)
10. Peffers, K., Rothenberger, M., Tuunanen, T., Vaezi, R.: Design science research evaluation. In: Peffers, K., Rothenberger, M., Kuechler, B. (eds.) DESRIST 2012. LNCS, vol. 7286, pp. 398–410. Springer, Heidelberg (2012)
11. Venable, J., Pries-Heje, J., Baskerville, R.: FEDS: A Framework for Evaluation in Design Science Research. Eur. J. Inf. Syst. (2014)
12. Lee, A.S.: Integrating Positivist and Interpretive Approaches to Organizational Research. Organ. Sci. 2, 342–365 (1991)
13. Mingers, J.: Combining IS Research Methods: Towards a Pluralist Methodology. Inf. Syst. Res. 12, 240–259 (2001)
14. Mingers, J.: Real-izing Information Systems: Critical Realism as an Underpin-ning Philosophy for Information Systems. Inf. Organ. 14, 87–103 (2004)
15. Wynn, D., Williams, C.: Principles for Conducting Critical Realist Case Study Research in Information Systems. Manag. Inf. Syst. Q. 36, 787–810 (2012)
16. Zachariadis, M., Scott, S., Barrett, M.: Methodological Implications of Critical Realism for Mixed-Methods Research. MIS Q. 37, 855–879 (2013)
17. Hirschheim, R., Klein, H.K.: Four paradigms of information systems development. Commun ACM 32, 1199–1216 (1989)

18. Venkatesh, V., Brown, S.A., Bala, H.: Bridging the Qualitative-Quantitative Divide: Guidelines for Conducting Mixed Method Research in Information Systems. MIS Q. 37, 21–54 (2013)
19. Stahl, B.C.: The Ideology of Design: A Critical Appreciation of the Design Science Discourse in Information Systems and Wirtschaftsinformatik. In: Becker, J., Krcmar, H., Niehaves, B. (eds.) Wissenschaftstheorie und gestaltungsorientierte Wirtschaftsinformatik, pp. 111–132. Physica-Verlag HD, , Heidelberg (2009)
20. Alvesson, M., Sköldberg, K.: Reflexive Methodology - New Vistas for Qualitative Research. Sage, London (2009)
21. Whetten, D.A.: What constitutes a theoretical contribution? Acad. Manage. Rev. 14, 490–495 (1989)
22. Weber, R.: Evaluating and Developing Theories in the Information Systems Discipline. J. Assoc. Inf. Syst. 13 (2012)
23. Chatterjee, S., Price, A.: Healthy Living with Persuasive Technologies: Frame-work, Issues, and Challenges. J. Am. Med. Inform. Assoc. JAMIA. 16, 171–178 (2009)
24. Maccani, G., Donnellan, B., Helfert, M.: Action Design Research in Practice: The Case of Smart Cities. In: Tremblay, M.C., VanderMeer, D., Rothenberger, M., Gupta, A., and Yoon, V. (eds.) Advancing the Impact of Design Science: Moving from Theory to Practice, pp. 132–147. Springer International Publishing (2014)
25. Jencks, C.: The language of post-modern architecture. Academy Editions, London (1987)
26. Chatterjee, S., Sarker, S., Fuller, M.: Ethical Information Systems Development: A Baumanian Postmodernist Perspective. J. Assoc. Inf. Syst. 10, 787–815 (2009)
27. Kreps, D.: My social networking profile: copy, resemblance, or simulacrum? A poststructuralist interpretation of social information systems. Eur. J. Inf. Syst. 19, 104–115 (2010)
28. Kroeze, J.H.: Interpretivism in Information Systems: A Postmodern Epistemology?, http://sprouts.aisnet.org/11-171/
29. Krupnick, M.: Introduction. In: Krupnick, M. (ed.) Displacement: Derrida and after. Indiana University Press, Bloomington (1983)
30. Derrida, J.: Writing and difference. University of Chicago Press, Chicago (1978)
31. Derrida, J.: Margins of philosophy. University of Chicago Press, Chicago (1982)
32. Lyotard, J.-F.: The Postmodern Condition: A Report on Knowledge. University Of Minnesota Press, Minneapolis (1984)
33. Feyerabend, P.: Against method: outline of an anarchistic theory of knowledge. New Left Books, London (1975)
34. Weedon, C.: Feminist practice and poststructuralist theory. B. Blackwell, Oxford (1987)
35. Foucault, M.: Power/knowledge: selected interviews and other writings, pp. 1972–1977. Pantheon Books, New York (1980)
36. Collinson, D.L.: Identities and Insecurities: Selves at Work. Organization 10, 527–547 (2003)
37. Willmott, H.: Bringing agency (back) into organizational analysis: responding to the crisis of (post)modernity. Postmodernism and organizations, pp. 114–131. SAGE Publications, London (1993)
38. Brown, R.H.: Rhetoric, textuality, and the postmodern turn in sociological theory. Sociol. Theory 8, 188–197 (1990)
39. Rosenau, P.V.: Post-modernism and the social sciences: insights, inroads, and intrusions. Princeton University Press, Princeton (1992)
40. Sköldberg, K.: The poetic logic of administration: styles and changes of style in the art of organizing. Routledge, London (2002)

41. Richardson, J.: Writing: a method of inquiry. In: Denzin, N.K., Lincoln, Y.S. (eds.) Handbook of Qualitative Research. Sage Publications, Thousand Oaks (2000)
42. Linstead, S.: From Postmodern Anthropology to Deconstructive Ethnography. Hum. Relat. 46, 97–120 (1993)
43. Peltzman, S.: The effects of automobile safety regulation. J. Polit. Econ., 677–725 (1975)
44. Pandza, K., Thorpe, R.: Management as Design, but What Kind of Design? An Appraisal of the Design Science Analogy for Management. Br. J. Manag. 21, 171–186 (2010)
45. Sein, M., Henfridsson, O., Purao, S., Rossi, M., Lindgren, R.: Action Design Research. MIS Q. 35, 17–56 (2011)
46. Seidel, S., Recker, J., Vom Brocke, J.: Sensemaking and sustainable practicing: functional affordances of information systems in green transformations. Mis Q. 37, 1275–1299 (2013)
47. Frank, U.: Die Konstruktion möglicher Welten als Chance und Herausforderung der Wirtschaftsinformatik. In: Becker, J., Krcmar, H., Niehaves, B. (eds.) Wissenschaftstheorie und gestaltungsorientierte Wirtschaftsinformatik, pp. 161–173. Physica-Verlag HD, Heidelberg (2009)
48. Hevner, A.R., Webb Collins, R., Davis, C., Gill, T.G.: A NeuroDesign Model for IS Research. Informing Sci. 17 (2014)
49. Boland, R., Collopy, F.: Managing as designing. Stanford University Press (2004)
50. Bunge, M.: Scientific Research II: The Search for Truth. Springer, Berlin (1967)

Agile Design Science Research

Kieran Conboy[1], Rob Gleasure[2], and Eoin Cullina[1(✉)]

[1]Lero, Business Information Systems, National University of Ireland, Galway, Ireland
{kieran.conboy,e.cullina2}@nuigalway.ie
[2]Department of Accounting, Finance and Information Systems, University College Cork,
Corcaigh, Ireland
r.gleasure@ucc.ie

Abstract. As design science has matured, prescriptive frameworks and best practices have been advanced to assist researchers and lay out the academic standards for the paradigm. We argue that the problem-solving model underlying much of this progress has limited the ability of researchers to produce creative artefacts. To address this, we propose an amended Agile Design Science Research Methodology (ADSRM). ADSRM draws upon breakthroughs made in industry by those adopting 'agile' perspectives on IT development. This agile perspective balances procedural rigour with the need to consider empirically-driven problem/solution coevolution, allowing development to hone in on the most meaningful and unanticipated of problems. ADSRM proposes amendments to several existing DSR best practices, as well as two entirely new components to be modelled in the design process, namely a problem backlog and a hardening sprint. The value of these additions is illustrated in two exemplar cases.

Keywords: Design science · Agile · Software development

1 Introduction

The need for design-oriented research within the Information Systems (IS) discipline has been discussed at length in recent decades e.g. [1-3]. The resulting calls to action have been positioned as design theory [4, 5], engaged scholarship [6], action/action-design research [7], and most commonly, under the umbrella term of design science research (DSR) [8, 9]. The motivations for DSR are two-part. Firstly, the type of knowledge that is required for design is often distinct from the explanation-based knowledge generated by traditional research [10], meaning design knowledge may remain at the level of a 'craft' without more deliberate theoretical analysis [11]. Secondly, by becoming more actively involved in the design of innovative artefacts, researchers can engage problems closer to the vanguard of industrial practice [12, 13].

Despite these motivations, recent work [14] suggests that while many DSR studies focus on 'improvement' (new solutions to old problems) and 'exaptation' (old solutions to new problems), few focus on 'invention' (new solutions to new problems). This failure has been attributed to difficulties in balancing traditional standards of academic rigour against the practicalities of real-world development [15]. Such

B. Donnellan et al. (Eds.): DESRIST 2015, LNCS 9073, pp. 168–180, 2015.
DOI: 10.1007/978-3-319-18714-3_11

difficulties have resulted in several high-level process models to guide development and design theorizing, e.g. [7, 8]. Yet the desire to impose rigid *a priori* idealized structures on design risks stifling creativity and encouraging incremental, rather than exploratory design [16-18].

These issues are not restricted to scholarly pursuits. Industrial IT development projects have also historically struggled to balance creativity and formal structure, as academic pressures are replaced by managerial and regulatory demands [19, 20]. One of the most successful solutions to this problem for industrial practitioners is that of *agile* development, in which design practices react and adjust to changing user requirements while maintaining more dynamic structures for managing resources and software quality [21-24]. Thus, in the spirit of learning from industry, the objective of this study is *to apply the principles of agile software development to DSR to create an adaptive and responsive design process capable of inventive IT artefact development.*

The remainder of the paper is structured as follows. In the following section we explore the theoretical foundations of DSR, particularly the concept of design-as-problem-solving that has informed much of design-oriented IS research. We then discuss existing research on agile software development, identify key principles, and use these principles to inform a revised DSR process that extends the design process model proposed by [8]. This revised DSR process is illustrated in two exemplary cases, validating the potential of the approach for further development. Finally, the conclusions of the study are presented and future research directions are laid out.

2   Design Science Research and Design as Problem-Solving

In practical terms, DSR approaches may be considered as Strategy 1 and Strategy 2, which are differentiated according to their deductive or inductive/abductive focus (though both strategies rely on each of the various reasoning types to some extent) c.f.[25]. Strategy 1 DSR approaches a design problem at an abstract and generalizable level, relying heavily on deductive reasoning. Strategy 2 DSR approaches design at a pragmatic level at an instance-level, whereby the abstract implications of the solution for the class of problems are considered reflectively through a process of inductive and abductive reasoning. Yet a third perspective on design also exists in which design is seen not as sequence of problem definition and solution, but rather as a bricolage-like exploration of evolving problem/solution pairings [26-28]. This idea has been illustrated using the metaphor from genetics research of 'survival of the fittest' [29], where (i) design solutions compete within the solution space according to pressures exerted from the design problem space (ii) design problems within the problem space compete according to selection pressures from the solution space. From this process of competition, stable problem/solution pairs begin to emerge through a mechanism of focus and fitness until a survivable pair emerges. This model was explored further by [30], who not only observed support for its descriptive accuracy, but also noted greater creativity among individual designers who maintained greater flexibility over their initial problem space. This flexibility meant new requirements could be discovered, so increasing competition in the problem space and accelerating the coevolution of problems and solutions. Such coevolution receives little attention in existing models of DSR and this failure to actively consider and document this process of change presents a significant limitation for two reasons. Firstly, valuable design knowledge is not captured in the discipline's shared knowledge base. Secondly and perhaps most importantly, prescriptive DSR frameworks that do support problem/solution coevolution may be actively discouraging an important aspect of creativity in design.

3   Agility in IT Development

The concept of *agile* IS development was formalised in the Agile Manifesto [31]. This manifesto rejected the highly-formalised software development methods common at the time for faster, user-centric, and more dynamic methods. Among other things, this meant early and continuous delivery of software, regular reflection, and actively seeking and welcoming changes in requirements, even late in development. A variety of *agile* methods subsequently emerged including extreme programming (XP), feature-driven development, scrum, and adaptive software development, to name a few (c.f. [32-34]). These methods were employed with success across a range of domains [32] even extending to heavily regulated environments such as biomedical software development (e.g. [35]), healthcare e.g.[36], and regulatory compliance software[37].

The methods referred to collectively as *agile* can vary according to values, practices, tools, and metrics [38]. However, an extensive review and synthesis of *agile* literature [22] suggested to be reasonably considered *agile*, an IS development component must meet three conditions.

The first condition requires that the IS development component must not detract from any of the following (a) perceived economy (b) perceived quality (c) perceived simplicity. *Perceived economy* describes the importance of the problem being solved, *perceived quality* describes the usefulness of the solution in solving that problem, and *perceived simplicity* describes the efficiency with which the solution solves the problem. Viewed in coevolutionary terms, this condition relates to the stability of the problem/solution pairing, as it ensures both the problem and solution are relevant and well aligned. The second condition requires that the IS development component must contribute towards one or more of the following: (i) creation of change (ii) proactivation in advance of change (iii) reaction to change (iv) learning from change. This condition captures the evolution and mutation of possibilities within the problem and solution space. The third condition requires that the IS development component must be continually ready i.e. minimal time and cost to prepare the component for use. This ensures that seemingly stable problem/solution pairs continue to suffer empirically-driven selection pressures capable of upsetting artificial equilibria.

This perspective explains some portion of the success of *agile* methods. Unlike traditional 'waterfall' IS development methods in which solutions are contrasted against a fixed problem, *agile* methods allow both problems and solutions to adapt and evolve. This enables greater flexibility and responsiveness in design, therefore more useful IS components. Like traditional waterfall models of industrial design, leading models of DSR also lack a dynamic coevolutionary view of design. Thus, just as industrial *agile* methods have enabled more inventive software development, so the application of an *agile* perspective to DSR may serve to increase the proportion of inventive IT artefacts.

4   Theoretical Model

The aim of the research herein is to develop an agile adapted version of the DSRM framework [8]. DSRM is selected both because it is established within the community, because it compartmentalises design in a way that lends to both atomic and high-level design, and because it is relatively prescriptive as regards the design process. These characteristics make it ideally suited to both represent existing DSR practice as well as to relate findings back to the broader DSR paradigm. The extended model (referred to hereafter as ADSRM) is outlined in the diagram presented in Fig.1. The following sections will present a brief overview of existing practices outlined by DSRM, which are then critiqued and amended to better facilitate agility.

4.1   Problem Identification and Motivation

The *problem identification and motivation* sub-process is the first step to be carried out in the design process once a project has been initiated (this initiation occurs either through 'problem-centred initiation' in which little is known about a design problem; 'objective-centred initiation' in which little is known about how an objective of a solution impacts on a problem; 'design/development centred initiation' in which little is known about how to create a design feature, and; 'client/context initiated' in which an industry partner invites collaboration). *Problem identification and motivation* performs two important functions in DSRM. Firstly, the problem defined at the outset of the study is used to guide development of subsequent design components, so bounding and directing design activities [4, 11]. Secondly, the defined problem is used to ensure industrial relevance by linking to blind spots in both the practitioner and academic knowledge base [13].

In practice the customer can start from a position of not knowing what they want. Further, scenarios exist whereby the customer cannot know desired software capabilities until an initial version or prototype has been prepared to make concepts and associated issues tangible. To better capture this, two changes are proposed for ADSRM. Firstly, a new component is added in the form of a *problem backlog*. This component represents the broader problem space from which individual problems can be identified and motivated. Secondly, feedback from the latter stages is modelled to this *problem backlog*, representing the ability of any such stage to provoke insights regarding the problem space.

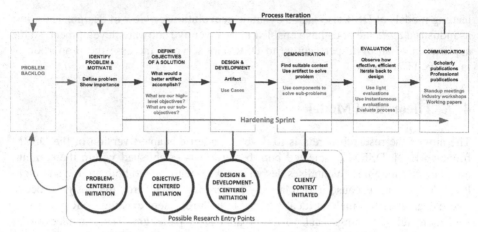

Fig. 1. Agile Design Science Research Model (*ADSRM*)

4.2   Define Objectives of a Solution

The next DSRM sub-process requires the *definition of the objectives of a solution*. These objectives define the characteristics of a solution that will address the defined design problem. In some studies this may be so sophisticated as to take the form of a separate embedded layer of causal explanatory theory, while in others it may be loosely formed or implicit [39]. These have been described as 'general components' of a solution, which break down a system in a way that lends itself to design [40].

Agility not only focuses on specific high level objectives but also breaks solution requirements into lower level 'digestible' user stories [41]. An Iteration Plan and subsequent solution is achieved "where through the communication among team elements and sequential iterations the problem is divided into sub-problems" [42] p.8. This allows objectives and sub-objectives to be identified that are somewhat stable, while still leaving space for objectives to emerge to the more uncertain, turbulent objectives. This gradation reduces resistance for vague but potentially competitive new problems and solutions. Consequently ADSRM is amended to consider (i) a high-level overall objective and (ii) lower-level sub-objectives of varying priorities and granularities.

4.3   Design and Development

The *design and development* sub-process creates the IT artefact comprising the key contribution of the study. Such artefacts may take different forms, e.g. constructs, models, instantiations [2], technological rules [43], and principles of implementation [11]. These prescriptive artefacts are ultimately functional and their justification stems from the problem and objectives identified earlier.

Agile methods expand on such a perspective by demanding mindfulness of non-functional requirements, such as reliability, testability, security and usability [44]. This allows quality-focused constraints to be implemented within the context of the project. Active user involvement throughout design iterations facilitates this mindfulness. In particular where use cases can identify anomalies not otherwise outlined in initial requirements[45] meaning solutions may be viewed holistically, rather than solely through the lens of a defined problem. Thus ADSRM is amended to explicitly consider non-functional requirements, e.g. through the addition of use cases during the *design and development*.

4.4   Demonstration

The *demonstration* sub-process identifies a suitable instance of the problem to solve using the proposed design, either by experimentation, simulation, case study, proof, or some other means. This sub-process translates reusable and abstract elements of the problem and solution into specific operational contexts, which allows theoretically situated elements of design greater 'empirical grounding' [46]. Further, providing examples of design prescriptions makes their intent more lucid and minimises the potential for misapplication [47]. Put differently, the *demonstration* acts an 'exposition' not only *that* a design can be implemented but also *how* it can be implemented [11]. Agile principles go one step further in that, not only must demonstration show that a design can be implemented and how this can take place, but some actual implementation must be produced. Such a strategy ensures there are no gaps between perception of validity and reality from the point of conception. This acts to test the stability of a problem/solution pair early, rather than allowing it to proceed unchallenged. Thus, ADSRM prescribes that early and frequent implementation should be considered for all design concepts (not just finished artefacts).

4.5   Evaluation

The *evaluation* sub-process determines how the proposed solution addresses or fails to address the defined problem. This corresponds roughly to the theory-testing component of traditional descriptive or explanatory research, though the emphasis is on the utility of the design, rather than its truthfulness [1, 2]. Evaluation can take place in 'artificial' settings, wherein variables can be controlled and participants are at low risk, and/or 'naturalistic' settings within real-world working environments, wherein embedded socio-technical effects and more diverse stakeholders can be observed [48, 49]. DSRM models this sub-process as feeding insights back to the sub-processes attempting to *define objectives of a solution*, as well as the *design and development*.

Agile views of evaluation differ in several ways. Firstly, there are *'light' evaluation methodologies and metrics* such as lean start up [50], which are less onerous and resource or time consuming, allowing more iterative and dynamic evaluation to take place. Secondly, many *agile* methods use instantaneous and automated testing to evaluate changes at a component-level [51, 52]. Thirdly, more recent research on *agile* evaluation advocates evaluation of not just an artefact but the agility afforded by the artefact (and the agility afforded by the process that creates it [22]). These practices increase the empirical selection pressure on problem/solution pairings, thus are also considered in ADSRM.

4.6   Communication

The *communication* sub-process represents the final stage of a DSR project, in which findings are shared with relevant audiences via publication, both scholarly and professional. Such dialogue with both scholars and professionals is vital if DSR is to properly integrate into the knowledge ecosystem [13]. To harness valuable feedback from audiences during *communication*, DSRM models this as informing ongoing efforts to *define objectives of a solution* and *design and development*.

Communication is central to agile practice [53] and notable points of relevance exist to be applied to DSR. Firstly, agile methods place increased emphasis on communication within the team, as opposed to the externally-facing view described in DSRM. Secondly, agile communication is a continuous and parallel process, whereas DSR is often communicated via more punctuated publication and distribution of findings. Thirdly, agile communication emphasizes the diversity of communication methods and interactions. Working papers, continuous seminars and live working artefacts all form part of additional communication methods used by Agile teams in achieving greater communication frequency and reach. These qualities allow agile communication a continuous flow of information that further resists artificial equilibria. Thus ADSRM is amended to consider the communication of findings frequently inside and outside the research team, and the utilisation of a range of outlets early in development, e.g. standup meetings, industry workshops, and working papers.

4.7   Balancing Agility and Rigour – 'Hardening Sprint'

DSR places significant emphasis on the rigor of the design process to differentiate itself from practice and ensure the reliability of findings [13, 49]. While we do not believe that the agility-based amendments to DSR practices presented in the previous section automatically detract from rigour, there are opportunities for this to happen. This is problematic, as doing so threatens to force a greater burden of rigor from the design process to the evaluation of the artefact, which may lead to less cutting-edge research [12]. Fortunately, the challenge of introducing agility without compromising procedural rigor has been explored and addressed in practice, e.g. in heavily regulated industries with high demands of transparency, documentation, and accountability during development [37]. Essentially a 'hardening' sprint is added every few iterations, with the goal of enhancing rigour that may be lacking during regular sprints. The frequency of these hardening sprints is very much context-based and dependent on the rigour or perceived lack thereof.

This concept of a *hardening sprint* is applied to ADSRM as an additional design component, although any DSR team should consider the full scope of the design process in this regard. This *hardening sprint* is based using several key mechanisms (1) Freeze the Problem. While the ability to deal with change afforded by agility is certainly in today's complex design environments, a level of rigour can be applied to a phase where no turbulence, dynamism or improvisation is allowed. If one thinks of trying to hit a continually moving target, a moment in time where the target is still can be a very valuable asset. (2) Freeze the Process. Agility encourages improvisation, underpinned by the 'people over process' principle of the Agile Manifesto. The concern from a rigor and regulatory point of view is that to be confident of rigour there are times when process must be valued over people. Again a single sprint that requires extra careful adherence to procedure, compliance checks and an absence of improvisation can be valuable in ensuring and maintaining rigour. (3) Add to the process. A third option to enhance rigour in this extra sprint is to add additional rigour-driven parts to the process. An obvious example of this would be to add extra measures or change the existing measures when conducting the evaluation phase.

5   Application of the Model

This section presents two DSR exemplars that demonstrate the need for an agile model that captures problem/solution co-evolution. The focus of these exemplars is the power of the two additional ADSRM components, a problem backlog and a hardening sprint.

Exemplar 1: The Value of a Problem Backlog.
The first project took place within a large US-based IT company offering cloud-based software and services to more than 500,000 customers worldwide and operating in more than 50 countries. This project was situated in one site in North-West Europe with over 700 employees. Technical support personnel in this location were creating semi-structured log files for each customer support request, detailing the nature of the query, customers' hardware and software configurations, and solutions offered. Management knew big data/predictive analytics techniques could be applied to log files to produce valuable insights, however they had no single defined 'problem' to be solved. Rather, they understood they had capabilities not currently being exploited. This dilemma is common for big data/predictive analytics projects, as the types of value that emerge are hidden until interesting correlations and patterns have been identified. Limited existing research was found to offer assistance with this scenario, so a DSR project was initiated.

One problem visible from the outset was to identify hardware and software configurations that occurred frequently in log files reporting errors. This problem appeared manageable and had limited institutional barriers to change, so became the focus of the first design iteration. A Hadoop MapReduce-based implementation identified correlations be-tween several problematic components that had previously gone unnoticed or unreported. The tangibility provided by this development fed engagement in the initiative across organisational and managerial functions, which resulted in the identification of new opportunities for its extension. The VP of Global Technical Support commented that the project "convinced me that this is what it's all about. There are algorithms and methodologies out there to decipher the huge amounts of data we have". An increasingly significant problem backlog began to emerge, including opportunities to pre-empt issues, reduce support re-quests and increase customer satisfaction.

This case illustrates how problem/solution coevolution can be driven by the solution-space, rather than problem-space. The interesting element of the case (and so the focus of theorising) was the search for problems that could produce stable problem/solution pairs where the solution was comparatively fixed. A design method emerged that pre-scribed finding problems that were technically manageable and lacking socio-political complexity, so enabling progressively more substantial problems could be integrated into the problem backlog. A traditional problem-driven DSR model applied deductively would have over-looked this opportunity, due to the lack of a defined problem at the outset. A traditional DSR model applied inductively/abductively would suggest the project was routine, obscuring and even discouraging re-flection upon the theoretically rich search of the problem-space.

Exemplar 2: The Value of a Hardening Sprint.
The second project took place within the early stages of a start-up company looking to develop a mobile application to assist home carers in managing general wellness. Existing research and a founder's personal experience providing home care indicated that carers were struggling to record and monitor specific health-related details, so inhibiting the timely introduction of medical interventions. This appeared to be because carers may not detect health deteriorations early enough to seek professional medical assistance. Further, when specific health deteriorations are reported, medical professionals have limited basis upon which to determine the origins, frequency, timeline, and so their trajectory. The lack of existing solutions allowing home carers to measure and track health-related details meant a DSR project was initiated. However, the fuzziness of the problem suggested several exploratory iterations would be needed before this problem could be defined clearly enough to allow more rigorous hardening to take place.

The first iteration of design assimilated existing survey-based measures of health into a crude mobile-friendly web interface. This interface was presented to the founder, who leveraged personal experience to act as product owner. The founder noted that the time required to fill out extensive surveys made the application impractical. The second iteration was more robust and focused on the speed and intuitive-ness of user interactions. Mechanics were implemented to shorten surveys and provide visual summaries and the maturing application was discussed with focus groups of carers. These carers reported that much of the problem lay in tracking wellness alongside specific interventions to better gauge their efficacy. Growing confidence led to a confirmatory hardening sprint in which new features were added and the application was released for beta-testing. Feedback from users supported the utility of the application, with several users initiating medical interventions to address areas of concern that had previously gone unnoticed.

This project illustrates the value of empirically-driven and evolving problem/solution spaces as enabled by progressively hardening design iterations. This resulted in a novel instantiation that modelled the role of carers as not only tracking health, but also proactively identifying, implementing and evaluating interventions independent of input from medical professionals. A traditional problem-driven DSR model applied deductively would have solved a problem that, though logically justifiable based on early research, was out of sync with actual practical needs. A traditional model applied inductively/abductively would have glossed over or omitted the initial positioning of the study and the rationale for problem redefinition. This would have isolated the project from existing research, making it difficult to relate and assimilate findings. It may have also resulted in emerging insights being misrepresented as known a priori design parameters, so focusing attention away from the most fundamental and interesting findings surrounding the proactivity and medical autonomy of carers. ADSRM allowed the problem and solution to gravitate towards the most stable pair, before latter more rigorous iterations ensured the validity of the final artefact.

6   Discussion and Conclusion

This study expands upon the view of DSR as problem-solving, in which problems are viewed as *a priori* inputs to the design process. This is contrasted with alternative perspectives from other disciplines, wherein the problem space is seen as emerging and evolving in tandem with the solution space. To better capture this emergence and evolution of problems, an agile perspective is adopted on the leading DSR process model, DSRM. A revised version is presented (ADSRM), as well as exemplars demonstrating the practical value of key amendments.

The first contribution of this study is a fundamental epistemological shift for DSR which encourages an agile approach to problem identification. We are aware that some researchers will argue such exploration already often occurs outside of the documented research process. However the explication and integration of this element of design into DSR allows for greater rigour and knowledge accumulation in how it is conducted, analysed, and reported. Moreover, it creates a more detailed and lucid understanding of the act of design for researchers.

The second contribution is the ADSRM model itself. In addition to amendments to existing practices, ADSRM offers two additional components in the form of a problem backlog and a hardening sprint. These additions draw upon tried and tested industrial practices that successfully balance exploration and procedural rigor during the design process. Further, the assimilation of such practices into an established model of DSR ensures changes come at minimal expense in terms of the progress already made to identify DSR best practices.

The third contribution is the increased potential for radical and innovative DSR in the future. The ability to reframe a problem has been positioned as a key dimension for creativity, vital for allowing for empirically-driven expansion of the parameters for design. ADSRM (and the agile philosophy that underlies it) gives researchers license to do this without compromising their academic standards, nor their ability to position their work against existing literature.

Acknowledgements. This work was supported, in part, by Science Foundation Ireland grant 10/CE/I1855 and by the Irish Research Government of Ireland 2013 Research Project Grants Scheme Council - RPG2013-6 (SFI/HEA).

References

1. March, S.T., Smith, G.F.: Design and natural science research on information technology. Decision Support Systems 15, 251–266 (1995)
2. Hevner, A.R., March, S.T., Park, J., Ram, S.: Design science in information systems research. MIS Quarterly: Management Information Systems 28, 75–105 (2004)
3. Baskerville, R., Lyytinen, K., Sambamurthy, V., Straub, D.: A response to the design-oriented information systems research memorandum. European Journal of Information Systems 20, 11–15 (2011)
4. Walls, J.G., Widmeyer, G.R., El Sawy, O.A.: Building an information system design theory for vigilant EIS. Information Systems Research 3, 36–59 (1992)
5. Kuechler, B., Vaishnavi, V.: On theory development in design science research: anatomy of a research project. European Journal of Information Systems 17, 489–504 (2008)
6. Mathiassen, L., Nielsen, P.A.: Engaged scholarship in IS research. Scandinavian Journal of Information Systems 20, 1 (2008)
7. Sein, M., Henfridsson, O., Purao, S., Rossi, M., Lindgren, R.: Action design research (2011)
8. Peffers, K., Tuunanen, T., Rothenberger, M.A., Chatterjee, S.: A Design Science Research Methodology for Information Systems Research. Journal of Management Information Systems 24, 45–77 (2007)
9. Hevner, A., Chatterjee, S.: Design Science Research in Information Systems. In: Design Research in Information Systems, vol. 22, pp. 9–22. Springer US (2010)
10. Nonaka, I., Toyama, R.: Strategic management as distributed practical wisdom (phronesis). Industrial and Corporate Change 16, 371–394 (2007)
11. Gregor, S., Jones, D.: The anatomy of a design theory. Journal of the Association for Information Systems 8, 312–335 (2007)
12. Iivari, J.: A paradigmatic analysis of information systems as a design science. Scandinavian Journal of Information Systems 19, 5 (2007)
13. Hevner, A.R.: A three cycle view of design science research. Scandinavian Journal of Information Systems 19, 4 (2007)
14. Gregor, S., Hevner, A.R.: Positioning and presenting design science research for maximum impact. MIS Quarterly 37, 337–356 (2013)
15. Österle, H., Becker, J., Frank, U., Hess, T., Karagiannis, D., Krcmar, H., Loos, P., Mertens, P., Oberweis, A., Sinz, E.J.: Memorandum on design-oriented information systems research. European Journal of Information Systems 20, 7–10 (2011)
16. Lee, J.S., Pries-Heje, J., Baskerville, R.: Theorizing in design science research. In: Jain, H., Sinha, A.P., Vitharana, P. (eds.) DESRIST 2011. LNCS, vol. 6629, pp. 1–16. Springer, Heidelberg (2011)
17. Fischer, C., Gregor, S., Aier, S.: Forms of Discovery for Design Knowledge. In: ECIS, pp. 64 (Year)
18. Gregor, S., Müller, O., Seidel, S.: Reflection, Abstraction And Theorizin. In: Design And Development Research. In: ECIS, pp. 74 (Year)
19. Brooks, F.P., Bullet, N.S.: Essence and accidents of software engineering. IEEE Computer 20, 10–19 (1987)
20. Boehm, B.: A view of 20th and 21st century software engineering. In: Proceedings of the 28th International Conference on Software Engineering, pp. 12-29. ACM (Year)
21. Beck, K.: Extreme programming explained: embrace change. Addison-Wesley Professional (2000)

22. Conboy, K.: Agility from First Principles: Reconstructing the Concept of Agility in Information Systems Development. Information Systems Research 20, 329–354 (2009)
23. Maruping, L.M., Venkatesh, V., Agarwal, R.: A Control Theory Perspective on Agile Methodology Use and Changing User Requirements. Information Systems Research 20, 377–399 (2009)
24. Sarker, S., Sarker, S.: Exploring Agility in Distributed Information Systems Development Teams: An Interpretive Study in an Offshoring Context. Information Systems Research 20, 440–461 (2009)
25. Iivari, J.: Distinguishing and contrasting two strategies for design science research. European Journal of Information Systems 24, 107–115 (2015)
26. Cross, N.: Designerly ways of knowing: Design discipline versus design science. Design Issues 17, 49–55 (2001)
27. Fallman, D.: Design-oriented human-computer interaction. In: Proceedings of the SIGCHI Conference on Human Factors in Computing Systems, pp. 225–232. ACM (Year)
28. Garud, R., Karnøe, P.: Bricolage versus breakthrough: distributed and embedded agency in technology entrepreneurship. Research Policy 32, 277–300 (2003)
29. Maher, M.L., Poon, J., Boulanger, S.: Formalising design exploration as co-evolution. In: Gero, J.S., Sudweeks, F. (eds.) Advances in formal design methods for CAD. IFIP, pp. 3–30. Springer, Boston (1996)
30. Dorst, K., Cross, N.: Creativity in the design process: co-evolution of problem–solution. Design Studies 22, 425–437 (2001)
31. Fowler, M., Highsmith, J.: The agile manifesto. Software Development 9, 28–35 (2001)
32. Boehm, B.: Get Ready for Agile Methods, with Care. Computer 35, 64–69 (2002)
33. Highsmith, J., Cockburn, A.: Agile software development: The business of innovation. Computer 34, 120–127 (2001)
34. Highsmith, J.: Agile software development ecosystems. Addison-Wesley Longman Publishing Co., Inc. (2002)
35. Kane, D.W., Hohman, M.M., Cerami, E.G., McCormick, M.W., Kuhlmman, K.F., Byrd, J.A.: Agile methods in biomedical software development: a multi-site experience report. Bmc Bioinformatics 7, 273 (2006)
36. Aronsson, H., Abrahamsson, M., Spens, K.: Developing lean and agile health care supply chains. Supply Chain Management: An International Journal 16, 176–183 (2011)
37. Fitzgerald, B., Stol, K.-J., O'Sullivan, R., O'Brien, D.: Scaling agile methods to regulated environments: An industry case study. In: Proceedings of the 2013 International Conference on Software Engineering, pp. 863-872. IEEE Press, (Year)
38. Dybå, T., Dingsøyr, T.: Empirical studies of agile software development: A systematic review. Information and Software Technology 50, 833–859 (2008)
39. Kuechler, W., Vaishnavi, V.: A framework for theory development in design science research: multiple perspectives. Journal of the Association for Information Systems 13, 395–423 (2012)
40. Baskerville, R., Pries-Heje, J.: Explanatory design theory. Business & Information Systems Engineering 2, 271–282 (2010)
41. Schwaber, K., Beedle, M.: Agile Software Development with Scrum. Prentice Hall PTR (2001)
42. Cossentino, M., Seidita, V.: Composition of a New Process to Meet Agile Needs Using Method Engineering. In: Choren, R., Garcia, A., Lucena, C., Romanovsky, A. (eds.) SELMAS 2004. LNCS, vol. 3390, pp. 36–51. Springer, Heidelberg (2005)

43. Aken, J.E.V.: Management research based on the paradigm of the design sciences: the quest for field tested and grounded technological rules. Journal of Management Studies 41, 219–246 (2004)
44. Glinz, M.: On Non-Functional Requirements. In: 15th IEEE International Requirements Engineering Conference, RE 2007, pp. 21–26 (2007)
45. Gayatri, V., Pammi, K.: Agile User Stories. Scrum Alliance, vol. 2015 (2013), http://people.scs.carleton.ca
46. Goldkuhl, G.: Design theories in information systems-a need for multi-grounding. Journal of Information Technology Theory and Application (JITTA) 6, 7 (2004)
47. Tetzlaff, L., Schwartz, D.R.: The use of guidelines in interface design. In: Proceedings of the SIGCHI Conference on Human Factors in Computing Systems, pp. 329-333. ACM (Year)
48. Pries-Heje, J., Baskerville, R., Venable, J.R.: Strategies for design science research evaluation (2008)
49. Venable, J., Pries-Heje, J., Baskerville, R.: A comprehensive framework for evaluation in design science research. In: Peffers, K., Rothenberger, M., Kuechler, B. (eds.) DESRIST 2012. LNCS, vol. 7286, pp. 423–438. Springer, Heidelberg (2012)
50. Ries, E.: The lean startup: How today's entrepreneurs use continuous innovation to create radically successful businesses. Random House LLC (2011)
51. Erculiani, F., Abeni, L., Palopoli, L.: uBuild: Automated Testing and Performance Evaluation of Embedded Linux Systems. In: Maehle, E., Römer, K., Karl, W., Tovar, E. (eds.) ARCS 2014. LNCS, vol. 8350, pp. 123–134. Springer, Heidelberg (2014)
52. Poppendieck, M., Poppendieck, T.: Lean software development: an agile toolkit. Addison-Wesley Professional (2003)
53. Hummel, M., Rosenkranz, C., Holten, R.: The role of communication in agile systems development. Business & Information Systems Engineering 5, 343-355

Data Mining and Analytics

NavigTweet: A Visual Tool
for Influence-Based Twitter Browsing

Chiara Francalanci and Ajaz Hussain[✉]

Department of Electronics, Information and Bio-Engineering,
Politecnico di Milano, 20133 Milano, Italy
{chiara.francala,ajaz.hussain}@polimi.it

Abstract. Directed links in social media could represent anything from intimate friendships to common interests. Such directed links determine the flow of information and hence indicate a user's influence on others—a concept that plays a vital role in sociology and viral marketing. Identifying influencers is an important step towards understanding how information spreads within a network. Social networks follow a power-law degree distribution of nodes, with a few hub nodes and a long tail of peripheral nodes. This paper proposes a novel visual framework to analyze, explore and interact with Twitter 'Who Follows Who' relationships, by browsing the friends' network to identify the key influencers based upon the actual influence of the content they share. We have developed NavigTweet, a novel visualization tool for the influence-based exploration of Twitter network. The core concept of the proposed approach is to identify influencers by browsing through a user's friends' network. Then, a power-law based modified force-directed method is applied to clearly display the graph in a multi-layered and multi-clustered way. To gather some insight into the user experience with the pilot release of NavigTweet, we have conducted a qualitative pilot user study. We report on the study and its results, with initial pilot release.

Keywords: Social Media Influencers · Social Media Influence · Twitter Analytics · Graph Visualization

1   Introduction

The social media literature makes a distinction between influencers and influence. Influencers are prominent social media users with a broad audience. For example, social users with a high number of followers and retweets on Twitter, or a multitude of friends on Facebook, or a broad connections on LinkedIn. The term influence refers to the social impact of the content shared by social media users. If social media users seem to be interested in something, they normally show it by participating in the conversation with a variety of mechanisms, mostly by sharing the content that they have liked. (Anholt 2006; Myers & Leskovec 2014) has noted that a content that has an impact on a user's mind is usually shared. Influencers are prominent social media users, but we cannot be certain that the their shared content has influence, as discussed by (Benevenuto et al. 2010).

© Springer International Publishing Switzerland 2015
B. Donnellan et al. (Eds.): DESRIST 2015, LNCS 9073, pp. 183–198, 2015.
DOI: 10.1007/978-3-319-18714-3_12

Social media have become pervasive and ubiquitous. There is a growing need for information visualization, which has recently become a popular subject of research (Fan & Gordon 2014; Klotz et al. 2014; Myers & Leskovec 2014). In general, information visualization aims at showing information in an easy, user-friendly and graphical way. However visualizing information properly is not trivial and becomes of challenge when the focus is social networks, such as Twitter. Twitter has been defined by many researches as the key role player of the change on how information dissemination is accomplished. Its influence on information dissemination has led to research exploring on how this is achieved. According to (Kwak et al. 2011) the unicity of direction in twitter connection provides the key driver of information dissemination via word of mouth (WoM) in retweets.

The ultimate goal of our research is to provide a novel visual framework to analyze, explore and interact with Twitter 'Who Follows Who' relationships, by browsing the friends' network to identify the key influencers upon the actual influence of the content they share. In this paper, we exploit a modified power-law based force-directed algorithm (Hussain et al. 2014) to clearly display the Twitter network graph in a multi-layered and multi-clustered way. NavigTweet aims to provide a visual interface to interact and explore the Twitter network. It helps to identify the key players or prominent Twitter users among Twitter browsed network based upon actual content they share and provides opportunity to follow them directly through application interface. The top-influencers are identified by both user-level (e.g. number of followers, number of tweets, etc.) and content-based (number of hashtags, number of URLs, etc.) influential parameters. The user can explore its own network and FOAF network in order to find out interesting people in the network and can directly follow or unfollow through application interface. The intended audience is people who want to find interesting information regarding their social network and empower them to enlarge their social network by providing interesting people to follow. The intended audience may find influencers among their own and as well as FOAF networks through a visual interface and can traverse the graph through visual interface to further explore networks at any depth level, to find out more influencers.

As part of this research, we have developed NavigTweet (Hussain 2015), a visual tool for the influence-based exploration of Twitter friends' network. It helps to identify the key players, and follow them directly through the NavigTweet. The user can explore its own Friend-of-a-Friend (FOAF) network in order to find interesting people to be followed. The top-influencers are identified by both user-level (e.g. number of followers, number of tweets, etc.) and content-based (number of hashtags, number of URLs, etc.) parameters, thoroughly described in Section 3. Based upon these parameters, the tool adopts the Analytical Hierarchy Process (AHP) technique, to rank Twitter users, as our NavigTweet user explores his/her FOAF network. The NavigTweet users can find influencers within their friends' network through a visual interface and iteratively explore FOAF network to find more influencers. To gather a preliminary feedback on the NavigTweet user experience with a pilot release of NavigTweet, we have conducted a survey targeting reference group of academic experts in the social media domain who have been asked to use the application in real time environment. This paper presents the results of Table 4 questionnaire collected through the survey.

The remainder of this paper is structured as follows. Section 2 discusses influence and influencers in social media, and provides insights about Twitter analytics and visualization tools. Section 3 presents our methodology. Section 4 discusses implementation aspects of NavigTweet. Section 5 presents the evaluation framework with pilot study and results. Conclusions are drawn in Section 5.

2   State of the Art

In this section, we will discuss about the concept of influencers and influence in social media. We also discuss insights about Twitter analytics and visualization tools.

2.1   Influencers and Influence in Social Networks

Traditionally, the literature characterizes a social media user as an influencer on the basis of structural properties. Centrality metrics are the most widely considered parameters for the structural evaluation of a user's social network. The centrality of a concept has been defined as the significance of an individual within a network (Fan & Gordon 2014). A node that is directly connected to a high number of other nodes is obviously central to the network and likely to play an important role (Barbagallo et al. 2012). In addition to degree centrality, the literature also shows other structural metrics for the identification of influencers in social networks. (Leavitt et al. 2009) presented an approach where users were identified as influencers based on their total number of retweets.

Several research works have addressed the need for considering content-based metrics of influence (Bigonha et al. 2012). Content metrics such as the number of mentions, URLs, or hashtags have been proved to increase the probability of retweeting (Bakshy et al. 2011). Twitter has been the most common dataset for researches on user influence. For example, (Chang 2014) and (Kwak et al. 2010) measure the influence of Twitter users based on the sheer number of retweets spawned from the users' tweets. Recently, (Wu et al. 2011) have studied the elite users who control a significant portion of the production, flow, and consumption of information in the Twitter network. In (Wu et al. 2011) a top-down approach is used by identifying top users based on how frequently these appear in user-generated lists.

2.2   Twitter Analytics and Visualization Tools

Twitter analytics tools generally aim at finding, analyzing and then optimizing a person's social growth. For example, `Twitonomy` (Twitonomy.com 2014) is an independent website, unaffiliated with Twitter that allows users to search for the Twitter history of accounts by entering a Twitter handle into a search box. Similarly, `Followerwonk` (Followerwonk.com 2014) is a web application which helps a user explore and grow his social graph. As discussed in (Klout.com 2014), `Klout` is a system-generated tool for measuring influence; in other words it is a potential rating system that can be used as a measure of credibility. A user's `Klout` score is measured based on three components: true reach (how many people a user influences), amplification (how much the user influences them), and network impact (the influence of the user's network) (about Klout.com, 2012). Klout scores have a range of 1–100, with a higher score indicating a higher level of influence. (Kilpatrick 2015) discusses additional analytics tools including The Archivist, SocialBro, Twenty Feet, TweetStats, Twitter Counter, Tweetstats, and TweepsMaps.

The literature on social network visualization tools indicate that there exist only a few visualization tools. (Kilpatrick 2015; Kujawski 2014) reviews existing tools, including TouchGraph, MentionMap, and Hashtagify. TouchGraph is a real-time web application which provides a cluster visualization of a user's Facebook network. It provides information for each friend and group of friends. The groups are clustered in different colors, but the representation is not friendly and a user cannot navigate or browse the network of other friends. Similarly, MentionMap provides a neat and interactive visualization, although sometimes it is hard to navigate due to ambiguous and cluttered graph layout, as shown in Figure 1 (a). It tends to discover the people who are more active in Twitter and the terms that they are talking about. The maximum depth of the graph is 2-level, as when a user browses another user's network, his/her own network disappears from visualization. Finally, Hashtagify allows a user to visualize a network based on a Twitter hashtag. Although the layout is not cluttered as compared to MentionMap, the tool does not allow the visualization of user's friends or followers.

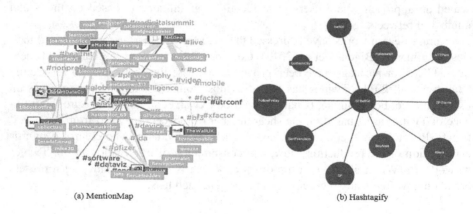

(a) MentionMap   (b) Hashtagify

Fig. 1. Twitter visualization tools

3   Design and Methodology

This section presents the network exploration approach and algorithms that are embedded in NavigTweet. First, we discuss the graph drawing algorithm that draws a Twitter network graph in an aesthetically pleasant and understandable way. Second, we discuss the ranking mechanism, that we adopted to identify influencers by using both user-level and content-based parameters.

3.1   Power – Law Algorithm (Graph Layout Technique)

This section summarizes the graph layout algorithm used in NavigTweet. Further details on the algorithm can be found in (Francalanci & Hussain 2014; Hussain et al. 2014). The power-law layout algorithm, shown in the following code snippet, belongs to the class of force-directed algorithms, see (Chan et al. 2004; Fruchterman & Reingold 1991). The proposed approach is aimed at the exploitation of the power-law degree distribution of Twitter users' nodes (N_s). Provided that the distribution of the degree of the nodes follows a power law, we partition the network into two disjoint sets of vertices N, i.e. the set of Twitter users' nodes N_s, and the set of friends' nodes N_f, such that $N = N_s \cup N_f$, with $N_s \cap N_f = \emptyset$.

Algorithm 1: High-level structure of power-law layout algorithm.

```
DATA:
  N  = User Nodes (Selected Users);
   s
  N  = Friend Nodes;
   f
  E = Edges connecting user and friend nodes.
  d = Node Degree, representing the number of connected friends;
  T = Energy / Temperature Variable;
  T  = Temperature threshold, to control simulation.
   h
BEGIN
1. NodePartition();
2. resetNodesSizes(Nf ,d);
3. InitialLayout();
       IF (T>Th) DO
            AttractionForce(N ,N );
                             s  f
            RepulsionForce(N ,E);
                           s
       ELSE
            AttractionForce(N ,N );
                             f  s
            RepulsionForce(N ,E);
                           f
4. LShellDecomposition(N ,N );
                        s  f
5. NodesPlacement  (N ,N );
                    s  f
6. TempCoolDown(T);
END
```

The `resetNodesSizes(Np,Nt,d)` method is responsible for resetting the size of each node in the graph, based upon their degree. The higher the degree of a node, the greater the size and vice versa. The `InitialLayout()` step calculates attraction and repulsion forces, based upon the value of T_h, which is a threshold value that can be tuned to optimize the layout, by providing maximum forces exerted upon hub-nodes N_h. The formulae of attraction and repulsion forces are similar to those used in traditional force-directed approaches, such as (Chan et al. 2004). In this paper, the forces formulae have been taken from the power-law based modified force-directed algorithm presented in (Hussain et al. 2014). The `LShellDecomposition(N_s,N_f)` method is responsible for the calculation of the l-shell value of friend nodes in N_f, in

order to create a multi-layered hierarchy of friends nodes around the user nodes. The
`NodePlacement(N_g, N_f)` step performs the placement of nodes on graph canvas
based on the computation of forces among nodes. Finally, the `TempCooldown(T)`
step is responsible for the control of the overall iteration mechanism. This step is responsible for cooling down the system temperature, in order to make the algorithm
converge. Moreover, the general workflow of the power-law algorithm is presented in
Figure 2.

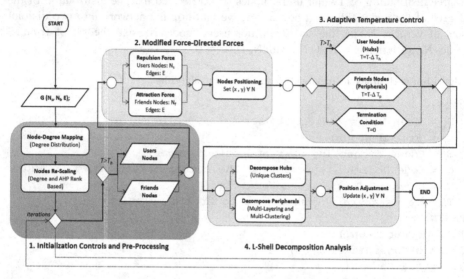

Fig. 2. Power–Law algorithm workflow

3.2   User Ranking Methodology

The ranking methodology that we have adopted in NavigTweet, is summarized in
Figure 3. NavigTweet initially collects influence parameters, at both user-level and
tweet-level. To weigh different parameters, based upon their relative importance, we
have adopted the Analytical Hierarchy Process (AHP) method proposed by (Saaty
1990; Saaty & Vargas 2001), which is widely used in the scientific community.

The outcome of AHP is a vector of weights of parameters. NavigTweet provides
aggregated score of each user, as a weighed sum of different parameters using the
weights obtained from AHP. The higher the score the higher the rank, and vice versa.
Figure 3 summarizes the methodology framework of user ranking adopted by
NavigTweet.

3.3   User Ranking Algorithm

Algorithm 2 outlines the user ranking algorithm adopted by NavigTweet. As an input,
the algorithm takes Twitter user node N, and object U provided by Twitter API, and,
as an output, it provides final ranking value of U.

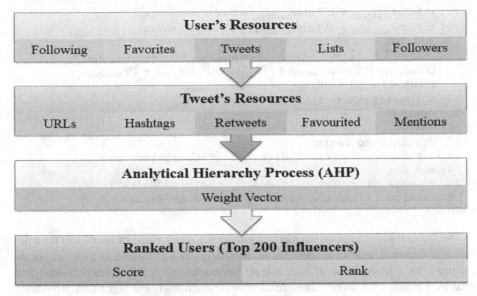

Fig. 3. User ranking methodology/workflow

Algorithm 2: User ranking algorithm of NavigTweet.

DATA
```
N = Twitter User Node
U = Twitter User Object, retrieved from Twitter API.
(AHP based Weight Vectors)
CONSTANT W_parameter as DOUBLE
```
INPUT
```
(N, U)
```
OUTPUT

Final Ranking value (Score) of each node n ∈ N.

BEGIN
1. **function** UserBasedScore(u) := **do begin**
2. (User-based influence parameters ranking)
3. (Product sum of weight and values)
4. $DOUBLE\ d \leftarrow \sum(W * U.Value) = (W_{favourites} * U.Value_{favourites}) +$ $(W_{followers} * U.Value_{followers}) + (W_{following} * U.Value_{following}) + (W_{listed} *$ $U.Value_{listed}) + (W_{tweets} * U.Value_{tweets});$
5. N.userRank ← d;
6. **return** d;
7. **end do**
8. **function** TweetBasedScore(u) := **do begin**
9. (Tweet-based influential parameters ranking)
10. (Summing up values for last 200 fetched-tweets)
11. **for** i:=1 **to** 200 **do begin**
12. $U.Value_{favourited} = U.Value_{favourited} + Tweet_i.favourited;$
13. $U.Value_{retweets} = U.Value_{retweets} + Tweet_i.retweets;$
14. $U.Value_{urls} = U.Value_{urls} + Tweet_i.urls;$

```
15. U.Value_hashtags = U.Value_hashtags + Tweet_i.hashtags;
16. U.Value_mentions = U.Value_mentions + Tweet_i.mentions;
17. end for
18.  DOUBLE f ← ∑(W * U.Value) = (W_favourited * U.Value_favourited) +
     (W_retweets * U.Value_retweets) + (W_urls * U.Value_urls) + (W_hashtags *
     U.Value_hashtags) + (W_mentions * U.Value_mentions);
19. N.tweetsRank ← f;
20. return f;
21. end do
22. ∀ u in U do begin
23. u.AHPScore = UserBasedScore(u)+TweetsBasedScore(u);
24. end for
25. ( Descending sort of nodes by their AHPScore )
26. (assign i^th indexed-value as node's AHPRank)
END
```

The `UserBasedScore(u)` method provides a score value of user-level parameters and returns a user-level score value. Similarly, `TweetBasedScore(u)` method provides a score value of tweets-level parameters (last 200 fetched-tweets) and returns a tweet-level score value. After scoring each user, the algorithm provides a rank value of each user by sorting all users based upon score value.

3.4 Application Workflow Architecture

The workflow of NavigTweet is provided in Figure 4. The basic building of the application are the following:

1. **Twitter Authentication:** NavigTweet uses OAuth protocol for Twitter user authentication, using the Pin-based mechanism provided by Twitter API. This module is responsible for handling user authentication for successful login.
2. **User Node:** After successful login, the application creates a user node on graph canvas, corresponding to the user who has logged in.
3. **Twitter Data Streaming:** This module is responsible for fetching the user's friends' data. Due to the rate-limit of Twitter APIs, we fetch a maximum number of 500 friend IDs and 100 User objects in once API call.
4. **Graph Model Processing:** This module creates nodes and edges for parsed friends on the graph canvas. As a result a local neighborhood cluster of friends' nodes around a user's node is created on graph canvas.
5. **AHP-Based Ranking:** This module provides each node's AHP-based score and rank, by using both user-level and tweet-level influence parameters provided by Twitter API, as shown in Figure 3.
6. **Graph Controller:** Finally, this module handles event related functionalities (e.g. mouse double-click event), and applies power-law based graph layout over graph nodes. Whenever, the user double-clicks on any node, the application repeats from the 3rd module of Twitter Data Streaming, in order to fetch clicked node's friends, and position them on the canvas.

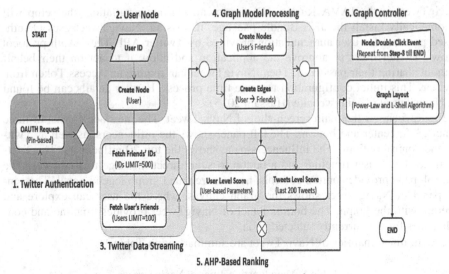

Fig. 4. NavigTweet Workflow

4   Implementation

We have implemented NavigTweet as a desktop application. The application is written in JAVA using Twitter4j (Twitter4j.org 2010) – a JAVA based Twitter Streaming API, and Piccolo 2D (Bederson et al. 2004) – a JAVA based 2D Graphics API. The application has a GUI compatible with multiple operating systems (Windows, MAC OS, and Linux/Unix) and contains a runnable JRE file. The only pre-requisite of

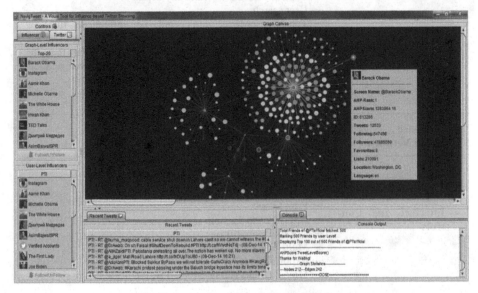

Fig. 5. Screenshot of NavigTweet Interface

NavigTweet is the JAVA Runtime Environment. During installation, the setup will automatically install the JRE Bundle package, if missing. NavigTweet uses OAuth-based protocol for user authentication provided by Twitter API. The OAuth protocol allows Twitter users to approve the application and allow it to act on their behalf without sharing their password. Then, NavigTweet can require an Access Token from Twitter. This initial configuration is a one-time process. Further details can be found on NavigTweet official website (Hussain 2015).

Figure 5 shows the main screen-shot of NavigTweet. The interface consist of three panels, left, center and bottom. The left panel shows the influencers, as well as Twitter and control options. The influencers-pane shows the top-20 influencers. The Twitter-pane shows user-timeline and a button to send direct message to followees. The control–pane provides button controls, node search, and graph legend panel. The center panel of NavigTweet shows the graph canvas, where the user can explore and interact with the graph. The bottom panel of NavigTweet provides timeline and console panes for the currently selected node.

The main functionalities of NavigTweet are summarized in Table 1.

Table 1. Main functionalities of NavigTweet

Categories	Features
• **User Profile Management**	— User Authentication — Access Token Generation for Login. — Profile information access
• **Interaction with Twitter**	— Follow / Unfollow user — Display friends' network graph. — View timeline — Post a tweet — Explore social network at any depth. — User search. — Top-20 user-level influencers (i.e. influencers that are selected among any node on canvas.) — Top-20 graph-level influencers (i.e. influencers that are selected among users connected with a followee relation with currently selected users). — View user analytics — Send direct messages
• **Influence – based Social Network**	— Perform ranking of each user — Show mutual-Follower(s) — Browse FOAF network.
• **Interface and Controls**	— Zoomable user interface — Node Tooltip and Show/Hide node labels — Bird's Eye View of Graph Canvas. — Print Graph. — Apply Power-Layout — Console Output/Log — Multi-Colour Clusters — Export Data (CSV) — Mouse Events (Drag, Scroll, Over, Click)

5   Evaluation and Results

In this section, we present a qualitative comparison between NavigTweet and existing applications. Later, we present the pilot execution and results.

5.1   Comparison Between NavigTweet and Existing Applications

As noted in Section 2, there exist a few visualization tools. Twitter changes its API periodically, which enforces developers to continuously update their tools. This represents the main reason why the number of tools are practically limited. Table 2 shows the highlights of the comparison between NavigTweet and the tools that we have been able to test.

Table 2. Features comparison

Features x Tool	TouchGraph	MentionMap	InMaps	NavigTweet
Real-time	No	Yes	No	No
Graph depth	1	2	1	Many
Response time	<5s	<5s	<5s	>5s
Initial load time	>5s	<5s	<5s	>5s
Open source	No	No	No	TODO
Pre/freemium	Both	Freemium	Freemium	Currently Freemium
Social Network	Facebook	Twitter	LinkedIn	Twitter
Platform	Web	Web	Web	Currently Desktop
Help and support	Feedback	Feedback	FAQ/Feedback	Feedback/Tutorial

Table 3 provides a more qualitative analysis of the usability of different tools, including NavigTweet. Note that clarity can be defined as the percentage of the amount of information displayed as perceived by human mind. The main difference among the tools is their ability to represent graphs. We have considered several aesthetics factors, such as color-scheme, distance between the nodes displayed, information amount displayed per node, zoom ability of graph canvas, node shapes, mouse controls, etc.

5.2   Pilot User Feedback Survey

The pilot activity aims to target expert user opinion, in order to get feedback and suggestions. Our goal was to finalize the application by incorporating their feedback, prior to an extensive survey research step which is still ongoing. The pilot was also meant as a technical test of NavigTweet multi-platform compatibility features.

Table 3. Clarity comparison

Clarity x Tool	TouchGraph	MentionMap	InMaps	NavigTweet
Network browsing	Self & Others	Self & Others	Self	Self & Others
Friendly colors	Somehow	Yes	Yes	Somehow
Clusters clarity	Yes	Yes	Somehow	Yes
Multi-color cluster	No	No	Yes	Yes
Zoom-able Interface	Yes	Yes	Yes	Yes
Pan & drag	Yes	Yes	Yes	Yes
Information quantity	A lot	Normal	Normal	Normal
Information placement	ToolTip	None	ToolTip	Tooltip
Default information	Name + Photo	Name + Photo	Name	Screen Name
Node shape	Circular	Rectangular	Circular	Circular

Pilot Participants: Initially, we targeted a reference group of 8 people from academia, who are expert in the domains of *Data, Web and Security, Information Systems, Advanced Software Architecture and Methodologies*, and *Social Network Analysis*. We intended to demonstrate the application in a real-time environment, to gather their feedback about the application.

Face-to-Face Interviews: During the pilot, we have performed one-to-one, face-to-face interviews. We had the opportunity to brief the interviewees about the application scenario, installation, and application flow. We obtained real-time feedback from each participant who was asked to run and use the application. The discussion and test sessions with each participant took around 1 – 1.5 hours. During each session, each participant tested the application thoroughly and provided us with open-ended feedback.

Feedback Survey: The pilot activity also involved a structured feedback survey, provided in Table 4, which have administered after the face-to-face meetings.

Pilot Results: We conducted briefing sessions with each pilot participant, where we discussed in detail the application scenarios. Each pilot participant evaluated existing requirements and features of the application and also proposed new requirements, including both functional and non-functional requirements. A technical issue identified during pilot activity was the *Installer Problem on MAC OS* (the application failed to install on MAC OS). Overall, the survey results were positive, as shown in Figure 6. Comments were generally favorable towards NavigTweet (*"Really useful, and aesthetically pleasant graphs with nice color-scheme"*, *"Innovative and Informative tool"*, *"User Ranking and Influencers Identification over graphs is quite wonderful!"*), which was especially praised for *User Interface, Graph Animated Layout, Multi-Colored Clustering Scheme, Dynamic Top-20 User- and Graph-Level panel, Browsing Friends' List, Mutual-Friends Identification*. Several participants pointed out that the tool identifies actual influencers that are visualized in a novel and easy-to-understand way. A pilot participant advised to reduce tool-tip contents, and to reduce some information panels, as the tool itself is self-explanatory and provides an understandable work-flow. Another pilot participant advised to introduce new panel of graph-level influencers, i.e. tool should show top influencers from overall graph of currently selected users and their followee relation connections. We also received advises on introducing other features like Data export, refined node search, and hence we also implemented these features prior to public release.

Table 4. Feedback Survey

QUESTIONS	ANSWER CRITERIA
Qualitative Analysis	
Do you find NavigTweet interesting? *(User Interest)*	• Funny • Boring • Helpful • Informative • Innovative • Useful • Usable
How would you rate the effectiveness of NavigTweet, as an interactive tool to explore your Twitter social networks? *(User Interaction)*	Low/High 5 point scale.
How would you rate the clarity for NavigTweet? *(Clarity Perception)*	Low/High 5 point scale.
Do you find NavigTweet helpful in exploring and identifying the influencers (prominent twitter users)? *(Influencers Identification)*	Yes/No/Somehow
Would you browse other users' friends' networks via NavigTweet? *(Network Browsing Level)*	Yes/No/Somehow
How would you rate NavigTweet overall? *(User Satisfaction)*	Low/High 5 point scale.
User Interface	
Do you like the User Interface of NavigTweet? *(Graphical User Interface)*	• Graph Representation. • Friendly color-scheme. • Cluster Clarity. • Informative node tooltip
Which color scheme in clusters you prefer? *(Clusters color-scheme)*	Same/Different
How much information is displayed per user node? *(User Information Quality)*	Too little/Normal/Too much

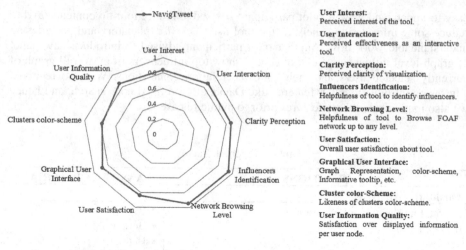

Fig. 6. User rating of the NavigTweet based on different criteria

6   Discussion

Identifying the most efficient 'influencers' in a network is an important step to-wards optimizing the use of available resources and ensuring the more efficient spread of information. Social media influencers are prominent users who share important contents and are most likely to be followed by intended audience, e.g. in Twitter, people with high number of followers seems to be prominent active users. The ultimate goal of our research is to provide a visualization framework to analyze, explore and interact with social network, specifically Twitter. We presented a power-law based modified force-directed algorithm to draw aesthetically pleasant multi-clustered and multi-layered graphs.

Moreover, we intend to identify prominent users in Twitter network, by investigating the influence of the actual content that social media users share. For that purpose, we collected both user-level and content-level (tweet-based) influence parameters provided by Twitter API and applied AHP technique in order to determine the score and rank of each user. We developed NavigTweet – a visual tool for exploring influence based Twitter browsing, in which user can explore and interact with his own and FOAF networks. NavigTweet identifies top-100 influencers among friends' network and provides users an opportunity to directly follow them via application interface.

The intended audience is people who want to find interesting information regarding their social network and empower them to enlarge their social network by providing interesting people to follow. User can explore his own and FOAF network at any depth-level to find influencers. NavigTweet provides a novel research dimension towards visualizing and exploring social networks to identify most prominent users, based upon the influence of their actual shared content, in the network.

We conducted pre-launch pilot activity via qualitative user-study, in order to get real-time feedback and suggestions. Comments from pilot were generally favorable.

We incorporated pilot comments by updating functionalities in NavigTweet, which is officially released and available to public users.

7   Conclusion and Future Work

This paper proposes a novel visual framework to analyze, explore and interact with Twitter '*Who Follows Who*' relationship, by browsing a user's friends' network to identify the key influencers based upon the influential content that they share on Twitter. We developed NavigTweet, which is able to visualize Twitter FOAF networks in aesthetically pleasant multi-clustered and multi-layered graphs, and helps to identify prominent users or top influencers from the network. We have reported on a qualitative analysis of our tool. We also reported on a pre-launch pilot test execution, by involving a qualitative user study, to get a feedback via survey. We found that pilot participants were positive about the functionalities and features of the tools along with novelty of the idea itself, and received favorable comments concerning NavigTweet. We have addressed the pilot comments by modifying and updating the tool accordingly. We are currently conducting an extensive survey.

Future work will consider detailed evaluation and implementation of web-based interface of NavigTweet, in which we intend to incorporate additional navigation and analysis features. Any suggestions or reviews received from end-users, as part of the ongoing extensive survey, will also be considered in this second release.

References

1. Anholt, S.: Competitive identity: The new brand management for nations, cities and regions. Palgrave Macmillan (2006)
2. Bakshy, E., Hofman, J.M., Mason, W.A., Watts, D.J.: Everyone's an influencer: quantifying influence on twitter. Paper presented at the Proceedings of the Fourth ACM International Conference on Web Search and Data Mining (2011)
3. Barbagallo, D., Bruni, L., Francalanci, C., Giacomazzi, P.: An empirical study on the relationship between twitter sentiment and influence in the tourism domain. In: Information and Communication Technologies in Tourism 2012, pp. 506–516. Springer (2012)
4. Bederson, B.B., Grosjean, J., Meyer, J.: Toolkit design for interactive structured graphics. IEEE Transactions on Software Engineering 30(8), 535–546 (2004)
5. Benevenuto, F., Cha, M., Gummadi, K.P., Haddadi, H.: Measuring User Influence in Twitter: The Million Follower Fallacy. Paper presented at the International AAAI Conference on Weblogs and Social, ICWSM 2010 (2010)
6. Bigonha, C., Cardoso, T.N.C., Moro, M.M., Gonçalves, M.A., Almeida, V.A.F.: Sentiment-based influence detection on Twitter. Journal of the Brazilian Computer Society 18(3), 169–183 (2012)
7. Chan, D.S.M., Chua, K.S., Leckie, C., Parhar, A.: Visualisation of power-law network topologies. The 11th IEEE International Conference on Paper presented at the Networks, ICON 2003 (2004)
8. Chang, J.-Y.: An Evaluation of Twitter Ranking Using the Retweet Information. Journal of Society for e-Business Studies 17(2) (2014)

9. Fan, W., Gordon, M.D.: The power of social media analytics. Communications of the ACM 57(6), 74–81 (2014)
10. Followerwonk.com (2014), https://followerwonk.com/
11. Francalanci, C., Hussain, A.: A Visual Approach to the Empirical Analysis of Social Influence. Paper presented at the DATA, - Proceedings of 3rd International Conference on Data Management Technologies and Applications (2014), http://dx.doi.org/10.5220/0004992803190330
12. Fruchterman, T.M.J., Reingold, E.M.: Graph drawing by force-directed placement. Software: Practice and Experience 21(11), 1129–1164 (1991)
13. Hussain, A.: NavigTweet (2015), http://home.deib.polimi.it/hussain/navigtweet/
14. Hussain, A., Latif, K., Rextin, A., Hayat, A., Alam, M.: Scalable Visualization of Semantic Nets using Power-Law Graphs. Applied Mathematics & Information Sciences 8(1), 355–367 (2014)
15. Kilpatrick, G.:(January 2, 2015), http://twittertoolsbook.com/10-awesome-twitter-analytics-visualization-tools/
16. Klotz, C., Ross, A., Clark, E., Martell, C.: Tweet! – and I can tell how many followers you have. In: Boonkrong, S., Unger, H., Meesad, P. (eds.) Recent Advances in Information and Communication Technology. AISC, vol. 265, pp. 245–253. Springer, Heidelberg (2014)
17. Klout.com (2014), https://klout.com/home
18. Kujawski, M.: (August 13, 2014), http://www.mikekujawski.ca/2014/08/13/two-free-twitter-network-visualization-tools/
19. Kwak, H., Lee, C., Park, H., Chun, H., Moon, S.: Novel Aspects Coming From the Directionality of Online Relationships: A Case Study of Twitter. ACM SIGWEB Newsletter (Summer 2011)
20. Kwak, H., Lee, C., Park, H., Moon, S.: What is Twitter, a social network or a news media? Paper presented at the Proceedings of the 19th International Conference on World Wide Web (2010)
21. Leavitt, A., Burchard, E., Fisher, D., Gilbert, S.: The influentials: New approaches for analyzing influence on twitter. Web Ecology Project 4(2), 1–18 (2009)
22. Myers, S.A., Leskovec, J.: The bursty dynamics of the Twitter information network. Paper presented at the Proceedings of the 23rd International Conference on World Wide Web (2014)
23. Saaty, T.L.: How to make a decision: the analytic hierarchy process. European Journal of Operational Research 48(1), 9–26 (1990)
24. Saaty, T.L., Vargas, L.G.: Models, methods, concepts & applications of the analytic hierarchy process, vol. 1. Springer (2001)
25. Twitonomy.com (2014), http://www.twitonomy.com/
26. Twitter4j.org (2010), http://twitter4j.org/en/index.html
27. Wu, S., Hofman, J.M., Mason, W.A., Watts, D.J.: Who says what to whom on twitter. Paper presented at the Proceedings of the 20th International Conference on World Wide Web (2011)

A Continuous Markov-Chain Model of Data Quality Transition: Application in Insurance-Claim Handling

Yuval Zak and Adir Even[✉]

The Department of Industrial Engineering and Management,
Ben-Gurion University of the Negev,
P.O.B. 653, 8410501, Beer-Sheva, Israel

Abstract. Data quality (DQ) might degrade over time, due to changes in real-world entities or behaviors that are not reflected correctly in datasets that describe them. This study presents a continuous-time Markov-Chain model that reflects DQ as a dynamic process. The model may help assessing and predicting accuracy degradation over time. Taking into account cost-benefit tradeoffs, it can also be used to recommend an economically-optimal point in time at which data values should be evaluated and possibly reacquired. The model addresses data-acquisition scenarios that reflect real-world processes with a finite number of states, each described by certain data-attribute values. It takes into account state-transition probabilities, the distribution of time spent in each state, the damage associated with incorrect data that fails to reflect the real-world state, and the cost of data reacquisition. Given current state and the time passed since the last transition, the model estimates the expected damage of a data record and recommends whether or not to correct it, by comparing the potential benefits of correction (elimination of potential damage), versus reacquisition cost.

Following common design science research guidelines, the applicability and the potential contribution of the model is demonstrated with a real-world dataset that reflects a process of handling insurance claims. Insurants' status must be kept up-to-date, to avoid potential monetary damages; however, contacting an insurant for status update is costly and time consuming. Currently the contact decision is guided by some heuristics that are based on employees' experience. The evaluation shows that applying the model has major cost-saving potential, compared to the current state.

Keywords: Data Quality · Accuracy · Continuous-Time Markov Chain · Design Science Research

1   Introduction

Organizations rely on data resources for supporting operations and decision making. As highlighted by a plethora of studies, degradation in data quality (DQ) can be associated with business-process deficiencies, flawed decision and major monetary damages. With the rapid growth in the magnitude of data resources, the task of maintaining high DQ level is becoming increasingly complex and costly, particularly when the detection and the correction of DQ defects require some manual intervention.

© Springer International Publishing Switzerland 2015
B. Donnellan et al. (Eds.): DESRIST 2015, LNCS 9073, pp. 199–214, 2015.
DOI: 10.1007/978-3-319-18714-3_13

DQ management is therefore in a growing need for tools and techniques that can aid and expedite detection and correction in scenarios where the task cannot be fully automated – e.g., by alerting on data items that are likely to be erroneous, predicting possible quality degradation, and improve the cost-effectiveness of manual interventions. The model developed in this study aims at making contribution to that end.

This study addresses scenarios in which data was acquired correctly, but the real-world entity described change over time. If the data is not updated accordingly, it may no longer reflect the real-world state, and becomes inaccurate. For example, if we fail to update a person's data for a while, some attribute might become inaccurate – e.g., the person may have changed address, marital status, or education level. Handling inaccuracies introduce inherent cost-benefit tradeoffs. On the one hand, relying on inaccurate data might lead to fault decisions, possibly associated with some monetary damage. On the other hand, not all accuracy defects can be handled automatically, and manual detection and correction is expensive and resource-demanding. Do the benefits from DQ improvement justify the associated costs? If yes, what is the optimal point in time at which data values should be evaluated and possibly reacquired?

The model developed in this study reflects data-values transitions as a dynamic process. Taking the continuous-time Markov chain approach, the model assumes a finite set of states, each reflecting a possible attribute value. The model also considers the damage caused by inaccuracies – i.e., cases where the data state does not meet the real-world value. As shown later – such formulation can help answer important DQ management questions: a) What is the likelihood that a certain existing data value is inaccurate? b) From the point of acquisition (or, reacquisition) – how long will it take a certain data item to become inaccurate? c) What is the economically-optimal point of time for auditing and possibly correcting a certain data item?

To demonstrate applicability and potential contribution, the model is evaluated with a real-world dataset that reflects insurance-claims handling. Much of the handling is done via phone calls, during which an employee must update the insurant's status. Insurants often neglect to report status updates; hence, the dataset is subject to inaccuracies that translate to major losses for the firm. Contacting all insurants regularly is infeasible, due to time and cost constraints, and currently contact-initiation decisions are guided by heuristics based on employees' experience. The evaluation shows that call-initiation could have substantially improved by applying the model.

In the remainder of this paper, we first review studies that influence our thinking and development. The model formulation is described next, followed by evaluation with real-world data, and discussion of the results. To conclude we summarize the study and its key contributions and highlights possible directions for future research.

2   Background

Data is often subject to quality defects – missing records or values, mismatches between values and real-world entities, outdated values that no longer reflect current behavior, and others. With the broad recognition of data as a critical resource, data quality (DQ) defects and their hazardous effect attract growing attention. Poor DQ may harm operational processes, decision-making activities, and cooperation within and between organizations (Batini, Cappiello et al. 2009). The task of DQ management may involve different perspectives: technical solution, functional requirements, management responsibility, organizational culture, economics, and others (Madnick et al., 2009). This study focuses on DQ assessment - a key DQ management activity (Wang, 1998; Pipino et al., 2002). Measuring DQ and sharing the results can raise awareness to DQ defects, prevent flawed decisions, and help reducing the magnitude of errors and the time spent on validation (Chengalur-Smith, Ballou et al. 1999; Cai and Shankaranarayanan; 2006). A plethora of studies addressed DQ assessment from many different perspectives. Here, we wish to highlight some key questions and insights that rise from a review of some previous works, and influence our study.

2.1   Orthogonal or Dependent DQ Dimensions?

DQ research broadly adopts the notion of DQ dimensions – the claim that DQ should not be assessed as a single "overarching" concept, but rather as a set of perspectives, or dimensions, each reflecting a different type of DQ defects or hazards (Pipino et al., 2002; Even and Shankaranarayanan, 2007) – e.g., Completeness, Accuracy, Currency, Timeliness, and Validity. The common measurement approach, along these dimensions, is a 0-1 ratio that reflects a proportion of non-defected items (1 – perfect DQ, no defects), and can be assessed at different levels - records, specific attributes, or entire datasets (Pipino et al., 2002; Even and Shankaranarayanan, 2007).

A first question that we raise is – should DQ dimensions be treated as orthogonal or dependent? So far, DQ dimensions were more commonly treated as orthogonal and assessed independently. This approach is apparent in works that discuss a specific dimension (e.g., Even et al., 2010; Fisher et al., 2009; Heinrich and Klier, 2011; Wechsler et al., 2013), or multiple dimensions, each measured independently (Pipino et al., 2002; Even and Shankaranarayanan, 2007). Some studies, however, look at possible mutual effect between DQ dimensions – how changes in one are reflected in others. Ballou and Pazer (1995; 2003) look into accuracy-timeliness and completeness-consistency tradeoffs. Parssian et al. (2004) analyze the evolvement of DQ defects along a multi-stage process, showing that defects of a certain type may evolve into defects of other types at later stages.

This study looks into the mutuality between currency and accuracy – the former reflects the extent to which data is up-to-date, while the latter reflects the extent to which the data is free of errors. It shows that as data becomes less current it is also likely to become less accurate. A similar proposition was made by Wechsler et al. (2012), who developed a model that highlights possible mechanism behind that mutual effect and demonstrated it with census data. This work will be discussed some more later, as it influenced the conceptualization the model development in this study.

2.2   DQ as a Static Snapshot or as a Dynamic Process?

DQ measurements serve as input for important DQ management tasks – analysis of current state, communicating DQ status to end-users, and directing improvement efforts (Wang, 1998). *A second question that we raise is – should assessment take a static ("Snapshot") view, or rather a dynamic view of DQ as an evolving process.*

Many works reflect a static view – assessment based on a "snapshot" of data, taken at a certain point of time (e.g., Ballou et al., 1995; Chengalur-Smith et al., 1999; Even et al., 2010). Some works introduce a probabilistic approach into their measurement schema, acknowledging the fact that the data sample available for evaluation does not necessarily provide a comprehensive and recent enough picture of the real-world state (e.g., Fisher et al., 2009, Heinrich, et al., 2009/2011). Regardless the probabilistic approach, this body of works still offers a static view, and provider measures that reflect the current DQ state.

A dynamic view is reflected to an extent in Pipino et al. (2002) – their software utility permits tracking progression of "snapshot" measurements over time. Even et al. (2010) show that DQ deteriorates over time, to a point where outdated data might become useless and no-longer worth fixing. Wechsler et al. (2012) model transitions between data values as a multi-stage dynamic process that explains DQ deterioration. An important motivation behind dynamic modeling is the possibility to turn it toward prediction of future DQ degradation. If predictions are reasonably reliable, managers can prepare for possible DQ hazard, act proactively, and take preventive measures.

2.3   Impartial or Value-Driven DQ Assessment?

A number of studies have highlighted economic aspects of DQ. A possible perspective for observing economic DQ issues is the value of information, as high-quality data is positively associated with higher value or utility (Haug et al., 2011, Even and Shankaranarayanan 2007). DQ defects might degrade the potential value, and cause monetary losses – e.g., by resulting-in sub-optimal decisions (Heinrich, Klier et al. 2009, Even et al. 2010). The other possible economic perspective is the cost associated with DQ improvement – manual handling of DQ defects typically require major time resources (Wechsler and Even, 2012), while automation require investment in IT resources (Cappiello et al. 2003, Eppler and Helfert, 2004).

Our third question – should the goal of DQ assessment be error-free data, or maximizing value and economic benefits? Even and Shankaranarayanan (2007) link this differentiation to impartial versus contextual DQ measurement. The former reflects stand-alone assessment of data and DQ defects, regardless of how data is used. The latter reflects the impact of DQ defects within a specific context of use. Their contextual assessment applies the concept of utility – a measure for the value stems for data usage that may vary, depending on the usage contexts. Impartial measurement is more common in earlier DQ works (e.g., Ballou and Pazer, 1995/2003, Chengalur-Smith et al., 1999; Parssian et al., 2004), while some more recent works look into linking DQ assessment to data utilization with the associated benefits (e.g., Even et al., 2010; Heinrich et al., 2009; Wechsler et al., 2013). This study links DQ assessment with the utility damage of inaccuracies and the cost of correction, toward economically-optimal prioritization of DQ improvement efforts.

3   Model Development

The model developed in this section addresses data management scenarios that adhere to the following characteristics and assumptions:

- A dataset, in which each record reflects a single instance (e.g., a list of customers).
- A target attribute, with value that reflects the real-world state of the associated instance (e.g., the customer's status). The model assumes a finite number of real-world states, each associated with a corresponding data value. Hence, the value domain of the target attribute is a discrete and finite set of possible values.
- When a dataset record is added or updated, the target attribute reflects correctly the real-world state. However, the real-world state may change, and if the target attribute is not updated accordingly, it no longer reflects the real-world state accurately.
- The target attribute is assumed to have significant business importance, with a certain cost or penalty in case of inaccuracies; hence, the motivation for maintaining target-attribute values as accurate as possible.
- Besides the target attribute, a record contains a number of additional attributes (e.g., the customer's gender, date of birth, or region of residence). Some of those attributes may have some association with the target attribute, and may help predicting transitions in the real-world state to an extent.

A modeling approach that may fit such scenarios is the Markov Chain (MC) model (Ross, 1996). The basic MC form considers a stochastic process of transitioning over time between a finite number of possible values $\{x_i\}_{i=1..N}$. Time is modeled as a discrete variable ($t = 0, 1, 2, ..$), where steps in $[t]$ are associated with equal time interval. The transition probability P_{ij} reflect the likelihood of transitioning from value x_i to value x_j within a single time interval. The MC assumes "memory-less" transitions – i.e., the transition probability depends only on the current value, and not on previous values, and does not change over time. The collection of transition probabilities forms the transition matrix, where $\sum_{j=1..J} P_{i,j} = 1$ for each $[i]$:

$$P = \begin{bmatrix} P_{11} & \cdots & P_{1n} \\ \vdots & \ddots & \vdots \\ P_{n1} & \cdots & P_{nn} \end{bmatrix} \tag{1}$$

P is assumed to be stationary; hence, $P(t)$, the t-steps transition matrix (i.e., the set of probabilities that a value will change from x_i to x_j after t periods) is the t-power of the transition matrix: $P(t) = P^t$.

A model for DQ assessment, based on the basic MC form, was introduced in (Wechsler and Even, 2012). The proposed model fits the characteristics and the assumption of the scenario described above. If a certain target-attribute value x_i was recorded at time $t=0$, it can be shown that its expected accuracy level (the likelihood to remain accurate) at a later time t is given by $A_i(t) = P_{ii}(t)$. The modeling approach proposed by that study had major influence on the approach applied in this study. However, that modeling approach poses a few major limitations, which are addressed by this study: fixed-length discrete time periods, possible dependencies between attributes, and the need to consider possible cost-benefit tradeoffs.

Notably, extended MC forms offer refined treatment of time (Ross, 1996). The *Continuous-Time Markov Chain* extends the MC to a continuous stochastic process. In the continuous-time MC the time spent in state x_i has the "memoryless" property as well. Let τ_i denote the time spent in state x_i before transitioning, then $P\{\tau_i > s + t | \tau_i > s\} =$

$P\{\tau_i > t\}$. The random variable τ_i must therefore be exponentially distributed. The transition probability from x_i to state x_j depends of the transition time: $P_{ij}(t) = P\{X(t + s) = j|X(s) = i\}$. This MC extension is used in the development of our model, which is described next.

3.1   Baseline Formulation: Optimal Data Reacquisition Time

Next, we present an analytical formulation, aimed at answering the question: given a record with a target-attribute value of x_i, what would be the optimal time for reacquisition of that record? The formulation, which considers the following factors, is first stated at a high-level, and further extended later:

- The time, denoted by (t), passed since the most recent data acquisition,
- The real-world property, reflected by the target attribute has N possible states. Accordingly, the target attribute has one among N possible values $\{xi\}_{i=1...N}$
- The data state, as reflected by a current target-attribute value x_i, (denoted by index $[i]$) vs. the real-world state, which should have resulted a target-attribute value x_j (denoted by $[j]$). The record is said to be accurate if $i=j$, and inaccurate otherwise.
- Inaccuracy may result in some monetary damage, which may change over time. The damage function $d_{ij}(t)$ reflects the damage that can be attributed to a record currently at state $[i]$, which should have been in state $[j]$. All $\{d_{ij}(t)\}$ are assumed to be non-negative, monotonic and non-decreasing with (t) (i.e., can be a constant). We also assume no damage when a record is accurate (i.e., $d_{ii}(t) = 0$). Since the assumption if that at the time of acquisition the data is accurate, $d_{ij}(0) = 0$.
- The cumulative damage function D_i reflects the accumulation of damage functions, weighted by the probability or transitions. $P_{ij}(t)$ reflects the probability that a record with state $[i]$ at $t=0$ has transitioned to state $[j]$ at time t. The cumulative function can therefore be expressed as $D_i(t) = \Sigma_{j=1..N}\left(P_{ij}(t) \cdot d_{ij}(t)\right)$. Since $D_i(t)$ is a linear combination of $\{d_{ij}(t)\}$ with non-negative weights, it is also non-negative, monotonic/non-decreasing with (t), and $D_i(0) = 0$.
- Reacquisition cost $C_i(t)$ depends on current state $[i]$ and on (t). As with the damage function, we assume that $C_i(t)$ is positive, monotonic, and non-decreasing with (t).

The optimal point of time for data reacquisition is (t) that solved the following:

$$C_i(t) = D_i(t) = \Sigma_{j=1...N}\left(P_{ij}(t) \cdot d_{ij}(t)\right) \tag{2}$$

In other words: data reacquisition should be performed at the first point of time where the potential damage is higher than the reacquisition cost.

- Since $C_i(t)$ and $D_i(t)$ are both monotonic and non-decreasing, there is at the most one optimal point of time t_{opt} that solves the equation (Fig. 1a).
- At the time of acquisition $(t=0)$, the cost is positive; hence, greater than the damage: $C_i(0) > D_i(0) = 0$. If for all (t) $C_i(t) > D_i(t)$ (Fig. 1b), no reacquisition will occur. This is particularly true if the record is at a state with no transitioning out (a "sink") – i.e., $P_{ij}(t)$ is 1 for $i=j$, 0 otherwise, and $D_i(t) = 0$ for all (t).

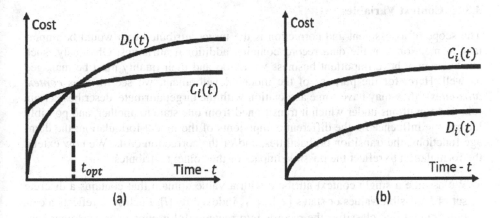

Fig. 1. Inaccuracy Damage versus Correction Cost

3.2   State Transitions as a Continuous-Time Markov Chain

Assuming that the transitions between states follow a Continuous-Time Markov-Chain (CTMC), the formulation in Eq. 2 can be further extended:

- The probability of transition $P_{ij}(t)$ from state [i] to state [j], as a function of time (t), is seen as assembled from two separate components: the probability of transition, and the time between transitions.
- Assuming a CTMC, the probability of transition from state [i] to state [j] is a constant P_{ij} - a component in the transition probability matrix P, described earlier in Eq. 1. This probability does not dependent on the previous states in which the records resided, other than the current state [i].
- Assuming a CTMS, the time between transitions is exponentially distributed, dependent on the current state [i], and the next state [j]. It is defined as $\sim\exp(\lambda_{ij}\alpha_{ij})$, where λ_{ij} is the transition rate from state [i] to state [j], and α_{ij} is an auxiliary parameter.
- Assuming an exponential distribution, the probability of a record to transition out of state [i] by the time (t), given target state [j], is $P(t|i \rightarrow j) = 1 - e^{-\lambda_{ij}\alpha_{ij}}$.
- The damage function $d_{ij}(t)$ is based on assessment of potential damages. The formulation has to be defined over the $[0, \infty]$ range, and adheres to the conditions defined earlier: non-negative, monotonic, and non-decreasing with (t)
- Since the damage function $d_{ij}(t)$ is zero at $t = 0$ ($d_{ij}(0) = 0$), the expected potential damage (i.e. the accumulative damage) at time (t) is defined as $E_D[t] = \int_0^t D_i(x)dx = D_i(t) - D_i(0) = D_i(t) - 0 = D_i(t)$

Based on these assumptions, the formulation presented in Eq. 2 of the optimal point for the time for data reacquisition, can be extended to:

$$C_i(t) = D_i(t) = \sum_{j=1...N}\left(P_{ij} \cdot \left(1 - e^{-\lambda_{ij}\alpha_{ij}}\right) \cdot d_{ij}(t)\right) \qquad (3)$$

3.3   Context Variables

The scope of assessment and correction is the target attribute but it would be important to mention that the data record contains additional attributes. Obviously, such attributes may have important business value too and their quality must be managed as well. Here, for the purpose of the model development, we see them as *context attributes* – they may have some association with the target attribute, describes certain relevant conditions under which it transitioned from one state to another, and possibly have some influence on the different components of the model formulation: the damage functions, the transition probabilities, and/or the correction costs. We now extend the formulation to reflect the possible impact of the context attributes:

- We assume a single context attribute with a value domain that contains a discrete set of L possible values or states $\{x_l\}_{l=1...L}$, indexed by $[l]$. Each state reflects a certain context that classifies the records into meaningful groups (e.g., customer segments, system of data origin, etc.).
  - A context variable defined over a continuous range (e.g., "annual salary"), can be transformed into a discrete set of ranges ("bins") that reflect meaningful business classification (e.g., "salary range", of "high", "medium", or "low").
  - Multiple attributes can be transformed to a single context attribute, in which each state reflects a combination of value. For example, a combination of {"marital status" and "salary range"} with possible value combinations of ("single", "low"), ("single", "medium"), ("married", "low"), etc.
- The assumption is that the context value of a record is set when the record is first acquired, and does not change over time. As discussed in the concluding section, later extensions to this work should look into modeling possible transitions in $[l]$.
- The specific context value $[l]$ may affect all the model components; hence, their annotation should be extended accordingly:
  - The correction cost function $C_{il}(t)$
  - The damage function $d_{ijl}(t)$ and the cumulative damage function $D_{il}(t)$.
  - The transition probability matrix P_l and its cells $\{P_{ijl}\}$.
  - The exponential distribution parameters: $\sim\exp(\lambda_{ijl}\alpha_{ijl})$.

Accordingly, the formulation in Eq. 3 should be extended to:

$$C_{il}(t) = D_{il}(t) = \sum_{j=1...N}\left(P_{ijl}\cdot\left(1 - e^{-\lambda_{ijl}\alpha_{ijl}}\right)\cdot d_{ijl}(t)\right) \tag{4}$$

The implication is that, given a context variable with a set of possible states, the model has to be evaluated separately for each state. This implies a need to establish L models, one for each context state, and for each record apply the model that matches the context group to which it belongs.

4   Empirical Evaluation

This study contributes a novel model for predicting economically-optimal data reacquisition cost. This contribution aligns with the design-science research (DSR) paradigm, which targets the creation of new artifacts (such as models) toward improving IS implementation. The success of DSR outcome is judged by its quality, contribution, and the impact of the developed artifacts (Hevner at al., 2004). The work described so far can be linked to the DSR steps defined in (Peffer et al., 2007):

1. *Identify Problem and Motivate:* data inaccuracies may cause substantial damages, and the cost of fixing them may turn out to be high, hence the need for solutions that may help predicting inaccuracies, assess the potential damage, and prioritize improvement efforts accordingly.
2. *Define Objectives and Solutions:* the proposed solution is an analytical model, based on the Markov-Chain approach, which helps predicting accuracy degradation, and help assessing the cost-benefit tradeoffs associated with fixing it.
3. *Design and Development:* the development of the proposed model was described in the previous section.

In this section we proceed to the next steps: demonstration of the model and evaluating its performance within a suitable real-world data management scenario.

4.1 Evaluation Setup – The Firm and the Business Process

Our evaluation site is a privately-owned service provider (referred to as the FIRM) that works in collaboration with leading Health Maintenance Organizations (HMO's) and handles insurance claim for customers who suffered work accidents (magnitude of 10,000's claims, annually). A person who suffers an accident is entitled for some benefits (e.g., monthly stipend for the recovery period, coverage of medical expenses, and help in transportation) from the National Insurance Organization (NIO). The process of applying for those benefits is long and complex, and required submission of applications, medical records, and specialist assessments. It is in the interest of the HMO's that a customer fills-in the application, otherwise medical expenses that could have been covered by the NIO, will have to be charged to the HMO's. The HMO's hire the FIRM to accompany the customer, assist them with the claim-application process and make sure that the required documentation is delivered. Customers are not charged for this service, and the FIRM is getting reimbursed for claims that ended-up being filed.

The process is mostly remote – i.e., almost no face-to-face meetings are required, and most of the status tracking is done via phone call with serviced representatives. The claims are filed either by FIRM representatives or by the customer. Customers are supposed to report FIRM representative on any progress. However, in practice, they often neglect to do so; hence, their data record often does not reflect correctly their actual status. Discrepancies as such might turn out to be costly – for example, if the customer has received the forms, but failed to complete and sign them, the processes might be substantially delayed, and the FIRM will not get reimbursed. To avoid possible discrepancies, FIRM representatives call customers that are still in the process eventually, and verify their status. Making such a call costs the service-representative time; hence, cannot be performed too often. To avoid too-high cost, the representatives call only a subset of the customers each month, where the choice is based on their current state, and other "heuristics" that have evolved in the firm over the years. Given this current situation of severe damages due to data inaccuracies, and high data reacquisition cost, the FIRM is currently looking into a solution that will help turning the customer calls into a more cost-effective process.

With the help of FIRM managers, the claim-handling was modeled as an 8-stage process with possible transitions among them.

1. *Customer data received*: data was received from the HMO, no contact with the customer was made yet.
2. *Customer is waiting for the forms*: first contact with the customer was made, and the customer is waiting for the forms.
3. *Customer is filling the forms*: customer has received the forms and needs to fill them and get his employer to sign.
4. *Customer had signed the forms*: customer had filled-in and signed the forms, and needs to deliver it back to the company.
5. *Claim was filed*: the claim was submitted to the NIO, and pending for processing and approval.
6. *Claim was filed independently*: the customer had chosen to file the claim independently, with only partial help of the company.
7. *Process is irrelevant*: the customer is either unreachable, had already filed in a claim, or is interested in filing a claim at all.
8. *Claim approved*: the claim processing by the NIO has been completed, and the application was approved.

From the FIRM's stand point – the hazardous states, with some potential damage, are 6 and 7. In all the stages the customer is associated with some cost (the time spent on calls so far), but the FIRM will see no revenue.

4.2   Data Collection and Preparation

The evaluation included a dataset with 14,209 customer records. The records were anonymized – Id's were converted to sequential numbers, and any detail that could have identified the customer was removed. The current process step (a value between 1 and 8) was defined as the target attribute. As context attribute we chose an attribute that reflected three forms ($L=3$) of how the contact with the customer is handled: phone calls ($l=1$, 7,513 records), field representative ($l=2$, 5,330 records), or a combination of both ($l=3$, 1,366 records). FIRM managers suggested that the contact form has important implications for the process, and significant impact on costs and potential damage; hence three models were developed, one for each context value.

Currently, the FIRM's customer database does not keep track of the changes, and does not record the exact date and time in which the status was updated. To track changes in status, we sampled the dataset periodically, and compared customer status and the beginning and at the end of each period. Overall, we sampled in periods, each reflecting a slightly different number of days (32, 31, 34, 30, 32, and 29). Transition matrices $\{P\}$ for all models were calculated for each period – we have verified and the transition probabilities were indeed similar between periods; hence, it was reasonable to assume that the transition matrices stay stationary over time. This sampling schema introduced some issues that had to be addressed in the evaluation:

- The dataset state the last date of contacting the customer. It is therefore possible to know whether or not the customer was contacted during the month, and if yes – whether or not the call resulted in a change in state. However, as only the last call is recorded, it is impossible to tell whether or not within a single period a customer received a few calls, and the status updated more than once. The evaluation therefor considered only the last transition within a period, if more than one occurred. Since the model assumes memoryless transitions, this approximation did not bias significantly the model outcomes.
- If a customer was not contacted during the period – it is impossible to tell whether or not the real-world state did change. In that case, a possible transition in the real world state had to be approximated – based on actual transitions of customers at similar states, who were contacted via the same contact form.

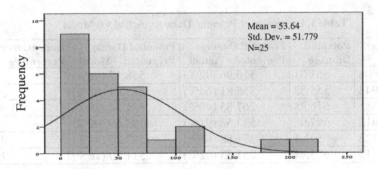

Fig. 2. Transition Histogram Example: From State 1 to State 8 under Contact From 1

The assessment of probability parameters was conducted for all 6 periods, where the estimation was conducted for customers who performed transitions. The transition probability matrices reflected, in general, the expected business process – for example, state 8 that was expected to be stationary, indeed did not have transitions out. However, the transitions did not always conform to the assumption of exponentially distributed transition time. Out of 132 transition rates, only 64 were shown to be exponentially distributed (using the K-S goodness-of-fit test, with significance level of 0.05). Some transition time distributions did not pass the test, but still appeared to have nearly-exponential characteristics (For example – the distribution shown in Fig. 2). Despite the misfit of some distributions to the model assumption, we chose to proceed with the model, in hope that when applied it can still yield better prediction results than current performance, in terms of cost-saving.

4.3   Evaluation Results

The model can help predicting the optimal time in which data should be reacquired. The potential damage of data inaccuracy is zero at $t=0$ and may grow over time. The evaluation was conducted, for each period, along the following steps:

- The customers who were evaluated were those with known state at the beginning of the period (i.e., not newly-added), and not stationary (i.e., state other than 8).
- Per customer, the model was used to predict the potential damage at the end of the period. From the FIRM's standpoint, the damage will realizes if the customer actually reached states 6 or 7 – but the data shows a different state, not perceived as hazardous. The potential damage was therefor set as the likelihood that a customer will reach one of the hazardous states at the end of a period, given current state. The records were there sorted by their potential damage – high to low.
- The evaluation compared the performance against the current heuristics-based calls by FIRM representatives. If at a certain period Y calls were made – the evaluation compared Y customers who were actually called to the Y customers that that were ranked as having the highest potential damage according to the model's prediction.

Table 1. Prevention of Potential Damage, Actual vs. Model

Pd.	Recor ds	Potential Damage	Potential Damage Prevented – Actual	Potential Damage Prevented – Model	Improvement Percentage
1	4608	561.01	516.96 (92%)	558.17 (99%)	8%
2	3943	555.32	355.81 (64%)	488.44 (88%)	37%
3	3385	676.98	267.85 (40%)	531.54 (79%)	98%
4	5412	597.92	543.53 (91%)	592.69 (99%)	9%
5	4123	592.4	371.88 (63%)	512.20 (86%)	38%
6	3315	673.94	285.35 (42%)	511.40 (76%)	79%

Table 1 compares the potential damage prevented, which is defined as the potential damage of a customer who were actually called by representatives (or recommended by the model). In all periods, the predictions made by the model could have prevented more potential damage. The margin is explained by the quality of recommendations made by the model – while both methods were evaluated with the same number of customers per period, the model could recommend customers with higher damage potential to be contacted.

Table 2 demonstrates how the suggested model prevents actual damage, by comparing model recommendation to the transition during the evaluated period.

- Damage prevented: customers who were actually called by representatives (or recommended by the model) and ended-up transitioning. When the customer's state is reacquired, if transitioned to states 6 or 7, the damage was considered as damage prevention.
- Damage inflicted: customers who were not called by representatives (or not recommended by the model), and ended-up transitioning to another state.
- Except for period 1, the model increased the damage prevented and reduced the damage inflicted. In some periods major improvements were made.

Table 2. Damage Analysis

Pd.	Recs.	Potential Damage	Damage Prevented – Actual	Damage Prevented – Model	Prevention Increase (%)	Damage Inflicted – Actual	Damage Inflicted – Model	Infliction Decrease (%)
1	4608	561.01	400.06 (71%)	394.51 (70%)	-1%	41.00 (7%)	46.55 (8%)	14%
2	3943	555.32	308.24 (51%)	329.29 (54%)	7%	216.35 (36%)	195.30 (32%)	-10%
3	3385	676.98	198.95 (27%)	311.51 (42%)	57%	335.70 (46%)	223.14 (30%)	-34%
4	5412	597.92	365.23 (61%)	386.68 (64%)	6%	56.23 (9%)	34.78 (6%)	-38%
5	4123	592.4	294.80 (45%)	354.48 (54%)	20%	239.30 (37%)	179.61 (27%)	-25%
6	3315	673.94	243.92 (33%)	326.84 (44%)	34%	329.27 (45%)	246.35 (34%)	-25%

The context attribute that we chose for evaluation is the form of contact, with 3 possible values. As suggested earlier (Eq. 4), the model parameters were developed for each form separately and the customer subgroups where evaluated each according to the associated model. The evaluation in Table 2 has been repeated, but disregarding the context-value. The results are summarized in Table 3.

The non-context-evalution results, as presented in Table 3, are fairly similar to the evalution that did consider the differences in context. In some periods the damage prevention was higher and the damange inflinction was smaller, but in average the preformacnce was similar, with no statistically-significant difference. Without contextual attribute the average damage prevention was 21.53% and the averatge damage infliction was -22.2%, while when splitting the customers into 3 groups the average numbers were 20.36% and -19.67%, respectively.

Overall, the evaluation results were encouraging. The use of the model was able to provide recommendations of customers with high probability of state transition that need to be contacted, with overall performance that was substantially higher than the current heuristics-based contact method. A key preliminary assumption, made prior to the model evaluation, was that the transition time has exponential distribution. This assumption was supported only partially by the actual data – some distributions confirmed this assumption but some did not. Regardless – the use of the model could provide good results, in terms of damage reduction, despite some mismatched with the assumption of exponential behavior. The further separation to different models, based on the values of the contact form as context variable, did not improve the results but did not harm them either. Notably the choice of context variable was based on a recommendation made by FIRM's managers. A more robust evaluation of context variable is needed, and a better choice could have possibly made a greater impact.

Table 3. Damage Analysis, Disregarding the Impact of Context Attribute.

Pd.	Records	Potential Damage	Damage Prevented – Actual	Damage Prevented – Model	Prevention Increase (%)	Damage Inflicted – Actual	Damage Inflicted – Model	Infliction Decrease (%)
1	4608	452.49	363.88 (80%)	363.81 (80%)	0%	39.79 (9%)	39.86 (9%)	0%
2	3943	451.37	281.41 (62%)	284.12 (63%)	1%	195.6 (43%)	192.89 (43%)	-1%
3	3385	517.28	182.47 (35%)	304.86 (59%)	67%	301.87 (58%)	179.48 (35%)	-41%
4	5412	523.15	333.86 (63%)	360.53 (69%)	8%	59.39 (11%)	32.71 (6%)	-45%
5	4123	513.21	269.84 (52%)	306.75 (60%)	14%	215.76 (42%)	178.85 (35%)	-17%
6	3315	520.55	223.75 (42%)	312.11 (60%)	39%	300.54 (58%)	212.18 (41%)	-29%

5   Conclusions

With the growing dependency of organization on their data resources, the issue of data quality defects and their potential damage is on the rise. Data quality management is in need for tools and techniques that will aid the associated decisions – which data items should be audited and possibly corrected, what is the optimal timing to do so, and how to do so in a cost-effective manner. This study contributes to that end by offering a model that can help predicting possible degradation in data quality and recommending the optimal time for requisition. The model, based on a continuous-time Markov chain, takes some novel approaches, compared to tools and techniques that were previously introduced in research. The study looks at a possible interplay of two DQ dimensions that are mostly treated independently – accuracy and currency. It observes quality degradation as dynamic process, and builds into the model possible cost-benefit tradeoffs, that can influence economically-optimal choices.

The application and the potential contribution of the model were demonstrated with a large dataset that reflects a dynamic real-world scenario with characteristics that justify, in general, the model formulation and assumptions. The results were encouraging, and the model indeed showed a potential to improve the data acquisition process and reduce damage. Obviously – some more evaluation and adjustments are required, before the model can turn into a tool that can be applied in practice.

While this study makes some contributions, it had some limitations that should be acknowledged, and possibly addressed in future research. The model relies on the assumption that the company reacquires the customers' current state without interfering with the natural course of their process. In practice, contacting a customer for data reacquisition may serve as an opportunity to make some offers and influence the customers' behavior. By that – the act of data acquisition does not only update the record to reflect the real-world state, but can also influence the real-world state and result in some changes to the data. Modeling reacquisition as a decision tree may help capturing this possibility. Another limitation is the underlying assumption of a memory-less transition time with exponential distribution. In this study, this assumption was applied even in cases where the actual transition time did not match an exponential behavior. In future extensions, the model can be further developed to deal with different type of distribution. A third limitation is the assumption that context variable are stationary – i.e., their value is set when the record is first acquired, and does not transition over time. Obviously, this assumption applied only with certain context attributes, but not with others. A future enhancement to the model can consider possible transitions in the values of context attributes, and assess the possible impact of such transitions on the ability to predict the transition time, and optimize the reacquisition decision accordingly. The improvements discussed here are currently under development and evaluation, and we plan to present them in a follow-up study.

References

1. Ballou, D.P., Pazer, H.L.: Modeling completeness versus consistency tradeoffs in information decision contexts. IEEE Trans. Knowledge and Data Eng. 15(1), 240–243 (2003)
2. Ballou, D.P., Pazer, H.L.: Designing information systems to optimize the accuracy-timeliness tradeoff. Information Systems Research 6(1), 51–72 (1995)
3. Batini, C., Cappiello, C., Francalanci, C., Maurino, A.: Methodologies for data quality assessment and improvement. ACM Computing Surveys (CSUR) 41(3), 16 (2009)
4. Cai, Y., Shankaranarayanan, G.: Supporting data quality management in decision-making. Decision Support Systems 42(1), 302–317 (2006)
5. Cappiello, C., Francalanci, C., Pernici, B.: Time-related factors of data quality in multi-channel information systems. J. of Management Information Systems 20(3), 71–92 (2003)
6. Chengalur-Smith, I.N., Ballou, D.P., Pazer, H.L.: The impact of data quality information on decision making: An exploratory analysis. IEEE Transactions on Knowledge and Data Engineering 11(6), 853–864 (1999)
7. Eppler, M., Helfert, M.: A classification and analysis of data quality costs. Paper presented at the International Conference on Information Quality (2004)
8. Even, A., Shankaranarayanan, G.: Utility-driven assessment of data quality. ACM SIGMIS Database 38(2), 75–93 (2007)
9. Even, A., Shankaranarayanan, G., Berger, P.D.: Evaluating a model for cost-effective data quality management in a real-world CRM setting. DSS 50(1), 152–163 (2010)
10. Fisher, C.W., Lauria, E.J., Matheus, C.C.: An accuracy metric: Percentages, randomness, and probabilities. Journal of Data and Information Quality (JDIQ) 1(3), 16 (2009)
11. Haug, A., Zachariassen, F., Van Liempd, D.: The costs of poor data quality. Journal of Industrial Engineering and Management 4(2), 168–193 (2011)
12. Heinrich, B., Klier, M., Kaiser, M.: A procedure to develop metrics for currency and its application in CRM. Journal of Data and Information Quality (JDIQ) 1(1), 5 (2009)
13. Heinrich, B., Klier, M.: Assessing data currency—a probabilistic approach. Journal of Information Science 37(1), 86–100 (2011)
14. Hevner, A.R., March, S.T., Park, J., Ram, S.: Design Science in Information Systems Research. MIS Quarterly 28(1), 75–105 (2004)

15. Madnick, S.E., Wang, R.Y., Lee, Y.W., Zhu, H.: Overview and framework for data and information quality research. J. of Data and Information Quality (JDIQ) 1(1), 2 (2009)
16. Parssian, A., Sarkar, S., Jacob, V.S.: Assessing data quality for information products: Impact of selection, projection, and Cartesian product. Management Science 50(7), 967–982 (2004)
17. Peffers, K., Tuunanen, T., Rothenberger, M., Chatterjee, S.: A Design Science Research Methodology for Information Systems Research. Journal of Management Information Systems 24(3), 45–77 (2007)
18. Pipino, L.L., Lee, Y.W., Wang, R.Y.: Data quality assessment. Communications of the ACM 45(4), 211–218 (2002)
19. Ross, S.M.: Stochastic processes, 2nd edn. Wiley, USA (1996)
20. Wang, R.Y.: A product perspective on total data quality management. Communications of the ACM 41(2), 58–65 (1998)
21. Wechsler, A., Even, A.: Assessing accuracy degradation over time with A Markov-chain model. In: The 17th Intl. Conference on Information Quality (ICIQ), Paris (2012)
22. Wechsler, A., Even, A., Weiss-Meilik, A.: A Model for Setting Optimal Data-Acquisition Policy and its Application with Clinical Data. In: The Intl. Conf. on Information System (ICIS), Milan, Italy (2013)

Enabling Reproducible Sentiment Analysis:
A Hybrid Domain-Portable Framework
for Sentiment Classification

Matthias Eickhoff[✉]

Georg-August University, Göttingen, Germany
matthias.eickhoff@wiwi.uni-goettingen.de

Abstract. In this paper a hybrid framework for Sentiment Analysis is presented. In the first part, dictionary based and machine learning based Sentiment Classification are introduced and the two approaches are contrasted. In the second part of the paper, the HSentiR framework, which combines the two approaches, is introduced. Consequently, the framework is evaluated regarding scoring accuracy and practical concerns.

Keywords: Sentiment analysis · Reproducible research

1   Introduction and Research Problem

Content and sentiment analysis as fields of study have intrigued researchers for a long time. As early as the nineteenth century, the quality of newspaper-articles was studied on a statistical basis [1]. However, due to the exponential increase in readily available digital texts that also has resulted from the rise of social media, sentiment analysis has become one of the most active data mining topics. Popular techniques include the use of (1) machine learning approaches, such as of Support Vector Machines (SVM) and naïve Bayes classification, or (2) scoring by comparing the words in a text with a dictionary of sentiment words of known polarity [2]. These two approaches to sentiment analysis have specific advantages and limitations. While dictionary based scoring methods offer a higher level of domain portability than machine learning based ones, their ability to detect sentiment in a document remains limited to the used dictionary and, for optimal scoring accuracy, a domain-specific dictionary is desirable nonetheless [3]. On the other hand, machine learning based classifiers are typically not domain-portable at all because they are based on different statistical measures of similarity and consequently perform much worse, if the documents at hand are not comparable to initial training data [4]. Due to these drawbacks of the individual approaches, researchers have combined them in hybrid models, which strive to combine advantages of both methods. It has been shown that the combination of two or more methods can improve scoring accuracy [5]. However, these models remain widely inaccessible to the scientific community at large. Thus, neither the validation of existing research, nor the application of existing implementations of these models, can be

© Springer International Publishing Switzerland 2015
B. Donnellan et al. (Eds.): DESRIST 2015, LNCS 9073, pp. 215–229, 2015.
DOI: 10.1007/978-3-319-18714-3_14

done easily. However, reproducible research has been identified as being key to build trust in the validity of empirical research [6], especially when it is computationally-assisted [7]. In order to be able to reproduce the results of sentiment analysis, both the data used for the study and the computational method used to calculate the results may need to be made available, at least to the reviewers of the paper, ideally to the general public. While the availability of data is a research project-specific problem and often hindered by licensing and privacy concerns, the methods used to perform the analysis should be made available whenever possible. The goal of this research is to combine the advantages of hybrid-classification methods with enabling reproducible research in sentiment analysis tasks. Due to this goal, the presented approach is implemented in R, is domain portable and improves scoring-accuracy over dictionary-based scoring alone. The proposed framework for hybrid domain-portable sentiment analysis is modular and can be easily reproduced or modified using the publicly available source code and R-script files.[1] The remainder of the paper is organized as follows: The first section gives a brief overview of sentiment analysis methods and their different prerequisites, as well as some of their strengths and limitations. The second part presents the developed hybrid sentiment analysis framework HSentiR as a framework to combine different approaches leveraging their individual strengths. The third part presents an empirical evaluation of the framework, using the popular movie-review polarity corpus by Pang and Lee [8]. Results show that the dictionary-based stage of the process performs comparably to other implementations, provided a domain-appropriate dictionary is used. The machine learning stage of the process improves the scoring accuracy. Whether this is a result of the machine-learning algorithm used in the example (k-NN) or a domain-specific result is an interesting question for further research. Apart from the slight increase in scoring accuracy, the machine learning stage offers the advantage of faster scoring of new documents and independence of sentiment-dictionaries.

2   Theoretical Background

Sentiment analysis, as a subcategory of opinion mining [2], describes the field of study that tries to summarize the emotional, or opinionated, contents of texts in a manner that allows for a quick grasp of these properties for arbitrary amounts of text. Practical sentiment analysis applications range from improving the quality of restaurant reviews [9], over stock market prediction [10, 11], to the classification of movie reviews [12], political analysis [13] or the measurement of consumer confidence [14]. As noted, the field has a long history. This hardly surprises, as the opinion of the masses have always been of interest to scientific scrutiny. However, in the past such studies had to concentrate on topics like newspaper articles [1], because the personal opinions of the individual were not available to researchers. Social Media has changed this data landscape fundamentally. Today, for every major public event, thousands if not millions of tweets, blog or forum posts are available online and often

---

[1] These files are available on: http://www.uni-goettingen.de/en/482273.html.

can be accessed through an Application Programming Interface (API) in real time to those willing to pay for the privilege. Due to this exponential increase in available data, sentiment analysis—yesterday's scientific curiosity—has become a necessity for businesses and the politically ambitious alike. The task of automated sentiment extraction from texts is not a trivial one, even if digital texts are as freely available as they are today. This is due to the fact, that unlike human readers, automated classification systems are not able to detect the subtleties of human communication by default. In example, while the sentence "I love chocolate" will easily lend itself to analysis, another example such as "Don't I just love politicians, they are all so honest!" obviously poses a number of challenges. In fact, the second example contains three major challenges to sentiment analysis; sarcasm (irony), negation and the use of sentiment words to express the opposite of their expected sentiment. A fourth such challenge is identified by Liu, who notes that superficially objective sentences, such as "My car's motor stopped working a week after I bought it", carry a sentiment that, while being obvious to a human reader, will be virtually undetectable through a pattern based analysis [2]. Another especially difficult problem is the use of the rrealis [15], e.g. "Had Rome not fallen, we might all be called Julius". While the use of a single grammatical phenomenon, such as the irrealis, might not seem problematic since the usage of the construct is relatively rare, these challenges to sentiment analysis have to be considered as a whole, as errors due to them will accumulate and skew the results of the analysis. While there are a number of publications on each of those specific problems, here the focus will remain on sentiment analysis in general. Still, the addition of mechanisms that deal with these problems would constitute worthwhile extensions to the processes described later on. Meanwhile, a possible way to mitigate such problems would be to analyze texts that are assumed to contain sentiment but employ factual language, such as governmental press releases.

2.1   Two Approaches to Sentiment Analysis

There are two popular approaches to sentiment analysis. One is to treat the analysis as a classification problem and use supervised or unsupervised learning methods to cluster texts, sentences or individual words into categories (e.g. positive and negative), while the other is to use sentiment lexica containing the semantic orientation of a given set of words [16]. Both approaches have a number of advantages and disadvantages and have been the subject of a variety of research, both for dictionary-based methods [17, 18] and machine learning based approaches [19, 20]. One major difference between the methods is portability, i.e. the ability to use a method established in one domain on text in another. While it is almost pointless to try to use the result of supervised learning outside of the domain used to train the classification algorithm [16], it is intuitive that the words contained in sentiment lexica will carry most of their semantic orientation across domains (and perhaps more importantly the orientation will seldom change to its opposite). Still, a dictionary intended for cross-domain use cannot be expected to perform as well as a domain-specific one because the choice of words that express a particular sentiment differs greatly from domain to domain. In example, a positive movie review might use words like "entertaining" or "stunning", while a positive analyst report regarding a company's financial performance might contain words like "continuity" or "increase". Thus, specialized dictionaries are, of course, ideal and are a core-requirement whenever a high scoring accuracy is desired. Another disadvantage of supervised learning approaches is their reliance on frequentist properties of the data. Frequentist properties denote properties related to the field of frequentist statistics, which focuses on relative frequencies [21]. For an introduction to such properties see Held or Mayo and Cox [22, 23]. In example, if a given corpus of reviews contains only one case of each positive and negative attribute expressed by the reviewers, there will be no statistical pattern to discern and the machine learning (ML) approach will fail. A similar argument can be made for Bayesian approaches. In either case, the models rely on a statistically discernable difference between the groups or categories of texts. A dictionary might still contain a large part of these attributes [16]. On the other hand, machine learning based classification can assign texts to categories, which are not "identical" to the training data used to create the classifier, while dictionary based scoring requires an absolute matching of terms. In a sense ML based methods capture the latent sentiment of words via their relation to one another, while dictionary based approaches rely on explicit mappings to categories. It is also important to remember that these two approaches are by no means mutually exclusive. Hybrid approaches have been successfully employed to combine the portability of dictionary-based approaches with some automation [16]. Examples include Read and Carroll, as well as Li et al. [24, 25]. Indeed, such a combined method is the basis for the HSentiR framework introduced here. Liu differentiates between three types of sentiment dictionaries [2]. At first, sentiment dictionaries were created manually, which of course takes time and cannot be done on a project specific basis [2]. The second approach is to create sentiment dictionaries from normal dictionaries and is called "The Dictionary based Approach" by Liu [2]. This approach will be used in the work at hand. When talking about it, it is important to remember that according to Liu the name refers to the (general) dictionaries used to create the sentiment dictionary, and not the newly created lists of sentiment words that will be called sentiment dictionaries. Since all dictionaries used in the paper will fit this description, here "dictionary-based" will simply refer to sentiment analysis using a dictionary instead of a machine learning approach. A third approach described by Liu is to create the sentiment dictionary-based on a specific corpus. This approach, while being attractive due to the perspective of creating a sentiment dictionary that is corpus specific, requires large corpora to function properly [2]. Any dictionary-driven content analysis approach is "[...] done on a hit-or-miss basis" [26]. Either the sentiment vocabulary used in the studied corpus is contained in the dictionary or it is not. Thus, a dictionary suited to the domain of interest could not be more critical to a study's success. Consequently, many different dictionaries have been developed since the early days of computer-aided content analysis. As there now are a great number of different dictionaries available from various publications, the following section will be restrained to giving an overview of possible ways to create dictionaries and listing some of the most commonly used in secondary research, thus being by no means comprehensive. The basic assumption made when using such dictionaries is that the words contained therein have a prior polarity [27], e.g. the word "good", when considered without context, will be perceived as positive by most people. This prior polarity is used to assign words to a sentiment category. Of course, a word's prior polarity will not always coincide with its contextual polarity, e.g. "fast" might be contained as a positive word in a dictionary for the automobile domain and a text might contain the phrase "it broke fast". Where such violations of the assumption occur, they introduce a bias to the analysis. Muhammad et al. propose a distant-supervision approach to generate domain specific dictionaries that mitigates this bias [3]. Such a method might be a prudent addition to dictionary bootstrapping techniques. Stone et al. pioneered the dictionary-driven approach and the work they started has been continually improved ever since [28]. The dictionary-based content analysis tool they created is commonly referred to as The General Inquirer (GI) and performs a variety of tasks from corpus pre-processing to result summarization [28]. The original goals of this tool are still relevant today. It was created to provide a possibility to operationalize theory, enable researchers to use a comparable and reproducible procedure and reduce the manual work required for content analysis [28]. For the purposes of this text, GI is considered mainly for its dictionary. For a more detailed description including the corpus pre-processing techniques and tagging procedures used by GI in its original version see [28]. Today, GIs dictionary has been extended to encompass a total of 175 categories and includes both The Harvard IV-4 categories (IV-4) and The Lasswell dictionary (Lasswell). The first two categories contained in the dictionary are positive and negative words with 1915 and 2291 entries respectively. For both types of sentiment classification, texts are commonly aggregated in a data-structure referred to as a corpus [29]. In addition to the texts themselves, this corpus can also contain metadata, such as authors, geo-locations or the time a certain text was created.

2.2   Requirements Facing a Sentiment-Classification Framework

As noted in the last section, both dictionary-based and machine learning based sentiment classification methods have a number of disadvantages. Therefore, combined methods are desirable because they can mitigate these disadvantages. What are the key issues researchers face when working with sentiment classification systems? When working with different solutions, data-formats can make it difficult to use the output of one tool as the basis for further analysis. In addition, most methods described in the literature are simply not available for research-use. When tools are available, they are generally not intended for hybrid use. Based upon these practical concerns, what requirements should a good framework for sentiment classification meet? First, it should be integrated into the research-workflow. This requirement can help to reduce the need for data-transformation and re-entry, thus reducing the likelihood of errors during these tasks. Due to the diversity of available statistics packages covering these and many other fields of interest, R offers a wide user base already familiar with a powerful statistical toolset and programming language. Furthermore, these existing packages can be used to perform the entire content analysis process, from data import to the statistical examination of the results, within one application framework. In addition, the framework should be modular, in order to allow researchers to use project-specific methods. This is a key requirement for research-purposes because only by allowing for the adoption of novel-methods, new knowledge can be incorporated in future research. In addition, ideally, the framework should be open and reproducible because "black-box" methods are undesirable in practical research. Most of all, the framework should be easy to use. Ideally, researchers would always use the most accurate classification solution, which reflects the latest advances in Sentiment Analysis. However, due to factors like time constraints and familiarity with certain software implementations, the best solution will not prevail if it is hard to use. Thus, ease of use and proper documentation are key features of content analysis software. Finally, the framework should provide the needed facilities needed in order to create reproducible research. While graphical user interfaces may be more intuitive for beginners, researchers have a need for script-based input formats because such scripts can easily be shared with reviewers and the public.

3   HSentiR: A Hybrid Sentiment Analysis Framework

Here, a two-staged hybrid framework for sentiment analysis using R is presented. Figure 1 shows a simplified illustration of the process.

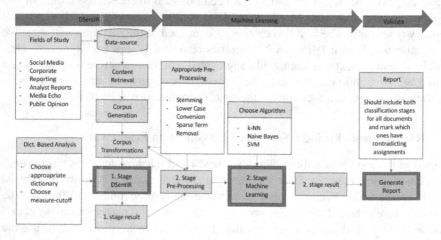

Fig. 1. The HSentiR Framework (Hybrid Sentiment Analysis in R)

The analysis process begins by importing text-data from a data source into R. Due to the large number of available R packages for such tasks, many APIs (e.g. Twitter) can be directly accessed for this purpose. Of course, data-import from a variety of file formats is also possible "out of the box". In order to be able to work with large amounts of text, a standardized storage format needs to be chosen. Such collections of text are commonly referred to as Corpora [29]. Here, due to the mutually exclusive needs of the two classification methods used throughout HSentiR, two storage formats are used. The dictionary-based classification uses a list-structure, which allows for corpus-wide transformations and cleanup tasks while retaining the input data in its original form. The machine learning stage utilizes the corpus class of the tm package available on the Comprehensive R Archive Network (CRAN). Note that the tm package also includes a variety of other text mining related tools, as well as pre-processing capabilities, such as stemming and the creation of term-document-matrices (TDM), which are a convenient basis for machine learning based analysis in R. This twofold storage structure enables custom pre-processing for the two stages of the analysis. Indeed, this possibility is needed because the pre-processing needs of the two stages are mutually exclusive. Pre-processing for a dictionary-based analysis should aim to increase the matching probability between the dictionary and the corpus, while machine learning based classification benefits from pre-processing tasks like sparse term removal, which would decrease matching probability with the dictionary. In the subsequent subsections, the two stages of the HSentiR framework will be described in more detail, before putting the framework to the test using movie-review data [8].

Step1: DSentiR – Dictionary Based Scoring

As shown in Figure 1, the dictionary based scoring phase of the process generates the training data for stage 2. Figure 2 gives a more detailed overview of the dictionary based classification process this stage of the HSentiR process.

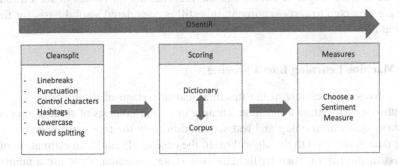

Fig. 2. The dictionary based stage of HSentiR: DSentiR

As the figure illustrates, the cleansplit function provided by the DSentiR package covers a number of common pre-processing tasks, such as removing characters from that data that might hinder the matching of words with the sentiment dictionary and splitting texts into individual words. This function is easily expandable using custom Regular-Expression (Regex) patterns and is therefore easily adapted to domain-specific pre-processing needs. Processing a text with this function results in a vector consisting of individual words. Afterwards, the scoring function is used to match this word-vector with the sentiment dictionary. The function returns the match-count between the dictionary and the supplied text. Optionally, the function can also return the matched words themselves if a "sanity check" is desired. Finally, the match counts are handed over to a function containing the chosen sentiment measures, which determine the classification of each text based on the scores. As is, the *sentiment.measures* function outputs the proportion of positive matches in relation to the total match-count as the default measure:

$$score = \frac{pos-neg}{pos+neg} \tag{1}$$

It is assumed that if this percentage exceeds 50 a text is of positive sentiment. Indeed, this intuitive cut-off value is very near to the empirical optimum determined in the validation section of this paper. Apart from this pos.-percentage measure the function is also able to return polarity (centered around 0). Furthermore, the function is easily adaptable to other measures should those be desired instead of the already available implementations. Finally, each document is assigned a sentiment category (e.g. positive or negative) based on the chosen sentiment measure. If a corpus is expected to contain neutral documents, adding a "dead zone" to the measure might be desirable. Consequently, the output of the first stage of HSentiR consists of category assignments for all documents, which contained at least one word present in the sentiment dictionary. Of course, the percentage of documents assigned a score using this method is a function of document length. However, the movie review corpus used to assess the method shows that for medium length documents, all texts were assigned a score. This can not be expected to be the case for shorter documents. In example, in a corpus of 7,000 tweets with hashtag "#google", 51% were assigned a score. Factoring in both the limited length of tweets and the fact that not all tweets in such a random sample are expected to carry sentiment, this still is considered a solid basis for further classification.

Step2: Machine Learning Based Scoring

Figure 3 gives an overview of the machine learning stage of the process. Typically, the input required to train a machine learning classifier consists of three components. The data is split into training and test sets, additionally the true classifications of the training data is supplied to the algorithm. In the case of HSentiR, an estimation of this true classification is supplied by the DSentiR stage. As noted, there are a number of different algorithms, such as naïve Bayes, k-NN or SVMs, which are known to perform well in text classification tasks. All of these (and more) are already available as R packages and can be utilized with the training data resulting from DSentiR. Choosing a suitable classifier for a given domain is not a trivial task and involves trial and error, i.e. trying a number of different algorithms on a given corpus. Thus, this flexibility is a prerequisite for domain-portability.

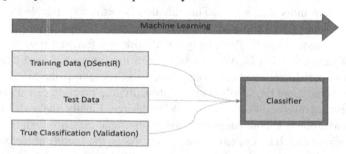

Fig. 3. The machine learning stage of HSentiR

4   Framework Evaluation

In this section, the HSentiR framework will be applied to a corpus of 2,000 movie reviews provided by the well-established movie review corpus 2.0, which has been the basis for over a hundred analyses to this date [8]. This corpus has been the subject of this many studies due to the fact that is has been manually pre-categorized, allowing for reliable process assessment and reliable comparison of different methods. The evaluation consists of three different assessments. First, the dictionary based scoring phase alone will be applied to the corpus, in order to provide an overview of the abilities and limits of this basic scoring method. Consequently, a k-NN classifier will be introduced and trained using the true (true label) training data given by the pre-classified movie-review data. This provides a baseline to compete against for another run of k-NN training using the DSentiR result as training data (estimated label), allowing for a comparison of accuracy within the movie-review domain. As previously discussed, using a domain-appropriate sentiment dictionary is key to dictionary based sentiment classification accuracy. Thus, in this section, different dictionaries will be used to score the documents contained in the movie-review corpus. It is expected that scoring-accuracy varies depending on the used dictionary. In particular, three dictionaries are used:

1: The positive and negative word categories from the current version of the General Inquirer (GI) dictionary [28], as available from the GI-Homepage.
2: The AFINN dictionary, created by [30] for use with form 10-K annual reports, which give an overview of a company's financial situation and its business(domain-inappropriate for movie-reviews).
3: The current version of the dictionary introduced by [31].

As the AFINN dictionary was created for the financial domain, it serves as an example of choosing the wrong dictionary. This should lead to a significant loss of scoring accuracy. The following table shows the classification accuracy for all three dictionary, for both positive and negative reviews, as well as the average across both categories.

Table 1. Percentages of correct sentiment classification within Movie-Review Data

	Positive	Negative	Average
Liu	59.5	77.2	68.35
AFINN	28.6	83.3	55.95
GI	70.2	50.5	60.35

Indeed, the AFINN dictionary results in 5-13% loss of average accuracy. Therefore, choosing the right dictionary for the domain is imperative. The GI has the highest success rate for positive reviews but hardly beats a coin flip for negative ones. Finally, the Liu dictionary seems to be most consistent for this dataset with 68.35% average accuracy. As mentioned before, these results are for positivity with 50% as cut-off value. Although cutting at this threshold seems intuitive, the reasoning behind this value is worth a closer look, as it might not be optimal. How does the cut-off value affect correct scoring in both negative and positive reviews? To answer this question, the percentages of correct scoring are calculated in 0.5% steps for cut-offs ranging from 0.05 to 1, which results in a 200-step distribution of results.

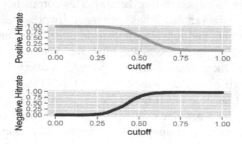

Fig. 4. Distributions of correct scoring for cut-offs 2 (0; 1], 200 steps for positive (upper) and negative (lower) reviews

As expected, all reviews are scored positive for cut-offs near zero and all negative for those near 1. More importantly, both distributions are symmetrical. While the distribution for positive reviews is centered on a value slightly higher than 0.5, the negative case is centered around a value smaller than 0.5. This should balance in the mean of both cases and allow 0.5 to serve as a reasonable cut-off. Figure 5 shows the mean of simultaneous correct scoring for both positive and negative reviews. The maximum of simultaneous correct scoring for both categories is close to 0.5. To be exact, it is found at the cut-off value 50.5% with 70.6% correct scorings, thus providing a 2.25% improvement over the original average.

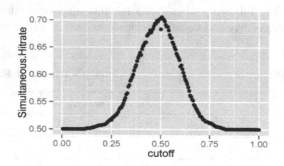

Fig. 5. Distribution of simultaneously correct scores

While this result should not be considered a general truth, it seems that at least in this dataset, positive reviews contain about as many positive matches with the dictionary as negative reviews contain negative matches. Whether this is due to good balancing in the Liu dictionary or a natural property of the dataset would be another interesting question for future research. Of course, such an analysis is only possible with pre-labeled data, which is generally not available when sentiment analysis is desired. However, the example shows that the proposed classification method works and offers up to 70% accuracy, even though the dictionaries were not specifically intended for use in the domain. Next, the accuracy of a k-NN classifier using the pre-determined classification of the movie-review dataset is assessed, in order to provide a baseline for the combined scoring approach of HSentiR. The k-NN classifier is only one of the possible classifiers available through various R-packages. Other options include SVMs or advanced methods like string-kernels [29]. A domain-appropriate classifier has to be chosen on a trial and error basis using the data in question. The "class" R-package provides the k-NN implementation used here. Pre-processing in this case includes the removal of all punctuation, white space, lower case conversion, as well as the removal of stop-words. Also, those words in the term-document-matrix, which occur not at least in half the documents are removed (sparseness factor 50%). A random sample of 70% of the data is used to determine the training data for the algorithm. The remaining 30% are used for validation. The table 2 shows the confusion matrix resulting from the process.

Table 2. Confusion Matrix for k-NN classification (true labels)

	Actual	
Prediction	Negative	Positive
Negative	288	69
Positive	21	222

Based on this confusion matrix, the overall accuracy of the k-NN classifier, trained with the actual categories of the data (true label), can be calculated as 85%. Although this scoring accuracy could certainly be improved by using alternate algorithms or fine-tuning of the input-parameters, it is sufficient to act as a benchmark for the hybrid approach, using the same parameterization. In addition, it is important to remember that this real label information would usually not be available in practical research, which is why hybrid approaches, such as the one introduced by the HSentiR framework, are needed in praxis. Using the estimated sentiment-classification, resulting from the DSentiR stage of the process, the same process as before is repeated, yielding the results portrayed in table 2.

Table 3. Confusion Matrix for k-NN (estimated labels)

	Actual	
Prediction	Negative	Positive
Negative	249	123
Positive	66	162

As the new confusion matrix illustrates, the accuracy drops to 68.5% using the esti-mated label information instead of the true label. Note that, due to the random sam-pling of the training and prediction cases, the accuracy varies between runs of the model. However, it is reasonably stable on a level comparable to the accuracy of the DSentiR stage. This raises the question of the benefit of the machine learning stage of the process. As described earlier, the machine learning stage allows to classify docu-ments not containing words included in the sentiment dictionary. The answer to this question also has to be answered on a project specific basis, depending on factors, such as the number of documents and their individual length. When very large corpora are analyzed, using the DSentiR stage on a subsample to create training data is computa-tionally preferable, while small corpora can be analyzed entirely using dictionary based scoring. Compared to the k-NN model trained with the real label information, 16.5% accuracy were lost by the label-estimation. Of course, if this is a reasonable price to pay for not having to manually create the training data, is project specific. While it is feasible to create training data manually in datasets like the movie-review example (n=2,000), larger corpora require an automated approach to the problem, like DSentiR. In addition, the k-NN method allows for the classification of documents that do not contain words included in the sentiment dictionary but are otherwise similar to those which do. Due to its modular nature, the HSentiR framework can be applied to both cases. In addition, the increase in scoring accuracy has to be determined on a corpus-specific level and different machine-learning algorithms, such as naïve Bayes or SVMs may increase accuracy even more. Since the goal of this research is to establish a framework for such optimizations, this will not be investigated here because there is no general answer to the question of the most suitable classifier.

5   Conclusions and Outlook

The goal of this research was to create an open, hybrid and domain-portable approach for sentiment classification that meets the requirements of domain-portability and public accessibility, while limiting the level of complexity in order to enable a large amount of users to make use of the process. The evaluation of the two stages of HSen-tiR shows that the dictionary based stage (DSentiR) performs well if an appropriate sentiment-dictionary is used. This confirms that dictionary based sentiment classifica-tion is only as good as the dictionary used to score the texts. The movie-review exam-ple shows that a k-NN classifier, when trained with the true classifications of the data, achieves ~85% accuracy in this domain. When using the estimated classifications from DSentiR, the accuracy drops to ~68%. Of course, this level of accuracy leaves room for further process refinements. These can be achieved in three key areas. First, the scoring accuracy of the DSentiR stage should be optimized. There are three possi-ble ways to expand upon the proposed techniques. First, the existing functionality could be made more performant, thus enabling usage on larger data quantities. There are several possible ways to achieve this goal. First, the code could be revised with the goal of vectorization. However, most of the functions used here already comply with this paradigm of R performance. Another way to improve performance could be making use of the existing interfaces between R and other programming languages, such as C++ (rccp) or the C interface that is part of the R-core. Especially the substitution tasks in the cleansplit function could benefit from implementation in those languages. A third possible way to optimize performance is making use of the compiler package and its Just In Time Compiler (JIT), which does not require code revision. The second possible addition to the proposed techniques is extending the existing process to address more of the specific challenges that sentiment analysis faces. An obvious addition would be to make use of the sentiment strength scores available in some sentiment dictionaries. In addition, the pre-processing techniques employed by the cleansplit function could be improved, in example by including a spell-checking and stemming stage to improve the chances of matching a word with the dictionary. Furthermore, the introduction of word sense disambiguation could improve result accuracy. Furthermore, automated translation of corpora and dictionaries could enable cross-language use of the process. Finally, the need for domain-specific dictionaries remains an issue. One approach to solving this problem is using a digital dictionary like WordNet [32] to bootstrap a dictionary for each dataset, using some of the domains most prominent sentiment-laden terms as seeds. Such bootstrapping approaches have been shown to effective [33] and a WordNet interface for R is already available. Apart from achieving scoring-accuracy, this research intended to create a reproducible and open framework for sentiment analysis, which enables researchers to produce peer-reviewable results. The HSentiR process relies on simple R-scripts, which can be shared with both reviewers and the public, ideally making the reproduction of results as easy as pressing as pressing a button. This combination of openness of method and ease of producing results for validation can help the scientific community to build public trust in empirical research. Furthermore, public validation of results can help researchers to correct mistakes, thus improving the quality of future publications. It is with these goals in mind, that the use of methods, such as the HSentiR framework, should be encouraged.

References

1. Speed, J.G.: Do Newspapers now give the News? Forum Fam Plan West Hemisph 15, 704–711 (1893)
2. Liu, B.: Sentiment analysis and opinion mining. Synth. Lect. Hum. Lang. Technol. 5, 1–167 (2012)
3. Muhammad, A., Wiratunga, N., Lothian, R., Glassey, R.: Domain-Based Lexicon Enhancement for Sentiment Analysis. In: BCS SGAI SMA 2013 BCS SGAI Work. Soc. Media Anal., pp. 7–18 (2013)
4. Aue, A., Gamon, M.: Customizing Sentiment Classifiers to New Domains: a Case Study. In: Proc. Recent Adv. Nat. Lang. Process RANLP, vol. 49, pp. 207–218 (2005), doi:10.1111/j.1745-3992.1984.tb00758.x
5. Prabowo, R., Thelwall, M.: Sentiment analysis: A combined approach. J. Informetr. 3, 143–157 (2009), doi: 10.1016/j.joi, 01.003
6. Gentleman, R., Temple Lang, D.: Statistical Analyses and Reproducible Research. J. Comput. Graph Stat. 16, 1–23 (2007), doi:10.1198/106186007X178663

7. Peng, R.D.: Reproducible Research in Computational Science. Science 334, 1226–1227 (2011), doi:10.1126/science.1213847
8. Pang, B., Lee, L.: A sentimental education: Sentiment analysis using subjectivity summarization based on minimum cuts. In: Proc. 42nd Annu. Meet. Assoc. Comput. Linguist., p. 271 (2004)
9. Blair-Goldensohn, S., Hannan, K., McDonald, R., et al.: Building a sentiment summarizer for local service reviews. WWW Work. NLP Inf. Explos. Era (2008)
10. Arnold, I.J.M., Vrugt, E.B., Arnold Ivo, J.M., Vrugt Evert, B.: Fundamental uncertainty and stock market volatility. Appl. Financ. Econ. 18, 1425–1440 (2008), doi:10.1080/09603100701857922.
11. Zhang, X., Fuehres, H., Gloor, P.A.: Predicting stock market indicators through twitter "I hope it is not as bad as I fear". Procedia-Social Behav. Sci. 26, 55–62 (2011)
12. Kennedy, A., Inkpen, D.: Sentiment classification of movie reviews using contextual valence shifters. Comput. Intell. 22, 110–125 (2006)
13. Baron, D.P.: Competing for the public through the news media. J. Econ. Manag. Strateg. 14, 339–376 (2005), doi:10.1111/j.1530-9134.2005.00044.x
14. Ludvigson, S.C.: Consumer confidence and consumer spending. J. Econ. Perspect. 18, 29–50 (2004)
15. Steele, S.: Past and irrealis: just what does it all mean? Int. J. Am Linguist. 41, 200–217 (1975)
16. Taboada, M., Brooke, J., Tofiloski, M., et al.: Lexicon-based methods for sentiment analysis. Comput. Linguist. 37, 267–307 (2011)
17. Hatzivassiloglou, V., McKeown Kathleen, R.: Predicting the semantic orientation of adjectives. In: Proc. 35th Annu. Meet. Assoc. Comput. Linguist. Eighth Conf. Eur. Chapter Assoc. Comput. Linguist., pp. 174–181 (1997)
18. Turney, P.D., Littman, M.L.: Measuring praise and criticism: Inference of semantic orientation from association. ACM Trans. Inf. Syst. 21, 315–346 (2003)
19. Pang, B., Lee, L., Rd, H., et al.: Thumbs up?: sentiment classification using machine learning techniques. In: Proc. ACL 2002 Conf. Empir. Methods Nat. Lang. Process., vol. 10, pp. 79–86 (2002)
20. Salvetti, F., Reichenbach, C., Lewis, S.: Opinion polarity identification of movie reviews. In: Comput. Attitude Affect Text Theory Appl., pp. 303–316. Springer (2006)
21. Everitt, B.S.: The Cambridge Dictionary of Statistics, 2nd edn. Cambridge University Press, Cambridge (2002)
22. Held, L.: Methoden der statistischen Inferenz. Likelihood und Bayes. Heidelb. Spektrum Akad. Verl. (2008)
23. Mayo Deborah, G., Cox David, R.: Frequentist statistics as a theory of inductive inference. Lect. Notes-Monograph Ser. 77–97 (2006)
24. Read, J., Carroll, J.: Weakly supervised techniques for domain-independent sentiment classification. In: Proc. 1st Int. CIKM Work. Top. Anal. Mass Opin., pp. 45–52 (2009)
25. Li, S., Huang, C.-R., Zhou, G., Lee, S.Y.M.: Employing personal/impersonal views in supervised and semi-supervised sentiment classification. In: Proc. 48th Annu. Meet. Assoc. Comput. Linguist., pp. 414–423 (2010)
26. Berelson, B.: Content analysis in communication research. Society 44, 220 (1952), doi:10.1086/617924
27. Wilson, T., Wiebe, J., Hoffmann, P.: Recognizing contextual polarity in phrase-level sentiment analysis. In: Proc. Conf. Hum. Lang. Technol. Empir. Methods Nat. Lang. Process., pp. 347–354 (2005)

28. Stone, P.J., Dunphy, D.C., Smith, M.S., Ogilive, D.M.: The General Inquirer. The M.I.T. Press, Cambridge (1966)
29. Feinerer, I., Hornik, K., Meyer, D.: Text Mining Infrastructure in R. J. Stat. Softw. 25, 1–54 (2008), doi: citeulike-article-id:2842334
30. Loughran, T., McDonald, B.: When is a liability not a liability? Textual analysis, dictionaries, and 10-Ks. J. Finance 66, 35–65 (2011)
31. Hu, M., Liu, B.: Mining and summarizing customer reviews. In: Proc. tenth ACM SIGKDD Int. Conf. Knowl. Discov. Data Min., pp. 168–177 (2004)
32. Miller, G.A.: WordNet: a lexical database for English. Commun. ACM 38, 39–41 (1995)
33. Baccianella, S., Esuli, A., Sebastiani, F.: SENTIWORDNET 3.0: An Enhanced Lexical Resource for Sentiment Analysis and Opinion Mining. In: Proc. Lr. Seventh Int. Conf. Lang. Resour. Eval., pp. 2200–2204 (2008)

Improving Customer Centric Design for Self-service Predictive Analytics

Colm Thornton and Brian O' Flaherty[(⊠)]

Business Information Systems Dept, University College Cork, Corcaigh, Ireland
thornton.colm@gmail.com, BOFlaherty@afis.ucc.ie

Abstract. Customer-centric design is critical to the success of delivering Predictive Analytics (PA) as a Self-Service Technology (SST), yet efforts to date have focused upon the related technical challenges. This research turns to the multidisciplinary field of Service Design to address this where its centerpiece Service Blueprint (SB) method has the potential to support such customer-centric design. However the fields' long-standing emphasis on traditional high-touch low-tech services limits its utility for the design of SSTs. This research adopts a Design Science approach to improve upon the SB to offer a more complete solution beyond these traditional boundaries. As output, a new multi-model is proposed with an enhanced SB at its center, enabling design practitioners to rise to the challenges of these technology-enabled services. Besides providing the necessary customer-focused design for PA SSTs, the research contributes to the development of a more holistic approach to the broader practice of Service Design.

Keywords: Service Blueprint · Self-Service Technology · Predictive Analytics · Service Design · Service Science · Design Science

1 Introduction

The importance of services within the global economy is widely recognised with long-standing trends of their increasing dominance and forecasts which only see point towards their continued growth [1, 2]. The convergence of two recent technologies, cloud computing and software-as-a-service, is giving rise to an innovative new class of service within the analytics domain referred to as Predictive Analytics as a self-Service (PAaaS) [3, 4]. Generally speaking, Predictive Analytics (PA) is the application of statistical models and analysis drawing upon existing and/or simulated future data in the provision of actionable insights for real-world problems [5]. A Self Service Technology (SST) is then any technology-enabled service which enables the user to avail of a service independent of direct service employee involvement [6]. The delivery of PA in this way offers such insights on a pay-per-user on-demand self-service basis allowing organisations which do not have the necessary infrastructure or expertise to exploit their potential benefits. The challenges in realising such a service are both broad and varied [7] with much of efforts to date having focused on the technical design [4 , 8]. Yet this technical focus threatens to neglect the user's perspective

B. Donnellan et al. (Eds.): DESRIST 2015, LNCS 9073, pp. 230–245, 2015.
DOI: 10.1007/978-3-319-18714-3_15

during design, which represents one of the key success determinants for any Self-Service Technology (SST) [9, 10]. As such, this research turns to the multidisciplinary field of Service Design to offer a customer-centric approach to the design of PAaaS.

2   Literature Review

Service Design is a multidisciplinary design field which sits at the intersection of service strategy, innovation and implementation [2, 11, 12]. It seeks to design service processes, interactions, features, systems and strategies in an orchestrated manner, where the principal objective is to offer superior customer experience and differentiate from service competitors [2, 12-16]. In spite of its steadfast customer focus and a myriad of tools and methods however, there is increasing recognition that it has failed to keep pace with the technology-driven evolution of services [2, 17, 18].

For Self-Service Technologies (SSTs) as well as many other services, technology and information systems have become essential foundations giving rise to conflicting design perspectives. This can give rise to service designers complaining that developers build systems which constrain their ability to deliver what the customer wants. Similarly developers may encounter difficulties where designers propose service aspects which the back-end system can't support [19]. A unified design perspective is needed which addresses the trade-offs and potential conflicts from both sides of the screen: where developers better understand customer needs and designers better appreciate the constraints, as well as the opportunities, of the underlying technology [1, 20, 21]. Yet the legacy of Service Design remains rooted in the traditional high-touch low-tech services where the focus largely remains on design of the service front stage, i.e. the service interface and corresponding interactions between service user and provider with some expansion to the surrounding context of a socio-material system [15, 22] in neglect of the corresponding back stage elements.

In fact amongst all the Service Design methods, the only exception to this is the Service Blueprint (SB) which offers a customer-focused process-orientated visualisation of service delivery [23, 24]. Along the horizontal axis, it represents the chronology of actions conducted during its delivery. Along the vertical axis, this is decomposed into five different rows or swimlanes: the Physical Evidence, i.e. what the customer sees, the Customer Actions, the On-Stage Employee Actions, the Back-Stage Employee Actions and Support Processes undertaken by non-contact employees. The SB has become fundamental to the practise of Service Design [25] and the literature refers to its use and adaptation in support of designing the service processes, customer experience, provider organisation and overarching strategy [23, 24, 26-30]. As the swimlane names may suggest however, the SB has predominantly only been applied to high-touch low-tech services where the technological dimension of design has been neglected [21, 31]. Furthermore, in spite of its potential, these previous explorations have focused upon the front stage design, discounting the importance of back stage service elements. This reflects a central shortcoming of traditional design understanding where service quality was commonly viewed as something which occurred at the service interface rather than determined by the entire service system and simply manifested there [19].

A more holistic approach is beginning to emerge within the broader context of Service Science. This global initiative spans academia, industry and government in seeking to unite the entire spectrum of service-related fields and is underpinned by a view of services as complex configurations of people, technology and other resources in the co-creation of value [1, 2, 32-34]. This has led to the development of the Service Experience Blueprint (SEB) method within Service Design in the first concrete step towards addressing the challenges of technology-enabled service innovations. It extended the design scope beyond the traditional single interface focus to allow for integrated customer experience design across multiple channels, where the traditional brick-and-mortar interface is complemented by SSTs such as on-line stores or telephone interfaces [9, 18, 21]. In doing so, it also explicitly incorporated technology actions in addition to human actions to the traditional SB format. In spite of this, the SEB remains focused on design of the front stage experience with minimal representation of the back stage technology.

Further efforts to advance Service Design under the umbrella of Service Science exhibit the same shortcoming. One of the most noteworthy examples, the Multi-level Service Design (MSD) method extends the traditional design scope upwards across three hierarchal levels [17]: the service concept: the benefits the service offers to its customer positioned with the value constellation [35]; the service system in accordance with the above definition [34]: and the service encounter: aligned with the historical design focus of the interactions setting and process. However whilst it offers an integrated view of a service across each of these levels, it propagates a neglect of the back stage design through incorporation of the SEB at the foundational service encounter level. Other research efforts such as Customer Experience Modelling have also explicitly focused on offering a more holistic view of the front stage experience [16, 36]. In fact, many of the concerns expressed in relation to the traditional SB remain unaddressed. These include the apparent restriction to represent only basic service systems [25-27, 31] as well as its application to isolated areas of improvement for existing services rather than the design of new more complex systems [37].

This paper argues therefore that Service Design is lacking a comprehensive and robust method enabling the integrated design across complex front-stage back-stage service system. In the case of PAaaS, the need for such a method to allow a unified design perspective is considered even more critical where in addition to collaboration between service designers and developers, the perspective of the analytics expert must also be incorporated. The objective of this exploratory research is therefore to **explore the use of the Service Blueprint to support the integrated design of a Self-Service Technology in Predictive Analytics**. This aligns with the call for its creative expansion within Service Science [2] as well as the many calls to extend upon its representation for all but the most basic of service delivery processes [25, 27, 31, 37].

3   Research Methodology

This research adopted a Design Science research approach where the IT artifact takes the form of a method [38]   to support the integrative design of Self-Service Technology (SST) in Predictive Analytics (PA). As such, the research can be regarded as an exploratory study contributing to the improvement of Service Design knowledge and practice where existing solutions for the design of SSTs are inadequate. The authors were also participants in developing the technology, which implies that this research is participatory in nature and may also be seen as drawing up on an Action Research oriented methodology paradigm [39].

The development of the artifact is informed by both existing literature from Service Design, as well as empirical evaluation from an exploratory case study. The former provides high-level guidance, the latter allows real-world complexities to be appreciated and close observation of the artifact's application in context.

Three research questions are formulated to guide the design and evaluation of the artifact: First, does the SB capture the creators' perception of the front-stage back-stage service system of the SST in PA? Second, does it support the design team in integrated design of the service system? Third, what improvements can be made to better support this? The first two questions address both sides of the coin where conceptual modelling is concerned, regarding both its creation and use, while the third question draws upon both of these to extend the model as necessary.

The selected case study was conducted under a long-standing industrial-academic collaboration partnership between the University College Cork (UCC) and a statistical software company for the development of a SST offering predictions of customer churn to business users. The PA SST was to allow non-expert users to upload historic customer data to a cloud service and generate predictions to identify those customers at greatest risk of ending their subscriptions. It also offered customised interactive visualisations surrounding the corresponding 'loyalty curve' to help define targeted marketing campaigns to increase retention amongst the identified high-risk customer segments. This type of capability empowers key decision makers in churn management, commonly regarded as one of the key application areas of PA [40]. The complexity of the SST delivery spanned several technologies such as C#.NET, SQL Server and IIS for the core information system, Fortran 77 for the analytics algorithms and EXTJS for the visualisations, all encapsulated as a web service. Accordingly, the service design team was a multidisciplinary group of experts spanning commercial, analytical and software development competencies. This team was jointly led by a project director and technical project manager, both of whom were supported by a business analyst, predictive analytics expert as well as a senior and junior software developer. Only the technical project manager had prior experience with the Service Blueprint (SB) model. The work was jointly sponsored by the software company together with the funding organisation as part of an industry innovation programme.

The evaluation was cross-sectional in nature allowing for three different design cycles at different snapshots during the 12 month period from October 2013 to September 2014. This enabled on-going knowledge sharing between the researcher and practitioners where both the evolving nature of the service together with the artifact could be accounted for in the collaborative development of an improved solution.

The artifact evaluation was driven by multiple data collection techniques in the different design cycles offering rich qualitative data. The first research question was addressed using informed argumentation [41], which evaluated the ability of existing methods to capture the needs of service design. The second research question concerning use of the service design model was addressed using focus group discussions with the service design team during the course of the project, together with participative observation by one of the authors. The third research question built upon consolidated observations from informed argumentation, focus groups, and participative observation to identify emerging themes and opportunities for improvement in the service design methods employed.

4   Artifact Description and Evaluation

In accordance with the iterative nature of Design Science, the following sub-sections describe the artifact and its evaluation across each of the three design cycles. Its application in the case study environment serves as illustration of use and proof-of-concept in support of the integrative design of a Self-Service Technology (SST) integrated design in Predictive Analytics (PA). Due to space limitations, the following section documents only the most important observations from the construction and evaluation of the artefact. However these observations are sufficient to demonstrate where the existing Service Blueprint (SB) method falls short and the evidence for proposed improvements.

4.1   First design Cycle

Context and Description. The first design cycle centered upon the launch of the case study project, wherein it was necessary to communicate the starting vision of the service to the newly-formed design team. This was needed to enable an overall project plan to be established identifying key areas for collaboration and allowing individual design activities to commence. To this end, the researcher created the first service design model drawing upon the traditional SB of Bitner, Ostrom [24] with the single modification that it allowed representation of technology actions in addition to human actions as in the more recent Service Experience Blueprint (SEB) method [21].

Evaluation. The SB demonstrated a capability to transform the initial textual service brief into a visual representation of the integrated front-stage back-stage service system. The chronological depiction of service delivery combined with its decomposition across the different 'swimlanes' offered an intuitive means with which to encapsulate the understood vision.

Evaluation via the focus group discussions saw mixed views expressed as to the degree to which the model supported the integrative design of the service system. On the one hand, the SB successfully offered a high-level representation of the service system "*effectively transforming the brief into a tangible vision*" as described by the project director. This instilled a shared mental model and provided a starting platform from which to discuss the design, as well as enabling participants to overcome their individual disciplinary silos and approach design from a unified perspective, i.e. from the service user. Participants described how it offered a "*crystallisation of the customer perspective*" where even the most technically-orientated PA expert and software developers noted how the SB helped maintain basic customer experience design at the forefront of consideration. The evaluation also newly highlighted the particular value of the SB for SST experience design. Its swimlane structure continually enforced conscious design decisions regarding what was made visible to the service user and what was hidden in addition to which actions were automated and which were realised by the user. These respective design concepts of service transparency and empowerment are central to self-service design but particularly so when dealing with the challenges of readily delivering the complexities of PA capabilities for the non-expert business user. On the other hand however, the lack of depth in the model was criticised by the software developers concerned with the technological aspect of design. The lack of process logic detail together with a complete absence of the information view inhibited the start of any development activities. Even basic representation of the user-interface was missing. This impacts both design of the technology solution and the customer experience. More generally, the team recognised that, in spite of its potential, the lack of detail in the SB limited its support for more meaningful multidisciplinary discussions.

Moving forward, two recommendations central to improvement of the SB were identified: First, the adoption of the Business Process Modelling Notation (BPMN) in place of the current free-form notation. This was intended to allow more detailed and complex process flow representation in addition to the introduction of the corresponding information flow. Second, the incorporation of a user interface storyboard in order to represent how the virtual service will look to the user. This was hoped to strengthen design of the customer experience as well as making tangible that which sits at the centre of integrative design between front and back stage.

4.2   Second Design Cycle

Context and Description. The second design cycle was conducted three months later when a more detailed vision for the service was beginning to take shape. Development of the service had not yet commenced, yet the maturing design knowledge presented an opportunity to evaluate the method under increasingly detailed conditions. A second model was created to incorporate feedback from the first iteration and implement the identified improvements (see example in Figure 2 below).

Evaluation. The refined SB model significantly extended the ability to both capture and elaborate a more complex service system design. The advance beyond the traditional format to representation of a technology-enabled service is reflected by the renaming of generic swimlanes to "Physical & Virtual Evidence" and "Support Processes & Systems". The service design storyboard [42] strengthened the link between what is visible and available to the user and the underlying complexity of the service delivery. This allowed a more complete representation via the process logic gateways and information flows enabled by BPMN, meaning greater integration of the customer experience and technology design. It also increases the level of detail in the model as the project progresses, further strengthening its support for integrative design.

Three further improvements of note were identified. The first two were implemented during the course of the model creation. First, a high-level delivery process framework was introduced in the form of the activity vectors located above the swimlane grid. These represent the primary stages in delivery of the PA process, drawing upon accepted PA process models [3, 43, 44], and facilitated the elaboration of an increasingly complex design in a modular fashion. Second, the notion of comment boxes was introduced. These captured identified gaps in the design and highlighted areas for future discussion. Both of these are anticipated to be of increasing benefit

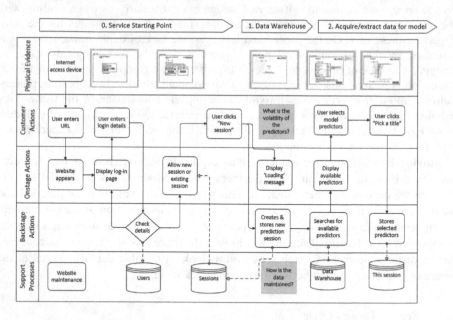

Fig. 1. Iteration 2 -   Improved Service Blueprint

as the SST design evolves. The third improvement, flagged for future evaluation, is the combined use of user personas with the improved SB model. Personas offer a precise description of a service user and what he or she wishes to accomplish [45]. These can offer an explicit representation of the user perspective which should drive detailed elaboration of the SST design.

4.3   Third Design Cycle

Context and Description. The third and final design cycle was conducted following a further four months as part of the projects Critical Design Review (CDR). The purpose of this was to establish a design baseline for a service prototype to be released to the prospective customer organization. Within this context, a further evolution of the design model took place to consolidate recent design team knowledge in respect of the SST and to address the increasing complexity and corresponding challenges. The result was a multi-model, as illustrated in Figure 3 below, comprising of a further enhanced SB, together with service user personas and a newly developed Service Blueprint Overview Map (SBOM) to be discussed below.

Evaluation. As the proposed SST service system became increasingly lucid, the refined SB from previous iterations struggled to capture all of the necessary information. Although the benefits of changes made to date (BPMN notation, interface storyboard, activity vectors, comment boxes, etc.) in the representation and elaboration of the design were re-affirmed, increasing complexity placed additional demands.

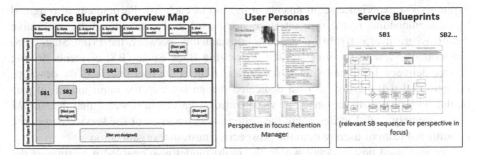

Fig. 2. Iteration 3 - Multi-model

The service now required a multi-provider offering where the data used to generate predictions was managed by a third party provider external to the prospective customer organisation. Further to this, it also evolved to a multi-user offering where different individuals within the organisation would be responsible for prediction data administration, prediction generation and subsequent strategy definition. The Service Blueprint Overview Map (SBOM) was developed in response to these emerging requirements. It allowed representation of the complete design of the service system across an interconnected constellation of SBs spanning the service delivery process within the high-level activity vector framework along the horizontal, as well as the multiple design perspectives of all the key delivery stakeholders along the vertical. The multi-user nature of the service also heightened the need to capture and differentiate between individual service user needs and preferences.

This was reinforced by further evaluation in focus group discussions. The design team regarded this multi-model as a significant improvement upon the traditional SB where it strongly supported the integrative design of the SST as part of the CDR. Central to this, the multi-model was observed to offer a more complete representation of the service. Participants described how for the first time they had an *"end-to-end 360° view"* of the service system where prior to the model design discussions had been fragmented or at best unstructured. The detailed representation offered by the improved SB combined with the top-level view of the SBOM was stated as helping to avoid risks associated with over-simplification or under-estimation of the work involved. This was evident in a number of instances where the model helped reveal the need for additional software modules and user interfaces previously unrecognized.

The new multi-model consolidated existing refinements as well as adding some additional features in support of customer experience design. Introduction of the personas offered an explicit description of the user perspective to be adopted. All participants described how this maintained a unified design perspective for even detailed discussions where a shared vision not just of the service system but of the design rationale behind it was made possible. In particular, the software developers explained how the persona-SB combination helped *"ground design ideas with respect to the service user, ensuring the technology is the means to an end, rather than an end to itself"*. The business analyst did comment however that the personas did sometimes remain disconnected from the SBs. To compensate for this, it was suggested to explicitly list experience requirements at the top of each SB. Participants also agreed that the embedding of the user interface storyboard further facilitated the integrative design where it effectively mandated a constant link between the Front Stage (FS) elements on view to the user and the underlying Back Stage (BS) elements driving service delivery. For a more detailed representation of the user interface, the developers agreed that it merited its own dedicated design layer in the multi-model, in particular with respect to the analytics visualizations. Participants stated that the SBOM was extremely useful in designing the collective experience of the service across the coordinated team of users within the prospective customer organization.

The increased design detail within the multi-model also enabled it to support design of the underlying technology solution and encompassed analytics. The design team described how representation of complex process logic, information flow and datastores allowed *"high-level conversations to take place whilst uncovering implications on software development"*. The model helped developers explain constraints relating to deep structure design elements such as datastores of the underlying database and also facilitated discussions for new design features providing a platform for greater description of what's required. The developers did suggest that a link to Data Flow Diagrams (DFDs) and Entity Relationship Diagrams (ERDs) would further embed use of the model for day-to-day usage.

Overall, the design team attested to the strength of the multi-model in newly supporting collaborative and iterative design efforts. Individuals described how it helped identify and highlight areas of collaboration and impart control over discussions, navigating the breadth and depth of design issues. Where some instances of confusion did occur as to the exact usage situation of use being modelled, it was proposed to explicitly identify and differentiate between different scenarios. Beyond this, the only other major drawback was the absence of software to support update of the multi-model during live discussions.

5   Discussion

5.1   Findings

This research offers several significant findings regarding the use of the Service Blueprint (SB) method for integrated design of a Self-Service Technology (SST) in Predictive Analytics (PA).

With respect to the first research question, it is found that the SB only allows the model creator to capture a high-level understanding of the SST front-stage back-stage service system. On the one hand, the customer-centric swimlane decomposition of the system provides an intuitive tool with which to depict design understanding. This is particularly relevant for self-service PA where it mandates an awareness of the degree of transparency and empowerment designed into the delivery of complex analytical capabilities to a non-expert user. On the other hand, the research underscores a number of shortcomings which limit the practical benefits of this. The absence of a formal notation means that the SB lacks the ability to represent detailed process flows necessary to capture understanding beyond anything but a nascent design vision. The process-orientated format of the SB also fails to address the information-intensive nature of the service where the storage and processing of analytics data, as part of the overall delivery process, are as important as the actions driving it. Similarly the lack of representation of virtual service evidence in complement to the traditional physical evidence, i.e. the user interface, limits the extent to design understanding can be captured. More significant perhaps, is the inherent restriction of the SB to single-user single-provider service systems which is more the exception than the rule in such technology-enabled service innovations. This all has significant implications on its wider use by a design team.

In relation to the second research question then, the SB can offer only limited support to the integrated design of a PA SST service system. The research shows that it can help a design team at the initial stage of a project to transform the starting design vision into something tangible, providing a discussion platform to stimulate design discussions. However this type of high-level representation, which exemplifies existing research efforts, restricts its potential to support the service design in a more meaningful way. First, support to customer experience design is limited to basic agreement of service transparency and empowerment. This is fundamentally affected by the absence of service virtual evidence where it does not depict what the user sees on-screen or how they interact with it. Furthermore, the customer perspective which the SB mandates is difficult to maintain when efforts turn to articulate a more indepth design of the service and underlying analytics. In this situation, the tendency to revert to a technology-driven rather than customer-driven solution dominates. Second, support to technology design is limited to offering developers a broad understanding of the service to be developed. The inability to represent a detailed process flow or the corresponding informational aspects means the SB cannot offer a more detailed conceptual design and in no way contributes to the logical or physical design of the technology solution. For these same reasons, neither can it support the necessary collaboration between developers and analytics experts concerning the detailed steps underlying the predictive analytics or the generation of the corresponding visualisations. Again the absence of the user interface inhibits such integrative design efforts where it is the central element bridging the front and back stage design. Overall, whilst the SB does provide an initial shared mental model for envisioning a SST, its lack of detail undermines its ability to offer any further design support.

In answering the third research question, the research identifies a broad gamut of improvements to address identified shortcomings. Focusing on the SB, the research proposes a number of adaptations significantly improving upon existing efforts. Key changes include: incorporation of Business Process Management Notation (BPMN) to allow representation of complex process and information flows; embedding of a user-interface storyboard to depict the virtual service evidence; introduction of activity vectors to offer a high-level delivery framework; inclusion of comment boxes to capture identified design gaps and flag areas for future work as part of an overall service development roadmap. Furthermore, in what is a significant step towards a holistic service design, the research proposes a multi-model approach to SST design integrating different design perspectives even further with this improved SB situated at its centre as illustrated in Figure 5 below. It explicitly captures the customer perspective to be adopted in design through service user personas. It provides a dedicated design space for the user interface through the designers' storyboard, itself linked to the SB virtual evidence. Notably, the multi-model also includes and consolidates multiple design perspectives for the service system via the Service Blueprint Overview Map (SBOM). It complements the process-orientated view of the SB with the Encounter Information flow (EIF). This is the software development Data Flow Diagram over-laid with the high-level activity representation. The model also explicitly identifies the different scenarios for which the SST is designed. This allows the corresponding different user-provider configurations, interfaces, SBs, etc. to be presented depending upon the specific scenario in focus. Underpinning all this and linked to the depicted SB data stores and information flows, the final model component is the Information System Architecture which represents the structure of the required database. This is the Entity Relationship Diagram from software development and naturally links to the datastores identified in the SB and the information flows but here and the EIF.

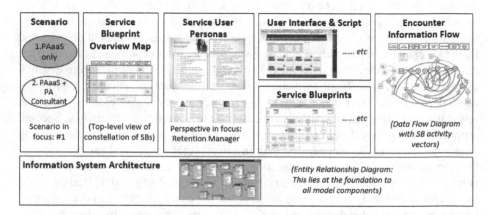

Fig. 3. Final artifact - multi-model

5.2   Theoretical Contributions

To the best of our knowledge, this is the first empirical study which evaluates the use of the Service Blueprint (SB) for the design of a new Self-Service Technology (SST). The vast majority of Service Design literature focuses upon the design of high-touch low-tech services. Several exceptions exist [17, 21], however those studies focus upon front stage design and are restricted to the improvement of existing service offerings. This research provides a number of other theoretical contributions. First, it presents a broader understanding of the service experience concept in reflection of multi-user service. Recent research extended the service experience beyond its singular focus at a single interface to its application across multiple channels [17, 21]. In a similar fash-ion, this research extends the concept from an organisation perspective, bridging across the coordination and/or collaboration of a team of service users. This further embeds the notion of service experience as an emergent property of the service system and, in doing, so opens up a new design space beyond the individual user ex-perience of particular importance to Business-to-Business (B2B) services where the traditional focus has been on Business-to-Consumer (B2C) services [2]. Second, it demonstrates a way in which academically rigorous Service Design research can be conducted using a design science approach. The lack of theoretical foundations within Service Design is widely recognised [15] and Design Science presents a natural means to address this within the field. In particular, it can help address the wicked nature of design where the problem, i.e. the service, to be designed for evolves as the research is conducted. Further, the use of Design Science becomes increasingly attractive where Service Science calls for the integration of language, concepts and models from different disciplines [1, 2] demanding a standardised solution-driven research approach across the research community .

5.3   Practical Implications

The primary contribution of this research lies within a number of significant advancements within the practise of Service Design. First, it has developed and demonstrated a model which can offer a customer-centric design approach whilst simultaneously integrating a technological perspective. This enables integrative design of both front stage and back stage service elements from multiple design perspectives and is a critical enabler for the successful design of technology-enabled innovations such as Predictive Analytics self-services.

Second, reflecting upon its broader utility, the research offers an enhanced Service Blueprint method relevant for the design of many service types (e.g. technology improved person-to-person, multi-channel or multi-provider services) and not just SSTs. The model enables representation of complex service delivery and explicitly addresses the infusion of technology in services. This responds to calls to address the many shortcomings associated with the traditional SB format [25-27, 31, 37] as well as for calls to extend its application to the design of new services rather than simply the improvement of existing services [37]. It builds upon the more recent SEB responding to calls for further research to extend its design focus beyond the front stage experience and explore its use for B2B services [21].

Third, the utility of the research extends even further with respect to the developed multi-model with this enhanced SB at its centre. This offers a comprehensive representation for the above mentioned service types, addressing both the breadth and depth of their complex design in a manner not previously seen. The multi-model helps design complex service delivery processes together with their corresponding information flows in the co-creation of value amongst multi-user/provider value configurations across different service scenarios. This contributes to the advancement of Service Design where the consensus is that it simply has not kept pace with the evolution of services in recent decades [2, 17, 20]. From a Service Science standpoint, it integrates methods from Service Design and software engineering bridging the disciplinary gap offering a platform for collaborative design efforts. This responds to the call for a unified design perspective [1, 2], where Glushko and Tabas [19] in particular emphasise the importance for the development of shared information flow and process models. As a whole, the multi-model answers the call for the creative expansion of the traditional SB in enhancement of Service Design, one of the ten identified research priority areas for Service Science [2]. The importance of adopting a holistic approach to design is also increasingly recognised [2 , 11] and the research further embeds this practise where it can improve the MSD by extending its design scope for the broader complexity of design at the service encounter level.

5.4   Limitations and Future Work

As with any study, this research has a number of limitations. Given the available resources and time constraints, the evaluation focused upon a single case study. As exploratory research, this facilitated a considerable depth of knowledge concerning the use of the SB and offered a practitioner-driven case for its extension to the developed multi-model. However this limited the opportunity to uncover additional improvements relevant to a wider audience and, to some extent, the degree to which the research results can be generalized to broader design efforts. It is recommended that further work be conducted leveraging the model in additional design engagements with different design teams and even to different service types or within different industries. Another limitation concerns the absence of an agreed approach for evaluating the quality of a conceptual models, in this case the SB. This is currently recognized as an on-going area of research [46] and any further exploration of the multi-model should seek to capitalize on accepted empirical evaluation criteria. Finally, it is recommended that any such exploration be conducted within the broader context of Patrício, Fisk [17]s' MSD method. This research focused upon the front-stage back-stage service system at the equivalent service encounter layer of the model. The possibility to further investigate MSD with the multi-model developed here situated at its foundation in place of the SEB presents a significant research opportunity for future work. Overall then, further validation of the proposed method is required to determine the generalizability where this research paves the way for future confirmatory research. This would both further enhance the application of the SB to self-service Predictive Analytics and help advance towards a generalizable theory.

5.5   Conclusions

This exploratory study concludes that, in spite of its customer focus, the traditional Service Blueprint (SB) model is insufficient for supporting the integrative design of a Self-Service Technology (SST) in Predictive Analytics (PA). It fails to capture anything more than a high-level representation for basic service systems and its use by design teams is therefore limited as a discussion platform for all but the most nascent of SST designs. An improved solution is presented in the form of a multi-model, with an enhanced SB at its core. This multi-model draws upon familiar concepts within both Service Design and software development to offer a more detailed and comprehensive model of the service system. This significantly improves upon a design team's ability to collaboratively design a SST in PA, or indeed any other domain of self-service. The resulting design knowledge includes the description of a method for supporting SST design, the associated constructs and model together with an instantiation for the case study SST. Accordingly, the research contributes to a nascent design theory for the design of SSTs in PA where further advanced can be achieved through its exploration for additional services and incorporation within broader holistic frameworks such as the Multi-level Service Design (MSD) model [17].

References

1. Chesbrough, H., Spohrer, J.: A research manifesto for services science. Commun. ACM 49(7), 35–40 (2006)
2. Ostrom, A.L., et al.: Moving forward and making a difference: research priorities for the science of service. Journal of Service Research 13(1), 4–36 (2010)
3. Kridel, D., Dolk, D.: Automated self-service modeling: predictive analytics as a service. Information Systems and e-Business Management 11(1), 119–140 (2013)
4. Demirkan, H., Delen, D.: Leveraging the capabilities of service-oriented decision support systems: Putting analytics and big data in cloud. Decision Support Systems 55(1), 412–421 (2013)
5. Cooper, A.: What is Analytics? Definition and Essential Characteristics. CETIS Analytics Series 1(5) (2012)
6. Meuter, M.L., et al.: Self-service technologies: understanding customer satisfaction with technology-based service encounters. The Journal of Marketing, 50–64 (2000)
7. Talia, D.: Toward Cloud-based Big-data Analytics. IEEE Computer Science, 98–101 (May 2013)
8. Kim, H., et al.: Online risk analytics on the cloud. In: 9th IEEE/ACM International Symposium on Cluster Computing and the Grid, CCGRID 2009. IEEE (2009)
9. Bitner, M.J., et al.: Implementing Successful Self-Service Technologies [and Executive Commentary]. The Academy of Management Executive (1993-2005) 16(4), 96–109 (2002)
10. Salomann, H., et al.: Self-service Revisited: How to Balance High-tech and High-touch in Customer Relationships. European Management Journal 25(4), 310–319 (2007)
11. Saco, R.M., Goncalves, A.P.: Service design: An appraisal. Design Management Review 19(1), 10–19 (2008)
12. Moritz, S.: Service design: practical access to an evolving field. Köln International School of Design, Cologne (2005)
13. Mager, B., Gais, M.: Service design. UTB vol. 3113 (2009)
14. Pine, B.J., Gilmore, J.H.: Welcome to the experience economy. Harvard Business Review 76, 97–105 (1998)
15. Alves, R., Jardim Nunes, N.: Towards a Taxonomy of Service Design Methods and Tools. In: Falcão e Cunha, J., Snene, M., Nóvoa, H. (eds.) IESS 2013. LNBIP, vol. 143, pp. 215–229. Springer, Heidelberg (2013)
16. Teixeira, J., et al.: Customer experience modeling: from customer experience to service design. Journal of Service Management 23(3), 362–376 (2012)
17. Patrício, L., et al.: Multilevel service design: from customer value constellation to service experience blueprinting. Journal of Service Research 14(2), 180–200 (2011)
18. Glushko, R.J.: Seven contexts for service system design. In: Handbook of Service Science, pp. 219–249. Springer (2010)
19. Glushko, R.J., Tabas, L.: Designing service systems by bridging the "front stage" and "back stage". Information Systems and E-Business Management 7(4), 407–427 (2009)
20. Glushko, R.J.: Designing a service science discipline with discipline. IBM Systems Journal 47(1), 15–27 (2008)

21. Patrício, L., Fisk, R.P., Cunha, J.F.: Designing Multi-Interface Service Experiences The Service Experience. Journal of Service Research 10(4), 318–334 (2008)
22. Yu, E., Sangiorgi, D.: Service design as an approach to new service development: reflections and futures studies. In: Fourth Service Design and Innovation Conference Service Futures, ServDes (2014)
23. Shostack, G.L.: Designing services that deliver. Harvard Business Review, 133–139 (January/February 1984)
24. Bitner, M.J., Ostrom, A.L., Morgan, F.N.: Service blueprinting: a practical technique for service innovation. California Management Review 50(3), 66 (2008)
25. Wreiner, T., et al.: Exploring Service Blueprints for Multiple Actors: A Case Study of Car Parking Services. In: DeThinking Service, ReThinking Design: The First Nordic Conference on Service Design and Service Innovation, Oslo, Norway (2009)
26. Polonsky, M.J., Garma, R.: Service blueprinting: a potential tool for improving cause-donor exchanges. Journal of Nonprofit & Public Sector Marketing 16(1-2), 1–20 (2006)
27. Spraragen, S., Chan, C.: Service Blueprinting: When Customer Satisfaction Numbers are not enough. In: International DMI Education Conference. Design Thinking: New Challenges for Designers, Managers and Organizations (2008)
28. Chuang, P.-T.: Combining Service Blueprint and FMEA for Service Design. The Service Industries Journal 27(2), 91–104 (2007)
29. Boughnim, N., Yannou, B.: Using blueprinting method for developing product-service systems. In: International Conference of Engineering Design (ICED) (2005)
30. Fließ, S., Kleinaltenkamp, M.: Blueprinting the service company: Managing service processes efficiently. Journal of Business Research 57(4), 392–404 (2004)
31. Milton, S.K., Johnson, L.W.: Service blueprinting and BPMN: a comparison. Managing Service Quality 22(6), 606–621 (2012)
32. Spohrer, J., Kwan, S.K.: Service science, management, engineering, and design (SSMED): an emerging discipline. International Journal of Information Systems in the Service Sector 1(3) (2009)
33. Ng, I., Maull, R., Smith, L.: Embedding the new discipline of service science. In: The Science of Service Systems, pp. 13–35. Springer (2011)
34. Maglio, P.P., et al.: The service system is the basic abstraction of service science. Information Systems and e-business Management 7(4), 395–406 (2009)
35. Normann, R.: Reframing business: When the map changes the landscape. Wiley (2001)
36. Teixeira, J.G., et al.: Dynamic Multi-interface Services: An Application to the Design of a Multimedia Service. In: 2013 Fifth International Conference on Service Science and Innovation (ICSSI). IEEE (2013)
37. Baum, S.H.: Making your service blueprint pay off! Journal of Services Marketing 4(3), 45–52 (1990)
38. Gregor, S., Hevner, A.R.: Positioning and Presenting Design Science Research for Maximum Impact. MIS Quarterly 37(2), 337–356 (2013)
39. Sein, M., et al.: Action design research (2011)
40. Hadden, J., et al.: Computer assisted customer churn management: State-of-the-art and future trends. Computers & Operations Research 34(10), 2902–2917 (2007)
41. Hevner, A.R., et al.: Design science in information systems research. MIS Quarterly 28(1), 75–105 (2004)
42. Stickdorn, M., Schneider, J., Andrews, K.: This is service design thinking: Basics, tools, cases. Wiley (2011)

43. Shmueli, G., Koppius, O.: Predictive analytics in information systems research. Robert H. Smith School Research Paper No. RHS, 2010: pp. 06–138 (2010)
44. Bose, R.: Advanced analytics: opportunities and challenges. Industrial Management & Data Systems 109(2), 155–172 (2009)
45. Cooper, A., Saffo, P.: The inmates are running the asylum. Sams (2004)
46. Cruzes, D.S., Vennesland, A., Natvig, M.K.: Empirical evaluation of the quality of conceptual models based on user perceptions: A case study in the transport domain. In: Ng, W., Storey, V.C., Trujillo, J.C. (eds.) ER 2013. LNCS, vol. 8217, pp. 414–428. Springer, Heidelberg (2013)

Emerging Themes

The Front End of Innovation: Perspectives on Creativity, Knowledge and Design

Shirley Gregor[1] and Alan R. Hevner[2(✉)]

[1]Australia National University, Canberra, Australia
shirley.gregor@anu.edu.au
[2]University of South Florida, Tampa, FL, USA
ahevner@usf.edu

Abstract. While the importance of innovation as a dominant driver of societal and economic progress is well established, the processes and outcomes of innovation remain distressingly ad-hoc and unpredictable. In particular, the Front End of Innovation (FEI) provides many open questions as innovators are challenged to understand the opportunity context, generate novel ideas, and evaluate these ideas for the implementation of solutions. We propose an original model of the FEI with a nascent theory base drawn from recent perspectives in the areas of innovation, creativity, knowledge, and design science. A key insight is the application of a knowledge maturity lens to distinguish four categories of innovation – invention, exaptation, advancement, and exploitation. We conclude with an agenda for future research to extend innovation theories and with actionable advice for improving current practices of innovation.

Keywords: Innovation · Front end of innovation · Design science research · Knowledge · Creativity

1 Introduction

Innovation's positive role in advancing economic growth and benefitting society has been long established [1]. However, recent studies have expressed concerns of an innovation slowdown with deleterious consequences (e.g. [2]). Chief among the challenges are the difficulty of measuring the novelty and impacts of innovation outcomes, the unpredictable nature of the innovation process, and the lack of strong, coordinated commitments by industrial, academic, and governmental stakeholders to enable a culture of innovation and risk-taking.

Innovation processes and outcomes are difficult to predict and understanding is hampered by the lack of clearly articulated concepts and theories that underlie effective innovation activities. In this paper, we focus on the *front end of innovation* (FEI). FEI encompasses the activities in the innovation process in which ideas are generated and evaluated before one or more selected ideas or prototypes continue on to the comparatively well-structured new product and process development (NPPD) activities. FEI is receiving increased attention because of a perception that there is a lack of high-profit ideas entering NPPD [3, 4]. Noting the lack of research into the

© Springer International Publishing Switzerland 2015
B. Donnellan et al. (Eds.): DESRIST 2015, LNCS 9073, pp. 249–263, 2015.
DOI: 10.1007/978-3-319-18714-3_16

FEI and believing that the FEI is not as mysterious as it has been portrayed; Koen et al. [5] developed a model for the FEI based on best practices in eight companies. However, the FEI is hardly studied at all in connection with IT innovations - an exception being Brem and Voigt [6]. Thus, we believe that innovation with IT offers a fertile ground for theorizing the FEI. Not only are "IT-innovations" ubiquitous, they come in many shapes and forms, including products, processes and services. In addition, the FEI is comparatively atheoretical [7] and current innovation models are not linked to the insights that can be gleaned from relevant underlying theories, including germane theories of creativity, knowledge, and design science.

The objective of the paper is to develop the initial base for a FEI theory with IT, drawing insights from the perspectives of creativity, knowledge, and design as surveyed in the next section. The nascent theory is based on an innovation model resulting from a synthesis of existing theory. As a key model component we adapt the Knowledge Innovation Matrix (KIM), a typology for innovations and design science contributions developed by Gregor and Hevner [8, 9]. Different patterns of effective FEI activities will depend on the type of innovation being explored – invention, exaptation, advancement (improvement), or exploitation. The KIM-FEI model posits that effectiveness and eventual success in each innovation category will require variations in innovation activities, organizational environment, team skills, and produced outcomes. The implications of this study are examined in the discussion section. The research contribution is a novel conceptual model (nascent theory) that integrates IT concepts and business innovation concepts to develop a fine-grained understanding of the front-end of product-process-service innovation, utilizing perspectives on the roles of creativity, knowledge, and design.

2   Grounding Perspectives

The territory covered by the term *innovation* is immense and crosses multiple disciplines. The human actors in this landscape are many and varied, including managers, inventors, creative employees, entrepreneurs, university researchers, and policy makers. With such a large landscape it is not surprising that it is hard to rise above one's immediate surroundings and take a global view of innovation. Thus, we bring together ideas from multiple perspectives on current research thinking and practice to inform and ground our nascent innovation theory development. While we cannot hope to perform an exhaustive survey here, our goal is to highlight several key research streams that ground the innovation model presented in the next section.

2.1   Innovation Perspective

We begin by examining perspectives that take an encompassing view of innovation. These broad innovation perspectives take a process view of innovation and study how innovation activities occur over time against a background of environmental and organizational conditions.

Van de Ven et al. [10] provide a comprehensive model for novel innovations developed from their work in the Minnesota Innovation Research Program. These authors question stage-wise (stage-gate) models that see the innovation process as progressing through a series of stages or phases, such as invention-development-testing-commercialization. Instead, they see a richer process that is more complex and uncertain than stage models. They believe that innovation can be accomplished in a number of different ways and that the *innovation journey* can unfold along many different paths. The period of the Van de Ven et al. [10] model that is of most interest to the current study is the initiation period which corresponds to the FEI. A key insight is that there are many possible FEI paths in the journey.

Work that focuses more specifically on the FEI is that of Koen et al. [3, 4] who study FEI activities through the lens of a New Concept Development (NCD) model. The NCD [5] divides the FEI into three key parts: the engine, the wheel, and the rim. The engine contains the core elements that give power to the front end process - organizational attributes (i.e. strategy, vision, resources, culture, teams and collaboration). The wheel, the inner part of the NCD, has five activity elements: opportunity identification, opportunity analysis, idea generation, idea selection, and concept definition. Ideas flow and iterate among these five activity elements. The third part of the NCD model is the rim, the environmental factors, such as the company's organizational abilities, regulatory changes, and worldwide trends, which influence the core elements and shape the five steps. The NCD focus is on the creation of "new" products and processes, rather than the creative "adoption" of the ideas of others. Given its firm grounding and wide acceptability as a model of the FEI, we use the NCD as a base for our current work.

2.2   Creativity Perspective

According to Burkus [11, p. 15], "creativity is the starting point for all innovation" where creativity is defined as "the process of developing ideas that are both novel and useful" [12]. We expect the role of human creativity to be especially salient in the FEI, where novel ideas are needed for an innovation process to begin. Here we briefly focus on Amabile's componential theory of creativity to inform our FEI model. Amabile [13, 14] posits that four components are necessary for a creative response:

- *Domain-relevant skills* include intelligence, expertise, knowledge, technical skills, and talent in the particular domain in which the innovator is working;
- *Creativity-relevant processes* include personality and cognitive characteristics that lend themselves to taking new perspectives on problems, such as independence, risk taking, self-discipline in generating ideas, and a tolerance for ambiguity.
- *Intrinsic task motivation* is a central tenet. "People are most creative when they feel motivated primarily by the interest, enjoyment, satisfaction and challenge of the work itself – and not by extrinsic motivators." [14, p. 3].
- *The social environment,* the only external component, addresses the working conditions that support creative activity. Negative organizational settings harshly criticize new ideas, emphasize political problems, stress the status quo, impose excessive time pressures, and support low-risk attitudes of top management. While positive organizational settings stimulate creativity with clear and compelling management visions, work teams with diverse skills working collaboratively, freedom to investigate ideas, and mechanisms for developing new ideas and norms of sharing ideas.

It is important to note that Amabile's work is based on two important assumptions. First, there is a continuum from relatively low, everyday levels of adaptive creativity to the higher levels of creativity found in significant inventions and scientific discoveries. Second, there are degrees of creativity exhibited in the work of any single individual at different points of time and circumstances [13]. Comparing Amabile's model with the NCD of Koen et al. [3, 4], it can be seen that there are some similarities. For example, Amabile's social environment construct is similar to the organizational attributes construct of the NCD. However, the NCD does not focus on the interpersonal components of skills and motivation that feature prominently in the Amabile [13] model.

2.3   Knowledge Perspective

The connections among existing knowledge sources and the generation of new ideas are fundamental to innovation. "Innovation is about knowledge – creating new possibilities through combining new knowledge sets" [15 p. 37]. Knowledge-intensive activities, such as innovation, are studied for their historical impacts on societies and cultures [16]. Broad theories are proposed around the efficient growth of economies based on their production, management, and consumption of knowledge. Key topics include appropriate incentives for the efficient production of knowledge and the trade-offs of public access to knowledge (e.g. open sources) vs. privatized exploitation of knowledge (e.g. proprietary patents).

Thus, we include a special focus on knowledge and knowledge flows as applicable to innovation. In academic-business settings, providing an identifiable contribution to knowledge, as in journal outputs or patents, is a key motivator for at least some of the individuals involved. Approximately two-thirds of leading innovations in recent years are estimated to have come from collaborative partnerships involving academia, business, and government, including government funded labs and university research [17]. These collaborative research ventures should yield dual outcomes, with both: (1) innovations in terms of products and processes with real-world impacts outside the development environment; and (2) formal knowledge production.

At the organizational level the work of Nonaka and colleagues on the "knowledge-creating" company depict the central importance of knowledge for innovation and focus on changes from tacit to explicit knowledge in a spiral process (e.g. [18, 19]. Nonaka [18] shows how innovations are linked to novel ideas, which can be gleaned from individuals' tacit knowledge. For example, the Matsushita product development company incorporated ideas obtained from careful observation of an expert human bread maker into the design of a superior bread making machine.

2.4   Design Science Perspective

The Design Science Research (DSR) paradigm has its roots in engineering and the sciences of the artificial [20] and is fundamentally a problem-solving paradigm. DSR seeks to enhance human knowledge with the creation of innovative artifacts. These artifacts embody the ideas, practices, technical capabilities, and products through which information systems can be efficiently developed and effectively used. The results of DSR include both the newly designed artifact and a fuller understanding of the theories of why the artifact is an innovation in the relevant application context [21, 22]. IT artifacts as composed of inherently mutable and adaptable hardware, software, and human interfaces provide many unique and challenging design problems that call for new and creative ideas. DSR in IT fields involves the construction of a wide range of *socio-technical* artifacts such as decision support systems, modelling tools, governance strategies, methods for software systems development and evaluation, and system change interventions.

Gregor and Hevner [8] develop a DSR framework to assist researchers in positioning knowledge contributions so that the significance and novelty of the contribution could be better recognized via academic publication. We believe that this framework can be modified and extended so as to provide a guide to understanding the impact of knowledge contributions and real-world outcomes in innovation for a broader audience.

2.5   Types of Innovation – The Knowledge Innovation Matrix (KIM)

The nature of the FEI is said to vary with the type of innovation. For instance, Koen et al. [4] show in an empirical study that processes for radical innovations differ from those for incremental innovations. Distinguishing more clearly between the processes and activities that occur with different innovation types is a core objective that drives our innovation model. Thus, we need to choose a categorization schema that is suitable for the FEI. There are many ways to classify innovations, as noted in reviews by Garcia and Calantone [23] and Miller and Miller [24]. Some basic dichotomous classifications include the distinction between *exploration* and *exploitation*, introduced by March [25] in relation to learning. March saw exploration as "search, variation, risk taking, experimentation, play, flexibility, discovery, innovation" [25 p. 71]. Exploitation was "refinement, choice, production, efficiency, selection, implementation, execution." Another important dichotomous classification is that between *radical* and *incremental* innovations. Rothwell and Gardiner [26 p. 16] see a radical innovation as a major advance in the technological state of the art, while an incremental or improvement innovation is the utilization of even small changes in technological know-how.

In our FEI model we use the Knowledge Innovation Matrix (KIM) as developed in Gregor and Hevner [9]. This 2x2 typology, as seen in Figure 1, offers a finer-grained view than simple dichotomous classifications and is firmly based in the fundamental differences in triggers of an innovation in the FEI, needs-pull (problem trigger) or technology-push (knowledge trigger) [15] and the combinations of these two triggers. KIM extends and combines prior work on classifying innovations on two dimensions (e.g. [24, 27, 28]).

The two dimensions that form the basis of the matrix are:

1.   The knowledge (solution) maturity dimension, which resonates with the key roles in innovation of new ideas [10, 29], new insights [30], new knowledge and skills [31], technological know-how [26], new knowledge [32], and learning [25].

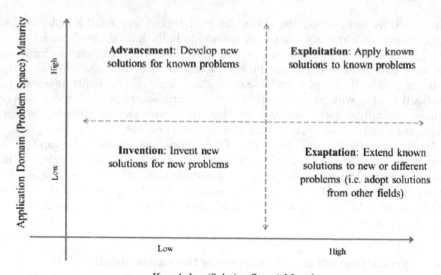

Fig. 1. Knowledge Innovation Matrix

2. The application domain (problem) maturity dimension, which resonates with the key roles in innovation of opportunities [15], tasks and problems [33], markets [34], needs [35] and fields [36].

The KIM quadrants are described here briefly and the reader is referred to Gregor and Hevner [8, 9] for further detail.

1. The *invention quadrant* includes very novel innovations that are seen as "new to the world", where both the both the idea of the problem or opportunity, and the knowledge to solve it, have not been recognized before. Recognition of the application domain and the related solution knowledge are both low.
2. The *exaptation quadrant* includes innovations where knowledge of how to satisfy one particular need or application function is applied to another need or market in a completely different field. Solution knowledge is well advanced, but recognition of how to apply that solution to the specific application area is low.
3. The *advancement (improvement) quadrant*[1] includes innovations where a better solution is developed for a known problem. The difference between this quadrant and the invention quadrant is that here the goal of the innovation effort can be specified at the outset. Solution knowledge is suboptimal, but recognition of the problem is high.
4. The *exploitation quadrant* includes innovations which are seen as "new-to-us" rather than "new-to-the-world." Known solutions are applied to known problems, possibly with some relatively minor customization. Innovative work in this

---

[1] In prior work the label "improvement" was used for this quadrant, rather than "advancement" [8, 9]. The label has been changed here to avoid confusion between "improvement" and the term "incremental improvement", which has a different meaning. The use of the stronger label "advancement" recognizes that in this quadrant knowledge is advanced to some significant degree.

quadrant can be seen as professional design and development and an organization could derive considerable value from the innovation.

3   New Front End of Innovation (FEI) Model

Drawing from the multiple perspectives of innovation surveyed above, we propose a novel, integrated model of the FEI. A driving insight is the use of the knowledge innovation matrix (KIM) as a prism to identify and distinguish the different innovation categories based on the objectives and characteristics of the innovation project. Figure 2 depicts the new KIM-FEI model graphically showing its main components.

3.1   Environmental Factors

An innovation project resides within an environmental context of competitor threats, diverse stakeholders (including customers), global conditions and trends, government regulations, and economic risk and uncertainty [3]. The ability to capture these *influences* defines the landscape for the activities to produce appropriate innovations. The current *knowledge base* includes the depth and strength of enabling sciences and technology [4]. The knowledge included can take the form of ideas that are passed formally or informally, accounts of case studies, reports, research publications, online information sources (an IT operand resource) and so on. The level of knowledge that exists in the problem and solution domains will determine the measurements of novelty and impact associated with the innovations [8]. In this sense the knowledge base is a communal knowledge base, accessible across organizations and individuals.

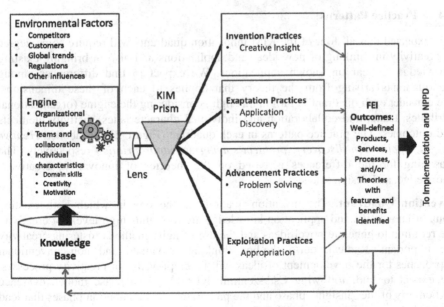

Fig. 2. The KIM-FEI Model

3.2   Engine

The engine gives power to the FEI and consists of [3]:

- *Organizational attributes* to include supportive and involved senior management, an innovation culture, a clear strategic vision of the project goals, a positive work environment, and adequate resource commitments [4, 14]. Resources can include internal knowledge resources and intellectual organizational capital.
- An innovation project *team* that is "collaborative, diversely skilled, and idea-focused" [14].
- Each team member must have the appropriate *individual characteristics* to be successful. Key characteristics include creativity, domain skills, and intrinsic motivation [14].

The innovation engine analyzes opportunities in the environment, accesses current knowledge from the knowledge base, and generates interesting ideas for further study. Then the results from the engine will be focused and sent through a lens to the KIM prism.

3.3   KIM Prism

The KIM prism identifies and distinguishes the innovation categories in the project. There may be one or more innovation opportunities in the four categories of invention, exaptation, advancement, or exploitation. As described in the previous section, these categories are defined by the levels of knowledge maturity in the application and solution contexts for the innovation opportunity.

3.4   Practice Patterns

It is expected that all four of the KIM innovation quadrants will require some degree of creativity in thinking of new ideas and applications and also in bringing existing knowledge to bear on known applications. We expect to find differences among the quadrants arising from the theory that applies to each of these dimensions. We consider each quadrant in turn in this light, considering the engine (organizational attributes, teams and collaboration and individual characteristics), activity elements and outcomes. The practice patterns in each quadrant (Figure 2) are labelled *creative insight, application discovery, problem solving* and *appropriation* respectively. The reasoning for the differences is based on the theories of innovation, creativity, knowledge, and design science.

Invention Quadrant. The invention quadrant is the one in which both existing domain knowledge and application knowledge are low, thus high levels of creativity are required to generate novel ideas and the use of agile methods fostering creativity are important. Radical, out-of-the-box thinking is valued and non-conventional approaches for the development of ideas will be employed. For creativity processes, we expect to find, following Csikszentmihalyi's [37] five phase model, evidence particularly of the "insight" phase and the preparation and incubation phases that lead up to it. Organization policies that foster creativity are key, particularly those that allow employees time to think and try out their own ideas. Outcomes from this phase include concepts that may be highly risky, as evidence of their utility and effectiveness may be scarce.

Exaptation Quadrant. In the exaptation quadrant a novel association is found between existing solution knowledge in one field and a challenging opportunity in another field. As in the invention quadrant, a relatively high level of creativity and associative thinking are required to generate the novel relationships between the existing knowledge and a new application. The important thing here is to conceptualize an association between the existing technology and some purpose that is different from what was originally envisaged. We want to find new niches for existing technologies in which connections are made between apparently disparate ideas, either from very creative individuals or a group with diverse ideas. Open innovation methods such as crowdsourcing are examples of ways in which exaptation can be encouraged. Crowdsourcing encourages a diverse range of people, including fringe experts, to contribute ideas. Organizations also make use of creativity, brainstorming, and ideation techniques to encourage creative connections between a technology (knowledge) and a new use for the technology. The process here is termed one of application discovery [38].

Advancement Quadrant. The advancement quadrant is the one in which there is less than optimal solution knowledge for achieving a relatively well-understood application. The goal is to achieve a significant advance on existing knowledge for solving a particular problem. People are needed who are experts with significant relevant domain knowledge. Methods in this quadrant include typical research and design activities, such as that described for design science research with IT [39]. Gregor and Hevner [8] show in an analysis of 13 design science articles in a leading journal that the majority (77%) fell into the improvement (i.e. advancement) quadrant.

Exploitation Quadrant. The exploitation quadrant is the one in which there is mature domain knowledge for achieving a well-understood application or function. The goal is then to optimize the functioning of a state-of-the-art technology in a new application environment. The innovation is new-to-me or new-to-us rather than new-to-the-world. Innovation in this quadrant can be cast in different lights and there is a wide range of theorizing. From ỏne viewpoint, exploitation within a firm is seen as a later stage of innovation after the FEI, where innovations are effectively and profitably deployed. From another viewpoint, the innovation is seen as adopted or appropriated from an outside source. We use the term "appropriation" for this process, to capture the idea that it is more than "adoption", but can include adaption, and re-design in order to capture value [40].

3.5   Outcomes

The innovation outcomes of all four KIM quadrants can be described as well-defined concepts, or demonstration prototypes, for products, services, and processes that are sent forward for further consideration and refinement in the implementation stages of innovation. In other words, the fully-formed new idea is moved from FEI to subsequent innovation stages of further demonstration (e.g. prototyping), new product (service, process) development, and, eventual commercialization [5]. Each outcome will be accompanied by a detailed features list, evidence of the benefits and costs, and identification of limitations and potential risks. Outcomes from the different innovation categories will be distinguished by the knowledge maturity gaps filled by the innovation activities performed. This new knowledge will also be contributed to the current knowledge base as shown in Figure 2.

4   Building Design Theory from the KIM-FEI Model

The KIM-FEI model provides the basis for the development of a nascent theory for the FEI with IT innovations [8].

4.1   Research Propositions

In order to gain more complete understanding of the FEI, here we advance some propositions based specifically on the unique aspects of the KIM-FEI model. These propositions point out some salient characteristics of each innovation quadrant that can lead to further research questions and nascent FEI theories. Note that we do not address propositions that apply across all innovation quadrants. Such general innovation theories are well-covered in the grounding perspectives literature. As noted before, with all innovations the individual characteristics and organizational conditions that allow human creativity and enhance the association between ideas will be important to some degree. Access to pertinent knowledge bases and the latest technology trends along with free flow of knowledge among collaborators will also be important across all quadrants.

Proposition Set 1: For *inventions*, the salient conditions are:
a) Organizational attributes that foster creativity, including policies that give freedom to employees to investigate problems of their own devising in free time, allowing innovators to incubate ideas (e.g. bootlegging policies);
b) Supportive teams with colleagues who encourage original thinking and tolerate eccentricities.
c) Individual characteristics that typify highly creative people, including strong intrinsic motivation. However the innovators may be fringe experts in so far as the innovation is concerned.
d) Activities as in the creative process: preparation, incubation, evaluation and elaboration.
   These propositions are advanced because the invention quadrant is the one in which high levels of creativity are expected, so theories of creativity are especially relevant [14, 37].

Proposition Set 2: For *exaptations*, the salient conditions are:
a) Organizational attributes that include resources to encourage contributions of diverse ideas and connections between these ideas, for example open innovation through crowdsourcing.

b) Collaborative teams with diversities in domain expertise and technical skill sets.

c) Individual characteristics that typify highly creative people, including strong intrinsic motivation in many cases. However the innovators may be fringe experts in so far as the innovation is concerned.

d) Activities termed application discovery, where individuals, teams or groups are encouraged to generate ideas for re-purposing existing knowledge (e.g. brainstorming, ideation exercises).

These propositions are advanced because the exaptation quadrant is the one in which knowledge and creativity across boundaries are expected, so theories of creativity [14, 37] and associative thinking [41], and concepts of open innovation [42, 43] and exaptation [38] are relevant.

Proposition Set 3: For *advancements*, the salient conditions include:

a) Environmental factors such as access to important knowledge sources in the knowledge base, including the latest scientific research. What advancement improvements will make a true difference in the current IT environment and how is that advancement measured?

b) Organizational attributes that include an open, innovative culture that allows experimentation and risk taking.

c) Research and development teams with collaborative, disciplined, and creative colleagues.

d) Individual characteristics that typify creative people, including strong intrinsic motivation. The innovators will require true expertise to fully understand the current state of knowledge and envisage potential solutions that will make a difference.

e) Activities as in problem solving, with heuristic search for a solution taking place in a problem space, with actions such as experiments.

These propositions are advanced because the advancement improvement quadrant is the one in which theories of human problem solving [44] and design science research [22] are more relevant.

Proposition Set 4: For *exploitation*, the salient conditions are:

a) Environmental factors such as competitor threats, customer trends, and regulatory changes that supply an innovator with an opportunity that could lead to value-added advantages. A knowledge base is required from which the ideas behind the innovation can be retrieved and applied.

b) Organizational attributes that include senior management vision and organizational strategy.

c) Development teams that can apply cutting-edge technologies to interesting problems.

d) Individual characteristics that typify creative people in a professional role with expertise in the restructuring and redefining of the innovation to fit a new context, e.g. software engineering or change management expertise.

e) Activities as in the innovation appropriation process: agenda-setting, matching, redefining/restructuring, clarifying, and routinizing.

These propositions are advanced because the exploitation quadrant is the one in which existing innovations are adopted, adapted and refined to suit a new context [29].

5   Discussion and Conclusions

This paper advances a theoretical model for the front end of innovation (FEI), showing the different conditions and activities that typify innovations of different types. Innovations are categorized according to their position in the Knowledge Innovation Matrix (KIM), being invention, exaptation, advancement or exploitation. Compared to the familiar exploration-exploitation dichotomy, invention, exaptation and advancement correspond to exploration modes, whilst exploitation remains exploitation. We have avoided the use of the radical-incremental distinction, as we argue that this distinction applies more to the depiction of innovations when they have reached the market, rather than the FEI.

Different patterns are expected in each quadrant, with respect to knowledge flows, level of expertise, individual creativity, working across boundaries and activities. The activity patterns in each quadrant are labelled *creative insight, application discovery, problem solving* and *appropriation* respectively. The reasoning for the difference in patterns is based on the perspectives and theories of innovation, creativity, knowledge, and design science. The research propositions in the previous section are meant to inspire research on these differences and, thus, establish a starting point for building theory in the FEI.

The FEI model has both theoretical and practical significance. Theoretically it provides a model for the FEI that is soundly based in prior theory, thus providing a valuable extension to prior work. Further, it shows that for innovations related to IT, which comprise a healthy proportion of all modern innovations, IT can have roles as both *operant* and *operand* [45]. As an operant, IT innovations trigger further innovation in an ongoing process. As an operand, IT provides for valuable tools that support innovation, such as knowledge support systems and open innovation platforms.

Practically, the FEI model provides opportunities for managers to plan and evaluate the strategies they use for innovation. The different patterns for the quadrants show how different strategies can be used for different ends. The thinking underlying the model has some resemblance with the Ansoff matrix that proposes strategies for growth around new product development [27] and has been used successfully in industry for many years. The FEI model is soundly based in theory and takes into account the changes in the way innovations occur, includes both process and product innovations, supports innovation across organizational boundaries, and involves the use of IT in both operand and operant roles.

We note that the differing innovation patterns in the model should not be expected to hold too strictly. Any one innovation is likely to involve occurrences of creative insight, application discovery, problem solving and appropriation and possibly will move between quadrants over time. What the patterns show is what is expected at a general level, showing archetypes of behavior for different categories. In fact, the "menu" of activities that are depicted may suggest possibilities to managers, rather than blindly following familiar patterns. Managers can map innovation practice in their organization and see if there are gaps and opportunities for doing things differently.

Our current study has limitations. We recognize that the landscape of innovation is huge and we are at risk in classifying all types of innovation in only four categories. More study is needed to validate our model. Another limitation is the lack of a fuller analysis on the role of government in innovation activity. The government (or public sector) perspective on innovation concerns the economic and societal welfare of the governed population. This is necessarily a 'big picture' view of the need for innovation to improve the human condition. Government can stimulate processes in which basic research is linked to utilization of innovations when forces within academia and industry are insufficient by themselves to achieve this goal.

In conclusion, the new KIM-FEI model provides exciting opportunities for much future work. The propositions can be tested empirically and the theoretical model developed further. The exaptation quadrant is one that is comparatively underdeveloped theoretically, with concepts from open innovation and need-solution pairs still not well integrated theoretically. More work can be done examining the roles of IT as both operant and operand and the IT systems such as knowledge sharing systems that are involved with IT as an operand resource. Work can also be done to investigate how organizations can use the model so as to behave multidextrously, being involved in multiple types of innovation at the same time. It has been shown that firms that can balance these activities well are nine time more likely to achieve breakthrough products and processes than others, even while sustaining their existing business [46].

References

1. Schumpeter, J.: Capitalism, Socialism, and Democracy. Harper Press, New York (1942)
2. Cowen, T.: The Great Stagnation. Penguin Books, London (2011)
3. Koen, P., Bertels, H., Kleinschmidt, E.: Managing the Front End of Innovation – Part I. Research-Technology Management 57(2), 34–43 (2014a)
4. Koen, P., Bertels, H., Kleinschmidt, E.: Managing the Front End of Innovation – Part II. Research-Technology Management 57(3), 25–35 (2014b)
5. Koen, P., Ajamian, G., Buirkart, R., Clamen, A., Davidson, J., D'Amore, R., Elkins, C., Herald, K., Invorvia, M., Johnson, A., Karol, R., Seibert, R., Slavejkov, A., Wagner, K.: Providing Clarity and a Common Language to the "Fuzzy Front End". Research – Technology Management 44(2), 46–55 (2001)
6. Brem, A., Voigt, K.: Integration of Market Pull and Technology Push in the Corporate Front End and Innovation Management – Insights from the German Software Industry. Technovation 29, 351–367 (2009)
7. Anderson, N., Potocnik, K., Zhou, J.: Innovation and Creativity in Organizations: A State-of-the-Science Review, Perspective Commentary, and Guiding Framework. Journal of Management 40(5), 1297–1333 (2014)
8. Gregor, S., Hevner, A.: Positioning and Presenting Design Science Research for Maximum Impact. Management Information Systems Quarterly 37(2), 337–355 (2013)
9. Gregor, S., Hevner, A.: The Knowledge Innovation Matrix (KIM): A Clarifying Lens for Innovation. Informing Science: The International Journal of an Emerging Transdiscipline 17, 217–239 (2014)

10. Van de Ven, A., Polley, D., Garud, R., Venkataraman, S.: The Innovation Journey. Oxford University Press, New York (2008)
11. Burkus, D.: The Myths of Creativity. Jossey-Bass (2014)
12. Amabile, T.: Creativity in Context: Update to the Social Psychology of Creativity. Westview, Boulder (1996)
13. Amabile, T.: The Social Psychology of Creativity: A Componential Conceptualization. Journal of Personality and Social Psychology 45, 2 (1983)
14. Amabile, T.: Componential Theory of Creativity, Working Paper, Harvard Business School (April 2012), http://www.hbs.edu/faculty/Publication%20Files/12-096.pdf (accessed March 10, 2014)
15. Tidd, J., Bessant, J.: Managing Innovation Integrating Technological, Market and Organizational Change, 4th edn. John Wiley & Sons, Chichester (2009)
16. Mokyr, J.: The Gifts of Athena: Historical Origins of the Knowledge Economy. Princeton University Press, Princeton (2002)
17. Block, F., Keller, M.: Where Do Innovations Come From? Transformations in the U.S. National Innovation System 1970-2006. The Information Technology and Innovation Foundation (2008), http://www.itif.org/files/Where_do_innovations_come_from.pdf (retrieved February 5, 2013)
18. Nonaka, I.: The Knowledge-Creating Company. Harvard Business Review, 96–104 (November-Dececember 1991)
19. Nonaka, I., Toyama, R., Nagata, A.: A Firm as a Knowledge-creating Entity: A New Perspective on the Theory of the Firm. Industrial and Corporate Change 9(1), 1–20 (2008)
20. Simon, H.: The Sciences of the Artificial, 3rd edn. MIT Press, Cambridge (1996)
21. Gregor, S., Jones, D.: The Anatomy of a Design Theory. Journal of the Association of Information Systems 8(5), 312–335 (2006)
22. Hevner, A., March, S., Park, J., Ram, S.: Design Science Research in Information Systems. Management Information Systems Quarterly 28(1), 75–105 (2004)
23. Garcia, R., Calantone, R.: A Critical Look at Technological Innovation Typology and Innovativeness Terminology: A Literature Review. The Journal of Product Innovation Management 19, 110–132 (2002)
24. Miller, L., Miller, R.: Classifying Innovation. International Journal of Innovation and Technology Management 9(1), 18 pages (2012)
25. March, J.: Exploration and Exploitation in Organizational Learning. Organization Science 2(1), 71–87 (1991)
26. Rothwell, R., Gardiner, P.: Invention, Innovation, Re-innovation and the Role of the User. Technovation 3, 168 (1985)
27. Ansoff, I.: Strategies for Diversification. Harvard Business Review 35(5), 113–124 (1957)
28. Danneels, E.: The Dynamics of Product Innovation and Firm Competencies. Strategic Management Journal 23, 1095–1121 (2002)
29. Rogers, E.: Diffusion of Innovations, 5th edn. Free Press, New York (2003)
30. Mascitelli, R.: From Experience: Harnessing Tacit Knowledge to Achieve Breakthrough Innovation. Journal of Product Innovation Management 17(3), 179–193 (2000)
31. Leonard-Barton, D.: Core Capabilities and Core Rigidities: A Paradox in Managing New Product Development. Strategic Management Journal 13, 111–125 (1992)
32. Levinthal, D., March, J.: The Myopia of Learning. Strategic Management Journal 14, 95–112 (1993)
33. Horenstein, M.: Design Concepts for Engineers, 2nd edn. Prentice-Hall, Upper Saddle River (2002)

34. Danneels, E.: Disruptive Technology Reconsidered: A Critique and Research Agenda. Journal of Product Innovation Management 21(4), 246–258 (2004)
35. von Hippel, E., von Krogh, G.: Identifying Viable Need-Solution Pairs: Problem Solving without Problem Formulation. DSpace@MIT. Massachusetts Institute of Technology. Engineering Systems Division (2013), http://hdl.handle.net/1721.1/82610 (accessed March 10, 2014)
36. Cropley, D., Cropley, A.: Functional Creativity "Products" and the Generation of Effective Novelty. In: Kaufman, J., Sternberg, R. (eds.) The Cambridge Handbook of Creativity, pp. 301–317. Cambridge University Press (2010)
37. Csikszentmihalyi, M.: Creativity, Flow and the Psychology of Discovery and Invention. Harper Perennial, New York (1997)
38. Andriani, P., Carignani, G., Kaminska-Labbe, R.: The Appearance of New Functions in Technological Innovation: The Role of Exaptation. In: Academy of Management Proceedings (January 2013)
39. Peffers, K., Tuunanen, T., Rothenberger, M., Chatterjee, S.: A Design Science Research Methodology for Information Systems Research. Journal of MIS 24(3), 45–77 (2008)
40. Carroll, J.: Completing Design in Use: Closing the Appropriation Cycle. In: ECIS 2004 Proceedings (2004)
41. Mednick, S.: The Associative Basis of the Creative Process. Psychological Review 69, 220–232 (1962)
42. Chesbrough, H.: Open Innovation: The New Imperative for Creating and Profiting from Technology. Harvard Business School Press, Boston (2003)
43. Dahllander, L., Gann, D.: How Open is Innovation? Research Policy 39(6), 699–709 (2010)
44. Newell, A., Simon, H.: Human Problem Solving. Prentice-Hall, Englewood Cliffs (1972)
45. Nambisan, S.: Information Technology and Product/Service Innovation: A Brief Assessment and Some Suggestions for Future Research. Journal of the AIS 14, 215–226 (2013)
46. O'Reilly, C., Tushman, M.: The Ambidextrous Organization. Harvard Business Review (April 2004)

Five and Ten Years on: Have DSR Standards Changed?

John R. Venable[✉]

School of Information Systems, Curtin University, Perth, WA, Australia
j.venable@curtin.edu.au

Abstract. It has been more than ten years since the publication of Hevner et al [1] and five years since Venable [2] surveyed editors and DSR researchers on standards and criteria for judging the quality and suitability of DSR submissions for publication. Since then, there has been much further discussion about evaluation, design theory, and standards for DSR publication. This paper attempts to answer the question of how standards for judging the quality (e.g., rigour and relevance) of DSR research publications have changed since 2010 and to develop a snapshot of the relative importance of different extant DSR publication criteria. To do so, the author surveyed editors of IS Scholars' "basket-of-eight" journals, DESRIST conference program committee members, and DESRIST (co-)authors. This paper compares the quantitative findings of the current survey to the 2010 survey.

Keywords: Design Science Research · Research Standards · Evaluation · Design Theory · Publication Criteria

1   Introduction

It has now been more than ten years since the publication of Hevner et al (2004), which set a de facto standard for the conduct and evaluation of Design Science Research (DSR), and five years since Venable [2] surveyed editors and DSR researchers on standards and criteria for judging the quality and suitability of DSR submissions for publication. Venable found a high level of disagreement about the different criteria or standards for DSR, such as adoption of the Hevner et al [1] guidelines, the suitable kinds and rigour with which evaluations should be conducted, and the development of design theory as a research outcome.

Since 2010, there has been much further discussion in the IS and DSR community about the application and applicability of the Hevner et al. guidelines (e.g. [3,4]), evaluation in DSR [5,6], design theory [7,8,9,10,11,12], and standards for DSR publication.

This paper attempts to answer the question of whether and how standards for DSR research publication have changed since 2010 and to develop a snapshot of the relative importance of different extant DSR publication/quality criteria.

To do so, in line with Venable [2], the author surveyed the editors of IS Scholars' "basket-of-eight" journals, DESRIST conference program committee members, and DESRIST (co-)authors. This paper compares the quantitative findings of the current survey to the 2010 survey.

© Springer International Publishing Switzerland 2015
B. Donnellan et al. (Eds.): DESRIST 2015, LNCS 9073, pp. 264–279, 2015.
DOI: 10.1007/978-3-319-18714-3_17

This paper is organized as follows. Following this introduction, section 2 introduces literature relevant to DSR standards and criteria. Section 3 describes the survey research method used and section 4 presents the quantitative findings. Finally, section 5 discusses the findings and concludes the paper.

2   Literature Review

There are several different areas relevant to DSR standards, including (1) extant guidelines for conducting DSR (e.g. the Hevner et al. guidelines), (2) papers expanding on the evaluation aspect discussed by Hevner et al. (e.g., [5,6,13,14,15]), and (3) papers discussing the need for and form for design theory (e.g., 7,8,9,10,11,12). Additionally, Venable [2] identified (4) several other potential criteria, both *a priori* and suggested by survey respondents. The next four subsections briefly discuss each of these four areas before the last subsection summarises and states the paper's research questions.

2.1   The Hevner et al. (2004) Guidelines and Recent Literature

Following DSR's perceived devaluation concomitant with the rise of behavioural research in Information Systems, Hevner et al. [1] advocated and rejuvenated interest in DSR. In their seminal MISQ paper, they discussed the nature and conduct of DSR and its importance in the field of IS. Among other things, they proposed seven guidelines for conducting and evaluating good DSR, as summarized below.

1. Design as an Artefact – An identifiable and viable design artefact, as in March and Smith [16], i.e. a construct, model, method, or instantiation, must be produced.
2. Problem Relevance – The design must address a relevant and important problem.
3. Design Evaluation – The utility, quality, and efficacy of the design artefact must be rigorously evaluated.
4. Research Contributions – The contribution must be clear and verifiable. Contributions are seen to arise out of the novelty, generality, and significance of the designed artefact. Contributions include the design artefacts themselves, new foundations (constructs, models, methods, and instantiations), and new [evaluation] methodologies.
5. Research Rigor – Research methods must be rigorously applied.
6. Design as a Search Process – Research must be conducted with knowledge of other, competing approaches and should approach the process as a cyclical problem solving process, in which solutions are tested against each other and against their efficacy for solving the full problem.
7. Communication of the Research – Presentation of results needs to address both the rigor requirements of the academic audience and the relevance requirements of the professional (e.g. managerial) audience.

Hevner et al. clearly intended these guidelines "to assist researchers, reviewers, editors, and readers" (p. 82), so their use in reviewing and editing papers is to be expected. However, they also cautioned against "mandatory or rote use of the guidelines" (p. 82). Nonetheless, anecdotal evidence from fellow design science researchers indicates that the guidelines are sometimes enforced quite strictly in reviewing and editing DSR papers.

Venable [2] examined DSR researcher and editor perceptions of these guidelines and found that addressing all of the guidelines was perceived as only of low importance (5.36 on a 0-10 scale), with guidelines 1-4 being individually rated as highly important and the other guidelines less so.

Arnott and Pervan [3] examined the application and fulfilment of the seven Hevner et al. guidelines in the Decision Support System (DSS) literature. The literature reviewed covered the period 1990-2005, so there was almost no opportunity for the Hevner et al. guidelines to influence the field at that point. They found that 31% of the journal DSS literature reported on DSR and a high percentage of that delivered different DSR artefacts (guideline 1), especially instantiations. They noted that Hevner et al.'s guideline 2 "provides no guidance on how to assess or categorize the 'importance' and 'relevance' constructs." (p. 931). For guideline 3, they found that (worryingly) the most common evaluation method was "None" (42.3%), although this had improved over the years. "None" was followed by Experimental Simulations (20.4%), Descriptive Scenarios (15.7%), and Observational Case Studies (11.6%). They found that, in almost all cases, guideline 4 (Research Contribution) was fulfilled by the design artefact. For guideline 5 (Research Rigor), Arnott and Pervan [3] found that over 80% of DSS DSR papers had adequate or strong theoretical foundations, but nearly 75% were coded as weak in the rigorous application of research methodology, particularly evaluation. Importantly, though, this guideline seems to overlap somewhat with guideline 3 (Design Evaluation). For guideline 6 (Design as a Search Process), they found "little support for an evident means-ends search process in published DSS design-science research" (p. 937), but also pointed out that journal articles tend to present a more linear, less iterative, and more structured process than the actual practice of a typical search might entail. Interestingly, in private conversation with one of the authors, he noted that it was particularly difficult to find or to develop a clear way to code guideline 6, indicating that it would be very hard to apply this criterion when reviewing paper submissions. Re. guideline 7, Arnott and Pervan [3] found that most DSR papers in the DSS literature were aimed at researchers, with 85.4% of publications being rated low in the effectiveness of their management-oriented communication. Most interestingly, Arnott and Pervan [3] did not report that the research contribution (guideline 4) was solving a problem or achieving a particular goal or purpose, presumably due to lack of emphasis on relevance (guideline 2), evaluation (guideline 3), and serving the needs of practitioners (guideline 7).

In their more recent paper, Arnott and Pervan [4] critically examined DSS literature up through 2010. This extra five years of publication data allowed them to assess the impact of the Hevner et al [1] paper and its guidelines. Among other things, Arnott and Pervan [4] identified an increase in the percentage of DSS papers following the DSR paradigm (or method as they call it) to nearly 50% of all DSS papers over the seven years since the publication of Hevner et al [1]. They also found that the rigor of DSS DSR research (guideline 5) has not improved. Re. guideline 7, they found that the relevance of publications to IT practitioners had declined, but relevance to management had increased.

2.2   Evaluation in the Recent DSR Literature

As stated earlier, Hevner et al.'s guideline 3 asserts that good DSR needs to include rigorous evaluation. Hevner et al [1] identify 5 classes of evaluation methods and 12 individual evaluation methods, but provide little or no guidance on when to use each and why.

Since 2010, Venable et al [5,6] have consolidated their earlier work on evaluation in DSR to identify purposes of evaluation (formative and summative), forms of evaluation (artificial and naturalistic), strategies for evaluation (combining the previous two into a 2x2 framework), guidance for choosing evaluation methods (based on the 2x2 framework), and trajectories for evaluation. Of these, we are most concerned here with summative evaluations (which are what are typically presented in DSR papers) and the choice between artificial and naturalistic evaluation. Artificial evaluations, particularly using empirical methods, are best for determining the efficacy of an artefact to achieve its purpose, i.e. controlling for external variables to determine the extent to which achievement of some desired purpose is due to the use of the artefact, not something else. Naturalistic evaluations are best for determining the effectiveness of an artefact to achieve its purpose, i.e. whether (or not) an artefact works within a normal, e.g. organisational, usage context. A fully naturalistic evaluation meets three realities – real users, using the real artefact, and on a real problem or an actual situation [17].

2.3   Design Theory in the Recent DSR Literature

Hevner et al[1] did not consider design theory, consistent with the earlier perspective of March and Smith [16]. However, others have argued in favour of Design Theory as an important output of DSR [7,8,9,10,11,12,18].

Since 2010, Baskerville and Pries-Heje [11] and Venable [12] have argued in favour of simpler formulations of Design Theory, in particular focusing on the artefact design and its utility for achieving its purpose or requirements. This is consistent with the recommendations from the prior study of community opinions on DSR standards by Venable [2].

2.4   Other Standards and Criteria in the Literature

Other standards and criteria for assessing good DSR work have been published in the literature. Venable [2] identified several other potential standards and criteria for assessing DSR work, including:

- Relevance of the problem to industry/society clearly established (note: expands on guideline 2)
- Significance of the problem to industry/society clearly established (note: expands on guideline 2)
- Depth of analysis and clarity of understanding of the problem and its causes
- Depth or profoundness of insight leading to the new design artefact
- Novelty of the new design artefact
- Size and complexity of the new design artefact
- Amount of effort that went into the development of the new design artefact(s)
- Elegance of the design of the new artefact(s) (mentioned in Hevner et al [1])
- Simplicity of the design of the new artefact(s)
- Clear understanding of why the new artefact works (or doesn't work)

Venable [2] also identified another potential criterion suggested by one of the survey respondents, which is whether an artefact was adopted and used by organisations. Such adoption would indicate a rational assessment of sufficient utility (i.e. satisficing). Adoption by many organisations of an artefact would be strong evidence of its (perceived) utility.

Building on the work of Avital and Te'eni [19], Gill and Hevner [20], and Gregor and Hevner [21], one can suppose that artefacts that are not yet mature, but promising, may also be able to inspire further innovation in other new artefacts or new uses of existing artefacts. This "generative potential" (inspired by the "generative capacity" in Avital and Te'eni) might also be considered as a potential positive criterion in assessing a DSR publication. [Note: The term "generative potential" (and its etymology) was used in an anonymous manuscript that the author reviewed.]

2.5   Summary and Research Question

As discussed earlier in this section, there has been ongoing discussion since the prior study by Venable [2] in the IS literature about standards for DSR literature, including about the Hevner et al. (2004) criteria, evaluation in DSR, design theory, and a few other potential criteria that may demonstrate value of a DSR publication (or submission).

The ongoing discussion then begs the question of how such discussion has affected the perceptions of the various standards and criteria by which the quality of DSR and DSR publication submissions might be judged or evaluated. More specifically, what and how much has changed since the survey and publication by Venable (2010)? This gives rise to the following research questions.

- Has the perceived importance of the various criteria changed since 2010?
- How do any new criteria fit in with other existing criteria?
- Which criteria are now considered to be the most important?
- Has there been a move away from the dissensus reported in Venable [2] toward consensus?

3   Research Method and Design

To address the research questions, an obvious choice is to conduct another survey of the same research participants using the same questionnaire instrument as in Venable [2]. However, some minor changes to the survey research design would be useful.

First, Venable [2] surveyed editors of the IS Senior Scholars' Basket of 8 journals, but those editors have changed over the last five years. Therefore, it would be useful in understanding current perceptions to survey the current editors. Journal websites were scrutinised and the respondent panel was updated, removing people who are no longer editors and adding people who are. Where email addresses were supplied, these were used. Where email addresses were missing, they were searched for and located online.

Second, Venable [2] surveyed DESRIST conference program committee members and (co-)authors, but there have now been five more years of DESRIST conferences, with more people serving on the program committees and more people having published papers at DESRIST. Therefore, it would be useful to survey all DESRIST participants, including those from the more recent conferences. Again, email addresses were obtained either from the conference website or proceedings, or located online.

Third, Venable [2] used an email survey to which respondents replied via email. Some respondents in 2010 indicted that they would prefer an online survey and there are advantages for automatically tracking and capturing survey responses with an online survey. Therefore, the survey was re-implemented online (using Qualtrics). Logic was included to ensure all quantitative questions were answered (required in order to meaningfully compare different criteria average ratings across all respondents). As mobile device use is now highly common, the online survey was also designed to allow easy completion using a mobile device.

Fourth, as noted in section 2.4, there are at least two new potential criteria for judging the value of DSR work that could be included in the survey. Therefore, the two new criteria ("adoption by industry" and "generative potential") were added under "Other" in the existing survey.

Fifth, the 2010 survey [2] contained an error in which evaluation of "effectiveness" was omitted and evaluation of "efficacy" was inadvertently described using the explanation for effectiveness. This error was rectified in the online survey version.

As in the 2010 survey [2], respondents were first asked to provide demographic information about their journal editor responsibilities (if any) and whether or not they had (co-)authored a published paper *about* design science or a paper *using* design science as its research paradigm. As the survey was not anonymous, data was not needed about (but did confirm) basket-of-eight journal editorships, DESRIST program committee membership, and DESRIST paper co-authorship.

Following the demographic data collection, the survey contained questions above about each respondent's opinion of the relative importance of various potential criteria for assessing the suitability of publication. As in the 2010 survey [2], the survey was divided into four parts. Part 1 included questions about the importance of the Hevner et al guidelines as standards or criteria, part 2 contained questions about various evaluation practices and standards, part 3 had questions about the relative importance of aspects of design theory, while part 4 contained questions about the relative importance of miscellaneous other potential criteria.

As in the 2010 survey [2], each part contained questions that asked respondents to rate the importance of each criterion on a 0-to-10 scale, with zero being "irrelevant" and 10 being "mandatory". Additionally, as in the 2010 survey, each part contained a question that asked for open comments about the potential criteria in each part.

4   Survey Results

The survey was distributed via email in January 2015 to 976 potential respondents. Of these, 384 (39.2%) were editors (editor-in-chief, senior editor, or associate editor) of one or more basket-of-eight journals, 135 (13.8%) had served on at least one DESRIST program committee (2006-2014), and 572 (58.4%) had authored or co-authored at least one paper at a DESRIST conference (2006-2014). The above categories of potential respondents are not mutually exclusive, so total more than 100%.

4.1   Response Rates and Possible Non-Response Bias

Of the 976 survey emails sent out, Qualtrics results indicate that 472 (48%) of emails sent were opened. 148 respondents completed the survey, giving a response rate of 148/472 or 31.3%.

35.1% of respondents were journal editors, 23.0% had served on at least one DESRIST programme committee, and 66.9% had (co-)authored a paper at a DESRIST conference. DESRIST co-authors and programme committee members are thus over-representative of the surveyed sample. A higher percentage of respondents than the sample also belonged to more than one of these roles. However, as described in the next paragraph, many of the journal editors did not feel they had sufficient DSR expertise to answer the survey.

Of the 324 potential respondents who read the email request but didn't complete the survey, 135 or 41.6% kindly replied by email to give a reason why they weren't completing the survey. By and large, the most common responses were that the respondent didn't have DSR duties at their journal, lacked expertise in DSR, or wasn't interested in DSR. These and other reasons given are unrelated to different criteria and do not indicate any non-response bias.

4.2   Detailed Results

Tables 1-4 show the detailed results for the criteria ratings in each area and compare the ratings of the 2010 and 2015 surveys. The wordings of the criteria are shortened from those in the actual survey. 2010 ranks were computed from the 2010 mean ratings. The change columns show the increase or decrease in each from 2010 to 2015. Increasing standard deviation indicates increasing disagreement about a criterion.

Table 1. Ratings, Standard Deviations, and Ranks of Criteria in the Hevner et al Guidelines

Hevner et al (2004) Guidelines	2010			2015			Change		
Survey Item	Mean	Std Dev	Rank	Mean	Std Dev	Rank	Mean	Std Dev	Rank
Addressing *all* of the guidelines given in Hevner et al 2004	5.36	3.00	39	5.23	2.72	42	-0.13	-0.28	-3
Presenting an identifiable and viable design artefact (Guideline 1)	8.39	1.78	4	8.12	2.20	4	-0.27	+0.42	0
- Presenting one or more clearly defined new concepts	6.52	2.47	20	7.16	2.18	14	+0.64	-0.29	+6
- Presenting one or more clearly explained new models	6.16	2.41	26	6.10	2.26	25	-0.06	-0.15	+1
- Presenting one or more clearly explained new methods for building the artefact	6.29	2.44	23	5.74	2.56	32	-0.54	+0.12	-9
- Presenting one or more example instantiations of the artefact	7.30	2.23	14	7.07	2.28	16	-0.23	+0.05	-2
Addressing a relevant and important problem (Guideline 2)	9.05	1.21	1	8.85	1.74	1	-0.20	+0.52	0
Evaluating the utility, quality, and efficacy of the designed artefact (Guideline 3)	8.31	1.61	6	7.86	2.07	7	-0.45	+0.46	-1
Clearly identifying the novelty, generality, and significance of the contribution (Guideline 4)	8.45	1.74	3	8.43	1.86	2	-0.01	+0.13	+1
Rigorous use of the research methods (Guideline 5)	7.33	1.90	13	7.30	2.24	12	-0.03	+0.33	+1

Table 1. (*Continued*)

Developing the design using a cyclical, problem solving search process (Guideline 6)	6.09	2.46	28	5.74	2.75	33	-0.35	+0.28	-5
Addressing both rigour for the academic audience and relevance for the professional audience (Guideline 7)	7.20	2.07	16	7.28	2.50	13	+0.08	+0.43	+3

[Note: In the following text, criteria names/descriptions are shown in italics.]

As shown in table 1, *Addressing a relevant and important problem* (Hevner et al guideline 2) is still the highest rated criterion across all areas, while guideline 4 (*Clearly identifying the novelty, generality, and significance of the contribution*) has increased in ranking to #2, even though its mean rating has decreased very slightly. Guideline 1 (*Presenting an identifiable and viable design artefact*) remains ranked at #4 overall. Importantly, meeting all of the Hevner et al criteria [1] continues to be rated very lowly, third from the bottom in both 2010 and 2015 (note that 3 new items were included in 2015). The big changes in table 1 are that *Presenting new concepts* has increased in importance while *Presenting a method* has declined substantially.

Table 2 shows the results for criteria relating to evaluation. *Conducting some sort of evaluation* remains very important, although its rank has declined from #2 to #3, while *Evaluating the utility of the designed artefact for solving the problem to be addressed* remains the fifth most important criterion across all categories. Importantly, *Conducting an artificial evaluation* and *Quantitatively measuring outcomes during evaluation* have both increased significantly in their rankings.

Table 3 shows the results for criteria relating to design theory. Almost across the board, design theory related criteria have declined in their perceived importance, often substantially. An important exception is that *Specifying constructs as representations of the entities of interest in the theory* has increased in its importance ranking (which can be interpreted as constructs in March and Smith [16]), as has *Specifying an expository instantiation* (from Gregor and Jones [10] and March and Smith [16]).

Table 4 shows the results for other, miscellaneous criteria. By and large there is little change in the results for these items. *Relevance of* and *Significance of the problem to industry/society clearly established* both remain highly ranked, in accordance with the #1 rank of Hevner et al guideline 2. *Novelty of the new design artefact* has increased somewhat in the ranking of its perceived importance. Of the two candidate criteria added in 2015, *Adoption and use of the new artefact by real organisations* is lowly ranked at #38 out of 45, while *The generative potential of the artefact for further development and transfer to other problem areas* is medium ranked at #21 of 45.

Table 2. Ratings, Standard Deviations, and Ranks of Criteria Relating to Evaluation in DSR

DSR Evaluation	2010			2015			Change		
Survey Item	Mean	Std Dev	Rank	Mean	Std Dev	Rank	Mean	Std Dev	Rank
Conducting some sort of evaluation, whether artificial or naturalistic	8.80	1.40	2	8.28	1.74	3	-0.52	+0.34	-1
Conducting an Artificial evaluation	6.11	2.35	27	6.29	2.30	22	+0.18	-0.04	+5
Conducting a Naturalistic evaluation	7.18	2.16	17	6.90	1.89	18	-0.28	-0.27	-1
Evaluating the artefact's *utility* for *solving the problem to be addressed*	8.35	1.59	5	8.11	1.79	5	-0.24	+0.20	0
Evaluating the artefact's *efficacy**	7.11	2.02	18	6.78	2.07	20	-0.33	+0.05	-2
Evaluating the artefact's *effectiveness**	7.11	2.02	18	6.81	2.12	19	-0.30	+0.10	-1
Evaluating the artefact's *efficiency*	6.35	1.88	22	6.26	2.03	23	-0.10	+0.16	-1
Quantitatively measuring utility, efficiency, efficacy	5.74	2.42	35	5.95	2.22	27	+0.20	-0.20	+8
Comparing the artefact to other extant solutions	7.37	2.18	11	7.08	2.07	15	-0.29	-0.10	-4
Evaluating for side effects	6.21	2.19	24	5.92	2.09	28	-0.29	-0.10	-4

* Note: The 2010 survey [2] item inadvertently and ambiguously combined efficacy (the term used) and effectiveness (the explanation provided), so the 2010 results [2] are repeated for these two items.

Table 3. Ratings, Standard Deviations, and Ranks of Criteria Relating to Design Theory

IS Design Theories	2010			2015			Change		
Survey Item	Mean	Std Dev	Rank	Mean	Std Dev	Rank	Mean	Std Dev	Rank
Specifying a full and complete design theory	5.72	2.68	37	5.03	2.59	43	-0.69	-0.09	-6

Table 3. (*Continued*)

Specifying the meta-requirements or purpose and scope	6.80	2.41	19	6.11	2.52	24	-0.69	+0.11	-5
Specifying a meta-design or principles of form and function for the design artefact product	6.49	2.43	21	5.76	2.52	31	-0.73	+0.09	-10
Specifying a design method for instantiating the meta-design or principles of form and function for the design artefact process	5.99	2.28	31	5.24	2.34	41	-0.74	+0.05	-10
Specifying kernel theory(ies) or justificatory knowledge relevant to how the meta-design meets the meta-requirements	6.21	2.64	25	5.61	2.61	34	-0.60	-0.03	-9
Specifying kernel theory(ies) or justificatory knowledge relevant to the design method	5.95	2.41	32	5.32	2.46	40	-0.64	+0.05	-8
Specifying testable hypotheses or propositions about how well the meta-design meets the meta-requirements	5.79	2.72	34	5.51	2.52	36	-0.28	-0.20	-2
Specifying testable hypotheses or propositions about how well the design method results in an artefact consistent with the meta-design	5.73	2.64	36	5.32	2.54	39	-0.40	-0.09	-3
Specifying constructs as representations of the entities of interest in the theory	6.06	2.79	30	6.05	2.36	26	0.00	-0.43	+4
Specifying principle(s) of implementation in specific contexts	6.09	2.46	29	5.92	2.27	29	-0.18	-0.19	0
Specifying an expository instantiation	5.91	2.63	33	5.83	2.37	30	-0.07	-0.25	+3

Table 4. Ratings, Standard Deviations, and Ranks of Other Potential Criteria

Other Potential Criteria/Standards	2010			2015			Change		
Survey Item	Mean	Std Dev	Rank	Mean	Std Dev	Rank	Mean	Std Dev	Rank
Relevance of the problem to industry/society clearly established	8.05	1.77	7	7.97	1.80	6	-0.08	+0.03	+1
Significance of the problem to industry/society clearly established	7.87	1.80	9	7.58	1.84	9	-0.29	+0.04	0
Depth of analysis and clarity of understanding of the problem and its causes	7.92	1.42	8	7.50	1.79	10	-0.42	+0.37	-2
Depth or profoundness of insight	7.35	1.61	12	7.01	1.86	17	-0.33	+0.25	-5
Novelty of the new design artefact	7.29	2.02	15	7.38	2.14	11	+0.08	+0.12	+4
Size and complexity of the new artefact	4.51	2.36	41	4.19	2.80	44	-0.32	+0.44	-3
Amount of effort to develop the artefact	4.25	2.29	42	3.90	2.72	45	-0.35	+0.43	-3
Elegance of the design	5.22	2.34	40	5.40	2.46	37	+0.18	+0.13	+3
Simplicity of the design	5.62	2.22	38	5.53	2.33	35	-0.09	+0.10	+3
Clear understanding of why the new artefact works (or doesn't work)	7.68	2.04	10	7.82	1.81	8	+0.14	-0.23	+2
Adoption and use of the new artefact by real organisations*	N/A	N/A	N/A	5.38	2.70	38	N/A	N/A	N/A
The generative potential of the artefact for further development / and transfer to other problem areas*	N/A	N/A	N/A	6.51	2.22	21	N/A	N/A	N/A

5   Discussion

Having examined the detailed results for 2015 and compared them to the 2010 results, this section will now consider answers to the research questions, overall trends, limitations, implications, and suggestions for future work.

First, we consider the first research question: *Has the perceived importance of the various criteria changed since 2010?* Clearly, looking at the detailed results, the answer is yes, but overall, two major trends are worth noting with respect to the increase and decrease in perceived importance of various kinds of criteria. One clear trend is the decline in the perceived importance of the provision of design theory as a criterion for publication of good DSR. Another trend is one toward increasing research rigour and taking a more positivistic stance, particularly considering the increased importance rankings of these criteria: Rigorous use of the research methods (Guideline 5), Conducting an Artificial evaluation (which commonly evaluates efficacy by controlling for confounding variables), Quantitatively measuring utility, efficiency, or efficacy, Presenting one or more clearly defined new concepts, and Specifying constructs as representations of the entities of interest in the theory.

The second research question is: *How do any new criteria fit in with other existing criteria?* As discussed earlier, the candidate criterion of Industry adoption received a relatively low importance rating on average and ranked #38 out of 45. The candidate criterion of Generative potential was better received, with a perceived importance ranking of #21 out of 45.

The third research question is: *Which criteria are now considered to be the most important?* Selected Hevner et al criteria continue to be of high importance, with four of them being in the top 10 most highly rated. #1 is guideline 2 (Addressing a relevant and important problem). #2 is guideline 4 (Clearly identifying the novelty, generality, and significance of the contribution), where significance partly overlaps with guideline 2. #4 is guideline 1 (Presenting an identifiable and viable design artefact). #7 is guideline 3 (Evaluating the utility, quality, and efficacy of the designed artefact). Other highly rated criteria are consistent with those guidelines. The criteria rated #3 (Conducting some sort of evaluation, whether artificial or naturalistic) and #5 (Evaluating the arte-fact's utility for solving the problem to be addressed) are consistent with guideline 3. The criteria rated #6 (Relevance of the problem to industry/society clearly established) and #9 (Significance of the problem to industry/society clearly established) are consistent with guideline 2, but relevance seems to be perceived as more important than significance.

Two other criteria rated in the top 10 are not clearly related to the Hevner et al. guidelines, but are worth discussing. First, the #8 rated criterion is: Clear understanding of why the new artefact works (or doesn't work). It seems unlikely that this criterion will be fulfilled through the use of a positivistic, quantitative, theory testing evaluation. Other methods would seem to be necessary to achieve this. Second, the #10 rated criterion is: Depth of analysis and clarity of understanding of the problem and its causes. Again, the research methods discussed in the DSR literature largely do not address this, with the exception of Venable [22].

The fourth and final research question is: *Has there been a move away from the dissensus reported in Venable (2010) toward consensus?* Two ways to measure consensus or dissensus are the range and the standard deviation of responses. Both measures indicate a decrease in consensus or agreement about standards and criteria. In the 2015 survey, all criteria were rated at zero (0) by at least one individual respondent and were also rated ten (10) by at least one other respondent. These are the maximum possible range. While many items in the 2010 survey received a minimum rating of zero, many did not. Moreover, one can also compute the average of the standard deviation across all items. For the 2010 survey, the average was 2.18 (across a closed-end range of 11 from 0 to 10). For the 2015 survey, the average is 2.25, which is an increase of 0.07. This difference is not large, but clearly there is no convergence toward consensus and dissensus remains quite high.

Another interesting finding is that, across all items, the average of all the average criteria ratings has decreased. In 2010, the average across all ratings was 6.72 out of 10. In 2015, the average is 6.47, which is a decline of 0.25. One possible explanation for this is that, overall across the respondents, the use of criteria is considered to be less important or is less likely to be mandatory, and hence is less likely to be rigidly enforced. Of course, this is just speculation.

From a methodological point of view, one limitation of this study is that the sample was formulated theoretically to include various stakeholders in DSR publication, but may not be representative of the overall population. E.g., editors of less highly ranked journals were not surveyed (although many respondents also served in such a role). Another potential limitation is that some of the different criteria are at different levels, which some respondents found hard to rate. Given that the precise findings are not that important, but the overall trends and areas of priority are of interest, these limitations are not significant for this particular piece of research.

Overall, while this research provides a snapshot, it does not make arguments for why various criteria are rated as more important that others, nor does it make an argument for which criteria *should be* considered to be more important than others. It merely suggests that a dissensus continues and that ongoing discussion and work is needed to achieve a suitable level of agreement and useful guidance for researchers.

Finally, further research is needed to address the qualitative comments provided by the respondents and to compare responses from different classes of respondents (e.g. journal editors vs DSR authors). More importantly, this study only highlights the uncertainty in the domain of DSR publication. To resolve such uncertainty and dissensus, it is important to revisit criteria to develop clear, agreed standards and criteria for DSR publications with a clear rationale to substantiate why they *should be* applied to reviewing and accepting DSR publications.

References

1. Hevner, A.R., March, S.T., Park, J., Ram, S.: Design Science in Information Systems Research. MIS Quarterly 28(1), 75–105 (2004)
2. Venable, J.R.: Design Science Research Post Hevner et al: Criteria, Standards, Guidelines, and Expectations. In: Winter, R., Zhao, J.L., Aier, S. (eds.) DESRIST 2010. LNCS, vol. 6105, pp. 109–123. Springer, Heidelberg (2010)

3. Arnott, D., Pervan, G.: Design Science in Decision Support Systems Research: An assessment using the Hevner, March, Park, and Ram guidelines. Journal of the Association for Information Systems 13(11), 923–949 (2012)
4. Arnott, D., Pervan, G.: A critical analysis of decision support systems research revisited: the rise of design science. Journal of Information Technology, 1–25 (2014)
5. Venable, J., Pries-Heje, J., Baskerville, R.: A Comprehensive Framework for Evaluation in Design Science Research. In: Peffers, K., Rothenberger, M., Kuechler, B. (eds.) DESRIST 2012. LNCS, vol. 7286, pp. 423–438. Springer, Heidelberg (2012)
6. Venable, J.R., Pries-Heje, J., Baskerville, R.: FEDS: A Framework for Evaluation in Design Science Research. European Journal of Information Systems (2014), advance online publication at http://www.palgrave-journals.com/doifinder/10.1057/ejis.2014.36
7. Walls, J.G., Widmeyer, G.R., El Sawy, O.: Building an information system design theory for vigilant EIS. Information Systems Research 3(1), 36–59 (1992)
8. Walls, J.G., Widmeyer, G.R., El Sawy, O.: Assessing Information System Design Theory in Perspective: How Useful Was Our 1992 Initial Rendition? JITTA: Journal of Information Technology Theory and Application 6(2), 43–58 (2004)
9. Venable, J.R.: The Role of Theory and Theorising in Design Science Research. In: First International Conference on Design Science Research in Information Systems and Technology (DESRIST 2006), Claremont, CA, USA (2006)
10. Gregor, S., Jones, D.: The Anatomy of a Design Theory. Journal of the Association for Information Systems 8(5), 312–335 (2007)
11. Baskerville, R., Pries-Heje, J.: Explanatory Design Theory. Business & Information Systems Engineering (5), 271–282 (2010)
12. Venable, J.R.: Rethinking Design Theory in Information Systems. In: vom Brocke, J., Hekkala, R., Ram, S., Rossi, M. (eds.) DESRIST 2013. LNCS, vol. 7939, pp. 136–149. Springer, Heidelberg (2013)
13. Venable, J.R.: A Framework for Design Science Research Activities. In: 2006 Information Resource Management Association Conference. Information Resource Management Association, Washington, DC (2006)
14. Baskerville, R., Pries-Heje, J., Venable, J.R.: Evaluation Risks in Design Science Research: A Framework. In: Baskerville, R., Vaishnavi, V. (eds.) 3rd International Conference on Design Science Research in Information Systems and Technology (DESRIST 2008), Atlanta, Georgia, USA (2008)
15. Pries-Heje, J., Baskerville, R., Venable, J.R.: Strategies for Design Science Research Evaluation. In: Golden, W., Acton, T., Conboy, K., van der Heijden, H., Tuunainen, V.K. (eds.) 16th European Conference on Information Systems (ECIS 2008), Galway, Ireland (2008)
16. March, S.T., Smith, G.F.: Design and natural science research on information technology. Decision Support Systems 15(4), 251–266 (1995)
17. Sun, Y., Kantor, P.B.: Cross-Evaluation: A new model for information system evaluation. Journal of the American Society for Information Science and Technology 57(5), 614–628 (2006)
18. Rossi, M., Sein, M.: Design Research Workshop: A Proactive Research Approach (2003), http://tiesrv.hkkk.fi/iris26/presentation/workshop_designRes.pdf (retrieved July 17, 2005)
19. Avital, M., Te'eni, D.: From generative fit to generative capacity: Exploring an emerging dimension of information systems design and task performance. Information Systems Journal 19(4), 345–367 (2009)
20. Gill, T.G., Hevner, A.: A Fitness-Utility Model for Design Science Research. ACM Transactions on Management Information Systems 4(2), 237–252 (2013)

21. Gregor, S., Hevner, A.: Positioning and presenting design science research for maximum impact. MIS Quarterly 37(2), 337–355 (2013)
22. Venable, J.R.: Using Coloured Cognitive Mapping (CCM) for Design Science Research. In: Tremblay, M.C., VanderMeer, D., Rothenberger, M., Gupta, A., Yoon, V. (eds.) DESRIST 2014. LNCS, vol. 8463, pp. 345–359. Springer, Heidelberg (2014)

Projecting the Future for Design Science Research: An Action-Case Based Analysis

Richard Baskerville[1](✉) and Jan Pries-Heje[2]

[1]Georgia State University, Atlanta, USA and Curtin University, Perth, Australia
baskerville@acm.org
[2]Roskilde University, Roskilde, Denmark
janph@ruc.dk

Abstract. Design science research should be relevant, valuable, purposeful and prescriptive. Its value as a relevant source of prescriptions implies the practical usefulness of its results beyond a single expository instantiation. But propagation of such design science products as design principles and theories appears to be a key challenge. In this paper we commence with a DESRIST paper from 2012 that instantiated design principles in an artifact for a bank. That paper included plans and techniques for future use of its principles (propagation), including prescriptions for a five-phase adoption process. In this paper we discuss the propagation issues around *generalizing* design science research across multiple contexts and propose alternative propagation concepts of *projectability* and *entrenchment*. The existing concepts around generalizability have issues that make them less suitable for design science research: context (local/possible worlds) and theoretical statements based on functional explanations. A *projection* is any relevant instance that supports a theory. Projectability involves defining the relationship between a base case or evidence and a projection. Entrenchment occurs when design principles or theories have stimulated many actual projections. We demonstrate these concepts in a case study of propagation: a chemical manufacturer and service provider that adopted the design principles arising from that 2012 DESRIST banking-based design science research. We conclude that generalizability is too well-oriented to descriptive research and argue that a more appropriate framing for design science research is projectability and entrenchment. The paper includes recommendations to increase the projectability of design science research.

1 Introduction

Everyday companies create business cases and cost-benefit analyses that involve prediction of the future. The near future is often predicted using cost forecasts and the more distant future is predicted on the assumption that benefits will loiter out there in the future. The process of design science research is somewhat similar. Develop an artefact, a design theory or some design principles. Evaluate it. Then try to predict other arenas in which it may also be useful. This is more than just generalizing from an instance … it is a prediction of how useful our future will be after we propel our products into it.

© Springer International Publishing Switzerland 2015
B. Donnellan et al. (Eds.): DESRIST 2015, LNCS 9073, pp. 280–291, 2015.
DOI: 10.1007/978-3-319-18714-3_18

Our current ability in predicting the future for design science research is as flawed and prone to errors as naïve attempts to predict potential benefits for a new product without knowing how the market could develop, how competitors could react, how and which user needs will develop, etc. In other words, we have limited knowledge about how design principles and theories propagate to settings other than the one in which they originated. This paper presents insights from an empirical design science research study that was presented at DESRIST three years ago [1]. This study developed design principles at two levels: (1) design principles for improving teams by systematically building social capital, (2) a method for propagating the design principles to other settings. It was grounded in a banking case (Danske Bank). The principles were embodied in a six-by-six, virtual project, social capital, team development framework [for details on the 6x6, see reference 1]. The DESRIST report considered a projection of potential future use: "Using a single case study we have confirmed the proposition and now need to consider what can be abstracted or generalized to other companies facing similar problems?" [1, p. 267]. The report proposed the following five-phase propagation process as a means for using the design science results in other, future organizational settings (p. 268):

1. Establish the challenges you are facing in your organization. This can be done through an interview study or through a survey using the seven problem areas that we identified.
2. If the challenges are similar you can benefit from adopting the six-by-six framework for systematically building social capital in projects.
3. Before you can adopt the framework you need to take each of the techniques mentioned in the framework (see appendix) and make sure that they are useful in your context or whether other techniques should be added. Consider experience from virtual projects in your organization and "harvest" positive results using different techniques.
4. When the framework has been locally consolidated, pilot it in five-to-seven projects.
5. When the pilot project has been evaluated and results taken into account then roll-out the six-by-six framework as adapted to your organization.

In the paper that follows, we present insights that follow from the experience of applying this five-phase process as a means of propagating the framework-based design principles developed in the 2012 bank case to another organization, a chemical manufacturer and service provider in 2014.

2   Issues with Generalizing in Design Science Research

Science aims "to discover and to formulate in *general terms* the conditions under which events of various sorts occur, the statements of such determining conditions being the explanations of the corresponding happenings" [2, p. 4, emphasis added]. We sometimes assume that the greater the generalizability of our research findings, the more important and intellectually useful is our accomplishment. But generalizability in science is a deeply value-laden concept. It can take different forms for different research designs [3]. Authorities debate how to distinguish its forms and attributes [e.g., 4, 5]. But given the high degree of practical relevance expected from design science [6], it seems that the greater the generality of any design study results, the greater the impact of the science.

Importing generalizability concepts from other sciences leads to issues in design science. The phenomena in the natural sciences "have an air of 'necessity' about them in their subservience to natural law." Instead, the phenomena in design science "have an air of 'contingency' in their malleability by their environment." Design scientists make general empirical propositions about designs that, "given different circumstances, might be quite other than they are" [7, p. xi].The practical value of design studies lies in their consideration for applicability beyond a single context-bound example [8]. For example, the findings of a past design study in information systems might offer useful knowledge for a future design study in urban design. In design, such usefulness should be able to cross such conceptually different contexts as information systems and urban planning.

2.1   The Issue of Context: Local Worlds

As with any other branch of science, the audience for design science may be more interested in useful future design prescriptions than they are in descriptions of a particular, past, local design. It is a sense of impact that design science research shares with experimental science. Like experiments, scientific designs "are highly local but have general aspirations" [9, p. 18]. It is an issue between the localized nature of the knowledge achieved in the actual empirical design process and the more generalized knowledge goals that science aims to achieve. This connection of design science results to broad future applicability is critical; otherwise the results are merely descriptive history of past design work. For future applicability, "generalization at the linguistic level of the constructs" is needed rather than a history of construct operationalization in a particular design [9, p. 18].

In design, it is not just the generalizability of findings from the study of one phenomenon to explain other phenomena; it also regards the usefulness of the knowledge across different contexts. Design findings propagate to other settings as a means of action, not description [10].

For example, consider studies that focus on a phenomenon in a sample of instances where that sample has been randomly selected from the population of such instances. Such studies will often adopt a statistical frame of generalizability that will project an expectation that characteristics found in the sample will also inhabit the population. For these studies, we assume that the relevant characteristics of the population are predictable or controllable. This assumption entails the assumption that the *context* of generalization is predictable or controllable.

But in design science the context can be unpredictable or uncontrollable because many design contexts do not yet exist. Design science is materially prescriptive in the sense that its theoretical statements prescribe as-yet unconstructed artifacts for as-yet non-existent contexts. In philosophical terms, design science operations span our actual world and possible worlds. "A possible world is a world that differs in some way from our 'actual world'" [11, p. 745]. Much of this philosophy is concerned with possible worlds that could have been, the degree to which such possible worlds are real, and the spatiotemporal distance between our actual world and possible worlds [12]. These concepts lead to our notion of a *local world*, the spatiotemporally closest possible world that constitutes "our" actual world. Design Science is concerned with possible worlds that could be, and the spatiotemporal distance between our actual world and a desirable possible local world: "Designers deal with possible worlds and with opinions about what the parts and the whole of the human environment should be." [13, p. 25] This aspect of design science creates fundamental issues in scientific generalization.

General statements in design science are prescriptive, functional, purposeful and future oriented [14]. For example, "all ship's clocks should be battery-driven" can be stated as an indicative conditional, "if the clock is for a ship, it should be battery-driven". This is a prescriptive generalization ("should") that proceeds from an environmental requirement (weight-driven clocks cannot work on board ships because the clock, as well as the weights move in relation to gravity). The counterfactual conditional is, "if the clock had been for a ship, it would have been battery-driven".

We can see from the nature of lawlike generalizations that generalized prescriptive statements confront the issue of their operation in contexts (i.e., local worlds) that have not yet been considered, and indeed may not yet exist. There will be new kinds of ships that could well introduce new requirements for clocks that demand new generalizations. Such new conditionals are non-existent in the logic because the contexts are as-yet non-existent. This consequence was among those that drove Simon to eschew imperative logics in favor of searching through a solution space comprised by declarative logics [7].

This issue also inhabits one of the existing alternatives to generalizability: Transferability. Transferability is associated with forms of naturalistic inquiry such as action research [15, 16]. In originating this concept of transferability, Lincoln and Guba indicate it requires a deep knowledge of both the "sending" and "receiving" contexts in order to determine adequate congruence in the contexts [16, p. 124]. It is grounded in "naturalistic generalizability" [17, p. 324], and like generalizability, transferability fits poorly with design science because it requires at least partial grounding in local worlds (contexts). The logical requirement means transferability is not an ideal conceptualization of how design theories are useful for designing as-yet immaterialized future artifacts in as-yet unknown contexts.

3   Projectability as a Design Science Alternative to Generalizability

The existing formulations of generalizability and transferability are not well-suited for situations involving future applicability inherent in the materially prescriptive nature of design science. Rather than inject yet another distant form of generalizability into this mix, we propose an alternative concept that fits the prescriptive nature of design science: *Projectability*. Nelson Goodman [18] originally developed this concept in the philosophy of science as a means to delimit and describe realized (factual) and unrealized (counterfactual) antecedents in making lawlike generalizations. Generalizability provides good framing for descriptive research that centralizes causal statements (e.g., X causes Y). But projectability itself provides good framing for prescriptive research (like design science) that centralizes purposeful statements (e.g., I want to achieve Y and therefore I will do X).

Generalization describes and explains the history of regularities or consistencies that have previously existed or currently exist. *Projection* can also prescribe and propose possible regularities or consistencies that could be created to construct future worlds. The term encompasses the action-oriented propagation of design principles and theory. A *projection* is any relevant instance that supports a theory:

> *The problem of confirmation, or of valid projection, is the problem of defining a certain relationship between evidence or base cases on the one hand, and hypotheses, predictions or projections on the other. [18, p. 87]*

> *A theory is projectable if it is capable of being projected, has no known violations (observations that oppose the theory), and not all possible instances have been examined. A theory is actually projected when some (but not necessarily all) of its possible instances have been examined. When the terms of the theory have been used in many projections, it is said to be entrenched [18, pp. 87-95, 19].*

Goodman's projectability concept provides an ideal alternative to generalizability in the case of design science research. For example, empirical design studies will typically instantiate an artifact, which means that such studies will *actually project* their design principles or design theory. These actual projections are known as expository instantiations [20]. The actual projections enable the empirical statements that are important for justifying the theoretical statements.

In Goodman's terms [18], many additional or future projections (instantiations) will serve to *entrench* the design principles or theory. We can expect that such projections will take the design principles or theory into different contexts. Another way of describing such projections would be to say that these additional or future projections may justify the design principles or theory in different possible worlds.

4   Research Method

Our work originated with a previous case – Danske Bank - where Design Science Research had resulted in the two levels of design principles mentioned earlier: a design of a six-by-six virtual team development framework and a process (method) for propagating this framework. To evaluate the promise of projectability we carried these principles into a subsequent case where we have combined intervention (using the both levels of design principles) with interpretation in order to achieve both improvement in the setting (e.g., better functioning virtual teams) and our own understanding of the nature of projectability of design principles and theory. This interpretive-intervention approach is known as an *action case* [17]. It entails the key factors characterized in Table 1 as situated in this research.

Table 1. Situated action case approach factors [adapted from 17]

Factor	Attribute	Action case concern	As situated in our research setting
Suitability	Research Design	A declared framework of ideas and methodology?	Invited by case hosts: The 6x6 virtual team development framework and propagation method.
	Researcher Skills	Experience and skills to make an intervention?	Sound: A researcher skilled experienced in design science and action research and a participant in the previous banking case.
Interpretation	Richness	Sufficiently rich context to yield understanding?	Quite rich: the subsequent case was a global firm with a large
	Focus	Clear research question or problem?	Aim: interpreting the intervention events using projectability
Intervention	Scale	A manageable scale?	Use an overall champion manager and collaborating project managers
	Participation style	Level of organization member participation?	Researcher-led workshops that propagate the framework through training and adoption
	Critical impact	Human/social issues?	Social capital aspect of framework could improve social setting by better awareness of social values
Practicability	Economics	Sufficient financial support & researcher time?	Corporate support from champion, researcher was available
	Access	Negotiable/feasible?	Directive by high level champion
	Politics	Conflict with organizational politics?	Conflict noted with existing project management practices.
	Control	Research projected controlled?	Use of a pilot study to build momentum.

The case setting was a company named Alpha Bravo (anonym), a chemical manufacturer and service provider that is a world leader chemical science. Alpha Bravo is an organization dedicated to helping their customers achieve optimal performance by maximizing the benefits of their chemical processes and products, using the least possible energy and resources, and operating in the most responsible way.

The empirical process was straightforward. The contact with Alpha Bravo arose when two managers attended a presentation of the six-by-six framework for virtual teams made in a meeting of the Danish Engineering Association. One of the managers was responsible for all projects and project managers at Alpha Bravo. He wondered, "Can we use this for our virtual teams?" Ultimately this contact led to a decision by Alpha Bravo to adopt the framework as a means to improve all virtual teams at Alpha Bravo.

Action case methodology embodies the combination of an interventional practice experience (change) and interpretation (understanding) of the experience. In this case the practice experience is based in applying in Alpha Bravo the propagation process and the virtual team development framework from the banking case. The interpretation and understanding of this experience resulted from the use of projectability concepts to explain the events in the practice experience.

5   Projecting the Five-Phase Framework

The Alpha Bravo adoption decision opened the process of making a new actual projection of the framework using the five-phase propagation process developed by Pries-Heje & Pries-Heje [1] and described in the introduction. After developing the five phase process in the banking case, the design principles were projected in a substantially different kind of organization.

In terms of possible worlds, the two organizational worlds involved were the banking setting and the chemistry setting. These two actual worlds were close in some regards, distant in others. The worlds were close because both organizations involve virtual teams operating across different countries, the virtual teams were developing software, the organizations included service missions, and the organizations were headquartered in Denmark. However, the worlds were also distant in other ways. One organization was producing commercial and retail banking services, developing banking software mainly in Denmark and India, and had extensive tele-presence and e-meeting support. The other organization was producing chemical equipment in Denmark, and other countries, and chemical and environmental engineering services all over the world. For the chemical equipment and the services embedded software and business software was developed as an important part of the whole product. Its teams were operating mainly across Denmark, Russia, India and China, and there was more limited virtual team meeting support technology. Could the five phase process enable the projection of the framework into this different context (this different "possible world")?

Phase 1. *Establish the challenges you are facing in your organization. This can be done through an interview study or through a survey using the seven problem areas that we identified.*

The design researchers used a workshop followed by individual interviews. The reason for the workshop can be understood as the need for the design scientists to understand the context at Alpha Bravo as well as the need for inventorying the challenges. In terms of projection, the design scientists needed to understand the spatiotemporal distance between the actual world on which the framework was based (the bank) and the actual world into which the framework was being projected (Alpha Bravo). The workshop was held in March 2013 with 20 participants from different places and countries within the company. The workshop used brainstorming, affinity analysis and dot vote to arrive at a list of challenges. The challenges identified were:

1. Challenges related to communication and interaction technology
2. The nature of the project life-cycle in Alpha Bravo. E.g. that the whole virtual team did not start at the same time
3. Cultural differences – E.g. virtual teams at Alpha Bravo included people from Russia, China, Denmark and often other countries
4. The central core with most relevant knowledge and experience always situated in Denmark

Phase 2. *If the challenges are similar you can benefit from adopting the six-by-six framework for systematically building social capital in projects.*

During summer 2013 the design researchers reviewed and compared the challenges from the bank study. These were:

1. Social ties take time to build – Just putting people from different places into the same team does not create social ties within the team.
2. Not enough trust in relationships especially across Denmark and India – To work well together trust is needed.
3. Lack of shared vision and common vocabulary – This is necessary to build parts of the same artifact or product at different places.
4. Cultural distance – meaning that the ways and means, traditions and expectations are highly different in different parts of the organization.
5. Communication Issues – Different backgrounds and different cultures often result in mis-communicate.
6. Lack of reciprocity between Denmark and India – The Danish project participants often reported that they were giving more to the projects than they received back.
7. Not sufficient team identification across sites – People in the same team distributed across different sites did not feel as if they were the same team.

The design researchers decided that the list of challenges was similar enough to support a reasonable belief in potential success from the implementation of the six-by-six framework for virtual teams within Alpha Bravo. In terms of projectability, this decision represented a belief that the two worlds were sufficiently close for the projection of the design principles. This focus on challenges, rather than the firms' products or culture is a critical aspect of projection. The two possible worlds were close in some ways; distant in others. This decision meant that the design researchers believed that the ways in which the two worlds were close were more important than the ways in which the two worlds were different. It portended a new possible world: one in which virtual teams in Alpha Bravo operated more effectively; and one that was close to the present actual world of Alpha Bravo. There was also the belief that the projection of the banking framework into the present actual world of Alpha Bravo would create the new possible world.

Phase 3. Before you can adopt the framework you need to take each of the techniques mentioned in the framework (see appendix) and make sure that they are useful in your context or whether other techniques should be added. Consider experience from virtual projects in your organization and "harvest" positive results using different techniques.

Design researchers adapted the 2012 six-by-six framework to Alpha Bravo (about 10% of the framework was changed). Changes were needed to account for the different level of virtual teamwork support technology available at Alpha Bravo. A few techniques were also removed because they were specific to Danske Bank. There was also a major addition to the framework. Unlike the bank, Alpha Bravo has many shorter, six-month projectS and many longtime (15-20 years) employees. As a result, many virtual team startups included reunions of former virtual team co-workers. To account for these prior project relationships, design researchers developed a *relationship matrix* of techniques that recorded the strong and weak social ties at project initiation. These techniques included patterns of risky relationships used to identify potential risks associated with these initial relationships existing at the beginning of a project.

These adaptations represented the actions needed to project the 2012 design principles into the actual world of Alpha Bravo. They account for the differences between the banking firm actual world (context) and the chemistry firm actual world with practical adjustments to the principles that include dropping some, adding some, and revising some as the actual world requires. Because the largest part of the framework was preserved, the Phase 3 results indicate that the design principles are projectable.

Phase 4. When the framework has been locally consolidated, pilot it in five-to-seven projects.

It was somewhat difficult to identify a pilot project in Alpha Bravo. Ideal projects for a pilot would be newly started or just about to start with a new virtual team. The design researchers tried different divisions without success. Finally in the beginning of 2014 the design scientists turned up a number of projects in the environmental division that were about to start new virtual teams with participants in Denmark and

China. A two-day facilitation workshop was held in January 2014 to train ten virtual team managers in the use of the revised framework. The ten participants learned how to facilitate the use of the techniques and the framework. The pilot began in three projects.

Two of the three projects in the pilot were cancelled for reasons unrelated to the framework. One of these two projects never materialized because the end customer simply never signed the contract. The second project was similarly cancelled halfway to completion. The manager for the third project was reassigned, and the newly assigned project manager had not been a workshop participant. As a consequence, the framework was either unused or it went unevaluated in the Alpha Bravo pilot.

The pilot was evaluated in August 2014. Experience with the pilot indicates that the projection of the design principles, in terms of the main framework, did not cross over from the actual world of the banking firm to develop a new possible world for the chemistry firm. Since the chemistry firm did not pursue any further attempt at the pilot (yet – February 2015), it suggests that the actual worlds of the two firms were too distant to enable the projection. This suggestion indicates that the Phase 2 results (similarity of challenges) may have been incorrect. One possible explanation is that the Phase 2 was made in a different division than that used for the pilot. This explanation may indicate that the actual worlds of the two divisions in Alpha Bravo are themselves distant, or at least that the Phase 4 division was more distant from the actual world of the bank than the Phase 2 division. In other words, the context of the Phase 2 division may have been suitable for the framework, but the context of the Phase 4 division was not. The results might have been different if the pilot had been conducted in the Phase 2 division.

Phase 5. *When the pilot project has been evaluated and results taken into account then roll-out the six-by-six framework as adapted to your organization.*

Since Alpha Bravo did not pursue the rollout, it is tempting to assume the projection failed and nothing was learned. However, three aspects of rollout are notable. First, there is an indication that the actual world of the Phase 2 division was close to the actual world of the bank, and that the actual world of the Phase 4 division was not that close. Had the pilot run in the Phase 2 division, it might have succeeded. In other words, an actual projection might have developed. However, the pilot indicates that, had there been further rollout in Phase 5, the projection to the Phase 4 division might not have succeeded. Running the pilot projection in the friendly context of the closest possible world is not the best predictor of how well the design principles will fit more distant worlds.

Second, the Phase 2 experience strengthens the 2012 banking experience in indicating that the design principles are projectable, although not yet actually projected beyond the original banking instance. We find strong projectability, but not yet actual projection. The design principles have not yet propagated.

Third, while the design principles embodied in the 2012 framework did not materialize an actual projection in 2014, there was a spurious propagation of design principles. The use of the relationship matrix that arose in Phase 3 itself propagated in Alpha Bravo and led to the reduction in virtual team problems in at least two projects.

Although not an intentional product of design science *per se*, we could regard it as projectable and actually projected. As a design principle, the relationship matrix is a product of the actual world of the chemistry firm, and its characteristic closeness to this world may explain its projectability.

6   Summary and Conclusion

This paper originated in the projection of a framework from DESRIST 2012. We have discussed the issues around *generalizing* design science research across multiple contexts and into the future: We have found that the existing concept of generalizability has issues that make it less suitable for design science research. Instead we have proposed alternative concepts: *Projectability* and *entrenchment*. Projectability involves defining the relationship between a base case or evidence and a projection. Entrenchment occurs when design principles or theories have stimulated many actual projections.

In an action case – Alpha Bravo – we have demonstrated the projection of the 2012 DESRIST framework. Furthermore we have shown that projection can use a five-phase method that we have detailed above (see discussion section).

Generalizability concepts are widely applicable across the many different forms of descriptive research. However, design science has features that make generalizability less suitable. Design science has a future orientation, explanations that are functional in nature, principles and theories that are descriptive, and an impact on the actual world that lead to as-yet unembodied possible worlds. A more appropriate framing for the design principles and theories that proceed from design science research is projectability and entrenchment.

References

1. Pries-Heje, J., Pries-Heje, L.: Designing a Framework for Virtual Management and Team Building. In: Peffers, K., Rothenberger, M., Kuechler, B. (eds.) DESRIST 2012. LNCS, vol. 7286, pp. 256–270. Springer, Heidelberg (2012)
2. Nagel, E.: The Structure of Science: Problems in Scientific Explanation. Routledge and Kegan Paul, London (1961)
3. Lee, A.S., Baskerville, R.L.: Generalizing Generalizability In Information Systems Research. Information Systems Research 14(3), 221–243 (2003)
4. Lee, A.S., Baskerville, R.L.: Conceptualizing Generalizability: New Contributions and a Reply. MIS Quarterly 36(3), 749–761 (2012)
5. Tsang, E.W.K., Williams, J.N.: Generalization and Hume's Problem of Induction: Misconceptions and Clarifications. MIS Quarterly 36(3), 729–748 (2012)
6. Hevner, A.R., et al.: Design Science in Information Systems Research. MIS Quarterly 28(1), 75–105 (2004)
7. Simon, H.A.: The Science of the Artificial, 3rd edn. MIT Press, Cambridge (1996)
8. Williams, R., Pollock, N.: Moving Beyond the Single Site Implementation Study: How (and Why) We Should Study the Biography of Packaged Enterprise Solutions. Information Systems Research 23(1), 1–22 (2012)

9. Shadish, W.R., Cook, T.D., Campbell, D.T.: Experimental and Quasi-Experimental Designs for Generalized Causal Inference. Houghton Mifflin, Boston (2002)
10. Bunge, M.: Scientific Research II: The Search for Truth. Studies in the Foundations Methodology and Philosophy of Science, vol. 3. Springer, New York (1967)
11. Crane, T.: Possible worlds. In: Honderich, T. (ed.) The Oxford Companion to Philosophy, p. 744. Oxford University Press, Oxford (2005)
12. Lewis, D.: On the Plurality of Worlds. Malden Mass, Blackwell (1986)
13. Buchanan, R.: Rhetoric, Humanism and Design. In: Buchanan, R., Margolin, V. (eds.) Discovering Design, University of Chicagor Press, Chicago (1995)
14. Baskerville, R., Pries-Heje, J.: Explanatory Design Theory. Business & Information Systems Engineering 2(5), 271–282 (2010)
15. Guba, E.G., Lincoln, Y.S.: Epistemological and Methodological Bases of Naturalistic Inquiry. Educational Communications and Technology Journal 30(4), 233–252 (1982)
16. Lincoln, Y.S., Guba, E.G.: Naturalistic Inquiry. Sage, Newbury Park (1985)
17. Hellström, T.: Transferability and Naturalistic Generalization: New Generalizability Concepts for Social Science or Old Wine in New Bottles? Quality & Quantity 42(3), 321–337 (2008)
18. Goodman, N.: Fact, Fiction, & Forecast. Harvard University Press, Cambridge (1955)
19. Baskerville, R., Pries-Heje, J.: Design Theory Projectability. In: Doolin, B., Lamprou, E., Mitev, N., McLeod, L. (eds.) IS&O 2014. IFIP AICT, vol. 446, pp. 219–232. Springer, Heidelberg (2014)
20. Gregor, S., Jones, D.: The Anatomy of a Design Theory. Journal of the Association for Information Systems 8(5), 312–335 (2007)

Design Practice and Design Thinking

Multi-criteria Selection in Design Science Projects – A Procedure for Selecting Foresight Methods at the Front End of Innovation

Patrick Brandtner[1(✉)], Markus Helfert[2], Andreas Auinger[1], and Kurt Gaubinger[3]

[1]University of Applied Sciences Upper Austria, Campus Steyr
{patrick.brandtner,andreas.auinger}@fh-steyr.at
[2]Dublin City University, Dublin, Ireland
markus.helfert@computing.dcu.ie
[3]University of Applied Sciences Upper Austria, Campus Wels
kurt.gaubinger@fh-wels.at

Abstract. In order to identify the best option(s) out of a set of alternatives selection procedures are used in many different fields of application. Depending on the respective setting and research domain, developing or selecting an appropriate selection procedure is a complex and challenging task. This paper proposes a procedure for selecting a set of options out of a large amount of alternatives. The procedure is used within a Design Science Context. It has been developed, applied and evaluated in the course of a current research project addressing the highly dynamic Front End of Innovation. This represents a classic "wicked" and challenging Design Science problem. The selection procedure proposed in this paper can serve as a reference framework for other Design Science based projects in similar "wicked" application domains, where a theory- and practice-based definition of selection criteria and a structured evaluation process requires comprehensive domain knowledge and deep practical insights.

Keywords: Selection procedure · Design Science Research · Front End of Innovation · Corporate Foresight · Focus Group Study

1 Introduction

Multi-criteria selection procedures are used in many different fields of application in order to select the best option(s) of a defined set of alternatives. In this context, it is often hard to define what "best" means. It is often challenging to define a procedure based on criteria to evaluate a set of alternatives. In literature, a broad variety of multi-criteria selection procedures for different kinds of purposes can be found: be it for selecting the most appropriate standard software out of many solution providers [1,2], be it for selecting the best of a set of alternative actions using simulation experiments [3,4], be it for selecting the most appropriate construction method in concrete building [5] or be it for selecting suppliers in an organizational context [6,7]. Depending on the respective application domain, the selection of a suitable selection procedure together

© Springer International Publishing Switzerland 2015
B. Donnellan et al. (Eds.): DESRIST 2015, LNCS 9073, pp. 295–310, 2015.
DOI: 10.1007/978-3-319-18714-3_19

with suitable selection criteria can be a very challenging and highly complex task. Applying an inappropriate or insufficient selection procedure has negative effects on the outcome of the whole selection process [8–11]. Selection processes have to be developed based on domain criteria considering frameworks and well know procedures, in order to provide transparency, reliability and validity in projects.

This is especially true in a Design Science context, where evaluation plays a key role in order to ensure that the results developed meet a defined purpose. Without evaluation, outcomes are unconfirmed declarations that an artifact meets the defined purpose [12] (i.e. be useful for selecting a set of methods in a given project setting). Design Science addresses research through the building and evaluation of artifacts, which have to be designed in order to meet an identified business need. Hence, utility can be regarded as the goal of Design Science research. The artifact should not only be able to be applicable in the respective environment (relevance) but also to provide additions to the knowledge base [13]. In the course of artefact design and development, divergent and convergent thinking is essential: while divergent thinking is highly innovative and generates multiple, alternative solutions to the problem identified, convergent thinking is essential for evaluating the different alternatives and selecting the most contextually relevant one(s) out of them. Hence, a structured, criteria-based evaluation and selection procedure is especially important in a Design Science context [14].

A core element of Design Science is practitioner insight – not only in the course of artifact development, but also in the course of artifact evaluation. In the current paper, a selection procedure will be presented, that helps to provide transparency. Development and evaluation of this procedure was done by applying it in the setting of a current Design Science research project "InnoStrategy 2.0". We specifically selected this project, as it addresses a wicked research problem [15,13] and provides a good setting for evaluating and testing the proposed procedure in an actual Design Science context. A wicked research problem is characterized by unstable requirements, complex relationships and interactions among subcomponents of the problem and constraints based upon ill-defined environmental contexts. Project success strongly depends on human social abilities (creativity, gut feeling) and effective solutions must address implicit knowledge as well as complex interaction processes in teams. The selected project aims at developing a process model addressing the highly volatile Front End of Innovation (FEI). The FEI includes the earliest stages and activities of the innovation process and usually starts with opportunity identification, opportunity selection and idea generation. In this application domain, uncertainty, gut feeling and creativity play a major role and managerial decisions have huge implications on the subsequent phases along the innovation process [16–18] (cf. section 4.2).

The reminder of the paper is structured as follows. In a first step, the research method of the paper (cf. section 2) followed by a general introduction regarding Design Science Research is presented, providing and summarizing the framework conditions of the research project InnoStrategy 2.0 (cf. section 3). Subsequently, the application and testing domain of the paper (Innovation Management and Corporate Foresight, cf. section 4) is discussed, and the procedure for selecting foresight methods at the Font End of Innovation in accordance with the framework conditions of the Design Science approach is presented in section 5. In this context, criteria-based selection is essential, as there is a wide variety of foresight methods available (cf. section 4.4). Identifying and selecting appropriate foresight methods out of this plethora of methods which are applicable at the Front End of Innovation and which fulfil the requirements at this stage of the innovation process is a challenging task, which has not yet been addressed - neither in innovation management nor in corporate foresight related literature. Finally, the paper concludes with the main findings and lessons learned in the course of the selection procedure development and application (cf. section 6).

2   Research Method

The research question underlying this paper is the following: How should a systematic selection procedure providing a clear evaluation structure and including key selection criteria look like? Applied to the research project InnoStrategy 2.0, the proposed selection procedure should be able to (a) fulfill theoretical implications and practical requirements at the Front End of Innovation and (b) to address the specific framework conditions of a Design Science project.

In order to develop our selection procedure we follow a Design Science Research approach using the Process Model proposed by Peffers et al. (2006) (cf. figure 1):

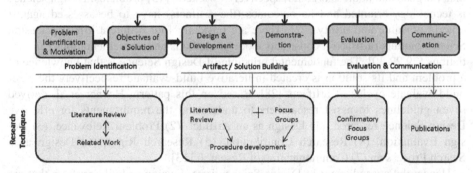

Fig. 1. Research Methodology of the Paper (adopted from Peffers et al. (2006))

Problem identification and motivation was done by conducting an extensive literature review regarding existing selection procedures in Design Science projects in general and for selecting foresight methods at the Front End of Innovation in specific terms. As discussed above, appropriate procedures for assessing and selecting various approaches are currently limited or not existing. However, literature presents us with a plethora of foresight methods that offer huge potential at this stage of the innovation process (cf. section 4.4).

As research context we use a research project, InnoStrategy 2.0. This offers us a suitable research environment to design and develop a structured, criteria-based procedure for selecting foresight methods to support strategic orientation at the Front End of Innovation.

3   Design Science Research

Research aims to find solutions and answers to questions concerning the un-known. In literature, research is defined as a logical process of steps applied to collect and analyze data in order to improve the knowledge and understanding of a topic or issue respectively to solve a problem perceived [19–21]. Solely focusing on the domain of information systems, a plethora of different approaches on conducting research can be found in literature. In information systems (IS), knowledge to date has been acquired by two complementary but distinct paradigms: behavioral or natural sciences and Design Sciences [22,23,13]. Originating from natural science paradigm, behavioral science aims at finding the truth by developing and justifying theories that explain or predict a specific phenomenon [24]. Usually starting with a hypothesis, behavioral science research collects data to either prove or disprove a defined hypothesis [25]. The Design Science paradigm on the other hand has its roots in engineering and the sciences of the artificial [26] and positions itself as a problem-solving paradigm [27]. Design Science can be defined as an attempt to create outputs that serve a particular human purpose with the objective of producing an artifact which must be designed and then evaluated thoroughly [12,23,22,28].

Design science focuses on creating "things" or artifacts that serve a particular human purpose and address urgent respectively "wicked" [15] problems. Design science is technology-oriented and its outcomes (the artifacts) have to be assessed against criteria of value and utility [22]. There are basically four different kinds of Design Science outputs (artifacts): constructs models, methods and implementations / instantiations [29,22,30]. The fundamental principle of Design Science is that knowledge of a problem and its solution is created in iterative build-evaluate respectively theorize-build-evaluate cycles of artifacts [28]. Based on this pattern, Hevner et al. derived seven guidelines to assist researchers to understand the requirements for effective Design Science research: (1) Design as an Artifact, (2) Problem Relevance, (3) Design Evaluation, (4) Research Contribution, (5) Research Rigor, (6) Design as a Search Process an (7) Communication of Research [13].

Hence, the core element of Design Science is to develop or build artifacts that are theoretically grounded (rigorous knowledge base) and to justify or evaluate those artifacts for the particular environment (relevance for application environment).

Many different methods and techniques can be found and applied in the context of Design Science to build, evaluate and improve artifacts, including experimental, observational, testing, descriptive and more recently action research methods [12,29,31,13,32]. Those methods can support divergent as well as convergent thinking.

In this paper the evaluation of different alternatives or options and selecting the most contextually relevant one(s) is in focus, and thus the current paper focuses on convergent thinking stream. In this context, the application of a structured, criteria-based evaluation and selection procedures offers huge potential [14]. The amount of publications regarding the development and application of selection procedure in a Design Science context is relatively low and often addresses sample selection or selection procedures applied in the course of a literature review, e.g. [33,34].

In reviewing relevant literature, we could not find suitable procedures that specifically address method selection based on criteria derived from theory and practice. The current paper addresses this research gap in Design Science by proposing a detailed and sequential procedure for selecting foresight methods at the Front End of Innovation. As discussed above, we conducted the research within this application domain as the use of foresight methods at the FEI and the FEI in general represents a "wicked" organizational problem. Also the requirement of assessing various foresight methods presented us with a useful research environment. Furthermore, the current research project InnoStrategy 2.0 (cf. section 1) offered the research environment necessary in order to develop, test and evaluate the proposed procedure. Thus, the project setting is regarded as suitable by Design Science research [15,13].

4   Innovation Management and Corporate Foresight

The background of this paper relates to the field of innovation management (cf. section 4.1, 4.2) and corporate foresight (cf. section 4.3) respectively the intersection between those two areas (cf. section 4.4). The procedure proposed will be developed, applied and tested in this particular research context.

4.1   Innovation Management

A global and volatile environment accompanied by constantly changing customer requirements and fierce competition poses huge challenges to organizations. Increased costs of raw materials, the recent economic crisis, high failure rates in New Product Development processes (NPD) and shorter innovation cycles further increase the difficulties and burdens organizations have to face. It is becoming increasingly difficult for companies to succeed in such a high velocity, uncertain and often highly unpredictable kind of environment without being able to quickly and flexibly react to potential or impending changes.

These developments and the resulting consequences clearly stress the necessity for strategically oriented and efficiently conducted innovation management [35–37].

The huge importance of innovation management has also been emphasized by Henry Chesbrough, who is often referred to as "the father of open innovation" [38,39]. According to Chesbrough *everyone knows that innovation is a core business necessity. Companies that don't innovate die."* [40].

Existing findings indicate that improving the FEI process offers the largest potential for improving an organization's innovation capability as a whole with the least effort [41,42]. Other authors found that the main differences between winners and losers in regard to innovation management can be found in the quality of their predevelopment activities [43], refer to the FEI as "the root of success" for organizations involved with discontinuous product innovation [44] and clearly state that high failure rates in the NPD process are often related to too little effort put in the FEI activities [16,45,46]. This indicates that the FEI is especially critical for innovatory success and long-term competitiveness [47].

4.2   The Front End of Innovation (FEI)

The Front End of Innovation (FEI) has received quite some attention in literature, nevertheless, a generally accepted definition is still missing [41], different authors disagree on its boundaries [48] and the terminology varies [42]. However, there is a broad consensus in scientific literature that the FEI is characterized by its ambiguous nature, a high degree of uncertainty or by ill-defined processes. Furthermore, it is highly dynamic, extremely error prone, fuzzy and troublesome [17,41,49].

Depending on the respective source, the FEI includes concept definition and its preceding stages (e.g. [50]), for others, business and programme planning should be included as well (e.g. [51], [16]). Most authors describe the process at the Front End of Innovation as a sequential process that consists of single sub-phases including iterations among and within them (e.g. [52], [46]). Other scholars do not particularly focus on the sequential order of the different activities and phases at the FEI, but rather concentrate on recurring key activities (e.g. [50], [53]. Many process models for the FEI start with an idea generation phase (e.g. [54], [55], [52]), but most began with an initial more or less strategically oriented scanning process (e.g. [47], [46], [56]) respectively with opportunity identification and analysis (e.g. [57], [58], [50]). Those definitions emphasize the importance of a strategic orientation at the FEI. In the course of the current paper, the New Concept Development model proposed by Koen et al. (2001) was used as a reference framework for the Front End of Innovation (cf. figure 2):

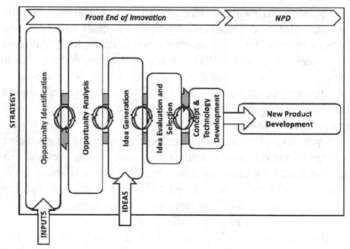

Fig. 2. The project relevant FEI process (adopted from Koen et al., 2001)

According to this process model, initial opportunity identification triggers the chain of activities at the FEI, which ends with transferring selected ideas in the form of first product concepts to the actual New Product Development process. Companies that are first to identify and contextualize emerging trends and issues are expected to be in a position to gain competitive advantages. The sooner a relevant development in the respective company environment is perceived and the better it is understood by an organisation, the faster and the more appropriate the response will be [59,18].

The discussion above demonstrates that the Front End of Innovation is an important research area that has already received quite some attention in scientific literature and plays an important role in organizational practice. Nevertheless, the amount of holistic and practical approaches on how to manage the FEI is relatively low [60] and there are still few empirical studies clarifying Front End practices [61,41]. Especially the need for a viable approach to implement strategic orientation at the FEI seems to be left unaddressed in literature as most publications mainly focus on the actual ideation process [55]. There is a need for further empirical research on the Front End of Innovation and the significance of developing new theories and proposals that support effective implementation of a strategic orientation at the FEI is immense – from a scientific perspective as well as from a practical one [47,44,62,56,45]. One approach that supports on the hand strategic orientation and strategic thinking and on the other hand is also able to create value at the Front End of Innovation is corporate foresight [63] (cf. section 4.3).

4.3   Corporate Foresight

Corporate Foresight has its roots in the term strategic foresight and lays a specific emphasis on foresight applied in private companies as opposed its application in a public domain. Many different definitions of the term can be found in scientific literature (e.g. [64], [65], [66,18]. According to von der Gracht, corporate foresight *"has become the prevalent term used by many companies for their futures research activities. The term stands for the analysis of long-term prospects in business environments, markets and new technologies, and their implications for corporate strategies and innovation [...] Hence, corporate foresight can be understood as an overarching futures orientation of an organization and is, therefore, considered a part of strategic (innovation) management"* [59]. Many different foresight frameworks and approaches can be found in literature, e.g. the foresight process by Horton [64], the Houston Foresight Framework by Hines and Bishop [67] or the generic foresight process framework by Voros [68].

4.4   Corporate Foresight at the Front End of Innovation

The link between foresight and innovation activities has already been analyzed in literature [63,18]. Rohrbeck [18] defined three main clusters of roles that foresight plays in regard to innovation management. Using a standard four-step innovation process, Rohrbeck positioned those three roles at the start of the innovation funnel (initiator role), outside the innovation funnel (strategist role) and along the innovation funnel (opponent role): As an important initiator for idea generation, corporate foresight is intended to deliver and identify new needs, technologies and developments in the relevant company environment. Furthermore, corporate foresight in its strategist-role provides the organisation with the possibility to create and maintain a strategically oriented Front End of Innovation and subsequently supports the further selection of the right ideas to be transferred into the actual NPD process. Thirdly, corporate fore-sight also acts as an opponent, meaning that it constantly challenges basic assumptions and current innovation activities and projects. This in turn can result in a higher level of flexibility and shortened reaction times to developments in the relevant company environment.

Corporate Foresight is a valuable approach to increase and systematically maintain the strategic orientation at the FEI. The concept of Corporate Foresight includes a wide array of methods and tools which can be applied in practice [69–71]. One of the most comprehensive empirical studies concerning the application of foresight methods in practice was conducted by Popper, who based his findings on a sample of 886 foresight studies [72]. He identified the top 25 methods used to support foresight activities (cf. figure 3):

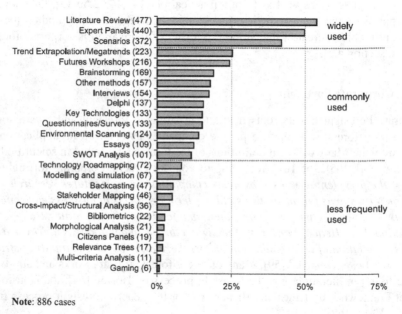

Note: 886 cases

Sources: EFMN and SELF-RULE (2008)

Fig. 3. Level of use of foresight methods

Identifying and selecting appropriate foresight methods which are applicable at the Front End of Innovation and which fulfil the requirements at this stage of the innovation process is a challenging task, which has not yet been addressed neither in innovation management nor in corporate foresight related literature. In the course of this paper, we propose a selection procedure for foresight methods applicable at the Front End of Innovation (cf. section 5).

5   A Procedure for Selecting Foresight Methods at the Front End of Innovation

As discussed in section 2, the core element of Design Science is to develop or build artifacts that are theoretically grounded (rigorous knowledge base) and to justify or evaluate those artifacts for the particular environment (relevance for application environment). In the specific context of this paper, this means that the selection procedure for foresight methods at the Front End of Innovation should not only be developed based on requirements respectively criteria derived from literature, but also has to address practitioners' needs. Subsequently, the evaluation of the procedure has to be done by applying it in practice, which in the present case took place in the course of the project InnoStrategy 2.0. In this section of the paper, the developed selection procedure will be presented. We propose a six-step procedure as visualized in figure 4, which was developed applying the Design Science procedure by Peffers [27] (left side of figure 4) discussed in section 2:

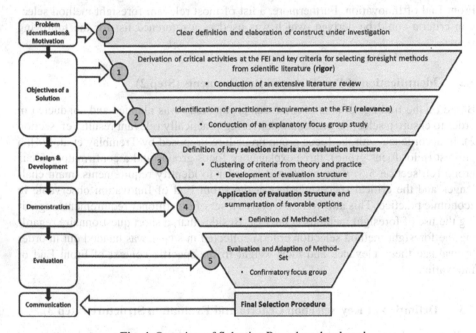

Fig. 4. Overview of Selection Procedure developed

The definition of the construct under investigation and an elaboration of a common understanding of it (**Step 0**) are the basis for initializing the selection procedure as depicted in figure 3. In this paper, the construct under investigation was the issues of how a procedure for selecting appropriate foresight methods applicable at the Front End of Innovation could look like (cf. section 4.1, 4.2, 4.3 and 4.4). The actual selection procedure proposed consists of five sequential steps (**Steps 1 to 5**) and specifically addresses theory and practice. **Step 6** is not part of the selection procedure, but relates to communication and its scientific dissemination [73]. In the following sections 5.1 to 5.5, those steps and its application within the research context are explained in more detail.

5.1 Creation of a Knowledge Base (Step 1)

In accordance with the Design Science approach (cf. section 2), the first step of the proposed selection procedure aims at laying the required knowledge base for the whole selection process. By that, a rigorous selection procedure, which also takes into account previous work in relevant literature, is ensured. In the current case, an extensive literature review regarding key activities, critical success factors and recommendations for a strategic orientation at the Front End of Innovation was conducted. Additionally, existing literature and case studies, regarding the application of foresight methods, their individual benefits and basic functions as well as classic selection criteria of such methods, were analyzed. This allowed us to derive a first set of theory-based requirements concerning the application of foresight methods at the Front End of Innovation. Furthermore, a list of most relevant foresight method selection criteria could be derived, which was used as a reference list for the following steps.

5.2 Identification of Practitioners' Requirements (Step 2)

Based on the findings of step one, a focus group study was planned and conducted in order to ensure a selection procedure delivering practically relevant results (cf. section 2). In accordance with the focus group procedure proposed by Tremblay et al. [74], a pre-test (pilot focus group), three explanatory focus groups and a confirmatory focus group (cf. section 5.5) were conducted in order to identify requirements, main challenges and the critical success factors at the Front End of Innovation observable in economic practice. This allowed us to derive a set of practitioner requirements regarding the use of foresight methods at the FEI. Besides that, a short questionnaire regarding the foresight method selection criteria collected in step 1 was handed out in order to evaluate their relevance and their weight in the specific context of Front End of Innovation.

5.3 Definition of Key Selection Criteria and Evaluation Structure (Step 3)

Building on the results of step one and two, we were able to combine theoretical and practical requirements respectively criteria in the form of a list of selection criteria for foresight methods at the Front End of Innovation. Two blocks of selection criteria where derived: The first set of criteria specifically addressed the Front End of Innovation as a whole and represented the basic requirements and key activities at the FEI. This list was defined in order to specifically select foresight methods applicable at the Front End of Innovation. The second list of criteria consisted of principles which explicitly addressed the issue of strategic orientation in order to integrate classical elements of strategic planning. Based on those two sets of criteria, a two-step evaluation structure for selecting foresight methods applicable at the Front End of Innovation was developed and applied in step 4 (cf. section 5.4).

5.4   Application of Evaluation Structure and Summarization of Favorable Options (Step 4)

The criteria based-evaluation of foresight methods respectively the method selection was done in two steps: First, the top 25 foresight methods according to Popper (cf. section 4.4) were analyzed in detail regarding their applicability at the Front End of Innovation. This was done using the list of basic requirements and key activities at the FEI, derived from literature and gained by conducting the focus group study (cf. section 5.3). By that, a list of top-ten methods best fulfilling the criteria regarding the FEI. Those ten methods were in a second step assessed based on the criteria regarding the principles of a strategic orientation respectively the integration of classic elements of strategy planning. According to Popper [72] an average foresight methods-set consists of 5 (with extreme cases) respectively six methods (without extreme cases). Based on the evaluation of the second criteria list, we selected the top six methods and used the foresight diamond to visualize the methods mix gained that way (cf. figure 5):

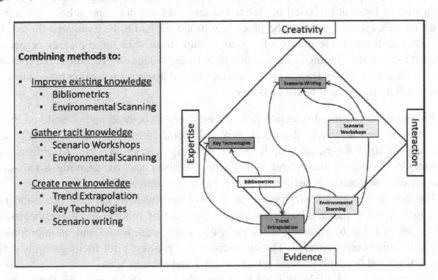

Fig. 5. The set of methods selected based on the proposed selection procedure

This set of methods was defined based on rigorous (cf. section 5.1) and relevant selection criteria (cf. section 5.2). In accordance with the Design Science research approach (cf. section 2) we evaluated the proposed method set in the course of a confirmatory focus group (cf. section 5.5).

5.5   Evaluation and Adaption of Selection Procedure

The final step of the selection procedure proposed aims at evaluating and if necessary adapting the steps and criteria sets of the selection process. In the current context, we decided to conduct a confirmatory focus group [74] concerning the foresight diamond developed based on the results of the third and fourth step (cf. section 5.3 and 5.4). The participants from the respective partner organisation were provided with a detailed introduction to the previous selection steps and the method set was explained in detail. Based on the outcomes of this focus group, we did not have to adapt the set of methods proposed, all participants considered the suggested foresight diamond relevant and valid in their respective application context. Nevertheless, the selection procedure raised some issues, which will be discussed in section 6.

6   Conclusion

In this paper, a selection procedure developed and evaluated addressing the specifics of a Design Science project was presented. The procedure was applied and testes within a suitable research environment, the research project InnoStrategy 2.0. We aimed to develop a procedure for systematically selecting foresight methods at the Front End of Innovation based on defined criteria. As current approaches are not existing for this specific context, the procedure proposed had to be evaluated thoroughly. This was done in the course of a focus group study with three partner organisations. Based on the findings of the application of the selection procedure, the following conclusions and key learnings for developing and applying selection procedures in a Design Science context could be derived:

- Although the proposed selection procedure is very structured and considered theoretical as well as practical criteria, it was difficult to ensure that we actually selected the right criteria and applied them in the right order. We tried to address this issue by clustering theoretical and practical criteria and by deriving a two-step evaluation structure (as seen in section 5.3).
- The conduction of focus groups was a valid approach to identify practitioners' requirements at the highly unstructured Front End of Innovation. Nevertheless, it was challenging to ensure that the right questions were asked and an appropriate questioning route was used. The conduction of a pre-test pilot focus group is definitely advisable in this context (cf. section 5.2 and section 5.5).
- The criteria-based evaluation of methods was very structured and transparent. However, some issues regarding the final selection of methods were encountered, as the evaluation results did not show significant differences. Hence, the final selection could not be done as clear as assumed initially. We addressed this issue by conducting a confirmatory focus group to validate and if necessary adapt the criteria as well as the evaluation structure of the procedure (cf. section 5.5).

In conclusion, we suggest that a reproducible selection procedure applicable in a Design Science context and set in a "wicked" application domain (cf. section 2) needs to emphasis on the combination of criteria derived from theory and practice. A systematic literature review (as presented in section 5.1) followed by a focus group study planned and conducted based on the results of the literature review (as presented in section 5.2) provides the possibility to address rigor as equally as relevance. As seen in section 5.5, we strongly suggest conducting a final confirmatory focus group regarding the results of the selection procedure in order to ensure valid selection outcomes. This does not only provide the possibility to adapt results if necessary, but also allows identifying weaknesses and shortcomings of the procedure itself respectively of the selection criteria and the evaluation structure used. Overall the paper provides a useful procedure for multi-criteria evaluation problems within Design Science projects. This can be applied to subsequent Design Science project. By this it not only assists researchers to conduct Design Science projects, it also helps to improve their transparency, validity and reliability.

References

1. Lai, V.S., Trueblood, R.P., Wong, B.K.: Software selection: a case study of the application of the analytical hierarchical process to the selection of a multimedia authoring system. Information & Management 36, 221–232 (1999)
2. Maiden, N.A., Ncube, C.: Acquiring COTS software selection requirements. IEEE Softw. 15, 46–56 (1998)
3. Nelson, B.L., Goldsman, D.: Comparisons with a Standard in Simulation Experiments. Management Science 47, 449–463 (2001)
4. Jack, C.E.: A revisit of two-stage selection procedures. European Journal of Operational Research 210, 281–286 (2011)
5. Chen, Y., Okudan, G.E., Riley, D.R.: Sustainable performance criteria for construction method selection in concrete buildings. Automation in Construction 19, 235–244 (2010)
6. Pal, O., Gupta, A.K., Garg, R.K.: Supplier Selection Criteria and Methods in Supply Chains: A Review. International Journal of Social, Management, Economics and Business Engineering 7, 1395–1401 (2013)
7. de Boer, L., Labro, E., Morlacchi, P.: A review of methods supporting supplier selection. European Journal of Purchasing & Supply Management 7, 75–89 (2001)
8. McDougall, A., Squires, D.: A Critical Examination of the Checklist Approach in Software Selection. Journal of Educational Computing Research 12, 263–274 (1995)
9. Waeber, R., Frazier, P.I., Henderson, S.G.: A Framework for Selecting a Selection Procedure. ACM Trans. Model. Comput. Simul. 22, 1–23 (2012)
10. Tahriri, F., Mousavi, M., Hozhabri, H.S., Zawiah, M.D., Dawal, S.: The application of fuzzy Delphi and fuzzy inference system in supplier ranking and selection. J. Ind. Eng. Int. 10 (2014)
11. Durst, C., Durst, M., Kolonko, T., Neef, A., Greif, F.: A holistic approach to strategic foresight: A foresight support system for the German Federal Armed Forces. Technological Forecasting and Social Change 8 (2014)
12. Helfert, M., Ostrowski, L.: Design Science Evaluation – Example of Experimental Design. Journal of Emerging Trends in Computing and Information Sciences 3, 253–262 (2012)
13. Hevner, A.R., March, S.T., Park, J., Ram, S.: Design Science in Information Systems Research. MIS Quarterly 28, 75–106 (2004)

14. Johannesson, P., Perjons, E.: An introduction to design science. Springer, New York (2014)
15. Rittel, H.W.J., Webber, M.M.: Dilemmas in a general theory of planning. Policy Sciences 4, 155–169 (1973)
16. Cooper, R.G.: Winning at new products: Creating value through innovation, 4th edn. Basic Books, New York (2011)
17. Akbar, H., Tzokas, N.: An Exploration of New Product Development's Front-end Knowledge Conceptualization Process in Discontinuous Innovations. Brit. J. Manage. 24, 245–263 (2013)
18. Rohrbeck, R.: Corporate Foresight. Physica-Verlag HD, Heidelberg (2011)
19. Creswell, J.W.: Educational research: Planning, conducting, and evaluating quantitative and qualitative research, 4th edn. Pearson, Boston (2012)
20. Ghauri, P.N., Grønhaug, K.: Research methods in business studies: A practical guide, 3rd edn. Financial Times Prentice Hall, Harlow (2005)
21. Johnston, A.: Rigour in research: theory in the research approach. European Business Review 26, 206–217 (2014)
22. March, S.T., Smith, G.F.: Design and natural science research on information technology. Decision Support Systems 15, 251–266 (1995)
23. Hevner, A.R., Chatterjee, S.: Design research in information systems: Theory and practice. Springer, New York (2010)
24. Devereux, G.: From Anxiety to Method: In the Behavioral Sciences. Mouton & Company, La Hague (1967)
25. Kerlinger, F.N.: Behavioral research: A conceptual approach. Holt, Rinehart, and Winston, New York (1979)
26. Simon, H.A.: The sciences of the artificial, 3rd edn. MIT Press, Cambridge (1996)
27. Peffers, K., Tuunanen, T., Rothenberger, M., Chatterjee, S.: A Design Science Research Methodology for Information Systems Research. J. Manage. Inf. Syst. 24, 45–77 (2007)
28. Goldkuhl, G.: Activity Cycles in Design Research: A Pragmatic Conceptualisation of Inter-related Practices. In: Helfert, M., Donnellan, B. (eds.) EDSS 2012. CCIS, vol. 388, pp. 49–60. Springer, Heidelberg (2013)
29. Goldkuhl, G., Lind, M.: A Multi-Grounded Design Research Process. In: Winter, R., Zhao, J.L., Aier, S. (eds.) DESRIST 2010. LNCS, vol. 6105, pp. 45–60. Springer, Heidelberg (2010)
30. Hevner, A., Chatterjee, S.: Design Science Research in Information Systems. In: Hevner, A., Chatterjee, S. (eds.) Design Research in Information Systems, pp. 9–22. Springer, Boston (2010)
31. Cole, R., Purao, S., Rossi, M., Sein, M.K.: Being Proactive: Where Action Research Meets Design Research. In: Avison, D.E., Galletta, D.F. (eds.) Proceedings of the International Conference on Information Systems (ICIS), December 11-14 (2005)
32. Baskerville, R., Myers, M.D.: Special Issue on Action Research in Information Systems: Making IS Research Relevant to Practice - foreword. MIS Q. 28, 329–335 (2004)
33. Ostrowski, Ł., Petkov, P., Helfert, M.: Process for Assessment Data Quality in Complex Service Oriented Architectures Using Design Science Approach. In: Helfert, M., Donnellan, B. (eds.) EDSS 2012. CCIS, vol. 388, pp. 76–87. Springer, Heidelberg (2013)
34. Van Looy, A., De Backer, M., Poels, G.: Towards a Decision Tool for Choosing a Business Process Maturity Model. In: Peffers, K., Rothenberger, M., Kuechler, B. (eds.) DESRIST 2012. LNCS, vol. 7286, pp. 78–87. Springer, Heidelberg (2012)
35. Schweitzer, F., Gabriel, I.: Action at the Front End of Innovation. Int. J. Innov. Mgt. 16 (2012)

36. Rejeb, H.B., Boly, V., Morel-Guimaraes, L.: Attractive quality for requirement assessment during the front-end of innovation. The TQM Journal 23, 216–234 (2011)
37. Filieri, R.: Consumer co-creation and new product development: A case study in the food industry. Marketing Intelligence & Planning 31, 40–53 (2013)
38. Munkongsujarit, S., Srivannaboon, S.: An integration of broadcast search in innovation intermediary for SMEs: A preliminary study of iTAP in Thailand. In: Proceedings of Technology Management for Emerging Technologies (PICMET), pp. 2117–2124 (2012)
39. Lindgren, P., Rasmussen, O.H., Poulsen, H., Li, M., Hinchley, A., Martin, A., et al.: Open Business Model Innovation in Healthcare Sector. Journal of Multi Business Model Innovation and Technology 1, 23–52 (2012)
40. Chesbrough, H.: Open business models: How to thrive in the new innovation landscape. Harvard Business School Press, Boston (2006)
41. Aagaard, A., Gertsen, F.: Supporting Radical Front End Innovation: Perceived Key Factors of Pharmaceutical Innovation. Creativity and Innovation Management 20, 330–346 (2011)
42. Nobelius, D., Trygg, L.: Stop chasing the Front End process - management of the early phases in product development projects. International Journal of Project Management 20, 331–340 (2002)
43. Cooper, R.G., Kleinschmidt, E.J.: Winning businesses in product development: The critical success factors. Research-Technology Management 39, 18–29 (1996)
44. Reid, S.E., de Brentani, U.: The Fuzzy Front End of New Product Development for Discontinuous Innovations: A Theoretical Model. Journal of Product Innovation Management 21, 170–184 (2004)
45. Verworn, B.: A structural equation model of the impact of the "fuzzy front end" on the success of new product development. Research Policy 38, 1571–1581 (2009)
46. Khurana, A., Rosenthal, R.: Towards holistic "front ends" in new product development. Journal of Product Innovation Management 14, 57–74 (1998)
47. Oliveira, M.G., Rozenfeld, H.: Integrating technology roadmapping and portfolio management at the front-end of new product development. Technological Forecasting and Social Change 77, 1339–1354 (2010)
48. Martinsuo, M.: Teaching the Fuzzy Front End of Innovation: Experimenting with Team Learning and Cross-Organizational Integration. Creativity and Innovation Management 18, 147–159 (2009)
49. Jörgensen, J.H., Bergenholtz, C., Goduscheit, R.C., Rasmussen, E.S.: Managing Inter-Firm Collaboration in the Fuzzy Front-End: Structure as a Two-Edged Sword. International Journal of Innovation Management 15, 145–163 (2011)
50. Koen, P., Ajamian, G., Burkart, R., Clamen, A., Davidson, J., D'Amore, R., et al.: Providing Clarity and a Common Language to the "Fuzzy Front End". Research Technology Management 44, 46–55 (2001)
51. Kim, J., Wilemon, D.: Strategic issues in managing innovation's fuzzy front-end. European Journal of Innovation Management 5, 27–39 (2002)
52. Griffiths-Hemans, J.: Setting the Stage for Creative New Products: Investigating the Idea Fruition Process. Journal of the Academy of Marketing Science 34, 27–39 (2006)
53. Bröring, S., Martin Cloutier, L., Leker, J.: The front end of innovation in an era of industry convergence: evidence from nutraceuticals and functional foods. R & D Management 36, 487–498 (2006)
54. Cooper, R.G.: Predevelopment activities determine new product success. Industrial Marketing Management 17, 237–247 (1988)
55. Alam, I.: Removing the fuzziness from the fuzzy front-end of service innovations through customer interactions. Industrial Marketing Management 35, 468–480 (2006)

56. Trotter, P.J.: A New Modified Total Front End Framework for Innovation: New Insights from Health Related Industries. International Journal of Innovation Management 15, 1013–1041 (2011)
57. Brem, A., Voigt, K.: Integration of market pull and technology push in the corporate front end and innovation management - Insights from the German software industry. Technovation 29, 351–367 (2009)
58. Whitney, D.E.: Assemble a Technology Development Toolkit. Research Technology Management 50, 52–58 (2007)
59. von der Gracht, H.A., Vennemann, C.R., Darkow, I.: Corporate foresight and innovation management: A portfolio-approach in evaluating organizational development. Futures 42, 380–393 (2010)
60. Markham, S.K.: The Impact of Front-End Innovation Activities on Product Performance. J. Prod. Innov. Manag. 30, 77–92 (2013)
61. Koen, P.A., Bertels, H.M.J., Kleinschmidt, E.: Managing the Front End of Innovation - Part I. Research Technology Management 57, 34–43 (2014)
62. Saetre, A.S., Brun, E.: Strategic management of innovation: Managing exploration-exploitation by balancing creativity and constraint. International Journal of Innovation & Technology Management 9 (2012)
63. Rohrbeck, R.: Trend Scanning, Scouting and Foresight Techniques. In: Gassmann, O., Schweitzer, F. (eds.) Management of the Fuzzy Front End of Innovation, pp. 59–73. Springer, Heidelberg (2014)
64. Horton, A.: A simple guide to successful foresight. Foresight 1, 5–9 (1999)
65. Slaughter, R.A.: A new framework for environmental scanning. Foresight 1, 441–451 (1999)
66. Battistella, C.: The organisation of Corporate Foresight: A multiple case study in the telecommunication industry. Technological Forecasting and Social Change 87, 60–79 (2014)
67. Hines, A., Bishop, P.C.: Framework foresight: Exploring futures the Houston way. Futures 51, 31–49 (2013)
68. Voros, J.: A generic foresight process framework. Foresight 5, 10–21 (2003)
69. Georghiou, L.: The handbook of technology foresight: Concepts and practice. Elgar, Cheltenham (2008)
70. Andersen, A.D., Andersen, P.D.: Innovation system foresight. Technological Forecasting and Social Change 88, 276–286 (2014)
71. Popper, R., Teichler, T.: 1st EFP Mapping Report: Practical Guide to Mapping Forward-Looking Activities (FLA) Practices, Players and Outcomes. European Foresight Platform (2011)
72. Popper, R.: How are foresight methods selected? Foresight 10, 62–89 (2008)
73. Peffers, K., Tuunanen, T., Gengler, C.E., Rossi, M., Hui, W., Virtanen, V., et al.: The design science research process: a model for producing and presenting information systems research. In: Proceedings of the First International Conference on Design Science Research in Information Systems and Technology (DESRIST 2006), pp. 83–106 (2006)
74. Tremblay, M.C., Hevner, A.R., Berndt, D.J.: Focus Groups for Artifact Refinement and Evaluation in Design Research. Communications of the Association for Information Systems 26, Article 27 (2010)

Design Science for Future AIS: Transferring Continuous Auditing Issues to a Gradual Methodology

Andreas Kiesow[✉], Novica Zarvić, and Oliver Thomas

Information Management and Information Systems,
Osnabrueck University, Osnabrueck, Germany
{andreas.kiesow,novica.zarvic,oliver.thomas}@uni-osnabrueck.de

Abstract. The tightened legal framework and technical evolution increase the relevance of effective *Accounting Information Systems* (AIS). In this context, researchers and practitioners predict the transition from traditional auditing to automated *Continuous Auditing* (CA). However, the organizational implementation of CA is still an unsolved problem in AIS research. To face this challenge, the authors of this paper used a *Design Science Research* (DSR) model considering the characteristics of CA. The proposed artifact in this paper is a gradual methodology which addresses general issues of CA implementation projects. The authors evaluate this artifact in an argumentatively descriptive way before stating limitations and giving an outlook on future research. Ultimately, the authors believe that the proposed methodology as well as the DSR approach for CA research contribute to the knowledge base and set the baseline for further investigations.

Keywords: Continuous Auditing · Accounting Information System · Design Science Research

1 Introduction

Throughout the last decades, there have been tremendous changes in the area of accounting-relevant processes and financial auditing. On the one hand, IT management and auditors are faced with complex legal frameworks, for example the Sarbanes-Oxley Act in 2002 [1], or the attempt to reform the audit sector in the European Union [2]. On the other hand, technical progress concomitantly affects both the innovation of new solutions for *Accounting Information Systems* (AIS) (e.g. [3], [4]) and the challenges of the increasing complexity of data generation and their processing (e.g. [5], [6]). The breadth of this discussion reaches from critical considerations about security and privacy (e.g. [7], [8]) to the question of how value and benefits can be generated from the ever-growing size of data (e.g. [9], [10]). Nevertheless, the development of appropriate AIS is gaining heavily in importance and becoming a reasonable challenge for the research community as well as for audit firms and IT management departments.

Design Science Research (DSR) enables the development of appropriate artifacts (e.g. constructs, models, methods, and instantiations) for human purposes [11], [12].

© Springer International Publishing Switzerland 2015
B. Donnellan et al. (Eds.): DESRIST 2015, LNCS 9073, pp. 311–326, 2015.
DOI: 10.1007/978-3-319-18714-3_20

Apart from the aforementioned evolution in technology, the main objective of the auditor is still to achieve an expression of an opinion on the fairness and truth of financial statements according to national and international law and accounting principles [13], [14]. Consequentially, the aim of this paper is to show *how* DSR can be applied in the area of AIS research to reach the highest level of *Information System* (IS)-based auditing activities: *Continuous Auditing* (CA). The *American Institute of Certified Public Accountants* (AICPA) stated in 2012 that CA "*consists of many diverse elements and may be implemented at various levels of sophistication*" [15]. The applied DSR-approach allows for the possibility to divide the work into consecutive steps. First, the audit of accounting-relevant processes was documented by interviewing experts; the applicability of *Computer-Assisted Audit Tools and Techniques* (CAATTs) was analyzed in prior work [16]. Through further investigations, the authors analyzed the practicability of these CAATTs from a theoretical perspective. Subsequently, the authors devised an audit concept based on CA [17]. The concept included the implementation of *Embedded Audit Modules* (EAM) along with accounting-relevant processes and the analysis of their results in a centralized application. Furthermore, this concept uses *Test Data* to test the functionality of key controls as well as instantiations of *General Audit Software* (GAS).

The implementation of CA is strongly affected by an organization's data, controls, and processes, in other words, the organization's architecture [6]. Thus, the implementation of CA is a long-term, complex task [15]. The proposed artifact in this paper is a gradual methodology which enables the implementation of CA considering these issues. To achieve the "maximum impact" of the DSR-approach applied in this paper, it is structured according to GREGOR and HEVNER (2013) [18]. The issues of implementing CA are analyzed in Section 2 by revisiting relevant literature. The research approach is described in Section 3, and the artifact itself is proposed in Section 4. Special attention is given to the choice of an appropriate architecture for using CA techniques; a conceptual three-tier architecture is proposed. Section 5 contains the descriptive evaluation of the method using information from the knowledge base. In Section 6, the results of the evaluation are summarized and discussed. This section contains an outlook which emphasizes the need for further work in this research area. Finally, the conclusions are presented in Section 7.

2   Theoretical Background on CA Implementation Issues

2.1   DSR in the Context of CA

The research literature in the field of CA is fairly extensive. Nevertheless, little attention has been given to DSR adoption in CA research. MAJDALAWIEH (2012) followed a DSR approach by identifying relevant problems from the knowledge base, defining the goals of the study, designing and developing a sophisticated CA concept, and evaluating the proposed model [19]. GEERTS et al. (2011) discussed the application of DSR on AIS research, which is strongly related to CA research, through "retroactive analysis" [20].

To build up an argument for an artifact's utility, it is necessary to analyze the information implied in the knowledge base (i.e. relevant research) [12]. This is in line with the analysis phase in the DSR approach stated by ÖSTERLE et al. [21] and needs to be performed prior to the creation of artifacts. It is on this basis that the research objective is specified and a research plan is defined (cf. Section 3). For identifying the issues of implementing CA in organizations, relevant literature from a variety of sources needs to be revisited. In order to include not only theoretical and scientific works but also the views of practitioners, the publications of professional organizations such as the *Information Systems Audit and Control Association* (ISACA) and the aforementioned AICPA were taken into consideration as well. This is important inasmuch as the topic under consideration has high practical relevance [22]. Moreover, experience from practitioners also needs to be derived from surveys (e.g. expert interviews). Finally, important issues regarding the implementation of CA are expected as results of CA projects which have been carried out in the past. Therefore, the essential literature for this paper needs to cover the investigations of professional organizations, expert surveys, and lessons learned from CA projects. However, the selection of the references requires an overall view of the state of the art literature in the field of CA as a first step and is presented in the following subsection.

2.2   Identifying Issues of Implementing CA in Organizations

First of all, prior to every financial audit project, the subject matter of the audit has to be defined (**i1**). In traditional auditing, the subject matter is usually a part of the audit assignment, which is agreed between the client and the audit board. In terms of CA, the subject matter of the audit is frequently discussed in literature. The aforementioned ISACA suggested the auditing of relevant data that has important value to its users [23]. The AICPA stated that the subject matter must have suitable characteristics to audit it via CA. Referring to this, business processes must provide real-time or close to real-time information shortly after the occurrence of accounting-relevant transactions [6]. These considerations are strongly connected with the nature of testing and controls (**i2**). For instance, the AICPA mentioned that effective controls within the systems providing the subject matter are necessary to assure the completeness and accuracy of accounting-relevant information [6]. In this context, ALLES et al. mentioned the issue of compensating controls, namely the problem that CA systems are not able to detect if compensating controls are in place [24]. Consequently, the success of CA depends on the adequacy and the effectiveness of all controls in the accounting-relevant process [23].

A significant prerequisite for the implementation of CA is the nature of the organization's environment (**i3**). The environment encompasses the whole socio-technical composition of an organization and thus has tremendous impact on audit routines [25]. Naturally, CA is easier to achieve if strong business processes and controls are already in place [23]. In this regard, environments with highly sophisticated Enterprise Resource Management Systems are the most likely to be able to translate CA into action [26], [24]. The spread of CA throughout the organization is a long-term project and requires comprehensive strategic planning [6]. In this context, one significant issue is the lack of management support (i4). Furthermore, AICPA pointed out that in past CA projects, the understanding of CA was still rather low, especially at the top management or board levels [15]. This results in a reduced likelihood that operational departments would turn CA projects into reality. The segregation of duties between management and audit departments are discussed in literature in this regard [27]. ALLES et al. pointed out that the biggest issue within their CA research project was the overlap between CA activities, which are usually performed by audit departments, and monitoring activities, which are usually performed by management [24]. Thus, the management must support the CA project from the very beginning, and the performance of monitoring activities must be declared when CA is implemented.

As mentioned above, CA is a highly sophisticated audit approach. Therefore, the employees involved, such as auditors and IT staff, must have an appropriate level of skills and knowledge in various disciplines [27]. Hence, lack of skill, knowledge, and employee training can raise a significant issue for CA projects (i5). The AICPA designated an extensive list of skills which auditors will need to have in the future, such as knowledge of business processes and controls, internal audit experience, and familiarity with statistics [15]. Most of all, reasonable IT skills are considered as essential [6]. Referring to this, SUN emphasized the interaction between audit and IT staff. Through interaction with each other, the mutual understanding of each other's domain could be increased [25].

The cooperation between involved departments is strongly connected with this issue. Hence, communication barriers and a lack of teamwork are considered to be significant hindrances to CA projects. (i6). In particular, the access to accounting-relevant data requires proper communication between the data owner and auditor [27]. This leads to another considerable issue: protectionism of data owners (i7). The AICPA stated that various businesses (e.g. in the financial sector) are very protective of their data. In this context, the data owner tends to prohibit comprehensive and on-going access to systems [15]. This can be problematic because a major requirement for CA systems is unconstrained access to accounting-relevant process data [24].

The aforementioned segregation of duties, the demand of training, and the real-time auditing of accounting-relevant data require a fundamental adjustment of audit procedures (i8). VASARHELYI et al. raise the question *how* existing audit procedures should be modified to increase the utilization of technology in auditing [27]. The distinction between the automation of existing audit procedures and their reengineering are also questioned by ALLES et al. [24]. The AICPA highlights the need for standard modification and formal endorsement of CA by setting standards [15]. Among practitioners, it is believed that a CA standard supports organizations in performing the change from traditional to continuous audit procedures. SUN shed light on the relationship between audit procedures and the documentation of auditing, because documentation supports the integration of computer audit procedures with manual processes and consequently empowers auditors to understand the procedures of automated programs [25]. Therefore, inadequate documentation is a crucial issue for CA projects (i9).

The adjustment of audit procedures depends largely on timing restrictions. Time periods need to be defined for the duration that audit reports cover (called the reporting period), or the time necessary to issue a report [23]. In this context, ALLES et al.

mentioned the problem of time lags between the occurrence of a finding and its reporting [24]. Additionally, the AICPA stated that associated audit reports have to be constantly available and accessible for the legitimate users. Moreover, the results of the audit procedures must be efficiently communicated via an electronic channel [6]. Consequently, the timing restrictions of auditing are a relevant issue to CA projects (**i10**).

Table 1. General issues of CA implementation derived from literature

No.	General Issues of CA Implementation	Reports of Professional Organizations			Expert Surveys		CA Projects
		ISACA (2002)	AICPA (Oct 2012)	AICPA (Nov 2012)	Sun (2012)	Vasarhelyi et al. (2012)	Alles et al. (2008)
i1	Defining the Subject Matter	x		x			
i2	Considering the Nature of Testing and Controls	x		x			x
i3	Analyzing the Organization's Environment	x		x	x		x
i4	Lack of Management Support		x	x		x	x
i5	Lack of Skill, Knowledge, and Employee Training	x		x	x	x	
i6	Lack of Communication/ Teamwork				x	x	
i7	Protectionism of Data Owner	x				x	x
i8	Adjustment of Audit Procedures	x			x	x	x
i9	Inadequate Documentation of CA Projects				x		
i10	Timing Restrictions of Audit	x		x			x
i11	Cost, Economic Implications	x			x	x	
i12	Technical Implementation Difficulties	x		x	x		x

The handling of costs and economic implications are important considerations in CA projects (**i11**). From interviews of internal audit department managers, VASARHELYI et al. learned that cost is not a major barrier for the adoption of CA technology [27]. Moreover, it is a common understanding in literature that the application of CAATTs, which sets the baseline for CA, could in fact result in future savings [25]. However, the general view among practitioners is still that the realization of CA systems is a costly undertaking. An important consideration in this context is when the payback period starts, or when the cost-benefit tradeoff becomes positive [15].

Finally, the implementation of CA systems is a recognized technical challenge, because it is composed of different elements which have to be combined [15]. Furthermore, audit evidence is provided via highly automated procedures [6]. Therefore, the technical implementation issues of CA projects (**i12**) are often mentioned in literature.

For example, the effort required to customize the software limits the outcome of the CA procedures [25]. Other technical issues are related to the choice of aggregation and universal data availability, parsing the output of the CA system, and, particularly, the phenomenon of "alarm floods", which is caused by the continuous monitoring of accounting-relevant procedures [24].

The challenges mentioned above were taken from the reviewed literature, evaluated according to their nature, and arranged into twelve categories. The results of this analysis are shown in Table 1. These categories also form the basis for the evaluation in Section 5.

3   Design Science Research Approach for Continuous Auditing

Generally, the authors of this paper pursue the design of IS-based solutions for accounting and auditing. The aim of this work is the development of artifacts which serve human purposes according to the definition of DSR [11]. Hence, this work is positioned in the Theory of Design and Action. This theory is characterized by the usage of *"principles of form and function, methods, and justificatory theoretical knowledge"* for the development of IS [28]. Moreover, the authors intend to demonstrate a complete DSR process by detailing all relevant phases and activities. However, being aware that this aim is quite ambitious for a single research paper and that, surely, every single activity cannot properly be described for space reasons, the authors do put a focus on specific phases that are fundamental to DSR. The selected DSR approach consists of four basic phases, namely: *analysis*, *design*, *evaluation*, and *diffusion*, according to ÖSTERLE et al. [21]. The main considerations and activities of the analysis phase were already described in detail in the previous section.

First, the requirements for the audit of accounting-relevant processes as well as the potentiality for the development of innovative CAATTs were collected and analyzed through expert interviews (*analysis*, [16]). Subsequently, the specific considerations were investigated, which lead to the conclusion that CA is an applicable approach. A conceptual IT architecture, which is essentially based on the implementation of EAM throughout the accounting-relevant processes, was presented (*analysis*, *design*, [17]). In the present paper, a methodology for the implementation of the concept (artifact) is proposed and descriptively evaluated by using information from the knowledge base [12], which is built on the issues discussed in the literature review in Section 2 (*design*, *evaluation*). Stronger evaluations such as experiments, testing and observation, as well as the *diffusion* of the concept and the methodology proposed in this paper are the subject matter of future work. As mentioned above, DSR is an iterative process; to illustrate this, the presentation of the four basic phases was extended into a circle. Moreover, the authors assume that the rigor of this approach increases with each iteration depending on the exchange with the knowledge base (Rigor Cycle). Additionally, the increasing relevance of research activities was motivated by the problems and challenges mentioned in the first section (Relevance Cycle) [29]. The results of these considerations are presented in the upcoming Fig. 1.

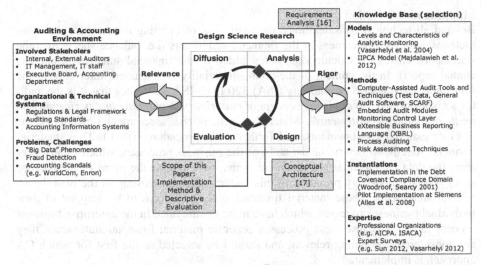

Fig. 1. DSR Approach for CA in the style of Österle et al. [21] and Hevner [29]

4   Methodology for the Implementation of Continuous Auditing

As mentioned in previous sections, the implementation of CA is a complex undertaking. According to common project management theory, such undertakings can be divided into individual phases to manage their complexity (e.g. [30]). However, the overall goal of the project must still be constantly pursued and monitored in spite of this subdivision. Therefore, a methodology is required which enables the implementation of CA along the accounting-relevant processes and provides for the correct order of tasks.

Previous considerations reasoned that the implementation of CA is comparable to a top-down transformation process, which affects major parts of the organization's architecture (e.g. accounting processes, AIS, and control environment). Consequently, the basic concept of the following methodology is to divide the implementation of CA into individual projects, which focus on financial statements, accounting-relevant processes, and AIS (see Fig. 2).

Adoption

Overall, the implementation of CA is a long-term decision which affects all business areas of the organization as well as supporting activities such as those of the financial and accounting department, the IT department, and the internal audit. Therefore, the decision to implement CA has to be made by management and can only be successfully accomplished if management supports the implementation throughout the whole process. To do so, the diffusion of the CA has to be incorporated into the business strategy, into the IT strategy, and, finally, applied on the operational level.

Mapping and Selection

Beyond all technical considerations, the main task of auditing is to ensure the completeness and the correctness of the financial statements (i.e. balance sheets, income statements, cash flow calculations, notes added to the financial statements, and the annual report). In the context of the audit, materiality is discussed, inter alia, in the *International Standard on Auditing* (ISA) 320 [31]. ISA 320 states that it is the auditor's responsibility *"to apply the concept of materiality in planning and performing an audit of financial statements"*. Materiality affects risk assessment procedures, the risks of material misstatements, and further audit procedures (ibid.). Thus, material financial statements determine the audit of the business processes, which finally generate the data for the financial statement items, for example the items of the balance sheet. The methodology proposed in this paper suggests focusing on the material financial statements. These material financial statements have to be mapped to their individual business processes, which have to be documented in the enterprise business process model. Because these processes generate material financial statements, they are considered accounting-relevant and should be selected as the first for which CA approach is implemented.

Identification

After the accounting-relevant sub-processes are selected, the existence and nature of the (application) controls in place have to be identified. The importance of controls to auditing is mentioned by experts, as for instance by SCHULTZ et al., who conducted expert interviews in this field: *"A process audit is mainly a controls audit, the process is just a link between controls"* [32]. The auditor's activities are prescribed in ISA 315.20: *"The auditor shall obtain an understanding of control activities relevant to the audit, being those the auditor judges it necessary to understand in order to assess the risks of material misstatement at the assertion level and design further audit procedures responsive to assessed risks"* [33]. Therefore, this step is part of every traditional audit and does not need further explanation in the context of CA. However, because the proposed CA architecture requires the results of controls to be in an electronic and analyzable form, the implementation of a CA approach requires the existence of automated controls. Hence, the nature of application controls, which is explained in ISA 315 A.105 [33], has to be evaluated.

Transformation

Afterwards, the complete transformation of manual application controls into automated application controls is required. This could imply the implementation of additional supporting systems such as Workflow Management Systems, or Document Management Systems. Lastly, all controls have to be suitable for integration into the EAM.

Integration

Finally, the EAM will be integrated into the controls level. This seems to be the most difficult part of the methodology, because controls are usually characterized by heterogeneity: systems can consist of standard software, customized software, or self-developed software. Consequently, the effort of the implementation depends on the controls environment. Furthermore, testing activities and approval procedures have to be considered. At the end of this phase, all application controls along the accounting-relevant processes (which generate material financial statements), that collect their results and make them auditable, will have been automated and integrated into the EAM.

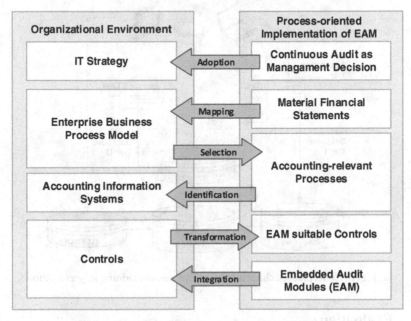

Fig. 2. Process-oriented Implementation of EAM

Architecture

The daily use of CA techniques requires the implementation of an appropriate architecture. A potential architecture was developed based on previous work [17] and is briefly described in this sub-section. This concept can be divided into several levels: *database tier*, *application tier*, and *presentation tier*. First, the activities of the auditors depend on the *Results* which are generated by the EAM (*application tier*) and stored in a relational database (*database tier*). The auditors need to be empowered to assess every single result of the EAM directly in real-time or nearly in real-time. Therefore, metadata (e.g. structure, frequency, or occurrence) has to be collected and stored in a separate *Data Inventory*. This allows for identifying the location of potential misstatements quickly. Additionally, information regarding the controls in place (e.g. frequency, nature of control, or supervisor) needs to be gathered and stored in a *Control Inventory* (*database tier*).

The *presentation tier* should encompass the visualization of the results on mobile and stationary devices via a *representation*. Additionally, the presentation tier has to provide functionality for managing *Test Data*, which can be used to test the accuracy of controls in place. Because the auditor created the Test Data, the outcome of passing this data through the control can be predicted and therefore allows for a statement about the accuracy of the control. Finally, the presentation should be connected with essential GAS to enable the development and execution of deeper data retrieval investigations. The proposed architecture is shown in the following Fig. 3.

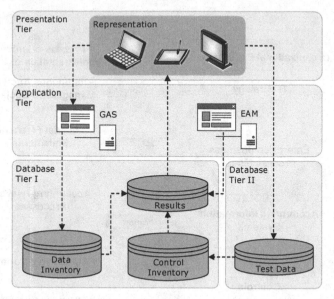

Fig. 3. Conceptual Architecture of a Continuous Auditing Representation

5   Evaluation

According to the third DSR guideline of HEVNER et al. (2004), an artifact needs to be evaluated in terms of utility, quality, and efficacy [12]. Consequentially, the general issues of CA implementation detailed in Section 2.2 are used to build a convincing argument for the methodology's utility. Hence, a descriptive evaluation was chosen.

The *definition of the subject matter* (**i1**) is characterized as a major issue in the context of CA. In the methodology proposed in this paper, the subject matter of audit is every single control, which ensures the completeness and accuracy of the processed data. It was demonstrated how the controls are determined by the materiality of the financial statements and the related business processes. The controls and their results are collected and monitored in a separate representation layer. In this context, the *nature of the controls and the testing procedures* (**i2**) have to be identified and documented in a Control Inventory so that this crucial information is available for audit. Moreover, because the CA approach requires the transformation of manual controls into automated controls, a sound exploration of the control environment is an essential step in the implementation. Controls, (business) processes, the enterprise business process model, financial statements, and existing audit procedures are part of the *organization's environment* (**i3**). Through the application of the proposed methodology, these subjects are concomitantly considered and analyzed.

Because the application of the methodology intends for the adoption of CA as a strategic decision, the top management imposes the implementation upon itself. Therefore, *the support of the management* (**i4**) is given from the outset. The methodology proposed in this paper does not directly affect the *education, training, skill, and knowledge of the employees* (**i5**). Furthermore, procedures to enable *communication and collaboration between the departments* (**i6**) as well as actions to lessen *protectionism of data owner* (**i7**) are not proposed either at the outset. The proposed methodology does not include explicit *adjustments of audit procedures* (**i8**) in terms of written organizational standards or policies. However, the representation should enable the monitoring of controls at any time. Moreover, the use of Test Data and GAS ameliorates the data assurance. Therefore, the application of the method indirectly indicates the necessity for adjustments to the audit procedures due to the increased flexibility of the audit.

The *documentation of the CA project* (**i9**) is partially provided by the usage of the construction of the Data Inventory, the Control Inventory, and, finally, the table Results. Further documentation actions are not directly covered by the methodology.

The frequency of audit activities or reports, and the reporting period (i.e. the time that the report covers) are considered to be major issues of CA by researchers. From a technical perspective, both the frequency of reports and the reporting period are easy to implement given that CA enables real-time, or nearly real-time, auditing of the subject matter. Additionally, the aforementioned representation ensures that the results of controls are visible at any time. Therefore, these *timing restrictions* (**i10**) are rather recognized as an organizational issue, which is strongly related to the internal audit standards (see i8).

Although research and practice have not provided evidence of cost savings resulting from CA [34], increasing efficiency is an assumed impact of CA among researchers and practitioners [27]. In this context, the methodology does not allow for any considerations about the *costs of implementation* (**i11**), because economic implications are neither calculable nor predictable for the time being. Ultimately, costs depend on the complexity of the implementation. The technical difficulties of implementation require a sound exploration and a reasonable solution. *Technical difficulties of the implementation* (**i12**) are to be expected in the transformation of manual controls into automated controls, and in the integration of the EAM. The methodology does not include specific actions for dealing with technical difficulties.

The issues discussed above were identified from the existing knowledge base (cf. Section 2.2) and have been used to build an argument. In our opinion, this can already be categorized as a convincing argument, because each issue (from Table 1) has been included in the discussion to some extent. Thus, from a completeness perspective, an informed argument was achieved.

6   Summary and Discussion

To bring this paper to an end, the essential results are briefly summarized and discussed within this section. Firstly, the need for innovative CAATTs, such as EAM,

Test Data, and GAS, as well as the need for CA, has been shown in prior publications. The intended prototyping raised the question of *how* the issues of CA projects can be addressed. Understandably, the development of a reasonable implementation methodology for CA seems to be a remarkable challenge. Revisiting the relevant literature, we were able to gain insight on issues regarding CA implementation from different perspectives (professional organizations, expert surveys, and lessons learned from CA projects) group them into twelve major categories (i1-i12). Considering the complexity of CA projects and their potential impact on an organization's architecture, the proposed methodology divides the implementation into smaller individual projects. According to the underlying research approach, which follows the DSR paradigm, the major issues (i1-i12), which are based on information from the knowledge base, were used to build an informed argument. Subsequently, the descriptive evaluation has shown that these issues are at least partially covered by the methodology.

The evaluation emphasized the salient position of management support given that the other issues (i5, i6, i7, and i8) are covered by the strategic diffusion of CA. In detail, top management has to delegate appropriate recruitment and training, and see to the establishment of an organizational culture which supports collaboration and the sharing of data. However, the proposed gradual methodology provides top management with an approach to implement CA step-by-step and thus with the opportunity to increase the awareness of affected departments.

A further major issue is the appropriate documentation of the CA project (i9), because documentation has a strong impact on the success of the methodology. However, the adoption of the CA approach as a management decision predicates the driving of appropriate actions, for example, documentation, to ensure the reasonable transition from traditional auditing to CA throughout the organization.

The investigations brought to light the limitations of the methodology, which have to be delved into in future work. First, the calculation of costs (i11) is impossible without a real implementation. However, through its gradual approach and the focus on materiality, the methodology enables at least the possibility to manage resources and monitor costs during the implementation. Second, technical difficulties of the implementation (i12) are not covered by the methodology. Otherwise, the gradual approach divides the overall question (i.e. true and fair view of financial statements) into sub-problems, making the complexity more manageable. Furthermore, the success of the methodology depends inter alia on an updated and correct enterprise business model and sophisticated change management, which enable the accurate transformation of controls as well as the integration of EAM in the accounting-relevant systems.

However, the authors are aware of the fact that a descriptive evaluation is only one of the evaluation methods proposed by HEVNER et al. (2004), the other types mentioned being namely observational, analytical, experimental, and testing [12]. Nevertheless, with respect to the nature of the research stage and output of this paper, the authors were of the opinion that an argumentatively descriptive evaluation fits best for the moment. The authors of this paper are aware that the proposed methodology is characterized by its theoretical nature and a high-level point of view. Therefore, deeper investigations related to the individual steps of the methodology are needed.

Additionally, a stronger evaluation is planned in future work. Most of all, the authors seek for the development of a prototype to enable the evaluation in terms of testing, experimental, and observational methods (e.g. traditional audit vs. CA). Moreover, the impact on IT-Governance frameworks (e.g. COSO, COBIT), and audit standards (e.g. ISA) in matters of CA also need to be soundly explored.

Nevertheless, the proposed methodology provides various solutions for recognized issues of CA implementations. First, it provides a holistic view of CA projects and their step-by-step implementation. Second, it considers the needs of auditors with respect to materiality and the organizational environment. Moreover, it focuses on controls and their improvement. It also combines the strengths of different audit techniques (EAM, Test Data, and GAS). A further argument is the proposed concept for the permanent visualization of the control procedures, which is characterized by the fast processing of structured and unstructured data, by means of a representation. To summarize, in spite of the limitations and requirements discussed, the proposed methodology is concomitantly unique and novel. Therefore, the authors believe that it contributes to both the research and practice of CA.

Table 2. DSR Guidelines according to HEVNER et al. 2004 [12] in the context of CA research

No.	Guideline	CA research proposed in this paper	Reference in this paper
1	Design as an Artifact	Gradual methodology plus architecture enable the implementation of CA throughout an organization.	Section 4
2	Problem Relevance	Computer-assisted auditing is a recognized and relevant business problem for both researchers and practitioners.	Section 1-2
3	Design Evaluation	The proposed artifact was descriptively evaluated by means of an informed argument. This evaluation showed the weaknesses of the proposed artifact.	Section 5
4	Research Contributions	The contributions to the CA research domain were clearly and verifiably presented in this paper.	Section 4-6
5	Research Rigor	The construction of the artifact as well as the evaluation rely upon methods which are accepted in IS research.	Section 2-5
6	Design as a Search Process	The construction of the artifact considers issues of the CA research domain. The evaluation showed the need for further research to create an artifact which finally achieves a solution.	All sections
7	Communication of Research	The DSR study proposed in this paper is condensed into an appropriate publication schema and contains implications for technology as well as managament audiences.	All sections

7   Conclusion

DSR contributes to the development of effective IS solutions. Regarding an appropriate artifact for the implementation of CA, it was necessary to use a DSR model that addressed the specific characteristics of CA research. To ensure the effectiveness of the study at hand, it was verified against the guidelines of DSR established by HEVNER et al. (2004). The results of this verification are shown in Table 2.

Subsequently, the paper was structured according to the publication schema of DSR [18]. Hence, researchers can use the schema applied in this paper to create their own DSR studies in the field of CA research. Moreover, practitioners will be empowered to discuss the major issues of CA implementations on various organizational levels. Future work will employ the next cycle in the DSR approach in terms of stronger evaluation, for instance testing, experiments, and observations. Additionally, a structured and systemized literature review—comprised of a more extensive selection of theoretically and practically relevant CA information—is required to assure that a wider and more complete range of potential issues for CA are considered. Hence, the subject matter of further research is at least the prototypic implementation of CA in a test system. Moreover, the individual steps of the approach, particularly the transformation of controls as well as the integration of the EAM, require deeper investigation and provide high potential for further research. Finally, future work could imply the transition from CA to an integrated audit service based on related methodologies, as for example by NIEMÖLLER et al. (2014) [35].

References

1. Sarbanes-Oxley Act: Public Law No. 107-204. Washington, DC Gov. Print. Off. 107 (2002)
2. European Commission: Commissioner Michel Barnier welcomes provisional agreement in trilogue on the reform of the audit sector, http://europa.eu/rapid/press-release_MEMO-13-1171_en.htm
3. Vasarhelyi, M.A., Chan, D.Y., Krahel, J.P.: Consequences of XBRL standardization on financial statement data. J. Inf. Syst. 26, 155–167 (2012)
4. Abbasi, A., Albrecht, C., Vance, A., Hansen, J.: Metafraud: a meta-learning framework for detecting financial fraud. MIS Q. 36, 1293–1327 (2012)
5. Fochler, K., Schmidt, A.H., Paffrath, R.: IT-Revision 3.0—Herausforderungen für die interne IT-Revision. HMD Prax. der Wirtschaftsinformatik 50, 20–30 (2013)
6. Byrnes, P.E., Al-Awadhi, A., Gullvist, B., Brown-Liburd, H., Teeter, R.: J. Donald Warren, J., Vasarhelyi, M.: AICPA: Evolution of Auditing: From the Traditional Approach to the Future Audit, New York (2012)
7. Rajan, S., van Ginkel, W., Sundaresan, N.: Cloud Security Alliance (CSA): Top Ten Big Data Security and Privacy Challenges (2012)
8. Bojilov, M., Chew, R., Kaitano, F., Zororo, T.: ISACA: Privacy & Big Data (Whitepaper), Rolling Meadows, IL, USA (2013)
9. Chew, R., Genicola, K., Li, B., Philip, J., Tichanona, Z.: ISACA: Big Data Impacts & Benefits (Whitepaper), Rolling Meadows, IL, USA (2013)
10. Bhagat, B., Chagpar, Z., Chapela, V., Gee, W., Marks, N., Pasfield, J.: ISACA: Generating Value from Big Data Analytics (Whitepaper), Rolling Meadows, IL, USA (2014)
11. March, S.T., Smith, G.F.: Design and natural science research on information technology. Decis. Support Syst. 15, 251–266 (1995)
12. Hevner, A.R., March, S.T., Park, J., Ram, S.: Design science in information systems research. MIS Q. 28, 75–105 (2004)

13. AICPA: Responsibilities and Functions of the Independent Auditor. SAS No. 1, section 110; SAS No. 78; SAS No. 82, United States of America (1972)
14. IFAC: International Standard on Auditing 200. In: Handbook of International Quality Control, Auditing, Review, Other Assurance, and Related Services Pronouncements, p. 74. International Federation of Accountants, New York (2013)
15. Byrnes, P.E., Ames, B., Vasarhelyi, M., Warren Jr., J.D.: AICPA: The Current State of Continuous Auditing and Continuous Monitoring (Whitepaper), New York, USA (2012)
16. Kiesow, A., Bittmann, S., Thomas, O.: IT Support through CAATTs - Systematic Requirements Analysis and Design for Process Audit. In: 20th Proceedings of the Americas Conference on Information Systems (AMCIS 2014), August 7-10, Association for Information Systems (AIS), Savannah (2014)
17. Kiesow, A., Zarvic, N., Thomas, O.: Continuous Auditing in Big Data Computing Environments: Towards an Integrated Audit Approach by Using CAATTs. In: Management of Complex IT-Systems and Applications (MITA) - INFORMATIK 2014, Stuttgart, Germany, September 22-26. Lecture Notes in Informatics (LNI), vol. 44.Jahrestagung der Gesellschaft für Informatik e.V, GI (2014)
18. Gregor, S., Hevner, A.R.: Positioning and presenting design science research for maximum impact. MIS Q. 37, 337–356 (2013)
19. Majdalawieh, M., Sahraoui, S., Barkhi, R.: Intra/inter process continuous auditing (IIPCA), integrating CA within an enterprise system environment. Bus. Process Manag. J. 18, 304–327 (2012)
20. Geerts, G.L.: A design science research methodology and its application to accounting information systems research. Int. J. Account. Inf. Syst. 12, 142–151 (2011)
21. Österle, H., Becker, J., Frank, U., Hess, T., Karagiannis, D., Krcmar, H., Loos, P., Mertens, P., Oberweis, A., Sinz, E.J.: Memorandum on design-oriented information systems research. Eur. J. Inf. Syst. 20, 7–10 (2011)
22. Rezaee, Z., Elam, R., Sharbatoghlie, A.: Continuous auditing: the audit of the future. Manag. Audit. J. 16, 150–158 (2001)
23. ISACA Standards Board: Continuous Auditing: Is It Fantasy or Reality? Inf. Syst. Control Journal 5 (2002)
24. Alles, M.G., Kogan, A., Vasarhelyi, M.A.: Putting continuous auditing theory into practice: Lessons from two pilot implementations. J. Inf. Syst. 22, 195–214 (2008)
25. Sun, C.-M.: From CAATTs Adoption to Continuous Auditing Systems Implementation: An Analysis Based on Organizational Routines Theories. MIS Rev. An Int. J. 17, 59–85 (2012)
26. Vasarhelyi, M.A., Alles, M.G., Kogan, A.: Principles of analytic monitoring for continuous assurance. J. Emerg. Technol. Account. 1, 1–21 (2004)
27. Vasarhelyi, M.A., Alles, M., Kuenkaikaewa, S., Littley, J.: The acceptance and adoption of continuous auditing by internal auditors: A micro analysis. Int. J. Account. Inf. Syst. 13, 267–281 (2012)
28. Gregor, S.: The nature of theory in information systems. MIS Q. 30, 611–642 (2006)
29. Hevner, A.R.: A three cycle view of design science research. Scand. J. Inf. Syst. 19, 4 (2007)
30. Meredith, J.R., Mantel Jr., S.J.: Project management: a managerial approach. John Wiley & Sons (2011)
31. International Federation of Accountants (IFAC): International Standard on Auditing 320. In: Handbook of International Quality Control, Auditing, Review, Other Assurance, and Related Services Pronouncements, pp. 21–329. International Federation of Accountants, New York (2013)

32. Schultz, M., Müller-Wickop, N., Nüttgens, M.: Key Information Requirements for Process Audits – an Expert Perspective. In: Proceedings of the 5th International Workshop on Enterprise Modelling and Information Systems Architectures, pp. 137–150. EMISA, Vienna (2012)

33. IFAC: International Standard on Auditing 315. In: Handbook of International Quality Control, Auditing, Review, Other Assurance, and Related Services Pronouncements, pp. 267–320. International Federation of Accountants, New York (2013)

34. Eulerich, M., Kalinichenko, A.: Die Continuous Auditing - Diskussion aus wissenschaftlicher Sicht. Zeitschrift Interne Revis. 49, 34–45 (2014)

35. Niemöller, C., Özcan, D., Metzger, D., Thomas, O.: Towards a Design Science-Driven Product-Service System Engineering Methodology. In: Tremblay, M.C., VanderMeer, D., Rothenberger, M., Gupta, A., Yoon, V. (eds.) DESRIST 2014. LNCS, vol. 8463, pp. 180–193. Springer, Heidelberg (2014)

Unpacking the Artifact Knowledge:
Secondary Data Analysis in Design Science Research

Mateusz Dolata^(✉), Mehmet Kilic, and Gerhard Schwabe

University of Zurich, Department of Informatics, Zurich, Switzerland
{dolata,kilic,schwabe}@ifi.uzh.ch

Abstract. Evaluation of design artifacts generates a set of scientifically valuable data, which is primarily used to prove the utility of the artifact or to identify potential for improvement. Extension of such studies by reanalyzing the same data set did not attract much attention in design-oriented research and design science. However, the reuse of this data with the secondary analysis approaches can provide valuable insights on artifact-based interventions. This paper aims at launching a debate on the role of secondary analysis in DSR. We argue that secondary analysis of evaluation data shall be granted respect within the DSR-IS community as a valuable method for scientific inquiry. By discussing role of data reuse in reference disciplines and showing how secondary analysis is understood within the IS, we argue that there is a need and great opportunity for reanalysis data originating from design experiments as a form of evaluation. With thin in mind, we provide guidance for conducting such analysis.

Keywords: Secondary data analysis · Evaluation · Methods · Design experiments

1   Introduction

Design Science Research (DSR) offers a framework to address practical problems while considering scientific rigor and contributing to the knowledge base. DSR projects are complex, require involvement of different stakeholders, and are time and money intensive. This is compensated, however, with their practical relevance. Within the field of Information Systems (IS), researchers apply DSR in socio-technical context, which recognizes the role of the interaction between people and technology in goal-oriented interaction. Due to the complexity of practical problems in this area, DSR-IS researchers produce large amounts of data, including: interviews and field-work observations from the preliminary phase, a number of solution ideas and proto-types, evaluation results, and implementation and acceptance reports. We argue that this data includes novel insights of high relevance, which, however, only seldom find their way into the scientific community, and propose reanalysis of design evaluation data as a way to bring this knowledge to the surface.

DSR has proven to produce valuable contributions in a range of contexts [1, 3, 19]. It is being listed in one line with other methods within the IS [49], but its impact may be limited by the predominant roles of artifacts. They are often presented as key

© Springer International Publishing Switzerland 2015
B. Donnellan et al. (Eds.): DESRIST 2015, LNCS 9073, pp. 327–342, 2015.
DOI: 10.1007/978-3-319-18714-3_21

elements in changing the routines, behaviors, and organizations. Pentland and Feld-man [46] point out, that artifact-perspective is not suited to describe human behaviors in organizational context. They complain about a naive mechanism of research within the DSR framework, which they describe as a mindless way along such steps as: re-quirements gathering, definition of principles, implementation, user training, and deployment. They may be right in multiple cases. Successful design-based interven-tions are frequently reported in such a way, while fostering the deterministic view on design. However, this view does much harm to the theoretical foundation of DSR.

In their seminal paper, Hevner et al. [29] present a view, that behavioral and design science, even if rooting in different disciplines have potential to co-exist and well complement each other. In particular, if socio-technical systems are considered, the interdependence between those inquiry modes becomes obvious. Recently, mixed method approaches try to bridge the divide between various research practices and receive growing attention in the IS community [57]. They see finding theoretically plausible answers to research questions as the goal of research. They call of accep-tance of a methodological mix as a legitimate way of inquiry [57]. This concept is motivates an approach in which a set of data is analyzed with multiple qualitative and quantitative techniques. We extend on this and suggest a bridge between the design-oriented and behavioral research – we recommend secondary analysis of evaluation data from DSR projects as a way of establishing that bridge.

Secondary analysis offers an opportunity to review raw data produced in a separate research project to answer a different research question [14, 18]. It is widely applied in a range of disciplines, including such reference disciplines of IS as social science, psychology, and economics. Data mining, as a subfield of computer science, provides tools to re-attend data sets, especially if provided as relational databases. In this paper, we want to start a debate on the secondary analysis as an inquiry method in DSR. In particular, we claim that extension of prior studies by reanalyzing their data set suits the DSR while being useful for providing insights on why particular design works.

Given that background, secondary analysis of data originating from evaluation of socio-technical systems has a great potential to produce novel knowledge: First, it lends itself to extend evaluation results and support their validity – evaluation forms a central element of DSR, while aiming at showing that the intervention works and why [29, 47, 56]. Second, it may inform subsequent designs and is in line with the view on design as a search process [28, 29, 33] that proposes utilization of available means on the way to find the optimal solution to the problem. Third, it is well suited to extend the behavioral basis and understanding of the problem – particularly, through comparison of states before and after the intervention in an explorative manner. DSR community provides guidance on how and when to plan evaluation episodes [56]. It, discusses the relation between search and design, and how improvements can be made along the way [30, 45, 52]. Finally, it provides insights on how theorizing shall be conducted [20] and how to present its outcome [22]. Nevertheless, little practical guidance is given on how to answer the "why" question of evaluation when joint ar-tificial and behavioral perspective is taken. In this paper we address this issue while pointing the secondary analysis of evaluation data as suitable way. Due to their popu-larity, precise definition, and rigor, we focus on the case of design experiments [37].

2 Secondary Analysis in Related Disciplines

Secondary data analysis has been widely discussed in other disciplines and results in domain-specific approaches, but also acceptance issues. In particular, in the reference disciplines of IS, access to previously collected data plays an important role: it is used there to synthesize the previous research, to reanalyze data with a novel perspective, and to discover unexpected regularities. To provide an understanding of key issues, we discuss position of secondary analysis in reference domains and in the IS.

2.1 Secondary Analysis in Cognitive Psychology and Health Studies

Starting in 1970-ies, reanalysis of data from psychological experiments have gained in importance, while leading some to the conclusion that it became more influential than the primary analysis [18]. This tendency comes back to the availability of novel statistical techniques and technological means to conduct complicated calculations with many examples. Already tested hypotheses could, then, be verified, and novel ones could be tested efficiently with use of existing data. Also, due to accumulation of fraud cases in psychological research [6], voices demanding access to data for replication reasons became louder. This tendency has resulted in calls for public or shared access to experimental and survey data in psychology and related fields [6].

In the same period of time, publication of contradictory or incompatible results in the broader area of health studies, drew Cochrane to propose use of randomized control trials to make medicine more effective and efficient [10]. His call up for systematic reviews of relevant randomized controlled trials did not remain without consequence and led to the development of Cochrane Library oriented at collection and provision of systematic reviews of trials to the researchers and public [8]. Based on this data, the evidence of effectiveness of interventions can be easily updated, thus making medical treatments more reliable and consistent. Meanwhile, this trend has transformed view on synthesis as a secondary analysis of data and *Cochrane review* became a synonym for systematic meta-analysis of relevant trial studies.

Psychology and health studies clearly have benefitted from secondary analyses of available data. Such approaches are well acknowledged in those fields as methods of scientific inquiry, with strong impact on the discipline (in 2013, Cochrane Database was ranked 10th among medicine journals by ISI Journal Citation Report [11]). Furthermore, extensive guidance is provided on how to conduct secondary analysis, both, as synthesis of previous research [31] and as re-analysis of previous experimental data [17]. We argue, that also in other fields, including design-oriented research, scientists may benefit from review of available studies or summary studies based on compilation of raw data: From the point of view of a particular researcher, knowing the knowledge base and its empirical background is necessary to make the next step on the way towards resolving a particular problem, including the practical ones. From the global point of view, synthesis of previous studies helps with building up a consistent knowledge base on a particular topic [35]. With this in mind, it may be also used to identify opportunities for research issues [4].

2.2   Secondary Analysis in Economics and Social Sciences

The popularity of secondary analysis in economics and social sciences has been primarily driven by the access to a whole range of publicly available statistics and other data, including census and annual reports of large market players [14]. In particular, when hypothesis to be tested require a large whole, such as, e.g., a nation, access to such data proves essential. Indeed, secondary analysis is said to provide a list of advantages compared to primary studies: resource savings, increased data quality, larger sample size, as well as access to topics and time ranges otherwise inaccessible [14, 54]. Additionally, as secondary analyses build upon the knowledge available at the time of analysis and not only at the time of collection, such studies may have further advantages [32]. Given this background, the fact that secondary analysis belongs to the canonical methods in social sciences and economics does not surprise [7].

While reuse of publicly available statistics and survey data causes hardly any controversies, reuse of qualitative data still triggers a discussion in social sciences [25]. In fact, an extensive scientific discourse addresses the ethics and pragmatics of reanalysis of data that are qualitative in their nature, ranging from ethnographical observations, over video or audio recordings, up to structured and semi-structured interviews [25, 26, 34]. Ethical issues, primarily, reflect the fact that qualitative data is generated in contexts where mutual trust between the subject and researcher plays an important role, and where the subjects are informed about the characteristics and goals of the ongoing study rather than possible topics that secondary analysis may or may not address [34]. Practical issues occur due to the character of the data and the situation of the original research project: since the original data is collected to address a particular research question, it will necessarily be influenced by the mindset of the original researcher at that time – understanding this mindset is essential to rework the data: more in case of ethnographical research, less in case of structured interviews [24, 34].

However, reanalysis of qualitative data with a novel perspective or while using new methods has potential to provide essential help to a researcher dealing with a complex research question [26]: it may be used to supplement, extend, or transcendent original findings, it supports validation of original statements, it can embrace several previously separated data sets, or it may inform a follow-up study. A particular researcher benefits from the efficiency of this course of action – he may produce novel knowledge and propose further hypotheses without collecting new data. By doing so he makes a step from proof-of-concept study to the stage of proof-of-value [39]. From the global point of view, the community is made aware of hidden facts discovered, possibly, through an unconventional approach towards available data.

2.3   Secondary Analysis in Computer Science

Whereas in the previous cases, a conceptual or topical switch motivated secondary analysis of existing data, data mining as a sub-discipline of computer science promotes another approach towards data analysis. We call it an *opportunistic search*. It starts solely with the data and methods to analyze them [15]. While application of such search is not limited to secondary data, and it can be seen as a method for one of the cases discussed above, we decide to present it separately in here due to its character that differs from the classical way of scientific inquiry starting with a hypothesis or research questions to be addressed. Given the extensive amount of data produced around the world, we estimate that application of data mining will gain in importance, not only in analytics companies, but also in research. As of today, access to unique data sets is considered to be an asset within the scientific community. Therefore, many of the contemporary findings, in particular from the field of social networks or other big data analytics, may follow from an opportunistic search for patterns. This trend comes in hand with the development of data mining approaches ranging from clustering and association rules to more recent subgroup discovery [23, 60]. While approaches from data science are widely accepted in the industry to provide novel insights, e.g., on the market situation [15], the research community in the IS still considers it at least "non-traditional", however recently efforts were made to establish data mining techniques as modes of scientific enquiry within this community [41].

Application of methods inspired by data mining to secondary data may lead to unexpected discoveries and identification of effects that are possibly stronger than the desired ones or the ones discovered in primary study. This makes data mining not only a tool to efficiently rework large amounts of data, but also a verification mechanism as well as a tool to find side effects and moderating conditions. However, while secondary analysis driven by hypothesis might well be used for confirmatory statements, data mining approaches support, primarily, exploratory purposes. Nevertheless, due to the recent popularity of *data science*, knowledge discovery in databases finds its way to other domains including the above ones [2, 15].

2.4   Secondary Analysis in Information Systems

As discussed above, secondary analysis of existing data has multifold character. We may differentiate various approaches based on the character of data (e.g., qualitative vs. quantitative), its type (e.g., reports, census, etc.), the availability of the data (e.g., public vs. private), or the way of data acquisition (e.g., formal or informal data sharing). While the reference disciplines listed above already possess a tradition of secondary analysis, and particularly, have dedicated effort to define standards for this kind of inquiry, information systems has not considered secondary analysis in a wider sense. As of 2003 and still in 2007, secondary analysis was, also, considered a minor issue and was not widespread in research practice, at least according to review of information management literature [43, 44]. This fact was put in relation with low availability of public data, in particular statistics and reports on IS-relevant topics.

In order to understand the nature of secondary analysis in the IS in recent years (2004-2014), we decided to conduct a keywords-driven systematic review of IS literature available in the Library of Association for Information Systems (AISeL: all journals and conferences such as ICIS, ECIS, AMCIS, and PACIS) and chosen proceedings series from Digital Library of Association for Computing Machinery (ACM DL: CSCW, CHI, GROUP, d.go, ICEGOV – according to the proficiency of the authors). We searched for such keywords "secondary data" and "secondary analysis"[1] in the above databases. Based on the title, abstract, method section, and paragraphs where words "reuse" or "secondary" occur, we identified a set of only 242 studies out of 326 for further analysis. Most of the disregarded papers include papers with keywords in the title in their bibliography, refer to another study using secondary analysis, or declare intention to use secondary data in future research.

Out of the 242 studies considered for this quick bibliographic study, 35 (14%) were meta-analyses of previous studies, 98 (40%) used analysis of secondary data as their main research method, and 109 (46%) supplemented other primary study with secondary analysis of data. Studies that use secondary data as their main or the only source of scientific inquiry rely mostly on publicly available data – 80 cases. In 3 other cases, a mixture of public and private data is used. Overall 83 studies make use of public data: 56 use published statistics, 26 use publicly available reports, 18 consider newspaper articles, 10 – user-generated content such as blog or Wikipedia entries, 8 – other archival material, and 4 – published case studies (some studies use more than one data source). Only 15 studies use private data as their empirical basis: 8 reanalyze documents or data collected in companies, and only 7 reanalyze experimental data. Nevertheless, as indicated above the dominating tendency is, clearly, to support a primary analysis with secondary data. This is a common strategy in case or field studies with use of ethnographic methods – in such studies use of many different data sources is considered as an asset, thus researchers provide long lists of documents, reports, and statistics they considered during their research.

Interestingly, based on the distributions of different types of secondary analyses in the IS field, we clearly see the strong influence of economics and social sciences on its methodological body. While this is not surprising, we stunned by little importance of methods inspired by data mining – even though we encountered many studies reusing quantitative data from publicly available statistics, none of them *discovers knowledge from data* but instead uses the data to *verify formulated hypothesis*. This approach reflects the strong tendency within IS to formulate theories, test them, and adjust them in consequence [21]. In a moderate importance of meta-reviews and meta-analyses we see the influence of psychology and health studies, but similar tendencies can be observed in other sciences too. However, the most important observation is that revisiting empirical and experimental data remains unpopular in the IS – out of thousands of papers in both libraries, only a fraction actually states to reuse data. Furthermore, only one study found by us reanalyzes data originating from evaluation of a system or set of systems. Of course, this may result from the limitation of keyword-based approach, and we are sure that many behavioral studies root in design-oriented projects, in particular given the growing importance of intervention based approaches [12, 59]. However, our analysis shows, at least, the tendency not to denote "secondary analyses" of evaluation data as such.

---

[1] Searches with other keywords, such as „data reuse" or „data reanalysis", as well as "data reuse" and "data re-analysis" yielded nearly 100% of false positives. Therefore, we decided to consider only two key phrases in our analysis: "secondary data" and "secondary analysis". Due to the page limitations of a conference paper, we do not provide the list of reviewed articles in here, but it is available upon request from one of the authors.

3   Secondary Analysis for DSR-IS

We think, that the little overlap between secondary analysis as an approach towards data and DSR as a scientific paradigm results from the definition of DSR provided by the available frameworks and definitions. Neither Peffers et al. [45], nor Hevner et al. [29], nor Sein et al. [51] explicitly refer to the possibility of data reuse as a way to produce valuable scientific inquiry within the DSR framework. Without an explicit guidance, studies using data obtained during evaluation of DSR artifacts remain in a methodological vacuum – somewhere in between behavioral science with its rigor on data collection and DSR with its engineering background and practical relevance criteria. In our opinion, this is a waste of potential: data showing complex, socio-technical or social processes, developed in a costly procedure, remains silent – it does not contribute to the knowledge base. In the following, we address exactly this issue by discussing position of secondary analysis in DSR and providing practical guidance. In order to keep our discussion focused, we limit our suggestions to the cases when socio-technical artifacts undergo evaluation in form of design experiments [37].

3.1   Position of Secondary Analysis within the DSR Paradigm

The three main frameworks in DSR, given the number of citations [13], include DSR in IS research by Hevner et al. [29], DSR Methodology for IS research by Peffers et al. [45], and Action Design Research by Sein et al. [51]. Additionally, recent elaborations and guidance include works by Gregor [21] and Gregor and Hevner [22]. Even though the frameworks differ in terms of focus and assumptions, they all provide models for design-based scientific inquiry. They commonly identify a set of activities that belong to a DSR project: (1) identification of a practically relevant problem, (2) definition of solution objectives, (3) consideration of existing body of knowledge to inform the solution, (4) iterative development of a solution, (5) definition of the solution, (6) demonstration and evaluation of the solution, and (7) contribution to the knowledge base. These elements can be ordered in a cycle and do not necessarily need to be approached each time. However, if one considers the guidance on positioning of DSR outcomes, it becomes clear that those activities shall get reflected in an optimal DSR paper [22]. Consequently, the reading of DSR as a straightforward engineering science approach emerges, as criticized by Pentland and Feldman [46] as too rigid to give the appropriate credit to the fragile nature of human behavior. However, this does not need to be the case – DSR includes mechanisms to deal with complexity.

In the very core of DSR paradigm, in particular in *Guideline 6* by Hevner et al. [29], design is described as a search process – through iterations in a build-evaluate cycle, the complexity can be added to the process, such that the *ends, means,* and *laws* addressed in the design, capture (to some feasible degree) the complex nature of the problem and the solution. For this mechanism to work, a proper application of evaluation in DSR is essential. Hevner et al. [29] as well as Peffers et al. [45] stress the primary goal of evaluation as justification of the designed artifact. They propose that utility, quality, and efficacy [29] or effectiveness and efficiency [45] of the artifact shall be tested against the predefined requirements and solution objectives. In fact, they even list a set of methods to be considered during evaluation: according to Hevner et al. [29] it ranges from observations, over analytical, experimental, and testing methods, up to descriptive methods. Beyond that, Hevner et al. point to the fact, that evaluation shall inform the subsequent iterations in the build-evaluate cycle. Peffers et al. [45] offer two kinds of evaluation: demonstration and evaluation. Whereas the first demonstrates that the artifact solves at least one instance of the problem, the latter is a more extensive and formal undertaking. It shall answer the question on "how well the artifact supports a solution to the problem" [45]. With regards to methods, he simply points to qualitative and quantitative methods, as well as simulations and logical proofs. Nevertheless, as pointed out by Venable et al. [55], there is lack of practical guidance on how to choose the appropriate evaluation approach. To answer this, Venable et al. [56] offer a framework to lead decisions on evaluation strategy. Recently, an instruction was published that has even a more hands-on and pragmatic character: Mettler et al. [37] introduce a concept of a design experiment as a counterpart of natural science experiment for DSR. Nevertheless, none of the above foresees the possibility of secondary analysis of data from evaluation and consequently none directly applicable guidance regarding execution and publication of such analyses exists.

While the above frameworks pay only little attention to the process of data analysis, they all stress the importance of explaining why the artifact works, as opposite to only showing that it works. We argue, that this implicates collection and analysis of additional data, beyond the metrics that measure the utility, quality, or efficacy of the artifact. In particular, for socio-technical systems answering the *why* question has a twofold character. On the one hand, it concerns the technical side, i.e., showing what are the qualities of the artifact that cause the desired effect. On the other hand, it addresses the social side, i.e., showing what are the qualities of human behavior or social interaction that cause the desired effect. While kernel theories may support answering those questions, in many cases the effects will result from a complex interplay of smaller behaviors. However, at latest then, when despite a good implementation of kernel theories the artifact fails, a deeper analysis of the reasons lying possibly outside the scope of kernel theories, may be necessary. For such cases, collection and analysis of lateral data is necessary. Again, DSR frameworks do not provide sufficient methodological guidance for such cases. This negatively affects young researchers, who, without reference to an established methodology, may find it difficult to publish their insights even if they are relevant to a wider audience and a valuable contribution. Publishing in accordance with DSR paradigm means, mostly, reporting on a successful design-based intervention. Publishing in behavioral sciences means, mostly, reporting on an insight obtained through rigorous and simplistic experimental design. Due to the complexity of DSR artifacts, the latter becomes a critical point, however secondary analysis is well suited to generate valuable insights from design failures.

Despite the listed difficulties, secondary analysis of evaluation data from DSR is being conducted. Moreover, insights resulting from such analyses find its way to primary conferences in the particular fields of research, as in the following examples.

Kjeldskov and Paay in a series of studies investigate the design of location- and context-aware mobile systems for navigation and guidance in social situations [36, 42]. In their original study, they [36] evaluate three system alternatives including a context-aware mobile system providing an informational overlay to the civic space of Federation Square in Melbourne, Australia, in a realistic scenario. Through their evaluation they show that given the context (defined by the location, physical context, and social context) and very short, *indexical*, data on the mobile device, the user is able to understand and process the information properly. They use the concept of indexicality to motivate their design. In the subsequent study, Paay and Kjeldskov [42], "unpack" the general findings while referring to the principles of proximity, closure, symmetry, continuity, and similarity, as described by the Gestalt theory [58]. By reanalyzing of the available video recordings in a qualitative manner, they are able to provide the answer to the question on *why* the users understand scarce information in the context. They report on findings for each of the principles given above, e.g., they conclude that proximity plays an important role, since users see the information on the mobile device as an annotation of the place that they are situated in. Importantly, they do not solely use the same data to tell a different story or use a different theoretical lens. Instead, they generate additional data through analysis of the available video material.

From the methodological point of view, Kjeldskov and Paay [36] or Paay and Kjeldskov [42], do not clearly show that they use DSR (e.g., through citation of one of the popular frameworks), but they follow a design-oriented research paradigm: they design an artifact to answer problem from practice and orient themselves at user needs and at available theoretical basis. Importantly, they directly state that they conduct a secondary analysis of data, specify what was the overall goal of the project, and what was the goal and conditions in the evaluation. They provide background to understand how the question asked in the secondary study fits into the whole project.

In our second example, Heinrich et al. [27] and Nussbaumer et al. [40] address the area of IT support for financial advisory service encounters. In the original study, Nussbaumer et al. [40] introduce two systems designed for a tabletop, but relying on two different metaphors: slideshow and widgets. They use the transparency concept as their kernel theory. They show that in a realistic scenario a system with a rigid slideshow metaphor enforces process transparency, while the flexible widget metaphor supports casual transparency. The findings indicate that, according to data from a survey, observations, and interview statements, the customers in fact consider the second solution more transparent and it leverages their satisfaction. In a subsequent study, Heinrich et al. [27] systematically code and analyze the eye gaze patterns in the videos, and show that when using the second prototype participants have more eye contact, and presumably build up a better relationship.

Heinrich et al. [27] clearly refer to the DSR framework of Hevner [29] and address all typical elements of the paradigm. They do not directly state to conduct a secondary analysis; they do not present their research as reanalysis[2]. They, however, provide information on the experimental design of the evaluation, list the treatments, etc. But they do not relate the new research question to the original one.

---

[2] In fact, the authors reported to us that they tried submitting this results as a secondary data analysis, but the paper got rejected due to an "unconventional argumentation" on experimental design. Reviews clearly suggested a publication strategy that ignores the fact of reanalysis. A careful reader will, however, find that they refer to the previous work.

3.2   Guidance for Secondary Analysis of Evaluation Data

As discussed before, answering the *why* question is an inherent element of the evaluation in the DSR. While, the desired outcome in the evaluation is assumed to follow from application of a kernel theory, we argue that a deeper and more extensive consideration of the collected data may provide more specific, concrete, or novel explanations apart from the existing theoretical bed. Since in the DSR, one conceptualizes, builds, and tests complex artifacts, one shall expect complex changes and effects. This is in line with adaptive theories from the IS stating that software as well as other artifacts are flexible and their nature is related to their use [48, 50]. Additionally to complex effects observable in artifact conditions, in design experiments the control treatments (i.e., those where the developed artifact is not used) can be considered a coherent and rich data source on existing practices. Such data may be interesting not only to DSR researchers, but also to social, communication, and behavioral scientists or may be approached with their respective perspectives. Furthermore, in a specific experimental design, when control treatments are conducted before and after the experimental one, observations on the influence of the intervention on the general mindset of participants can be observed. Often, through confrontation with socio-technical artifact participants become more aware of their previous practices and behaviors, such that the intervention changes their post-experimental behavior. Observing such effects within the DSR project is possible, primarily, through secondary analysis.

In general, reanalysis of evaluation data is not without challenges. The most important risk is the de-contextualization. When referring to evaluation data from a DSR project, one needs to consider and be open about the original purpose of the data, namely, the measurement of utility of an artifact. Even though reanalysis of the data follows a behavioral mode of scientific enquiry, the data mostly has not been acquired in the same way as in other behavioral studies. The difference becomes prominent in the case of experiments: in behavioral experiments like in physics the researcher tries to isolate the measured effect from any external influence – he tries to manipulate a single independent variable and measure dependent variables expected to change, while controlling for other variables. The complexity of a DSR artifact makes this procedure impossible, so that wide range of moderating effects has to be considered and addressed in the analysis. Therefore, we formulate the first guideline as follows: *put your secondary analysis in context.* For an extended discussion on design experiments we point to Mettler et al. [37]. While DSR argues for the need of developing generalizable artifacts [22], one cannot assume that the results obtained through secondary analysis has exactly the same scope of generalization. The scope should be defined properly to assure internal and external validity of the results. The second guideline says: *formulate a focused research question.* Focus of data reanalysis is often stressed in the context of publicly available statistical data in economics and social sciences. In fact, census and other large surveys may entice to look for correlations and some may be indeed found, but many of them will simply lead to discovery of accidental subgroups of no theoretical value [38].

As a researcher designing an evaluation study, which later shall supplement a secondary analysis, taking future reuse of data into consideration is a wise decision nowadays and many act accordingly: First, in particular in early phases of DSR projects, one can assume unexpected effects to occur – capturing them with rich data collection methods, e.g., with video, data logs, etc., may have essential value for detecting failures. Second, such data may inform the subsequent iterations in the build-evaluate cycle. Third, generation of such data is inexpensive and does not involve much effort, while guaranteeing for enough data to be available and, additionally, extensively documenting knowledge about the evaluation design. Apart from such documentation, all data produced during preparation of the experiment shall be collected, including the motivation for particular decisions. Also, possible consent issues shall be resolved prior to the experiment or evaluation period, if users are involved. In many cases, the access to data may be limited by the agreements with industrial partners or with the study participants. Furthermore, the design of the study itself shall consider the best scientific practices for a given type of study. For instance, in case of a design experiment issues related to the choice of study subjects (e.g., representative vs. convenience sampling), experimental setting (e.g., control group vs. manual matching), artifact characteristics (e.g., poor usability may impede any social situation), manipulation procedure (e.g., artifact against artifact vs. artifact against baseline), evaluation metrics (e.g., solely fulfillment of requirements vs. extended set of features), experimental results (e.g., definition of evaluation criteria in advance) [37]. Overall, we therefore propose a third guideline: *prepare for secondary data analysis.* In medicine, proper preparation of data is for secondary analysis is key issue to be included in shared repositories of data, which in turn influences citation numbers [31].

As a researcher who is given the opportunity to work with secondary data collected in a DSR project, one shall consider the availability of an extensive documentation regarding the design of the artifact as well as the design of the study – understanding the rationale behind the two may be essential for the interpretation of the results. In an optimal situation, there shall be a direct contact to the researcher who conducted the DSR study. One shall also consider the quality of the available data, and possibly have an opportunity to test applicability of the desired analysis technique on a limited sample. This implies choice of an appropriate method: Qualitative data may be extensively coded and used for qualitative and quantitative reasoning, but requires post-processing. Quantitative data can be mostly used out of the box, however the constructs used have to be well understood to support any conclusion found, e.g., through regression. Importantly, data inherited from older projects shall be reconsidered with regard to its *age* – older data may simply be outdated due to changes in the society and technology: today nobody would seriously take a study that reports on mobile phone usage patterns based on the data from 2000, however a comparison of the patterns from 2000 and 2015 may result in interesting findings and attract large attention in the community. Consequently, we introduce the fourth guideline: *be critical in use of secondary data.* What quality criteria can be employed for secondary data assessment was extensively addressed in social and statistics research [38].

Last but not least, we argue for rigorous and transparent reporting on the whole procedure – we formulate the fifth guideline: *respect the audience.* If the secondary analysis of data leads to scientifically valuable insights characterized by their novelty, contra-intuitiveness, and rigor with regard to the data analysis, one shall consider publication of such results. Communication, as an important element of scientific undertaking, poses additional requirements. First, when describing a secondary analysis study, the relation between this study and primary analysis shall be clarified. To answer this, one shall provide the original solution objective, original research question, and the new research question as well as explicate the relationship between them (independent, extension, verification). Process of data collection shall be described clearly – for design experiments this concerns the experimental design including characterization of treatments and randomization strategies [37]. This description shall also include information on dependent and independent variables: inquiry based on relation between dependent variables may be good for explorative purposes, but it will be difficult to produce a standalone generalizable insight. This fact needs to be considered when choosing and reporting on data analysis method: conversation analysis may better suit an explorative study than, e.g., statistical regression. Finally, the original context of the study needs to be considered and clearly specified – it mostly well describes the scope of the study. Generalization that goes beyond it may be a quite dangerous and simply false assumption. For further guidance on publication strategies and methodological issues regarding reuse of data, we suggest consulting guidance from reference domains [9, 16, 26, 54].

We conclude that unpacking DSR artifact knowledge is a challenging, but valuable approach. In particular, it goes in line with the recent arguments for leaving behind the black box view on IT artifacts and their effects [20, 52]. Even though publishing secondary analyses of evaluation data may be an obstacle, we are strongly convinced of their scientific value, confirmed by the examples provided above, as well as our own extensive experience with DSR projects and publication of their results.

4   Discussion

As shown, secondary analysis of evaluation data offers a great opportunity to DSR researchers. It is in line with Hevner's et al. [29] vision of co-existence and mutual benefit of behavioral and DSR paradigms of scientific inquiry. Secondary analysis provides a rich methodological toolset widely used in behavioral sciences, while it only finds little attention in DSR. We argue, that this toolset can be easily transferred to the design-oriented research. And so, DSR researchers shall also be able to benefit from this rich and elaborated toolset. As we show in the examples, secondary analysis in DSR can lead to novel, unexpected insights that bring forward the design of an artifact as well as provide valuable findings regarding the artifact use. In DSR we have the great opportunity to reanalyze very rich raw data, apply new perspectives to it, and address particular aspects of the complex socio-technical situation. By doing so, we generate, in fact, new data. For instance, through coding of video material, new observations can be made. In that sense, we do not promote a method for "slicing the salami" – we do not encourage the researchers to reuse the same data all over again for telling a different story. Instead, we call on for a perspective change.

Our proposition is, also, in line with the mixed method approach [57]. For some readers, we may go even further: while mixed method focuses on applying multiple data analysis methods to a data set, we see this publication as an attempt to bridge two research paradigms in IS: DSR and behavioral approach. With this in mind, secondary analysis is not only another method that could or could not be applied in course of DSR projects – we claim, that it shall have a permanent and prominent place in this paradigm. In fact, we argue that secondary analysis of evaluation data shall be the culmination of a DSR project – secondary analysis of available data shall be considered due to the following reasons: (1) to deepen the understanding of why an artifact works (or not), (2) because of research and funds management. Eventually, it is inefficient if rigorously, costly generated and possibly valuable data is simply not used.

Our elaboration is strongly related to the evaluation discourse in the DSR community [37, 47, 55, 56]. While secondary analysis is definitely a way to deeply motivate the success of an intervention, it needs also to be considered when preparing the evaluation strategy, e.g., designing the experiment. The available frameworks necessarily address the question on whether and how to plan evaluation based on the stage of the project, the desired outcome, and the setting. We add to it, by claiming that the future use of data shall be considered too. We, also, extend the view on secondary analysis within the IS, to date dominated by reuse of publicly available statistics and reports, and by supplementary analysis within the case study approach. We propose inclusion of secondary analysis of evaluation data, in particular, from design experiments into the canon of acknowledged methods. By doing so, we enhance the role of design experiments as an evaluation approach [37]. However, we can also easily imagine that secondary analysis of data from other evaluation forms can be easily conducted and lead to new, valuable knowledge. For instance, rich log-data from a pilot study is well predestinated to undergo extensive reanalysis in the context proposed in this paper.

We argue that secondary analysis of secondary data is, particularly, well suited to support exploratory purpose of DSR. It can be used to discover and describe new phenomena, as well as correlate them to other phenomena and contexts of their occurrence [5, 53]. As exploratory research does not require resulting in causal explanations, use of data showing complex situations, such as those generated through complex artifacts in DSR evaluations, is possible. Inversely, use data generated in realistic context may be even beneficial for exploratory research: such data is rich in novel, unexplained phenomena that can be later approached one by one in separate projects. In other words, secondary analysis may well deal as a method to generate hypothesis for forthcoming studies. Experience of doing secondary analysis may be a particularly helpful and influential task for young researchers. In the field of DSR, they often consider their artifact to be the ultimate goal of their research project – most of the time is spent on designing, building, and adjusting the artifact. However DSR implies a dichotomy between building and evaluating not without a reason – it is namely the rich and realistic evaluation where novel insights about the world come to the light. Sometimes, they are not obvious and deeper look into the collected data is necessary. However, to attract young researchers, wider acceptance of secondary analysis in the DSR community is necessary, so that insights obtained through secondary analysis do not have to be covered in the fear that such method will be considered too problematic for publishers and editors at journals, and chairs at conferences.

With this in mind, this paper is a call for acceptance: after acceptance of DSR as a methodology of IS, and acceptance of design experiments as a method of scientific inquiry, acceptance of secondary analysis based on this experiments is the next logical step of a scientific community – inspired by the developments in reference disciplines we shall make the next step better now than later – it may generate valuable knowledge worth spreading. We agree, that experiments are not comparable to the ones in Cochrane's Library, but nevertheless, or exactly because it is so, they provide a rich picture of the situation and can significantly contribute to the scientific inquiry.

In this context, the issue of sharing data plays an important role – as shown by reference disciplines initiative to make data publicly available resulted in popularization of secondary analyses. Many of them provide valuable insights and form basis for reliable synthesis. We argue that with popularization of DSR, more and more parallel projects will approach similar topics and therefore sharing data between them may benefit both sides. However, we also understand the point that access to valuable data is expensive and provides an asset to the particular researcher.

In this paper, we argue for necessity of data reuse in DSR and present benefits that it may bring. We aim at launching a broad debate on the related methodological issues. Through establishing secondary analysis as an approach towards data within the DSR-IS, researchers who applied this method in the past will receive proper methodological foundation and recognition. Furthermore, those, who see an opportunity in applying secondary analysis in the future, will receive methodological assistance and can hope for an attentive and well-meaning audience for their novel insights.

References

1. Albert, T.C., et al.: GIST: A model for design and management of content and interactivity of customer-centric web sites. MIS Q., 161–182 (2004)
2. Arzberger, P.W., et al.: Promoting Access to Public Research Data for Scientific, Economic, and Social Development. Data Sci. J. 3(29), 135–152 (2004)
3. Ayanso, A., Lertwachara, K., Vachon, F.: Design and behavioral science research in premier IS journals: Evidence from database management research. In: Jain, H., Sinha, A.P., Vitharana, P., et al. (eds.) DESRIST 2011. LNCS, vol. 6629, pp. 138–152. Springer, Heidelberg (2011)
4. Brereton, P., et al.: Lessons from applying the systematic literature review process within the software engineering domain. J. Syst. Softw. 80(4), 571–583 (2007)
5. Briggs, R.O., Schwabe, G.: On Expanding the Scope of Design Science in IS Research. In: Jain, H., Sinha, A.P., Vitharana, P. (eds.) DESRIST 2011. LNCS, vol. 6629, pp. 92–106. Springer, Heidelberg (2011)
6. Bryant, F.B., Wortman, P.M.: Secondary analysis: The case for data archives. Am. Psychol. 33(4), 381–387 (1978)
7. Bryman, A.: Social Research Methods. Oxford University Press (2012)
8. Chalmers, I., et al.: Getting to grips with Archie Cochrane's agenda. BMJ 305(6857), 786–788 (1992)
9. Church, R.M.: The Effective Use of Secondary Data. Learn. Motiv. 33(1), 32–45 (2002)
10. Cochrane, A.L.: Effectiveness and efficiency: Random reflections on health services. Nuffield Provincial Hospitals Trust, London (1972)
11. Cochrane Library: The Cochrane Library 2013 Impact Factor and usage report. Cochrane Library (2013)
12. Cornwall, A., Jewkes, R.: What is participatory research? Soc. Sci. Med. 41(12), 1667–1676 (1995)

13. Cronholm, S., Göbel, H.: The Need for Empirical Grounding of Design Science Research Methodology. In: Intl. Works. on IT Artefact Design & Workpractices Impr., Friedrichshafen, Germany (2014)
14. Devine, P.: Secondary Data Analysis. In: The A-Z of Social Research. SAGE (2003)
15. Dhar, V.: Data science and prediction. Commun. ACM. 56(12), 64–73 (2013)
16. Donnellan, M.B., Lucas, R.E.: Secondary analysis of datasets in multicultural research. In: Leong, F.T.L., et al. (eds.) APA Handbook of Multicultural Psychology, Vol. 1: Theory and Research, pp. 161–175. American Psychological Association, Washington, DC (2014)
17. Ebrahim, S., et al.: Reanalyses of Randomized Clinical Trial Data. JAMA 312(10), 1024 (2014)
18. Glass, G.V.: Primary, Secondary, and Meta-Analysis of Research. Educ. Res. 5(10), 3–8 (1976)
19. Goes, P.B.: Design Science Research in Top Information Systems Journals. MIS Q. 38(1), iii–viii (2014)
20. Gregor, S., et al.: Reflection, Abstraction And Theorizing In Design And Development Research. In: Proc. ECIS (2013)
21. Gregor, S.: The nature of theory in information systems. MIS Q., 611–642 (2006)
22. Gregor, S., Hevner, A.: Positioning and Presenting Design Science Research for Maximum Impact. Manag. Inf. Syst. Q. 37(2), 337–355 (2013)
23. Hand, D.J.: Data mining: statistics and more? Am. Stat. 52(2), 112–118 (1998)
24. Heaton, J.: Reworking qualitative data. SAGE, London (2004)
25. Heaton, J.: Secondary Analysis of Qualitative Data. In: The A-Z of Social Research. SAGE (2003)
26. Heaton, J.: Secondary Analysis of Qualitative Data: An Overview. Historical Social Research 33(3), 33–45 (2008)
27. Heinrich, P., et al.: Enabling relationship building in tabletop-supported advisory settings. Presented at the (2014)
28. Hevner, A., Chatterjee, S.: Design Science Research in Information Systems. In: Design Research in Information Systems, pp. 9–22. Springer US, Boston (2010)
29. Hevner, A.R., et al.: Design Science in Information Systems Research. MIS Q. 28(1), 75–105 (2004)
30. Hevner, A.R.: The three cycle view of design science research. Scand. J. Inf. Syst. 19(2), 87 (2007)
31. Higgins, J.P.T., Green, S. (eds.): Cochrane handbook for systematic reviews of interventions. Wiley-Blackwell, Chichester (2008)
32. Hinde, A.: Secondary analysis. In: Graham, A., Skinner, C. (eds.) Handbook for Research Students in the Social Sciences, p. 205. Falmer Press (1991)
33. Iivari, J.: Twelve Theses on Design Science Research in Information Systems. In: Design Research in Information Systems, pp. 43–62. Springer US, Boston (2010)
34. Irwin, S.: Qualitative secondary data analysis: Ethics, epistemology and context. Prog. Dev. Stud. 13(4), 295–306 (2013)
35. King, W.R., He, J.: Understanding the role and methods of meta-analysis in IS research. Commun. Assoc. Inf. Syst. 16(1), 32 (2005)
36. Kjeldskov, J., Paay, J.: Indexical Interaction Design for Context-aware Mobile Computer Systems. In: Proc. Australia Conf. Computer-Human Interaction: Design: Activities, Artefacts and Environments, pp. 71–78. ACM, New York (2006)
37. Mettler, T., et al.: On the Use of Experiments in Design Science Research: A Proposition of an Evaluation Framework. Commun. AIS 34(1), 223–240 (2014)

38. Van Nederpelt, P., Daas, P.: 49 Factors that Influence the Quality of Secondary Data Sources. Statistics Netherlands, The Hague/Heerlen (2012)

39. Nunamaker Jr., J.F., Briggs, R.O.: Toward a broader vision for Information Systems. ACM Trans. Manag. Inf. Syst. 2(4), 1–12 (2011)

40. Nussbaumer, P., et al.: "Enforced" vs. "Casual" Transparency – Findings from IT-Supported Financial Advisory Encounters. ACM Trans. Manag. Inf. Syst. 3(2), 11:1–11:19 (2012)

41. Osei-Bryson, K.-M., Ngwenyama, O.K.: Advances in Research Methods for Information Systems Research - Data Mining, Data Envelopment (2014)

42. Paay, J., Kjeldskov, J.: Drawing From a Larger Canvas-a Gestalt Perspective on Location-Based Services. In: Proc. ACIS, p. 34 (2006)

43. Palvia, P., et al.: A profile of information systems research published in Information & Management. Inf. Manage. 44(1), 1–11 (2007)

44. Palvia, P., et al.: Management information systems research: what's there in a methodology? Commun. Assoc. Inf. Syst. 11(1), 16 (2003)

45. Peffers, K., et al.: A Design Science Research Methodology for Information Systems Research. J. Manag. Inf. Syst. 24(3), 45–77 (2007)

46. Pentland, B.T., Feldman, M.S.: Designing routines: On the folly of designing artifacts, while hoping for patterns of action. Inf. Organ. 18(4), 235–250 (2008)

47. Pries-Heje, J., et al.: Strategies for Design Science Research Evaluation. In: Proc. ECIS (2008)

48. Richter, A., Riemer, K.: Malleable End-User Software. Bus. Inf. Syst. Eng. 5(3), 195–197 (2013)

49. Riedl, R., Rueckel, D.: Historical Development of Research Methods in the Information Systems Discipline. In: Proc. AMCIS (2011)

50. Riemer, K., Johnston, R.: Artifact or Equipment? Rethinking the Core of IS using Heidegger's ways of being. In: Proc. ICIS (2011)

51. Sein, M., et al.: Action design research (2011)

52. Sonnenberg, C., vom Brocke, J.: Evaluations in the Science of the Artificial – Reconsidering the Build-Evaluate Pattern in Design Science Research. In: Peffers, K., Rothenberger, M., Kuechler, B. (eds.) DESRIST 2012. LNCS, vol. 7286, pp. 381–397. Springer, Heidelberg (2012)

53. Stebbins, R.A.: Exploratory research in the social sciences. Sage Publications, Thousand Oaks (2001)

54. Vartanian, T.P.: Secondary data analysis. Oxford University Press, New York (2011)

55. Venable, J., Pries-Heje, J., Baskerville, R.: A Comprehensive Framework for Evaluation in Design Science Research. In: Peffers, K., Rothenberger, M., Kuechler, B., et al. (eds.) DESRIST 2012. LNCS, vol. 7286, pp. 423–438. Springer, Heidelberg (2012)

56. Venable, J., et al.: FEDS: A Framework for Evaluation in Design Science Research. Eur. J. Inf. Syst. (2014)

57. Venkatesh, V., et al.: Bridging the qualitative-quantitative divide: Guidelines for conducting mixed methods research in information systems. MIS Q. 37(1), 21–54 (2013)

58. Wertheimer, M., et al.: Gestaltpsychologie. Einfuhrung Neuere Psychol. AW Zickfeldt Osterwieck Am Harz (1927)

59. Whyte, W.F.E.: Participatory action research. Sage Publications, Inc. (1991)

60. Wrobel, S.: An algorithm for multi-relational discovery of subgroups. In: Komorowski, J., Żytkow, J.M. (eds.) PKDD 1997. LNCS, vol. 1263, pp. 78–87. Springer, Heidelberg (1997)

Artifact-Centered Planning and Assessing of Large Design Science Research Projects – A Case Study

Gerald Daeuble$^{(\boxtimes)}$, Michael Werner, and Markus Nuettgens

Hamburg Research Center for Information Systems (HARCIS), University of Hamburg,
Max-Brauer-Allee 60, 22765 Hamburg, Germany
{gerald.daeuble,michael.werner,markus.nuettgens}
@wiso.uni-hamburg.de
http://www.bwl.uni-hamburg.de/harcis

Abstract. Design science research has gained increased attention in the academic research community in the past decade. Several authors have published useful guidelines for conducting and publishing design science-oriented research. But little attention has yet been paid to the set-up and planning of design science research projects. Design science research is different compared to other research approaches due to the duality of the epistemological and the design objective. We investigate how a framework that was developed for the structuring of large design science projects by focusing on research artifacts can be used for the planning and assessment of such projects. We use a case study to demonstrate the application of the framework and discuss what kind of conclusions can be drawn on the applicability of the used framework. We also provide suggestions that might be useful for other scholars when assessing their projects.

Keywords: Design Science Research · Management of Research Projects · Critical Analysis

1 Introduction

Design Science Research (DSR) is an important research approach that has gained increased attention over the last decade in the international scientific community [1]. DSR differs from other research approaches because of the duality of the epistemological and the design objective [2]. It intends to create research outputs that are on the one hand useful for the application domain and that on the other hand contribute to the scientific knowledge base [3]. DSR has to align with both, business needs to create useful research artifacts and research rigor for sound scientific outputs [4]. The objective to create artifacts that are valuable for practical purposes requires the involvement and participation of project members from the application domain. Evaluation is an essential component in design science-oriented research projects [2, 5]. The instantiation of designed artifacts is commonly a time-consuming task that requires different skills compared to those that are necessary in the design phase. To carry out all different research phases and the duality of the research objectives commonly

© Springer International Publishing Switzerland 2015
B. Donnellan et al. (Eds.): DESRIST 2015, LNCS 9073, pp. 343–357, 2015.
DOI: 10.1007/978-3-319-18714-3_22

results in large research projects. Those projects usually include the participation of multiple researchers, research assistants, different scientific institutions and partner companies from the application domain. The interaction of multiple researchers and participation of different interest groups contribute to the complexity of these projects.

Little attention has yet been paid to the question of how large research projects can actually be structured, planned and managed. The risk exists that projects get out of control, out of budget, out of time and consume valuable research resources without achieving the intended research objectives if they are not managed appropriately.

The presented research work is guided by the question as to how scientists can be supported in structuring, planning and assessing large design science oriented research projects. We focus on a case study to find answers to this question. The case study describes a successful DSR project. This project was planned in the initiation phase by using simple work packages for the structuring of the research tasks without any further formulated planning procedure. Although the project was finished successfully several problems occurred during its life-time. We intend to analyze if these problems could have been prevented if they had been identified and taken into account appropriately in the project planning phase. We use a framework for this purpose that was developed for the structuring of the content of large DSR projects [6]. The aim is to investigate how it can be used as a tool to plan design science-oriented projects or to assess, adjust and manage already running projects. The framework provides different dimensions that can be used to identify separate research segments and artifacts. We call using this framework an artifact-centered approach because it enables researchers to identify relevant artifacts and associated analysis, design, evaluation and diffusion methods for a specific research project. We focus on design science-oriented research projects in the information systems science discipline because of their aforementioned idiosyncratic characteristics compared to other research approaches. The overall goal of our investigation is to provide researchers a useful tool and a method for its application to improve their research processes and to yield better research results from their projects.

2   Methodology and Research Structure

The overall research objective of the presented work is the improvement of the planning activities for the management of large DSR projects or the assessment of already running projects. We aspire to provide tools and methods for scientists to improve the management of such projects. DSR addresses research problems that originate from the application domain and aim to develop useful artifacts that can be applied in practice [3]. It was therefore chosen as the primary research approach to achieve the stated objective.

Different frameworks can be used to structure design-oriented research activities [7–11]. The presented research covers different DSR phases. It provides empirical information on a selected DSR project - the provided case study – for analysis purposes. The analysis of the problem domain as a first step in DSR is partly covered in the introductory section. It is also discussed in the context of the specific case at the beginning of the Case Study section which also covers the aforementioned evaluation and design aspects. The paper closes with a brief discussion, summary and outlook to future research. The diffusion of our research results as the last phase in DSR is already addressed by the publication of this article.

Necessary data was collected by conducting structured workshops. We relied on procedures that are recommended for semi-structured interviews [12] to carry out the workshops. This included the preparation and test of discussion guidelines, transcription and analysis of transcribed information. Case study research is commonly criticized for the lack of generalizability due to the uniqueness of the investigated case and it could be argued that using a single case is not sufficient for evaluation purposes. But Yin points out that similar concerns can, for example, also be applied in the contexts of single experiments [13]. Another aspect that should be considered is the fact that empirical data on large DSR projects is extremely difficult to collect due to the long life span of those projects and the limited public access to relevant data. The selected framework did not exist when the case study project started. It was therefore not possible to evaluate its application in its natural life-cycle. We instead used an artificial ex post examination by applying the framework from a retrospective point of view. This approach allows us to examine if the framework could have been applied and if problems that occurred in the project could have been prevented. It also allows us to identify the reasons why certain aspects of the project were very successful and others not.

The presented research results should not be considered as a complete research project management framework because project management has to take into account a variety of different processes and aspects. We instead focus on the planning phase of a research project life-cycle to stay in reasonable limits and for being able to provide a level of detail that is helpful for scientists in day-to-day work. We use a case study to investigate the applicability of the used framework, to assess the selected research project and to demonstrate a method for using the framework for these purposes. The case study describes a public funded collaborative project that aimed at increasing productivity within technical customer service processes and empowering technical service staff. Three scientific institutions, two partner companies from industry, a national standard setting institution and an industry association participated in the project that ran over a period of three years.

3   Related Work

A major challenge in scientific endeavors is the selection of adequate research methods [14]. A variety of well-established research methods is available for researchers in information systems science [15–19]. The need for structured and commonly agreed upon research processes has been mentioned by several scholars from the DSR community [20]. A variety of different approaches have been suggested to structure design science-oriented research activities. Peffers et al. present a research methodology for DSR in the information systems community [10, 11]. The authors present a research framework that consists of six phases: (1) identify problem and motivate, (2) define objectives of a solution, (3) design and development, (4) demonstration, (5) evaluation and (6) communication. Their framework is based on a review of existing scientific publications on the research process in the information systems and related research disciplines. They take into account process elements that have been identified by different scholars working in the information systems [3, 21–24] and engineering [25, 26] discipline. It is interesting that the continental European research community is mostly neglected by the authors although the design science discipline has a long lasting tradition especially in German speaking countries [27]. Österle et al. as representatives of this community suggest four phases for DSR: (1) analysis, (2) design, (3) evaluation and (4) diffusion [9]. March and Storey describe five different phases: (1) identification and description of a relevant IT problem, (2) demonstration that no adequate solutions exist, (3) development and presentation of a novel IT, (4) rigorous evaluation of the IT artifact, (5) articulation of the value added to the knowledge-base and to practice, and (6) explanation of the implications [28]. Gregor and Baskerville examine the research process from a philosophy of science perspective with the objective to provide a framework for the combination of design science and social science research.

The previously describes literature focusses on the different activities, steps, phases and principles that should be taken into account to carry out design science-oriented research. But little attention has yet been paid to the question of how these activities and research projects should be managed. Vom Brocke and Lippe are among the few authors that build the bridge between research processes and project management. They point out the need to tailor existing project management guidelines for research projects and identify eight characteristics that distinguish design science-oriented research projects from traditional project types [4]. We are not aware of quantitative research on project management in the field of information systems science. Researchers from the information systems discipline rarely refer to project management literature although mature knowledge on project management is available in international [29], national [30, 31] or industry [32, 33] standards and guidelines.

The aforementioned literature provides useful insights into the research processes in design science-oriented research. But little has yet been published that provides guidance on how large DSR projects can effectively be structured and set up. To do exactly that is what we intend with the presentation of the research results in this article.

4   Case Study

4.1   Research Project Description

The research project described in this section aims to increase the productivity in technical customer service processes and to empower technical service staff. The combination of products and services (product-service systems) has an impact on the product life-cycle and affects the overall cost and revenue structure. The case study describes a public funded collaborative research project with the overall objective to support and empower service technicians in the context of after-sales services.

The goal was to design and implement a mobile support system to assist technical service staff. This was achieved by proactively providing functional information and to automate administrative processes for improving the productivity of maintenance and repair processes. The project involved a commercial enterprise operating in the machine and plant construction industry, scholars from different research institutions, a commercial software development company and a national standardization organization. The project in sum involved seven partners and was scheduled for a three year period. The overall research questions were formulated as follows:

- How can the productivity of technical customer service processes be improved by IT-based support systems?
- How can the technical customer service staff be empowered by IT-based support systems?

The research activities in the project followed the phases for design-oriented research: (1) Analysis, (2) Design, (3) Evaluate and (4) Diffusion [9]. Work packages were defined to divide the scope and assign responsibilities to the different project partners. The data collection was part of the analysis phase. Five researchers were responsible in a field study with partner companies in two different European countries for *shadowing* service technicians in their day-to-day operations. The observation was accompanied by expert interviews and an extensive literature review to identify requirements, information needs and productivity measures for service processes. The identified requirements were transferred during the design phase into conceptual models as well as functional and technical specifications. Several artifacts were instantiated and evaluated in two prototypes (one for technical service staff and one for the management) operating on the same database. The diffusion phase consisted of publishing articles for different artifacts and evaluation results. The research results also severed as input for a national standard that was published as a part of the research project.

The project was able to answer the research questions from a scholar's and a practitioner's perspective and can be considered successful in terms of time, budget, quality and the funding organization's assessment. Although the project team achieved the overall goal, minor and major obstacles surfaced during the three year period. In order to investigate those issues and to improve further research projects, expert interviews and workshops were initiated after filing the final project report. Issues were individually described in a written form by the involved parties and consolidated in workshops. The following issues for improvement were identified:

- A design science researcher's goal to create artifacts relevant to both, scholars and practitioners, was not well supported by the work package structure.
- There was a structural difference between the documented target outcome per work package and desired artifacts (from a scientific perspective).
- The assignment of methods (for the phases analysis, design, evaluation and evaluation) to each artifact was not well supported by the work package structure.
- An artifact-centered and structured research process was not well supported by the work package description especially in larger work packages with more involved parties.

- The chronology of the research process as well as the collaboration structure of the parties regarding DSR artifacts changed in contrast to the initial planning. This shift also had implications on the time and resource planning.
- The publication process – focusing on design science research – was not well supported by work package planning due to the fact that publishable artifacts were not equal to work package results.

The initial work package description was referenced frequently during the ex post discussing of the consolidated issues. Despite having a common, inter-coordinated foundation (work package description defining scope, responsibilities and resources) the identified issues seemed not to be covered by the applied method.

Overall two questions emerged from the ex post analysis of the project: (A) Does the initial planning method based on the definition of work packages address the identified issues and (B) how could those issues have been identified at an earlier stage of the project?

4.2   Segmentation Framework

Work packages and Gantt charts are one way to describe projects and communicate among involved parties. The results from the case study showed that certain obstacles surfaced in the project that were not prevented by the simple separation into work packages. We introduce in this section a segmentation framework that was developed to support the structuring of large design science-oriented project. This framework is used as an alternative approach to view the project from a different perspective [34] and to analyze if these obstacles could have been prevented.

The design of the framework is extensively described in [6]. A full description would go beyond the scope of this paper. We therefore only provide a brief summary.

Each research project addresses an overall research question. The research questions in large research projects are, as a rule, complex. Otherwise it would be questionable if such a project indeed exhibits the characteristics of a large project. Complex research questions can usually be divided into detailed lower-level research questions. These research questions can be used as a categorization criterion for a third Research Question Dimension (RQD). Fig.1 shows the segmentation framework with all three dimensions. It illustrates how separate segments emerge based on the different dimension categories. Each segment can be referenced by using its x- (RQD), y- (RCD) and z-coordinates (HTD) in the cube.

Fig. 1 also illustrates a single segment from the overall model. The division into research segments can be seen as a 'divide and conquer' approach. The overall research project is broken into manageable components that can be conquered individually. For each segment it is now possible to identify and describe the relevant artifact(s), the research methods for the analysis, design and evaluation as well as the diffusion type. A template for such a description is illustrated in Table 1. Evaluation methods for a single artifact can, for example, be chosen by relying on available frameworks [5], whereas the type of diffusion can, for example, be determined by referring to the knowledge contribution level of design science-oriented research [35]. Each segment

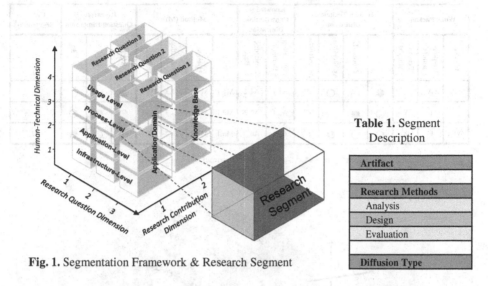

Fig. 1. Segmentation Framework & Research Segment

Table 1. Segment Description

Artifact
Research Methods
Analysis
Design
Evaluation
Diffusion Type

should be associated with one (or more) artifact. March and Smith define four types of research artifacts: constructs, methods, models and instantiations [3]. Gregor argues that design theories should also be regarded as an important outcome of design science-oriented research [36]. Many research methods exist for analysis, design and evaluation purposes. A summary of exemplary research methods is for example available in [16–19].

4.3   Applying the Segmentation Framework to the Research Project

We used the previously described framework to analyze the case study project in order to gain a different perspective (ex post) on the completed research project. The 3-dimensional model was first transferred into a 2-dimensional table. The aim was to map the project work packages to the different segments in the framework. The transformation facilitates this mapping. The corresponding dimensions of the cube - research questions dimension, human-technical dimension (layers) and research contributions dimensions - represent the columns in the table. The assignment can be done by using Harvey balls. A full ball represents an assignment of a research question or a cube dimension (layer) to a work package. An empty ball represents no correlation between them. The research methods can be listed for each research phase (analysis, design, evaluation and diffusion). Fig. 2 shows the table structure for matching the cube dimensions. By filling out the table, work packages can be mapped to the different dimension categories from the segmentation framework. The mapping can be used to gather, represent and explicate tacit knowledge from the project participants.

Work Package			Human-Technical Dimension				Knowledge Contribution Dimension		Method (M)				Research-Question Dimension			Cube Segment(s)
WP-No.	Respons-ability	Person Months	Usage-L	Process-L	Application-L	Infrastruct.-L	Application Domain	Knowledge Base	Analysis	Design	Evaluation	Diffusion	RQ 1	RQ 2	RQ 3	
WP1	A	X	●	○	○	○	A1.1	A1.2	M1.1	M1.2	M1.3	P1.1	●	○	○	I
WP2	B	Y	○	●	○	○	A2.1	A2.2	M2.1	M2.2	M2.3	P2.1	○	●	○	II
WPn	C	Z	○	○	●	○	An.1	An.2	Mn.1	Mn.2	Mn.3	Pn.1	○	○	●	III

● equals "correlation"   ○ equals "no correlation"

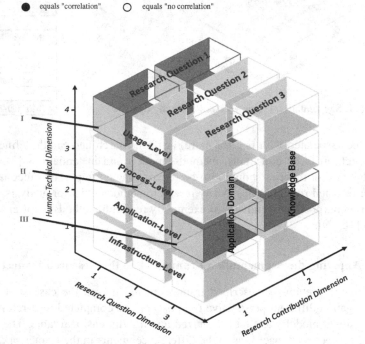

Fig. 2. Mapping of Work Packages to the Framework Dimensions

Fig. 2 conceptualizes how the mapping works. We used this mapping for the case study project. The project was divided into nine work packages. They are listed in the first left columns. Additional data for each work package is included that provides information of the planned resources and responsibility for each work package. The results were discussed among the project members in detail with the aim to consolidate the results and to reach consensus and a common perspective on the research project. Consensus was achieved to a large extend in regard to the assignment of layers – just WP5 brought up controversy (considering if the prototype also has to be assigned to the infrastructure layer). For this reason a half-filled Harvey ball was recorded. It indicates a partial correlation.

The assignment of artifacts was difficult and resulted in controversial and extensive discussions. The matching of documented work package outcomes and actual research project outcomes with the distinct definition of DSR artifacts was difficult. It became obvious that WP2-4 did not have a clear contribution to the knowledge base and – consequentially – had no direct related artifact and publication output. It also became obvious that publications only occurred where the artifact related to both, the application domain and knowledge base (WP1, WP5, WP6, WP8).

Table 2. Case Study Work Package Mapping

Work Package				Human-Technical Dimension				Knowledge Contribution Dimension		Method (M)				Research-Question Dimension	
WP-No.	Description	Respons-ability	Person Months	Usage-L	Process-L	Application-L	Infrastruct-L	Application Domain	Knowledge Base	Analysis	Design	Evaluation	Diffusion (References)	Productivity	Empower-ment
WP1	State-of-the-art and Requirements Analysis	A	13	●	●	●	●	construct	construct	literature review, interview, field study	qualitative & quantitative analysis	interview	[37]	●	●
WP2	Productivity Measures and Metrics	A	21	●	●	○	○	model		(cf. WP1 results)	modeling	case study (cf. WP7)		●	○
WP3	Functional Specification of Information System	B	19	●	●	○	○	model		(cf. WP1 results)	modeling	case study (cf. WP7)		●	●
WP4	Technical Specification of Information System	B	10	○	●	●	○	model		(cf. WP1, WP3 results)	modeling	case study (cf. WP7)		●	●
WP5	Implementation of Prototype	D	4	●	●	●	◐	instantiation	instantiation	(cf. WP1, WP3, WP4 results)	prototyping	(cf. WP6)	[38, 39, 42]	●	●
WP6	Evaluation	A	9	●	●	●	●	model	model		modelling	lab experiment (eye tracking)	[40]	●	●
WP7	Use Case (continuous)	B	22	●	●	●	●					case study		●	●
WP8	Standardization	C	15	●	●	●	○	construct, model, method	construct, model, method	meta analysis of project results	modelling	expert workshop	[41]	●	●
WP9	(Project Management & Public Relations)	A	27	○	○	○	○							○	○

● equals "correlation"   ○ equals "no correlation"   ◐ equals "partial correlation"

Several research methods were used during the project to analyze the requirements as well as to design and to evaluate the listed artifacts. It became apparent that several analysis methods used in WP1 related to a large extent to artifacts that were designed in other work packages. Likewise, WP7 contributed in terms of evaluation to three other work packages. Having a clear view on applied methods, phases and overall chronology is necessary to organize and direct the involved project partners in large research projects. Table 2 provides information on which partner actually contributed to the analysis, design and evaluation of the created artifacts. Table 2 also shows that

that every work package addressed both research questions except WP2 and 9. This could be an indication that the work packages were initially designed too broad.

In a next step the consolidated table is transferred back into the cube. The graphical three-dimensional representation makes it even more obvious that a work package often related to various segments while segments frequently relate to more than one work package vice versa. Fig. 3 illustrates that WP1 affected all 16 segments. This indicates that work packages might have been defined too broad. Fig. 4 represents two segments that referred to six different work packages. This indicates several interconnections between work packages. There is a risk of redundancy in not recognizing the interconnections to already existing project results. This corresponded with the previously identified problem statement that work packages do not support an artifact-centered approach lacking the required structure and granularity.

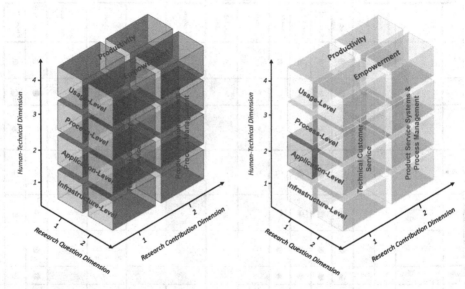

Fig. 3. Related Segments to a single Work Package (WP1)

Fig. 4. Segments related to six Work Packages

In the following the initially stated project issues are recapitulated. We investigate if these issues can be explained by using the segmentation framework.

1. *A design science researcher's goal to create artifacts relevant to scholars and practitioners was not well supported by the work package structure and described rather implicitly.*

2. *There was a structural difference between the documented target outcome per work package and desired artifacts (from a scientific perspective).*

The duality of epistemological and design objectives [2] is not necessarily inherent using a work package structure in combination with Gantt charts which are commonly used techniques for the planning of projects. A differentiation between "application in the appropriate environment" and "addition to the knowledge base" [3] is not part of these project planning techniques. It is therefore reasonable that the project participants perceived a lack of support to organize the development of artifacts. Such a constellation could have been prevented if the different research contribution domains would have been taken into account in the initial project planning phase.

3. *The assignment of methods (for the phases analysis, design, evaluation and evaluation) to each artifact was not well supported by the work package structure.*

4. *An artifact-centered and structured research process was not well supported by the work package description especially in larger work packages with more involved parties*

5. *The chronology of the research process as well as the collaboration structure of the parties regarding DSR artifacts changed in contrast to the initial planning. This shift also had implications on the time and resource planning.*

The described work packages were interrelated in regard to inputs, used research methods, outputs, chronology and involved parties. Table 2 shows that this constellation leads to overlaps regarding the separate research artifacts. The results from analysis phase in WP1 served as the input for the design of artifacts in in WP2 to 5. Different research partners were responsible for these work packages. But the interrelation of the involved artifacts and research methods was not obvious in the simple work package planning. Such dependencies could have been taken into account for the assignment of the different artifacts to specific project members and for planning the project time schedule. Redundancies in work efforts to create a specific artifact could have been prevented.

6. *The publication process – focusing on design science research – was not well supported by work package planning due to the fact that publishable artifacts were not equal to work package results.*

Table 2 shows that seven created artifacts contributed to the application domain but only four artifacts where perceived as contributions to the overall knowledge base. This implies an imbalance of the project and explains why the project participants state a missing support for the development and publication of researched artifacts. The activities for the analysis, design and evaluation of artifacts that primarily contribute to the knowledge base was not well supported.

The results of the assessment can be summarized by recapitulating the two research questions: (A) Does the initial planning method based on the definition of work packages addresses the identified issues and (B) how could those issues have been identified at an earlier stage of the project?

(A) Structural problems emerged because of the differences between the work package based project planning and the application of the design science paradigm.

Work package based project planning and scoping is a simple and broadly accepted and established approach and provides a common vocabulary. The aim is to expatiate and operationalize an artifact-centered approach in the initial planning and scoping phase. A planning approach on the basis of work packaged for large and complex DSR projects is prone to generate gaps in the research scope and redundancies especially in regard to cooperative projects that involve several parties. (B) The definition of the content and scope of a research project by using work package descriptions and Gantt charts is a basic project management technique. But such a planning does not take into account certain aspects that are vital to design science-oriented research projects. This especially relates to the necessary consideration of the duality of the research objectives of such projects. The presented framework is a useful tool to identify such an imbalance and it is likely that its application might have prevented several shortcomings that have been stated by the project participants.

4.4   Recommendations for Applying the Framework in the Initial Planning Phase

In this case study a project was analyzed ex post. In order to benefit from the perspective offered by the framework the integration in the initial planning phase (ex ante) is recommended. Based on the conducted interviews the following process is recommended to scope and plan research projects: (1) Definition of research question(s), (2) development of artifacts corresponding with the research question(s) and analysis if the artifacts correlate with the duality of DSR, (3) assignment of related layers (human-technical dimension) in order to adjust the scope and (4) assignment of methods to create the relating artifact. The graphical representation in form of the cube promotes an overview to identify redundancies, white spots and interfaces between project partners.

5   Discussion

The previous section described the application of a framework for the structuring of large research projects for a specific case study. Several project issues that were identified by interviewing the project members were the starting point for investigation. The project was initially planned primarily by defining work packages. The application of the introduced segmentation framework proved to be useful for revealing why certain shortcomings occurred. It revealed that certain aspects should have been taken into account in the planning phase of the project. A simple project planning on the basis of work packages neglects requirements that are relevant for design science-oriented research projects. The analysis of the case study showed that especially the contributions to the scientific knowledge base are at risk of being misrepresented. An artifact-centered planning approach by using the presented segmentation framework narrows the gap between work package planning and the research processes in design science-oriented research. Work packages are nevertheless necessary to plan projects but their definition should follow an artifact-centric planning approach that is necessary for DSR project to prevent imbalances in the project layout.

Providing a graphical representation proved to be valuable for identifying redundancies, gaps and interdependencies among artifacts, research methods and responsibilities. A common terminology also furthered a common understanding of important project aspects among project members.

6   Summary and Outlook

The aim of this paper is the presentation of an artifact-centered approach to plan and assess DSR projects. The planning, set up and management of large design science-oriented research projects has not been investigated yet in the scientific community. We referred to a public funded cooperative research project that was analyzed from a retrospective point of view. The identification of issues and obstacles that surfaced during the project were the starting point of investigation to find out if the identified shortcomings could have been prevented in the planning phase. We used a specific framework for this purpose that was especially designed for the structuring of large DSR projects. The described research project was planned using work packages and Gantt charts. These planning techniques are widely accepted and a prerequisite to acquire public funding. Using an alternative artifact-centered approach can be seen as a means of scientific triangulation to create novel insights from the observed subject. Our research work shows that the framework can be applied successfully and that it is helpful to assess large DSR projects and to find aspects for improvement.

The presented research just deals with a single case study. It might be questioned if this is a solid foundation for rigorous scientific contributions. But the same question can, for example, also be asked for in the context of single experiments (Yin, 2008). Empirical data for large research projects is difficult to collect because of their long lifespans and the limited public access to relevant information. Observing such research projects over their whole life-cycles would require a comparatively very long observation time. Further empirical studies are nevertheless planned for strengthening the results presented in this paper. The results from our case study illustrate that the planning and set up of large DSR projects is a difficult task. The used framework covers three different dimensions. Simple tables can be used as a means to reduce the level of complexity but at the cost of an adequate graphical representation. Using the presented framework could be supported by providing a web-based tool. The development of a software tool that implements the presented framework and the suggested procedure for its application is the goal of future research.

References

1. Vaishnavi, V., Kuechler, W.: Design research in information systems (2004)
2. Riege, C., Saat, J., Bucher, T.: Systematisierung von Evaluationsmethoden in der gestaltungsorientierten Wirtschaftsinformatik. In: Becker, J., Krcmar, H., Niehaves, B. (eds.) Wissenschaftstheorie und Gestaltungsorientierte Wirtschaftsinformatik, pp. 69–86. Physica-Verlag HD (2009)

3. Hevner, A.R., March, S.T., Park, J., Ram, S.: Design Science in Information Systems Research. MIS Q. 28, 75–105 (2004)
4. vom Brocke, J., Lippe, S.: Taking a Project Management Perspective on Design Science Research. In: Winter, R., Zhao, J.L., Aier, S. (eds.) DESRIST 2010. LNCS, vol. 6105, pp. 31–44. Springer, Heidelberg (2010)
5. Venable, J., Pries-Heje, J., Baskerville, R.: A comprehensive framework for evaluation in design science research. Des. Sci. Res. Inf. Syst. Adv. Theory Pract., 423–438 (2012)
6. Werner, M., Schultz, M., Müller-Wickop, N., Nüttgens, M.: Who Is Afraid of the Big Bad Wolf - Structuring Large Design Science Research Projects. In: Proceedings of the 22nd European Conference on Information Systems (ECIS 2014), Tel Aviv, Israel, pp. 1–16 (2014)
7. Alturki, A., Gable, G.G., Bandara, W.: A design science research roadmap. Service-Oriented Perspectives in Design Science Research. In: Jain, H., Sinha, A.P., Vitharana, P. (eds.) DESRIST 2011. LNCS, vol. 6629, pp. 107–123. Springer, Heidelberg (2011)
8. March, S.T., Smith, G.F.: Design and natural science research on information technology. Decis. Support Syst. 15, 251–266 (1995)
9. Österle, H., Becker, J., Frank, U., Hess, T., Karagiannis, D., Krcmar, H., Loos, P., Mertens, P., Oberweis, A., Sinz, E.J.: Memorandum on design-oriented information systems research. Eur. J. Inf. Syst. 20, 7–10 (2010)
10. Peffers, K., Tuunanen, T., Gengler, C.E., Rossi, M., Hui, W., Virtanen, V., Bragge, J.: The design science research process: A model for producing and presenting information systems research. In: Proceedings of the 1st International Conference on Design Science Research in Information Systems and Technology (DESRIST), pp. 83–106 (2006)
11. Peffers, K., Tuunanen, T., Rothenberger, M.A., Chatterjee, S.: A Design Science Research Methodology for Information Systems Research. J. Manag. Inf. Syst. 24, 45–77 (2007)
12. Gubrium, J.F., Holstein, J.A.: Handbook of Interview Research: Context and Method. SAGE (2002)
13. Yin, R.K.: Case Study Research: Design and Methods. Sage Publications (2008)
14. Galliers, R.D., Land, F.F.: Viewpoint: choosing appropriate information systems research methodologies. Commun. ACM 30, 901–902 (1987)
15. Chen, W., Hirschheim, R.: A paradigmatic and methodological examination of information systems research from 1991 to 2001. Inf. Syst. J. 14, 197–235 (2004)
16. Palvia, P., Mao, E., Salam, A.F., Soliman, K.S.: Management Information System Research: What's There in a Methodolgy? Commun. Assoc. Inf. Syst. 11, 289–309 (2003)
17. Palvia, P., Leary, D., Mao, E., Midha, V., Pinjani, P., Salam, A.F.: Research methodologies in MIS: An update. Commun. Assoc. Inf. Syst. 14, 526–542 (2004)
18. Wilde, T., Hess, T.: Methodenspektrum der Wirtschaftsinformatik: Überblick und Portfoliobildung. Arbeitspapiere Inst. Für Wirtsch. Neue Medien LMU Münch, 2 (2006)
19. Wilde, T., Hess, T.: Forschungsmethoden der Wirtschaftsinformatik. Wirtschaftsinformatik 49, 280–287 (2007)
20. Leist, S., Rosemann, M.: Research process management. In: Proceedings of the 22nd Australasian Conference on Information Systems (ACIS) 2011-Identifying the Information Systems Discipline, pp. 1–11 (2011)
21. Cole, R., Purao, S., Rossi, M., Sein, M.K.: Being Proactive: Where Action Research Meets Design Research. In: Proceedings of the 26h International Conference on Information Systems (2005)
22. Nunamaker, J.F., Chen, M., Purdin, T.D.M.: Systems Development in Information Systems Research. J. Manag. Inf. Syst. 7, 89–106 (1991)

23. Takeda, H., Veerkamp, P., Yoshikawa, H.: Modeling design process. AI Mag. 11, 37 (1990)
24. Walls, J., Widmeyer, G., El Sawy, O.: Building an information system design theory for vigilant EIS. Inf. Syst. Res. 3, 36–59 (1992)
25. Archer, L.B.: Systematic method for designers. Developments in Design Methodology, pp. 57–82. John Wiley, London (1984)
26. Eekels, J., Roozenburg, N.F.M.: A methodological comparison of the structures of scientific research and engineering design: Their similarities and differences. Des. Stud. 12, 197–203 (1991)
27. Winter, R.: Design science research in Europe. Eur. J. Inf. Syst. 17, 470–475 (2008)
28. March, S.T., Storey, V.C.: Design science in the information systems discipline: An introduction to the special issue on design science research. MIS Q. 32, 725–730 (2008)
29. International Organization for Standardization: ISO 21500 2011 Guidance on project management (2012)
30. British Standards Institute: BS 6079: 2000 Project Management. BSI Standards, London (2000)
31. Deutsches Institut für Normung: DIN SPEC 69901 - Projektmanagement. Beuth Verlag GmbH, Berlin (2009)
32. Great Britain, Office of Government Commerce: Managing successful projects with PRINCE2. TSO, London (2009)
33. Project Management Institute: A guide to the project management body of knowledge (PMBOK Guide). Project Management Institute, Newtown Square, Pennsylvania (2013)
34. Denzin, N.K.: The Research Act: A Theoretical Introduction to Sociological Methods. Transaction Publishers (2009)
35. Gregor, S., Hevner, A.R.: Positioning and Presenting Design Science Research for Maximum Impact. MIS Q. 37, 337–355 (2013)
36. Gregor, S.: The nature of theory in information systems. MIS Q. 30, 611–642 (2006)
37. Matijacic, M., Fellmann, M., Özcan, D., Kammler, F., Nuettgens, M., Thomas, O.: Elicitation and Consolidation of Requirements for Mobile Technical Customer Services Support Systems - A Multi-Method Approach. In: ICIS 2013 Proc. (2013)
38. Özcan, D., Niemöller, C., Fellmann, M., Matijacic, M., Däuble, G., Schlicker, M., Thomas, O., Nüttgens, M.: A Use Case-driven Approach to the Design of Service Support Systems: Making Use of Semantic Technologies. In: Proceedings of the International Symposium on Services Science (ISSS 2013), pp. 105–116 (2013)
39. Däuble, G., Schlömer, I., Böttcher, B., Nüttgens, M.: Supporting Technical Customer Service Processes: A Design-Centered Approach. In: Tremblay, M.C., VanderMeer, D., Rothenberger, M., Gupta, A., Yoon, V. (eds.) DESRIST 2014. LNCS, vol. 8463, pp. 408–412. Springer, Heidelberg (2014)
40. Däuble, G., Schlömer, I., Müller-Wickop, N., Schultz, M., Werner, M., Nüttgens, P.D.M.: Usability Evaluation – Messung, Bewertung und Verbesserung der Gebrauchstauglichkeit von Informationssystemen. In: Nüttgens, M., Thomas, O., Fellmann, M. (eds.) Dienstleistungsproduktivität, pp. 140–154. Springer Fachmedien Wiesbaden (2014)
41. DIN: DIN SPEC 91294: Anwendungsfälle Für Mobile Assistenzsysteme Im Technischen Kundendienst (2014)
42. Fellmann, M., Özcan, D., Matijacic, M., Däuble, G., Schlicker, M., Thomas, O., Nüttgens, M.: Towards a Mobile Technical Customer Service Support Platform. In: Daniel, F., Papadopoulos, G.A., Thiran, P. (eds.) MobiWIS 2013. LNCS, vol. 8093, pp. 296–299. Springer, Heidelberg (2013)

Prototypes

icebricks

Mobile Application for Business Process Modeling

Jörg Becker, Nico Clever[✉], Justus Holler, and Maria Shitkova

European Research Center for Information Systems, University of Muenster,
Leonardo-Campus 3, 48149 Muenster, Germany
{joerg.becker,nico.clever,justus.holler,
maria.shitkova}@ercis.uni-muenster.de

Abstract. In times of demanding requirements for BPM projects, providing an additional access point from a mobile device to the process modeling tool for efficient communication of process models and distributed modeling is of high importance. In this article, we present a mobile application (app) prototype for the web-based business process modeling tool icebricks. The app is realized as a hybrid app for the Google Android and Apple iOS operating systems. As such, it makes use of the advantages of mobile websites – single code repository for software updates – and native apps – device-specific functionality. The app is integrated with the icebricks web application, so redundancies in the data management are avoided. The design of the app adheres to the previously compiled usability guidelines and ensures, amongst others, the same look-and-feel for both the web application and the mobile app. The app was shaped in a design thinking workshop with developers, BPM consultants, who are using the tool, and academic BPM and usability domain experts. The functional range of the app is a subset of the web application functionality and was worked out as part of the design thinking workshop. The app was successfully evaluated by the product owner and target users, a BPM consultancy and its employees.

Keywords: Prototype · Modeling Tools · Business Process Management · Building Block Based Modeling · Mobile Application

1 Introduction

Business process management (BPM) in enterprises is an increasingly important topic and complex undertaking [1, 2]. One of the main concerns, in BPM generally, and for BPM tools specifically, nowadays is the distributed accessibility of process models, whether for documental, informational or modeling purposes [2]. Such a distributed accessibility can be ensured by providing an additional possibility for stakeholders such as consultants, process modelers, or department workers to access the respective models via a mobile device like a smartphone or a tablet next to a desktop or web application. This is due to the fact that the professional world is becoming faster and faster and people are required to react quicker to changing circumstances. Thus, in

© Springer International Publishing Switzerland 2015
B. Donnellan et al. (Eds.): DESRIST 2015, LNCS 9073, pp. 361–365, 2015.
DOI: 10.1007/978-3-319-18714-3_23

this article, we present the prototype of a mobile application for the BPM tool *icebricks*[1] [3].

2   Significance to Research

icebricks is a business process modeling tool which enables efficient and effective creation and management of process models. It adheres to and enforces several guidelines of modeling already at the time of model creation [4, 5]. Certain rationales, stemming from this adherence to modeling guidelines, are presented in the following.

By the strict use of four layers of abstraction, the complexity of modeling projects is rendered manageable as opposed to generic modeling languages like EPC or BPMN [1]. The four layers of icebricks are process frameworks, main processes, detail processes, and process building blocks. The process framework provides a general overview of an enterprise's main processes. On the lower layers, subsequently, the processes are described in ever more detail. By the use of comprehensive attribution on every layer of the process landscape, detailed in-depth information can be provided for every model element. Such semantic annotation functionality renders enhanced branching methods superfluous. This leads to an even more reduced complexity of the resulting models.

Enforcing the modeler to stick to a semantically standardized way of labeling the process elements increases comparability and enables reusability and automated analysis of process models [1, 6]. Thus, icebricks provides a glossary of business objects and related activities. These predefined valid combinations of business objects and activities can be used for labeling the elements, ensuring semantic standardization of the resulting models.

icebricks is realized as a web application based on the Ruby on Rails-Framework and JavaScript, strictly encapsulating the business logic, data management and presentation. Its modular nature facilitates the integration with a mobile application for the presentation and altering of the process models within a shared database. In the following section, the design of the mobile icebricks app is laid out in detail. While designing the app, several scientifically compiled usability guidelines for mobile websites and applications were taken into account [7].

3   Design of the Artifact

The mobile icebricks app is realized as a hybrid app for mobile devices using either the Google Android or the Apple iOS operating system. As such, it combines advantages from both mobile websites and native applications and gets rid of some of the disadvantages of either implementation. Direct use of the icebricks web application on mobile devices is not possible due to scaling impediments and other technical reasons, e.g., JavaScript functionality. A hybrid app can make use of the code written for the web application (HTML and JavaScript) and when it comes to updates, only one

---

[1] http://presentation.icebricks.de

code repository has to be maintained. If a native implementation was chosen, for an update many code repositories would have to be maintained (web application repository plus one for each mobile operating system (OS)). Moreover, unlike a mobile website, a hybrid app allows for utilizing device-specific functions, e.g. pull-to-refresh or breadcrumbs. Apparently, more device-specific functionality could be employed if a native implementation was chosen. However, for mobile apps it is crucial that the look-and-feel is the same for all OS [8]. This also holds true for different versions of the same product, i.e., desktop/web application and mobile app. Use of numerous device-specific functions leads to an increased maintenance effort and can lead to an unmanageability of the code repositories.

The development of the hybrid icebricks app was a six months long project divided into a design and an implementation phases. The design phase encompassed a design thinking workshop which lead to a paper-based prototype of the artifact. In this workshop, the developers, together with two BPM consultants (six to seven years of BPM experience; also product owners w. r. t. the BPM tool) and three academics (three to four years of BPM and usability research experience) shaped the design of the app according to the previously determined usability guidelines for mobile websites and applications [7]. For example, a crucial success factor of developing a mobile app for a web application is to stick to a uniform design of both representations of the same product [8]. Furthermore, as the app handles sensitive data, passcode functionality and simple passcode entering are of importance [9], as well as the use of breadcrumbs for quick and easy navigation within the app [10–12]. For a comprehensive compilation of all guidelines adhered to in the design phase, see [7].

 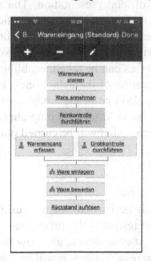 

Fig. 1. Design and functionality of the icebricks app (on Apple iOS)

In order to satisfy the needs of the target users (BPM consultants), they were involved in the definition of the functional spread of the application. Due to particularities of mobile devices, such as limited screen size and instable internet connection, just a part of the original web tool functionality could be transferred to the mobile app. This functionality included: display and basic modeling of the processes (extensive modeling prohibited by small screen size), display and editing of the glossary, display of the attributes of a process element, display of hierarchies (an icebricks construct to depict hierarchical structures like organizational charts, IT architectures etc.), and access to administrative functionality.

During the implementation phase of the app, regular meetings (mostly weekly) between the stakeholders were held to ensure the correct application of the usability guidelines and the accuracy of the implemented functionality. In **Fig. 1**, the design and some functionality of the icebricks app (Apple iOS version) are presented. Here, the passcode entering screen, a main process in edit mode, and the breadcrumb navigation are shown.

4   Significance to Practice and Evaluation of the Artifact

As mentioned in the previous sections, the decision to implement a mobile version of the BPM tool icebricks stemmed directly from the practice, namely the everyday needs of the consultants using the tool. Therefore, the significance to practice is inherent in the app. The product owner (consultancy company), represented by two BPM consultants, was an integral part of the development project. This provided the developers with a direct access to the practice requirements. When the end product was first officially presented, the product owner highly appreciated the results. Moreover, the CEO of the consultancy and the consultants' colleagues were immensely satisfied with the app during the first official presentation. The app is now used in real-life BPM projects. Although, this utilization is not a scientifically grounded evaluation, it can be said that the app is a helpful instrument for the consultants w. r. t. the communication possibilities in workshop/interview situations. With it, a quick look to reference or actual enterprise processes can be taken, enabling either an easy adaptation of the reference models or verification of the actual ones. Moreover, basic, unobtrusive modeling during interviews is also one of the advantages coming along with the app, which is currently verified in the field use. A comprehensive, scientific evaluation of the app is part of future research which will be carried out contemporarily.

5   Outlook

In the near future, studies will be carried out measuring the fitness for use of the icebricks app. This means both testing if the functionality provided by the app is sufficient for the everyday work of consultants, and how the usability of the app is perceived generally. Based on the results, the app will be adapted to the emerging needs. The studies are planned as interview-like app usage scenarios by BPM consultants/experts on the one hand, and by random people to determine the general usability on the other hand. Moreover, it is planned to extend research on the need and functional range of mobile versions of desktop/web applications in the context of BPM with the help of the icebricks toolset (web application and mobile app).

References

1. Becker, J., Kugeler, M., Rosemann, M.: Process Management: A Guide for the Design of Business Processes. Springer, Berlin (2011)
2. Scheer, A.-W., Klueckmann, J.: BPM 3.0. In: Dayal, U., Eder, J., Koehler, J., Reijers, H. (eds.) Business Process Management SE - 2, pp. 15–27. Springer, Heidelberg (2009)
3. Becker, J., Clever, N., Holler, J., Shitkova, M.: icebricks - Business Process Modeling on the Basis of Semantic Standardization. In: vom Brocke, J., Hekkala, R., Ram, S., Rossi, M. (eds.) DESRIST 2013. LNCS, vol. 7939, pp. 394–399. Springer, Heidelberg (2013)
4. Mendling, J., Reijers, H., van der Aalst, W.M.P.: Seven Process Modeling Guidelines (7PMG). Inf. Softw. Technol. 52, 127–136 (2008)
5. Becker, J., Rosemann, M., von Uthmann, C.: Guidelines of Business Process Modeling. In: van der Aalst, W.M.P., Desel, J., Oberweis, A. (eds.) Business Process Management. LNCS, vol. 1806, pp. 30–49. Springer, Heidelberg (2000)
6. Delfmann, P., Herwig, S., Lis, L.: Unified Enterprise Knowledge Representation with Conceptual Models - Capturing Corporate Language in Naming Conventions. In: 30th International Conference on Information Systems (ICIS 2009), Phoenix, Arizona, USA (2009)
7. Shitkova, M., Holler, J., Heide, T., Clever, N., Becker, J.: Towards Usability Guidelines for Mobile Websites and Applications. In: Proceedings of the 12th International Conference on Wirtschaftsinformatik, Osnabrück, Germany (2015)
8. Cooharojananone, N., Kongnim, P., Mongkolnut, A., Hitoshi, O.: Evaluation Study of Usability Factors on Mobile Payment Application on Two Different Service Providers in Thailand. In: IEEE/IPSJ 12th International Symposium on Applications and the Internet, pp. 233–238. IEEE (2012)
9. Bao, P., Pierce, J., Whittaker, S., Zhai, S.: Smart phone use by non-mobile business users. In: Proc. MobileHCI 2011, p. 445. ACM Press, New York (2011)
10. Dias, A.L., Fortes, de Mattos, R.P., Masiero, P.C., Watanabe, W.M., Ramos, M.E.: An approach to improve the accessibility and usability of existing web system. In: Proc. SIGDOC 2013, p. 39 (2013)
11. Nivala, A.-M., Brewster, S., Sarjakoski, T.L.: Usability Evaluation of Web Mapping Sites. Cartogr. Journal 45, 129–138 (2008)
12. VandeCreek, L.M.: Usability analysis of Northern Illinois University Libraries' website: A case study. OCLC Syst. Serv. 21, 181–192 (2005)

Supporting LIFE: Mobile Health Application for Classifying, Treating and Monitoring Disease Outbreaks of Sick Children in Developing Countries

Yvonne O' Connor[1(✉)], Victoria Hardy[2], Ciara Heavin[1], Joe Gallagher[3],
and John O' Donoghue[4]

[1]Health Information Systems Research Centre, University College Cork, Corcaigh, Ireland
{y.oconnor,c.heavin}@ucc.ie
[2]Department of Family Medicine, University of Washington, Seattle, USA
vhardy4@uw.edu
[3]gHealth Research Group, University College Dublin, Dublin, Ireland
joejgallagher@gmail.com
[4]Global eHealth Unit, Department of Primary Care and Public Health,
Imperial College London, London, UK
j.odonoghue@imperial.ac.uk

Abstract. This paper presents the Supporting LIFE (**L**ow cost **I**ntervention **F**or dis**E**ase control) project. Supporting LIFE applies a novel combination of Android based smartphone technology, patient vital sign sensors and expert decision support systems to assist Community Health Workers in resource-poor settings in their assessment, classification and treatment of seriously ill children, more specifically children from 2 months to 5 years of age. The application digitises widely accepted WHO/UNICEF paper based guidelines known as Community Case Management. The project also facilitates for disease monitoring and surveillance via a reporting website.

Keywords: Mobile Health · Developing Countries · Community Health Workers

1 Introduction

In the last decade, the diagnosis and treatment of childhood illness in developing countries has received immense attention (Hazel et al., 2015). The underlying rationale for this increased awareness may stem from the establishment of the eight Millennium Development Goals by the United Nations in 2001, more specifically the fourth goal which focuses on reducing under-five child mortality rates in developing countries.

The World Health Organisation (WHO) and United Nations Children's Fund (UNICEF) introduced a community-based initiative to assist Community Health Workers when delivering paediatric healthcare services in rural, remote areas of developing countries. This initiative, known as Community Case Management (CCM), employs clinical guidelines which aim to reduce death, illness and disability while promoting improved growth and development among children under five years of age

B. Donnellan et al. (Eds.): DESRIST 2015, LNCS 9073, pp. 366–370, 2015.
DOI: 10.1007/978-3-319-18714-3_24

(WHO, 2013). CCM is an algorithm to guide Community Health Workers through a series of clinical questions and assessment items; capturing socio-demographic and clinical information regarding the presence/absence and duration of symptoms, to classify illness and elicit treatment recommendations for sick children. Numerous countries in low-and-middle income countries employ CCM guidelines (Diaz et al., 2014; Rasanathan et al., 2014). Yet, these guidelines are customised on an individual country basis based on national child health indicators. For example, malaria, infantile diarrhoea and pneumonia are prevalent in Malawi so the CCM guidelines are custom-ised towards theses illnesses. In South Sudan, CCM guidelines have been customised to some extent to focus on malnutrition.

Existing research argues that correct implementation of CCM leads to improved child survival (Mugeni et al., 2014). Yet research has emerged showing that the CCM guidelines are often not correctly implemented (Amouzou et al., 2014) thus, poten-tially endangering the life of a sick child. A lack of knowledge and medical equip-ment is often reported as the key reasons for incorrectly implementing CCM during sick patient visits (c.f. Kallander et al., 2006; Druetz et al., 2013). To address the chal-lenges faced by Community Health Workers in developing countries an artefact (known as Supporting LIFE) is developed.

2   Design of the Artefact

2.1   Overview of Supporting LIFE

The overall goal of Supporting LIFE is to improve standards of care and to establish ways to overcome many of the existing barriers to healthcare delivery in resource-poor settings using low cost interventions.

The Supporting LIFE technological artefact is developed based on widely accepted and validated clinical guidelines known as CCM which comprises 34 questions. It is a smartphone application developed for Andoid 3.0 (Honeycomb) or above which is not only built upon the paper-based system but has also developed a guideline agnostic decision-support rule engine which operates on XML-based definitions of specific guideline instances. Developing the artefact in XML allows the application to be scal-able to other countries allowing the rules to be customised on a per-country basis. Based on the assessment data entered into the application, classification(s) of illness(es) and treatment(s) is/are recommended to the Community Health Worker (see Figure 1). As Community Health Workers only receive six days of formal educa-tion pertaining to the implementation of CCM the rules-engine developed as part of SL reduces uncertainty surrounding assessing, classifying and treating sick children. Noteworthy, to enhance knowledge of Community Health Workers training material is also available to them.

Location awareness is also incorporated within the application, which facilitates geographic tracking and monitoring of CCM patient classifications enhancing auto-mated disease monitoring and notification of disease outbreaks (Figure 2). A website has also been developed; into an infrastructure for the execution of medical-based reports, to facilitate disease surveillance, to identify and monitor disease outbreaks,

Fig. 1. Sample Screen Shots

and to enable administrative support of medical-based users. This website is constructed using Java Server Pages (JSP), Bootstrap, JQuery, HTML 5.0 and CSS 3.0.

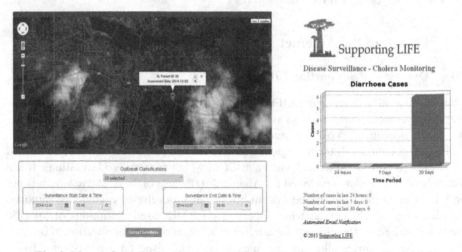

Fig. 2. Disease Surveillance Monitoring (left) and Notification of Outbreaks (right)

Aforementioned, a lack of medical equipment (i.e. stopwatch for measuring breathing rate) restricts Community Health Workers from performing CCM in accordance with procedure. To assist in overcoming this issue Supporting LIFE also includes an electronic breath counter and by tapping on the screen in unison with observed inhalation allows Community Health Workers to measure breathing rate.

2.2   Design Science Considerations

Hevner et al., (2004, p. 82) propose seven guidelines "to assist researchers, reviewers, editors, and readers to understand the requirements for effective design-science research." The application of these guidelines to the Supporting LIFE project are outlined as follows:

- *Guideline 1: Design as an Artefact* - A prototype is nearing end of development which can be utilised and customised in resource-poor settings.
- *Guideline 2: Problem Relevance* - To develop a fully functional technology-based solution to help address the issue of child morbidity and mortality in resource-poor settings.
- *Guideline 3: Design Evaluation* - The prototype is currently on release Version 5.0. An agile methodology approach, with a three monthly release cycle, was employed to facilitate for regular feedback from various stakeholders (e.g. both technical and clinical expertise). It is envisioned that Supporting LIFE will be evaluated initially vis-à-vis a feasibility study prior to a Randomised Control Trial in Malawi, Africa. The study will focus on functionality (i.e. mobile application), completeness (e.g. syncing of records to the cloud), consistency with existing approach, accuracy in terms of classifications and treatment of sick children, performance (e.g. speed), reliability (e.g. battery, solar panel chargers), usability (e.g. ease of use) and fit.
- *Guideline 4: Research Contribution* - Supporting LIFE is an open-source project which encourages other people outside of the consortium to become involved in the initiative. Our knowledge repository provides clear guidelines on how to build and contribute to the Supporting LIFE codebase. The source code is stored and shared through a GitHub repository.
- *Guideline 5: Research Rigor* - The prototype to date is predominantly developed based on widely validated paper-based CCM guidelines, with inputs from both clinical and technical personnel both on and off the ground of Malawi, Africa. Furthermore, when designing Supporting LIFE the contextual (e.g. requirements, constraints, technical, organisational and cultural) factors were considered.
- *Guideline 6: Design as a Search Process* - Preliminary testing to date in Malawi reveals that Supporting LIFE does indeed operate on the ground. Further testing is required to see what are the existing problems faced by people in Malawi and how Supporting LIFE can continuously attempt to solve these issues.
- *Guideline 7: Communication of Research* - The plan is to hold workshops before, during and/or after any Supporting LIFE testing in Malawi to inform community members about the motivation of the project, the need for and outcomes of the project. The findings will be disseminated to the Malawian Ministry of Health and in both clinical and technological academic outlets.

3   Forthcoming Evaluation of the Artefact

Malawi is ranked as one of the ten poorest countries in the world with a high rate of child mortality and morbidity (Callaghan-Koru et al., 2013). As a result, our research attentions and any forthcoming evaluations of Supporting LIFE will be conducted in Malawi, Africa.

Acknowledgement. The Supporting LIFE project (305292) is funded by the Seventh Framework Programme for Research and Technological Development of the European Commission www.supportinglife.eu.

References

1. Hazel, E., Amouzou, A,, Park, L., Banda, B., Chimuna, T., Guenther, T., Nsona, H., Victora, C.G., Bryce, J.: Real-Time Assessments of the Strength of Program Implementation for Community Case Management of Childhood Illness: Validation of a Mobile Phone-Based Method in Malawi. The American Journal of Tropical Medicine and Hygiene 14-396 (2015)
2. Diaz, T., Aboubaker, S., Young, M.: Current scientific evidence for integrated community case management (iCCM) in Africa: Findings from the iCCM Evidence Symposium. Journal of Global Health 4 (2014)
3. Rasanathan, K., Bakshi, S., Rodriquez, D., Oliphant, N., Jacobs, T., Brandes, N., Young, M.: Where to from here? Policy and financing of integrated community case management (iCCM) of childhood illness in sub–Saharan Africa. Journal of Global Health 4 (2014)
4. Mugeni, C., Levine, A.C., Munyaneza, R.M., Mulindahabi, E., Cockrell, H., Glavis-Bloom, J., Nutt, C., Wagner, C., Gaju, E., Rukundo, A., Habimana, J., Karema, C., Ngabo, F., Bingagwaho, A.: Nationwide implementation of integrated community case management of childhood illness in Rwanda. Global Health: Science and Practice 2, 328–341 (2014)
5. Amouzou, A., Morris, S., Moulton, L.H., Mukanga, D.: Assessing the impact of integrated community case management (iCCM) programs on child mortality: Review of early results and lessons learned in sub–Saharan Africa. Journal of Global Health 4 (2014)
6. Källander, K., Tomson, G., Nsabagasani, X., Sabiiti, J., Pariyo, G., Peterson, S.: Can community health workers and caretakers recognise pneumonia in children? Experiences from Western Uganda. Transactions of the Royal Society of Tropical Medicine and Hygiene 100, 956–963 (2006)
7. Druetz, T., Siekmans, K., Goossens, S., Ridde, V., Haddad, S.: The community case management of pneumonia in Africa: A review of the evidence. Health Policy and Planning, 1–14 (2013)
8. Hevner, A., March, S.T., Park, J.: Design science in information systems research. MIS Quarterly 28, 75–105 (2004)
9. Callaghan-Koru, J.A., Gilroy, K., Hyder, A., George, A., Nsona, H., Mtimuni, A., Zakeyo, B., Mayani, J., Cardemil, C., Bryce, J.: Health systems supports for community case management of childhood illness: lessons from an assessment of early implementation in Malawi. BMC Health Services Research 13, 55 (2013)
10. World Health Organisation (WHO) Report. WHO/UNICEF Joint Statement Integrated Community Case Management (iCCM) (2012),
    http://www.who.int/maternal_child_adolescent/documents/statement_child_services_acces s_whounicef.pdf?ua=1 (accessed September 12, 2013)

A Prototype for Supporting Novices in Collaborative Business Process Modeling Using a Tablet Device

Christian Ritter[✉], Josef-Michael Schwaiger, and Florian Johannsen

Chair of Business Engineering, University of Regensburg, Regensburg, Germany
{christian.ritter,josef-michael.schwaiger,
florian.johannsen}@wiwi.uni-regensburg.de

Abstract. Business process modeling is a decisive task as process models prepare the ground for business transformation and process improvement initiatives. However, modeling projects fall short of their initial aim when process participants are not involved in the act of model creation. The employees' individual process knowledge has been recognized as a crucial success factor to define high-quality process models that reflect a company's working procedures correctly. This paper introduces a prototype supporting collaborative modeling of business processes on tablet devices aimed at process modeling novices.

1   Introduction and Problem Statement

In today's fast-changing markets, companies are struggling to keep pace with constantly changing customer requirements [1]. New technologies (e.g. Web 2.0) lead to a high market-transparency, providing consumers with up-to-date information on product reviews, prices and alternative offers [2]. To face these challenges, companies are increasingly performing business transformation and business process improvement projects [3]. In this context, business process modeling is a decisive task. Process models do not only prepare the ground for process redesign initiatives but also foster the communication about working procedures amongst others [4]. However, enterprises encounter several obstacles during process modeling.

At first, process modeling is usually believed to be the responsibility of a few specialists only, rather than being recognized as an organizational task. If these specialists lack skills in translating staff comments and workshop documentations into proper process models, modeling initiatives will inevitably fall short of their initial aim [5]. We need to keep in mind that the process of model creation is highly subjective (cf. [6]). Second, employees' tacit process knowledge is essential to design process models that reflect a company's real working procedures (cf. [7]). Employees, having explicit knowledge of how business processes are executed on a daily basis, need to be involved in modeling projects [5]. This is especially relevant for inter-organizational business processes as companies tend to have isolated views only on processes within their own organization (cf. [8]). Thus, a collaborative (cf. [9]) and subject-oriented (cf. [10]) modeling approach, that integrates the process participants in model creation, is required. Instead of a specialist modeling a process end-to-end from an outsider's perspective, employees capture their specific work tasks as corresponding partial models [10]. As tablet devices are gradually adopted in the business

© Springer International Publishing Switzerland 2015
B. Donnellan et al. (Eds.): DESRIST 2015, LNCS 9073, pp. 371–375, 2015.
DOI: 10.1007/978-3-319-18714-3_25

world, they can support collaborative business process modeling (CBPM). They can be easily shared within the workforce and thus help to consolidate employees' isolated views on a business process into one integrated process model [9], [11].

The aim of the paper is to introduce a prototype for CBPM using a tablet device. The prototype allows to collaboratively design process models using an intuitive user interface that is easily comprehensible even by process modeling novices. It supports the user to capture process-related knowledge (e.g. activities to be performed, roles etc.) in an intuitive way without requiring in-depth knowledge of specific modeling guidelines. However, all captured information can be automatically transformed and exported as BPMN (Business Process Model and Notation [12]) models.

The contribution of this research is twofold: at first, we introduce a concept supporting process modeling novices in transforming their tacit process knowledge into explicit models, a central success factor in modeling initiatives (cf. [5]). Second, we provide a prototype to foster collaborative and subject-oriented process modeling.

Our research follows the design science research methodology proposed by Peffers et al. [13]. This section describes the problem and motivates the context. In the next section, the objectives and the design of the artifact (prototype) are presented. A first demonstration of the prototype is described in section 3. Section 4 highlights the significance of the research. The paper is rounded off with a conclusion and an outlook.

2   Design of the Artifact

Several requirements derived from the problem statement and backed by literature arose on the prototype, a tablet application for process modeling by novice users:

(I) The first requirement of novice users visualizing business processes without having advanced knowledge in process modeling is an easy-to-understand user interface (UI) (cf. [14]). A process participant without any previous process modeling experience should be able to capture the main steps of his or her daily work without the help of a modeling specialist. Besides a well-designed UI, the modeling notation used by the prototype should be subject-oriented and easy to understand.

(II) The second requirement represents the prototype's support of CBPM (cf. [9], [15]). The user should be able to gather process information on her/his own, by interacting with coworkers on the same tablet, or by interacting with other users on different tablets. The information gathered by all users needs to be consolidated in a central database and made available to everyone involved in the modeling initiative.

(III) While the modeling approach is subject-oriented, process models are usually required to display the control flow using standard notations (e.g. BPMN) to comply with company regulations (cf. [16]). Thus, transforming the gathered process activities into BPMN syntax and exporting it in a standardized way is the third requirement.

(IV) The fourth requirement concerns the actual organizational use of the process model (cf. [5]). The prototype should enable process experts to adjust the BPMN model to fit the company's modeling rules and integrate it into the process repository.

With the implementation of our prototype, we developed an approach for fulfilling the presented requirements. A major challenge for tablet applications is to provide a slim and easy to use UI and simultaneously deliver a wide range of functionality [11]. Consequently, it is necessary to build on a modeling notation that is suitable for the restricted modeling knowledge of novice users (requirement I). In that context, BPMN has emerged as a widely accepted industry standard. According to Recker [14], the existing amount of BPMN elements offers a huge diversification, which challenges novices to use it in the right way. As a result, we only picked the mostly used BPMN elements to be supported by our prototype: *start, end, activity, gateway, control flow, lane, and message flow.* We redesigned the selected elements to simplify them and to provide an easy-to-understand UI for unexperienced users (see Fig. 1). Users can name the current activity, attach a detailed description, and select internal or external preceding and succeeding activities. The number of possible predecessors and successors depends on the chosen connector. The description enables the user to include additional information (e.g. rules, input or output documents).

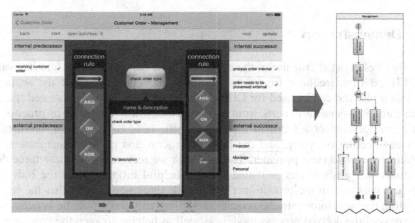

Fig. 1. Screenshot of the prototype and example export to BPMN via GraphML

Requirement II is the support of collaborative modeling. We achieve this by a client-server-architecture of the prototype that consists of three components (see Fig. 2): (1) A tablet application written in objective-C for use on iOS devices, (2) a PHP backend-server to manage the central database including user/role access and synchronize data on different devices, and (3) an export interface to convert the collected data into a BPMN model using GraphML as an exchange format. The architecture offers the possibility to work simultaneously on process models. To avoid concurrency conflicts, we prevent access to already opened processes temporarily, ensuring that only one user can edit a specific lane at a time. As users model their own view on the process only, lanes in the resulting process model are determined by the role of the user in the access management database (e.g. a user in the marketing department can only model a process in the marketing lane). To offer cross-system compatibility, we chose the open format *GraphML* (graphml.graphdrawing.org) for exporting the model as it provides the possibility to create models in BPMN notation (requirement III). The export is performed on the server and transforms the captured activities and dependencies stored in the database into proper BPMN syntax. The user can trigger the creation of an export file for each process lane on the tablet device when the lane is modeled completely (= has no

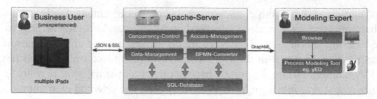

Fig. 2. Architecture of the prototype

undefined activities or 'dead ends'). The modeling expert can then download the file(s) from the server and view, edit, or combine the BPMN models (one lane per file) with the free software *yED* (www.yworks.com/en/products/yfiles/yed) (requirement IV).

3   Demonstration

Following Peffers et al., the use of the artifact is to be demonstrated before its evaluation [13]. At first, feedback from four Master's students proved that the artifact is fully functional and can be used for CBPM. As a next step, we demonstrated the artifact to three independent experts from different industries: The head of process and quality management of a German direct bank, the head of HR of an international power engineering company, and the head of process and quality management of a German financial services provider. The feedback we received from these three demonstrations was positive and provided us with helpful insights about the individual needs and wants from the practitioner's side. All three pointed out that the idea of integrating the workforce into the process modeling activities would be beneficial for correctness of the derived process models as well as helping to keep the process models up-to-date. Additionally, the 'fun' aspect of using a tablet was seen as a good way to motivate employees to engage in process modeling activities, which is usually seen as 'imposition'. However, some minor limitations of our prototype were seen as challenging for modeling very complex business processes. As a final step of the demonstration the prototype was presented at a conference for practitioners in the banking industry in front of an audience of approx. 30 professionals on the management and executive level. The discussion afterwards was positive and the feedback went along with the three interviews before. The idea of involving the individual employees on the operational level in process modeling was seen as very promising.

4   Significance of the Research

Our prototype is highly significant for research as well as for practice. At first, we provide a subject-oriented modeling approach which supports the transfer of employees' individual process knowledge into a corresponding process model building on an easy-to-use UI. Novices in process modeling may thus participate in modeling projects providing their valuable in-depth knowledge on working procedures (cf. [5]). In addition, our approach contributes to current research on how to support modelers during the process model creation (cf. [6]). Further, by using a tablet device, practitioners profit from the advantages of mobile solutions as these can be shared among employees.

A user then captures those parts of the holistic process (s)he is responsible for. This helps to gather models representing the actual working procedures.

5   Conclusion and Outlook

This paper presents a prototype for CBPM using a mobile tablet device. The usability of the prototype was demonstrated in expert interviews and a live presentation at a practitioner conference in the banking industry. The positive feedback received so far encourages us to develop the prototype further. In a next step, the prototype will be evaluated in a real world context by using it in modeling projects at companies of different size and branch. The insights gained will serve as base for refining the proto-type to better match practitioners' specific needs. More information about the proto-type can be found at: *http://www-be.uni-regensburg.de/Projekte/BPMN-Tool.html.en*

References

1. Greenberg, P.: The impact of CRM 2.0 on customer insight. Journal of Business & Indus-trial Marketing 25, 410–419 (2010)
2. Bruhn, M.: Qualitätsmanagement für Dienstleistungen. Springer, Berlin (2013)
3. Davis, D.: 3rd Biennial PEX Network Report: State of the Industry - Trends and Success Factors in Business Process Excellence (2013)
4. Harmon, P., Wolf, C.: Business Process Modeling Survey. BPTrends (2011)
5. Rosemann, M.: Potential pitfalls of process modeling: part A. BPMJ 12, 249–254 (2006)
6. Pinggera, J., et al.: Styles in business process modeling: an exploration and a model. Soft-ware & Systems Modeling, 1–26 (2013)
7. Seethamraju, R., Marjanovic, O.: Role of process knowledge in business process im-provement methodology: a case study. BPMJ 15, 920–936 (2009)
8. Gordijn, J., Akkermans, H., van Vliet, H.: Business modelling is not process modelling. In: Mayr, H.C., Liddle, S.W., Thalheim, B. (eds.) ER Workshops 2000. LNCS, vol. 1921, pp. 40–51. Springer, Heidelberg (2000)
9. Scholtz, B., Calitz, A., Snyman, I.: The usability of collaborative tools: application to business process modelling. In: Proceedings of the South African Institute for Computer Scientists and Information Technologists Conference, pp. 347–358. ACM (2013)
10. Fleischmann, A., Kannengiesser, U., Schmidt, W., Stary, C.: Subject-Oriented Modeling and Execution of Multi-agent Business Processes. In: Web Intelligence and Intelligent Agent Technologies Conference, pp. 138–145 (2013)
11. Kolb, J., Rudner, B., Reichert, M.: Towards Gesture-Based Process Modeling on Multi-touch Devices. In: Bajec, M., Eder, J. (eds.) CAiSE Workshops 2012. LNBIP, vol. 112, pp. 280–293. Springer, Heidelberg (2012)
12. OMG: Business Process Model and Notation (BPMN) - Version 2.0 (2011)
13. Peffers, K., Tuunanen, T., Rothenberger, M.A., Chatterjee, S.: A design science research methodology for information systems research. Journal of MIS 24, 45–77 (2007)
14. Recker, J., Safrudin, N., Rosemann, M.: How novices design business processes. Informa-tion Systems 37, 557–573 (2012)
15. Riemer, K., Holler, J., Indulska, M.: Collaborative process modelling-tool analysis and de-sign implications. In: Proceedings of ECIS 2011, paper 39 (2011)
16. Wohed, P., van der Aalst, W.M., Dumas, M., ter Hofstede, A.H., Russell, N.: Pattern-based Analysis of BPMN (2005)

CollaborGeneous: A Framework of Collaborative IT-Tools for Heterogeneous Groups of Learners

Amir Haj-Bolouri[✉], Lennarth Bernhardsson, and Patrik Bernhardsson

Institute of Economy and Informatics, University West, Trollhättan, Sweden
{amir.haji-bolouri,lennarth.bernhardsson,
patrik.bernhardsson}@hv.se

Abstract. In this paper, we present our designed prototype: *CollaborGeneous*. *CollaborGeneous* is a framework of collaborative IT-tools for heterogeneous groups of learners in Civic Orientation. It is designed to serve different types of activities for producing, maintaining, distributing and presenting digital learning-material within Civic Orientation. The significance of introducing our prototype is relevant for both practitioners and researchers within Design Science Research. The novelty of our artifact lies in its characteristic of use in the intersection between Civic Orientation and Information Systems, providing different groups of learner's necessary tools to collaborate and create an open digital experience of Civic Orientation.

Keywords: Heterogeneous Groups · Civic Orientation · IT-Tools · Learning · Design Science Research · CollaborGeneous

1 Introduction

Increased throughput of immigrants and newcomers has grown in Europe and Sweden [1]. From the perspective of UN (United Nations), the dimension of citizenship and human kinship is seen as a means for discussions about integration in the Swedish society. More specifically, the discussions emphasize how municipalities shall operate in order to learn immigrants and newcomers about the Swedish laws, culture, democratic values, education and more [2]. Therefore, a research team from University West, together with the municipality of Gothenburg, was in 2013 appointed by the Swedish government to digitalize a Civic Orientation program for immigrants and newcomers.

One purpose with digitalizing the program was to introduce, design and develop collaborative IT-tools for clerks and teachers to support their local activities at the municipality (production and maintenance of learning material) [3]. Another purpose was to develop and distribute online learning material for the participants (immigrants and newcomers) in the civic orientation program [4]. Together, these two purposes formed needs and requirements for a framework of collaborative IT-tools for heterogeneous groups of learners in Civic Orientation. In this paper, we will present our designed, developed and implemented prototype called *CollaborGeneous*. We call the prototype *CollaborGeneous* because it is intended to serve and support three different

© Springer International Publishing Switzerland 2015
B. Donnellan et al. (Eds.): DESRIST 2015, LNCS 9073, pp. 376–380, 2015.
DOI: 10.1007/978-3-319-18714-3_26

groups of learners with functionality for collaboration and distribution of learning material in Civic Orientation. More specifically, the learners are specified as learners, both in the context of Civic Orientation, but also in the context of the prototype and it's features. Therefore, we define the learners as heterogeneous groups of learners, meaning that they are all learners but for heterogeneous purposes.

The remainder of the paper is organized as follows: *Section 2* describes the design of the IT-artifact in terms of heterogeneous groups of learners, system layers, and the technical architecture. *Sections 3* report on the significance of the IT-artifact to researchers and practitioners respectively. *Section 4* summarizes the evaluation-process.

2   Design of the Artifact

2.1   Heterogeneous Groups of Learners

The core requirement of *CollaborGeneous* is to provide heterogeneous groups of learners, with supportive IT-tools for collaboration in terms of producing, maintaining and distributing learning material in Civic Orientation. The heterogeneous groups of learners are as follows:

- **Clerks:** are responsible for production and quality assurance of learning material. Clerks use *CollaborGeneous* to produce, maintain, and distribute the learning material. They have different roles in the system according to their IT-skills. Some of the clerks are explicitly responsible for distributing learning material, while others are responsible for updating and maintaining learning material, but also updating system-functionality, which distributes the learning material. Clerks have formally the highest level of authority in *CollaborGeneous*

- **Tutors:** are responsible for planning and conducting civic orientation activities in various modes of delivery (e.g. distance education, blended learning, classroom environment). Tutors use *CollaborGeneous* in connection with their teachings. They are responsible for their so-called *course-sites* (see next sub-section) and the additional learning material, which they distribute for their group of participants (immigrants and newcomers).

- **Participants:** are immigrants and newcomers attending the Civic Orientation program. They register themselves according to their native language (e.g. Arabic, Russian, Somali) and are thereafter obligated to participate in 60 hours of teachings, in order to receive their diploma. No exams are held during the civic orientation program. Therefore, the participants only need to be present during the teachings, which can be held both on distance and in the classroom. The participants use *CollaborGeneous* to interact with the distributed learning material.

2.2   System Layers

CollaborGeneous comprises the following system layers with their respective system features:

1. **Open Layer**: the open layer is an open entry-point for the public, which means that it is accessible regardless of login-credentials. This layer comprises system features for presenting general information about the civic orientation program, news in terms of RSS-feeds, Google translate for translating the information on the page, and links to the specific course-sites. Clerks are responsible for maintaining and updating the open layer.

2. **Presentation Layer**: the presentation layer is used in connection with the course-sites. The course-sites are maintained in terms of design, layout and content (learning material). Clerks instantiate course-sites from a general template with a standardized design and layout. Tutors use the course-sites in their teaching. Each tutor is together with a clerk, owner of a course-site, but a participant can interact with the presentation layer through the course-sites. Features for this layer support the interaction between tutors, participants and the distributed learning material.

3. **Content Layer**: the content layer is maintained by clerks and comprises the produced and distributed learning material, which is generally divided into different modules (e.g. course material, advanced learning features, course book) with relevant themes of content in civic orientation. However, tutors have also the authority to modify the content of their own course-sites, meaning that each tutor is justified to add learning material in addition to the pre-defined learning material.

4. **Production Layer**: a handful of selected clerks use services from Google Drive to collaborate with each other and produce, maintain and distribute the learning material. For example, when the course material is updated in the production layer, the update gets instantly established and published in the content layer.

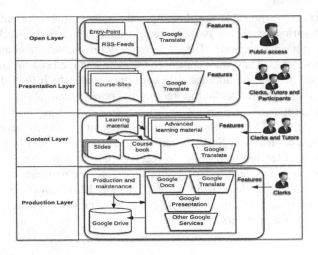

Fig. 1. Schematic of System Layers for *CollaborGeneous*

2.3   Technical Architecture

Technically, *CollaborGeneous* is based on two different platforms:

1. **WordPress Multisite:** WordPress is generally used as web-software to create a website or blog [5]. However, WordPress Multisite is used to create a network of multiple websites all running on a single installation of WordPress [6]. The open layer and the presentation layer are based on WordPress Multisite to distribute a network of course-sites. A handful of selected clerks are appointed as administrators and super-admins, and they are responsible for maintaining the websites in terms of functionality, adding users, changing design and layout etc.

2. **Google Drive:** *CollaborGeneous* uses the services provided by Google Drive for collaboration purposes regarding activities such as, producing, maintaining and distributing learning material. Clerks share a common Google-account and use services such as Google Presentation, Google Docs, and Google Sheets to distribute relevant learning material and present it through the presentation layer. Furthermore, a YouTube-channel has been created to distribute and embed relevant video-clips on the course-sites for the participants. Activities in Google Drive are a part of the production layer, and are only relevant for the clerks as groups of learners. They learn how to use the tools provided by Google and collaborate online with each other, through workshops together with the research team from University West.

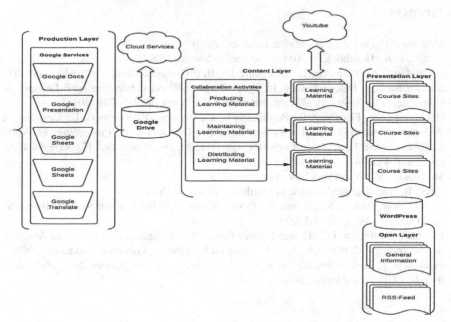

Fig. 2. Technical Architecture for *CollaborGeneous*

3   Significance for Practice and Research

Our work is significant for both practice and research in terms of Design Science Research [7][8] and civic orientation. We have designed and introduced a framework of IT-tools for a heterogeneous group of learners in civic orientation. The significance of this is important in terms of learning new technologies and using it for different modes of distributed learning material. The knowledge provided through such an innovation is relevant for both practitioners and researchers in the field of Information Systems, but also relevant and useful for the purpose of distributing the Civic Orientation program in Sweden.

4   Evaluation of the Artifact

We have done observational forms of evaluation [7] by simply observing how clerks and tutors use *CollaborGeneous*. Our observations have resulted into feedback and ideas for our forthcoming evaluation processes. Initially, we will use a web-questionnaire to evaluate how clerks and tutors experience *CollaborGeneous* in their daily work activities. More specifically, we will formulate a strategy for evaluation [9], which will test our tentative design principles formulated in a previous paper [3]. Doing so, we believe that we can re-evaluate our design principles and shape them according to the results gathered from the evaluation.

References

1. SCB: the division for the population statistics (2013)
2. Abraha, G.A.: Handbook for Asylum Seekers in Sweden (2007)
3. Haj-Bolouri, A., Svensson, L.: Designing for Heterogeneous Groups of End-Users - Towards a Nascend Design Theory. In: Proceedings of World Conference on E-Learning in Corporate, Government, Healthcare, and Higher Education, pp. 765–776 (2014)
4. Haj-Bolouri, A., Flensburg, P., Bernhardsson, L., Winman, T., Svensson, L.: Designing a Web-based Education Platform for Swedish Civic Orientation. In: Proceedings of World Conference on E-Learning in Corporate, Government, Healthcare, and Higher Education, pp. 755–764 (2014)
5. Mullenweg, M.: WordPress Now Available (2003)
6. Casel, B.: The Beginner's Guide to WordPress Multisite (2012)
7. Hevner, A.R., March, S.T., Park, K.: Design Research in Information Systems Research. MIS Quarterly 28(1), 76–105 (2004)
8. Indulska, M., Recker, J.C.: Design Science Research in IS Research: A Literature Analysis. In: Proceedings 4th Biennial ANU Workshop on Information Systems Foundations (2008)
9. Pries-Heje, J., Baskerville, R., Venable, J.: Strategies for Design Science Research Evaluation. In: ECIS Proceedings (2008)

InsightGame: Designing a Market Research Game to Gain Better Insights into Purchase Decision Processes

Silke Plennert[(⊠)] and Susanne Robra-Bissantz

Chair Information Management, Technische Universität Braunschweig, Braunschweig,
Germany
{s.plennert,s.robra-bissantz}@tu-braunschweig.de

Abstract. InsightGame is a serious game developed as an innovative qualitative
market research method. It can be used to gain valuable insights into purchase
decision processes by letting probands play their information search. The artifact uses the positive effects of games to gain better results than classical
market research methods. It is composed as a board game combined with a
smartphone application.

Keywords: Serious Games · Market Research Game · Purchase Decision
Process · Customer Insights · Game Design

1 Introduction

Gaining relevant insights into the customer journey – i.e. the purchase decision
process – is becoming more and more relevant. Many companies struggle with this
task and are unable to cope with the increasing influence of digital touch points [1].
They need to understand which touch points are relevant to their customers and what
information needs they have during their purchase decision [2].

The market research methods currently used have several weaknesses. For example, probands often give socially desirable responses during interviews or focus
groups [3], or the test persons are not able to properly remember their decision
process retrospectively [4].

This paper shows a new approach to this topic – the use of a serious game ("InsightGame") instead of classical market research methods. The research follows the
design science requirements proposed by March and Storey [5].

A game can be described as a „problem-solving activity, approached with a playful
attitude [6]". Serious games are games that have another purpose than entertaining the
players, like teaching them something [7], or in this case, to bring the players to reveal insights into their purchase decision process. Games can have several positive
impacts on players, which are crucial for market research. Amongst others, playing
games can have the following advantages: The players are more motivated and creative [8], they keep interest and concentration [9, 10], they immerse deeply into the
topic and thus give more valid answers [11, 12], they can show their emotions and
therefor be more authentic [7], [11].

© Springer International Publishing Switzerland 2015
B. Donnellan et al. (Eds.): DESRIST 2015, LNCS 9073, pp. 381–385, 2015.
DOI: 10.1007/978-3-319-18714-3_27

2   Design of the Artifact

2.1   Requirements

For the implementation of the market research game, the customer journey of buying a new car was chosen. In this case, buyers run through an extensive decision process, i.e. a comprehensive process with high involvement and relatively great risk [13].

The designed game needs to represent this customer journey and especially the information search in some degree. Additionally, the game has to be fun to play, in order to achieve the intended positive effects for gaining valuable insights. Also, it requires some possibility to collect data.

2.2   Game Design

InsightGame is composed of a board game and a smartphone application. It is played in a laboratory setting with three or four probands.

While designing the game, game design guidelines from Schell as well as Salen and Zimmerman have been applied [6], [14]. For example, the four basic game design categories – story, mechanics, aesthetics and technology – have been adopted and refined to create a positive player experience and thus a fun game [6].

Fig. 1 shows the game board on which the players move their tokens. They start in the corners and move their cars on the roads, trying to approach the information fields (the round fields with an "I") and ultimately the parking spaces in the middle of the board.

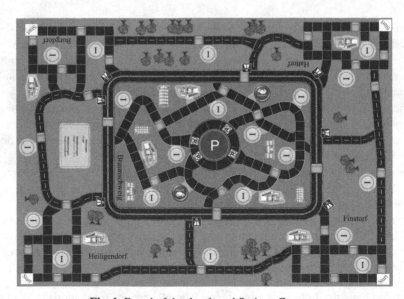

Fig. 1. Board of the developed Serious Game

2.3   Smartphone Application

In addition to the game board, an application has been implemented for Android smartphones to be used during the game. The app includes several features that are needed for the game, for example a dice and a deck of cards, as well as the collection data for the researcher. Fig. 2 shows six screenshots of the application.

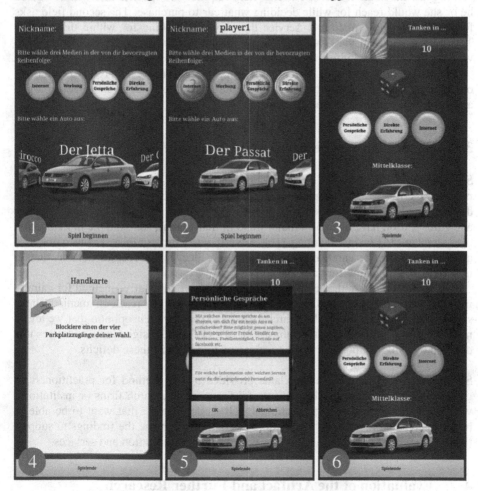

Fig. 2. Screenshots of the InsightGame application

On the start screen (1) the player has to type in a nickname and make two important decisions. First, he or she has to choose their favored type of information source when buying a new car, i.e. three out of four given categories (Internet, personal conversations, direct experience and advertising) and bring them in a preferred order. Second, the player can swipe through a carousel of cars and chose one. Screen (2) shows the completed start screen. The data is sent via E-Mail to the researcher. It is also saved in the app and transferred to the main game screen (3). There, the player can roll the digital dice, click on the car to view its specific features or draw a card (left top corner). Screen (4) shows an example of a drawn card. In the middle of (3) are three buttons displaying the information source categories the player chose at the beginning. They determine in which order the player has to reach the different information fields on the board. When reaching the first one, the player can click on the first button and the dialog in (5) appears. Here, the player has to answer two questions concerning his information needs. The first field requires the specific information source he or she would reach for while deciding what car to purchase. The second field asks for the detailed information or service the player is looking for within that source. This data is also sent via E-Mail to the researcher. Screen (6) shows the main screen with the first collected information, illustrated by the check mark in the background.

In addition to writing the answers in the app, the players are supposed to read them out loud to the others players, who are encouraged to ask questions (or even argue against it) by certain game design elements.

3   Significance to Research and Practice

Significance to Research. Two different research fields benefit from the developed market research game – game thinking and market research. In the game thinking domain, the artifact provides a new application for serious games. Recently, games and gamification have become a major trend in many areas, for example in innovation management [15] or in e-learning [16]. Nevertheless, the use of a serious game as a qualitative market research method for purchase decision processes demonstrates a new field of application for games.

For market research, the artifact offers an innovative qualitative method for gaining insights into purchase decision processes. Current market research methods have shown many deficits. Several researchers have expressed their opinion that we are in need for new approaches for the subject [3], [4], [17]. The InsightGame addresses this demand by using the positive impacts of games to minimize these deficits.

Significance to Practice. InsightGame provides a new method for practitioners to gain valuable customer insights. It is useful for market research firms or institutions, which want to expand their portfolio, as well as companies, that want to be able to better understand their potential customers. The latter can use the findings to support their customers at the right touch points with relevant information and services.

4   Evaluation of the Artifact and Further Research

Evaluation. To evaluate the artifact, playtests have been designed based on Fullerton and Schell [6], [18]. In addition to the data collected through the app, the players have been taped during the whole session as well as questioned afterwards.

In total, 37 so-called tissue testers have participated. The questionnaire after the playtests included mainly questions about the whole game and about the smartphone application. To name two examples, most players had fun playing the game and found the app to be supporting the game process. The tests also showed that in addition to the revealed insights during the play sessions, most probands were keen to join in further discussions afterwards.

Further Research. The next step will be to evaluate the game as a market research method. In order to do so, an experiment will be conducted. A classical and popular qualitative market research method – namely a form of the qualitative interview – and the InsightGame will be directly compared based on several criteria.

References

1. Munzinger, U., Wenhart, C.: Markenerleben messen, managen, maximieren. In: Munzinger, U., Wenhart, C. (eds.) Marken Erleben im Digitalen Zeitalter, pp. 147–167. Springer, Wiesbaden (2012)
2. Case, D.O.: Looking for Information: A Survey of Research on Information Seeking, Needs, and Behavior. Emerald Group Pub., Bingley (2012)
3. Boateng, W.: Evaluating the Efficacy of Focus Group Discussion (FGD) in Qualitative Social Research. Int. J. Bus. Soc. Sci. 3, 54–57 (2012)
4. Wellner, A.S.: The New Science of Focus Groups. Am. Demogr. 25, 29–33 (2003)
5. March, S.T., Storey, V.C.: Design Science in the Information Systems Discipline: An Introduction to the Special Issue on Design Science Research. MIS Q. 32, 725–730 (2008)
6. Schell, J.: The Art of Game Design: A Book of Lenses. Morgan Kaufmann, Amsterdam (2008)
7. Abt, C.C.: Serious Games. University Press of America, Lanham (1987)
8. Witt, M., Robra-Bissantz, S.: Sparking Motivation and Creativity with "Online Ideation Games". In: Goltz, U., Magnor M., Appelrath H.J., Mathies H., Balke W.T., Wolf L. (eds.) Informatik 2012. LNI, P-208, pp. 1006–1023 (2012)
9. MacElroy, W., Gray, M.: IMRO Online Survey Satisfaction Research: A Pilot Study of Salience-based Respondent Experience Modeling. J. Online Res., 1–17 (2003)
10. Singer, E., Groves, R.M., Corning, A.D.: Differential Incentives: Beliefs About Practices, Perceptions of Equity and Effects on Survey Participation. Public Opin. Q. 63, 251–260 (1999)
11. Füller, J., Hutter, K.: Im Spiel liegt die Wahrheit – Games zur Insights-Generierung. Mark. Rev. St Gallen. 29, 26–32 (2012)
12. Janke, K.: Die neue Lust am Mitmachen. mafo 2012, 8–10 (2012)
13. Diller, H.: Grundprinzipien des Marketing. GIM-Verl., Nürnberg (2007)
14. Salen, K., Zimmerman, E.: Rules of Play: Game Design Fundamentals. MIT Press, Cambridge (2004)
15. Witt, M., Scheiner, C., Robra-Bissantz, S.: Gamification of Online Idea Competitions: Insights from an Explorative Case. In: Heiß, H.U., Pepper, P., Schlingloff, H., Schneider, J. (eds.) Informatik 2011. LNI, vol. 191, pp. 392–394 (2011)
16. Cheong, C., Cheong, F., Filippou, J.: Quick Quiz: A Gamified Approach for Enhancing Learning. In: PACIS 2013 Proceedings, Paper 206 (2013)
17. Belz, C., Huber, D., Okonek, C., Rutschmann, M.: Reales Kundenverhalten – reales Marketing. In: Belz, C. (ed.) Innovationen im Kundendialog, pp. 35–67. Gabler, Wiesbaden (2011)
18. Fullerton, T.: Game Design Workshop: A Playcentric Approach to Creating Innovative Games. Morgan Kaufmann, Amsterdam (2008)

The Social Newsroom:
Visual Analytics for Social Business Intelligence
Tool Prototype Demo

Christopher Zimmerman[1(✉)] and Ravi Vatrapu[1,2]

[1]Computational Social Science Laboratory (CSSL) Copenhagen Business School,
Frederiksberg, Denmark
{cz.itm,rv.itm}@cbs.dk
[2]Westerdals Oslo School of Arts, Communication and Technology, Oslo, Norway

1 Introduction

Today, businesses are utilizing social media as part of their strategy for communicating with and understanding the behaviors of their consumers. The widespread public use of social media is a relatively new phenomenon that presents an ongoing, ever-changing challenge to companies and creates a unique set of risks as well as advantages to decision-makers. At the same time expansion into the online social space offers tremendous potential strategic advantages including demographic targeting from a new, pervasive reflection of consumers and brand advocates. Social media thus takes on a new relevance in forging relationships of brand co-creation. The research project, in its entirety, seeks to derive business value from social data by designing and developing a series of dashboards for those who struggle to interpret and keep up with the social data created around a brand and marketing campaign.

The following prototype demo demonstrates how the tool is theoretically informed (in a theory of social data), technically robust and sound (via visual analytics), methodologically rigorous (following Action Design Research), and empirically evaluated (in real-world campaigns and trainee evaluations). We first outline the foundation of tool development with focus on the main perspectives guiding the research. A presentation of the actual tool development is subsequently put forward highlighting the main components of the tool.

2 Tool Development

The practical challenge for social media marketers has been the need for data to support decision-making in the creation and curation of real-time content and community management. Creating a discourse through planned communication and strategic use of language is a way of attempting to lead followers and affect organizational culture (Alvesson et al 2011). Motivating consumer engagement through content creation must be undertaken with more uncertainty since language is socially constructed and context specific, and hence will change more online from one person to the other, than it would in physical and organizational network contexts, (Kelly, 2008), (Li, 2011). The design

© Springer International Publishing Switzerland 2015
B. Donnellan et al. (Eds.): DESRIST 2015, LNCS 9073, pp. 386–390, 2015.
DOI: 10.1007/978-3-319-18714-3_28

of a social media dashboard to that end has led to several outcomes in the form of dedicated interface designs. Current development of the platform is taking place within a research environment as well as a social media marketing agency. It has thus far combined six individual interfaces that serve specific social business purposes for practitioners. They are each designed with a primary visualization and supported by supplemental gauges to provide additional contextual background. The six interfaces that can be separated into three "pillars" for insights and three "dashboards" for monitoring. The following demonstration of interfaces for the Social Newsroom BI tool (Table 1) subsequently details each individual design and purpose. These interactive displays can be sharply contrasted with commonplace static examples, such as word clouds for topic discovery, line graphs for performance, and tables ranking people.

Insights Pillars: The three pillars for insights are intended to give the practitioner an ability to learn about story performance, important people and relevant topics respectively with interactive charts. This allows them to follow an information scent, or insight, and then have the possibility of leveraging it to inform other investigations within the other interfaces. The user has a hypothetical opportunity to shift content strategy in posting and re-assess performance gauges in a cyclical usage pattern of the dashboard. An information foraging path is evaluated during and after deployments.

Table 1. Six Interfaces Designed for The Social Newsroom / Project Baboon (Beta)

Insights Pillars		
Story Performance (P1)	Relevant Topics (P2)	Key Contributor Network (P3)
Monitoring Dashboards		
Channel Cockpit (D1)	PR Newsdesk (D2)	Campaign Overview (D3)

Performance Insights Pillar I (Story Performance) - Measuring success of content :
In order to continuously improve and create more engaging and relevant content for a given community, the case company needs to measure how the content is performing and to analyze the reasons why content is (or is not) performing. The Story Performance pillar is a self-reflective view of the campaign's own posting performance on Facebook, Twitter and Instagram, using multi-dimensional visual representations. Currently this displays how well individual stories, themes, and timings are being received by social media communities along four dimensions, including Action-Reaction Ratios, Affinity, Amplification, and Commentary magnitude. A primary bubble graph portrays amplification and affinity metrics of stories on either access while bubble size reflects

the amplitude of story commentary. The ultimate success of each piece of content is immediately visible, while clustering effects can shed light on patterns of content type, topic, and language. Finally, a glanceable calendar heatmap (not pictured) contrasts proportions between publishing actions and fan reactions.

Social Text Insights Pillar II (Topic Discovery) - Detecting related "trending topics":
In order to be able to produce relevant, real-time content for the brands it supports, a company monitors trending topics and uncovers new topics from within its community. This information may also potentially informs campaigns, services or even the physical design of future products. The socially-constructed folksonomies of a brand offer an unbiased definition by the community. The Topic Discovery pillar includes a selection of tools that provide insights on the hashtags that people associate with and use with when talking about a specific brand or topic on Twitter. This dashboard was designed to intuitively act as a radar for common words that exist around several brands or topics of interest. The interactive radar graph leverages language from raw tweets in Twitter datasets to identify related topics that revolve around given keywords or brands. Topics have been implemented including a brand, keyword topics and a celebrity (actor) whose mentions are mined and archived to then allow this tool to identify related words with the greatest frequency. When several topics are selected simultaneously, the keywords on the radar are overlapping volumes of harmonized interest areas. Each color-coded language footprint can also be manipulated to filter out any irrelevant terms that may surface and drill-down to the most relevant representation for analysis. The design also includes several contextual graphs. For example, each topic repository are represented in a venn diagram revealing actual volumes and overlaps embedded in the conversation.

Social Graph Insights Pillar III (Key Contributors) – Detecting relevant people:
In order to create relevant content it is also necessary to gain an in-depth understanding of the community. By isolating clusters, interventions can alter the course of a conversation as sentiments are disseminated through the network graph of the brand page. The People Pillar (Key Contributors) includes a selection of tools that show individual users who are talking about a chosen brand, campaign, or topic as well as how much they are talking. It currently leverages Twitter activity to find influential and interesting people around brands and topics. The contributor treemap graph shows the users who tweet the most within a given campaign keyword dataset. By further drilling into the graph, the user navigates the combination of chatter volume and followership. Size and shading allow quick identification of the most important people based on their degree of involvement and following. Additional graphs show the share of voice of top contributors as well as volumes of hashtag usage.

Monitoring Dashboards
A second set of dashboards provide monitoring functionality to serve real-time needs of a campaign newsroom that must constantly monitor exposure on social channels.

The 'Cockpit' – Dashboard I: The campaign cockpit design currently enables the manager or business leader to take the temperature of the current brand situation on four channels in the same dashboard (Facebook, Twitter, YouTube and Instagram) to monitor performance on a high level. Social media channels are color-coded within the gauges to contrast standard performance metrics within three combinable, cross-channel dimensions: Reach, Engagement and Buzz.

The Social PR Newsdesk – Dashboard II: Two subsequent interfaces for the social newsroom have been added in response to feedback from the first campaign, as well as design needs to monitor the launch of new products. The first was a simple newsdesk of mentions on news sites outside of social media. A repository was built using pre-directed RSS feeds from Google Alerts. This piping offers automatic population of relevant news stories to practitioners who then manually use the newsdesk to mark-up the article with context, such as levels of sentiment and number of social shares, and flag content for taking action by community managers. The supplemental impact from the periphery of social channels is thus included.

The Campaign Overview – Dashboard III: In further listening to these end-users, a final Social Newsroom interface was established that combines a three-part overview of campaign exposure. A primary map display of graduated symbols reflect a global volume of campaign mentions that are currently emanating around the world. This can be toggled from user-selected historical windows to "live mode". A time series graph plots total volume of posts (mentions) and a second line for potential reach of posts on a dual axis. Finally a timeline of alerts for posts from influential people (with high follower levels) or key influencers such as journalists and bloggers from press materials and PR outreach. The combined effect provides a contextual interface where a user in a control room setting can notice a spike in volume, refer to the map for its origination, and also see that any major actors (celebrities, etc) in the alert feed who mentioned campaign or brand topics. Several orders of this scenario will be tested in a controlled environment. The alert feed also includes an audio cue to grabs the user's attention (who is often multitasking across screens and reports) to take immediate notice of important involvement and take direct action.

3   Discussion and Concluding Remarks

Current state-of-the-art social media tools provide data collection, aggregation and analysis into KPIs. However when represented in dashboards for business intelligence, they lack visualizations that can facilitate meaning making opportunities and action taking possibilities. The visualization of social media data and subsequent monthly reporting therefore suffer from a lack of standards and design principles. Current tools either require a data science team of complementary competencies or supplementary tools to design, develop, evaluate and use the actionable data from social channels. This tool prototype summary illustrates that the design of the Social Newsroom Dashboard is not simply product development, but an IT artifact that seeks to be theoretically informed, methodologically built and empirically tested towards facilitating social business intelligence competencies. Several trial licenses to real-world companies have been granted during development and will lead to further empirical testing within a real world context; that is to say by the actions of real-world users generating real-world usage data. This is soon to be verified in lab study simulations and validated by further real-world practitioner cases.

References

1. Asur, S., Huberman, B.: Predicting the Future with Social Media. In: 2010 IEEE/WIC/ACM International Conference on Web Intelligence and Intelligent Agent Technology (WI-IAT), pp. 492–499. IEEE (2010)
2. Card, S.K., Mackinlay, J.D., Shneiderman, B.: Readings in Information Visualization: Using Vision to Think. Morgan Kaufmann (1999)
3. Cha, M., Haddadi, H., Benevenuto, F., Gummadi, K.P.: Measuring User Influence in Twitter: The Million Follower Fallacy, p. 8 (2010)
4. Chen, H., Chiang, R.H., Storey, V.C.: Business Intelligence and Analytics: From Big Data to Big Impact. MIS Quarterly 36(4), 1165–1188 (2012)
5. Dill, J.: Expanding the Frontiers of Visual Analytics and Visualization. Springer, London (2010)
6. Dinter, B., Lorenz, A.: Social Business Intelligence: A Literature Review and Research Agenda (2012)
7. Gallaugher, J., Ransbotham, S.: Social Media and Customer Dialog Management at Starbucks. Mis Quarterly Executive 9(4), 197–212 (2010)
8. Haugtvedt, C., Machleit, K., Yalch, R.: Online Consumer Psychology: Understanding and Influencing Consumer Behavior in the Virtual World. Lawrence Erlbaum Associates (2005)
9. Keim, D.A., Andrienko, G., Fekete, J.-D., Görg, C., Kohlhammer, J., Melançon, G.: Visual Analytics: Definition, Process, and Challenges. In: Kerren, A., Stasko, J.T., Fekete, J.-D., North, C. (eds.) Information Visualization. LNCS, vol. 4950, pp. 154–175. Springer, Heidelberg (2008)
10. Li, H., Leckenby, J.: Examining the Effectiveness of Internet Advertising Formats. In: Schumann, D., Thorson, E. (eds.) Internet Advertising: Theory and Research, pp. 203–224. Lawrence Erlbaum Associates (2007)
11. McAfee, A.: Enterprise 2.0: New Collaborative Tools for Your Organization's Toughest Challenges. Harvard Business School Press (2009)
12. Robertson, S., Vatrapu, R., Medina, R.: Online Video "Friends" Social Networking: Overlapping Online Public Spheres in the, U.S. Presidential Election. Journal of Information Technology & Politics 7(2-3), 182–201 (2010)
13. Romero, D.M., Galuba, W., Asur, S., Huberman, B.A.: Influence and Passivity in Social Media, Machine Learning and Knowledge Discovery in Databases. In: Gunopulos, D., Hofmann, T., Malerba, D., Vazirgiannis, M. (eds.) ECML PKDD 2011, Part III. LNCS, vol. 6913, pp. 18–33. Springer, Heidelberg (2011)
14. Schumann, D., Thorson, E.: Internet Advertising: Theory and Research. Lawrence Erlbaum Associates (2007)
15. Sein, M., Henfridsson, O., Purao, S., Rossi, M., Lindgren, R.: Action Design Research (2011)
16. Tapscott, D., Williams, A.D., Herman, D.: Government 2.0: Transforming Government and Governance for the Twenty-First Century, New Paradigm's Government 2.0: Wikinomics, Government and Democracy Program (2007)
17. Vatrapu, R.: Understanding Social Business. In: Akhilesh, K.B. (ed.) Emerging Dimensions of Technology Management, Springer, New Delhi (2013)
18. Vollmer, C., Precourt, G.: Always On: Advertising, Marketing and Media in an Era of Consumer Control. McGraw-Hill Professional (2008)
19. Zhang, Q., Segall, R., Cao, M.: Visual Analytics and Interactive Technologies: Data, Text, and Web Mining Applications. Information Science Reference, Hershey (2011)

A Mobile Cloud Workforce Management System for SMEs

Leonard Heilig[✉] and Stefan Voß

Institute of Information Systems (IWI),
University of Hamburg, 20146 Hamburg, Germany
{leonard.heilig,stefan.voss}@uni-hamburg.de

Abstract. The application of innovative technologies for advancing mobile workforce management often represents a considerable financial barrier, especially for small and medium enterprises. In this paper, we propose an on-demand and multi-tenancy cloud-based workforce management system utilizing state-of-the-art mobile and non-mobile technologies and vehicle routing methodologies. The prototype includes functionality to manage customer data, track and communicate with mobile workers, and to efficiently plan routes by solving vehicle routing problems with different metaheuristics in a highly scalable cloud environment using the Google App Engine. The cloud-based solution can be flexibly used "as a service" by different organizations and thus enables smaller enterprises to utilize innovative technologies for low variable expenses in order to improve their competitiveness. To the best of our knowledge, the proposed prototype is the first integrative approach to support the management of mobile workforces in the cloud. The generic architecture builds a foundation for implementing cloud-based real-time decision support and communication in other appropriate application areas.

Keywords: Mobile workforce management · Cloud computing · Google App Engine · Cloud-based decision analytics · Vehicle routing problem

1 Introduction

The ubiquity of cloud and mobile technologies fosters innovative applications to better support the planning and execution of activities being carried out by mobile workforces [9, 11]. Mobile workers, who work outside the business premises as part of a mobile workforce, are increasingly dependent on accurate and current information to efficiently complete their tasks at several customer locations. Therefore, it becomes more important for enterprises to share data between local information systems and their mobile workers as well as to apply means of decision analytics (for an extensive overview on the application of decision analytics in cloud computing see, e.g., [4]). Thereby, planning data that optimizes the allocation of mobile workers to customers, using optimization techniques, can be used as a basis to reduce operational costs, improve service quality, and become more eco-friendly. Many organizations with mobile workers are seeking to adopt information and communication technologies (ICT) to

© Springer International Publishing Switzerland 2015
B. Donnellan et al. (Eds.): DESRIST 2015, LNCS 9073, pp. 391–395, 2015.
DOI: 10.1007/978-3-319-18714-3_29

efficiently manage their mobile workers, meet new demands and encounter the increasing cost-pressure [9]. However, the related investments and operational costs of such systems often represent a considerable barrier for many organizations, in particular for small and medium enterprises (SMEs) or in developing countries. The concept of cloud computing may facilitate a more flexible and economic alternative for those organizations. Cloud computing, widely recognized as a paradigm shift in the way ICT services are invented, developed, deployed, scaled, updated, maintained and paid for [10], offers computing resources that complement mobile technologies by means of elastic storage and processing capabilities. Furthermore, cloud computing uniquely addresses specific business demands, in particular inquired by SMEs, by promoting specific characteristics, such as no upfront investments and flexible pricing schemes, elasticity and scalability as well as ubiquitous and interoperable access [5, 10].

In this paper, we present a prototype of *JobRoute*, which is an integrative solution to utilize cloud characteristics for providing an affordable on-demand mobile workforce management system for SMEs. The prototype represents an artifact in the sense of design science research [7, 8] contributing a framework for applying decision analytics based on mobile and cloud-based technologies as well as a valuable solution to be applied in other application environments. A demo of the web and mobile application can be tested on http://job-route.com.

2 Design of the Artifact

The proposed artifact primarily supports mobile workforce management. The multi-tenancy cloud solution provides several on-demand cloud services, a mobile application for mobile workers, and a web application for dispatchers to efficiently plan and organize jobs being carried out by mobile workers. To increase the customer satisfaction and simultaneously reduce time and costs needed to complete jobs, mobile workers are supported with real-time data based on a central cloud platform. The computation of routes, for solving the underlying vehicle routing problem (VRP), is executed in a highly scalable cloud environment and is available "as a service" for multiple SMEs. In the following, we present a generic system architecture as well as main features of the proposed artifact.

The system architecture describes the integration of web applications and mobile applications. Generally, the system architecture facilitates the outsourcing of data- and computationally intensive system components into the cloud and supports dynamic scaling mechanisms to adjust computational resources based on computational requirements (a respective provisioning and deployment process for elastic cloud services is described in [6]). It consists of three main environments, briefly explained in the following.

Cloud Environment. To integrate the web and mobile environment, three main service types are deployed in the cloud environment. Interface services ensure that communication hubs are available for the interaction with web and mobile environments as well as for external environments. Logical services manage the interaction between both sides, interact with external environments or services, and provide algorithms to solve optimization problems. Persistence services interact with the remaining services in order to persistently store the exchanged data in a database. The implemented services are executed in isolated containers providing a runtime environment so that multiple organizations can use the services in parallel. Service container are dynamically deployed to several virtual server instances in order to balance the load and to process multiple service requests in parallel.

Web Environment. The web environment consists of a rich web application providing functionality that is hosted in a scalable cloud environment. Core components of the web application are the job entry and route planning functionality. After job data (e.g., job type, priority, and expected duration) is recorded, it can be used to determine routes for available mobile workers. The underlying planning problem in its basic form may be modeled as a VRP [3]. In that respect we have applied a simple two-phase heuristic to solve the VRP with different heuristics in a cloud environment. For the first stage, we have implemented a nearest neighbor heuristic and a cheapest insertion heuristic. In the second stage a meta-heuristic is applied in order to enhance the search strategy and thus explore the search space more elaborately. The cloud-based mobile workforce management system currently implements simulated annealing (SA) and a genetic algorithm (GA), which consider the maximum capacities of each mobile worker. After the jobs are planned, resulting in an optimal or near-optimal route for each vehicle (as shown in Fig. 1 based on the results of SA), route instructions are automatically sent to mobile workers. Moreover, the web application allows to track the position of mobile workers and to communicate with them in real-time.

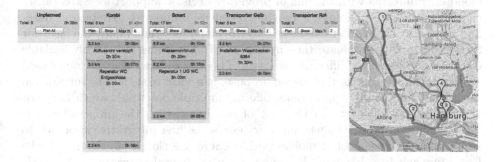

Fig. 1. Vehicle routing results (Google Maps API)

Mobile Environment. The mobile environment encloses the totality of all mobile applications being executed on mobile devices providing functionality to support mobile workers of different organizations by interacting with the cloud services. This includes functionality to receive job routes and descriptions, to write and receive messages, and to report the fulfillment of jobs. To enable real-time communication, data is frequently synchronized between the cloud and the mobile environment.

3   Significance to Practice and Research

To demonstrate the advantages of a cloud-based workforce management system for SMEs, we have implemented a prototype system supporting mobile workforces according to an exemplary business process. The process includes order processing, route planning (i.e., vehicle routing), job execution, and job completion. Consequently, the artifact contains key components to support important organizational problems in the area of workforce management systems and extends common capabilities by enabling a real-time communication and decision support based on a highly elastic and scalable cloud platform, mobile technologies, and a web-based backend application. Due to economies of scale, the proposed artifact represents an affordable solution, in particular for SMEs that are not able to invest in on-premise solutions and required computational resources. It implies no upfront investments, flexible use options and pricing schemes as well as a highly scalable computing infrastructure for enabling real-time decision support. As such, the artifact represents a starting point for developing a new generation of workforce management systems. Further, the generic architecture of the artifact can be used for other application areas. In the domain of maritime shipping and especially in port areas, for instance, the generic artifact can be applied to enhance the planning and communication between the port authority and drayage companies in order to reduce congestion and vehicle emissions based on real-time data and an integration of port-related information systems like traffic control systems.

This paper may be seen as complementing work of applying algorithms within cloud environments with the aim of providing decision support for SME rather than advancing methodology. It provides a generic framework to outsource data- and computationally intensive tasks into the cloud and thus builds the basis for further research to evaluate the application of algorithms in a highly scalable cloud environment for different use cases. This work shows that a cloud-based system architecture, like the one we propose, is a vital basis for the integration of rich web and mobile applications, offering multiple potentials which have not been fully exploited yet. To the best of our knowledge, the proposed cloud-based mobile workforce management system is the first integrative approach to support the management of mobile workforces in the cloud. Moreover, it is the first approach to solve the VRP based on a configurable two-phase heuristic solution in a cloud environment. As indicated, this work shall be considered as a starting point for further research in the area of mobile workforce management and, in particular, to further explore the impact of a cloud-based solution on the performance of algorithms.

4   Evaluation

As envisaged in the design science research paradigm, the evaluation of our artifact is divided into qualitative and quantitative approaches. A field experiment examines the application of the proposed artifact for a mobile nursing service. The experiment investigates, for instance, the usability of both the web and mobile application based on questionnaires. The quantitative evaluation of the artifact includes an assessment of costs by estimating the total cost of ownership for different scenarios. For this, we intend to simulate the proposed cloud architecture and different processing workloads by using CloudSim [1]. Further, we plan to extend the cloud-based planning functionality by applying advanced methods from operations research. Moreover, the problem settings that are addressed should be extended towards technician routing with load balancing constraints as well as issues related to workgroups diversity maximization [2].

References

1. Calheiros, R.N., Ranjan, R., Beloglazov, A., De Rose, C.A.F., Buyya, R.: CloudSim: a toolkit for modeling and simulation of cloud computing environments and evaluation of resource provisioning algorithms. Software: Practice and Experience 41(1), 23–50 (2011)
2. Caserta, M., Voß, S.: Workgroups diversity maximization: A metaheuristic approach. In: Blesa, M.J., Blum, C., Festa, P., Roli, A., Sampels, M. (eds.) Hybrid Metaheuristics 2013. LNCS, vol. 7919, pp. 118–129. Springer, Heidelberg (2013)
3. Golden, B., Raghavan, S., Wasil, E. (eds.): The Vehicle Routing Problem: Latest Advances and New Challenges, Operations Research/Computer Science Interfaces, vol. 43. Springer, New York (2008)
4. Heilig, L., Voß, S.: Decision analytics for cloud computing: a classification and literature review. In: Newman, A., Leung, J. (eds.) Tutorials in Operations Research – Bridging Data and Decisions, pp. 1–26. INFORMS, Catonsville (2014)
5. Heilig, L., Voß, S.: A scientometric analysis of cloud computing literature. IEEE Transactions on Cloud Computing 2(3), 266–278 (2014)
6. Heilig, L., Voß, S., Wulfken, L.: Building clouds: An integrative approach for an automated deployment of elastic cloud services. In: Chang, V., Walters, R., Wills, G. (eds.) Delivery and Adoption of Cloud Computing Services in Contemporary Organizations, IGI Global (to appear, 2015), doi:10.4018/978-1-4666-8210-8.ch011
7. Hevner, A.R., Chatterjee, S. (eds.): Design Research in Information Systems, Integrated Series in Information Systems, vol. 22. Springer, New York (2010)
8. Hevner, A.R., March, S.T., Ram, S.: Design science research in information systems research. MIS Quarterly 28(1), 75–105 (2004)
9. Lehmann, H., Kuhn, J., Lehner, F.: The future of mobile technology: Findings from a European Delphi study. In: Proceedings of the 37th Annual Hawaii International Conference on System Sciences (HICSS 2004), pp. 1–10 (2004)
10. Marston, S., Li, Z., Bandyopadhyay, S., Zhang, J., Ghalsasi, A.: Cloud computing – the business perspective. Decision Support Systems 51(1), 176–189 (2011)
11. Viehland, D., Yang, C.: Bringing the mobile workforce to business: A case study in a field service organization. In: International Conference on the Management of Mobile Business (ICMB 2007), pp. 39–44 (2007)

Smart City App

Promoting Community Engagement and Collaboration for a Sustainable Future

Joana Monteiro(✉), Matthew Austin, Gaurav Mandilwar, and Raj Sharman

State University of New York at Buffalo, Buffalo, NY, USA
{joanaalu,matthewa,mandilwa,rsharman}@buffalo.edu

Abstract. Collaboration is fundamental for cities and regions to meet the combined economic, environmental and social challenges of the 21st century. A broad array of stakeholders including citizens, non-profit organizations, private businesses, foundations, academic institutions and local governments, will need to make decisions together in order to realize a sustainable future for their communities. Our artifact was developed for the Western New York community as part of One Region Forward's planning process, developing a single portal for all stakeholders involved to continue collaborating on the plan. We developed an application that will serve as a forum to allow citizens that are passionate about sustainability to express their ideas to other citizens and plan stakeholders to build capacity and turn their ideas into action. The artifact acts as a multi-sided platform that promotes crowdsourcing for a variety of agents to come together and participate on sustainability related projects.

Keywords: Sustainability · Smart City · Green IS · Activity Theory · Design Science · Community Engagement · Climate Change · Environment · Urban Planning

1 Introduction

Smart City is a term that is gaining popularity. Smart Cities are cities that use Information Technology to improve the effectiveness and efficiency of their services. This is especially important as cities are increasingly being asked to become more sustainable, as well as provide better services to their citizens with strained resources. By using digital technologies and green information systems, cities can move towards becoming Smarter and more Sustainable. Our artifact was developed in anticipation of the conclusion of One Region Forward (1RF), a broad-based, collaborative effort to promote more sustainable forms of development in the Buffalo Niagara Region – in Land Use, Transportation, Housing, Food Systems, and Climate Change and Energy.

Our artifact takes form as a single portal that can be used by all community stakeholders; citizens, non-profit organizations, private businesses, foundations, academic institutions and local governments, to collaborate on community related projects that will help create more sustainable and smarter cities.

© Springer International Publishing Switzerland 2015
B. Donnellan et al. (Eds.): DESRIST 2015, LNCS 9073, pp. 396–400, 2015.
DOI: 10.1007/978-3-319-18714-3_30

2   Design of the Artifact

The operating goal of a Multi Sided Platform is to maximize the positive externality effects [6] between the various groups of users that the MSP brings together. By providing this "matching" service, the search costs are reduced for the sides involved in each transaction [6] The Smart City platform also identifies citizen education as well as some social objectives.

Even though the Smart City platform's objective is not to maximize profit [5], some consideration must still be made on the impact of each service provided on social welfare. Pricing considerations [3] can still be made, and concepts like price discrimination can still be applied [9] and, charging or subsidizing different sides involved might even be dependent on the characteristics of the region. The Smart City artifact is designed as a multi-sided platform that allows different stakeholders to play different roles with the system such as project initiators, skill providers, subject matter experts, city government administrators, etc. The design of the artifact includes a workflow for each stakeholder by type and role based access control. The system architecture include a core data store in the cloud, middleware and frontend on multiple platforms.

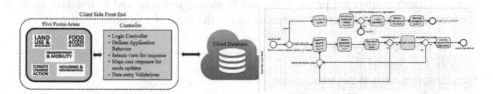

Fig. 1. System Architecture   **Fig. 2.** UML Process Flow

3   Significance to Research

The increase in concerns on sustainability and optimizing available resources [10] has shone a light on the lack of green IS solutions. The IS research community has the responsibility [2] of informing IS professionals of the most efficient and effective tools to promote the goals of sustainability. The artifact addresses the need for solutions that will turn ideas into action, provides a theoretical framework for building and evaluating green artifacts, and informs communities of the resources available to them. This artifact fills a need in Western New York of bringing together those interested in community development with different skills to different projects that benefit the society.

Using Hevner et al [7] guidelines for Design Science Research we identify the following aspects that break the paradigms identified by this body of literature:

- Design as an Artifact (G1): The artifact creates a collaboration instantiation that provides an MSP, through the use of both the front end application and the algorithm for the creation of new projects. A back end database will be updated in real time.
- Problem Relevance (G2): There is a lack of a holistic approach to community collaborative efforts for projects in sustainability, which has become a main stream interest and model of future regional development. This artifact is not only implementable but also provides relevance [1]
- Design Evaluation (G3) : The evaluation elements were identified by fitting the system into an Activity Theory framework, and relies on existing methods.
- Research Contributions (G4): The proposed artifact provides a move from planning and discussion into a plan of action through an Activity Theory framework for identifying the design elements, and following DSR guidelines [7]
- Research Rigor (G5): The construction of this artifact relies not only on the implementation of existing strategies and toolkits, but also on the adaptation of the existing Activity Theory as a way to identify design and evaluation elements.
- Design as a search process (G6): The system design allows each project to have a unique bio-system without compromising the set strategies for each focus area. All of the elements in the design process are clearly identified by the framework.
- Communication (G7): The artifact will be presented to the Design Science community through conference proceedings and academic journals, and to the 1RF communities through the evaluation process and in the form of a working prototype.

We are using Activity Theory [4] to describe the Smart City "ecosystem", where the emphasis is put on community collaboration to achieve common outcomes, which might otherwise not be achievable as effectively with only individual efforts. We used the Activity Theory to inform both the Design and the Evaluation elements described below.

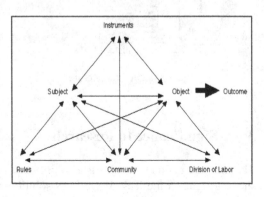

SUBJECT: System User
- Design Elements: The system users are identified as Citizens, Organizations, or Governmental agencies
- Evaluation Elements: User identifying elements ex. Name, email, address, etc.
OBJECT: Focus Areas
- Design Elements: Smart City is comprised of 5 focus areas: Land Use, Transportation, Housing, Food Systems, and Climate Change. Each area has different strategies for realizing the desired outcomes.
- Evaluation Elements: The strategies for each area that need to be tracked
COMMUNITY: Project Participants and Stakeholders
- Design Elements: Each participant brings different interests and skills to a project
- Evaluation Elements: Stakeholder profiles (skills, interests, experience)

INSTRUMENT: Resources
- Design Elements: Providing stakeholders with Toolkits, Case Studies, Best Practices, Guidelines and Examples
- Evaluation Elements: White papers, instruction manuals and guidelines
RULES: Plan Goals and Objectives
- Design Elements: Standards and strategies created by the steering committee, create a scope and boundary for each project that is initiated.
- Evaluation Elements; Documents derived from the regional plan
DIVISION OF LABOR: Standard responsibilities in each project
- Design Elements: The nature (Focus area + Strategy + Toolkit + guidelines) of each project. For example: can follow a standard project charter structure, or have a more fluid organization.
- Evaluation Elements: Tasks, categories, descriptions
The system outcome can be generally described as the completion of a community project in one of the 5 focus areas outlined by the Smart City application.

4   Significance to Practice

The Smart City application will serve as a forum to allow citizens that are passionate about sustainability, to express their ideas to other citizens and plan stakeholders to build capacity and turn their ideas into action, and move the regions into a future of Smart Cities through the use of Green IS. The system will act as a multi-sided platform that will bring together a multitude of agents who have a common sustainability oriented goal. The focus of Smart City is to have a positive impact on social welfare, enabling any member the community to start improving it, thus increasing the efficiency and capacity of One Region Forward.

The system can grow to include other focus areas, different strategies for each one of those areas and change to fit needs of the community as it evolves in its quest for sustainability. The system can also be customized taking into consideration the economic, social, geographical characteristics of a region to promote the same objectives in a different community and strategies to implement the artifact

5   Evaluation of the Artifact

The evaluation elements are derived from Activity Theory [4]. The elements identified for evaluation are listed in Section 3 (see above). The evaluation process includes both naturalistic and artificial methodologies. The artifact has also been validated during its creation (ex-ante evaluation) through literature referencing, expert evaluation, and potential system users. The evaluation of the completed prototype (ex-post evaluation) includes further technical experiments and illustrative scenarios (most appropriate for instantiations [8]). Due to the nature of the artifact, action research and case studies are part of the evaluation process of future developments of the artifact and the system as a whole [11].

6   Screen Shots

References

1. Benbasat, I., Zmud, R.: The identity crisis within the IS discipline: defining and communicating the discipline's core properties. MIS Quarterly 27(2), 183–194 (2003)
2. vom Brocke, J., Seidel, S.: Environmental Sustainability in Design Science Research: Direct and Indirect Effects of Design Artifacts. In: Peffers, K., Rothenberger, M., Kuechler, B. (eds.) DESRIST 2012. LNCS, vol. 7286, pp. 294–308. Springer, Heidelberg (2012)
3. Eisenmann, T., Parker, G., Van Alstyne, M.: Strategies for Two-Sided Markets. Harvard Business Review, 10 (2006)
4. Engeström, Y.: Activity Theory and Individual and Socila Transformation. Perspectives of Activity Theory, 19–38 (1999)
5. Evans, D.S.: Some Empirical Aspects of Multi-sided Platform Indiustries. Review of Network Economics 2(3), 191–209 (2003)
6. Hagiu, A.: Multi-Sided Platforms: From Microfoundations to Design and Expansion Strategies. Working Paper, Harvard Business School (2008)
7. Hevner, A., March, S., Park, J., Ram, S.: Designe Science in Information Systems Research. MIS Quarterly 26(1), 75–105 (2004)
8. Peffers, K., Rothenberger, M., Tuunanen, T., Vaezi, R.: Design Science Research Evaluation. In: Peffers, K., Rothenberger, M., Tuunanen, T., Vaezi, R. (eds.) Design Science Research Evaluation, vol. 7286, pp. 398–410. Springer, Heidelberg (2012)
9. Rysman, M.: The Economics of Two-Sided Markets. Journal of Economic Perspectives 23(3), 125–143 (2009)
10. Seidel, S., Recker, J., van Brocke, J.: Sensemaking and Sustainable Practicing: Functional Affordances of Information Systems in Green Transformations. MIS Quarterly 37, 1275–1299 (2013)
11. Venable, J., Pries-Heje, J., Baskerville, R.: A Comprehensive Framework for Evaluation in Design Science Research. In: Peffers, K., Rothenberger, M., Kuechler, B. (eds.) DESRIST 2012. LNCS, vol. 7286, pp. 423–438. Springer, Heidelberg (2012)

Considering Risks in Planning and Budgeting Process – A Prototype Implementation in the Automotive Industry

Tobias Knabke[1(✉)], Sebastian Olbrich[1], and Lars Biederstedt[2]

[1] Mercator School of Management, University of Duisburg-Essen, Duisburg, Germany
`tobias.knabke@stud.uni-due.de`,
`sebastian.olbrich@uni-due.de`
[2] PricewaterhouseCoopers cundus AG, Duisburg, Germany
`lars.biederstedt@de.pwc.com`

Abstract. Corporate budgeting, planning and risk management are crucial functions in today's organizations. Yet, these important functions are often separated in different departments although both rely on similar information. This paper suggests connecting the underlying data structures by means of a software prototype. The suggested solution is based on a planning and budgeting solution running in a major European automotive company. The current Business Intelligence system is extended by hierarchical risk and value driver model that follows the organization's structure. It utilizes a risk-adjusted corridor planning approach based on Monte Carlo simulations. Instead of common point estimates the approach uses ranges that consciously represent uncertainty. As a result budgeting and forecasting are informed by additional knowledge. Hence, behavioral risk that is immanent in any planning activity can be managed.

Keywords: Corridor Planning · Risk Management · Business Intelligence · In-Memory · Prototype · Monte Carlo Simulation

1 The Missing Link Between Planning and Risk Management

"It's hard to make predictions, especially about the future" is a famous allegation by physician Niels Bohr. Yet, when it comes to corporate planning and budgeting, organizations seem to do just that as the planning is mostly executed by doing point estimates. Those estimates represent rather personal targets than a sound approximation. Let's say it is agreed to reach a % increase in turnover to Y million by the end of the year or to reach an overall headcount of Z employees which means Z/A in department A. This common practice can lead to high risks, i.e. uncertainties with unmanaged consequences and systematically include behavioral risk of the individuals that are responsible for the estimates [1].

Of course, the planning process is initially designed to minimize the risk of decision making through limiting uncertainties and include risk. Yet, such planning procedures can be found in most organizations, regardless of the industry or the size. It contains strategic planning for a multi-year horizon as well as tactical or operational planning, is conducted top-down or bottom-up and may vary from department to department.

© Springer International Publishing Switzerland 2015
B. Donnellan et al. (Eds.): DESRIST 2015, LNCS 9073, pp. 401–405, 2015.
DOI: 10.1007/978-3-319-18714-3_31

Information systems (IS) such as business intelligence (BI) are designed to support planning [2]. BI can be defined as "*a broad category of applications, technologies, and processes for gathering, storing, accessing, and analyzing data to help business users make better decisions*" [3]. Hence, BI is an umbrella term for systems and processes that turn raw data into useful information [4, 5]. The underlying technical concept of BI is usually a data warehouse (DWH). It systematically transfers data from source systems and reflects the organizations' single point of truth [6, 7]. Although BI and DWH are an appropriate basis for planning, organizations insufficiently use them for this purposes [2] and it is questionable whether this would be enough to support the process for assessing risks.

To identify risks and make appropriate decisions many organizations have implemented dedicated risk management departments. During risk assessments internal and external risks and their potential impact are analyzed. It seems obvious that risk management and planning need to be connected. But, risk management is usually executed in departments different from planning. This may result in strategic decisions without considering identified risks. In a nutshell: Organizations often base their planning processes on neoclassical economic positions, i.e. an in theory rationally acting Homo Economicus. But in reality individuals act differently. Especially, as cognitive or social effects as well as emotional factors influence economic decisions (e.g. the targets in their daily business) and "*most human decision-making uses thought processes that are intuitive and automatic rather than deliberative and controlled*" [8]. This phenomenon is commonly described as behavioral economics [9]. We believe that the understanding of behavioral economics and "behavioral biases" [8] gains many insights for individuals and organizations to improve planning and risk management. Currently, BI does not support these processes in a sufficient, integrated way. We address this shortcoming by the following design assumptions:

- DA1: Facilitate planning and risk assessment by providing the same information to both processes, i.e. share each other's information base.
- DA2: Functionally integrate planning and risk management in a way that behavioral effects are addressed.

2   Use Case from a Global Player in the Automotive Industry

Our use case describes a European, globally operating automotive company with more than 100,000 employees. It is composed of several subsidiaries that develop and construct cars and utility vehicles in locations on every continent. Moreover, it offers financial and leasing services. During the recent market turbulences the company realized that their actual performance as well as strategic and operational planning showed room for significant improvement. Volatile financial markets had unforeseen impacts on the company's financial service offerings. Additionally, technical innovations of competitors gained market shares in the upper and luxury class, particularly in developing markets. This was even increased by volatile commodity prices. Although some risks were identified by the firm's risk managers, they have not been incorporated in planning decisions. Instead, only scenarios (best/worst/expected) based on the opinion of planning experts were taken into account. The planning process itself is executed with the help of the organization's DWH-based BI system. Risks are assessed by separate actuarial software which is flanked by several statistical software and spreadsheets. Summarizing, the company lacks an integrated risk and planning process e.g. by the organization's BI. Moreover, it uses single point estimates that may be influenced by emotions, cognitive or social effects; particularly in the times of recent crisis.

3   Instantiation of the Artifact

The presented solution addresses this integrational challenge. It combines the domains of risk management and planning. All calculations are based on Monte Carlo simulations (MCS) with a configurable number of simulations and ranges instead of point estimates. A MCS generates a large number of scenarios to obtain the distribution for a probabilistic problem for which a deterministic solution is infeasible [10]. Using ranges to represent uncertainty is much more realistic than giving point estimates for plan or risk management key figures [10]. For each value driver of the organization that is in scope of the planning process ranges are collected and a suitable distribution is assigned to best estimate the ranges. The identified risks, e.g. growing competition in new markets or volatile currency exchange rates, are then mapped to the value driver model. Finally, risks and value drivers are aggregated by using MCS. The prototype includes historical information from the company's DWH, e.g. key figures of the last three years. To further minimize behavioral risk, the past risks are quantified by actual occurrence. Fig. 1 depicts the concept of this approach.

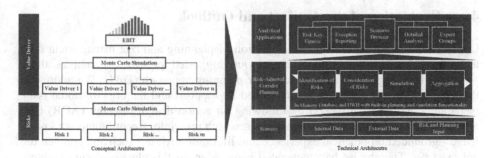

Fig. 1. Conceptual structure and technical architecture of the prototype

Fig. 1 also shows how the conceptual design is mapped to the technical architecture of the prototype. The implementation[1] is based on an in-memory (IM) appliance. This combination of hard- and software provides out-of-the-box functionalities for analytical and statistical calculations that have been adopted and extended in the prototype.

---

[1]   The artifact was implemented with SAP (BW on) HANA 7.4 using SAP BO Analysis (Edition for MS Office) 1.4 and Xcelsius 2008 as frontend tools. The MCS was executed by R scripts in SAP HANA. Data transfer and consolidation were done within SAP with ABAP.

Fig. **2** gives an impression of the result of the risk-adjusted corridor planning solution[2]. It shows the hierarchical decomposition of the organization's value drivers (here sales regions) and the high level distributions for the products for Asia Pacific. Additionally, the figure compares the deterministic plan value achieved from last year's actuals (Plan 2014) to the plan achieved with MCS (MCS result).

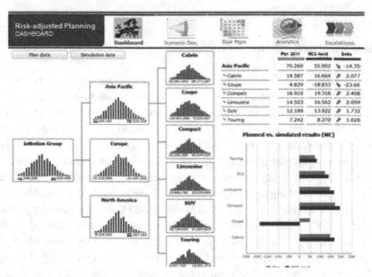

Fig. 2. Screenshot of the prototype

4   Evaluation of the Artifact and Outlook

Our overall aim is to facilitate the integration of planning and risk management on a technological and organizational basis. Our suggested prototype combines these processes by using a risk-adjusted corridor planning approach (DA1). We addressed the technical (insufficient and not integrated IS support) and the organizational issue (separately acting departments) by following an action design research (ADR) [11] approach focusing on the practice-inspired research principle. According to our knowledge - grounded on practical experience and literature review - such an approach did not exist yet. Thereby we have generated knowledge for this class of design problem within the automotive industry. With regard to practice, organizations benefit from a structured process across borders of single departments. The usage of distributions along the value driver hierarchy gathers significant insights through suitable granularity to better steer the organization. The approach consciously respects uncertainties as a characteristic of planning and risk management. It methodically reduces behavioral biases that influence decisions of human beings by using ranges and MCS (DA2). IM technology allows for processing of huge amounts of data and executing complex simulation methods that were not possible at all or inadequate in the past.

---

[2]   For a screencast demo of the running prototype please contact the authors.

We evaluated our solution innovated through ADR with experts from the automotive industry as well process experts from the areas of planning, risk management and simulation (MCS). In their opinion the usage of value drivers and hierarchical aggregation increases transparency and reliability. It thus improves the planning process and the quality of decisions as the focus is channeled to the most important value drivers. For further evaluation we plan to analyze if and to what extend key figures such as planning accuracy improved quantitatively. Yet, for a broader evaluation of business impact the concept should be observed in different organizational settings. As other industries, e.g. banking or reinsurance, have different requirements to and approaches to planning and risk management, we intend to broaden the scope of evaluation in the future. Another limitation is that the current solution depends on quantifiable risks with manageable complexity as a prerequisite. It uses corridor planning as methodology and can therefore hardly cope with, for instance, regulatory risks and compliance which are hard to quantify. We aim to address these challenges in our prospective research agenda.

References

1. Hillson, D., Murray-Webster, R.: Understanding and Managing Risk Attitude. Gower, Aldershot (2005)
2. Chamoni, P., Gluchowski, P.: Integrationstrends bei Business-Intelligence-Systemen - Empirische Untersuchung auf Basis des Business Intelligence Maturity Model. CG 2004 46, 119–128 (2004)
3. Watson, H.J.: Tutorial: Business Intelligence – Past, Present, and Future. Communication of the AIS 25, 487–511 (2009)
4. Wixom, B., Watson, H.: The BI-Based Organization. International Journal of Business Intelligence Research 1, 13–28 (2010)
5. Chen, X., Siau, K.: Effect of Business Intelligence and IT Infrastructure Flexibility on Organizational Agility. In: Proceedings of the International Conference on Information Systems, ICIS 2012. Association for Information Systems, Orlando (2012)
6. Rifaie, M., Kianmehr, K., Alhajj, R., Ridley, M.J.: Data warehouse architecture and design. In: Proceedings of the IEEE International Conference on Information Reuse and Integration, IRI 2008, pp. 58–63. IEEE Systems, Man, and Cybernetics Society, Las Vegas (2008)
7. Watson, H.J., Wixom, B.H.: The Current State of Business Intelligence. Computer 40, 96–99 (2007)
8. Erta, K., Hunt, S., Iscenko, Z., Brambley, W.: Applying behavioural economics at the Financial Conduct Authority, London (2014)
9. Mullainathan, S., Thaler, R.H.: Behavioral Economics (2000)
10. Hubbard, D.W.: How to measure anything. Wiley, Hoboken (2010)
11. Sein, M., Henfridsson, O., Purao, S., Rossi, M., Lindgren, R.: Action Design Research. MIS Quarterly 35, 37–56 (2011)

ITSM ProcessGuide – A Process Guidance System for IT Service Management

Stefan Morana[1,2(✉)], Timo Gerards[1], and Alexander Mädche[1,2]

[1] Chair of Information Systems IV, University of Mannheim, Mannheim, Germany
[2] Institute for Enterprise Systems, University of Mannheim, Mannheim, Germany
{morana,gerards,maedche}@es.uni-mannheim.de

Abstract. Process Guidance aims at increasing the process model understanding and effective and efficient process execution. In this paper we present the context, design, implementation, and ongoing evaluation of a Process Guidance System instantiation in an organizational setting. The system is used to support the IT Service Management processes within the case company. It is used productively in the case company of this research and this article describes how the system's features are designed for the evaluation.

Keywords: Process guidance · Longitudinal study · Organizational evaluation

1 Introduction

In order to handle the offered Information Technology (IT) services, many organizations refer to the ITIL framework [1] to define their IT Service Management (ITSM) strategy. With respect to the organization's ITSM strategy, organizations define processes to specify the handling of services and requests. In addition, they implement IT tools, e. g. ticket systems, to support their users in executing these processes. In order to achieve a high service quality and to ensure the proper operation of the provided IT services, the users are required to comply the defined processes and use the ticket systems as intended. But still, users have difficulties in using such systems and being compliant to organizational defined processes in many contexts. With respect to the ticket processing context there exist various challenges addressing the usage of such systems and the compliant execution of the underlying processes. Users may not know the defined ticket processes, how to execute a certain step of the ticket processes, or how to use the ticket systems. In order to address these challenges, the users require support in the execution of the processes in the ticket systems as well as the learning of the underlying ticket processes. Process Guidance Systems (PGS) address these challenges [2]. Building on the decisional guidance [3], explanations [4], and decision aids [5] research, PGS support the user in the understanding of the process models and the execution of processes by providing information about the process. While we reported the conceptualization of PGS in another paper [2], in this paper we shortly present the design, implementation, and ongoing evaluation of a PGS instantiation in an organizational setting. This research is part of our ongoing Design Science Research (DSR) project following the guidelines by

© Springer International Publishing Switzerland 2015
B. Donnellan et al. (Eds.): DESRIST 2015, LNCS 9073, pp. 406–410, 2015.
DOI: 10.1007/978-3-319-18714-3_32

Kuechler & Vaishnavi [6]. For the entire project, we collaborate with our industry partner which also serves as a case company. The company is a global supplier, development, and service partner for customers in many various sectors such as automotive, civil aviation, and mechanical engineering. In 2013, it employed 13.301 employees and had sales of more than 1.7 billion €. Overall, the DSR project consists of three design cycles. The first cycle served for the conceptualization of PGS, the derivation of three theory-grounded Design Principles (DPs), and the qualitative evolution of the DPs in our case company [2]. In the second cycle, we adapted the DPs to the results of the first cycle's evaluation and conducted an experiment to evaluate the DPs. The findings are currently under review in another outlet. In the third cycle, we implemented a PGS prototype to support the handling of IT ticket processes in our case company. In the following sections, we describe the use case, the design of the PGS, and the ongoing evaluation of the prototype.

2   ITSM ProcessGuide in an Organizational Setting

2.1   Ticket Processing Context

Following the suggestions by the ITIL framework [1], the case company's IT Governance team defined four types of tickets for the business and the IT users: Service Request, Incident, Request for Change, and Non-Standard Demand. These ticket types are used to classify and handle requests from the business and IT departments regarding the offered IT services. A Service Request ticket, for example, is created when a user needs a new Windows account. If there are issues with an application, the employee has to create an Incident ticket. For all these ticket types there exist distinct, specified processes defining how these tickets have to be processed. The company uses an IT tool to support the handling of these processes. This tool implements the four main ticketing processes of the case company, and the employees are required to use the tool and to comply with the defined processes. Nevertheless, the IT Governance team reports that specifically the IT department users have difficulties in handling these processes due to missing process knowledge and difficulties in using the tool. The business departments use the tool only for creating new requests, which is working as intended. Therefore, the focus is on the IT department users. In order to address these issues, the IT Governance team agreed to design and develop a PGS for the ticketing processes to support the IT departments.

2.2   Prototype Design

Based on our prior research, PGS should base on three theory-driven DPs [2]:

- **DP1:** Provide user-requested, pre-defined, and suggestive process guidance based on the monitoring and the analysis of the user's business process context
- **DP2:** Visualize lean and precise process guidance based on process standards integrated into the user's work environment
- **DP3:** Integrate detailed information about process standards and required process resources into the provided process guidance individually adapted to the user

For the implementation of the new PGS, we used the six Design Decisions (DDs) from the first PGS prototype [2] as a baseline, but modified them and added new DDs in order to develop the PGS for its intended purpose. In order to realize the PGS in the case company, we applied the following approach: First, we discussed the intended system and process context with the IT Governance team in two workshops. In the first workshop, we presented the existing DPs, DDs and the PGS prototype. Next, the IT Governance team explained the ticket processes and the used ticket tool. As a result, we agreed that the adapted PGS needs to be accessible from the rich client and the web client of the ticket tool. Therefore, we decided to develop a web-based PGS (DP2). The integration of the PGS into the ticket system is done by realizing a help button which opens the web-based PGS and passes all required process context information in the URL (DP1). As the ticket processes are very complex and broad, we decided to display only a subset of the whole process to the user. The PGS shows the current process status and the subsequent mandatory and optional process steps (DP2). In addition, a simplified overview of the overall process is visualized (DP2). For each process step, the PGS provides detailed information and – if required – images or links to documents or other applications (DP3). In the second workshop, we presented the developed PGS to the IT Governance team and discussed some minor changes in the layout and the backend of the PGS. **Fig. 1** shows the developed PGS and highlights the main features with respect to the DPs:

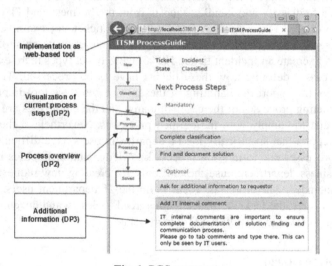

Fig. 1. PGS prototype

2.3   ITSM ProcessGuide Use Cases

The developed ITSM ProcessGuide serves for two main use cases. On the one hand, the provision of the process guidance as described and depicted in the previous section forms the primary use case of the system. On the other hand, the PGS instantiation also supports the long-term evaluation of our PGS by realizing two functionalities: First,

ITSM ProcessGuide gathers direct feedback from its users. In order to do so, the PGS is able to show a link to the feedback module (see **Fig. 2**). Within this module, the user is asked four questions addressing the usefulness of the provided information and the ITSM ProcessGuide related to the DPs.

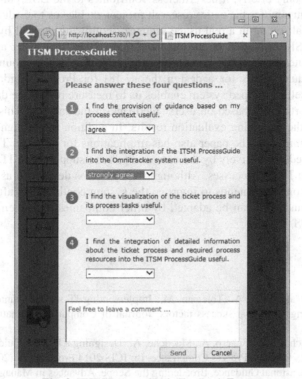

Fig. 2. ITSM ProcessGuide Feedback Feature

Second, the system is logging usage data providing us information about the anonymized user, the current ticket, the application of the PGS, and the kind of requested information.

2.4   Real-World Evaluation of the Prototype

The ITSM ProcessGuide is evaluated in a longitudinal manner. In addition to the objectively measured data gathered by the system, we are collecting user feedback within three surveys (three months before go-live, directly after go-live, and three months after go-live). This will enable us to analyze the users' feedback data based on self-reported perceptions in combination with objective usage data gathered by the system itself. We plan to combine all data sources in order to evaluate whether the ITSM ProcessGuide has an effect on users' process execution and process model understanding of the four ticket processes.

3   Conclusion

This paper reports the problem statement, the design and implementation of a PGS instantiation of our ongoing DSR project. Although the paper describes the artifact and its features only briefly, it nevertheless contributes to the DSR community. Having our case company for the entire research project enables us to evaluate our DPs in an organizational setting in a real usage scenario. Following the call by Peffers et al. [7] for more DSR evaluation in an organizational setting, this paper and the overall project contributes to the DSR community by proposing theory-grounded and multiple times evaluated DPs for a design theory [8] for Process Guidance Systems. Moreover, the self-developed system enables us to measure real usage data rather than purely self-reported data based on users' feedback in the surveys. This will enhance the validity of the upcoming evaluation results. In addition to the high relevance for the research community, the paper also has implications for practice. The ITSM ProcessGuide is used productively by the case company to support their IT worker in the execution of the ITSM processes. Although the system is developed as an evaluation prototype, the company intends to improve the system continuously after the evaluation. The DPs and DDs can be adapted by other companies to implement their own version of a PGS.

References

1. Tan, W.-G., Cater-Steel, A., Toleman, M.: Implementing IT service management: a case study focussing on critical success factors. Journal of Computer Information Systems 50, 1–12 (2009)
2. Morana, S., Schacht, S., Scherp, A., Maedche, A.: Designing a Process Guidance System to Support User's Business Process Compliance. In: ICIS 2014 Proceedings (2014)
3. Silver, M.: Decisional Guidance. Broadening the Scope. Advances in Management Information Systems 6, 90–119 (2006)
4. Gregor, S., Benbasat, I.: Explanations from Intelligent Systems: Theoretical Foundations and Implications for Practice. MIS Quarterly 23, 497–530 (1999)
5. Todd, P., Benbasat, I.: An Experimental Investigation of the Impact of Computer Based Decision Aids on Decision Making Strategies. Information Systems Research 2, 87–115 (1991)
6. Kuechler, B., Vaishnavi, V.: On theory development in design science research: anatomy of a research project. Eur. J. Inf. Syst. 17, 489–504 (2008)
7. Peffers, K., Rothenberger, M., Tuunanen, T., Vaezi, R.: Design Science Research Evaluation. In: Hutchison, D., et al. (eds.) Design Science Research in Information Systems. LNCS, vol. 7286, pp. 398–410. Springer, Heidelberg (2012)
8. Gregor, S.: The nature of theory in information systems. MIS Q 30, 611–642 (2006)

Short Papers

IS Success Awareness in Community-Oriented Design Science Research

Dominik Renzel[✉], Ralf Klamma, and Matthias Jarke

Advanced Community Information Systems (ACIS) Group
Chair of Computer Science 5, RWTH Aachen University
Ahornstr. 55, 52056 Aachen, Germany
{renzel,klamma,jarke}@dbis.rwth-aachen.de

Abstract. Design efforts on innovative IS artifacts are increasingly taking place in agile, small, and specialized long-tail communities supported by academic research. Long-tail communities need to reflect and develop awareness for the success of *community-specific IS (CIS)* artifacts in their particular practice context in an ongoing manner. In *community-oriented DSR*, researchers participate as active community members contributing *CIS success awareness* with the help of *CIS success models* resulting from ongoing CIS evaluation. However, CIS success awareness is challenging to achieve compared to organizational IS due to diversity, dynamicity, informal structures and permeable boundaries. In this paper, we emphasize the benefits of ongoing CIS success awareness with the help of custom-tailored CIS success models in community-oriented DSR contexts. We demonstrate our approach in a longitudinal case study of designing and evaluating therapeutic tools in an aphasia community.

1 Introduction

People naturally organize in communities around particular interests, practices, and goals. Governed by power-law distributions, a large number of agile, small, and specialized *communities of practice (CoP)* [23] in the distribution's *long tail* enable the current innovation culture shift from mass markets to millions of niches [1]. Continuous innovation efforts are important drivers to community sustainability and long-term success [23,18]. Modern ICT fosters the pervasive online organization, communication and collaboration of such CoP in *community information systems (CIS)*. Piloting innovative CIS artifact inventions, exaptations or improvements for long-tail CoP qualifies for academic DSR research [13]. *Community-oriented DSR* conceives the researcher as active community member contributing *CIS success awareness* as a result of ongoing community evaluation and *reflection* on CIS quality and impact [12].

In this paper, we contribute a perspective of DSR evaluation in long-tail community contexts, focusing on the researcher's role of contributing CIS success awareness with the help of *CIS success models*. To this respect, we contribute a long-tail community specific view on CIS success awareness to the body of DSR knowledge in contrast to organizational views on IS success predominant in IS

B. Donnellan et al. (Eds.): DESRIST 2015, LNCS 9073, pp. 413–420, 2015.
DOI: 10.1007/978-3-319-18714-3_33

and DSR literature. In Section 2, we discuss CIS success awareness as important prerequisite to community reflection contributed by community-oriented DSR researchers. In Section 3, we present a collection of principles specific to CIS success modeling in long-tail community contexts. In Section 4, we demonstrate the benefits of CIS success modeling and the resulting awareness in a long term case study of developing and evaluating the therapeutic tool SOCRATES in an aphasia community with patients and researchers as stakeholders.

2   CIS Success Awareness in Community-Oriented DSR

CIS success awareness is a necessary prerequisite for reflecting overall community success in presence of CIS artifacts supporting community practice. Only with ongoing awareness for CIS success in terms of quality and impact[12], long-tail communities can systematically guide the design of innovative CIS artifacts. IS success is already a highly complex and context-dependent construct, established by multiple factors in various dimensions [7,8]. Achieving CIS success awareness is even more challenging in long-tail community contexts due to inherent *diversity* in terms of domains, practices, and goals; *dynamicity* in terms of community life cycles [14]; *informal structures* involving multiple stakeholder perspectives [7,3]; and *permeable boundaries* given by individuals' membership in multiple communities. In contrast to business organizations, economic success is often of secondary importance in long-tail community contexts. Communities rather require multiple holistic stakeholder views on CIS success (beyond economic benefits), capturing human [3,2,12], technical [9] and community-specific [16] factors. We argue that a general model of CIS success can thus not exist. Instead, communities must be enabled to continuously explore, validate, refine, and share CIS success models relevant to specific practice and employed CIS artifacts. As such tasks are rooted in scientific work, researchers can make valuable contributions to ongoing CIS success awareness with the help of CIS success models in a similar fashion as actionable real-time business intelligence for data-driven businesses [5]. Given that CIS are inherently socio-technical systems, CIS success modeling must rather pursue naturalistic evaluation approaches focusing on efficiency and internal validity in real-life community practice than on strongest rigor in terms of repeatability [22], which is inherently challenging to achieve across diverse community contexts.

3   CIS Success Modeling as Formative Index Construction

Communities are mainly interested in the characteristics *defining* CIS success. Thus, CIS success is efficiently modeled as multi-dimensional formative index [12,15] using formative index construction methods [11,10,15]. Conceptually, we start with a sufficiently generic *CIS success model template* (cf. Figure 1) and successively populate its dimensions with factors and measures relevant for the CIS artifact and community context under consideration. As structural template, we deliberately employ a modification of the IS-Impact model accounting

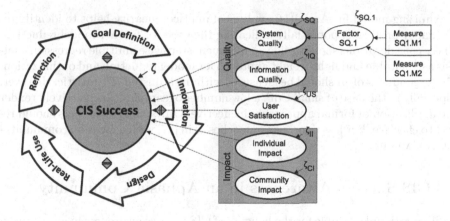

Fig. 1. CIS success model as central means for producing CIS success awareness

for system and information quality, user satisfaction, and impacts for individual members and the community as a whole. CIS success models act as central means for producing ongoing CIS success awareness during building and evaluating CIS artifacts. Starting with the formulation of non-functional requirements for a CIS artifact and continued during the whole design process, individual factors and their determining data-derived measures derived are assigned to the respective conceptually fitting model dimensions. Each CIS success model thereby composes survey items and usage data-based metrics, aggregated in a given community context and for a given CIS artifact. The presence of a mandatory overall CIS success indicator in any model enables correlation and regression analysis between multiple independent success factors and the single dependent variable *overall success*.

Success factors should be actionable and driven by community stakeholder goals, as widely agreed in practical business intelligence [5]. In general, CIS success models should balance parsimony and completeness [4], since *"[formative] index construction discourages redundancy among indicators"* [10]. For the collection of data driving CIS success models, we recommend a mixed-method approach governed by the principle of *"observe, where possible; only survey, where inevitable"*, thus contributing to unobtrusiveness and the avoidance of excessive evaluation overhead and bias in a naturalistic community context. Data collection should not substantially interfere with actual community practice to avoid evaluation entry barriers perceived by community members. Observational machine-collected CIS usage data should be preferred given their inherent objectiveness [9]. Survey data should be collected in repeated short online surveys administered to community members. Any CIS success model should make use of rigorously validated constructs, where possible [12]. However, community-specific constructs are often not covered by the literature. CIS success modeling thus requires the differential application and combination of established and new constructs [21]. This necessity should not be seen as detrimental to model quality. Any candidate CIS success model should minimize the number of model elements, while at the same time maximizing model fit. An initial analysis of multicollinearity helps to identify redundancy problems, potentially indicating the need for further model reduction. These considerations should guide a subsequent step-wise multiple regression analysis as a suitable and light-weight approach for model reduction and optimization. Model goodness-of-fit should be measured with the adjusted R^2 statistic. However, especially in the case of small CoP, a low number of samples can effectively render the application of formal approaches ineffective. Only then researchers should resort to effective, but less rigorous approaches as in [17] with a focus on community-internal validity.

4   CIS Success Awareness in an Aphasia Community

As illustrational example for the benefits of CIS success awareness in community-oriented DSR, we present a longitudinal study of designing a therapy tool in a German aphasia therapy community over almost a decade. Aphasia [6] results from lesions in the left brain hemisphere responsible for language-related tasks, thus causing impairments in speaking, understanding, writing and reading. The community consisted of 200 aphasia patients as well as therapists, linguists and computer scientists, distributed across Germany. Primary goal was the design of SOCRATES, an online chat platform for the effective and efficient support of ongoing aphasia therapy.

4.1   Designing the SOCRATES Chat Tool

As a supplement to the limited availability of physical therapy sessions in medical institutions, the community designed SOCRATES as a chat tool custom-tailored to conversation training in aphasia therapy [20]. In case of difficulties, patients could ask for in-conversation help by peers and therapists in real-time. Therapists had access to conversation transcripts for in-depth discourse analysis of aphasia patient communication as part of their researh. Although SOCRATES was found to effectively supplement aphasia therapy, the evaluation revealed several issues. Patients reported cognitive overload regarding user interface complexity and fast-paced conversations with more than one partner. In particular, the in-conversation help by peers and therapists was found problematic. Peers and therapists were often not online at the same time or able to assist. Aphasia patients conceived survey completion as painful exercise, effectively leading to frequent drop-outs from evaluation activities. For subsequent evaluations, survey overhead should be avoided and replaced by measures derived from SOCRATES usage data. The community derived concrete requirements from these goals for a next version of SOCRATES: *(R1) provision of automated patient help in absence of therapists; (R2) massively reduced user interface complexity;.* In order to provide CIS success awareness, the researcher team employed the methods and principles from Section 3.

To realize *R1*, community developers designed an automated word completion module available in any SOCRATES chat session. To realize *R2*, community developers followed a rapid UI prototyping approach. Complex overloaded UIs were known to induce a pathological lock state of repeated uncontrolled clicking on arbitrary UI elements. Central design effort was thus to reduce UI complexity to the barest minimum possible. The final prototype only included a conversation window, a text input field, a list of chat partners and a word completion list. The research team developed and employed a CIS success model specific to the aphasia community context to evaluate the CIS success of SOCRATES in supporting aphasia therapy.

4.2   Evaluation with SOCRATES CIS Success Model

The improved SOCRATES chat tool was evaluated in therapy sessions and informal remote communication with over 200 aphasia patients. We collected usage data including timestamped conversation transcripts on the keystroke-level, interactions with the word prediction module and related technical metadata. As part of the ongoing evaluation in community-based DSR, we posed the research question of how to measure CIS success for SOCRATES in a widely unobtrusive manner to avoid cognitive overload, frustration and drop-outs on aphasia patient side. As such, our case study is an extreme case in terms of anticipating drop-outs as usual consequence of excessively obtrusive evaluation overhead.

For an initial exploration of CIS success factors and indicators relevant in the aphasia context and for SOCRATES in particular, therapists, linguists and computer scientists defined an initial a-priori CIS success model, based on the structural template model in Figure 1. The selection of factors and indicators was grounded in UX theory, statistical discourse analysis and information retrieval, but sometimes required strong simplifications, given aphasia-caused patient impairments. Guided by requirements R1 and R2, quality and impact factors of the SOCRATES CIS success model focused on UI complexity and word prediction. Impact factors mainly reflected direct and indirect therapy success. Quality factors regarding user interface complexity could not build upon validated user experience constructs, since these were not designed for evaluation with aphasia patients. Instead, the research team had to include strongly simplified survey items. Factors and indicators on direct therapy success were computable from usage data (e.g. increase in words/sentences typed, decrease in typing errors, increase in conversations held, increase in contacts). Indirect therapy success in terms of achieving social integration as indicator for community impact was derivable from usage data by analyzing contact relationships over time.

The a-priori SOCRATES CIS success model included 76 potential usage data-derived measures and additional 14 five-level Likert items for yet missing, however relevant subjective factors, that were not derivable from usage data. For ongoing quality measurements of the word prediction module, we included measures such as *average hit rate (HR)*, *average number of keystrokes until prediction (KUP)* and *keystroke-saving rate (KSR)*. The constant awareness of these measures helped to tune the system to an HR of 91% with a low KUP of 1.5 and a good KSR of 60%. In the other direction, prototype development also had direct influences on the ongoing CIS success model building process. In particular the step-wise reduction in UI complexity implied a reduction in feature-richness, in richness and amount of available usage data and finally in the extent of derivable CIS success measures. After the final UI complexity reduction step, the previously 76 potential usage data-derived measures in the a-priori model were reduced to only nine measures.

The resulting SOCRATES CIS success model was implemented in the ongoing evaluation of the tool with aphasia patients, including the automated collection of usage data. In the first weeks after deployment, patients used word prediction in the anticipated manner, i.e. auto-completing word prefixes. However, usage data-based measures revealed that with word prediction the delay between patient's key presses unexpectedly increased. Patients reported that word candidate lists presented immediately after a key press irritated them. and thus requested a five seconds delay. With such a delay, we could effectively solve the issue. Weeks later, usage data and our a-priori success model revealed word prediction being used in an unanticipated manner. Subjects first scanned the word completion list and - instead of using auto-completion - completed typing the words on their own. Word prediction was rather used as learning tool to train correct spelling instead of a convenience function to type faster. The early discovery of such unanticipated consequences is essential for the guided emergence of CIS [19]. In our case, the availability of a CIS success model, including respective indicators computed from conversation transcripts made unanticipated use visible in near real-time, in contrast to survey-based assessment.

Most of the aphasia patients had decided to continue using SOCRATES, but only few committed to surveys, being painful tasks for aphasia patients. Although plenty of valuable usage data was recorded, the lack in survey data rendered a validation using regression analysis ineffective. Instead, we validated the model in collaboration with all therapists and a small group of patients as in [17]. The resulting model is depicted in Figure 2. We observe, that three of the six measures in the model could be purely derived from usage data, thus effectively lowering evaluation overhead and bias. We furthermore observe that none of the community impact factors from the a-priori model were sufficiently

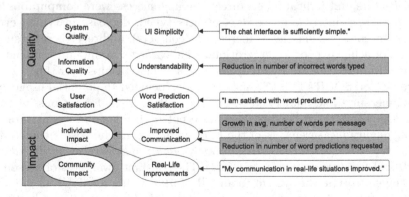

Fig. 2. The final SOCRATES CIS success model

significant to be retained in the final SOCRATES CIS success model. The final model was found to capture the most important success factors of SOCRATES for the aphasia community.

5 Conclusions

In this paper, we discussed DSR in the context of designing and evaluating CIS artifacts for long tail Communities of Practice in comparison to DSR in organizational contexts. In particular, we emphasized the role of researchers in community-oriented DSR with strong focus on participation instead of separating research and practice. This participation is a symbiotic joint enterprise of mutual efforts, as researchers gain access to the innovation potential of communities, while communities profit from the researchers' contribution of CIS success awareness. We discussed the benefits of ongoing CIS success awareness during the whole community life-cycle, mediated by community-specific CIS success models. With a focus on evaluation, we contributed practical guidelines for modeling CIS success in long-tail community contexts as multi-dimensional formative index. Finally, we demonstrated the application of our community-oriented DSR approach on the example of SOCRATES, a chat tool artifact supporting therapy in a German aphasia community. With our contribution, we address researchers and long-tail communities to make use of the symbiotic effects in joint community-oriented DSR. Community-based DSR should help communities to build and evolve their own awareness for CIS success to support ongoing learning and to sustain long-term success.

Acknowledgement. This research was supported by the European Commission in the 7th Framework Programme project *Learning Layers*, grant no. 318209.

References

1. Anderson, C.: The Long Tail: Why the Future of Business is Selling Less of More. Hyperion, New York (2006)
2. Ballantine, J., Bonner, M., Levy, M., Martin, A., Munro, I., Powell, P.L.: The 3-D Model of Information Systems Success: the Search for the Dependent Variable Continues. Information Resources Management Journal 9(4), 5–14 (1996)
3. Brynjolfsson, E.: The Productivity Paradox of Information Technology. Communications of the ACM 36(12), 66–77 (1993)
4. Burton-Jones, A., Straub, D.W.: Reconceptualizing System Usage: An Approach and Empirical Test. Information Systems Research 17(3), 228–246 (2006)
5. Chaudhuri, S., Dayal, U., Narasayya, V.: An Overview of Business Intelligence Technology. Communications of the ACM 54(8), 88–98 (2011)
6. Damasio, A.R.: Aphasia. New England Journal of Medicine 326(8), 531–539 (1992)
7. Delone, W.H., McLean, E.R.: Information Systems Success: The Quest for the Dependent Variable. Information Systems Research 3(1), 60–95 (1992)

8. Delone, W.H., McLean, E.R., Sedera, D.: Future of Information Systems Success: Opportunities and Challenges. In: Topi, H., Tucker, A. (eds.) Computing Handbook, 3rd edn. Information Systems and Information Technology, pp. 70: 1–19. CRC Press (2014)

9. Devaraj, S., Kohli, R.: Performance Impacts of Information Technology: Is Actual Usage the Missing Link? Management Science 49(3), 273–289 (2003)

10. Diamantopoulos, A., Siguaw, J.A.: Formative Versus Reflective Indicators in Organizational Measure Development: A Comparison and Empirical Illustration. British Journal of Management 17(4), 263–282 (2006)

11. Diamantopoulos, A., Winklhofer, H.M.: Index Construction with Formative Indicators: An Alternative to Scale Development. Journal of Marketing Research 38(2), 269–277 (2001)

12. Gable, G.G., Sedera, D., Chan, T.: Re-conceptualizing Information System Success: the IS-Impact Measurement Model. Journal of the Association of Information Systems 9(7), 377–408 (2008)

13. Gregor, S., Hevner, A.R.: Positioning and Presenting Design Science Research for Maximum Impact. MIS Quarterly 37(2), 337–355 (2013)

14. Iriberri, A., Leroy, G.: A Life-Cycle Perspective on Online Community Success. ACM Computing Surveys 41(2), 1–29 (2009)

15. Jarvis, C.B., Mackenzie, S.B., Podsakoff, P.M.: A Critical Review of Construct Indicators and Measurement Model Misspecication in Marketing and Consumer Research. Journal of Consumer Research 30, 199–218 (2003)

16. Leimeister, J.M., Sidiras, P., Krcmar, H.: Success Factors of Virtual Communities from the Perspective of Members and Operators: An Empirical Study. In: HICSS 2004: Proceedings of the 37th Annual Hawaii International Conference on System Sciences (HICSS 2004) - Track 7, p. 70194–1. IEEE Computer Society, Washington, DC (2004)

17. Moore, G.C., Benbasat, I.: Development of an Instrument to Measure the Perceptions of Adopting an Information Technology Innovation. Information Systems Research 2(3), 192–222 (1991)

18. Mustaquim, M.M., Nyström, T.: Designing Information Systems for Sustainability – The Role of Universal Design and Open Innovation. In: Tremblay, M.C., VanderMeer, D., Rothenberger, M., Gupta, A., Yoon, V. (eds.) DESRIST 2014. LNCS, vol. 8463, pp. 1–16. Springer, Heidelberg (2014)

19. Sein, M.K., Henfridsson, O., Purao, S., Rossi, M., Lindgren, R.: Action Design Research. MIS Quarterly 35(1), 37–56 (2011)

20. Spaniol, M., Springer, L., Klamma, R., Jarke, M.: SOCRATES: Barrier Free Communities of Aphasics on the Internet. In: Miesenberger, K., Klaus, J., Zagler, W.L., Burger, D. (eds.) ICCHP 2004. LNCS, vol. 3118, pp. 1024–1031. Springer, Heidelberg (2004)

21. Straub, D.W., Hoffman, D.L., Weber, B.W., Steinfield, C.: Measuring e-Commerce in Net-Enabled Organizations: An Introduction to the Special Issue. Information Systems Research 13(2), 115–124 (2002)

22. Venable, J., Pries-Heje, J., Baskerville, R.: A Comprehensive Framework for Evaluation in Design Science Research. In: Peffers, K., Rothenberger, M., Kuechler, B. (eds.) DESRIST 2012. LNCS, vol. 7286, pp. 423–438. Springer, Heidelberg (2012)

23. Wenger, E.: Communities of Practice: Learning, Meaning, and Identity. Learning in Doing. Cambridge University Press, Cambridge (1998)

Decision Support for Succession Management Conferences Using Mobile Applications – Results from the 3rd Iteration of a Design Science Research Project

Christian Tornack[✉], Björn Pilarski, and Matthias Schumann

Chair of Application Systems and E-Business, Georg-August-University Göttingen,
Göttingen, Germany
{ctornac1,bpilars,mschuma1}@uni-goettingen.de

Abstract. Although succession management can be supported through DSS, the final decision regarding succession candidates is made by managers and HR professionals within conferences. In practice, conferences are supported by paper-based information about employees, positions, and development measures. This approach has two major drawbacks: First, additional effort is needed, as all information must be prepared prior to conference. Second, additional information isn't available, if previously unconsidered candidates were suggested so that decisions are based on incomplete information. Our goal is to address these problems by developing a mobile application for tablet PCs which supports succession decisions by distributing necessary information. We identify requirements for such applications based on theoretical and practical insights, which we transform into design principles. Finally, these principles inform the construction of an instantiation that can support succession conferences.

Keywords: Design science research · Succession management conference

1   Introduction

"If you are in a discussion and have a portfolio of potential successors, it is likely that the participants have different knowledge about them. [...] I can imagine that we are going to use mobile applications in future conferences to reduce the amount of paper." (Exp 20; Quote from empirical study)

In order to improve efficiency and effectiveness of their succession management, organizations use decision support systems (DSS) to identify succession candidates and visualize domino effects of succession decisions [1, 2]. However, our prior research reveals that final decisions regarding succession candidates (**decision 1**), development measures for candidates (**decision 2**), and priority of successions (**decision 3**) are made by managers and HR professionals in a conference setting. Thus, decisions based on single opinions can be avoided. But these decisions entail the problem (see introductory quote) that managers and HR professionals usually have different knowledge regarding succession candidates (e. g. manager A knows his subordinates better than manager B's), development measures, and upcoming vacancies. Currently, there are two options: First, every manager has only his prior information and must rely on the

© Springer International Publishing Switzerland 2015
B. Donnellan et al. (Eds.): DESRIST 2015, LNCS 9073, pp. 421–429, 2015.
DOI: 10.1007/978-3-319-18714-3_34

opinion of managers who know the candidates. This can lead to wrong decisions as candidates cannot be compared objectively. Second, potential candidates and development measures must be named prior to the conference so that the required information can be printed on paper for all conference participants. Thus, the participants need an opportunity to access the required information during the conferences. Since the use of mobile devices in meetings is more suitable than the use of laptops or stationary systems [3, 4] and there is no existing literature regarding the design of mobile succession management applications, our goal is to examine the design of such an application for tablet PCs to support conferences. Hence, we ask:

RQ1: How should a mobile application be designed that supports decision making in succession management conferences?

Based on the derived design principles, we develop a mockup design of such a mobile application to verify the feasibility of the principles. Thus, we ask:

RQ2: How can a mobile application be implemented that supports decision making in succession management conferences?

The paper is organized as follows: Section 2 contains basics and related research for succession management. Afterwards, the research design is outlined in section 3 before design principles for mobile succession management applications are derived in section 4. Section 5 entails a mockup design of such a mobile application. Subsequently, we discuss our findings and reveal the contributions of our work in section 6.

2   Background

We define **succession management** as a systematic process with which re-staffing can be ensured so that positions in an organization are refilled with qualified employees prior to or shortly after a vacancy appears [2, 5]. Hence, succession plans are created (e. g. by DSS) and finalized by managers and HR professionals in conferences. *Before such conferences*, information about key positions and employee profiles must be gathered [5, 6] so that succession candidates can be suggested based on their competences and position requirements [2]. *During the conferences*, these suggestions and related information are discussed to find the most suitable candidates and finally decide, who should be entailed in succession plans (**decision 1**) [5–7]. Thereby, it must be avoided that the same employees are considered for almost every position [2]. Afterwards, these succession plans are utilized to identify gaps between position requirements and competences of the succession candidates [7] and decisions about individual development measures are made (**decision 2**) [7]. Beyond that, conference participants also discuss upcoming vacancies to make decisions regarding the priority of the succession of these positions (**decision 3**) [8]. *Subsequent to the conferences*, the development of succession candidates takes place and the succession plans are employed in the selection of successors for upcoming vacancies [5].

The results of a previous literature review show that there is only few research examining succession management conferences [7, 8]. Furthermore, there is some research regarding IS support of succession management [1, 2], but the knowledge base lacks of requirements and design principles for IS support of the conferences. The use of mobile applications (i. e. applications on smart phones or tablet PCs) to support meetings is also only partially covered in the existing literature [3, 4]. Scholars revealed that interaction between meeting attendees was enhanced [4] and that tablet based mobile applications depict a "social medium rather than [a] barrier" (p. 12) compared to the use of laptops in those meetings [3], which other studies found to be disturbing [9]. Hence, mobile applications can be a way to use technologies for displaying information and enhancing interaction without being considered to be rude [4]. However, only few articles cover the design of applications for meeting support [10, 11]. Thus, we transform the design principles for stationary succession management systems [2] and adapt them to the context of succession conferences.

3   Research Design and Previous Research

We use design science (DSR) [12] to structure our research and thus consider both, rigor and relevance. Within the first two parts of our research (see Figure 1) [2], we went through the whole DSR methodology process [12] (**1-6**) and provided empirically verified design principles (**6**) [2].

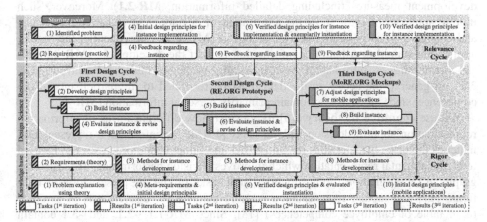

Fig. 1. The research design (based on [2])

Within the evaluation of the stationary system RE.ORG (**6**), the decision problems of HR conferences (see section 1) were identified so that we conduct a third iteration [13] which again starts with the suggestion step (**7**) and consists of three parts: First, we transfer the previously developed design principles [2] to the context of succession conferences to derive new meta-requirements and adapt them to the context of mobile applications by using cognitive fit theory [14]. Second, we use an exploratory interview study to ensure the relevance and to complement the meta-requirements from a practitioner's view. We then derive design principles for mobile succession management applications which we employ to develop a mock-up design (development step; **8**), since it constitutes the simplest type of instantiation while all physical aspects of the final system are entailed [13]. Finally, the instantiation is descriptively evaluated (**9**) before we reveal the contribution of our work in the conclusion (**10**).

4   Deduction of Design Principles

4.1   Meta-Requirements from Decision Perspective

The mobile succession management application should be used in conjunction with a stationary application and focus on decisions that are relevant for conferences. Based on [2], we deduce the following requirements: For *decision 1*, the mobile application must provide employee information (e. g. competences) and position information (e. g. requirements; **Meta-Requirement-1.1**) for the succession plans, which are prepared prior of the conference. To support the consideration of new suggestions, the mobile application should be able to determine the fit of employee profiles and position requirements (**MR-1.2**). Also, succession plans should be adjustable (add/remove employees and change the order) before they are finalized (**MR-1.3**). For *decision 2*, a mobile succession management application should provide suggestions for suitable development measures (including detailed information; **MR-2.1**). Moreover, such mobile applications must allow the adjustment of development plans (add measures and change the order) before they are finalized (**MR-2.2**). Subsequently, the mobile application should distribute this information to start the development (**MR-2.3**). To support *decision 3,* information about upcoming vacancies must be displayed (**MR-3.1**). In general, the access to the data must be restricted to the participants of the conference, since all decisions contain primarily personal information (**MR-4**).

We use **cognitive fit theory** [15] to consider how different forms of information representation support decision making tasks [15]. If the information representation matches the task characteristics (cognitive fit), the same mental processes can be used to create a mental representation which improves decision performance [16]. Thereby, graphical representation forms support spatial tasks (allow the preservation of relations) [17] and tabular representation is more suitable for discrete sets of symbols (e. g. table of employee competences) [18]. Since **MR-1.1, -2.1,** and **-3.1** contain primarily detailed (discrete) information, the representation should be in tabular form, in order to allow an easy comparison. Furthermore, the small screens of mobile devices can only display one or two employee profiles so that a graphical overview of suitable candidates is required (order of candidates; **MR-1.1**). Second, such mobile applications should display suitable development measures for candidates in a graphical overview, to display their connection to competence gaps (**MR-2.1**).

4.2   Meta-Requirements from Exploratory Interviews

In order to complete the requirements for IS support of these conferences, we performed semi-structured, exploratory interviews [19]. Thereby, we conducted interviews with 24 experts (HR professionals like HR division heads or succession management process managers) from 21 organizations (ranging from 1,000 to more than 100,000 employees).

The interviews were conducted by two interviewers via phone and lasted between 30 and 60 minutes. All interviews were recorded on tape, constantly transcribed and translated using contextual comparison [20], and coded.

The results of the interview study reveal the relevance of such conferences, since 15 of 21 organizations use them for the finalization of decisions. Thereby, the experts verified the meta-requirements **MR-1.1**, **MR-1.2**, **MR-1.3**, **MR-2.1**, **MR-2.2**, **MR-2.3**, **MR-3.1**, and **MR-4** (see Table 1) and identified one additional functional requirement: The selection of suitable candidates *(decision 1)* requires further support through an overview of all final succession plans to identify gaps (i. e. positions without successors; Exp 17; new **MR-1.4**). To achieve cognitive fit, the succession plans should be represented in graphical form to illustrate relationships in the data [15].

Table 1. Meta-requirements for mobile succession management applications

	Meta-Requirement	Exemplarily Quotes
decision 1	**MR-1.1** Possibility to access candidate information (competences, potential assessment, curriculum vitae) and positions requirements in detail (tabular form) and in an overview of suitable candidates for positions (graphical form)	*„There are conferences, where managers and HR professionals discuss suggested succession candidates. Thereby, supervisors get feedback regarding their suggestions. Thus, decisions are based on the appreciation of a group and not only a single person." (Exp 14)*
	MR-1.2 Possibility to match candidates and positions and determine the positions for which an employee is listed as succession candidate (tabular form)	*„There are HRD conferences, where managers and HR professionals discuss succession planning. Which employees match the requirements of the position?" (Exp 20)*
	MR-1.3 Possibility to adjust succession plans (add, remove and change order of candidates) and save the final plans	*"Based on the discussion [...], we change succession plans. Some candidates don't match and other candidates were suggested. Results of this conference are final succession plans." (Exp 1)*
	MR-1.4 Possibility to display an overview of all final succession plans (graphical)	*"We look at positions of a division in order to identify gaps in the succession plans so that we can address them, e. g. through external recruiting." (Exp 17)*
decision 2	**MR-2.1** Possibility to access information about development measures in detail (tabular form) and suitable development measures in an overview (graphical form)	*"At the end of these conferences, there are discussions about general development measures for whole areas of a division." (Exp 20)*
	MR-2.2 Possibility to adjust development plans (add, remove, or change order of measures) and save the final plans	*"We also discuss possible development measures based on competence gaps of candidates in order to create a development plan for the next year." (Exp 21)*
	MR-2.3 Possibility to provide information to start the development of candidates immediately	*"It is important that the results, the selected development measures, are conducted immediately." (Exp 7)*
decision 3	**MR-3.1** Possibility to access information about upcoming vacancies (date, actual incumbent, succession plan for this position; tabular form)	*„Another subject of the conferences is upcoming vacancies, which are discussed by the managers and HR professionals. For example, if the plan for this position entails gaps." (Exp 20)*
All	**MR-4** Possibility to restrict the access to employee information for participants	*"The access must be restricted so that the participants can't access all employees." (Exp 24)*

4.3   Design Principles for Mobile Succession Management Applications

From the meta-requirements, we deduce seven design principles for mobile succession management applications (see Table 2). They focus on conditions, where the assignment of positions and employees is complex so that manual effort and wrong decisions can cause great costs. We presume that a competence catalog with relations to employees, positions (requirements), and development measures exists.

Table 2. Design principles for mobile succession management applications

Design principles and propositions for mobile application
MR-1.1 ➜ **Design principle (DP)-1.** Provide functionalities for displaying position requirements (experience and competences) and information about employees (competences, potential assessment, preferences, and curriculum vitae) together (overview: graphical form; in detail: tabular form)
Proposition (P)-1: Providing required position and employee information increases the quality of succession decisions.
MR-1.2 ➜ **DP-2.** Provide functionalities for processing employee profiles and position requirements to determine the fit and for processing the actual succession plans to inform about the number of succession plans, in which a candidate is entailed (tabular form).
P-2: Displaying the fit and common succession candidates increases the efficiency within decision making due to avoided manual effort and quality of succession decisions due to avoided multiple nominations of one candidate.
MR-2.1 ➜ **DP-3.** Provide functionalities to suggest suitable development measures for the competence gaps of succession candidates and to access information about development measures (overview: graphical form; in detail: tabular form).
P-3: Revealing suitable development measures increases the efficiency within decision making due to avoided manual effort and the quality of succession decisions due to provided information about every development measure.
MR-1.3+1.4+2.2 ➜ **DP-4.** Provide functionalities for adding and removing candidates from succession plans and measures from development plans, for changing the order within plans, for saving the final succession and development plans, and displaying an overview of final succession plans.
P-4: Allowing the immediate transfer of discussion results to the application and the look at final succession plans for divisions increase the efficiency due to reduced manual post processing and the quality of succession decisions due to avoided gaps in the succession planning of a division.
MR-2.3 ➜ **DP-5.** Provide functionalities for the immediate distribution of information to managers and HR professionals, when development plans are specified, to start the development of the successors.
P-5: Functionalities for system controlled triggers decrease reaction times of process participants and thus increases the efficiency of the succession management conferences.
MR-3.1 ➜ **DP-6.** Provide functionalities for displaying detailed information about upcoming vacancies (date, actual incumbent, succession plan: tabular form).
P-6: Providing information about upcoming vacancies increase effectiveness of succession preparations.
MR-4. ➜ **DP-7.** Provide functionalities for restricting the access of conference participants so that they can access the functionalities above only for positions in their own area of responsibility (Exception: Employee information from suggested succession candidates from other areas).
P-7: Functionalities for rights within roles increase the quantity of users, which can access information, while ensuring data privacy and thus increase the efficiency within succession management conferences.

5   Instantiation moRE.ORG

Based on the design principles, we developed a mockup design of a mobile succession management application for tablets, which complements the stationary succession management system RE.ORG [2]. The application requires interfaces to the RE.ORG system and the HR master data system. Thereby, we distinguish between the conference chair (responsible manager/HR professional) who can use more functionalities, and conference participants (other managers and HR professionals). Thereby, the access to employee information is restricted to the users own area (except for suggested candidates; *DP-7*). To support decisions about succession candidates (**decision 1**), our instance includes an overview (see Figure 2), which provides information about the position (e. g. actual incumbent and requirements) and aggregated information about succession candidates (*DP-1*). Moreover, HR professionals and managers can access detailed candidate information (Figure 2, A) and compare them (Figure 2, B; *DP-1*). The position requirements always remain on the left side of the application so that a constant comparison with candidate profiles is possible (*DP-1*). The overview also includes an icon that displays the number of positions, for which the employee is succession candidate (Figure 2, C; *DP-2*). For Further information about these positions, the participants can click on the icon (Figure 2, C). Our instance also enables managers and HR professionals to add other employees to their own list (Figure 2, D; *DP-4*) and thereby determine the fit between the requirements and the employee profile (*DP-1*). Subsequently, participants can suggest employees as additional candidates and the conference chair can decide, whether the suggested employees will be available for all participants (Figure 2, E; *DP-4*). At the end of a discussion, the chair can select candidates (Figure 2, F) and save the succession plan (Figure 2, G; *DP-4*). The selection of development measures (**decision 2**) is supported by suggesting suitable development measures for candidates based on their competence gaps (Figure 2, right side; *DP-3*). By clicking on the link (Figure 2, H) detailed information about measures are displayed (Figure 2, I; DP-3). Then, these measures can be discussed, selected (Figure 2, J), and saved as a development plan for each candidate by the chair (Figure 2, K; *DP-4*). Subsequently, the stored information can be distributed to start the development of candidates (*DP-5*). To allow decisions regarding the priority of upcoming vacancies (**decision 3**), information about the date of the vacancy, the actual incumbent, and the succession plan for this position is provided (*DP-5*).

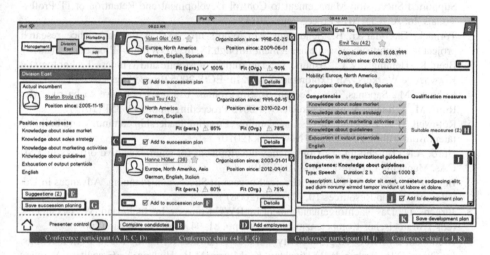

Fig. 2. Overview of succession candidates in MoRE.ORg

6 Discussion and Conclusion

According to the DSR paradigm, we descriptively evaluate our artifact [14]: The decisions regarding succession candidates (*decision 1*) and development measures (*decision 2*) are supported, since the conference participants can access information about positions, employees, and development measures independently via moRE.ORG so that the knowledge base of the participants is enhanced and the decision quality should be increased. Second, decisions regarding upcoming successions (*decision 3*) are supported by providing information about vacancies, which allow the participants to judge the preparation status and initiate corrective actions (if necessary) so that the quality of succession preparation is increased.

Overall, we presented seven design principles for mobile succession management applications (**RQ1**). We verified the feasibility of these principles by developing an instantiation and outlined (see above) how positive effects on decision making are achieved (**RQ2**). The next step in our research is to create an actual prototype which can be empirically evaluated to verify or revise our proposed design principles.

Our research contributes to a domain, which is highly relevant for organizations. We expand the existing knowledge base in the domain of succession management by providing an instantiation (level one), meta-requirements, and design principles (level two) for mobile succession management applications [14]. The design principles can also guide the implementation of such applications in organizations to improve decision quality and efficiency of succession conferences.

References

1. Tornack, C., Pilarski, B., Schumann, M.: How to Avoid Empty Chairs in IT Divisions? IS Supported Succession Management to Control Development and Retention of IT Professionals. In: AMCIS 2014 Proceedings (2014)
2. Tornack, C., Pilarski, B., Schumann, M.: Who's up Next? A design science research project to support succession management through IS. In: ADWI 2014 Proceedings (2014)
3. Breu, K., Hemingway, C., Ashurst, C.: The Impact of Mobile and Wireless Technology on Knowledge Workers: An Exploratory Study. In: ECIS 2005 Proceedings (2005)
4. Böhmer, M., Saponas, T.S., Teevan, J.: Smartphone use does not have to be rude. In: Rohs, M., Schmidt, A. (eds.) Mobile HCI 2013 Proceedings, pp. 342–351 (2013)
5. Rothwell, W.J.: Effective succession planning. Ensuring leadership continuity and building talent from within. AMACOM, New York (2010)
6. Hurd, A.R., Buschbom, T.: Competency development for chief executive officers in YM-CAs. Managing Leisure 15, 96–110 (2010)
7. Barnett, R., Davis, S.: Creating Greater Success in Succession Planning. Advances in Developing Human Resources 10, 721–739 (2008)
8. Jurgens, D.: Das Nachfolgemanagement im RWE-Konzern. In: Jochmann, W., Gechter, S. (eds.) Strategisches Kompetenzmanagement, pp. 81–94. Springer, Berlin (2007)
9. Kleinman, L.: Perceived productivity and the social rules for laptop use in work meetings. In: Olsen, D.R., Arthur, R.B., Hinckley, K., Morris, M.R., Hudson, S., Greenberg, S. (eds.) The 27th International Conference Extended Abstracts, pp. 3895–3900 (2009)
10. Huseman, R.C., Miles, E.W.: Organizational Communication in the Information Age: Implications of Computer-Based Systems. Journal of Management 14, 181–204 (1988)
11. Phillips, L.D.: A theory of requisite decision models. Acta Psychologica 56, 29–48 (1984)
12. Vaishnavi, V., Kuechler, W.: Design science research methods and patterns. Innovating information and communication technology, Boca Raton (2008)
13. Baskerville, R., Pries-Heje, J., Venable, J.: Soft design science methodology. In: Proceedings of the 4th International Conference on Design Science Research in Information Systems and Technology, pp. 1–11 (2009)
14. Gregor, S., Hevner, A.R.: Positioning and presenting design science research for maximum impact. MISQ 37, 337–355 (2013)
15. Vessey, I.: Cognitive Fit: A Theory-Based Analysis of the Graphs Versus Tables Literature. Decision Sciences 22, 219–240 (1991)

16. Sinha, A.P., Vessey, I.: Cognitive fit: An empirical study of recursion and iteration. IIEEE Trans. Software Eng. 18, 368–379 (1992)
17. Larkin, J.H., Simon, H.A.: Why a Diagram is (Sometimes) Worth Ten Thousand Words. Cognitive Science 11, 65–100 (1987)
18. Speier, C.: The influence of information presentation formats on complex task decision-making performance. Int. J. Hum.-Comput. Stud. 64, 1115–1131 (2006)
19. Myers, M.D.: Qualitative research in business & management. Sage, London (2013)
20. Suh, E.E., Kagan, S., Strumpf, N.: Cultural Competence in Qualitative Interview Methods with Asian Immigrants. Journal of Transcultural Nursing 20, 194–201 (2008)

Guidelines for Establishing Instantiation Validity in IT Artifacts: A Survey of IS Research

Roman Lukyanenko[1(✉)], Joerg Evermann[2], and Jeffrey Parsons[2]

[1] College of Business, Florida International University, Miami, FL USA
roman.lukyanenko@fiu.edu
[2] Faculty of Business Administration, Memorial University, St. John's, NL Canada
{jevermann@mun.ca,jeffreyp}@mun.ca

Abstract. The centrality of information technology (IT) artifacts in Information Systems (IS) research makes it important to understand the relationship between artifacts and the theoretical constructs they purport to instantiate. Despite the central role of the IT artifact in IS research, there are no generally accepted principles for establishing *instantiation validity* – the extent to which an artifact is a valid instantiation of a theoretical construct or a manifestation of a design principle. We survey relevant knowledge in IS and identify potential guidelines that may address threats to instantiation validity. The guidelines are intended for researchers and reviewers when using IT artifacts in theory testing and when evaluating design science artifacts.

Keywords: Instantiation validity · IT artifact · Design science research · Methodology

1 Introduction

Information Systems (IS) research routinely conceptualizes properties of IT artifacts as theoretical constructs that impact human behavior of interest, or as manifestations of design principles intended to achieve some outcome. Properties of IT artifacts are central to design science research (DSR) in IS, which develops and evaluates constructs, models, methods, implementations, and design theories.

A common practice in IS research is manipulating features of an IT artifact to evaluate theoretical models. For example, Komiak and Benbasat [1] investigate how "personalization" and "familiarity" affect IT adoption. They selected two existing software systems (recommendation agents) assumed to correspond to different levels of perceived personalization and familiarity. They conducted an experiment demonstrating that different levels of perceived personalization and familiarity engender different levels of intention to adopt. According to Lukyanenko et al. [2], the validity of this conclusion (i.e., that personalization of an IS leads to its increased adoption) "depends critically on whether the chosen artifacts faithfully instantiated the underlying theoretical construct of personalization and levels thereof" (p. 322). Lukyanenko et al. introduce the notion of ***instantiation validity*** (IV) to denote "validity of IT artifacts as instantiations of theoretical constructs" (ibid).

© Springer International Publishing Switzerland 2015
B. Donnellan et al. (Eds.): DESRIST 2015, LNCS 9073, pp. 430–438, 2015.
DOI: 10.1007/978-3-319-18714-3_35

In a similar vein, design science research is concerned with the construction of IT artifacts that manifest certain design principles intended to solve particular problems. In that case, instantiation validity is the extent to which the artifacts are consistent with the design principles. For conciseness, in this paper we intend the phrase "theoretical constructs" to include design principles where appropriate.

Instantiation validity is fundamentally concerned with the relationship between *abstract* theoretical constructs and IT artifacts - *concrete* software systems that are intended to instantiate (levels of) one or more constructs or design principles. IV takes on aspects of internal and construct validity, but the uniqueness of IV that arises from distinctive properties of IT artifacts and characteristics of the IS domain (e.g., relentless technological progress) limits the useful guidance from traditional research on validity [3, 4].

While Lukyanenko et al. [2] discuss IV in the context of IS theory testing, we believe this concept also applies to other types of knowledge contribution in IS research. Instantiation validity plays a role in evaluating design knowledge when this knowledge is used to instantiate properties of an IT artifact. Indeed, Venable et al. [5] note that, in evaluating an artifact for its utility, a researcher also evaluates the design theory that the artifact is based on. Rossi and Sein [6] suggest that evaluation should include assessing the match between an "abstract idea" and the artifact. Venable at al. [5] provide a comprehensive framework for artifact evaluation. Hevner and Chatterjee [7] classify evaluation into analytical modeling, simulation and measurement-based strategies. Of these, simulation (writing software code to mimic behavior of the proposed system) and measurement (e.g., experimentation using human participants and real systems) may result in a "medium shift" when abstract design principles are transformed into concrete forms, [2] thereby creating IV challenges.[1] Design science researchers increasingly call for a more transparent DSR process. Specifically, an evaluation stage has been suggested not only after the artifact is built, but also before and during development [8, 9]. IV can be conceptualized at the core of the design process as it ensures that the design process is transparent and justified.

Further, IV is a challenge for practitioners looking to build systems based on design knowledge. While design knowledge is generated in some specific context, once it is finalized or deemed sufficiently complete [10], researchers strive to generalize beyond the specific context of creation to inform development in other settings. The final product of design theorizing aims to solve some class of real-world problems [11, 12] by virtue of causal impact of artifact properties on features of the environment [13]. Chandra et al. [14] note that IV answers the question of whether a real-world artifact that adopts some design theory "indeed proffers the action described by the design principle" (p. 4046). Similar to theory testing, failure to build an artifact sufficiently similar to the one envisioned by the researcher may result in failure to solve the problem for which the artifact is built. Unless practitioners are aware of IV as a threat, this failure could undermine the **perceived** credibility of design knowledge.

---

[1] Note, analytical modeling may also involve a medium shift if the original design knowledge is expressed in natural language and is transformed into a symbolic representation.

In summary, the need to establish or demonstrate IV arises during: *theory testing*, when IS artifacts are used to manipulate theoretical constructs [2]; *evaluation* of a design science artifact, if the evaluation relies on a concrete instantiation [5, 14]; and the *application* of IS design knowledge by the practitioner community.

Despite the importance of IV, there are no generally accepted principles for establishing and demonstrating it. Lukyanenko et al. [2] call for establishing such principles. This paper attempts to answer this call. We synthesize relevant knowledge accumulated in IS to address the five threats to IV proposed in [2]. A review of IS reveals potentially useful recommendations that can guide researchers, reviewers and practitioners in theory testing, design science theorizing and evaluation and real software development.

2   The Instantiation Validity Problem in IS Research

IS researchers have long emphasized methodological rigor, in which establishing and demonstrating validity plays an important role. Commonly, rigor is demonstrated with respect to validity notions in social sciences (e.g., internal, construct, content, predictive) [3, 15], without specifically considering the validity of the artifact itself [2]. In particular, a seminal paper on the "state-of-the-art" of validation in IS by Boudreau et al. [3] conceptualized validity as internal, content, and construct validity. In the context of DSR rigor, Hevner at al. [11] likewise do not discuss the validity of an IT artifact as embodiment of a construct.

A major approach to validation in IS is to demonstrate validity post hoc using manipulation checks and statistical techniques. The idea of a manipulation check is to ensure that research subjects have perceived the intended manipulation of a theoretical construct [4], i.e. to assess the extent to which they have received the intended experimental treatment. For Boudreau et al. [3] manipulation checks are "critical tests of instrumentation" [i.e., the artifact] (p. 5). Unfortunately, however, manipulation checks can only be used once the system is built – they offer no guidance for developing valid instantiations. This is particularly problematic given the cost of artifact development. Furthermore, when the construct affects "hidden" features, such as an underlying algorithm, a manipulation check based on perceptions may not be possible. Manipulation checks may also "frame" the problem by providing research subjects with cues that lead them to answers they may not otherwise provide.

As using real or realistic software systems is costly (an IV threat [2]), IS research has proposed a number of potentially applicable strategies for pre-development validation. Notably, Benbasat [16] discusses the properties of experimental stimuli under the label "research design" and characterizes a design as faulty when a stimulus does not clearly separate the focal theoretical construct from others. Benbasat [ibid.] suggests that "the major point ... is to first determine precisely on what basis the stimulus materials are to be different" (p. 42) and that "once this is known, it becomes easier to determine if equivalency, except for the stimulus in question, was achieved" (p. 42).

While some research distinguishes between evaluating features of an artifact before and after instantiation [e.g., 5, 17], others, including Sein et al. [18], Eriksson et al.[9]

and Abraham et al. [19] argue for evaluation conducted during development. We adopt the recommendation of concurrent evaluation as it helps to address the threats to IV posed due to high cost of development and artifact complexity.

Another guideline is to re-use existing measurement items or employ standardized items (e.g., [20, 21]) or standardized stimuli (e.g., [22]). Stimuli standardization is less common in IS, but common in reference disciplines, such as psychology (e.g, [22]). While standardization has been popular in survey and experimental research, IT artifacts are frequently modified in response to rapid technological progress (an IV threat [2]), thereby limiting the extent of artifact standardization in IS research.

Another important concept found in IS research is that of traceability of theoretical constructs from more general to more specific ones. The DSR community has proposed approaches to link theoretical propositions from reference theories (known as justificatory knowledge or kernel theories) to design principles [11], recognizing the need to make a given theory and its constructs more concrete if these are to inform the construction of an artifact. While the focus has been on design principles or survey of reference disciplines (e.g., [23]), rather than the implemented artifact and its relationship with the design principles, the recommendation to provide a transparent link between different levels of abstraction apply to the concept of IV.

The long tradition of experimenting and building IT artifacts by IS researchers has produced a number of valuable strategies for both pre-development and post hoc validation of artifacts and measurement items. IS researchers clearly demonstrate awareness of the potential problems with using complex software systems as scientific instruments but, at the same time, lack widely-agreed criteria for the demonstrating and establishing IV. To develop such guidelines , in the next section we apply the suggestions from previous research to specific validity threats introduced in [2].

3   Addressing Threats to Instantiation Validity

In this section, we use the *five-threat IV framework* [2] to develop guidelines for establishing and demonstrating IV based on existing thinking in IS research.

Artifact Cost. The construction of typical IT artifacts is relatively more expensive than survey instruments. As a result, researchers may have the resources to create only a single artifact with limited functionality (e.g., in contrast to multiple measurement items). This limits the ability to control for confounding effects, to demonstrate validity and reliability by comparing multiple implementations, and to test multiple (especially extreme) levels of a construct.

One way of addressing this challenge is to implement features in a flexible, parameterized way. This allows researchers to vary only selected features of the artifact while keeping the rest of the architecture constant. Ideally, these variations are controlled by parameters in the instantiated software itself. For example, researchers interested in the impact of information representation (e.g., tables vs. graphs) may, instead of producing different software systems, produce variations of tables and graphs by parameterizing this construct through software settings that control aspects such as the presence of headers or the presence of row highlights in the artifact.

Additionally, such parameterization addresses the recommendation of traceability from construct to features, in that it can be shown clearly how different levels of a construct affect the relevant features of the artifact [2]. And while such an instantiation cannot demonstrate that each feature represents only one construct, it allows the researcher to keep the remaining design (e.g., data or data model of the information system) constant, thus reducing the confounding influences on the feature.

Reusing existing instantiations is an ideal way to reduce artifact cost. However, a theoretical challenge is that artifacts in IS research are typically constructed for specific research questions, thus limiting their reusability in different circumstances. A pragmatic challenge of reusability is that artifacts created for research are not typically shared in the IS design research community. This issue comprises both legal aspects of licensing, as well as technical aspects of hosting source code or entire projects. To address the former, various types of licenses exist that differ in their degree of permissiveness, such as the GPL, BSD or Apache style licenses. To address the latter, open-source repositories, such as GitHub or SourceForge, exist to host a project. We encourage researchers to avail themselves of these options.

Artifact Instantiation Space. Most IS theories are moderately abstract (mid-range theories [24]). A challenge, therefore, is to account for the consequences of the chosen implementation and ensure that they do not interact with the variables of interest in unpredictable ways. Ideally, this requires a level of theoretical understanding of software construction that we currently do not possess. However, researchers should be able to identify at least some of the theories that relate to features of their artifact, and to explicate possible factors that could influence the artifact's features [25].

Once the relevant constructs are identified, researchers need to trace their effects on the instantiated features of the artifact to identify if, how, and under what conditions they affect the features. For example, a particular user interface button may be placed to enhance personalization, but at the same time the button may also increase complexity of interaction. This can confound any conclusions drawn from the study if it is unclear whether complexity has a causal effect on a dependent variable.

Another way to address the instantiation space is to construct multiple instantiations. If it is difficult to choose one valid instantiation or if there is conflicting theoretical guidance regarding a given property, a researcher can develop multiple artifacts, each corresponding to a different way of instantiating a construct. These different instantiations should behave identically with respect to the study's dependent variable (e.g., see [26]). This may be viewed as similar to convergent validity (all survey items should behave similarly) or predictive validity (valid survey items behave as expected with respect to a criterion variable) in survey research. Additionally, this can show the robustness of a theory to different implementations [24].

Artifact Complexity. In contrast to many simple experimental stimuli (e.g., line drawings [22]) or questionnaire items, a software system is a complex entity with many interacting parts. We recommend that user studies such as focus groups [17] and pretests be conducted during multiple stages of artifact design and development [9, 18] to identify confounding emergent properties early in the research cycle. To the extent possible, researchers need to ensure ceteris paribus equivalence across conditions when instantiating different levels of the focal construct [16]. When artifact features interact, especially through technical constraints, it may be that equivalence [27] cannot be established, in which case this threat cannot be addressed with experimental designs. It is important that researchers identify possible interaction effects and address them either through artifact design or the larger research design.

To reduce artifact complexity, we recommend that researchers should not embody the artifact with more features than required. While a minimal artifact may affect the ecological validity of the research, there is little to be gained by conducting work that lacks IV in a realistic setting. This also implies that researchers who employ existing artifacts should choose the "simplest" one, or limit users' exposure to the complete artifact, for example through training, disabling of functions, or access control.

Artifact Medium and Distance. In survey research the theoretical construct and the items intended to measure it are expressed in the same medium – natural language, so that validity may be established in part by using terminology from a construct's theoretical definition for questionnaire items. In contrast, instantiated IT artifacts are expressed in a different medium than the theoretical construct.

Part of this distance can be bridged by the creation of design principles, as proposed in [25, 28]. Such principles can make the focal theoretical construct more concrete. However, considerable distance remains to be bridged from design principles to instantiations [24]. We recommend making explicit the translation between the two media by establishing traceability in their research and demonstrating how the distance is bridged. Additionally, focus groups [17] at various stages can be used to ensure that the artifact design remains congruous with the theoretical definition of the construct (or at least the perception of the construct in the target population). Finally, parameterization of the software artifact can help impose a metric on the design space and thus allow a comparison with the theoretical space. For example, when personalization of the artifact can be controlled by varying a software parameter between the values 0 and 1, the resulting features show low and high personalization. These can then be compared with theoretical ideals of different personalization levels.

Technological Progress. IT artifacts continuously change their form and behavior due to relentless progress in computing power, emergence of new development methods, and new ways of interacting with systems. This means the validity of an instantiation may change over time and requires that validity be re-established or re-demonstrated for every instantiation that is used in a different way or context. Although, as noted earlier, we agree in principle with the idea of instrument re-use and standardization (in this case of software artifacts) [20], this can be challenging in the context of IS. For example, giving research participants a character and command-based interface to support their virtual collaboration in the age of sophisticated 3-D interfaces may create negative reactions not present when such interfaces dominated the IT landscape. We caution researchers in reusing of IS artifacts to evaluate the extent to which the context has changed and may no longer be appropriate.

4   Conclusion

The technology focus inherent in the IS discipline gives rise to unique validity challenges. Ignoring concerns related to instantiation validity can have significant negative consequences for knowledge contributions in IS and application of IS design knowledge in practice. This makes establishing principles of IV both important and urgent. In this paper we begin addressing the lack of established principles by turning to the IS discipline itself for guidance. A review of the IS discipline revealed valuable recommendations that we use to address the threats to IV. These recommendations can be used by researchers and reviewers in: testing; design science theorizing; evaluation of IT artifacts; and building real-world software systems based on IS design knowledge.

To ensure increased attention to the problem of IV, we recommend a new **"Instantiation Validity"** section be included in research papers. This section should link features of the artifact to the underlying theoretical constructs and attempt to demonstrate instantiation validity. Authors should take full advantage of different presentation modes made available by the publisher. With the growing popularity of online supplementary materials, researchers may share the artifact itself to aid other researchers, reviewers and practitioners assess the validity of the artifact.

This paper is an early attempt to generate guidelines for IV. We do not claim to provide a comprehensive set of recommendations. For example, we focused primarily on positivist aspects of IV, ignoring the relationship between artifact and the context in which it is built as well as how it may be interpreted by people in that context. Our intent was to initiate a dialogue and propose a direction that more comprehensive research on IV can take. Thus, future studies should look beyond IS and consider guidance from other domains with a design focus. Finally, as science in general, and standards of validity in particular, are socially agreed-on ideas, future work should engage IS researchers in a dialogue (e.g., using conference panels, survey and Delphi study methods) to expand, refine and prioritize guidelines for addressing threats to IV.

References

1. Komiak, S.Y.X., Benbasat, I.: The effects of personalization and familiarity on trust and adoption of recommendation agents. MIS Q. 30, 941–960 (2006)
2. Lukyanenko, R., Evermann, J., Parsons, J.: Instantiation validity in IS design research. In: Tremblay, M.C., VanderMeer, D., Rothenberger, M., Gupta, A., Yoon, V. (eds.) DESRIST 2014. LNCS, vol. 8463, pp. 321–328. Springer, Heidelberg (2014)
3. Boudreau, M.-C., Gefen, D., Straub, D.W.: Validation in Information Systems Research: A State-of-the-Art Assessment. MIS Q. 25, 1–16 (2001)
4. Straub, D., Boudreau, M.-C., Gefen, D.: Validation guidelines for IS positivist research. Commun. Assoc. Inf. Syst. 13, 1–63 (2004)
5. Venable, J., Pries-Heje, J., Baskerville, R.: A comprehensive framework for evaluation in design science research. In: Peffers, K., Rothenberger, M., Kuechler, B. (eds.) DESRIST 2012. LNCS, vol. 7286, pp. 423–438. Springer, Heidelberg (2012)

6. Rossi, M., Sein, M.K.: Design research workshop: a proactive research approach. Present. Deliv. IRIS. 26, 9–12 (2003)

7. Hevner, A., Chatterjee, S.: Design Research in Information Systems: Theory and Practice. Springer (2010)

8. Sonnenberg, C., vom Brocke, J.: Evaluations in the science of the artificial – reconsidering the build-evaluate pattern in design science research. In: Peffers, K., Rothenberger, M., Kuechler, B. (eds.) DESRIST 2012. LNCS, vol. 7286, pp. 381–397. Springer, Heidelberg (2012)

9. Eriksson, C., Åkesson, M., Kautz, K.-H.: Authentic and Concurrent Evaluation: Refining an Evaluation Approach in Design Science Research. In: PACIS 2011 Proc., pp. 1–13 (2011)

10. Purao, S.: Truth or dare: The ontology question in design science research. J. Database Manag. JDM. 24, 51–66 (2013)

11. Hevner, A., March, S., Park, J., Ram, S.: Design science in information systems research. MIS Q. 28, 75–105 (2004)

12. Walls, J.G., Widmeyer, G.R., Sawy, O.A.E.: Building an information system design theory for vigilant EIS. Inf. Syst. Res. 3, 36–59 (1992)

13. Gregor, S., Hovorka, D.S.: Causality: The elephant in the room in information systems epistemology. In: 19th Eur. Conf. Inf. Syst. (2011)

14. Chandra, L., Seidel, S., Gregor, S.: Prescriptive Knowledge in IS Research: Conceptualizing Design Principles in Terms of Materiality, Action, and Boundary Conditions. In: Hawaii Int. Conf. Syst. Sci., pp. 4039–4047 (2015)

15. Venkatesh, V., Brown, S.A., Bala, H.: Bridging the qualitative-quantitative divide: Guidelines for conducting mixed methods research in information systems. MIS Q. 37, 21–54 (2013)

16. Benbasat, I.: Laboratory experiments in information systems studies with a focus on individuals: a critical appraisal. Harvard Business School, Cambridge (1989)

17. Tremblay, M.C., Hevner, A.R., Berndt, D.J.: Focus Groups for Artifact Refinement and Evaluation in Design Research. Commun. Assoc. Inf. Syst. 26, 599–618 (2010)

18. Sein, M., Henfridsson, O., Purao, S., Rossi, M., Lindgren, R.: Action design research. MIS Q. 35, 37 (2011)

19. Abraham, R., Aier, S., Winter, R.: Fail Early, Fail Often: Towards Coherent Feedback Loops in Design Science Research Evaluation. In: Int. Conf. Inf. Syst., pp. 1–12 (2014)

20. Moore, G.C., Benbasat, I.: Development of an Instrument to Measure the Perceptions of Adopting an Information Technology Innovation. Inf. Syst. Res. 2, 192–222 (1991)

21. Jarvenpaa, S.L., Dickson, G.W., DeSanctis, G.: Methodological issues in experimental IS research: experiences and recommendations. MIS Q. 141–156 (1985)

22. Snodgrass, J.G., Vanderwart, M.: A standardized set of 260 pictures: Norms for name agreement. J. Exp. Psychol. 6, 174–215 (1980)

23. Lukyanenko, R., Evermann, J.: A survey of cognitive theories to support data integration. In: AMCIS 2011 Proceedings, pp. 1–15 (2011)

24. Lukyanenko, R., Parsons, J.: Reconciling theories with design choices in design science research. In: vom Brocke, J., Hekkala, R., Ram, S., Rossi, M. (eds.) DESRIST 2013. LNCS, vol. 7939, pp. 165–180. Springer, Heidelberg (2013)

25. Arazy, O., Kumar, N., Shapira, B.: A theory-driven design framework for social recommender systems. J. Assoc. Inf. Syst. 11, 455–490 (2010)

26. Lukyanenko, R., Parsons, J., Wiersma, Y.: The IQ of the Crowd: Understanding and Improving Information Quality in Structured User-generated Content. Inf. Syst. Res. 25, 669–689 (2014)
27. Burton-Jones, A., Wand, Y., Weber, R.: Guidelines for Empirical Evaluations of Conceptual Modeling Grammars. J. Assoc. Inf. Syst. 10, 495–532 (2009)
28. Kuechler, W., Vaishnavi, V.: A Framework for Theory Development in Design Science Research: Multiple Perspectives. J. Assoc. Inf. Syst. 13, 395–423 (2012)

Analyzing Corporate Social Responsibility Reports Using Unsupervised and Supervised Text Data Mining

Monica Chiarini Tremblay[1(✉)], Carlos Parra[2], and Arturo Castellanos[1]

[1]Decision Sciences and Information Systems, Florida International University, Miami, USA
[2]Department of Marketing, Florida International University, Miami, USA
{tremblay,cmparra,aancaste}@fiu.edu

Abstract. The literature shows that companies have matured on how they see and understand CSR—even to the extent of seeing it as an essential element of the firm's strategy. As part of a comprehensive research agenda, we investigate CSR reports from seven Dow Jones companies to assess the embeddedness of Environmental Sustainability considerations into their Core Business discourse. We leverage the use of supervised and unsupervised Text Data Mining (TDM) techniques to analyze data from these seven companies. To our knowledge, this is one of the first attempts to apply TDM processing to analyze unstructured data from CSR reports. The process we outline should facilitate pattern discovery in documents, minimizing or eliminating the need for time-consuming content analysis that is frequently used in qualitative research.

Keywords: Corporate social responsibility · Sustainability · Text mining · STM

1 Introduction

This paper examines the extent to which environmental sustainability has become embedded in corporate policy and core business discourse by analyzing CSR Reports of a sample of large, publicly traded Dow Jones companies using Text Data Mining (TDM). Most academic contributions have assessed this level of embeddedness from a theoretical perspective—by looking at the stages of consciousness development in relation to action logics (Boiral, Cayer et al. 2009), by using quantitative approaches using primary information (e.g. surveys) (Boiral, Baron et al. 2012) or have relied on the use of secondary data (Gao and Bansal 2013). Within the overarching Corporate Social Responsibility (CSR) integration discussion, of particular interest to this study is the debate around the level of environmental sustainability considerations included in the core business discourse of firms.

1.1 Finding Patterns in CSR Reports

Text categorization can be defined as the assignment of natural language texts to one or more predefined categories based on their content (Dumais, Platt et al. 1998). The most common technique used to analyze text is content analysis, which requires independent

© Springer International Publishing Switzerland 2015
B. Donnellan et al. (Eds.): DESRIST 2015, LNCS 9073, pp. 439–446, 2015.
DOI: 10.1007/978-3-319-18714-3_36

coders to read through the data and assign parts of the document to predefined codes. The evolution of techniques used for CSR Report analyzing has evolved from simple word counting to Text Data Mining (TDM). From the corporate communications perspective, past studies have focused on relating word frequency counts to affective management practices (Saito, Tang et al. 2012), brand differentiation (Gill, Dickinson et al. 2008), or concentrated on a particular industry, such as oil and gas (Dickinson, Gill et al. 2008).

Barkemeyer, Figge, Hahn, and Holt (2009) conducted an automated approach on articles published from January 1990 to July 2008. They analyzed 20 million newspaper articles that mentioned to sustainability issues. The goal was to measure the frequency of use of sustainability related terms in media coverage. They found news articles referred to Sustainable Development and CSR, rather than Corporate Citizenship or Corporate Sustainability. The next logical extension of this approach is to explore concept associations and knowledge discovery utilizing Text Data Mining (TDM).

1.2   Text Mining

Eighty percent of business-relevant information originates in unstructured form, and primarily from text (Grimes 2008). Text mining is a process of knowledge discovery, which allows the organization extract implicit and potentially useful information from textual data using statistical methods (Feldman and Dagan 1995). Typical text mining tasks include text categorization, text clustering, concept extraction, sentiment analysis, and document summarization (Dörre, Gerstl et al. 1999). In this study we use two approaches for our analysis. The first approach uses an exploratory approach to uncover patterns in the reports. The second approach uses a supervised learning technique in which we use a training set previously validated by a subject matter expert.To our knowledge, this is one of the first attempts that use TDM techniques to analyze the embeddedness of environmental sustainability in CSR reports. In the subsequent sections we discuss text categorization, our methodology, present our results and analysis, and discuss these results and propose some avenues for future work.

2   Methodology

Shmueli and Koppius (2011) propose (see Figure 1) the model building steps in explanatory and predictive modeling.   These steps were not created for mining unstructured data, but can however be utilized for this purpose.

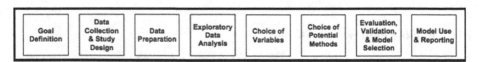

Fig. 1. Modeling Approach

2.1   Goal Definition and Data Collection and Data Preparation

Our goal is to analyze CSR Reports of a sample of large, publicly traded Dow Jones companies to examine the extent to which environmental sustainability has become embedded in core business discourse. We download complete CSR reports in PDF format from the corresponding official corporate websites. In total we download 20 reports from 2004, 2008 and 2012. These reports are then manually scrubbed in order to obtain the main text. We partition each report into 5 CSR dimensions that are based on the Sustainability Accounting Standards Board (SASB) (2014). This guideline contains 5 dimensions: business, governance, environment, human capital and social capital. We ask a subject matter expert to divide each report into 5 partitions corresponding to each sustainability dimension.

Not all reports are used. Citi's 2008 CSR report had security settings that prevented us from obtaining the main text, while Microsoft's 2008 and McDonalds' 2012 CSR reports were too short to obtain meaningful partitions. Thus, out of the 17 reports used in the analysis a total of 85 partitions were obtained - 35 partitions from 7 reports for 2004, 20 partitions from 4 reports for 2008, and 30 partitions from 6 reports for 2012.

2.2   Exploratory Data Analysis and Choice of Variables

We run the unsupervised TDM on 85 partitions to identify words do not add value to term groupings and that should be included in the stop list. For example, consider the words "Intel" or "Microprocessor" as terms with high weights associated to *Intel's 2004 social capital partition*. These words receive high weights because they appear frequently. However, they do not add value and could overshadow less frequent yet important words.

2.3   Choice of Methods

Data mining tasks can be broadly categorized into either supervised or unsupervised learning tasks. We utilize supervised TDM on the whole corpus to verify whether deductive machine learning would perform as well as humans at the task of classifying contents from CSR reports. We evaluate our supervised TDM results against that of independent coders and show how to streamline content analysis of CSR reports by *exaptation* of existing TDM techniques (Gregor and Hevner 2013).We then use unsupervised TDM to look at how these partitions group and explore whether environmental sustainability considerations are part of the core business discourse for the firms analyzed.

2.4   Supervised TDM

For the supervised component of this study we use the labels assigned by a subject matter expert, such that each text file in the input data is associated to a partition type. Input data are divided into a *training set* and a *validation set*. Sixty percent of the documents in the input data are used to train several supervised learning algorithms. The remaining 40% are used to validate and test the performance of the text classification models by having it assign labels to the remaining documents (the set of files not used during training).

We train several models to compare the classification accuracy of several algorithms; this allows us to select the best model for the task. We describe the results of our three best models: a decision tree model, a neural network model and a memory-based reasoning model. We evaluate the these models using common standard metrics such as accuracy, precision, recall, F-measure, sensitivity and specificity (Jurafsky and Martin 2009) (see Tables 1 and 2). The accuracy of a classifier is calculated by dividing the correctly classified instances by the total number of instances.

Table 1. Formulas for Evaluation

Precision	Recall	F-measure	Accuracy
$P = \dfrac{TP}{TP+FP}$	$R = \dfrac{TP}{TP+FN}$	$F = \dfrac{2(P*R)}{P+R}$	$A = \dfrac{TP+TN}{TP+TN+FP+FN}$
Sensitivity	**Specificity**	**Misclassification**	
$TPR = \dfrac{TP}{TP+FN}$	$SPC = \dfrac{TN}{TN+FP}$	$M.R. = \dfrac{FN+FP}{TP+TN+FP+FN}$	

Since we were dealing with a multi-class problem in which the target variable can have five different levels, we calculated the macro-average and the micro-average (Yang 1999) in addition to standard metrics such as precision, recall, and F-measure. Macroaveraging gives equal weight to each class and gives a sense of effectiveness on small classes, whereas microaveraging gives equal weight to each per-document classification decision (Manning, Raghavan et al. 2008). On average, the absolute differences between both calculations do not exceed two percent. Table No. 2 below compares model statistics for the three algorithms used.

Table 2. Evaluation metrics for the three supervised models

Model	Accuracy	Precision	Recall	F-Measure	Sensitivity	Specificity	Misclassification Rate
Neural Network	90.19	93.33	73.57	78.48	66.67	97.50	10.00
MBR	89.19	91.11	71.07	75.54	64.81	96.88	12.50
Decision Tree	86.17	82.02	62.50	69.82	59.62	94.38	17.50

Our results indicate that for the supervised TDM classifications are equivalent to the work of the subject matter expert. We explored the results of each of our supervised models. We describe the results of our Neural Network model, which has the lowest misclassification rate of 10%. The Neural Network algorithm mislabels "business" partitions as "environmental" partitions. All other partitions are correctly classified. This demonstrates that our supervised TDM classifies documents as accurately as the subject matter expert. We now investigate the use of unsupervised learning techniques to explore alternative document classifications.

2.5   Unsupervised Learning Strategy

Cluster analysis encompasses a number of different classification algorithms that can be used to develop natural groupings among the data (typically as part of exploratory data analysis) (Jain, Murty et al. 1999). In our study we utilize the expectation-maximization algorithm. We report unsupervised learning strategy for 30 partitions from the 2012. We identify six clusters : oil extraction firm grouping, environmental grouping with business partitions from General Motors and Intel, governance grouping (with Citi's business and social capital partitions), social capital grouping, beverage firm grouping, and human capital grouping. The Euclidean distance between the clusters, as seen in figure 2, indicates the clusters are sufficiently different (low intra-cluster similarity).

2012 Document Groupings

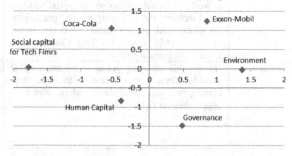

Fig. 2. Text Cluster analysis on 2012 partitions

Table No. 3 shows 2012 iteration's cluster name, description and files grouped in each cluster (Parra and Tremblay 2014). Of particular interest is the fact that General Motors' 2012 and Intel's 2012 business partitions grouped in the environmental cluster when using unsupervised learning techniques. This indicates that these business partitions contained various environmental sustainability considerations. These findings are intuitive. One firm produces cars (which consume fuel and contribute to greenhouse gas emissions). The other firm likely deals with electronic waste. Thus, environmental sustainability considerations are likely included in their core business discussion.

Table 3. Document Groupings Description

Cluster	Cluster Name	Description	Files Grouped
1	ExxonMobil	Grouping points to **ExxonMobil considerations**, this cluster groups all ExxonMobil partitions except governance and points to firm specific issues such as: upstream lines, gas, plans, projects, operations, conditions, international, design.	em2012biz em2012env em2012humk em2012sock
2	Environment	Grouping alludes to **environmental** issues (i.e. air, carbon, power, waste, drive, water, cost, energy, etc.). It is important to note that General Motors and Intel business partitions also grouped here, indicating that the descriptive terms are increasingly relevant for these firms' business activities.	citi2012env gm2012biz gm2012env intel2012biz intel2012env ms2012env

Table 3. (*Continued*)

3	Governance	Grouping includes most **governance** partitions and mentions: conduct, directors, compensation, independent, legal, principles, review, compliance, risk, etc. Citi's business and social capital partitions also grouped here, evidencing that governance topics were a priority for Citi in 2012.	citi2012biz citi2012gov citi2012sock coke2012gov em2012gov gm2012gov ms2012gov
4	Social Capital for Tech Firms	Grouping brings up **social capital considerations for Tech firms** insofar as it groups Microsoft and Intel partitions alluding supply chain issues (i.e. cash, central, campaign, audits, future, serve, conditions, china, centers, etc.).	intel2012sock ms2012sock
5	Coca-Cola	Grouping includes most of Coca-Cola's partitions (business, environment and social capital) – as well as General Motors social capital partition - and includes the following terms: "grant, Brazil, water, fund, partner, china, campaign, waste, partners, etc." Thus, this Text Cluster raises **Coca-Cola considerations.**	coke2012biz coke2012env coke2012sock gm2012sock
6	Human Capital	Finally, this grouping points to **human capital considerations** across industries through: "top, culture, women, workplace, safety, directors, people, human rights, etc."	citi2012humk coke2012humk gm2012humk intel2012gov intel2012humk ms2012biz ms2012humk

3   Conclusion and Future Work

We investigate the use of TDM to help us understand, classify and characterize the contents of CSR reports. In particular, we use supervised TDM to compare labels classified by TDM and classification algorithms to those labeled by a subject matter expert. We found that for most of text files in the validation set, supervised TDM is similar to expert labeling. The misclassifications by the best performing classification algorithms (Neural Network and Memory-based Reasoning) were somewhat explained by the results of our cluster analysis which indicated that indicated that CSR report partitions focusing on core business discussion (in the case of ExxonMobil) and social capital themes (in the case of General Motors) contained enough environmental sustainability considerations to be classified as environmental partitions.

The unsupervised TDM (Text Cluster analysis) on 2012 CSR report partitions to explore groupings resulted in six text Clusters: *oil extraction firm* grouping, environmental grouping with business partitions from General Motors and Intel, governance grouping (with Citi's business and social capital partitions), social capital grouping, *beverage firm* grouping, and human capital grouping. Of particular interest to us was the fact that the environmental grouping (cluster No. 2 in table No. 3) also grouped two business partitions (General Motors' and Intel's). Thus, providing additional justification for environmental sustainability embeddedness. Finally, it makes sense for companies like ExxonMobil and General Motors to have business and social capital partitions be reclassified by supervised TDM as environmental ones, evidencing a logical evolution for firms whose products must consume natural resources and contribute to global warming.

References

Barkemeyer, R., Figge, F., Holt, D., Wettstein, B.: What the papers say: trends in sustainability. A comparative analysis of 115 leading national newspapers worldwide. Journal of Corporate Citizenship 2009(33), 68–86 (2009)

Boiral, O., Baron, C., Gunnlaugson, O.: Environmental Leadership and Consciousness Development: A Case Study Among Canadian SMEs. Journal of Business Ethics: 1–21 (2012)

Boiral, O., Cayer, M., Baron, C.M.: The action logics of environmental leadership: A developmental perspective. Journal of Business Ethics 85(4), 479–499 (2009)

Dickinson, S.J., Gill, D.L., Purushothaman, M., Scharl, A.: A web analysis of sustainability reporting: an oil and gas perspective. Journal of Website Promotion 3(3-4), 161–182 (2008)

Dörre, J., Gerstl, P., Seiffert, R.: Text mining: finding nuggets in mountains of textual data. In: Proceedings of the fifth ACM SIGKDD International Conference on Knowledge Discovery and Data Mining. ACM (1999)

Dumais, S., Platt, J., Heckerman, D., Sahami, M.: Inductive learning algorithms and representations for text categorization. Proceedings of the Seventh International Conference on Information and Knowledge Management. ACM (1998)

Feldman, R., Dagan, I.: Knowledge Discovery in Textual Databases (KDT). In: KDD (1995)

Gao, J., Bansal, P.: Instrumental and integrative logics in business sustainability. Journal of Business Ethics 112(2), 241–255 (2013)

Gill, D.L., Dickinson, S.J., Scharl, A.: Communicating sustainability: a web content analysis of North American, Asian and European firms. Journal of Communication Management 12(3), 243–262 (2008)

Gregor, S., Hevner, A.R.: Positioning and presenting design science research for maximum impact. MIS Quarterly 37(2), 337–356 (2013)

Grimes, S.: Unstructured Data and the 80 Percent Rule (2008), http://breakthroughanalysis.com/2008/08/01/unstructured-data-and-the-80-percent-rule/ (2014)

Jain, A.K., Murty, M.N., Flynn, P.J.: Data clustering: a review. ACM Computing Surveys (CSUR) 31(3), 264–323 (1999)

Jurafsky, D., Martin, J.H.: Speech and Language Processing: An Introduction to Natural Language Processing. In: Computational Linguistics, and Speech Recognition. MIT Press (2009)

Manning, C.D., Raghavan, P., Schütze, H.: Introduction to information retrieval. Cambridge University Press, Cambridge (2008)

Parra, C.M., Tremblay, M.C.: Analyzing US Corporate Social Responsibility (CSR) Reports using Text Data Mining. In: Ninth International Design Science Research in Information Systems and Technologies (DESRIST), Miami, FL (2014)

Saito, M., Tang, Q., Umemuro, H.: Text-Mining Approach for Evaluation of Affective Management Practices. World Academy of Science, Engineering and Technology 72, 129–136 (2012)

Shmueli, G., Koppius, O.R.: Predictive Analytics in Information Systems Research. Mis Quarterly 35(3), 553–572 (2011)

Sustainability Accounting Standards Board, Sustainability Accounting Standards Board (2014), http://www.sasb.org/

Yang, Y.: An evaluation of statistical approaches to text categorization. Information Retrieval 1(1-2), 69–90 (1999)

Extending Battery Management Systems
for Making Informed Decisions on Battery Reuse

Markus Monhof[✉], Daniel Beverungen, Benjamin Klör, and Sebastian Bräuer

European Research Center for Information Systems (ERCIS), University of Münster,
Münster, Germany
{markus.monhof,daniel.beverungen,benjamin.kloer,
sebastian.braeuer}@ercis.uni-muenster.de

Abstract. A battery management system (BMS) is an embedded system for
monitoring and controlling complex battery systems in high-tech goods, such as
electric vehicles or military communication devices. BMSs are often designed
for simplicity and cost efficiency, storing few crucial data on the condition of
batteries. With an increasing trend to reuse batteries, BMSs face a need to implement additional functionality to support decision-making tasks. This functionality requires rich data on the structure, usage history, and condition of a
battery that is not supported by current BMS type series. Based on expert interviews and document analyses, we sketch a design theory for implementing
BMSs that supply the data required for making decisions on how to best reuse
battery systems.

Keywords: Design theory · Battery management system · Embedded system ·
Decision support system · Condition monitoring

1   Introduction

Since their commercial introduction in 1991, lithium-ion batteries have become a
widespread technology for supplying mobile devices and high-tech goods with energy
[1] and often account for a major share of the initial costs of the devices in which they
are applied [2]. One strategy for reducing the systems' total costs of ownership is to
reuse a battery for another application after it has completed its first lifecycle. For example, electric vehicles (EVs) require batteries with high energy density to provide for
a range that is accepted by drivers [3]. While it is assumed that these batteries are no
longer usable for EVs when their capacity drops to around 70-80% of their original
capacity [4], they might still be usable in stationary applications after their removal [5].

A crucial prerequisite for reusing a battery system is to accurately assess its condition and usage history. Since the procedures to obtain these data by manually testing
the battery are complex, resource intensive, and may lead to further cell degradation
[6], we propose that the data should be stored and made available by the battery management system (BMS) without conducting additional testing procedures.

BMSs are embedded systems that provide basic functions for operating a battery
system. Having been designed as low-cost systems with minimal hardware capabilities,

© Springer International Publishing Switzerland 2015
B. Donnellan et al. (Eds.): DESRIST 2015, LNCS 9073, pp. 447–454, 2015.
DOI: 10.1007/978-3-319-18714-3_37

they usually do not store data on the level of detail that is required for making decisions on reusing a battery. To identify this gap and present some first ideas on how to design the next generation of BMSs, the research question addressed in this paper is: In what way must BMS be extended to support decision-making on the reuse of battery systems, in addition to monitoring and controlling their basic operations?

The paper is organized as follows. In Section 2, basic principles of lithium-ion battery systems and BMSs are reviewed and second life applications are reviewed. In Section 3, the research method is exemplified. In Section 4, a first design theory for a class of BMSs that support decision-making on reusing battery systems is sketched. Section 5 concludes the paper.

2   Theoretical Background

2.1   Fundamentals of Lithium-Ion Battery Systems

Lithium-ion batteries are used as energy storages in many electric devices, ranging from small battery packs used in cell phones or cameras to large battery systems for EVs or temporary energy storages for photovoltaic systems. Advantages of li-ion batteries include "high energy and power densities, long life, and lack of memory effect" [6].

In general, larger battery systems follow a modular design and usually consist of a battery pack, battery case, battery management system, and thermo system [7]. A battery pack is an energy storage device that comprises several battery modules that again are composed of battery cells [8]. For increasing total voltage, battery cells are connected in series into battery modules, while for increasing total amperage a couple of modules are connected in parallel. Smaller batteries usually consist of one cell only. The inner components are protected by a solid case. The battery management system is an embedded system to monitor and control the battery. Finally, due to battery cells' temperature sensitivity, larger lithium-ion battery systems contain a thermo system for heating and cooling the cells that is controlled by the BMS [9].

Lithium-ion batteries suffer from cell aging, which mainly depends on the cell chemistry and operation conditions [6] and results in decreased performance. Battery aging can be divided into cycle aging and calendar aging [10]. While calendar aging describes the degradation of a battery during storage (i.e. while the battery is not in use), cycle aging denotes the degradation during charging or discharging operations [10]. Rezvanizaniani et al. [11] identify the five most significant factors for degradation in automotive applications: environment temperature, discharging current rate, charging rate, depth of discharge, and time intervals between full charge cycles. Due to initial variance of the cells and different temperatures occurring at different locations inside the module [12], cells might degrade unequally [13]. Since aging depends on "chemistry, design parameters and battery usage" [12], those aspects have to be considered for explaining battery aging. Even cells manufactured in the same production lot might show a variance in their aging behavior [12]. Therefore, Brand et al. [14] state that the prediction of a module's remaining useful life (RUL) requires knowledge about its previous usage history.

2.2   Battery Management Systems as Embedded Systems

Embedded systems are microprocessor-based systems performing dedicated tasks as part of another system. They commonly feature combinations of hardware and software, have few dedicated functions, are integrated in larger systems, and possess limited hardware resources regarding computing power and memory. Often, real-time constraints exist and the system's correctness is a compulsory design requirement [15].

A BMS is an embedded system to operate a battery, to prevent malfunction, and to extend the battery's lifetime. It is typically designed for three main goals. First, it ensures the safe and reliable operation of the battery. Second, it performs electrical management for optimized battery performance and acts as an interface between a battery and the device. Third, it controls the temperature of the battery [9]. To account for these goals, a variety of sensors are implemented into the battery, providing data about electric and environmental characteristics. Typical characteristics measured by a BMS include cell voltages, cell temperatures, and charge and discharge currents [16]. The sensor data are used to calculate or estimate a variety of metrics on the battery's status.

The most commonly used parameters are the state of charge (SOC) and the state of health (SOH). The SOC describes the "reversible" [17], while the SOH describes the "irreversible changes" experienced by a battery [17]. The SOC is defined as the ratio of remaining capacity to the capacity when fully charged [16], or the actual amount of charge divided by the total amount of charge [18]. In EVs, the SOC can be used as a kind of fuel gauge, as known from conventional combustion engines. Since the SOC cannot be measured directly, many different methods for SOC estimation have been proposed [16]. SOC and SOH estimation can be based on data that is stored in a bookkeeping systems that holds historical data such as the number of cycles [19]. An estimation model is stored in the BMS that is used for calculating the SOC or SOH [16].

Apart from estimating a battery's SOC and SOH the measured data are also required to ensure a battery's safe and reliable operation. Common safety features exist to prevent overcharges and deep discharges by controlling the electric currents and temperature [17], as lithium-ion cells may explode at high temperatures and their degradation highly depends on the battery's operating temperature. Therefore, a BMS operates a thermal management system in larger battery packs [20], shielding the battery from adverse environmental conditions to minimize its degradation and to avoid overheating [13]. Smaller batteries usually do not contain a dedicated heating and cooling device.

To extend the battery's lifetime, the SOC of all cells should be kept as equal as possible [20]. To achieve this objective, the BMSs contain active or passive mechanisms for cell balancing.

Depending on the size and complexity of a battery, a BMS can be implemented on all levels of a battery, such as cells, modules, and packs. Chatzakis et al. [21] state that "a BMS has to be 'cell based' in order to be effective". Hierarchical BMSs can be implemented by designating BMSs as masters and slaves, such that a battery's operations can be monitored on all levels of detail [19].

Data exchange between the BMS and the device is usually established using a communication bus (e.g. CAN-bus for EVs [20], system management bus (SMBus) for smaller devices [19]).

2.3   Second Life Applications of Used Batteries

Like any other product, a battery passes through different stages during its lifetime, including manufacturing, shipping, installation, useful life, dismantling, and disposal [22]. In addition to these lifecycle phases, batteries might be reused in second life applications to increase their sustainable use and generate additional revenues.

Second life applications may be viable if individual usage scenarios require disparate properties of a battery. For instance, electric vehicle batteries (EVBs) have to provide high discharge currents to provide decent acceleration capabilities, a high energy density, and slow cycle aging [23]. A degraded EVB that, due to an increased internal resistance, can no longer provide the necessary peak loads required in a car might still be usable in stationary applications that do not have such high power demands. Hence, reusing EVBs in stationary applications is explored in current projects [5].

Since every battery ages differently, information about the battery is needed to identify the best scenario for its reuse. Furthermore, to compile a new battery pack out of several used battery cells with an equal level of quality, information about each individual cell in a used battery pack are required. Following propositions of battery experts, this includes information about the individual cells' age, since cells with different aging histories should not be used in the same pack. While this information can be gathered by performing physical tests on the battery, these tests have been found to be complex, stressful, and lead to an increased cell degradation. To identify the aging mechanism of a cell, destructive methods like "X-ray diffraction (XRD) and scanning electron microscopy (SEM)" [6] are used frequently. While information about the current status can also be acquired with non-destructive methods, such as cyclization, these methods often increase the battery's cycle age due to the charging and discharging cycles carried out in the course of conducting the procedure. Thus, there are good technical and economic reasons to store more data about the battery's condition in a BMS.

3   Research Method

Design has been proposed to be a science of the artificial that differs from research on natural phenomena [24]. Gregor [25] proposed five types of IS theory, including prescriptive theories for design and action that convey knowledge on how artifacts ought to be, instead of explaining, analyzing, or predicting their behavior. Later, Gregor and Jones [26] conceptualized these five types of theories as 'design theories' and proposed eight components based on which design theories can be communicated.

To identify the current properties of BMS, we analyzed two battery systems based on document analyses and informal discussions with experts from two companies that manufacture battery packs and BMSs. The first battery pack is used in communication devices in a military context. The second battery pack is used in EVs.

Based on this assessment, we conducted informal discussions with battery researchers and manufacturers and analyzed the literature to advance BMSs into systems that inform decision making on reusing batteries. Based on these results, we sketched a design theory for a class of BMSs that do not only provide the usual features for monitoring and controlling the battery, but also make available the data that are required to enable decision making on how to best reuse the battery in other application scenarios.

4   Extending BMSs for Making Decisions on Battery Reuse

Our discussions with battery researchers and manufacturers as well as the literature analyses led to three types of data about a battery that are needed to make an informed reuse decision. First, data about the current condition of the battery is needed, especially the SOH regarding the capacity and the internal resistance are required to identify valid reuse applications. Second, transaction data are required, including the charging and discharging cycles of the battery. Third, to estimate the remaining useful life for different reuse scenarios and to assess whether a recombination of battery modules is possible the detailed usage history is needed, including basic condition data such as voltage, current and temperature experience by the battery as functions of time [27].

Based on the data that is needed for making informed reuse decisions, three aspects present themselves to advance BMSs into systems to obtain, store, and evaluate these data along the battery's first life.

First, the decision task might demand more data than is currently made available in a BMS. To acquire more data, additional sensors for measuring currents, voltages, and temperatures might be integrated into the battery. The frequency in which the parameters are measured and stored has to be adjusted to an adequate level of granularity to limit the data storage requirements and thus avoid an escalation of costs for data storage. For recombining and predicting the future performance of cells or modules, data on the usage history has to be identified on a cell or a module level, respectively.

Second, the hardware and software capabilities of BMSs need to be extended, since the data gathered by the sensors have to be processed for calculation or estimation of specific values that represent, e.g., the degradation of the battery. As regards the storage of a BMS, data that defines the history of the battery has to be stored for a sufficient period of time. An important observation is that while data storage prices are decreasing, storage space in embedded systems is still very costly, especially in automotive applications, because of high safety standards and cost pressure [28]. In these scenarios, data on selected parameters, such as cycle life or the maximum remaining capacity [29], might be saved as histograms.

Third, the – external – interfaces of the BMS have to be refined, since the recorded data has to be made available to a decision maker faced with the task of reusing a battery. The data can be communicated to an external system like a maintenance device or a superior system inside the same device, such as a vehicle management system in an electric vehicle, or read out after the end of the first lifecycle of the battery.

The identified aspects become manifest as additions to the design theory that underlies current implementations of BMSs as embedded systems (Table 1).

Table 1. Extended design theory for BMSs to foster decision-making for battery reuse

Components	*Additions to the current design theory underlying BMSs*
Purpose and scope	To obtain data for making decisions on battery reuse, including transactions and errors experienced by a battery and gradients of important battery parameters along the entire battery lifecycle.
Constructs	Physical components: Additional sensors, extended hardware capabilities, extended interfaces. Abstract components: Gradient of important battery parameters; transaction data on charging/discharging events; data on unusual events (e.g. extreme temperatures, unusual high energy requests, major physical shocks).
Principles of form and function	Acquisition and storage of transaction data affecting the battery, condition data on the battery, and evaluation of historical data to assess and predict the battery's condition.
Artifact mutability	To adapt to new models for evaluating battery data, so as to assess and predict the condition of the battery with greater accuracy.
Testable propositions	(1) The condition of the battery can be assessed more comprehensively than with conventional BMSs; (2) the future condition of the battery can be predicted based on historical data; (3) the selection and implementation of an adequate reuse scenario is fostered.
Justificatory knowledge	Decision theory [30], theory on predicting the future condition of a battery based on current data [31], IS design theory [26], [32].
Principles of implementation	The implementation needs to be able to monitor and control a battery, and to assess and predict the condition of the battery. It needs to be embedded into a decision support system to enable decisions on using the battery in suitable application scenarios.
Expository instantiation	To convey a BMS as an embedded system and (a) extend the sensors, memory, and processing capabilities of the BMS or (b) connect the BMS to an external information system to which crucial data are transmitted regularly to monitor the battery's lifecycle.

5   Contribution and Research Outlook

The contribution offered in this paper is to provide some first ideas on developing a design theory that describes a class of Battery Management Systems (BMS) that are capable of informing decision making on the reuse of batteries. BMSs are currently applied at the interface between the battery and its ambient device and control basic functions such as charging and discharging the battery, temperature management, and maintain safe operating conditions. We identified a lack of available data to be provided by BMSs to support decisions on the reuse of battery cells, battery modules, and battery packs. Subsequently, we identified a need to add additional sensors, hardware capabilities, and interfaces to BMSs and sketched a design theory for a class of BMSs that can inform decision making on reusing batteries in addition to operating the battery itself.

A limitation of the paper is a potentially incomplete appraisal of the current features of BMSs, which was done based on a literature analysis and a review of two expository instantiations. While this approach has enabled us to summarize the crucial characteristics of BMSs, additional BMSs might have to be reviewed to more fully explore the range of functions provided by current BMSs. In addition, further research is warranted to increase the completeness and level of generalization of the proposed design theory.

Acknowledgements. This paper was supported by a grant from the German Federal Ministry of Education and Research (BMBF) for the project 'EOL-IS' (promotion sign 01FE13023).

References

1. Winter, M., Brodd, R.J.: What are batteries, fuel cells, and supercapacitors? Chem. Rev. 104, 4245–4269 (2004)
2. Dinger, A., Martin, R., Mosquet, X., Rabl, M., Rizoulis, D., Russo, M., Sticher, G.: Batteries for Electric Cars Challanges, Opportunities, and the Outlook to 2020. Technical Report, The Boston Consulting Group (2010)
3. Herb, F.: Alterungsmechanismen in Lithium-Ionen-Batterien und PEM-Brennstoffzellen und deren Einfluss auf die Eigenschaften von daraus bestehenden Hybrid-Systemen. Dissertation, University of Ulm (2010)
4. Neubauer, J., Pesaran, A.: The ability of battery second use strategies to impact plug-in electric vehicle prices and serve utility energy storage applications. J. Power Sources 196, 10351–10358 (2011)
5. Sachenbacher, M., Mayer, T., Leucker, M., Brand, M., Jossen, A.: Towards 2nd-Life Application of Lithium-Ion Batteries for Stationary Energy Storage in Photovoltaic Systems. In: Proceedings of the International Conference on Solar Energy for MENA Region (INCOSOL), Amman, Jordan, pp. 22–23 (2012)
6. Han, X., Ouyang, M., Lu, L., Li, J., Zheng, Y., Li, Z.: A comparative study of commercial lithium ion battery cycle life in electrical vehicle: Aging mechanism identification. J. Power Sources 251, 38–54 (2014)
7. Schlick, T., Hertel, G., Hagemann, B., Maiser, E., Kramer, M.: Zukunftsfeld Elektromobilität–Chancen und Herausforderungen für den deutschen Maschinen-und Anlagenbau. Roland Berger Stragey Consultants VDMA, n/s (2011)
8. Amirault, J., Chien, J., Garg, S., Gibbons, D., Ross, B., Tang, M., Xing, J., Sidhu, I., Kaminsky, P., Tenderich, B.: The Electric Vehicle Battery Landscape: Opportunities and Challenges (2009),
   http://www.funginstitute.berkeley.edu/sites/default/files/The Electric Vehicle Battery Landscape - Opportunities and Challenges.pdf
9. Bitsche, O., Gutmann, G.: Systems for hybrid cars. J. Power Sources 127, 8–15 (2004)
10. Barré, A., Deguilhem, B., Grolleau, S., Gérard, M., Suard, F., Riu, D.: A review on lithium-ion battery ageing mechanisms and estimations for automotive applications. J. Power Sources 241, 680–689 (2013)
11. Rezvanizaniani, S.M., Liu, Z., Chen, Y., Lee, J.: Review and recent advances in battery health monitoring and prognostics technologies for electric vehicle (EV) safety and mobility. J. Power Sources 256, 110–124 (2014)

12. Baumhöfer, T., Brühl, M., Rothgang, S., Uwe, D.: Production caused variation in capacity aging trend and correlation to initial cell performance. J. Power Sources 247, 332–338 (2014)
13. Young, K., Wang, C., Wang, L.Y., Strunz, K.: Electric Vehicle Battery Technologies. In: Garcia-Valle, R., Peças Lopes, J.A. (eds.) Electric Vehicle Integration into Modern Power Networks, pp. 15–56. Springer, New York (2013)
14. Brand, M., Quinger, D., Walder, G.: Ageing inhomogeneity of long-term used BEV-batteries and their reusability for 2nd-life applications. EVS 26, 1–7 (2012)
15. Camposano, R., Wilberg, J.: Embedded system design. Des. Autom. Embed. Syst. 1, 5–50 (1996)
16. Waag, W., Fleischer, C., Sauer, D.U.: Critical review of the methods for monitoring of lithium-ion batteries in electric and hybrid vehicles. J. Power Sources 258, 321–339 (2014)
17. Jossen, A., Spath, V., Doring, H.: Reliable battery operation — a challenge for the battery management system. J. Power Sources 84, 283–286 (1999)
18. Meissner, E., Richter, G.: Battery Monitoring and Electrical Energy Management. J. Power Sources 116, 79–98 (2003)
19. Bergveld, H.J.: Battery Management Systems Design by Modelling. Dissertation, University of Twente (2001).
20. Xing, Y., Ma, E.W.M., Tsui, K.L., Pecht, M.: Battery Management Systems in Electric and Hybrid Vehicles. Energies 4, 1840–1857 (2011)
21. Chatzakis, J., Kalaitzakis, K., Voulgaris, N.C., Manias, S.N.: Designing a New Generalized Battery Management System. Trans. Ind. Electron. 50, 990–999 (2003)
22. Fecher, D.B.: Wireless monitoring of battery for lifecycle management. Patent, US20120038473A1, USA (2012)
23. Chalk, S.G., Miller, J.F.: Key challenges and recent progress in batteries, fuel cells, and hydrogen storage for clean energy systems. J. Power Sources 159, 73–80 (2006)
24. Simon, H.A.: The sciences of the artificial. MIT Press, Cambridge (1996)
25. Gregor, S.: The Nature of Theory in Information Systems. MIS Q. 30, 611–642 (2006)
26. Gregor, S., Jones, D.: The Anatomy of a Design Theory. J. Assoc. Inf. Syst. 8, 312–335 (2007)
27. Meissner, E., Richter, G.: Battery Monitoring and Electrical Energy Management. J. Power Sources 116, 79–98 (2003)
28. Sagstetter, F., Lukasiewycz, M., Steinhorst, S., Wolf, M., Bouard, A., Harris, W.R., Jha, S., Peyrin, T., Poschmann, A., Chakraborty, S.: Security Challenges in Automotive Hardware/Software Architecture Design. In: Design, Automation & Test in Europe Conference & Exhibition (DATE), pp. 458–463. IEEE Conference Publications, New Jersey (2013)
29. Pop, V., Bergveld, H.J., Danilov, D., Regtien, P.P.L., Notten, P.H.L.: Battery Management Systems - Accurate State-of-Charge Indication for Battery-Powered Applications. Springer (2008)
30. Simon, H.A.: The new science of management decision. Prentice Hall, Englewood Cliffs (1977)
31. Saha, B., Goebel, K., Christophersen, J.: Comparison of prognostic algorithms for estimating remaining useful life of batteries. Trans. Inst. Meas. Control. 31, 293–308 (2009)
32. Gregor, S., Hevner, A.R.: Positioning and Presenting Design Science Research for Maximum Impact. MIS Q. 37, 337–356 (2013)

How Can We Design Products, Services, and Software That Reflect the Needs of Our Stakeholders? Towards a Canvas for Successful Requirements Engineering

Christian Ruf[⊠] and Andrea Back

Institute of Information Management, University St. Gallen, St. Gallen, Switzerland
{christian.ruf,andrea.back}@unisg.ch

Abstract. Current research in the requirements engineering (RE) domain is extensive. However, despite increased efforts from both practitioners and researchers to make RE more successful, the implied link to project success is questionable. Consequently, to address this gap, researchers propose a new paradigm in the domain of RE, namely the artefact orientation. Based on this new research field, this study introduces a requirements engineering canvas (REC) which we developed based on model requirements (MRs) derived from a literature review. Moreover, we confirmed these MRs with findings from interviews involving 7 domain experts. In particular, the REC addresses the 7 MRs: goal orientation, documentation, integration, agility, continuity, adaptability, and responsibilities.

Keywords: Requirements engineering · Artefact orientation

1 Introduction

In recent years, requirements engineering (RE) has gained more attention. This becomes visible when we consult Google Trends with the keyword "requirements engineering". There is a 26% increase in search requests between 2013 and 2015 [1]. Not only practitioners, but also researchers have greatly increased their efforts in proposing new models, theories, and guidelines which should facilitate more successful RE [2,3]. However, despite increased efforts to improve RE and consequently project success, studies still report several difficulties. For example, findings suggest that only 48% of projects meet pre-defined time schedules, 45% stay within the budget constraints, and 21% achieve the goals [4].

This mismatch of greater suggested relevance and research compared to project success gives rise to a new paradigm in the domain of RE. The literature has introduced the artefact orientation which differs from the activity orientation [5]. While activity orientation discusses process models, techniques, and methods as to how RE should be done, the artefact orientation emphasises the output or artefacts. Such artefacts might include high-level goals or software specifications.

This study aims at consolidating recent research in the domain of artefact orientation by deriving model requirements (MRs). Based on these MRs, we build a requirements

© Springer International Publishing Switzerland 2015
B. Donnellan et al. (Eds.): DESRIST 2015, LNCS 9073, pp. 455–462, 2015.
DOI: 10.1007/978-3-319-18714-3_38

engineering canvas (REC), which consequently should lead to more successful RE. Hence, the research question of this study is the following: *How should we design the requirements engineering canvas (REC) to meet the derived model requirements (MRs) in the domain of artefact orientation and consequently lead to more successful RE?*

We organise the reminder of this study as follows. First, we elaborate on the relevant terms of RE and suggested artefact orientation in Section 2. Subsequently, Section 3 covers the design science research approach of the research project and explains how we conducted the literature review and expert interviews. After introducing the MRs in Section 4, we introduce the REC in Section 5 and guide future research endeavours in Section 6.

2   Related Work

2.1   Requirements Engineering (RE) and Model Requirements (MRs)

Requirements engineering (RE) addresses the process of eliciting, documenting, analysing, negotiating, and validating requirements, which represent the needs of customers and stakeholders [6]. According to the literature, RE should contribute to more successful project management [7]. A more extensive definition of the RE process is provided by Boehm [8]: *"Requirements engineering is the discipline for developing a complete, consistent unambiguous specification – which can serve as a basis for common agreement among all parties concerned...."* Hence, the success of the RE process might be assessed with the quality of the elicited requirements. In this study, we aim at identifying requirements, or in particular model requirements (MRs) which address how an artefact-oriented RE model should be designed.

2.2   Artefact Orientation

The literature differentiates between activity and artefact orientation. The artefact orientation refers to the output and results of the RE process and introduces specific categories and abstraction levels for documenting, analysing and validating requirements [9]. Activity orientation, on the other hand, emphasises techniques, methods, and process models, and thus, describes how the team should conduct the RE process. Researchers suggest that the artefact orientation should lead to increased project success [10]. This study aims at consolidating MRs to design an artefact-oriented RE model of this relatively young research domain of RE. The subsequent section elaborates on how we proceed with deriving and validating the MRs.

3   Research Approach

Design Science Research (DSR) consists of 6 distinctive activities, as suggested by Peffers et al. [11]. In Sections 3.1 and 3.2 we explain how we conducted the literature review and the expert interviews to derive the MRs, as well as how we developed the REC. Section 4 elaborates on the MRs (Activity 2) and in Section 5, we discuss the

REC (Activity 3). Finally, with regard to Activities 4 and 5, demonstration and validation, we shed light on how we plan to validate the proposed REC in future research projects in Section 6.

3.1 Literature Review

In our literature review, we followed the procedure recommended by Vom Brocke et al. [12] and Webster and Watson [13]. We used the search string "requirements engineering" in the titles of publications and searched the databases AIS Electronic Library, EBSCOhost, Emerald Insight, IEEE Explore Digital Library, Science Direct, and SpringerLink. Furthermore, we limited our search to journal articles and the top three ranked information management conferences, as suggested by the WI-Orientierungsliste [14]. We started with the search in November 2014 and finished in December 2014. Overall, we received 768 hits including a backwards and forwards search. We only considered papers which were published after the year 2000. The title needs to contain the relevant keyword "requirements engineering", and the paper needs to be peer-reviewed. Due to the page limit in this research paper, we only cite a representative number of articles. If requested, we are more than happy to provide a more extensive list of the identified conference and journal articles.

3.2 Expert Interviews

For validating the MRs from the literature review, we also conducted interviews with 7 domain experts (each of the interviewees has at least 4 years of domain experience). The expert interviews lasted between 35 and 58 minutes and followed a semi-structured guideline. Overall, we interviewed 3 Senior Consultants, 1 Senior Principal Consultant, 1 Product Manager, 1 Senior Supply Chain Director and 1 Consultant from different national and multinational organisations. First, we were interested in the backgrounds of the experts. Second, we asked the experts to elaborate on their previous experience with respect to a specific RE project. Third, we asked questions regarding how the experts would improve RE practices in the future. Furthermore, we transcribed the interviews and put the documents in a central database. Two researchers independently coded the transcripts. Prior to the coding process, we agreed on the particular coding schema based on the MRs identified in the literature review. We measured the intercoder reliability with Cohen's Kappa [15] as 0.65, exceeding the recommended threshold of 0.6 [16].

4   Identified and Validated Model Requirements (MRs)

The first **(MR1) goal orientation** was widely discussed in the literature. This requirement refers to both the goals of the service provider, and the goals of customers and stakeholders [17]. Notably, all of the interviewed experts confirmed this MR with the following representative statement: *"We needed to evaluate features... We used the pre-defined goals to do that..."*

With regard to **(MR2) documentation** and traceability, the literature emphasises the importance of documenting requirements on the same abstraction level in order to allow for comparison among the requirements [18]. Particularly, high-level goals should not be mixed with very specific software requirements. With the exception of Expert 6, all interviewees confirmed this MR. The following was a quote from Expert 3: *"We have a wiki where we document the use cases and scenarios."*

We propose **(MR3) integration** as the next MR. This MR refers to combining different views of RE, particularly in the domains of product, service, and software engineering. The combination of these three disciplines leads to the design of a hybrid product which consists of product, service, and system (PSS) components [19]. Expert 6 mentioned these different views which should be addressed in RE projects: *"There are all of these different competing types of requirements that are coming to fruition..."*

Following (MR3) integration, we introduce **(MR4) agility**. With agility we specifically address the importance of a fast throughput time of the RE process. Such agile practices have mainly been discussed in the domain of software engineering, e.g. with the agile manifesto [20]. The literature states that conducting the RE process parallel to the development process facilitates a much faster time to market [21]. Five of the domain experts also emphasised the relevance of agility, as Expert 6 suggested: *"What we do is that the product owner is iteratively and constantly modifying and validating the structure [of requirements]."*

Following (MR4) agility, we introduce **(MR5) adaptability**. Both researchers and practitioners agree that artefact-oriented RE models should be flexible, meaning that they should be adaptable to different RE processes and procedures. Furthermore, depending on the organisational or project characteristic, the model should be adaptable [22]. Expert 2 elaborates on the difficulty faced if the organisation has fixed structures and does not allow for adaptability: *"The problem is usually the following: the management of the organisation defines something and the team needs to do it. It is sink or swim..."* Overall, 3 experts discussed this MR.

Regarding **(MR6) continuity**, we suggest that, in line with (MR4) agility, elicited and documented requirements should be challenged constantly within and beyond the project at hand [23]. Depending on the abstraction level, from high-level goals to very specific software requirements, different evaluation techniques and procedures should be chosen. All of the interviewed practitioners confirm this MR, as Expert 4 stated: *"...we constantly checked the requirements with the customers..."*

Finally, **(MR7) responsibilities** introduces the relevance of involving particular roles in the RE artefact model. Such roles might include the Domain Expert, the System Designer, the Business Analyst, and the System Analyst [24]. As with (MR6) continuity, all domain experts confirmed this MR. Expert 7, for example, clearly stated that such responsibilities were missing in previous projects. Thus, this would be something that he would improve in future endeavours: *"I would introduce the role of a decision maker. Sometimes it is necessary [to] make quick decisions in the requirements engineering process..."*

The results from the literature review and the validation involving 7 domain practitioners confirm the 7 MRs from both theoretical and practical points of view.

5   Introducing the Requirements Engineering Canvas (REC)

We propose the REC which consists of three building blocks: (1) *Goals and Visions*; (2) *Continuous Evaluation*; and (3) *Flexible Adaption*. These building blocks do not suggest a chronological order. Rather, the RE team should be able to combine and use these building blocks flexibly. Notably, we highlight how each building block addresses the previously identified and validated MRs. Figure 1 depicts the REC, the three building blocks (right and left circles, and the pyramid), and the 9 distinctive steps.

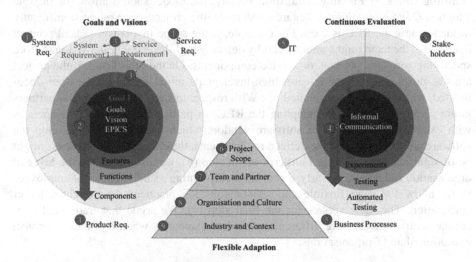

Fig. 1. Towards the Requirements Engineering Canvas (REC)

Building Block 1: Goals and Visions. The first building block of the REC consists of steps 1-3. (1) First, the RE experts should structure the requirements in product, service, and system requirements (*MR3 integration*). (2) Second, with four abstraction levels, goal, feature, function, and components, we differentiate between high-level artefacts and specific requirements (*MR1 goal orientation*). These different abstraction levels are similar to the "Requirements Abstraction Model" [25]. As a third step (3), we propose visualising the relationships between requirements on the same abstraction, and across different abstraction levels. We propose three notations, a link, a synergy, and a conflicting relationship (*MR2 documentation*). With regard to documentation, we also suggest that the RE team uses a separate database or collaboration tool to track requirements, and establish a common backlog for assigning tasks and responsibilities (*MR7 responsibilities*). This requirement is not particularly addressed in the model of this research in the progress paper.

Building Block 2: Continuous Evaluation. The second building block addresses steps 4-5. Furthermore, the artefacts in this block describe the evaluation in the RE process. With step (4), depending on the artefact level introduced in the previous building block (goals, features, functions, or components), an evaluation technique should be mapped (*MR6 continuity*). For example, for more high-level goals, informal communication such as expert interviews or focus groups might be chosen. For validating more specific software components, on the other hand, an automated testing procedure might be more appropriate. By defining these evaluation artefacts, we encourage parallel and agile RE and development processes (*MR4 agility*). Furthermore, step (5) addresses different stakeholders and customers, and the environment that should be involved. Hence, the evaluation artefacts of the previous step correspond to these stakeholder groups.

Building Block 3: Flexible Adaption. Finally, the model should allow for flexible adoption (*MR5 adaptability*). Regarding step (6), the project scope might significantly influence how the REC is used. For example, if the scope involves a radical product innovation, the team might want to start by defining high-level goals and visions before specifying software, product, or service components. On the other hand, if the project aims at developing a new release, high-level goals might already have been documented, which should be accounted for. With respect to step (7), the team and partners might also have reasons for adapting the REC. In particular, if the team cooperates with external organisations or software vendors which implement and develop the software artefacts based on the defined requirements, the documentation process might be of significant importance. Furthermore, in step (8), we also introduce the layer of organisation and culture. Clearly, a start-up incorporating a small number of employees might allow for more flexible and spontaneous RE practices than might a larger corporation. The same applies for the final step (9). We argue that traditional telecommunication might have different established standards, when it comes to project execution, than IT organisations.

6   Conclusions, Limitations, and Future Research

In this study, we consolidated MRs for developing an artefact-oriented RE model, goal orientation, documentation, integration, agility, adaptability, continuity, and responsibilities. Based on these 7 MRs, we introduced the REC, which incorporates 3 core building blocks: (1) *Goals and Vison*; (2) *Continuous Evaluation*; and (3) *Flexible Adaption*.

In future studies we will validate the REC in several projects involving graduate students, practitioners and researchers alike. In the student projects, we will ask the project teams in a graduate university course to work on several case studies for developing mobile business solutions. Additionally, we plan to conduct several in-depth case studies which should provide us with feedback from practitioners. Overall, we believe that the proposed REC should foster more thorough documentation, evaluation, and negotiation of requirements. Specifically, the REC might be used in workshop settings involving different stakeholders; it should allow for an iterative process.

Regarding the limitations of this study, we mainly involved experts from consultancy firms. Thus, by instantiating the model in a practical environment, we might challenge not only the REC but also the previously identified MRs more thoroughly. This addresses the different evaluation strategies in DSR; in particular, naturalistic ex post evaluations involving diverse stakeholders and real users [26]. Furthermore, we also plan to further highlight how the REC relates to existing artefact-oriented models. By doing so, we would like to further demonstrate the utility of the REC [27]. Moreover, despite the increasing popularity of canvas-based approaches for solving complex problems (e.g. the business model canvas by Osterwalder et al. [28]), this approach comes with some limitations, e.g. hidden complexities. Notably, our future research should address these challenges and limitations.

Acknowledgements. We would like to thank Alexander Müdespacher and Patrick Schenker for contributing to the project. Furthermore, we also appreciated the reviewer's comment, which we tried to incorporate in the final version of this paper.

References

1. Google Trends: Web Search Interest: Requirements Engineering, http://goo.gl/51fvRJ
2. Méndez Fernández, D., Wagner, S.: Naming the pain in requirements engineering: A design for a global family of surveys and first results from Germany. Inf. Softw. Technol. (2014)
3. Broy, M.: Requirements Engineering as a Key to Holistic Software Quality. Springer, Heidelberg (2006)
4. Kassab, M., Neill, C., Laplante, P.: State of practice in requirements engineering: contemporary data. Innov. Syst. Softw. Eng. 10, 235–241 (2014)
5. Méndez Fernández, D., Penzenstadler, B., Kuhrmann, M., Broy, M.: A meta model for artefact-orientation: Fundamentals and lessons learned in requirements engineering. In: Petriu, D.C., Rouquette, N., Haugen, Ø. (eds.) MODELS 2010, Part II. LNCS, vol. 6395, pp. 183–197. Springer, Heidelberg (2010)
6. Radatz, J., Geraci, A., Katki, F.: IEEE Standard Glossary of Software Engineering Terminology. IEEE Std. 610121990, 121990 (1990)
7. Hall, T., Beecham, S., Rainer, A.: Requirements problems in twelve software companies: An empirical analysis (2002)
8. Boehm, B.W.: Verifying and Validating Software Requirements and Design Specifications. IEEE Softw. 1, 75–88 (1984)
9. Penzenstadler, B., Mendez Fernandez, D., Eckhardt, J.: Understanding the Impact of Artefact-Based RE – Design of a Replication Study (2013)
10. Méndez Fernández, D., Penzenstadler, B.: Artefact-based requirements engineering: the AMDiRE approach. Requir. Eng (2014)
11. Peffers, K., Tuunanen, T., Rothenberger, M.A., Chatterjee, S.: A Design Science Research Methodology for Information Systems Research. J. Manag. Inf. Syst. 24, 45–77 (2007)
12. Vom Brocke, J., Simons, A., Niehaves, B., Reimer, K., Riemer, K., Plattfaut, R., Cleven, A.: Reconstructing the Giant: On the Importance of Rigour in Documenting the Literature Search Process. In: ECIS (2009)
13. Webster, J., Watson, R.T.: Analyzing the Past to Prepare for the Future: Writing a Literature Review. MIS Q. 26, xiii–xxiii (2002)
14. WKWI: WI-Orientierungslisten (2008), http://goo.gl/IL41Hz
15. Dewey, M.E.: Coefficients of agreement. Br. J. Psychiatry 143, 487–489 (1983)
16. Cohen, J.: Weighted kappa: nominal scale agreement with provision for scaled disagreement or partial credit. Psychol. Bull. 70, 213–220 (1968)

17. Paetsch, F., Eberlein, A., Maurer, F.: Requirements Engineering and Agile Software Development. In: Eberlein, A., Maurer, F. (eds.) 2012 IEEE 21st International Workshop on Enabling Technologies: Infrastructure for Collaborative Enterprises, p. 308 (2003)
18. Winkler, S., von Pilgrim, J.: A survey of traceability in requirements engineering and model-driven development. Softw. Syst. Model. 9, 529–565 (2009)
19. Berkovich, M., Esch, S., Mauro, C., Leimeister, J.M., Krcmar, H.: Towards an Artifact Model for Requirements to IT- enabled Product Service Systems. Wirtschaftsinformatik Proceedings 2011 (2011)
20. Fowler, M., Highsmith, J.: The Agile Manifesto. Softw. Dev. Mag. 9, 28–32 (2001)
21. Hickey, A.M., Davis, A.M.: Requirements elicitation and elicitation technique selection: model for two knowledge-intensive software development processes. In: Proceedings of the 36th Annual Hawaii International Conference on System Sciences, p. 10. IEEE (2003)
22. Valenca, G., Alves, C., Heimann, V., Jansen, S., Brinkkemper, S.: Competition and collaboration in requirements engineering: A case study of an emerging software ecosystem. 2014 IEEE 22nd International Requirements Engineering Conference (RE), pp. 384–393. IEEE (2014)
23. Pohl, K.: Requirements Engineering: Fundamentals, Principles, and Techniques. Springer (2010)
24. Poelmans, J., Dedene, G., Snoeck, M., Viaene, S.: An iterative requirements engineering framework based on Formal Concept Analysis and C–K theory. Expert Syst. Appl. 39, 8115–8135 (2012)
25. Gorschek, T., Wohlin, C.: Requirements Abstraction Model. Requir. Eng. 11, 79–101 (2006)
26. Venable, J., Pries-Heje, J., Baskerville, R.: A Comprehensive Framework for Evaluation in Design Science Research. In: Peffers, K., Rothenberger, M., Kuechler, B. (eds.) DESRIST 2012. LNCS, vol. 7286, pp. 423–438. Springer, Heidelberg (2012)
27. Gregor, S., Hevner, A.R.: Positioning and Presenting Design Science Research for Maximum Impact. MIS Q. 37, 337–356 (2013)
28. Osterwalder, A., Pigneur, Y., Tucci, C.: Clarifying business models: origins, present, and future of the concept. Commun. Assoc. Inf. Syst. 15, 1–43 (2005)

Impact of Text Mining Application
on Financial Footnotes Analysis

Research in Progress

Maryam Heidari[(⊠)] and Carsten Felden[(⊠)]

TU Bergakademie Freiberg, Freiberg, Germany
{maryam.heidari,carsten.felden}@bwl.tu-freiberg.de

Abstract. In recent decade and with the advent of the eXtensible Business Reporting Language (XBRL), financial reports have a great mutation in terms of a unified reporting process. Nevertheless, the unstructured part of financial reports, so called footnotes, remains as barrier facing an accurate automatic and real-time financial analysis. The purpose of this paper is to investigate whether the text mining approach is an appropriate solution to assist analyzing textual financial footnotes or not. The implemented text mining prototype is able to classify textual financial footnotes into related pre-defined categories automatically. This avoids manually reading of the entire text. Different text classification supervised algorithms have been compared, where the decision tree by 90.65% accuracy performs better rather than other deployed classifiers. This research provides preliminary insights about the impact of using a text mining approach on automatic financial footnote analysis in terms of saving time and increasing accuracy.

Keywords: Financial footnotes · Text mining · Prototyping · Classification algorithms

1 Introduction

It is recognized that results from financial analysis have impacts on financial decisions [10]. The emphasis of financial statement analysis is using a variety of analytical techniques in order to identify company's financial performance and support business decisions [3]. In this regard, footnotes, as inseparable parts of financial reports, play a critical role to enable and support the financial analysis process [17]. A careful review of a company's footnotes is necessary to reveal and explain identified values within the financial report's main body. However, their unstructured format is an obstacle to analyze them automatically. There are no standards for clarity or conciseness among them [14] and a labor intensive manual content analysis is needed. Therefore, the paper's goal is to design a text mining solution to perform financial footnotes analysis automatically by applying text classification techniques to accelerate financial analysis.

Previous studies have shown the relevance of footnotes and information demand, which resides in footnotes lines [11]. Based on different use cases, the main method

© Springer International Publishing Switzerland 2015
B. Donnellan et al. (Eds.): DESRIST 2015, LNCS 9073, pp. 463–470, 2015.
DOI: 10.1007/978-3-319-18714-3_39

for analyzing footnotes is still manually reading [11]. Furthermore, in spite of using XBRL as a unified data exchange standard for financial reporting [15] and even with the footnote detailed tagging, the automatic analysis of narrative information among footnote lines is not possible. Moreover, in terms of financial narratives analysis, coding procedures are used to identify financial patterns in textual financial parts [2]. However, this does not offer any benefit for analyzing financial footnotes automatically, because of manual code assignment to the texts [13]. In this regard, we suggest a text mining design toward facilitate automatic footnote analysis by performing different text classification algorithms. Therefore, we express the following research question:

RQ: Does proposed text mining solution facilitate financial footnote analysis in an automatic fashion to save time and accuracy?

The paper's structure is as follows: Section 2 discusses the related work in terms of financial analysis and unstructured data integration. In Section 3, we introduce the research design. Sections 4 and 5 present the proposed framework and the prototype implementation phases, respectively. Finally, after discussion about obtained results, the conclusion section summarizes further research and implication of the research results.

2   Related Work

According to [17], financial analysis without considering textual parts of financial reports is incomplete and might be a misleading task. However, manually analyzing financial footnotes is still a limitation and a time consuming issue in terms of an accurate financial analysis. A previous study [11], identified existing research papers (approximately 45), where each one relates to an issue in context of financial analysis. The study results demonstrated the importance and the effect of financial footnote information on financial analysis processes. It is indicated that existing methods for financial footnotes analysis rely on a manual process. As an example, Franceschetti et al. proposed a method to recognize insolvency in business transactions. Based on this method, there is a need to extract assets' elements manually from footnotes [8].

In this regard, since financial footnotes have textual format, existing literature in terms of text mining for financial predictions are studied as well. Beattie et al. introduced a comprehensive four dimensional coding system for content analysis of accounting narratives [2]. The limitation of this method is manually assigning the financial codes every time to each accounting report. According to Hussainey, this approach can be extremely time-consuming and error-prone because human coders could make mistakes and overlook some relevant content [13]. Brent and Atkisson built a coding scheme by training pre-defined categories, which assign codes to text documents automatically in order to analyze economic crises through newspaper articles [5]. Neumann et al. [9] design a text classification approach to process financial news to automate stock price prediction. It is based on three main text processing step: Dataset step as a base for the classification, feature processing step to extract different features and machine learning step which uses subset of data to train a classification algorithm to be able to classify financial news into positive and negative categories.

According to reviewed articles, it can be summarized that based on critical impact of footnotes on financial analysis process It is necessary to find an automatic-based solution to overcome this gap and facilitate financial analysis process, reliably and accurately. Moreover, according to related research in terms of using text classification approach in financial domain, it seems developing such a text classification approach for financial footnotes analysis has benefit to recognize hidden patterns in the narrative part of financial reports and facilitate financial footnote analysis considerably.

3   Research Design

In this chapter, we explain the basis of our proposed solution relying on existing text classification approaches to create and evaluate an artifact in order to solve the identified problem. The purpose of this solution is to demonstrate the benefit of an automatic text-analytics approach for financial footnote analysis. To this, we are supposed to classify particular sentences, which carry out soft information in textual parts of financial reports regarding the identification of required financial categories, which are relevant for financial analysis.

In order to have a systematic design, we applied the Cross-Industry Standard Process (CRISP) framework [7], which is one of the accepted frameworks in data/text mining domain [16] and has six phases. In the initial phase, business understanding, all our effort is to recognize the business case regarding the existing gap in the financial footnote analysis and the study aims to accomplish. Within the data understanding phase, we concentrated on the financial footnotes, which are available in financial report files of different companies. The database to get financial footnotes of company filings is Edgar online of U.S. SEC allowing quick research on companies' financial periodic reports like 10-K (annual reports) and 10-Q (quarterly reports). The next two phases, data preparation and model development, are focused on all activities with the aim of constructing the initial proposed text-mining artifact. In the evaluation step, we concentrate on a quantitative evaluation as a first evaluation phase to apply statistics to generalize the findings and to process data in a numerical way. However, further research is necessary to evaluate the obtained results by a qualitative approach to achieve business value as well. In the deployment phase, the outcomes will be deployed into a real information system [16].

In this regard, we develop our proposed solution based on existing methods in terms of text classification in financial area [9], which has three main steps: dataset, feature processing and machine learning. As a result, we train an example data set including the numbers of financial footnotes, first, to be able to recognize and classify different identified classes in financial footnotes. Afterwards, we deploy machine learning algorithms on our training documents to recognize the impact of using text classification approach on financial footnote analysis. Later on, the recognized algorithm will be used for new and untrained financial footnotes.

4   Proposed Framework

Figure 1 shows the workflow of the proposed approach.

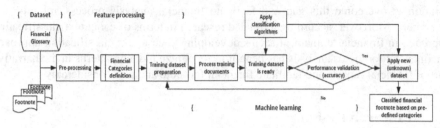

Fig. 1. Proposed framework

Dataset

The used dataset in this research step is comprised of income tax footnotes from financial reports (10k and 10Q) of 120 different companies in different work fields. We chose income tax as one of the identifiable footnotes, which carries important financial issues. We also applied the financial glossaries in order to facilitate the process of identified classes through income tax footnotes.

Feature Processing

In this step the primary task is to delineate between unstructured text and a set of predefined classes. According to the fact that in the financial footnote domain there are not any identified previous categorized trained patterns, we started to extract rule-based financial categories manually. First we read financial footnote samples from different companies in details and extracted related key terms out of the footnotes' lines. Afterwards, the key terms are compared with existing financial glossaries to prove the importance of the terms in financial analysis process. We recognized initial 31 categories in income tax footnotes. After reviewing related footnotes, six of these identified categories have to be removed from our initial categorization, because they are rarely used in context of income tax. Furthermore, in order to facilitate the classification process and increase the level of accuracy as well, we integrated the sub-categories in their main categories. Basically, there are two main reasons behind this integration. First, based on reviewing different financial footnotes, these sub-categories are not repeated consequently in every financial report. Moreover, by reducing the number of classes, the classification errors are decreased as well. As a result, twelve classes remain, finally, wherein six categories have a stronger effect on financial analysis. Figure 2 shows the categories identification process related to income tax footnotes.

Fig. 2. Categories identification process related to income tax footnote

Machine Learning

The training dataset process started with the data preparation process. The preparation process encompasses ordinary text mining pre-processes such as lower case transformation, stop words filtering, and tokenization. It should be considered that the major difference between the proposed methods is that it is not just sufficient, to recognize some rates and trends in footnotes' lines. A recognition of soft information through sentences and their relations is of importance, too. As a result, the whole income tax texts are tokenized into sentences, not just into terms. Therefore, we have 1,724 example sentences, where each one belongs to one or more particular pre-defined income tax categories. In the next step and when the training dataset is prepared, we applied the supervised algorithms such as K-NN, Naïve Bayes, Decision tree, and Support Vector Machine (SVM), which are typically used in supervised text classification area [1], [4], [6], and [18]. The reason behind using different algorithms is to observe the performance results, which help users to apply the more appropriate algorithm for a financial footnote analysis [12]. It should be noted, although unsupervised algorithms do not require pre-training process and provide high accuracy in clustering projects, but for classification purposes, which is the aim of this research, supervised algorithms yield better performance than unsupervised ones [18]. Since applying classification algorithms, their performance in terms of accuracy is validated in order to recognize an appropriate text classification algorithm. Subsequently, the more accurate algorithm will be selected for automatic classification of unknown and untrained income tax footnote. The implementation and results will be discussed in the next section.

5   Implementation and Results

The implementation of the proposed workflow as an artifact makes text-mining algorithms available to extract financial footnote classification using the open source software component Rapid Miner as an open source tool for machine learning purposes. It comprises different procedures including data loading and transformation, pre-processing and visualization, modeling, evaluation, and deployment. According to the proposed solution, all three main phases are implemented successfully and each algorithm is applied separately to the dataset. In all these classifiers, in order to evaluate the performance, the operator *split validation* with 0.7 split ratio splits up the example set randomly into 70 percent training set and rest remain as a test set to assess the robustness and validity of the classifiers in order to estimate, how accurately a model performs in practice. The performance of the model is also measured during the testing phase. In order to evaluate the performance of the trained model, the prediction accuracy, other statistic criterion such as precision, recall, absolute error, and root mean squared error (RMSE) of each algorithm are calculated. Table 1 shows the obtained results from applying these algorithms on the example set.

Table 1. Performance result of performing algorithms

Algorithm	Run time	Accuracy	Absolute error	Precision	Recall	RMSE
K-NN	7s	81.82%	0.183	82.34%	80.92%	0.362
Naïve Bayes	4s	82.86%	0.171	78.48%	77.85%	0.414
SVM	28s	79.22%	0.784	80.37%	78.46%	0.786
Decision tree	1m 45s	90.65%	0.136	91.38%	90.82%	0.280

6   Results and Discussion

By implementing a unified platform in Rapid Miner, we demonstrated the application of the proposed text classification solution and therefore the classification of income tax financial footnotes into identified categories.

As a result, among applied text classification models, a decision tree presents more reliable results in terms of accuracy and other statistic criteria except run time with 90.65%. In other words, 90.65% of income tax footnote sentences are classified correctly based on the defined six categories. An analyst, who is interested in getting knowledge about one category in income tax footnote could directly extract related sentences out of that category. This can facilitate and accelerate the financial footnote analysis process significantly instead of reading entire income tax footnote. However, the decision tree takes more time to run in comparison with other classifiers. In this regards and due to the reason that we have more than two classes, the often stated SVM algorithm has a weak performance and it is not appropriate for the applied approach of financial footnote analysis.

Regarding the proposed research question and the identified gap with the existing literature, it can be stated that using the proposed text mining solution offers an appropriate approach to overcome difficulties through manual analysis of financial footnotes. The contribution of using text mining techniques in financial footnote analysis is summarized in Table 2 by comparing it with selected existing methods.

Table 2. Comparing the proposed solution with existing financial footnotes analysis methods

Approach for textual part of financial report	Type of financial report	Financial footnotes analysis process	Challenges and benefits
Traditional approach	Traditional reports	Manual process	Time consuming and error-prone
Block and detailed tagging	XBRL reports	Tables and numbers are tagged but narrative information through footnotes lines should be analyzed manually	Both tagging procedures help just to have a unified structure in financial reports. / Textual parts of footnotes are still read manually which it is time consuming and error-prone.
Content analysis based on coding systems	Traditional reports	Manual code assignment to the text	Codes should be assigned manually to the text every time for each repot /Mistakes of human coders / More accurate in comparison with manual processing
Text classification method	Applicable for both traditional and XBRL reports	Automatic classification of financial footnotes based on pre-defined categories	Footnotes are classified automatically/ Textual part of footnotes are accessible through pre-defined categories/ Time saving/ More accurate in comparison with manual process/ Training documents process have been done manually/ Increasing the number of categories reduces the accuracy of the model

During the implementation phase, we encountered issues and limitations such as the challenge of manual process of training documents regarding improve the accuracy of classification. Another limitation is the number of classes through each footnote. In this research, we focused just on one of the footnote item (income tax). However, due to a great deal of classes, it is not possible to put all the footnotes' items in a single classification process.

In a nutshell, the results show that applying a text classification method we are able to classify textual parts of financial reports automatically into manually pre-defined classes. A financial analysis process can be done, to some extent, automatically, by breaking down a textual footnote to sentences with pre-processing operators. With an appropriate trained classification model, we classify sentences into related categories. Thus, analysts can directly access required sentences of related categories instead of reading the entire text document.

The next step of this research is a further development to address identified challenges in order to apply the process steps to an unknown data set classifying a new financial footnote document automatically.

7 Conclusion

The last decade has witnessed a great development in the field of financial analysis concerning XBRL. However, textual parts of financial reports, which carry critical and relevant information, are still a barrier for financial analyst and someone who cares about accurate and timely financial analysis as well.

We address this limitation by applying a text classification approach in order to improve financial footnote process. Referring to our stated research question: Does proposed text mining solution facilitate financial footnote analysis in an automatic fashion to save time and accuracy, we introduced a useable solution as an artifact to be able to determine, to which extent the usage of text classification algorithms is beneficial to gain a meaningful automization. The method can facilitate the time consuming and rigid manual processing of financial footnotes by using manually categorized footnotes examples to train classification algorithms. In terms of the chosen algorithms, the decision tree obtained a reliable result with an output of 90.65 % accuracy rate. However, in terms of run time, which is an important issue in this research, Naïve Bayes performs better than the other classifiers. A next step is to apply new and unlabeled footnotes to this framework in order to see a classified footnote as an output for further financial analysis. The major contribution of this paper is to support the analysis of financial footnotes in an alternative and more automated way, which facilitates existing manual analysis. However, the proposed solution is still tentative and further research is necessary to extend and develop the idea in a qualitative way in order to evaluate the business value of this method by verifying the results with experts' knowledge.

References

1. Baharudin, B., Lee, L.H., Khan, K.: A Review of Machine Learning Algorithms for Text-Documents Classification. Journal of Advances in Information Technology 1(1), 4–20 (2010)
2. Beattie, V., McInnes, B., Fearnley, S.: A methodology for analysing and evaluating narratives in annual reports: a comprehensive descriptive profile and metrics for disclosure quality attributes. Accounting Forum 28(3), 205–236 (2004)
3. Beretz, P.: Financial statement analysis, http://de.slideshare.net/anscers/financial-statement-analysis-i-session-2
4. Botzenhardt, A., Witt, A., Maedche, A.: A Text Mining Application for Exploring the Voice of the Customer. In: AMCIS 2011 Proceedings (2011)
5. Brent, E., Atkisson, C.: A standard-based automated coding program for unstructured text" Veyor ® Survey presentation, University of Surrey, USA (2011)
6. Chaovalit, P., Zhou, L.: Movie review mining: A comparison between supervised and unsupervised classification approaches. In: Proceedings of the 38th Annual Hawaii International Conference on System Sciences, HICSS 2005 (2005)
7. Chapman, P., Clinton, J., Kerber, R., Khabanza, T., Reinartz, T., Shearer, C., Wirth, R.: CRISP-DM- step by step data mining guide. SPSS, Chicago (2000)
8. Franceschetti, B.M., Koschtial, C., Felden, C.: Break-up Analysis: a method to regain trust in business transaction. In: IX Conference of the Italian Chapter of AIS, Rome, Italy, pp. 28–29 (2012)
9. Hagenau, M., Liebmann, M., Neumann, D.: Automated news reading: Stock price prediction based on financial news using context-specific features. In: 2012 45th Hawaii International Conference on System Science (HICSS). IEEE (2012)
10. Haskins, M.E., Ferris, K.R., Selling, T.I.: International financial reporting and analysis: A contextual emphasis. Irwin, Chicago (1996)
11. Heidari, M., Felden, C.: Toward Supporting Analytical Tasks in Financial Footnotes Analysis- A State of the Art. In: MKWI 2014, Paderborn, Deutschland, pp. 26–28 (2014)
12. Hotho, A., Andreas, N., Paaß, G., Augustin, S.: A Brief Survey of Text Mining, 1–37 (2005)
13. Hussainey, K.S.M.: A study of the ability of (partially) automated disclosure scores to explain the information content of annual report narratives for future earnings,Doctoral dissertation, University of Manchester (2004)
14. Investopedia, http://www.investopedia.com
15. Janvrin, D., Mascha, M.: The process of creating XBRL Instance document: A research framework. Review of Business Information Systems 14(2), 11–34 (2010)
16. Miner, G., Elder, J., Nisbet, B., Delen, D., Fast, A., Hill, T.: Practical text mining and statistical analysis for non-structured text data applications. Elsevier, Massachusetts (2012)
17. Putra, L.D.: Understanding footnotes to financial statements, http://accounting-financial-tax.com/2008/08/understanding-footnotes-to-financial-statement
18. Reinberger, M.-L., Spyns, P.: Unsupervised text mining for the learning of dogma-inspired ontologies. Ontology Learning from Text: Methods, Applications and Evaluation 123, 29–43 (2005)

Empirical Grounding of Design Science Research Methodology

Stefan Cronholm[✉] and Hannes Göbel

University of Borås, Allégatan 1, 501 90 Borås, Sweden
{stefan.cronholm,hannes.gobel}@hb.se

Abstract. The purpose of this paper is to empirically ground design science research methodology (DSR). We claim that popular DSR methodologies lack solid empirical grounding since they are based on reconstructions of studies conducted for other purposes. Thus, we have systematically collected methodology users' empirical experiences and reflections from DSR projects. The overall findings show that the experiences are mainly positive. However, there are negative experiences such as the guidelines' granularity, lack of rigorousness concerning evaluation of new knowledge, and support for collaboration.

Keywords: Design science research · Design science research methodology · Empirical grounding · Empirical validation · Secondary analysis

1 Introduction

The purpose of this paper is to empirically ground design science research (DSR) methodology. DSR is widespread and often viewed as the paradigm in the discipline of Information Systems (IS) (e.g. [9]). One purpose of DSR is to guide design and evaluation of artifacts (e.g. [6], [18]). The popularity of DSR calls for a methodology to serve as a commonly accepted framework [14]. In our literature review, we identified three DSR methodologies that, according to their number of citations, are well-known in the IS society: Design Science Research in Information Systems Research (DSRISR) (Hevner [5] and Hevner et al. [6]), A Design Science Research Methodology (DSRM) (Peffers et al. [14]), and Action Design Research (ADR) (Sein et al. [18]).

According to [4], methodologies need to be theoretically, internally and empirically grounded. The purpose of grounding is to provide arguments for specific method knowledge and to make actors more confident in using this knowledge [4]. External theoretical grounding means to relate method knowledge to relevant theoretical knowledge. Internal grounding means to eliminate internal contradictions and check that there is meaningful and logical consistency [4]. Our reading of these three popular DSR methodologies has shown that the authors have done an excellent theoretical and internal grounding. However, the methodologies do *not* rest on a solid empirically grounding. Empirical grounding means to investigate whether the prescribed methodology is successful in practice. It means: *to use and reflect upon the methodology, to observe the prescribed actions in relation to their results and consequences, and to*

© Springer International Publishing Switzerland 2015
B. Donnellan et al. (Eds.): DESRIST 2015, LNCS 9073, pp. 471–478, 2015.
DOI: 10.1007/978-3-319-18714-3_40

give a reference to empirical findings [4]. Important questions to ask in an empirical grounding process are: "Is the prescribed action in the methodology really successful in practice?" and "Will it lead to desired consequences?" [4]. The empirical evidence of DSRISR, DSRM and ADR are based on *reconstructions* of previous studies conducted for other purposes. Our criticism is supported by the authors' own words: a) "To illustrate the application of the design-science guidelines to IS research, we have selected three exemplar articles for analysis" [6] (p. 90); b) "To demonstrate the use of the DSRM, we apply it retroactively to four already published IS research projects." [14], (p. 57); and c) "... we illustrate how ADR can be applied by describing a research project conducted at Volvo IT" [18], (p. 45). Moreover, "... the VIP [Volvo Information Portal] project was not conducted explicitly as ADR ..." [18], (p. 52).

To use an existing data set, such as reconstruction of previous studies, to answer new or extended research questions is often referred to as secondary analysis. According to [7], two methodological issues can be raised when conducting a secondary analysis of a qualitative data set: a) the degree to which the data generated are amenable to a secondary analysis, and b) the extent to which the research purpose of the secondary analysis can differ from that of the primary analysis without invalidating the findings. That is, to use data for other purposes means that there is a need for a number of methodological considerations. In [6], [14] and [18] there are no such methodological discussions. We are not saying that the reconstructions of the studies have invalidated the results. However, we claim that these popular and widely accepted DSR methodologies should rest on a solid empirical grounding. Our claim is supported by other scholars, who also recognize the need for proper grounding of DSR (e.g. [1], [4]). The following section includes a description of related work. In section 3, we describe the research method and in section 4 we present the findings. Finally, in section 6 conclusions are drawn.

2   Related Work

We have analyzed the literature in order to describe the state-of-the-art concerning empirical grounding of DSR methodology. An impressive literature analysis concerning the proliferation, nature and quality of DSR in IS conferences since the publication of Hevner et al. [6] is reported in [10]. They have analyzed 142 articles published at five major IS conferences in the years 2005-2007, and they report that only a small percentage of the papers discuss a concise and consistent implementation of the design science methodology as suggested by [6]. According to the categorization of the articles, none is explicitly discussing DSR methodology from the perspective of empirical grounding. We have also searched articles related to Design Science Research on Google Scholar. We used the search words "design science research" and "design science research methodology". All together, these searches resulted in over 7 000 hits. To read and analyze this vast amount was not possible. Therefore we searched for empirical grounding of DSR methodology in specific IS journals and conference proceedings. We have, similar to [10], found that several studies report the use of DSR methodologies in order to develop design principles of some kind. There are also papers that suggest extensions to DSR methodologies (e.g. [3], [19]). Our conclusion is that none of these studies has had an explicit purpose to empirically ground DSR methodology. We have found several studies that provide fragmented important methodological insights based on experiences. These fragments stem predominantly from use of DSRISR.

3   Research Method

Our research question reads: "What is the empirical evidence that DSR methodologies work in practice?" In order to answer the question, we needed to decide: what is the analysis unit? (all the three DSR methodologies or a selection) and what is the data source? (own empirical experiences or other scholars' empirical experiences). Regarding the analysis unit, we decided to analyze empirical experiences concerning DSRISR. The reasons are: 1) DSRISR is the most cited DSR methodology and thus has had a large impact on the IS discipline; and 2) it is the most used DSR methodology and consequently there should be good conditions to collect experiences. Regarding the data source, we have chosen to analyze other scholars' experiences since our research is still in progress.

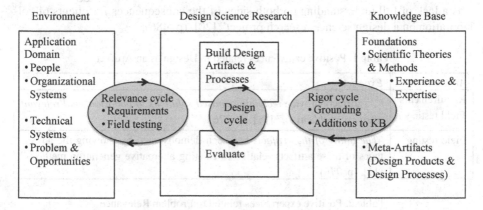

Fig. 1. Design Science Research Cycles [5]

We have collected empirical experiences by studying popular information systems journals and conference proceedings. We have searched in: European Journal of Information Systems (years 2006-2014); special issues on design science research in Management Information Systems Quarterly (vol. 32, no 4), Scandinavian Journal of Information Systems (vol. 19, no. 2), Organization Studies, (vol. 29, Issue 3); and conference proceedings in Design Science Research in Information Systems and Technology (years 2006-2013). The collected experiences have been ontologically anchored to each cycle in the Three Cycle View of Design Science Research [5] (see Fig. 1). The experiences have also been related to the seven DSR guidelines [6]: Design as an Artifact, Problem Relevance, Design Evaluation, Research Contributions, Research Rigor, Design as a Search Process, and Communication of Research. Moreover, in order to provide a good overview, we have classified the experiences as positive or negative. Due to limited space, we have presented a selection of the collected empirical experiences.

4   Analysis of Empirical Experiences

4.1   The Relevance Cycle

The relevance cycle relates the design science research domain to the environment domain. The overall question for the relevance cycle reads, "Does the design artifact improve the environment and how can this improvement be measured?" [23, p. 89]. We have related positive experiences to the guidelines Design as an Artifact (see table 1), Problem Relevance (see table 2) and Research Contribution (table 3). We have identified negative experiences for the guidelines Problem Relevance (see table 4). The negative experiences are mainly not contradicting the positive experiences. Rather, they focus on other aspects such as the need for more procedural guidelines. There are negative experiences related to the relevance cycle which we could not relate to a specific guideline. These experiences concern lack of guidelines for collaboration with practitioners and examples of quotes read: "The single biggest problem was a lack of full understanding on both sides of the consequences for clients of collaboration on a design science research project" [20], (p. 486);

Table 1. Positive experiences related to Design as an Artifact

Action	Experience
Requirements Field testing	"… artifacts provide *technology-based solutions to important and relevant business problems* …" [11], (p. 776).
Field testing	"*The utility of the artifacts* has been demonstrated by showing the advantages of these artifacts relative to existing alternative generation methods" [11], (p. 776).

Table 2. Positive experiences related to Problem Relevance

Action	Experience
Requirements	"… excellent approach for addressing practitioners' needs" [16], (p. 46).
Requirements Field testing	"Employing DSR in the IS discipline increases the relevance of IS research … by helping solve industry's problems" [1], (p. 311).

Table 3. Positive experiences related to Research Contributions

Action	Experience
Field testing	" … the empirical testing provided evidence that the design propositions are fulfilled and the goals are achieved" [15], (p. 56).
Requirements Field testing	"It was very useful to develop the artifact by prototyping because each version was tested so that errors and improvements were identified and addressed," [16], (p. 44).

Table 4. Negative experiences related to Problem Relevance

Action	Experience
Requirements	"... it is argued that scholars pursuing DSR has [sic] paid insufficient attention to the type of change necessary in the local practice" [17], (p. 153).
Requirements	"... the existing statement of guideline #2 [Problem Relevance] is that ... it tends to constrain the time horizons for design research. We often cannot foresee what problems will be relevant for the future of IT" [3], (p. 5:18).

4.2   The Design Cycle

In the Design Cycle activities iterate rapidly between the construction of an artifact, its evaluation, and subsequent feedback to refine the design further. This iterative process continues until a satisfactory design is achieved. We have found positive and negative experiences related to the guideline Design Evaluation (see table 5 and 6).

Table 5. Positive experiences related to Design Evaluation

" ... design science research with its iterative solving process allowed us to adjust and refine the focus of our research in an unconventional manner" [2], (p. 304).
"We noticed the value of real-world simulations for evaluating design artifacts" [2], (p. 304).

Table 6. Negative experiences related to Design Evaluation

"What is missing is guidance for how to perform the evaluation, more specifically, what evaluation methods to use with specific DS research outputs" [13], (p. 398).
"... yet there is surprisingly little guidance about designing the DSR evaluation activity, beyond suggesting possible methods that could be used for evaluation" [19], (p. 423), and "This state of affairs in DSR constitutes what we can call an 'evaluation gap' " [19], (p. 424).

4.3   The Rigor Cycle

The purpose of the Rigor Cycle is to connect the research project with the knowledge base. The purpose of the knowledge base is to inform the research project with scientific theory and methods. One purpose of the research project is to extend the knowledge base [5]. We have identified positive and negative experiences related to the guidelines Design as a Search Process (see table 7), to Research Rigor (see table 8 and 9) and to Research Contribution (see table 10). There are positive experiences in respect of the knowledge base as a support for explanation and justification. The negative experiences are mainly criticizing the methodology for not providing a rigor evaluation support. Research Contribution is discussed in terms of additions to the knowledge base (see table 10.) In relation to this guideline, we have only found negative experiences that discuss the quality of the evaluation process and suggested design principles.

Table 7. Positive experiences related to Design as a Search Process

Action	Experience
Grounding	"Reflecting on our experience in designing the Demand Response system, we appreciate design science research as it assisted us in the search process to discover an effective solution to our problem" [2], (p. 304).

Table 8. Positive experiences related to Research Rigor

Action	Experience
Grounding	"... when knowledgeable users are not available, previous research is a very useful source of information so that the critical requirements can be identified" [16], (p. 45).
Grounding	"... the method on hand offers greater rigor than action research does" [12], (p. 287).

Table 9. Negative experiences related to Research Rigor

Action	Experience
Add. to KB	" ... justification for design principles is often focused on specific aspects of the problem space and important principles are not explicitly identified in the design theory [8], (p. 239).
Grounding	"A final example for the need of rigour improvement in IS design science research is the lack of commonly accepted, specific evaluation guidelines for the different artefact types" [21], (p. 471).

Table 10. Negative experiences related to Research Contribution

Action	Experience
Add. to KB	"... evaluations of the design theory are compromised, as testing is less likely to examine the veracity of principles which are not stated in the theory. This limits the contribution of design evaluations to the knowledge base" [8], (p. 239).

5   Conclusions

We can conclude that the empirical experiences reported from scholars are fragmented. Thus we have: presented a structured wholeness and ontologically anchored the empirical experiences to the major constructs in DSRISR.

Relevance Cycle: The purpose of the Relevance Cycle is to answer the following questions: "Does the design artifact improve the environment and how can this improvement be measured?" Based on the empirical experiences, we can conclude that this purpose is fulfilled in respect of the actions Requirements and Field testing. However, there are negative experiences concerning the guidelines' granularity, procedural support and support for collaboration. We have not found any experiences related to the measurement of how the design artifact has improved the environment.

Design Cycle: The purpose of the Design Cycle is to iterate between the construction of an artifact, its evaluation, and subsequent feedback to refine the design further. Based on the empirical experiences, we can conclude that the purpose is fulfilled in respect of its iterative character. We can also conclude that there are mixed experiences concerning the guideline Design Evaluation. The main criticism addresses the "evaluation-part" and the lack of guidance.

Rigor Cycle: The purpose of the Rigor Cycle is to connect the research project to the knowledge base and to provide past knowledge to ensure innovation. Based on the empirical experiences, we can conclude that the purpose is fulfilled in respect of the action Grounding. The purpose is not fulfilled in respect of the action Additions to KB since there is s a lack of rigorousness concerning the evaluation of new knowledge such as design principles. One explanation might be found in Hevner et al. (2004): "… the principal aim is to determine how well an artifact works, not to theorize about or prove anything about why the artifact works" [6], (p. 88).

The overall conclusion is that DSRISR is experienced as a useful methodology that can be followed in practically relevant studies. Our conclusions refine and extend what is claimed in [22]. They contend that DSR in general "… has yet to attain its full potential impact on the development and use of information systems, due to gaps in the understanding and application of DSR concepts and methods" (p. 337). We have systematically and ontologically anchored positive and negative experiences in a way that has not been done before. We believe that our findings can be interesting in two ways: a) we have contributed with empirical grounding DSRISR; and b) the identified lacks in DSRISR can be used a base for redesign. As further research, we suggest an empirical grounding of other DSR methodologies and of DSRISR based on experiences from own research projects.

References

1. Alturki, A., Bandara, W., Gable, G.G.: Design science research and the core of information systems. In: Peffers, K., Rothenberger, M., Kuechler, B. (eds.) DESRIST 2012. LNCS, vol. 7286, pp. 309–327. Springer, Heidelberg (2012)
2. Bodenbenner, P., Feuerriegel, S., Neumann, D.: Design science in practice: designing an electricity demand response system. In: vom Brocke, J., Hekkala, R., Ram, S., Rossi, M. (eds.) DESRIST 2013. LNCS, vol. 7939, pp. 293–307. Springer, Heidelberg (2013)
3. Gill, T.G., Hevner, A.R.: A fitness-utility model for design science research. ACM Transactions on Management Information Systems (TMIS) 4(2), 5 (2013)
4. Goldkuhl, G.: Design Theories in Information Systems - A Need for Multi-Grounding. Journal of Information Technology Theory and Application (JITTA) 6(2), 59–72 (2004)
5. Hevner, A.: A Three Cycle View of Design Science Research. Scandinavian Journal of Information Systems 19(2), 87–92 (2007)
6. Hevner, A.R., March, S.T., Park, J., Ram, S.: Design Science in Information Systems Research. MIS Quarterly 28(1), 75–105 (2004)
7. Hinds, P.S., Vogel, R.J., Clarke-Steffen, L.: The possibilities and pitfalls of doing a secondary analysis of a qualitative data set. Qualitative Health Research 7(3), 408–424 (1997)

8. Hovorka, D.S., Pries-Heje, J.: Don't Ignore the Iceberg: Timely Revelation of Justification in DSR. In: vom Brocke, J., Hekkala, R., Ram, S., Rossi, M. (eds.) DESRIST 2013. LNCS, vol. 7939, pp. 228–241. Springer, Heidelberg (2013)
9. Iivari, J.: A Paradigmatic Analysis of Information Systems as a Design Science. Scandinavian Journal of Information Systems 19(2), 39–63 (2007)
10. Indulska, M., Recker, J.C.: Design Science in IS Research: A Literature Analysis. In: Proceedings 4th Biennial ANU Workshop on Information Systems Foundations, Canberra, Australia (2008)
11. Lee, J., Wyner, G.M., Pentland, B.T.: Process grammar as a tool for business process design. MIS Quarterly, 757–778 (2008)
12. Mayer, J.H.: Managing the Future—Six Guidelines for Designing Environmental Scanning Systems. In: Jain, H., Sinha, A.P., Vitharana, P. (eds.) DESRIST 2011. LNCS, vol. 6629, pp. 276–290. Springer, Heidelberg (2011)
13. Peffers, K., Rothenberger, M., Tuunanen, T., Vaezi, R.: Design science research evaluation. In: Peffers, K., Rothenberger, M., Kuechler, B. (eds.) DESRIST 2012. LNCS, vol. 7286, pp. 398–410. Springer, Heidelberg (2012)
14. Peffers, K., Tuunanen, T., Rothenberger, M.A., Chatterjee, S.: A Design Science Research Methodology for Information Systems Research. Journal of Management Information Systems 24(3), 45–77 (2008)
15. Piirainen, K.A., Briggs, R.O.: Design theory in practice – making design science research more transparent. In: Jain, H., Sinha, A.P., Vitharana, P. (eds.) DESRIST 2011. LNCS, vol. 6629, pp. 47–61. Springer, Heidelberg (2011)
16. Reynoso, J.M.G., Olfman, L., Ryan, T., Horan, T.: An information systems design theory for an expert system for training. Journal of Database Management (JDM) 24(3), 31–50 (2013)
17. Rudmark, D., Lind, M.: Design Science Research Demonstrators for Punctuation – The Establishment of a Service Ecosystem. In: Jain, H., Sinha, A.P., Vitharana, P. (eds.) DESRIST 2011. LNCS, vol. 6629, pp. 153–165. Springer, Heidelberg (2011)
18. Sein, M.K., Henfridsson, O., Purao, S., Rossi, M., Lindgren, R.: Action Design Research. MIS Quarterly 35(1), 37–56 (2011)
19. Venable, J., Pries-Heje, J., Baskerville, R.: A Comprehensive Framework for Evaluation in Design Science Research. In: Peffers, K., Rothenberger, M., Kuechler, B. (eds.) DESRIST 2012. LNCS, vol. 7286, pp. 423–438. Springer, Heidelberg (2012)
20. Weedman, J.: Client as designer in collaborative design science research projects: what does social science design theory tell us. European Journal of Information Systems 17(5), 476–488 (2008)
21. Wilson, J.: Responsible Authorship and Peer Review. Science and Engineering Ethics 8(2), 155–174 (2002)
22. Gregor, S., Hevner, A.R.: Positioning and presenting design science research for maximum impact. MIS Quarterly 37(2), 337–356 (2013)

Supporting Participatory Innovation Through Introductory Tools

Muhammad Mustafa Hassan[1(✉)], Andrés Moreno[1], Erkki Sutinen[1], and Abdul Aziz[2]

[1] School of Computing, University of Eastern Finland, Joensuu, Finland
{mhassan,amoreno,sutinen}@cs.uef.fi
[2] Faculty of Information Technology, University of Central Punjab, Lahore, Pakistan
abdul.aziz@ucp.edu.pk

Abstract. Recently, participatory design is gaining popularity in designing usable novel systems. A participatory design activity typically starts with presenting the participants with introductory tools. These tools provide the participant with the required background knowledge and also trigger their creative process. Thus, the right choice of introductory tools is a determinant of participants' creativity, and hence innovative output. In this work, the authors analyze the impact of various introductory tools on the overall innovation. To test the hypothesis, a series of participatory workshops were conducted to design a novel mleaning tool. Each workshop enrolled the real users of the system and was staged with a different combination of introductory tools. The participants' output in the form of innovative design artefacts was collected and behavior during workshops was noted. The authors analyzed the results to find the relation between the choice of introductory tools and the participants' innovative output.

Keywords: Participatory design · Innovation · Introductory tools · mLearning

1 Introduction

Participatory Design (PD) has recently gained popularity in designing innovative products [1]. An innovative product "brings people and technology closer in meaningful ways" [1] by introducing "novel combinations of new or existing tools" [2]—consistent with the Euro Comm definitions [3]. Innovations are the flash of a genius mind, however ignited mostly on the basis of background knowledge: a critical ingredient to initiate creative process and to bring quality in innovation [4,5,6]. Nonetheless, this ingredient is missing in the case of PD where designers (real users) lack domain knowledge and design expertise. To fill in this gap—and to ignite participants' creativity—PD facilitators conduct introductory inspiration sessions [7]—also termed as priming [8], scaffolding [1] or anchoring [9]—before a design activity. The tools employed in such sessions are called introductory tools or starting points.

A well designed introductory tool fills the background knowledge gap and provides abstract inspirations to ignite the creative process. The extent to which it is able to influence the participants' creativity determines the level and quality of innovation produced [10]. Hence, the scientific study of such knowledge inducting introductory

© Springer International Publishing Switzerland 2015
B. Donnellan et al. (Eds.): DESRIST 2015, LNCS 9073, pp. 479–487, 2015.
DOI: 10.1007/978-3-319-18714-3_41

tools is an important theme of research. Albeit a myriad of such tools is in use by PD community, but few are studied for their impact—to the best of authors' knowledge.

In this work, the authors report on the impact of various introductory tools on participants' creativity and innovation. The authors hosted a series of workshops, each starting with a different set of introductory tools. The participants were asked to design Jeliot Mobile (JM), an mlearning tool framed in socio-constructivist learning paradigm. The development of JM is in initial phase and the authors have adopted Reeves' Design-Based Research (DBR) methodology [11]. Due to the application of DBR, the workshops served two purposes in parallel, 1) designed JM in a participatory fashion, and 2) evaluated the impact of different introductory tools.

The authors collected two types of data from the experiment. First, the qualitative data noting participants' behavior was collected with diary writing during the workshops. Second, at the end of each workshop, the participants' output in the form of innovative ideas was collected and classified. The authors assessed the innovation of generated ideas and analyzed the impact of various combinations of introductory tools on participants' creativity and behavior.

In the following, the authors present the related work followed by research design in section 3. The results of the workshops are illustrated in section 4 and discussed in section 5. Finally, the authors present the conclusion and propose the future work.

2   Related Work

Three main studies have been reported on the impact of introductory tools on participants' creativity. Marois et. al. [10] staged three workshops to test three starting points: introductory games, interactive illustrations, and storyboards. They enrolled 93 students with computer science or health, safety and environment background. Their study concludes that storyboards work better.

Pommeranz et. al. [12] conducted four PD sessions to test three starting points, namely simple prototype, elaborate prototype, and interface elements. They recommend the use of elaborate prototypes to trigger participants' creativity. Kwiatkowska et. al. [13] compared the impact of structured and unstructured tools. They staged two workshops with 39 participants, concluding that the unstructured tools are preferable.

3   Research Methodology

The authors staged three workshops enrolling 80 participants—12 females and 68 males—from HCI course at the University of Central Punjab, Pakistan. The workshops were facilitated by Muhammad Mustafa Hassan and Abdul Aziza—both have jointly taught HCI several times.

3.1   Participants

The population was uniform—in skills learned and courses taken—and satisfied two required characteristics, 1) being real users of the system, and 2) being familiar with the notion of participation in design. The population was randomly divided into three groups, namely A, B, C with 31, 23 and 26 participants respectively. Each group was further divided into sub-groups of 3 to 6. The sub-group size varied because the participants were free to form their own groups.

3.2   Procedure

The workshops were divided into four stages, namely *probing*, *priming*, *understanding* and *generating*, as suggested by Sanders et. al. [8]. Table 1 summarizes the complete protocol. All workshops proceeded similarly in stages 1, 3, and 4, however differently in stage 2.

Table 1. Protocol used at the workshops

Stage	Activities	Duration (min)
1. Probing	Start	10
2. Priming	Starting Point(s) presentation	30
	Prayer Break	20
3. Understanding	Evaluation	10
	Participants ask questions	15
4. Generating	Brainstorming	30
	Design Scenarios	30
	Sketching	40
	Review	15
	Closing	

The purpose of the probing stage was to let the facilitators and participants get familiar with each other. It did not take much time because the facilitators and the participants were already familiar with each other.

The priming stage was the researchers' focus, in which the participants were prepared for the design activity by employing different introductory tools in different

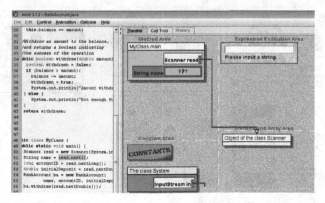

Fig. 1. A snapshot of exploratory prototype used at the workshops

workshops. The workshop A was started with an exploratory prototype with use scenarios. First, the facilitators used Jeliot 3 desktop version as the exploratory prototype—or interactive illustration—to co-discover the problem domain with participants. The participants ran animations of the sample programs shipped with Jeliot, similar to the one depicted in Fig. 1. The discovery was supplemented with little elaboration by facilitators. After exploratory prototype was discovered, the facilitators presented the participants with three use scenarios of the desired system. An example of such scenario is "Collaborative Learning: using Jeliot Mobile to run one animation across the class, centrally controlled by the teacher". The example use scenarios did not detail the idea. The tool only presented the participants with the initial thought of how the target system can be used, leaving the room for self-directed exploration and innovation. This approach helped the facilitators to keep the bias at the minimum.

The workshop B's introductory tool was storyboards. First, the facilitators elaborated the concept of software visualization, and the intention of developing a new mlearning SV tool. Then, the storyboards presented examples of use stories woven on the same use scenarios presented in workshop A. The difference between both tools was in the level of details and the form of presentation. The use scenarios presented with the exploratory prototype were verbally communicated with no details—only the idea was communicated to the participants. Contrary to this, storyboards took a pictorial form and communicated an entire use story consisting of several use cases. Despite being detailed than use scenarios, the storyboards were designed to be fairly simple. They showed only relevant details and contained some ambiguity, conforming to the attributes provided by Buxton [17]. Fig. 2 depicts an example storyboard.

The priming phase of workshop C started with a combination of exploratory prototype and storyboards—both of which are described in previous. First, the participants and the facilitators co-discovered the exploratory prototype in a fashion similar to workshop A. Once, the participants were prepared for the problem domain, they were presented with the storyboards of innovative use scenarios of the target system. This discovery was lightly supplemented verbally by the facilitators. This starting point varied from the first two in the form of combination of tools.

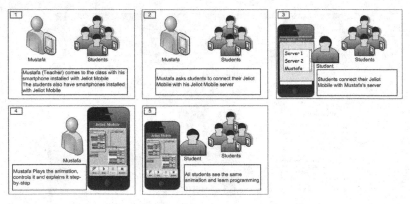

Fig. 2. Collaborative learning storyboard

In understanding stage, all three workshops proceeded in a similar manner. The facilitators used the Q/A tool to evaluate the participants if they have correctly discovered the concept and understood what output they are expected to produce. Afterwards, the participants asked questions to remove any remaining ambiguities. The facilitators kept flexibility in schedule of this stage to allow all the participants satisfy their questions and ambiguities, as suggested by Pommeranz et al. [18].

The last stage was the generation of innovative design artefacts, sub-divided into four activities. First, each sub-group brainstormed and documented ideas textually. Second, the sub-groups designed novel use scenarios. Third, each sub-group created design sketches. Finally, the participants reviewed their work.

The participants' output was mostly handmade. All sub-groups were given three days to digitalize their output, however told not to include any further ideas. The authors only considered design artefacts generated during the workshops and used digital copy when some text / figure in the hand-made version was difficult to read.

The facilitators also wrote a research diary throughout the workshops. They wrote down everything noticeable, from motivation to excessive time-consumption, and from inter/intra group communication to the number of questions asked by a particular group. At the end of each workshop, the notes were compiled in a report. This data helped in analyzing the impact of introductory tools on the participants' mindset.

3.3   Materials

The authors primarily used six tools, namely use scenarios, storyboards, exploratory prototype, sketches, participatory envisioning, and Q/A (question/answer tool). Storyboards, use scenarios and exploratory prototype were used as introductory tools to serve the *priming* purpose. Nonetheless, some participants also used storyboard and use scenario tools in *generation* of design ideas. The sketches and participatory envisioning were used for *generation* of innovative design artefacts by the participants. Finally, the Q/A tool was used for two purposes, 1) to *probe* the participants whenever needed, and 2) after *priming* to assess the understanding of participants.

4   Results

During the last stage of the workshops, the participants generated innovative design artefacts in form of textual ideas, use scenarios and sketches. Fig. 3 shows total artefact generation for each workshop. However, the authors do not treat the sketches, use scenarios or textual ideas differently. They consider all type of design artefacts similarly and rate them on the basis of innovation. The authors—aligning with the European Commission's definition on innovation [3]—consider a thought innovative if it new to the conceiving person and relates to the target design problem [19].

Mostly, the frameworks for innovation assess it in terms of economical growth. However, in this study, the authors are interested in assessing the quality of an innovative thought that is not yet realized as a product. Hence it cannot be evaluated in terms of economic growth. Thus, the authors use a simple four index—*Basic*, *Innovative*, *Incremental*, and *Disruptive*—scale to rate the innovative thought.

Table 2. Innovative design artefacts generated by sub-groups at workshops A, B, and C

Group	Basic	Innovative	Incremental	Disruptive	Total innovation (excludes Basic)
A	28	74	13	7	94
B	52	60	25	6	91
C	21	68	26	14	108

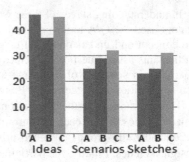

Fig. 3. Total innovative design artefacts produced at workshop A, B, C

The *Basic* design ideas are those already implemented in Jeliot 3, or presented in the workshops by the facilitators. The authors consider such ideas non-innovative and do not add them to the total innovative production of a group, as calculated in Table 2. An example of such idea is controlling animation speed. The *innovative* ideas novel interaction modes, use scenarios, use cases etc, but not new features. These ideas are neither implemented in Jeliot 3 nor presented by the facilitators in the workshops. An example is showing only that statement(s) of code which is/are highlighted to maximize the use of limited screen. The *incremental* ideas add new features to the system. An example is controlling the animation through gesture recognition. The *disruptive* category consists of ideas extending beyond the scope of software visualization, but still related to the target system. An example is quiz management system. The authors also use an additional class *Redundant* to mark and remove the ideas repeating inside a sub-group, however not across the sub-groups.

5   Discussion

The group A (exploratory prototype with use scenarios) and C (exploratory prototype with storyboards) had a combination of introductory tools. The interactive illustration (exploratory prototype) helped participants quickly discover the problem domain. However, the facilitators noted—by Q/A—that the participants were confused about what kind of innovative output they were expected to produce. The second introductory tool helped them in clarifying "the facilitators' expectations" and "what innovation means". During the later stages of understanding, and generation activities, the facilitators noted better response in C in terms of questions and confusion. Moreover, in group B (storyboards), the participants found the starting point more challenging, spent more time and asked more questions in discovering the problem domain than the interactive illustration groups. However, once they completed the discovery, they developed a better understanding of "the facilitators' expectations" and "what innovation means". Overall, the facilitators noted the group C achieved the best understanding, followed

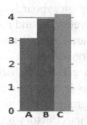

Fig. 4. Mean design artefacts generation

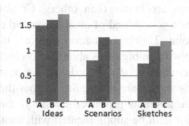

Fig. 5. Mean design artefact generation per artefact type

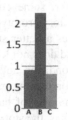

Fig. 6. Mean of basic design artefact generated

by group B, and worst in group A. The qualitative observation was reflected in quantitative data as well, as presented in the following.

The participants of the workshops C produced the most innovative ideas. However, the authors did not take the bigger number as an indicator of better performance because the workshops enrolled varying number of participants. To eliminate the group size bias, the authors calculated mean idea generation per participant—as illustrated by Fig. 4, however still found better results in group C.

The authors also analyzed the averages for each type of design artefact, that is, for ideas, use scenarios and sketches as depicted by Fig. 5. These parameters showed better productivity in group C with a slight variation in use scenarios where group B (storyboards) performed better. The reasons behind this are unidentified and the authors speculate that it was a random spike.

Moreover, the group C produced the least non-innovative ideas, as presented by Fig 6. The highest scoring subgroup in this category was B2 with 19 basic ideas, and the highest mean value was also scored by group B. The authors analyzed that it was due to the abstraction of group B's starting point (storyboards) which left participants with fewer details, more ambiguities, and the gaps to be filled by themselves.

Analyzing the group performance in general, the people at workshop C performed better, with the best scoring sub-group C6 producing 32 innovative design artefacts. The sub-group with the lowest production was A3 with 7 design artefacts. The participants of workshop A generally performed lesser in comparison with B and C.

The statistical parameters as well as behavioral analysis provide the evidence that combining exploratory prototype with storyboards impacts positively on participants' creativity and innovation. However, combining exploratory prototype with use scenarios does not bring any benefits, and has a lesser impact when compared to storyboards alone.

6   Conclusions and Future Work

The authors conclude two different aspects from this study. First, they conclude that combining multiple introductory tools as starting points does not necessarily bring the benefits in terms of innovative ideas, as supported by the results of workshop A.

However, some combinations are better than others. Combining storyboards with exploratory prototype creates a good blend of abstraction and concreteness, and hence becomes a better starting point. This combination supports the participants' innovation and does not leave them with ambiguities about the problem domain.

Second, the authors conclude that storyboards, albeit being a good introductory tool, confuse the participants and create ambiguities about the problem domain. The large number of basic design artefacts produced by storyboards group points to this fact. Thus, the storyboard tool shall be supplemented with another introductory tool to introduce the participants with the problem domain. It is especially important in the case of novel systems.

In the future, the authors plan to conduct further experiments 1) to re-validate the results presented here, and 2) to test the combinations of other introductory tools.

References

1. Buur, J., Matthews, B.: Participatory Innovation. International Journal of Innovation Management 12(3), 255–273 (2008)
2. Schumpeter, J.A., Opie, R.: The Theory of Economic Development: An Inquiry Into Profits, Capital, Credit, Interest, and the Business Cycle. Harvard University Press, Cambridge (1934)
3. EUROPEAN COMMISSION. Green Paper on Innovation (Dec 1995), http://europa.eu/documents/comm/green_papers/pdf/com95_688_en.pdf (accessed, February 2015)
4. Zhao, M.: Seek it or let it come: how designers achieve inspirations. In: Proc CHI 2013 Extended Abstracts on Human Factors in Computing Systems, Paris, France, vol. 13, pp. 2779–2784 (2013)
5. Drucker, P.F.: The Discipline of Innovation. Harvard Business Review 80, 8 (2002)
6. Bernard, C.: Cultural innovation in software design: the new impact of innovation planning methods. Journal of Business Strategy 30(2/3), 57–69 (2009)
7. Sanders, E.B., Stappers, P.J.: Co-creation and the new landscapes of design. International Journal of CoCreation in Design and the Arts 4(1), 5–18 (2008)
8. Sanders, E.B.-N., Brandt, E., Binder, T.: A framework for organizing the tools and techniques of participatory design. In: Proc PDC 2010, Sydney, Australia, pp. 195-198 (2010)
9. Bødker, K., Kensing, F., Simonsen, J.: Participatory Design in Information Systems Development. In: Reframing Humans in Information Systems Development. Springer, London (2011)
10. Marois, L., Viallet, J.-E., Poirier, F., Chauvin, C.: Experimenting Introductory Tools for Innovation and Participatory Design. In: Proc PDC 2010, Sydney, Australia, pp. 259–262 (2010)
11. Reeves, T.C.: Design Research from a Technology Perspective. In: Van den Akker, J., et al. (eds.) Educational Design Research. Routledge (2006)
12. Pommeranz, A., Ulgen, U., Jonker, C.M.: Exploration of Facilitation, Materials and Group Composition in Participatory Design Sessions. In: Proc ECCE 2012, Edinburgh, pp. 124–130 (2012)
13. Kwiatkowska, J., Szostek, A., Lamas, D. (Un)structured sources of inspiration: comparing the effects of game-like cards and design cards on creativity in co-design process. In: Proc PDC 2014, Windhoek, Namibia, pp. 31–39 (2014)

14. Buxton, B.: Sketching User Experiences: Getting the Design Right and the Right Design. Morgan Kaufmann Publishers Inc. (2007)
15. Pommeranz, A., Ulgen, U., Jonker, C.M.: Exploration of facilitation, materials and group composition in participatory design sessions. In: Proc ECCE 2012, Edinburgh, pp. 124–130 (2012)
16. Warr, A., O'Neill, E.: The effect of group composition on divergent thinking in an interaction design activity. In: Proc DIS 2006, University Park, PA, pp. 122–131 (2006)

Development of Augmented Reality Application on Android OS

Ondrej Bilek and Ondrej Krejcar[(✉)]

FIM, Center for Basic and Applied Research, University of Hradec Kralove,
Rokitanskeho 62, 500 03, Hradec Kralove, Czech Republic
Ondrej.Bilek@uhk.cz, Ondrej.Krejcar@remoteworld.net

Abstract. Augmented reality is one of the current mobile trends, while the main development has not yet come. It complements properties around the user for additional software added elements whose goal is to further expand the user possibilities to real reality. Many of augmented reality applications apply a wide range of sensors, because it is necessary to accurately identify the surrounding reality in order to be properly extended. Paper deals with use of embedded sensors of mobile devices. Selected examples of specific procedures and algorithms are described on currently the most widely used mobile platform Android OS. Design of application, implementation with class descriptions as well as interesting algorithms and testing of final application is also described.

Keywords: Sensor · Mobile · Device · Embedded · Augmented · Reality

1 Introduction

As power and possibilities of mobile devices rapidly grown with massive extension of smart devices such as smartphones or tablet computers, many sensors were integrated to extend possibilities and mainly, to help users with common use of smart devices [4-9].

Smart devices also integrate functions of some other devices [11-13]. Few years ago users need phone for calling or texting, camera for taking photos, MP3 player for listening music, GPS navigation or map to planning their trips [12, 13, 17], computer to opening documents etc. Nowadays, all these functions can be handled with single device, which offer great computational power with many possibilities in body of mobile phone or tablet computer. A brief comparison of supported and mandatory sensors is presented inside this paper on one case study example of augmented reality [1] application.

While several existing platforms on which the mobile smart devices are based, there is a one leading – Android OS [9-11] which is described in this paper in more detail, as well as conditions for developers to use these embedded sensors are outlined. Android OS is the most used mobile platforms of these days and it's still rapidly growing and expanding to other markets. Another great benefit of developing app for Android OS is multiplatform developer tools, relatively cheap app publishing on platform store and much information around web.

© Springer International Publishing Switzerland 2015
B. Donnellan et al. (Eds.): DESRIST 2015, LNCS 9073, pp. 488–495, 2015.
DOI: 10.1007/978-3-319-18714-3_42

After first part of a paper - introduction, the practical parts follows. Sample application uses principles of augmented reality, where view from device camera is used to include data from sensors, what can be enhanced to defect management system [2] or some kind of advisory solution [3, 15].

2 Design and Implementation of Augmented Reality Application

To demonstrate the possibility of using the built-in sensors of mobile devices, it will be described one of the possible - sample cases of their use in appropriately selected case study. Functions of this sample application was defined as follows:

1. Show data from GPS and sensors of environment
   a. (temperature, humidity, atmospheric pressure)
2. Show tilt of device towards water level and direction from north
3. Implement simple GPS navigation, this navigation should show distance and direction to coordinates, which should by user enterable
4. Application should run on majority part of existing smart devices with Android OS

UML diagram of developing application structure can be seen on (Fig. 1). Proposal of structure application counts on component architecture. There is component manager, interface to define components and components itself. Each component should prepare some data to show to user.

Sample application is using principles of augmented reality. Basic stone of application is real-time view from device's back camera. This view is enriched by overlay with sensor data. Firstly we focused on practical part in the sense of GUI design prior to final definition of UML and all functions as in classical way of application design [4-5], [9-11].

Application uses for communication between all parts sending of messages, so services sends messages while the class *MainActivity* receiving all messages sent to individual services and their data. On the service side sending is as follows:

1. Firstly, we declare the ability to sending messages to defined events (by Intent class instance). String which play as action is stored in a static variable of the public service.
2. Then the sequence of methods *putExtra(key, data)* attached to the message an individual data to be sent.
3. Finally, a message is sent by method *sendBroadcast()*. So the message is not directly addressed to *MainActivity* class, but class itself need to catch the message.

The procedure on the class MainActivity is a little more complicated. First, it is necessary to set an instance of IntentFilter that determines which messages are received. Action that identifies the message is gradually sets to this instance by calling addAction() method. Events are stored for each service as static variables. Receiving of messages is finished by setting of the recipient, which forms the interface instance created a BroadcastReceiver interface and IntentFilter is created by calling the registerReceiver (BroadcastReceiver, IntentFilter). Subsequent processing of received messages follow as the creation of an BroadcastReceiver interface instance, which is based on events in the report to determine its purpose and performs the processing of the message (usually displaying of data, or sending for further processing).

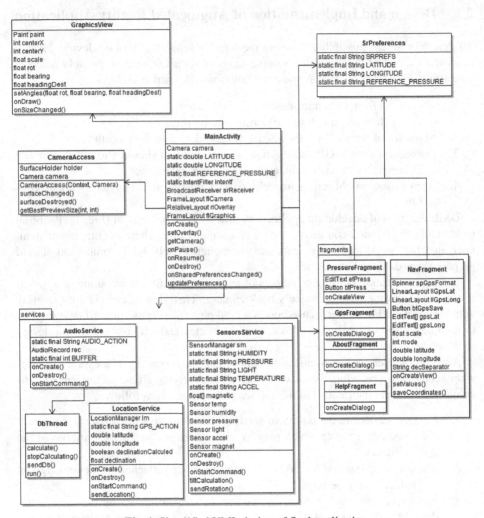

Fig. 1. Simplified UML design of final application

2.1   Selected Algorithms for Sensors Implementation

Developed solution cover operating with several important sensors using interesting algorithm like: Coordinates saving, converting and validation; Tilt calculation towards water level; Azimuth east from north calculation; and Calculation of direction to coordinates. As example we will describe several of these.

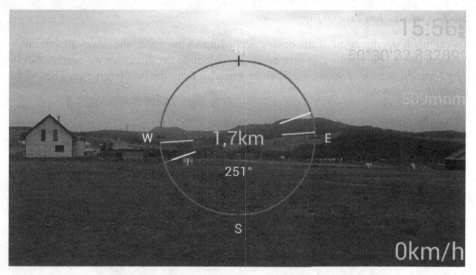

Fig. 2. Final GUI of developed augmented reality application

2.1.1 Tilt Processing

The tilt calculation is based on the modified procedure published in [18]. The first step of the calculation is a transfer of acceleration vector (array of values g) from the accelerometer to normalized ones. This is done by dividing of individual components by the square root of the sum of the components squares:

```
float n=(float)Math.sqrt(g[0]*g[0]+g[1]*g[1]+g[2]*g[2]);
g[0] = g[0]/n;   g[1] = g[1]/n;   g[2] = g[2]/n;
```

Another necessary data is to calculate the inclination, which indicates how the device screen is rotated relative to the ground. Tilting of the device can be calculated only when the display device is vertically to the ground. This is also supported by the fact that the laying device is in a horizontal level of the screen surface what cannot be displayed.

```
int inclination = (int) Math.round(Math.toDegrees(Math.acos(g[2])));
```

The last step is a computation of the device tilt according to water level:

```
//computation will run only until 30° from upright – 90°
if (inclination < 120 && inclination > 60)
{    int rotation = (int) Math.round(Math.toDegrees(Math.atan2(g[0], g[1])));
}
```

2.1.2 Orientation Processing

To calculate the direction of the device according to the north, the development environment has a better ability to process it. To calculate the direction we need not only data from the sensor of geomagnetic field, but also from the accelerometer. The calculation is as follows:

float[] rotMat = new float[9];   *//preparation of field for matrix of rotation devices*
SensorManager.getRotationMatrix(rotMat, null, magnetic, accel);
     // Acquisition of matrix, matrix is prepared by parameters, null (or matrix of inclination), a vector of the geomagnetic sensor and accelerometer vector
float[] orient = new float[3];   *// preparation of orientation vector of device*
SensorManager.getOrientation(rotMat, apr);   *//acquisition of orientation vector*
bearing = apr[0]+(float)(1.5*Math.PI);
     // direction is the first component of the vector, the possible transfer of the range 0 to 360 ° (the result is in radians)

2.2   Important Parameters of Developed Solution

Application is used to add sensor information to camera view. You can see various sensor information on sides of camera view and multifunctional circle indicator at middle of view, which contain:

Compass - yellow indicator, magenta end towards to north
Spirit level - green indicator
Azimuth - yellow text, degrees from magnetic north
Navigator - distance at middle of circle, cyan indicator show direction
Application could be used for simple GPS navigation. Some text fields are also clickable:

Time shows main menu
GPS longitude shows actual GPS coordinates in other formats
SET or distance open coordinate settings dialog. For coordinates on west or south hemisphere, use - before degrees.
Atmospheric pressure open reference pressure dialog (in hPa). This pressure is used to calculate altitude from barometer. If 0 is set, standard pressure is used.

3   Testing of Augmented Reality Application

For testing purposes of application we used few devices with different hardware configurations and different version of operational system (Table 1). On all devices application ran correctly, even on the weakest LG Optimus One. For user interface scalability tests was added also some emulator configurations, one with very low resolution 320x240 and second with high tablet resolution 1280x800. Application is usable on all resolutions, except lowest (320x240), where the quality of compound indicator is very low. Functions of application was tested by few users, who did not find some important bugs and application did not crashed.

Table 1. Testing devices (Senzors: T – temperature, P – atmospheric pressure, H – humidity, L – light)

Device	Ver.	Processor	Memory	Resolution	Missing Sensors
SE Xperia Neo	4.2.2	1GHz Arm7	380MB	854x480	T,P,H
SE Xperia Neo	4.0.4	1GHz Arm7	335MB	854x480	L,T,P,H
LG Optimus One	4.0.4	600MHz Arm6	414MB	480x320	L,T,P,H
LG Optimus Black	4.0.4	1GHz Arm7	440MB	800x480	L,T,P,H
HTC Desire Z	2.3.5	800MHz Arm7	368MB	800x480	T,P,H
Samsung G. S3	4.1.2	4x1,4Ghz Arm7	694MB	1280x720	T,H

Some information from sensors could not be tested, because there are almost no devices (related to end of 2013), which have sensors to provide it. These sensors are humidity and ambient temperature sensors. At the end of testing was also considered memory consumptions and number of threads in Eclipse IDE.

3.1 Testing of Speed and Memory Occupation

Augmented reality applications put the strong demand on the running speed and also on fluency, where user don't want to be disturbed by application breaking [14]. To ensure these requirements application need to be fully optimized for all parts, module and even for each thread! Our solution meet all these requirements while it can be also tested to document this capability.

Developed augmented reality application running on the mobile devices with activated navigation system (according to the debugging tools available in the development environment) use during the process 8 running threads (+ some support system threads of which the performance is almost not involved). The most exacting thread is one which take care of rendering the user interface and basic operation of application. This thread use over 90% CPU resources used by the application. In addition, each service has created a special thread. In the case of AudioService service a thread is added which calculate noise, while AudioRecord class thread record a sound. Custom thread has also a class SensorManager which serving the most sensors at the system level. Regarding the memory usage of the application variables allocates 7.5 megabytes of memory, of which approximately 2.5 megabytes is really used as shown (Fig. 3, 4).

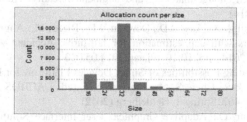

Fig. 3. Memory occupation by developed application

ID	Heap Size	Allocated	Free	% Used	# Objects	
1	7,512 MB	2,448 MB	5,064 MB	32,59%	41 999	Cause GC

Display: Stats ∨

Type	Count	Total Size	Smallest	Largest	Median	Average
free	1 608	4,928 MB	16 B	1,179 MB	288 B	3,138 KB
data object	24 858	761,820 KB	16 B	672 B	32 B	31 B
class object	2 805	816,945 KB	168 B	40,500 KB	168 B	298 B
1-byte array (byte[], boolean[])	88	23,742 KB	24 B	8,023 KB	32 B	276 B
2-byte array (short[], char[])	9 815	602,258 KB	24 B	28,023 KB	48 B	62 B
4-byte array (object[], int[], float[])	4 370	298,188 KB	24 B	16,023 KB	40 B	69 B
8-byte array (long[], double[])	19	2,117 KB	24 B	248 B	136 B	114 B
non-Java object	91	4,430 KB	16 B	480 B	32 B	49 B

Fig. 4. Memory occupation by developed application

4   Conclusions

Main goal of this work was to show possibilities in using of modern mobile devices as a tool which can help the user better recognize and grasp the reality around. We described several sensors, which are embedded in modern mobile devices. We also described a development process of a sample application for augmented reality, which is using these sensors. Paper covers only main information about selected sensors, while we focus on practical use of these sensors. Practical demonstration presented in this paper provide some basic exploration of the possibility to integrate different sensors to enhance user experience.

Acknowledgement. This work and the contribution were supported by project "SP-103-2015 - Smart Solutions for Ubiquitous Computing Environments" Faculty of Informatics and Management, University of Hradec Kralove, Czech Republic.

References

1. Daponte, P., De Vito, L., Picariello, F., et al.: State of the art and future developments of the Augmented Reality for measurement applications. Measurement 57, 53–70 (2014)
2. Kwon, O.S., Park, C.S., Lim, C.R.: A defect management system for reinforced concrete work utilizing BIM, image-matching and augmented reality. Automation in Construction 46, 74–81 (2014)
3. Rusch, M.L., Schall, M.C., Lee, J.D., Dawson, J.D., Rizzo, M.: Augmented reality cues to assist older drivers with gap estimation for left-turns. Accident Analysis and Prevention 71, 210–221 (2014), doi:10.1016/j.aap.2014.05.020
4. Krejcar, O.: Threading Possibilities of Smart Devices Platforms for Future User Adaptive Systems. In: Pan, J.-S., Chen, S.-M., Nguyen, N.T. (eds.) ACIIDS 2012, Part II. LNCS, vol. 7197, pp. 458–467. Springer, Heidelberg (2012)
5. Behan, M., Krejcar, O.: Adaptive Graphical User Interface Solution for Modern User Devices. In: Pan, J.-S., Chen, S.-M., Nguyen, N.T. (eds.) ACIIDS 2012, Part II. LNCS, vol. 7197, pp. 411–420. Springer, Heidelberg (2012)

6. Vanus, J., Novak, T., Koziorek, J., Konecny, J., Hrbac, R.: The proposal model of energy savings of lighting systems in the smart home care. In: IFAC Proceedings, vol. 12 (PART 1), pp. 411–415 (2013)
7. Vanus, J., Koziorek, J., Hercik, R.: Design of a smart building control with view to the senior citizens' needs. In: (2013) IFAC Proceedings Volumes (IFAC-PapersOnline), vol. 12 (PART 1), pp. 422–427 (2013) ISSN: 14746670. ISBN: 9783902823533
8. Machacek, Z., Slaby, R., Hercik, R., Koziorek, J.: Advanced system for consumption meters with recognition of video camera signal. Elektronika Ir Elektrotechnika 18(10), 57–60 (2012) ISSN: 1392-1215
9. Behan, M., Krejcar, O.: Modern Smart Device-Based Concept of Sensoric Networks. EURASIP Journal on Wireless Communications and Networking 2013(1), No. 155 (June 2013), doi 10.1186/1687-1499-2013-155, ISSN 1687-1499
10. Gantulga, E., Krejcar, O.: Smart Access to Big Data Storage – Android Multi-language Offline Dictionary Application. In: Nguyen, N.-T., Hoang, K., Jędrzejowicz, P. (eds.) ICCCI 2012, Part I. LNCS, vol. 7653, pp. 375–384. Springer, Heidelberg (2012)
11. Krejcar, O., Jirka, J., Janckulik, D.: Use of Mobile Phone as Intelligent Sensor for Sound Input Analysis and Sleep State Detection. Sensors 11(6), 6037–6055 (2011), doi 10.3390/s110606037, ISSN: 1424-8220
12. Benikovsky, J., Brida, P., Machaj, J.: Proposal of User Adaptive Modular Localization System for Ubiquitous Positioning. In: Pan, J.-S., Chen, S.-M., Nguyen, N.T. (eds.) ACIIDS 2012, Part II. LNCS, vol. 7197, pp. 391–400. Springer, Heidelberg (2012)
13. Michal, M., Peter, B., Machaj, J.: Modular Localization System for Intelligent Transport. In: Badica, A., Trawinski, B., Nguyen, N.T. (eds.) Recent Developments in Computational Collective Intelligence. SCI, vol. 513, pp. 115–124. Springer, Heidelberg (2014)
14. Dey, A., Sandor, C.: Lessons learned: Evaluating visualizations for occluded objects in handheld augmented reality. International Journal of Human-Computer Studies 72(10-11), 704–716 (2014), doi 10.1016/j.ijhcs.2014.04.001
15. Leu, J.S., Su, K.W., Chen, C.T.: Ambient mesoscale weather forecasting system featuring mobile augmented reality. Multimedia Tools and Applications 72(2), 1585–1609 (2014), doi 10.1007/s11042-013-1462-4
16. Cerny, M., Penhaker, M.: Wireless Body Sensor Network in Health Maintenance Systems. Elektronika Ir Elektrotechnika, 113–116 (2011), doi: 10.5755/j01.eee.115.9.762, ISSN: 1392-1215
17. Penhaker, M., Darebnikova, M., Cerny, M.: Sensor network for measurement and analysis on medical devices quality control. In: Yonazi, J.J., Sedoyeka, E., Ariwa, E., El-Qawasmeh, E. (eds.) ICeND 2011. CCIS, vol. 171, pp. 182–196. Springer, Heidelberg (2011)
18. Rumi, S.M.I., Hossain, M.F., Shanamul Islam, I.S.M., Rahman, M.K.: System design of two wheeler self-balanced vehicle. In: 10th France-Japan/ 8th Europe-Asia Congress on Mecatronics (MECATRONICS 2014), pp. 331–336 (2014), doi:10.1109/MECATRONICS.2014.7018582
19. Kay, M., Rector, K.I., Consolvo, S., Greenstein, B., Wobbrock, J.O., Watson, N.F., Kientz, J.A.: PVT-touch: Adapting a reaction time test for touchscreen devices. In: 7th International Conference on Pervasive Computing Technologies for Healthcare (PervasiveHealth 2013), pp. 248–251 (2013)

Toward a Taxonomy of Wearable Technologies in Healthcare

Mayda Alrige[✉] and Samir Chatterjee

Claremont Graduate University, Claremont, California
{Mayda.alrige,Samir.Chatterjee}@cgu.edu

Abstract. Wearable Technologies continue to dramatically change healthcare system in various ways. The proliferation of these wearable technologies used in healthcare has made the emerging discipline confusing to understand. To better understand the rapid, fast-moving change, we propose a taxonomy to classify wearable technologies in terms of three major dimensions: application, form, and functionality. This taxonomy is evaluated by conducting both literate and market mapping. By doing so, we were able to classify a number of existing wearable technologies in light of the taxonomy dimensions. This DSR project concludes with some practical implications as design principles.

Keywords: Wearable computing · Wearable technology · Smart devices · Taxonomy · Classification framework

1   Introduction

As technology advances, miniaturization along with mobile computing are giving rise to a new form of computing that we call "wearable computing technology". Interesting applications of wearable technology in healthcare is beginning to appear. Wearable Technology holds a great promise not just to boost clinical applications but also to advance the general health and well-being of people across the globe.

Many forms of wearable technologies continue to evolve and have the potential to revolutionize healthcare in various ways. Several terminologies have been coined, such as unobtrusive sensing, edible capsules, smart tattoos for glucose monitoring or skin-stretchable materials such as the CNT-based strain sensor for human motion monitoring[1]. The proliferation of a variety of wearable technologies used in healthcare has made the emerging discipline confusing to understand. This calls for a classification scheme to explain the state-of-the-art, specify the underlying principles, and establish the major criteria to categorize wearable devices in healthcare. Designing a taxonomy that not only helps to better understand the phenomenon, but also provides tools to categorize concepts in an emerging field is an essential first step towards broader understanding.

Given the enormous contribution of wearable technologies in healthcare, some previous attempts have been made to summarize the recent developments in wearable sensors and devices for various medical applications[1–4] . Each attempt focuses on one aspect of wearable computing. Nevertheless, little attention has been given to designing a comprehensive taxonomy of wearable technologies in healthcare.

© Springer International Publishing Switzerland 2015
B. Donnellan et al. (Eds.): DESRIST 2015, LNCS 9073, pp. 496–504, 2015.
DOI: 10.1007/978-3-319-18714-3_43

In this paper, we present a taxonomy to classify wearable technologies in healthcare in terms of three dimensions: the application, form, and functionality. We adopt the design science research approach [5]. Following the DSR approach, a rigorous multi-step building process is carried out to illustrate the steps of designing the taxonomy, starting from the conceptual definition to coming up with the taxonomy criteria.

By designing a wearable computing taxonomy, our goal is to help researchers and designers understand the major dimensions that are critical in their work. The value of such taxonomy includes:

- An easy to understand classification framework which can assist novice scholars to gain a deeper understanding of the emerging phenomenon.
- Explain the underlying principles behind wearable technologies and clear the ambiguity around all forms of wearable technologies, whether implantable, such as smart adhesives and tattoos, or edible such as endoscopy capsules.
- Assist designers and researchers to either add novel products to the existing base or extend the possibilities of wearable computing by using the taxonomy.

The rest of the paper is organized as follows. Section 2 presents the related work. Section 3 specifies the research method, including the build process and how each dimension is arrived at. In Section 4, we present the entire taxonomy followed by the evaluation of the artifact in Section 5. Section 6 is to conclude our work and discuss some implications and limitations of the taxonomy.

2   Literature Review

Constructing a taxonomy scheme aims to classify wearable devices as well as pinpoint the principles underlying such a phenomenon. McKelvey in his seminal book: "*Organizational Systematics: Taxonomy, Evolution, Classification*" explains how to establish a taxonomic theory, for which constructing a taxonomy is the starting point. He contends that taxonomies and classification frameworks are extremely beneficial to gain more insight into the underlying constructs and how they relate to one another. The classification of differences into categories can produce knowledge about certain phenomenon (wearable computing) by understanding the relationship among its constructs.

In the body of literature, prior attempts have been made to summarize recent developments in wearable technologies [1–4]. While the aforementioned attempts contribute to the wearable technologies body of knowledge, they fell short to provide a comprehensive taxonomy to classify wearable technology in healthcare. The present paper aims to fill this gap and improve our understanding by proposing such a broad classification framework.

3   Method

In this study, the design science research methodology (DSRM) was adopted [6]. The research team met regularly for 10 weeks to brainstorm on various aspects of the taxonomy. The resultant artifact we designed is a classification framework for wearable technologies in healthcare. The following sub-sections elaborate on the challenges we faced during the build phase of the design project.

3.1   Challenges with Defining Wearable Technology

Our first challenge was to arrive at a comprehensive definition of wearable technology and clarify what constitutes a wearable computing device. In order to do so, forming a definition statement is always the first preliminary step. According to the authors in [3], they define wearable technology as: the intelligent, low-cost, ultra-low-power sensor networks that are designed to help provide services to dependent persons and can collect a huge amount of health information from dependent individuals. We simply decided to augment this definition to include wearable technologies or sensors that can be placed either on-body or inside-body (implantable and edible). In addition, Research has shown that ambient sensors can often complement wearable sensors, especially in applications of rehabilitation [2]. However, we decided to exclude such ambient sensing from the taxonomy.

To meet the growing societal challenges of chronic diseases, aging and public health disparities, acquisition of health-related information by unobtrusive sensing and wearable technologies has become a new trend in health informatics [1]. "Sensors can be weaved or integrated into clothing, accessories, and the living environment, such that health information can be acquired seamlessly and pervasively in daily living"[1]. We include in our taxonomy such unobtrusive sensors and wearable clothing devices. But wearable devices should also embrace five main key enabling technologies in the acronym "MINDS" (Miniaturization, Intelligence, Networking, Digitalization, and Standardization) [1, 7].

3.2   Establishing Criteria for the Taxonomy

Our team started with a clean slate. We placed known wearable computing products (either commercially available or research-based) on to the design board. Our team started analyzing what themes are common in them. We soon started to identify a pattern. The first theme we noticed was the form. We noticed that some devices were carried as *accessories* while others were *portable*. Some were embedded inside clothing (or *garment*) while a few were *implantable* (or edible).

An immediate second theme that we noticed was the fact that each device or technology had an application purpose. For example we found that Fitbit is exclusively used for monitoring physical steps while Google glasses have been used for communication by medical professionals. Another interesting thing that we noticed was that certain wearable technologies were being used by real patients (clinical) while a number of them were being used by consumers (non-clinical). Hence our team did a further sub-classification of the application into: patients were either using them for *monitoring* and *assistive* technology (for disabled), and consumers were primarily using them for *communication* or *prevention* purposes.

Besides the application and form dimensions, we also noticed that some devices had a single function while others exhibited multiple functions. Hence our team decided to add a third dimension to the taxonomy, that of functionality. This would include a single-sensor or multi-sensor wearable devices. This led us to the final structure of the taxonomy: a 4*4*2 cuboid as can be seen in Figure 1.

3.3   Overcoming Technologies that Span Multiple Cells

Once our taxonomy cuboid was in place, we faced a new challenge with some devices. Initially, cells of the taxonomy were thought to be mutually exclusive. That is, the wearable device should not span more than one cell. However, as we did further analysis, some technologies naturally seemed to overlap multiple cells. In fact, if we look at the commercially designed wearable devices, we can see that designers are intentionally designing their devices to serve more than one application. For example, Google glasses [8] are designed to aid both clinical applications targeting healthcare professionals, and non-clinical applications targeting consumers. Moving toward research-based wearable devices, one can see that these devices are designed for solely one application for the whole research project. Hence we allow application overlaps.

We found that the four forms (accessory, garment, implantable and portable) are independent in their own existence but there are some systems where a garment may be interoperating with a portable device such as a smartphone. So we are not stating that there is form overlap but there are specific instances of smart systems where various form components depend on each other.

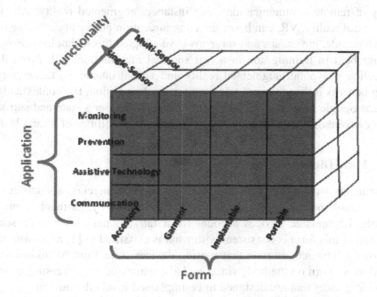

Fig. 1. 3-Dimensional Taxonomy of Wearable Technology in Healthcare

4   The Taxonomy Description

4.1   Application Dimension

This dimension is meant to address the main purpose of the wearable technology, and it consists of four levels. First two levels are monitoring and assistive technology mainly used by patients. The other two levels, namely, prevention and communication are typically for healthy population. We can also refer to them as consumers who are motivated to use wearable health devices and technology.

Remote monitoring has proved beneficial for chronic diseases management, such as diabetes, COPD , Parkisnon's and Cardiac patients. Early detection, daily monitoring and rehabilitation are all common activities for these applications. In addition, a number of wearable devices that are used as an assistive technology are available today. Recently, technology has been harnessed to assist elderly, and physically disabled individuals. The industry has shown great examples of these technologies, such as Muse headband and eSight glasses.

The third application is the use of wearable technology for prevention. Majority of wearable devices are designed targeting healthy population either to maintain a healthy behavior such as weight management wristbands or to keep them safe from unanticipated events. Wearable sensors can protect in disaster situations, such as fire, or earthquake. In addition, wearable sensors have the potential to build motivation to maintain a healthy lifestyle, and create what is called user-centric health management.

The fourth and last application level is the use of wearable technology for communications. We are seeing how recent forms of wearable technology improve the efficiency of remote communications. For instance, augmented reality, AR, that stems from virtual reality, VR, can boost the communication power in certain settings. Over the past decade, physicians and surgeons have adopted this technology using heads-up displays both in training and in actual surgical interventions [8]. From the clinical application viewpoint, augmented reality and virtual interactive technology are providing benefits in live surgical tele-monitoring. In addition, the contextualization, for instance Google Now feature, taking into account the user's state and surroundings is another advantage that adds to the communication capabilities of wearable devices.

4.2   Form Dimension

Our scanning of the literature and the available commercial products revealed that most wearable technologies exist in four forms: accessory, garment, implantable and portable. Implantable devices account for a fair amount of wearable sensors. The inclusion of this form is consistent with what is classified in [1] as a form of wearable technology. The authors state that sensing devices should not be limited to those designed to be worn on the body since we have witnessed an increasing number of implantable sensors that are designed to be implanted inside the human body. Examples include, but are not limited to: glucose-biosensor tattoos and CardioMEMO.

The second form of wearable technologies is portable in nature. These can be smartphones, video camera with microphone, or PDAs. This form is in line with what has been identified as smart wearable systems [3]. The third form of wearable technology is as a smart garment or e-textile that can be worn as a jacket to sense different kinds of physiological and motion data, and provide a holistic state of the wearer. The final form of wearable technology is accessory, which can supplement daily style such as a smart watch, smart glasses, or a smart shoe.

4.3   Functionality Dimension

Since some technology measures one parameter and does a single function while others measures more and do multiple functions, we added functionality as our third dimension to the taxonomy. This dimension can also impact the size of the wearable device.

5   Evaluation

To evaluate the utility of the taxonomy, we mapped to the taxonomy both publications from the literature and also commercially available products from the market. Keeping in mind that it is a taxonomy, we wanted to ensure that it can be applied effectively to both literature and market landscape. For each identified wearable computing product or literature, we applied the taxonomy criteria to illicit the applicable dimensions. Moreover, since we are focusing on health technologies, we also added a column at the end to discuss actual health outcomes reported by the use of the wearable technology. Appendix 1 shows how the taxonomy applies to various wearable products while in the next sub sections we provide detailed categorization analysis for two wearable devices, one for prevention while the other as an assistive technology.

5.1   Muse

Muse *accessory* is a brain training tool designed to help *prevent* stress and anxiety. The initial brain readings assist Muse to calibrate and adjust to the wearer state of thinking. In the long run, identifying the states of distractions and accordingly suggesting new mechanisms for focused attention would increase the level of productivity, and hence happiness and satisfaction. In terms of *functionality*, Muse consists of seven finely calibrated sensors that detect and measure the activity of the brain from outside the body.

5.2   eSight

This digital *eyewear* aims to enhance the vision for legally blinded individuals. It can be worn as an *assistive technology* accessory, enabling the user to magnify and view close and distant objects. It consists of an HD camera to capture ahead, and a head-mounted display to project the pictures in real-time[9]. eSight embraced high value for visually impaired people. Compared to prior eyewear for visual aids, eSight weighs lighter and can substitute prescription lens.

6   Discussion and Conclusion

While evaluating this taxonomy, we found that the monitoring application, among other applications, has predominated wearable technologies. This can be attributed to the complex challenges faced by healthcare, at the top of which is the skyrocketing healthcare cost. Wearable technologies, thus, seek to reduce the cost of hospitalization, and alter the healthcare model, especially for elderly and other chronically ill populations.

In order to address the utility of this taxonomy, we sought to generalize the design principles for constructing a taxonomy in three main principles, as outlined in Table 1. These principles, if followed correctly, can guide the process of designing a taxonomic tool for any focal concept of interest.

Table 1. Design Principles for Constructing a Taxonomy

• **Define the term for which the taxonomy will be constructed.**
• **Establish the major dimensions of the taxonomy that characterize the focal concept.**
• **Define the rule of overlap between the taxa or taxonomic unit.**

The present study pinpoints the phenomenon of the emergence and proliferation of wearable technologies by designing taxonomy of wearable technologies in healthcare in terms of the application, forma and functionality. While the taxonomy is meant to classify any wearable technology in healthcare, there is no absolute guarantee to achieve holism. In fact, holism can never be claimed by any classification scheme. Further underlying criteria, such as internet of things, security and privacy, interoperability, and maintainability could be incorporated into this taxonomy. However, for the sake of simplification, we confine it to three major dimensions: application, form, and functionality, and sidestep other underlying technical and economic dimensions.

References

1. Zheng, Y.-L., Ding, X.-R., Poon, C.C.Y., Lo, B.P.L., Zhang, H., Zhou, X.-L., Yang, G.-Z., Zhao, N., Zhang, Y.-T.: Unobtrusive Sensing and Wearable Devices for Health Informatics. IEEE Trans. Biomed. Eng. 61, 1538–1554 (2014)
2. Chan, L., Rodgers, M., Patel, S., Park, H., Bonato, P.: A Review of Wearable Sensors and Systems with Application in Rehabilitation (2012)
3. Chan, M., Estève, D., Fourniols, J.-Y., Escriba, C., Campo, E.: Smart wearable systems: Current status and future challenges. Artif. Intell. Med. 56, 137–156 (2012)
4. Ananthanarayan, S., Siek, K.A.: Persuasive wearable technology design for health and wellness. In: 2012 6th International Conference on Pervasive Computing Technologies for Healthcare (PervasiveHealth), pp. 236–240 (2012)
5. Hevner, A., Chatterjee, S.: Design Science Research in Information Systems, pp. 9–22. Springer US, Boston (2010)

6. Peffers, K., Tuunanen, T., Rothenberger, M.A., Chatterjee, S.: A Design Science Research Methodology for Information Systems Research. J. Manag. Inf. Syst. 24, 45–77 (2007)
7. Poon, C.C.Y., Zhang, Y.-T.: Perspectives on High Technologies for Low-Cost Healthcare. IEEE Eng. Med. Biol. Mag. 27, 42–47 (2008)
8. David, G., Armstrong, T.M.R.: A Heads-Up Display for Diabetic Limb Salvage Surgery: A View Through the Google Looking Glass. J. Diabetes Sci. Technol. (2014)
9. Holton, B.: eSight Eyewear and Smart Glasses from Assisted Vision (2014)
10. Curone, D., Secco, E.L., Tognetti, A., Loriga, G., Dudnik, G., Risatti, M., Whyte, R., Bonfiglio, A., Magenes, G.: Smart garments for emergency operators: the ProeTEX project. IEEE Trans. on Inf. Technol. Biomed. 14, 694–701 (2010)
11. Puiatti, A., Mudda, S., Giordano, S., Mayora, O.: Smartphone-centred wearable sensors network for monitoring patients with bipolar disorder. In: 2011 Annual International Conference of the IEEE Engineering in Medicine and Biology Society, EMBC, pp. 3644–3647. IEEE (2011)
12. Introducing our smart contact lens project, http://googleblog.blogspot.com/2014/01/introducing-our-smart-contact-lens.html
13. Adamson, P.B., Abraham, W.T., Aaron, M., Aranda, J.M., Bourge, R.C., Smith, A., Stevenson, L.W., Bauman, J.G., Yadav, J.S.: CHAMPION trial rationale and design: the long-term safety and clinical efficacy of a wireless pulmonary artery pressure monitoring system. J. Card. Fail. 17, 3–10 (2011)

Appendex 1

Wearable device	Application	Form	Functionality	Health Outcomes
[10]ProTEX	*Prevention*: safety monitoring	Full *Garment* (inner and outer garment – boat)	*Multi-sensor*: Physiological parameters and external environmental sensors (presence of toxic gases: CO2, external temperature, heat flux)	ProeTEX is designed for emergency-disaster personnel, by constantly monitoring vital signs and environmental parameters to process data and remotely transmit them to the operation manger. ProeTEX have proved promising for firefighters, soldiers, and others in life endangered situations.
[11] MONORCA	Mental *Monitoring* for early sign of depression	*Accessory* Sock- wrist band	*Multi-sensor*: GPS sensor, accelerometer, social-interaction sensors, other sensors for the wristband and sock	The main responsibility for the wearable system is to recognize the early warning signs of Bipolar disorder or depression. This will helps recognize early warning signs and predict manic/depressive episodes, and adjust the therapy accordingly.
[12]Google Contact Lens	*Monitoring*: early detection	*Implantable* lens	*Single-sensor*: miniaturized glucose sensor	Given the high frequency of glucose fluctuation level, the tiny pinhole in the lens allows for tear fluid to seep into the sensor and read blood sugar level every second, and provide early warning when the glucose level exceed predefines thresholds.
[13]CardioMEMS	*Monitoring*: HF monitoring	*Implantable*	*single-sensor*: pressure sensitive capacitor	CardioMEMS implantable monitoring system can provide long-term measurement of pulmonary arterial pressure of patients with heart failure. It is the only FDA system for HF monitoring. This device is proved to reduce hospitalization.
SIGMO	Communication	*Portable*	*multiple-sensor*: microphone-speaker	One of the potential applications of this language translator is to facilitate the communication and overcome language barriers among healthcare professionals.

Author Index